THE GREENHOUSE AND NURSERY HANDBOOK

A Complete Guide to Growing and Selling Ornamental Container Plants

Francis X. Jozwik

ANDMAR PRESS
Mills, Wyoming 82644

Library of Congress Catalog Number 91-76059
ISBN: 0-916-781-23-2
Printed in the United States of America

CIP

Jozwik, Francis X.
    The greenhouse and nursery handbook: a
complete guide to growing and selling ornamental
container plants / Francis X. Jozwik -- 2nd ed.

    p. cm.
    Includes bibliographical references and index.
    LCCN: 91-76059
    ISBN: 0-916781-23-2

    1. Greenhouse management--Handbook, manuals,
etc. 2. Nurseries (Horticulture)--Management--
Handbooks, manuals, etc. 3. Potted plant industry--
Handbooks, manuals, etc. 4. Ornamental plant
industry--Handbooks, manuals, etc. I. Title.

SB415.J68 2000   635.9'86
                   QBI99-1197

CONTENTS

ABOUT THE AUTHOR

Francis Jozwik received a Ph.D. in Plant Science from the University of Wyoming in 1966. He began his professional career lecturing in plant physiology with the University of Wisconsin System and later was appointed to the position of Arid Lands Research Scientist in the Commonwealth Scientific and Industrial Research Organization of Australia.

In addition to his scientific and academic background, Dr. Jozwik has become active in commercial horticulture as the owner of a successful greenhouse and nursery business. The wide experience Dr. Jozwik has acquired both as a scientist and in private industry assure that his books and articles are technically correct while possessing a down-to-earth style.

Who's Who In America and *Who's Who in the World* have honored Dr. Jozwik for his professional accomplishments by repeatedly including his biography in those publications. The National Science Foundation has supported some of his basic research in the field of biosystematics.

Ordering information for the *Greenhouse and Nursery Handbook* and for other titles by Dr. Jozwik is available near the back cover.

DISCLAIMER

This book is intended to present information about commercial activity within certain subject areas of horticulture. While the author and publisher have carefully attempted to make this information reliable and timely, readers should note that a good deal of it is based upon personal experiences and observations of the author. The validity of the information and viewpoints can differ with circumstances; therefore, neither the author nor publisher guarantees the accuracy of the text material under all situations.

No attempt has been made to make the present book a final and ultimate source of information about the subject matter involved. Readers should always study further sources in order to complement, amplify, and confirm the present text.

Beginning a business in specialized horticulture is not a get rich quick scheme. Although many people have become extremely successful in this field, most have accomplished the feat only after working hard and smart.

The author and Andmar Press shall have no liability or responsibility to any individual or entity experiencing loss or damage, or alleged loss or damage, thought to be caused directly or indirectly by information presented in this book.

Readers who have purchased this book directly from Andmar Press and who do not wish to accept the above conditions in full may feel free to return the book to the publisher for a refund of the purchase price. The original Andmar Press invoice along with the customer's name and address must accompany all refund requests.

If you purchased the book from any independent agent other than Andmar Press, you must follow their refund policies.

PREFACE

This book contains the basic technical information necessary to produce containerized crops of flowers, foliage plants, trees, and shrubs. It is aimed primarily at those people who already are or who would like to become commercial growers of these crops. Secondary users of this book might be park and grounds personnel, students and teachers, and amateur enthusiasts who require more detailed information than is available from consumer oriented literature sources.

The information presented will typically be most useful in small or medium sized commercial greenhouses and nurseries. While a good deal of the subject matter is applicable to larger operations, readers must be aware that some modification in interpretation and employment of information might be necessary in the latter case. Producing several million containerized plants a year is a somewhat different task than when the objective is ten thousand or one hundred thousand.

Most of the technical recommendations contained in the following pages result directly from over thirty years of the author's daily experience as a commercial grower. Minimal compilation of information from alternative sources is practiced; and then only when further viewpoints might lean towards clarification of the subject. Due to the preponderance of original material contained in *The Greenhouse and Nursery Handbook*, citations of literature are omitted.

Each grower will face unusual circumstances, and no book can claim to meet the exact needs of everyone in every instance. Growers must use this book as a guide rather than following each recommendation religiously as one might when using a recipe. Ultimately the individual grower is responsible for retailoring the generalized information presented here to fit the specific situation.

The author and publisher disclaim any present or future responsibility for assuring the applicability of information in this book to the particular circumstances of individual growers. Every recommendation, whether arising from this present book or from other sources, should be verified by preliminary testing before being employed on a larger scale. Basic procedures and objectives are similar for almost all types of container grown plants. Only small alterations of cultural methods are required to make them pertinent to any crop grouping. Container growing practices, whether indoors in the greenhouse or outdoors in the nursery, should be based upon the same principles (but with some consideration given to obvious environmental differences). An exact differentiation between greenhouse and nursery culture cannot be made; suffice it to say that greenhouse culture usually occurs indoors and focuses principally upon herbaceous species while nursery culture takes place outdoors primarily and focuses chiefly upon woody species.

A good deal of effort has been extended in *The Greenhouse and Nursery Handbook* toward balancing general concepts with specific information. A reference work of this nature is of little use unless it provides a theoretical background which can be employed to interpret the discussion of individual topics. Hopefully, the author has accomplished this task in a manner which most readers will find satisfactory.

Please note that production of hydroponic food crops, cut flowers, and field nursery stock are not covered in the present book. First, production in these crops is often dominated by larger businesses. In addition, the cultural methods employed for hydroponics, cut flowers, and field nursery stock are sometimes quite different than for container production; adequate coverage would require further enlargement of scope in an already lengthy book. Finally, these crops are, for various reasons, not generally high profit products which offer easy entry to beginners or those who lack extensive capital resources.

Although this book is compiled principally from a North American perspective, some effort is made to relate topics to other geographic and cultural areas of the globe. This practice will perhaps allow international readers to more easily utilize the specific information presented.

Adopting a totally consistent method of use for scientific and common names in this book is most difficult. In general, the name most commonly in use within the trade is employed (whether it be common or scientific, or whether the scientific and common name are identical. The author is well aware of taxonomic principles, having been active for years as a systematic botanist. I have chosen the somewhat haphazard nomenclatural process with full knowledge that certain experts will find it lacking in precision. Hopefully, the general audience will accept it as a reasonable compromise.

8

Part I
Introduction

In this section of *The Greenhouse and Nursery Handbook* the basic features of container plant production are investigated. Cultural guidelines presented here must be regarded by growers as only a starting point to aid in the eventual development of their own plant culture programs. Each growing operation will face situations caused by climate, business conditions, or other factors which necessitate some modifications to the general principles related in the following pages.

The interrelatedness of plant growth processes should be kept firmly in mind as production programs are developed and employed. Each factor which influences plant growth is in turn affected by other factors and by the totality of the plant organism. Seemingly small variations in cultural practices can often produce vast changes in the effectiveness and suitability of the entire program.

The Greenhouse and Nursery Handbook is meant to help growers in their daily work. Therefore, some suggestions are offered concerning fertilizer, soil, and other cultural programs which might be employed. These suggestions must be viewed with a full realization that they represent only a small sample of the many alternatives available.

An important point to remember when studying greenhouse crop production is that the growing temperature mentioned refers to the night temperature at plant level. When temperatures are mentioned in other situations, the reader must be careful to note the specific conditions. This caveat applies not only to the present book but also to most other literature sources.

A sound understanding of the basic principles which affect plant growth and development is not easily acquired but it is essential if growers are to deal effectively with the many unexpected situations which arise in the production process. Anyone who wishes to become a professional grower must become aware of the dynamic nature which living organisms exhibit as they respond to internally directed growth mechanisms and the external environment.

Success in the commercial greenhouse and nursery business is highly dependent upon developing a well planned and integrated crop culture program which favorably fulfills the final marketing and financial needs of the operation. This objective is realized not only from information available in sources such as the *The Greenhouse and Nursery Handbook* but also from practical experimentation under actual circumstances. Such experience is a critical factor in the long term viability of any plant growing operation. In recognition of this fact, every grower must from the start implement a documentation program aimed at recording and retrieving important cultural and marketing information as it becomes available from the results obtained each season.

Chapter 1

INTRODUCTION TO
THE GREENHOUSE
AND NURSERY INDUSTRY

The greenhouse and nursery industry had its earliest beginnings when man developed a material civilization which allowed free time for activities not concerned with immediate survival. Artwork and other records from ancient cultures suggest that at least the upper classes of the Near East, Egypt, Greece, India, China, Rome, and Meso-America pursued horticultural interests in those times. Even more primitive cultures were acutely interested in the medicinal and other powers associated with plants. It is entirely possible that Stone Age people developed rudimentary horticulture practices to augment plant products which were especially important.

This preoccupation with plants expanded gradually through the centuries until a considerable body of general knowledge was amassed concerning the subject. Much new information about plants and many exotic species were imported to those nations which participated in the discovery of new lands through sea voyages. When the scientific revolution in human thought emerged, horticulture was transformed from being mainly an art form into an organized discipline which relied principally upon the new scientific method as a means of providing further technical advancement. Although horticultural knowledge was growing quickly, this knowledge was typically employed mostly to aid in food and fiber production or to benefit the leisure interests of the privileged classes. The general populace, however, was exposed to horticultural progress through the establishment of numerous botanical and public gardens in almost every civilized corner of the world.

After the establishment of a truly affluent middle class in industrialized countries, horticultural pastimes were taken up by a significant part of the population and a widespread nursery and greenhouse industry began to develop. This development progressed moderately but steadily until approximately the early 1960's when numerous advances in plant variety offerings, cultural methods, marketing, and distribution combined to act as a springboard for unprecedented growth in the industry. Continued technical progress has added fuel to the fire.

As we enter a new century, the greenhouse and nursery industry appears poised to enter a second phase of accelerated growth caused primarily by demand for the product. This demand is being created particularly by a widespread public awareness of the practical and esthetic benefits which plants can add to human life and to the environment. Reinforcing this basic mental attitude is the fact that generally both husband and wife now work outside the home (at least in the United States), thus increasing household purchasing power but reducing the time available for other activities. People want to enjoy plants and flowers more but they have less time to do it and must consequently purchase ready to use horticultural products rather than growing the necessary plant material themselves.

Another factor which will contribute to world demand for ornamental plants is the rapid economic growth which seems likely to continue in emerging countries. The populations of these expanding areas will almost certainly follow similar trends as occurred in previously developed nations.

Conditions seem favorable for a continuation of rapid growth in the greenhouse and nursery industry, both in North America and globally. It is difficult to accurately state the total worldwide value of these products. So much depends upon whether the quotes refer to wholesale or retail sales and the amount of services included. One hundred billion U.S. dollars is perhaps a low estimate if one is speaking of retail products and services. Some sources indicate expenditures approaching $50 billion in the United States alone.

PATTERNS OF INDUSTRY DEVELOPMENT IN NORTH AMERICA

Until recently most nursery and greenhouse products were both grown and sold at the same location by relatively small neighborhood operations.

The introduction of new varieties, such as these magnificent "Inca" marigolds, has encouraged healthy growth in the horticultural industry.

True, there were some large wholesale oriented businesses but their number and influence in the trade were limited.

As with many other aspects of American commercial life, the neighborhood greenhouse and nursery has tended to be replaced since World War II by businesses which exhibit a different method of operation. Many readers will be able to remember a similar process which brought about the near total demise of the corner grocery store. However, the decline of neighborhood greenhouses and nurseries began at a later date and has not progressed so quickly or to so great an extent as did that of corner grocery stores.

Although extremely large greenhouses and nurseries now account for a great deal of plant production and chain store type plant outlets market about one half of total crops, independent neighborhood garden centers and plant and flower stores are still numerous and mostly in healthy condition.

The nursery and greenhouse industry in North America today exhibits a more or less two tier organization composed of relatively few large producers and marketers coexisting with numerous smaller operations which have carved out profitable specialized niches. Significant differences in the horticultural industries of Canada, Mexico, and the United States

Most homeowners realize that tasteful landscaping is the most economical means of adding value to their property. And they can enjoy their investment each day.

still exist, but the North American Free Trade Agreement has and will continue to cause a narrowing of these differences.

The ability of smaller independent businesses to service and prosper in this industry is perhaps due mainly to the high degree of artistry often associated with ornamental plant use. Larger, more impersonal businesses often lack the degree of flexibility and creativity necessary to deal with this type of situation.

The larger producers and chain type outlets usually specialize in those horticultural products which can be grown and sold in a large enough volume to warrant establishment of standardized cultural and marketing methods. Smaller operators often concentrate upon handling and providing service for more unusual products which cannot be adequately addressed by mass production and mass marketing.

Although there are numerous individuals who are not happy with the change which has taken place in the industry, the facts suggest that on the whole, it has been both beneficial and necessary. Painful adjustments were required in some cases but anyone who was willing to progress with the times has been well rewarded.

The greenhouse and nursery industry now seems to be in a reasonable state of equilibrium with abundant opportunities for diverse interests. If

A neighborhood greenhouse and nursery which has successfully survived competition from chain outlets. Service and selection are the main attraction here.

anything, the larger mass market oriented businesses and smaller service oriented operations complement one another to provide the public with a complete range of horticultural products. It cannot be denied that the present organization of the industry is allowing profitable expansion to continue through many different avenues.

Greenhouse and nursery businesses now have a wide array of options available for future development. This situation provides a stimulating atmosphere for those who wish to be commercial growers. The United States is a net importer of greenhouse and nursery products. While this fact indicates that there is a strong competition from foreign sources, it also shows there is room for expansion by U.S. growers if they can develop efficient methods of production. Two of the largest suppliers of imports are Canada and the Netherlands; neither of these countries are inherently favored by low wages or climatic advantages. On the other hand, Columbia, Mexico, and Ecuador (also large sources of horticultural imports) possess some climatic and labor advantages when compared with U.S. growers.

Along with the basic changes in industry organization described above, other developments have occurred. Specialization in particular crops and in crop phases is presently more common than in the past. Many growers limit production to a single or very few groups of plants while others produce only starter plants or only finished crops. And due to several factors, sunbelt geographic areas have become more popular for location of larger facilities. In numerous cases, larger specialist growers have relocated their entire operation or certain segments of it out of their native countries into areas with ideal natural climatic conditions.

There are two principal questions which must be asked when locating any ornamental horticultural business: 1) Does a viable market exist within the local area or is there a competitive and reliable means of transport to a good market? 2) Are the climate and geography suitable for profitable culture of the chosen crops (especially important with outdoor crop production)?

Technology and precise planning are now more a part of every successful greenhouse and nursery operation. The competitive nature of the industry requires growers to utilize every technological and informational advantage possible if a healthy business is to be maintained. The days of simply sticking a few seeds or cuttings in the soil and hoping for a successful outcome are long past. Efficient methods which yield

Table 1

Ten states in the United States of America account for more than two-thirds of U.S. floriculture and nursery production.

State	Rank	% of U.S. Production
California	1	20
Florida	2	11
N. Carolina	3	8
Texas	3	8
Ohio	4	5
Oregon	4	5
Michigan ⎫		
Pennsylvania ⎬ 5		2-4 each
Oklahoma ⎭		
New York		

From: Floriculture and Environmental Horticulture Yearbook. U.S. Department Horticulture, Economic Res. Service. 1996.

A chain outlet plant display which exhibits careful attention to cleanliness and merchandise upkeep – often rare qualities under these circumstances.

predictable results are now essential to a profitable operation. Even smaller seasonal growers must keep on top of new methods, technology, and information if they expect to remain competitive.

A good number of large wholesale nurseries and greenhouses have been established in the recent past to supply the rising tide of retail horticultural outlets which are totally lacking of any production facilities. This trend has undoubtedly increased production efficiency but it results in growers having less control over the final marketing of crops and lessens the profit potential which exists when both production and retail aspects are closely integrated.

Public corporations which retail to mass markets have been selling a wide array of plants for many years. Only recently, however, have a significant number of grower organizations offered stock shares on registered financial exchanges. It is too early to assess whether or not this means of financing and management will prove widely successful in the ornamental horticulture industry, but one must expect that it will at least be applicable in specific situations.

The existence of markets independent of production facilities and the trend towards larger facilities has in some cases resulted in situations where nursery and greenhouse products become dangerously close to

This greenhouse specializes in azalea production only. Over 1,000,000 square feet of well grown uniform plants produced under standardized conditions.

being simply a commodity. In such cases, growers often have little control over the pricing and profit structure of crops; the buyers and the marketers are generally more powerful financially and virtually dictate the conditions of sale. Fortunately, the very nature of living plants helps prevent this scenario from developing to an extreme degree.

Although specific countries, such as Israel, New Zealand, Australia, Japan, and those of Europe, possess their own individual character, the ornamental horticulture industry in highly developed countries outside of North America has progressed in a generally similar fashion as described above. In emerging market countries the evolution of ornamental horticulture is progressing more or less as it did in developed lands with the exception that a previously established technological base is available to draw upon. Here again, each country develops within the particular constraints of climate, culture, and available resources.

NURSERY AND GREENHOUSE TECHNOLOGY

The world we live in is one which measures progress primarily in terms of technological advance. Until recent years, greenhouses and nurseries could not be said to have participated fully in the application of modern scientific methods to practical problems. But the industry is now quickly making up for lost time. Virtually every month witnesses significant new advances in plant varieties, knowledge, products, and machinery which can be employed in daily operations.

Many of the most successful varieties (such as maple and ash trees) now in production were not commercially available only two or three years ago. Even some totally new crops (wild land restoration crops as fully commercial ventures) have been developed within the past ten years. The horticultural industry is fortunate in that the living plants we work with offer an unlimited variety of potential products for development. Sufficient knowledge is now available to utilize existing genetic diversity and also to create additional diversity while directing its utilization towards useful goals.

Basic research into details of plant growth and development is giving us a much better understanding of how to manage greenhouse and nursery production. A good number of the methods and products which we now employ on a routine basis have been introduced on an important scale only in the past decade. Many present uses of fertilizers, soil, and pest control technology are of recent introduction while modern methods of gene alteration, conservation, and rearrangement have progressed very rapidly and represent one of the most significant possibilities for profit improvement within the horticultural industry.

Much original biological and physical research information which promotes practical applications in the horticultural field has been available in abundant supply for many years, although sufficient means of translating and communicating this information to the commercial grower have not generally been realized. This situation is improving rapidly as government and private research institutions make more of an effort to insure that information is directed to the ultimate user. Trade magazines, books, grower organizations, trade shows and conferences, and the internet are the chief means of disseminating new information to growers. Every production operation must take advantage of these informational sources or risk being relegated to the dust heap of the past. No amount of hard work can take the place of advanced knowledge.

In the not too distant past a grower would have to visit numerous plant production operations and supply houses to become familiar with recent developments in the field. Now a person can skim through the latest

In contrast to the preceding photo, this successful greenhouse range occupies less than 30,000 square feet and grows well over 200 plant varieties.

magazine issues and visit one or two trade shows to accomplish the same objective. This represents a vast improvement in efficiency.

STRUCTURES AND RELATED EQUIPMENT

Nurseries and greenhouses have traditionally been dependent upon cheap sources of energy and labor. This equation has changed dramatically in the past few years. Now it is essential for every grower to devise cultural plans which utilize as little as possible of both ingredients.

This objective is realized by employing modern materials, controls, and design to provide efficient structures and equipment. Greenhouses are now available which can save one half and more of the fuel which was formerly used. And new machinery on the market is capable of performing almost every nursery and greenhouse task previously performed by hand. Of course, every section of the globe faces not only different technological capabilities but also diverse cultural and economic priorities regarding the application of new technology.

Not only is efficiency improving at the primary level where actual work is done but the secondary level of task integration and control is being modernized through the use of automatic control systems which are often monitored and directed by computers.

THE INFLUENCE OF
MODERN TRANSPORTATION

Few factors have affected the greenhouse and nursery trades as significantly as the development of a fast and economical transportation system. Plant products are constantly being moved all around the world in response to market needs. Intercontinental transport of some items is becoming commonplace and leads to an industry which is much more interconnected than in than past.

Not only finished products are benefiting from modern transport methods. A very large amount of starter plants are shipped from specialist growers to others who finish growing the plants into a completed product.

Much of the basic nursery and greenhouse industry pattern of organization is due in part to the influence of transportation. Present marketing structures, geographic distribution of operations, and crop specialization by growers are only a few of the more important factors which are often determined by transportation considerations. Plant pests and diseases also are increasingly becoming more cosmopolitan as a result of plant shipments between countries and continents.

INDUSTRY MARKETS AND ECONOMICS

The general economic outlook for nurseries and greenhouses appears to be positive. There are, of course, certain product areas (large commodity crops) and specialized situations (grower consolidation) which are cause for concern but, by and large, demand for the product seems likely to continue strong if the industry takes care to provide high quality merchandise and bring along new products on schedule.

Production costs and adequate profit margins will possibly be more of a problem for growers than is a scarcity of actual demand. This is not to say that a strong marketing effort by growers is unnecessary. Anyone who expects to survive in this business must realize that modern commerce is heavily reliant upon well planned and rigorously executed marketing programs.

Nurseries and greenhouses have been lucky in the immediate past because market expansion was accomplished without any great effort on the part of the industry. Demand materialized and was utilized mostly to good advantage. Although some of the forces which create demand can be expected to continue, it would be foolish not to establish programs which insure further market expansion. In short, both individual businesses and the industry as a whole must take a more active part in creating a demand.

Most nurseries and greenhouses will be forced to accept the absolute necessity of devoting considerable time and effort towards making sure their crops are sold at a desirable profit level. Each passing year sees a continual growth in the importance of marketing programs to the overall success of plant growing businesses. The days when growers could at least survive comfortably without giving much thought to active product marketing are long gone.

Whether a grower is supplying the new chain type outlets or competing against them, it is essential to realize that these organizations have an enviable track record of being able to move all types of merchandise. Plant suppliers must learn to deal effectively and profitably with the chains while independent retailers must devise strategies for competing successfully against them.

The new realities of the marketplace cannot be ignored by continuing to rely upon timeworn platitudes and outdated methods of doing business. The challenge must be met with well thought out plans which anticipate and solve problems before they assume critical proportions.

BASIC INDUSTRY CONCERNS

A few of the main problems and issues facing the nursery and greenhouse industry have already been touched upon in previous introductory remarks. A short summarization of these points and some others not specifically mentioned earlier will perhaps help readers focus attention upon key problems as the basic growing methods presented throughout this book are studied. Technical information is of little value unless it is directed towards achieving broader strategic business goals.

Maintaining and developing markets must be the overriding goal of everyone in the industry. We cannot simply grow plants and hope they sell. Numerous unrelated products actively compete against plants for the consumer's dollar. If we do not present our product to customers in the proper manner, they will find business persons in other fields who are eager to provide alternatives.

The markets we develop must be profitable for our industry. There is no use in working to expand the use and production of plant products if we allow outside interests to be the primary beneficiaries of our efforts. A clear sense of purpose and direction along with some degree of solidarity amongst growers will be necessary to prevent an excessive concentration of power over markets in the hands of only a few national chain marketing outlets. This goal will be realized chiefly through a commitment to the profit principle; growers must learn to participate only in business transactions which insure an adequate profit for their operations. It is better to be out of business than to continually accept orders which only permit a subservient level of economic participation.

The development of new products and cultural methods is an important requirement in our effort to create markets; growers must continually seek innovative ways to produce better plants with less expenditure of time and resources. The profit principle will again generally dictate how well this goal is realized. Individuals and firms whose business is innovation will not provide this service unless growers are supportive of new methods and new products. An overly conservative approach will not allow the incentive necessary for fresh ideas to prevail.

Plant growers are now beginning to face some issues which will be even more crucial to profitable crop production in the years ahead. Dealing with governmental regulations, foreign plant imports, and energy price and availability issues will require producers to plan and operate with these concerns in mind.

Imports affect only a few segments of the industry in North America at present but are almost certain to assume greater importance. Some of the effects of imports are good in the immediate time frame while some are less desirable. But the question of good or bad is mostly irrelevant, the primary issue is how each individual grower learns to adapt and manage with imports being a fact of life.

Energy prices and availability are largely out of the grower's control and there is no reasonable means of predicting what gyrations may occur in this field. Individuals must learn to cope with this situation as best as possible. Everyone should assume that there will be surprises in store and plan with this uncertainty in mind.

Government regulations, particularly as they relate to environmental concerns, are perhaps the most potentially troublesome area facing growers in the near future. Sane and equitable policy solutions to environmental issues will undoubtedly be worked out by give and take over the long term but there will be numerous instances where growers encounter unreasonably punitive regulatory action simply because the rules are new and have not been fine tuned to deal with real world situations. The rules will often be based initially upon theoretical assumptions which do not fairly take account of legitimate grower concerns.

Here again, individual growers must plan for a very uncertain scenario. On the one hand, some strong regulations must be expected, but on the other hand, it would be foolhardy to commit excessive resources towards compliance procedures which may eventually be found unnecessary or ineffective.

Increasing global interaction between both producers and marketers of horticultural goods will certainly obligate participants to recognize the serious impact which macroeconomic events and trends can have on individual businesses. Currency gyrations, trade agreements, and banking policies have all shown the potential to affect even locally based nurseries and greenhouses.

Chapter 2

STRUCTURES AND EQUIPMENT
FOR
CONTAINER PLANT PRODUCTION

The purpose of a greenhouse, cold frame, or shade house is to provide conditions in which the life processes of plants can be carried on at the particular time desired. Architectural forms of structures are unimportant as long as they accomplish their purpose in a suitable fashion. The following discussion will deal mainly with factors which must be controlled and methods of accomplishing this rather than with specific architectural details. Any structure manufacturing company will supply prospective customers with construction plans of their models. They will also have information and prices for all the accessories. Many manufacturing companies have engineers available to design complete structures; this service is usually free.

If a person understands how plants grow, it should come as no surprise that the most important considerations in greenhouse and shade house construction are to provide proper light and temperature conditions for economical culture of crops. An adequate but not excessive exchange of air is also a primary consideration but normally this is easily accomplished and can be taken care of without much special design. All commercial greenhouses and shadehouses are a compromise between providing the very best conditions for plant growth while still being economical. There is a point beyond which it does not pay to provide the ultimate in growing conditions. One important factor which must be taken into account when building a growing structure is adequate space for workers to care for plants.

Before making any decisions about building a structure, the grower should have a firm idea of the crops to be specialized in and at what times of the year they will be grown. It makes no sense to design greenhouses to withstand -40^0 F if they will only be used in the late spring when temperatures never drop below 25^0 F. Provisions for heating are expensive and heat sources should be sized carefully to the particular purpose of each greenhouse. Similar caution is necessary when relating structural design to other crop growth or environmental factors.

Growing structures may be simple without heating or cooling or they can be very complex with all environmental factors precisely controlled by computers. The more sophisticated operations are generally those whose owner is committed to servicing a wholesale market over a period of years. More primitive facilities are usually those whose owner is new to the business or is unwilling to commit capital to long term ventures. It is common in the trade to hear these extremes termed high investment and low investment construction. The type of building constructed will depend partly on how much money is available but it should also be determined by the length of time and at what seasons one plans to be in business. There may be no need to build facilities which will last fifty years if a person wishes to retire within ten years. It is important to be sure of business objectives before deciding what type of construction methods to use.

A thorough knowledge of local weather extremes is necessary before selecting a building design. Structures must be equipped for the extreme weather likely to be encountered rather than for normal conditions. There are three primary weather factors which should be considered: minimum yearly temperature, maximum likely wind speeds, and maximum snowload. If the locality has very low light intensities during growing seasons, it may also be necessary to focus attention on greenhouse construction details which will maximize light transmission. Low winter light can be an extreme problem in such areas as the Pacific Northwest of the United States.

Of course, there are other less continually occurring natural factors such as flooding, hailstorms, and atmospheric humidity which must be kept in mind as the site and structural design are chosen. Conditions other than weather are also important (soil properties and ground water levels, etc.).

Equipment and control mechanisms for plant growing facilities should be chosen with similar practical applications in mind as were discussed for the basic structures. The major factor used to determine the need for equipment and other devices in nursery and greenhouse production should be whether or not they accomplish intended tasks efficiently. Efficient, as described here, takes into account not only the work produced but purchase and upkeep costs, safety considerations, and any other factor which relates to the economics of production.

Most nurseries and some greenhouses usually require some open air grounds which are modified to facilitate container production. The amount of modification necessary is often minimal and generally relates to ground preparation but can occasionally include more extensive facilities.

No matter whether structures, equipment, or grounds are being considered, adequate planning must be done to determine how each particular improvement may affect all levels of production and how each improvement will integrate into the entire business operation.

Too often, growers spend large amounts of capital upon improvements which are not needed or which cannot properly serve the task at hand. Most of these mistakes result from a poor initial analysis of the situation, or no analysis at all. In many cases the improvements function well for a short time but become quickly outdated because expansion and changes in business operation were not anticipated in the planning stages.

GREENHOUSES

Greenhouse covering materials

The material used to cover a greenhouse is, in many cases, the only thing standing between the grower and disaster. The skin of a greenhouse is quite vulnerable because it must be made of relatively flimsy, transparent material in order for light to be admitted in sufficient quality and quantity. Other factors may affect decisions somewhat, but a greenhouse cover should be chosen primarily on the basis of crop safety, light transmission, and economy.

There are three main types of covering utilized for greenhouses: glass, plastic films, and semirigid fiberglass or plastic panels. Glass was used almost exclusively until the 1950's when fiberglass panels became available. Fiberglass enjoyed a period, before the steep rise in energy prices, when it was the chief covering material utilized. After the energy scare of the early 1970's, new construction was heavily slanted toward double layer inflated polyethylene houses because they are more energy efficient and very inexpensive to erect.

The need for energy efficient greenhouses which are covered with more lasting materials than polyethylene film has led to adaptations where glass

These greenhouses were originally covered many years ago with glass. Now the roof is skinned with semirigid double layer plastic sheets. The sidewalls remain in glass.

and fiberglass houses are provided with movable curtains inside. Another material introduced in this vein is double faced plastic sheeting with insulating air spaces between the layers.

   Glass is still frequently used in construction of new greenhouses and, if anything, has been increasing in popularity during the past few years. It is the most permanent covering available, unless damaged by hail, and retains its light transmission capabilities longer than any other material. The only logical situations where glass should be used is if the structure is to be used more than twenty-five years, if extremely good light transmission is necessary, or if appearance is a critical factor. Glass is expensive to install and maintain. Larger panes are more resistant to hail damage than smaller ones and square panes will withstand more abuse than rectangular ones. A 20 inch x 20 inch pane is often used because it is large enough to withstand damage but small enough to handle with ease when installing. Glass quality is an important consideration in greenhouses. Growers should make certain that the glass they purchase is the highest quality recommended by reputable supply firms. Glazing techniques are available which allow houses to have an insulating layer of air between two panes of glass.

High quality quonset style greenhouses with fiberglass endwalls, poly roofs, and large overhead doors for easy mechanical movement of crops.

When compared to glass, fiberglass is more economical, requires less initial maintenance, and is more energy efficient. The biggest drawback of fiberglass has been the loss of light transmission and material degradation over time. Improvements in manufacturing techniques and protection from surface degradation by special coating preparations has increased the life of fiberglass but it still cannot compete with glass in this respect. A word of caution: many types of fiberglass sold at general retail outlets are of low grade and unsuitable for greenhouse construction. Panels should be purchased from reputable greenhouse supply firms and even then specifications and guarantees must be carefully analyzed. Brand names are not sufficient proof of quality since some companies manufacture several grades of material.

Fiberglass will prevent the loss of crops from all but the most violent hailstorms. Light transmission properties are, however, seriously impaired by hail damage and the covering must often be replaced even though there are no actual holes in it. Although fiberglass transmits somewhat less light than glass, many growers believe it grows better crops, at least initially, because light is diffused as it enters and is more evenly distributed to all sections of the greenhouse.

A typical greenhouse natural gas heater.

Double-faced acrylic and polycarbonate sheeting with air spaces between the layers has been introduced recently. The chief advantage of these rigid materials is the insulation provided and resultant savings in heating costs; but they are relatively expensive. These plastic-like panels have replaced fiberglass panels in popularity to a large degree during the last few years. Physical properties vary greatly with the base material used for manufacture, and care should be taken to adequately understand the implications of these differences. There is a significant difference in cost between types of plastic sheeting, depending mainly upon the base material utilized and the thickness of spaces between layers.

Plastic film has been used for quite some time as a greenhouse covering but it was not until the 1970's that the use of it became widespread. The development of stronger, longer lasting films, improvements in fastening systems, and the design of greenhouse frames to accept film easily are some of the technical advances which led to the popularity of polyethylene (the most widely used type of plastic) houses. The increasing importance of spring bedding plants led growers to seek a greenhouse inexpensive enough to be used only for one or two spring crops. Polyethylene had not been in widespread use for long before the energy crisis arrived; at that time it became common to install two layers of plastic and inflate the airspace between them with small blower fans. This innovation saved 30-40% on fuel costs and many growers began to operate double layer plastic houses through the winter months.

Technical improvements in film technology are still occurring at a steady pace so that the product is even more durable, more energy efficient, and easier to install. Quality control from batch to batch is also much better than in earlier days.

Poly greenhouses are the logical choice for growers who want low investment houses. If materials are chosen and installed carefully, there is no reason to be apprehensive about growing through the winter in them. Polyethylene covers are inexpensive, will protect crops from hail damage, save fuel when used as a double layer, and, if replaced every three to four years, will provide excellent light transmission throughout the life of a structure. The principal disadvantages of plastic film are the near impossibility of recovering a large house unless winds are very calm and the high humidity which builds up under the air tight cover unless excellent ventilation is provided. Growers who are accustomed to outside air infiltration through glass or fiberglass houses (which usually have significant air leakage between panels) will have to adjust their cultural practices in polyethylene houses. Inside relative humidity must be reduced to a point low enough so that crop quality is not reduced and diseases which reproduce and grow under high humidity do not become rampant.

If polyethylene is to be used for more than a few months, it must be manufactured with ultraviolet inhibitors added; this process slows down material degradation dramatically. Films on the market are usually rated for three or four years of use but sometimes may last a year or two longer when properly installed and maintained. The author has personally used films rated for a three year life-span for up to six years, even in high light and high wind environments. Certain plastic films can be *seriously* damaged through contact with various materials such as some types of construction and mending tapes, chemicals, volatile compounds, and even other plastic materials. Care must be taken to investigate potential hazards in this respect. Tears and holes can be easily and safely repaired on most films with a high quality silicon sealant from tubes. Larger rips may need to be patched with special greenhouse tape which is then covered with a liberal layer of silicone. This two-stage method of repairing large holes is

Table 2
General properties of greenhouse covers

*Ratings may not apply under all circumstances. For example, fiberglass and polyethylene are moderately resistant to hail damage but must generally be replaced totally if a significant reduction of light transmission occurs.

Cover	Light Transmission	Cost of Material
Glass (Non-tempered)	Best	High
Fiberglass	Moderate	Moderate
Polyethylene (Double)	Moderate	Low
Acrylic Panels	High	High
Polycarbonate Panels	Good	Moderate

Cover	Resistance to Hail	Heat Retention	Flammability	Lifespan
Glass (Non-tempered)	Moderate	Least	No	Longest
Fiberglass	Moderate	Low	Yes	Moderate
Polyethylene (Double)	Moderate	Good	Moderate	Shortest
Acrylic Panels	Good	Excellent (Double wall)	Yes	Long
Polycarbonate Panels	Best	Excellent (Double wall)	No	Moderate

much stronger and long lasting than simply using tape alone.

The numerous benefits of polyethylene greenhouse covers must be balanced with problems which occasionally arise. Ice storms, when accompanied by moderate to high winds, often cause serious tear damage in a matter of minutes. Although most holes can be mended when good weather returns, the cold and wet conditions associated with such storms generally preclude effective immediate repairs. Newer energy efficient films which restrict heat movement from the interior greenhouse to outside film surfaces may sometimes allow snow and ice build up on the roof to a dangerous point (this is in addition to the normal snow load which could be expected). Another catastrophic event which occurs (although rare) is a total "blow up" of the polyethylene cover (much like a balloon being "popped"). Perhaps this uncommon phenomena may be caused by too much inflation pressure in combination with other seldom achieved factor thresholds. The few cases which the author has observed have little in common except that the weather was cold at the time of "blow up" and each house was not being heated to any significant degree. Each event also occurred at night. A simple explanation for and preventive action against "blow ups" may exist although it has escaped being widely publicized in grower publications.

The wide array of greenhouse coverings which have become available in the past several decades makes it difficult to present definite recommendations as to what choices a grower should or should not make in this area. So much depends upon the exact performance needed by growers, finances, energy costs, and other pertinent factors that an individual determination is necessary in each specific case.

Growers must study the options available and make a choice of coverings only after a careful analysis of how each possibility will integrate into the total greenhouse plan of culture and management. Particular attention is necessary to evaluate technical, safety, and durability specifications which manufacturers present.

First hand inspections of installations similar to the one planned and recommendations of growers who have experience with the material under consideration should take precedence over any claims made by manufacturers or salespersons. Guarantees normally cover only the purchase price of material, not all the considerable related expenses which may arise as a result of poor performance or suitability.

Greenhouse heating systems

A heating system is composed of two essential parts: the heat generation component and the heat distribution portion. The most common sources of heat are central hot water or steam boilers with a heat distribution system or unit heaters. The configuration and fuel sources of heat generators is extremely flexible and many choices are available to meet the particular needs dictated by different conditions.

Hot water and steam boilers are more commonly used in larger greenhouses but there are small boilers available. The heat from steam or hot water is usually distributed throughout the greenhouse by a system of metal pipes located around the perimeter of the house and under benches. Heat is transferred passively from the pipes to the surrounding air. Metal unit radiators are sometimes used as heat exchangers and will normally be equipped with a fan to aid in heat transfer and distribution. A newer concept in heat distribution for hot water is the use of closely spaced, small diameter plastic hoses on bench tops. This system concentrates heat more in the immediate vicinity of plants and can be designed so that individual benches may be left unheated if they are empty. Larger diameter tubes can be alternatively or additionally imbedded in the greenhouse floor during construction. Boilers are not intrinsically more economical than unit heaters, but, because many of them burn coal, it often happens that they are cheaper to run than unit heaters which seldom have coal burning capability. Coal is normally the most economical fuel available. The high cost of installation, expensive heat exchange systems, and pollution concerns outside the greenhouse often offset the lower fuel costs associated with coal.

Unit heaters are most often fired by natural gas but can be operated with propane, fuel oil, or even coal and wood. The unit is a combination heat generator and exchanger. A fan or blower is usually attached to distribute heat away from the immediate vicinity. The self-contained nature of these units makes them especially useful for small greenhouses. Installation is simple and can be accomplished with little previous experience.

Since a unit heater is usually located in the greenhouse, there are several safety precautions which should be observed. Always be sure heaters are properly vented and fuel lines do not leak. Even small amounts of flue gases or fuel vapors can damage crops. Observe the manufacturer's specifications for clearance from combustible materials when installing a heater. Heat exchangers must be fabricated from aluminum or stainless steel; ordinary steel heat exchangers will rust out quickly in the humid greenhouse atmosphere. Pilot lights should be well protected by a series of shields to prevent their being blown out by cooling and air distribution fans. Newer heater models are generally available with electronic ignitions which require no pilot. Fuel combustion consumes oxygen. In relatively air tight polyethylene houses it is not uncommon for a heater to "flame out" when the oxygen supply is depleted. Normally the manufacturer's installation directions will specify how large an air opening must be provided for proper combustion.

Energy efficient unit heaters which have enhanced fuel burning and heat exchange features and forced air vent systems are now commonplace. They should be used in all new construction and can often easily justify their cost if older heaters are replaced to increase fuel efficiency.

It is extremely important to provide good air circulation in greenhouses, not only to distribute heat evenly but also to lessen the high humidity which can build up around plant surfaces when air is stagnant. Fans are the normal means of providing heat distribution. Careful placement is necessary to achieve the desired results. The distance a fan will throw air should be known and if more than one fan is used; they should be placed so that the air movement provided by each fan complements that of others. The area directly under unit heaters is usually the coldest spot in a house and provision must be made to circulate heat to this area. The best means of providing air circulation is to install a large diameter perforated plastic tube the length of a greenhouse. Air is blown into this tube and circulated out the perforations (which can be placed in any desired pattern). Often the tube is located overhead and the perforations direct air toward the sides of the greenhouse and slightly downwards. Heaters may be located to discharge warm air into these tubes.

In earlier years, unit heaters were almost universally installed overhead so that valuable floor space was not occupied and heaters were not subjected to the water and dirt present at floor level. Many specially enclosed units are now installed on the floor with the heat distribution ducts running underneath benches. This saves fuel because the warm air rises to heat plants rather than being circulated above plant level. An alternative arrangement is to place the heaters overhead and install rigid ducts directing heated air to ground level. Care must be taken to assure the ducts are large enough to prevent dangerous heat backup into the heater.

Solar heat systems are normally restricted to those houses where crops require little additional heat and the design is usually of a passive nature. Heat requirements of warm greenhouses are so large that the cost of a solar system to provide total heat is prohibitive in colder climates. Unit heaters are now marketed which direct heat via infrared rays to the plant surfaces, thus eliminating the need to heat large air masses. If personal experience with these units is lacking, you should visit installations where they are in use in order to make certain they will function properly for the use under consideration.

The heating system chosen should be carefully sized to the greenhouse it will service. Too large a heating capacity is a waste of money and one that is too small will result in poor crops. The number of BTUs (British Thermal Units) needed to maintain the desired inside temperature is calculated by using an equation which takes into account the outside climatic conditions, area of exposed greenhouse surface, and type of construction materials. Firms which specialize in supplying greenhouse heating components can readily calculate your needs or supply data which will enable you to do it yourself.

Heating systems should be designed to maintain the desired crop temperature except on the very coldest nights expected. Crops will generally not be harmed if the temperatures fall 15-20^0 F below the optimum for 1 or 2 nights. If at all possible, it is a good idea to provide heat from 2 units, either one of which is capable of maintaining the inside temperature above freezing on the coldest nights. Growers sleep better when they know a back up heater is available to prevent crop failure. Of course, a reliable temperature and power outage alarm system is essential for alerting growers to possible problems. Most modern heating systems rely on electricity to power fans and controls; it is therefore essential to provide an emergency generator since power failures are relatively common. This is one reason electricity should not be used as a heat source. Backup generators to power only air circulation fans and controls need not be very large; if they were used to provide electricity for heat, the size and cost would escalate out of bounds.

Higher and wildly gyrating energy costs have led to a dramatic reevaluation of how things are done in the greenhouse industry. Prior to

A low cost double poly greenhouse range which has survived for years in some of the windiest, coldest winter weather in North America.

1973 fuel costs were a significant but not crucial cost of doing business. This cost was also rather stable from year to year. Due to sometimes higher fuel costs and the unpredictable nature of costs after this date, many growers of marginally profitable crops have switched to more profitable crops or have gone out of business. Greenhouse construction methods now emphasize energy conservation and a great deal of research is focused on methods of raising plants with less energy.

As mentioned previously, one way to save 30-40% on fuel costs is to grow in inflated double-poly houses or to use double glazing techniques when employing plastic panels or glass. Many growers who already have fiberglass or glass houses have taken to covering the outside with a layer of poly and inflating the air space between. Special fastener systems are sold for this job. Probably the best long term solution to high energy costs is to provide a movable system of insulation curtains within houses. Curtains are mechanically operated and drawn shut in the evening and opened in the morning. This method of fuel conservation has a high initial cost but admits more light to greenhouses than double cover techniques. Curtains not only provide insulation but also save an additional 10-20% on fuel since they normally block off the upper one third of ceiling space. The curtains can be programmed to operate automatically. A similar effect is accomplished by utilizing inflatable banks of clear plastic tubes in the ceiling. When inflated, the tubes fit tight against one another, thus preventing the rise of warm air higher into the ceiling. The presence of plastic tubes overhead limits light intensity and it is very difficult under most types of greenhouse construction to get a good heat seal. The main advantage of this method is the low initial cost. Growers should be aware that heat must be admitted to the outside greenhouse skin when heavy snow accumulations might cause the roof to collapse.

There are many other ways to save energy in the greenhouse but they are generally common sense applications such as closing up cracks and insulating any sidewall which does not admit light. Some methods of modifying the greenhouse skin which are in the developmental stages or have limited potential have not been mentioned. When modifying the greenhouse structure to save fuel, one should always take note of the effect it might have on crop growth. Fuel economy at the expense of crop quality is no bargain.

One means of energy conservation every grower can practice is to select crops that will flourish at lower temperatures. Of course, one cannot dictate what crops the market will accept but there is some latitude of choice. Research has indicated that it may be possible to lower the temperature each night on some crops for specified periods of time without affecting crop quality or timing. Many crops will tolerate colder temperatures at different stages of growth so that the grower need not maintain higher temperatures during the entire crop cycle. It is the grower's responsibility to know the requirements of each crop and maintain the greenhouse temperature at the most economical level. When a temperature is quoted in the industry, it is commonly accepted to mean night temperature unless otherwise qualified. Automated climate control systems using computer technology are available at reasonable cost, and they should be investigated for use in all but the most simple or smallest greenhouses.

The greenhouse heating system normally entails considerable initial installation expense and the efficiency with which it provides heat through the years will significantly influence operating costs. Deciding which type of heating system or which type of fuel to use is not an easy matter since the entire set of circumstances which prompt a particular decision may change quickly. A change in fuel prices or availability and alteration of pollution guidelines might render previous decisions less desirable or perhaps even unworkable.

A heating system which offers some flexibility in fuel sources is preferable but is not often a practical possibility. The next best alternative is to construct a heating management plan which produces the most stable and predictable set of circumstances which is realistically possible. Growers are better able to cope with a reasonably well known heating cost (although it may be somewhat higher on average) than one which fluctuates wildly. It sometimes happens that the most economical heating system may not always be the most desirable choice.

The corrosive nature of the greenhouse atmosphere must be evaluated when a heating system is being installed. The high humidity and frequent use of pest control chemicals and plant fertilizers may require that special attention be focused upon preventing failure of the combustion unit, controls, or delivery systems through corrosive degradation. Under certain low use or climatic conditions, the extra expense involved to protect equipment is not justified. Only an analysis of the specific situation will provide suitable answers to this question.

Greenhouse cooling systems

Most growers in cooler geographic regions realize the need for adequate heating but fail to attach the same importance to cooling systems. This is an especially common fault among inexperienced personnel. Even at northern United States latitudes, midwinter greenhouse temperatures will rise to unacceptable levels on a clear day unless some ventilation is provided. By mid spring the same greenhouse would be completely useless without a well designed cooling mechanism.

The traditional method of cooling when most houses were covered with glass was to have vents at the roof apex, they allowed rising warm air to escape. As summer approached and light intensity was not so critical, shade compounds would be applied to the greenhouse covering in order to further reduce greenhouse temperatures. Additional vents were sometimes located in sidewalls, facilitating the entry of cool air. This system was generally adequate until the hottest months arrived, at which time crop quality suffered because greenhouse temperatures could not be lowered adequately.

Today, many greenhouses are equipped with thermostatically controlled fans to evacuate warm air. This method, if properly sized, will reduce air

Evaporative pads manufactured from treated paper material are an effective and long lasting component of many modern greenhouse cooling systems.

temperatures 5-10^0 F more than can be accomplished with older convection type roof vents. Draft-free ventilation during the colder months can be accomplished with exhaust fans by attaching perforated polyethylene tubes to the fresh air inlets. The tube is suspended overhead by a support system and runs the length of the greenhouse. When exhaust fans begin to run, a vacuum is created in the greenhouse and the tube inflates. Air is discharged into the greenhouse atmosphere through the perforations. The fan, tube, perforation, and inlet sizes should be carefully correlated and the entire system must be adequate for the greenhouse volume. Many first time growers fail to install large enough exhaust fans. It usually takes a summer of intolerable temperatures to convince neophytes about the importance of cooling. A system of fans should be

Mechanical shade system inside of the greenhouse.

designed so that air intake can vary from about 20% up to a full load; this enables the grower to ventilate steadily on cool days.

A basic principle of physics states that as water evaporates, heat is absorbed. It is not surprising then that water evaporation plays an important part in greenhouse cooling. The most common method of evaporating water for cooling is to install large porous pads at the end of the greenhouse opposite exhaust fans. Water is circulated onto these pads when exhaust fans are running, causing rapid water evaporation as outside air is drawn through the pads. The addition of wet pads will permit a further 5-10° F cooling of the greenhouse air as compared with fans alone. The degree of cooling will vary depending on outside relative humidity and light intensity. The biggest advantage of fan and pad cooling systems is that little or no shading is required, which usually results in improved crop quality in areas where light intensity is a problem. Fan and pad cooling also renders a greenhouse reasonably impermeable to larger insects in the warmer months when insect populations reach epidemic proportions outside. Proper correlation of the fan, pad, and water supply size is important in obtaining effective cooling. Most greenhouse manufacturers can supply a properly designed cooling system with any greenhouse ordered. Evaporative cooler units meant for mobile home service can be used in very small greenhouses, although they are quite expensive for the amount of cooling received.

Another method of evaporating water to cool greenhouses is the high pressure mist system. It is used in greenhouses with vents or fans. Very fine mist at pressures of 500-1000 pounds per square inch is sprayed into the air above plants; most or all of the mist evaporates before reaching plant level. Temperatures comparable with fan and pad cooling are obtained but the water supply must be regulated carefully to prevent accumulations on floors and plants. Mist cooling is very effective if the system is designed and maintained properly. Both types of evaporative cooling work best in areas where relative humidity is low; if incoming air is dry, more water evaporates and more cooling takes place. Drier outside air can enter the structure through vents or the use of fans.

More flexible misting modules which cool a restricted area can also be employed by providing mist emitters on or near high discharge fans. These modules often do not employ high water pressure, relying more upon air discharge to break up water droplets.

Shading is an obvious method of reducing greenhouse temperatures, but it can result in decreased productivity due to reduced light intensity. Evaporative cooling permits the grower to vary the temperature independently of light. Shade compound is readily available as a liquid concentrate which is diluted with water and sprayed on. A homemade shade can be prepared by diluting 1 part latex paint with 5 to 10 parts water. All shade compounds, whether homemade or manufactured commercially, should be adequately tested before they are put into general use. They must stick adequately to accomplish the purpose but allow for removal if necessary. Shading is normally removed in the fall. It is quite difficult to adequately clean shade compounds from fiber glass and plastic so that some compound generally remains on the covering during winter. This can be very deleterious if high light requirement crops are being grown at this time. Shade compounds should always be white since this color reflects a great deal more sunlight than any other.

On smaller greenhouses, outside lath shading made from bamboo, wood, aluminum, or shade cloth is sometimes used. This permits some flexibility in the amount of light admitted. The cost is much higher than for shading compounds and strong winds may cause damage to both greenhouses and lath. Shade cloth used inside the greenhouse may reduce the temperature of plant parts and greenhouse fixtures but does not significantly alter the air temperature. Inside shading will not reduce the amount of radiant energy which penetrates the greenhouse covering.

The type of cooling systems used in greenhouses varies from time to time but generally the systems installed are only variants of those basic types described above. At the present time, the widely popular exhaust fan with accompanying wet pad system is giving way to a return of improved revisions of roof vent and mist evaporation systems. This turnabout is due in part to newer, more effective greenhouse and misting mechanism designs but also to the realization that exhaust fans require considerable energy input.

New research findings indicate that night temperatures and day temperatures which closely approximate one another result in shorter, more compact plants in many crops. This knowledge will undoubtedly place a greater emphasis upon finding cooling methods which can reduce greenhouse day temperatures even more reliably and inexpensively. Formerly, growers were interested mainly in bringing down day temperatures only to a tolerable level where suitable total crop growth could be maintained. Now they will aim not only towards maximum total growth but also towards improved quality through precise control of day temperatures. Further discussion of day/night temperatures as they affect plant height is presented in Chapter 9.

Both the heating and cooling systems in greenhouses need a thorough preseason checkup and repair program. Systematic checks made throughout the cropping season help uncover potential problems before they occur in full force.

Extensive shade systems placed outside the greenhouse are now being employed in special situations where additional cooling is necessary. These systems can also be mechanized and automatically controlled to vary the amount of light energy reaching plants, even when cooling is not necessary or is not the principal objective. Such an arrangement essentially results in a greenhouse within a shadehouse. An additional benefit can also be protection of crops and expensive greenhouses from some hail damage.

Basic greenhouse construction considerations

The choice of a greenhouse site depends on what resources are available, the nature of the business, and several construction related factors. Wholesale greenhouses need not be located on a prime traffic site but should be within easy reach of nearby main roads. Retail sales are highly correlated with visibility, nearness to potential customers, desirability of surrounding neighbors, and ease of access and parking. The property, in either case, must be well-drained to prevent mud and water buildup and the possibility of major flooding. There should be no large trees or buildings which shade the greenhouses. External light sources such as street lights, car headlights, and sign lighting should be evaluated carefully. Extraneous light can seriously upset flowering schedules. Level ground permits easier construction and facilitates the movement of materials and people when the greenhouse is in production. An adequate supply of high quality water which is free of toxic materials and relatively low in soluble salts must be available. In some areas of the country attention may need to be focused on potential pollution problems. Since higher wind speeds significantly increase the heating load of greenhouses, it is helpful if there are nearby natural or man-made wind barriers.

The site a grower chooses to build upon will be a significant part of his or her life; careful evaluation is therefore necessary before selection. If a greenhouse is planned on land adjacent to the grower's home, the site should be reasonably suitable for this business purpose. As long as adequate personal privacy is maintained, it is handy if a grower can live and work on the same property. About 300 hours a year would be consumed in transit if it takes the average worker 1 hour each day going to and from work. At $20 per hour, this is a waste of $6000, not counting vehicle use.

Whether growers choose to buy manufactured greenhouses or construct their own, there are many details which should be planned in advance. Some of the important points which can save time and money later on are listed below. These examples relate only a few points which may not be obvious to first time builders. There are certainly many more items to be considered.

1. If the site is at a latitude closer to the North or South pole than

A galvanized metal greenhouse post corroded with rust under the ground surface. Extra protection at critical points is essential.

approximately 35^0 N or S and the greenhouse will be used in winter, it should be oriented longitudinally from east to west. Greenhouses with more light admitting area on one side than the other should have that side facing the direction from which the winter sun shines. Both of these orientations provide more winter light and, in general, steeper roof slopes will do the same.

2. Roof slopes of less than 25^0 do not allow snow to slide off readily and inside condensation will drip on plants rather than run to the sidewall.

3. Greenhouse roof beams or trusses should be engineered to support extreme local snow loads plus the anticipated load of wet hanging baskets.

4. Extremely small greenhouses are difficult to heat and cool evenly. If possible, have a floor area of at least 500 square feet.

5. Endwalls, doors, utility service, and venting are major expenses in greenhouse construction; it therefore is usually less costly per square foot to build larger and longer greenhouses.

6. Plan for efficient material and personnel movement in the greenhouse structure. Head space and aisle space must be adequate for free movement at a fast pace.

7. Provide a separate storage shed for potentially dangerous fertilizers, chemicals, and pesticides. Plan for plenty of general storage also.

8. The ability to add to facilities without major disruption should be planned

An outdoor shade house.

in advance.

 9. Critical water, fuel, and electric supply avenues must be sized to allow for expansion of facilities without major disruption of services.

10. The water supply system will be much easier to service if plenty of shut off valves, unions, and backflow prevention devices are installed.

11. Water filtration devices are necessary to protect certain in-line systems. Install as required.

12. All structural members must be of aluminum, galvanized steel, or properly painted or treated lumber. The constant presence of water and the high humidity of greenhouses accelerates corrosion of metals and decay of wood. Extra protective material should be applied to both metal and wood at critical points, especially where posts are in or contact soil.

13. Use the very highest quality paint possible; repainting in a high humidity greenhouse is extremely difficult and paint fumes can be damaging to crops.

14. Never use pentachlorophenol or creosote as greenhouse wood preservatives. The fumes are deadly to plants and may last for years. An acceptable wood preservative should contain copper naphthenate or a suitable substitute which has been proven beyond question to be safe for use in greenhouse construction.

15. Heating and cooling possibilities are greatly influenced by basic building

A container nursery complete with roadways and an irrigation pond used for sprinkling systems in the background.

design and layout. Proper integration must begin in the early planning stages.

16. Provide an efficient general work area and make it accessible to all growing areas. If one plans to retail plants, customer comfort must be considered. People buying plants do not appreciate muddy walkways and clothes catching snags.

17. Air inlets are necessary for fuel combustion, especially in polyethylene houses. Heaters and boilers should be vented according to specifications and clearance from combustible materials must be observed.

18. Locate fan exhaust areas and major door entries in the opposite direction of prevailing winds.

19. Construct ventilation systems so that they can be operated at several levels of capacity.

20. If possible, distribute heat near ground level so that it rises to the plants.

21. Purchase greenhouse covering materials from reputable supply firms and, if possible, inspect the material under actual use conditions before buying.

22. Benching arrangements for plants should utilize every available square foot of space but still accommodate easy movement by workers. Install benches at a height from which workers can comfortably work on plants.

23. Insects eventually become a problem in any greenhouse. Do not attach a greenhouse to your home. This arrangement makes it very dangerous to apply poisons for pest control.

24. Plan to have a relatively pest free (no weeds, insects, or trash) perimeter zone which is maintained as bareground or paved.

25. Once established, weeds are difficult to eradicate from greenhouses. During construction avoid bringing soil or materials onto the site if they have been located in a weed patch.

26. Be sure any weed killers used previously on the site or during construction have completely dissipated or will be harmless in their present combination with soil underlying the site.

27. Install an alarm system to warn of power outages and temperature problems in the greenhouse which occur after working hours. The emergency electrical source must integrate properly with essential service equipment and controls.

28. Motors, controls, and some basic parts may be interchangeable in mechanical systems. This possibility should be an important consideration when choosing various systems.

29. Check regulations concerning access requirements for the disabled. It may be necessary to provide special entry and walkway modifications.

30. Always check local zoning codes carefully before any type of development is planned.

Technical manuals and catalogs published by greenhouse and equipment manufacturers are usually the most up to date sources of information concerning greenhouse materials and construction methods. The data and specifications in this area change so frequently that general greenhouse books can only hope to provide an outline of common practices. As an example, retractable roof greenhouses, which allow crops to be grown in a more or less open air environment during favorable weather, have been offered by manufacturers only in the last few years.

Books published before the turn of the century may not even mention this new development.

Information provided by manufacturers must always, to a certain degree, be regarded as promotional material. It should not be accepted without critical evaluation. Putting together the various elements which make up a reliable and efficient greenhouse package is not an easy task. Growers are ultimately the ones who must work each day in the greenhouse and they should accept responsibility for final design decisions. A good deal of searching through data sources is necessary before informed choices can be made.

SHADEHOUSES

The chief function of a shadehouse is to provide some shade and wind protection for crops, either at critical production stages or year around. With shadehouses, these functions are served in a basically outdoor environment, the covering material generally being fairly pervious to moisture and air. Another name often given to these structures is lath house; this term is perhaps less suitable since it infers the use of particular construction materials.

Shadehouses may also serve aesthetic and convenience purposes when they are utilized at retail plant selling sites. A well designed shadehouse can add architectural interest and focus to a sales area while also providing a more comfortable shopping climate.

Growers of both herbaceous and woody crops may have need of shade facilities, depending upon the particular cultural practices used. Certain crops require shade for their entire production cycle while protection is afforded to others mainly during periods of establishment or acclimatization. In certain cases, mist evaporation cooling may be provided to artificially lower temperatures during extremely hot temperatures or in critical stages of plant development.

Although we normally think of protection as being necessary during the actively growing stages of plants, shade houses can be even more helpful for both evergreen and deciduous nursery stock during winter weather. The alternate freezing and thawing of plant material exposed to full sun is partially avoided in shadehouses while a reduction in wind velocity helps prevent tissue desiccation and encourages snow and dead leaf accumulation over the root mass.

Because there is usually no attempt to control environmental factors beyond a mere passive modification, the initial cost of shadehouses is generally rather moderate. This often causes growers to be more lackadaisical in their construction planning, leading to careless choice of materials, poor construction methods, improper location and ground preparation, and poor design. Most of the construction considerations just listed for greenhouses would apply to shadehouses.

Shadehouse frames

The frames of shade structures were previously made mostly of wood but galvanized steel structural members are now frequently utilized. Although a large number of prefabricated models may be exactly the same product offered as a greenhouse frame, shadehouse versions are often manufactured with lighter grade materials since less roof and sidewall strength is generally needed when compared to a greenhouse.

Wood is entirely satisfactory as a frame but warping and decay may occur if high quality material is not used and weatherproofed carefully. Whether wood or metal is used, enough structural strength is necessary to account for construction material dead loads, maximum snow loads, and maximum windloads. Too often, shadehouses are constructed so that they can scarcely stand up under their own weight; apparently because the builders fail to realize that snow and wind affect these structures in the same way as any other building, only to a lesser degree. It is not uncommon to see numerous poorly designed shadehouses caved in after a heavy spring snowfall.

Adequate overhead clearance is necessary in shadehouses to allow the tallest anticipated crops to be moved in and out. Large doorways located opposite one another provide easy entry and exit for nursery transport equipment.

Shadehouse coverings

Wood and various types of plastic netting are the materials most commonly used as covering for the shadehouse frame. The material must be durable enough to provide the degree of sun and wind protection desired for the length of time necessary. The aesthetic appearance of the structure also sometimes has an influence upon the selection of covering materials.

When used as a shadehouse cover, wood is usually applied in the form of a woven wire lath or as larger dimensional lumber. Neither method is inherently more suitable or more economical. The choice will depend on the price and availability of materials and upon the preferences of the builder. Dimensional lumber as a covering can often provide a more visually pleasing appearance if it is arranged properly.

Woven wire lath varies greatly in quality. Some grades are woven carefully from high quality decay resistant wood while the more commonly available grades are made with less desirable materials. The poorer grades are adequate for short term structures where appearance and durability are of little importance but only the better quality is suitable for shadehouses which will be used for longer than 3 or 4 years. Suppliers of nursery grade woven wire lath may also have several lath spacings available to provide different degrees of shade.

Plastic net fabric is not generally so permanent as are wood coverings but it is usually cheaper in the short run, easier to apply, and quickly movable from structure to structure. It is also widely available in a range of shade percentages. These plastic materials may be extremely resistant to degradation due to sunlight and weather or they can be susceptible to damage from these factors. If durability is important, this aspect of quality must be checked out carefully. Growers should also find out if the material they purchase tends to shrink after installation. This can be an important factor to consider in the application process.

Plastic netting is often the only practical means available for shading large metal quonset style frames if a covering permeable to water and air is desired. White plastic film may be used for shade on quonset frames when an impermeable material is preferred. In sunny weather, heat can build up quickly under the film if plenty of air flow is not allowed at the base and both ends. Plastic films must be adequately secured at the ends and lower edges in order to avoid wind damage.

WINTER PROTECTION SHADEHOUSES

Woody plants and perennials in containers often must be held over the winter for one reason or another. Depending upon the species and climatic conditions, it is frequently desirable to provide protection from the elements for plants being overwintered. Modern nurseries often find this protection is most economically provided by storing plants in an unheated structure which is covered with white plastic film.

The object is to prevent desiccation by wind, reduce alternate freezing and thawing caused by winter sun, and to moderate exposure to low temperatures. The latter two objectives are sometimes also aided by placing various insulation materials over the tops of shorter plants or over the containers if plants are placed on their side in the shadehouse.

These closed winter protection structures must be opened up if extremely clear and warm winter weather is encountered. The benefits of winter protection houses are quickly nullified if plants are placed in storage too early or removed too late, these conditions cause damage due to excessive heat build up in the house. In areas where winter sun is often intense, nursery managers need to critically evaluate whether or not an impermeable cover is desirable. The best means of analyzing the situation is to visit neighboring installations and rely upon their experience.

Open air growing areas

In areas where the winter climate is severe, open air container plant growing grounds are typically utilized only during the warmer seasons. Growers in more moderate climates may grow hardier crops outside without protection through the entire year while allowing tender crops to remain outside only during the frost free season.

A wide range of ornamental container crops are grown outdoors in different climatic regions. People from colder areas may be familiar with only woody plants and hardy perennials being grown in this manner but a full spectrum of woody plants, bedding plants, foliage, and cut flowers is grown outdoors in more moderate climates.

Principal growing area requirements

The chief considerations (other than general climatic suitability) in choosing an outdoor area for growing container plants are: is it level enough to permit easy movement of people and machines and to allow plants to be placed level on the ground?; is it well drained so that excess irrigation and storm waters quickly flow off roads and growing grounds?; is it located so that cold air does not drain into the area from the surrounding topography?; is it free of trees and other obstructions which may hamper work operations and shade crops more than desirable?; is it located where both actual and perceived environmental concerns can be addressed adequately?

All of these factors are self explanatory except perhaps the last one. Heightened public concern with the environment places some restrictions upon container plant growers. They must, at the very least, prevent any movement of toxic chemicals and fertilizers off of the property or into the ground water. Some governmental agencies also require that there be absolutely no irrigation water runoff to surrounding land and water courses.

Additionally, growers would be wise to plan plant culture and grounds development so that even hints of undesirable environmental activities are less likely to draw attention. The best way of accomplishing this goal is to locate facilities away from heavily populated or heavily traveled areas. Close proximity to people naturally brings more curiosity from them. The objective is not to subvert legitimate environmental laws but to draw less attention to practices which are perfectly legal but may engender some controversy from surrounding neighbors.

A holding and recycling pond for irrigation runoff is required in many localities at the present time and this requirement is likely to become more widespread. The pond must not only prevent surface runoff to surrounding areas but it must prevent seepage to the ground water table.

If open air growing grounds are also to serve as a retail location, it is likely that specific display areas should be developed to allow customers to shop more comfortably without walking long distances in order to select plants.

Roadways, drainage, and irrigation systems

Outdoor container growing areas receive a good deal of foot and vehicle travel, much of it while the ground is wet from irrigation or spring storms. Careful ground preparation and adequate drainage will insure that movement is not hampered by muddy conditions. Both the growing areas and roadways should be constructed so that they have a small slope towards the drainage courses. In areas where the soil lacks natural drainage capability, drain tiles may be required below ground level in addition to surface drain systems.

After adequate drainage is assured, roadways especially and growing grounds to a lesser extent, will generally need at least some modification to prevent muddy conditions. Different types of suitable road construction materials are available but pure sand or gravel are seldom a good choice.

A well-drained and surfaced roadway through outdoor growing areas is essential for movement of people and machinery.

A road base material must first be laid down before any gravel surface is applied. Local sand and gravel companies should be able to advise what the best road base mixture is for the area.

A thin layer of road base is also necessary for growing grounds if light machinery will enter the areas. When no vehicle traffic is expected, only superficial modification of the ground surface is required. Commercial weed mats made of various woven materials may be sufficient ground cover for light foot traffic.

Several irrigation methods are used for outdoor container crops. Hand held hose watering is labor intensive but often used in smaller operations or where labor is inexpensive. Sprinkler systems are perhaps the most commonly used irrigation method but they are wasteful of water resources and necessitate greater attention to drainage and groundwater pollution problems. These considerations are combining to render sprinkling a less viable irrigation method than in previous years.

Drip irrigation of containers is perhaps the most desirable and flexible method from a cultural and environmental standpoint but proper installation and maintenance of the system is expensive.

Drip systems also require that the sizes and numbers of containers within a particular area remain reasonably constant if the full benefit of the system is to be realized.

Various flood irrigation methods are frequently used in greenhouses and the practice is now being employed to a limited extent outdoors. The main problem of this method outdoors is the necessity of having extensive areas precisely leveled and then made watertight so that a uniform layer of water can be introduced to the growing grounds and be allowed to stand for the necessary period of time to saturate containers. A good deal of water recycling capacity must also be designed into the system.

Environmental concerns are causing extensive changes to be made in the way crops are irrigated. Due to this fact, growers should anticipate that larger capital outlays will be necessary in order to provide adequate water application in an environmentally acceptable manner.

Site protection and maintenance

Even if care is taken during construction to prevent weed contamination in the growing area, this problem will eventually surface and cause considerable cultural problems unless it is dealt with in a timely and thorough fashion. Although most weeds can be easily controlled with chemical treatments, it is preferable to lay out the grounds so that as much weed control as possible can be efficiently performed mechanically. Weeds should also be meticulously controlled on the periphery of the growing area so that less seed is readily available to infest both the grounds and containers.

Fencing of the growing grounds may be a necessity to protect crops, people, and the improvements. In many areas of North America door damage to crops is the principle motivation behind fence construction. Other parts of the world may have different pests to protect against. Although security fencing is expensive and a nonproductive aspect of grounds construction, it may be a requirement in order to obtain liability and property theft insurance in some areas.

EQUIPMENT AND CONTROLS

The greatest expansion of greenhouse and nursery activities has taken place in a time when labor costs are escalating quickly. Qualified and willing workers are not always available even when wages are generous. This situation, along with the often seasonal business cycle of the industry provides a very fertile setting for the introduction of labor saving equipment and devices.

Labor is generally the largest expense at a greenhouse or nursery. Reducing this expense is often the surest and quickest way to improve business profits. Labor costs can be reduced by utilizing personnel more efficiently, either through improved work management or through expanding worker output with machines.

Machines and equipment are welcomed by workers because they reduce the amount of monotonous and heavy labor required to perform tasks. Efficiency brought about through work management programs is not always received so willingly since it usually involves regimentation of and additional effort by the work force. Thus, machines are often the most painless means of bringing about improved efficiency in the greenhouse or nursery.

It must be remembered, however, that most equipment is expensive and its use must be managed effectively in order to justify the cost. As has been mentioned previously, a good deal of thought should be put into the purchase and proper employment of machinery. Some businesses become tremendously overburdened with equipment because it is unquestionably assumed that every modern device is both cost efficient and convenient. Some managers are simply equipment freaks; they feel the need to purchase every new gadget which comes along. Neither of these situations is healthy. Machinery is an advantage only when it is purchased and managed for the efficient and economical production of work.

The following summary of different equipment categories will allow readers to gain an overall perspective concerning the topic. More details about particular machines will be given when the factors or process they relate to are discussed.

Equipment associated with structures

It is often difficult to determine where the dividing line should be drawn between what part of an operation is considered as a basic structural member and what is considered as ancillary equipment. The distinction is not especially important except as it provides a convenient basis of arrangement for discussion. Structurally related equipment in this book will mostly deal with the basic heating and cooling systems of greenhouses, along with a few specialized machines which often perform a building related function.

The fundamental aspects of heating and cooling equipment were described previously but some brief mention of them here will serve to emphasize that since they are composed of various machines and controls which work in an integrated fashion, they should be maintained and repaired on a regular basis. Many greenhouse managers become so accustomed to the heating and cooling systems operating in a monotonously efficient manner that they begin to take these machines for granted and expect that they will always serve reliably without interruption.

This attitude must be overcome since only a few moments reflection reveals the overwhelmingly important role which heating and cooling equipment plays in greenhouse operation. Each component of the systems must be meticulously inspected, serviced, and repaired as frequently as is necessary to provide uninterrupted and efficient service. Once a year service before the major season of use is the absolute minimum service schedule.

Although the plant growing benches in most greenhouses are stationary structures which are rarely, if ever, moved; many new greenhouses are equipped with benching systems which can be moved, rearranged, or modified in one or several manners. Newer types of benches are constructed and installed in such a way as to minimize or eliminate the need for aisle space in greenhouses and to sometimes serve as a mobile growing platform which can be moved easily into special areas for plant treatments, transplanting, or shipment. These new bench systems are expensive but can provide important labor savings. They are employed chiefly in high production wholesale ranges where crop benching arrangements remain fairly constant from season to season and where entire benches can often be marketed as a unit. Benches are often designed to serve also as a watering system or to aid in the process.

The amount and duration of light in greenhouses is sometimes controlled by various lighting and shading equipment. Artificial light may be provided for the purpose of promoting more total plant growth or it may be required only to trigger particular physiological processes in plants. In the first case, considerable intensity of appropriate quality is needed to accomplish the purpose while in the second case, only relatively weak light intensities are usually necessary and the exact spectral qualities are often not so important. Thus the systems necessary to perform different functions are quite dissimilar.

Mechanical shading systems often serve a double purpose. The amount of natural daylight reaching plants may be precisely controlled to suit crop needs and night time heat loss can be reduced if desired by pulling the shade fabric to close off the upper portions of the greenhouse.

Transport, loading, packing equipment

One of the major labor consuming activities in any container plant operation involves the various tasks related to simply handling crops and moving them from place to place as the need arises. A greenhouse or nursery manager who wishes to maximize efficiency in this area must not only employ modern equipment but also provide the conditions under which it can perform adequately.

Too often, transport equipment in the greenhouse or nursery is expected to operate efficiently in cramped or muddy conditions which prevent full utilization. Although there are many operations which would benefit from upgrading their transport and handling equipment, there are also a large number which could increase productivity more significantly by providing optimum conditions for existing machines to operate properly.

Not every greenhouse or nursery requires sophisticated machinery to handle crops economically. Smaller operations may find that several well maintained hand carts are perhaps a better investment than a single motorized cart which is bigger than necessary for the crops being handled and too large to work within confined areas.

Transport and handling needs should be evaluated carefully before any attempt to select equipment is made. A few hours spent studying the various movement and handling requirements present in a growing operation will usually result in a much improved appreciation of exactly what the problems are and how they may be solved.

Not only the need to handle materials and crops efficiently is at question when mechanization of the operation is being considered. The impact upon the human workforce must also be evaluated.

Most efforts to save labor by moving or handling crops and material mechanically will also result in improved employee morale and productivity above and beyond the savings directly attributable to any particular task. Employees who are physically worn out from moving plants all day cannot function properly to carry out duties which require either manual dexterity or mental alertness.

Sometimes, selected operational aspects of the greenhouse or nursery must be modified in order to efficiently synchronize with mechanical handling and moving. Certain crops are more easily handled by equipment than are others and particular cultural methods may be more easily adapted to mechanization.

New transport and handling equipment is being developed every day specifically for use in greenhouses and nurseries. Growers would be well advised to visit a nearby trade show or inspect the latest lines offered by distributors before design and purchase of equipment is initiated. The combination bench, moving, and packing system described in the previous section is but one of the options available. Overhead monorail transport systems are proving well adapted to greenhouse use and, as they become more common, manufacturers are able to offer less expensive yet dependable systems.

Most of the especially monotonous and physically tiring work connected with handling or moving container plants can be eliminated with only a few basic pieces of relatively inexpensive equipment. A plan for saving on labor costs should reflect implementation priorities since it is unlikely that unlimited funds will be available to purchase every piece of equipment considered desirable.

Managers should lean towards first acquiring machinery which will be used frequently and result in the greatest savings but they should also give some consideration to the flexibility inherent in particular machines. Items like simple hand or motorized carts, conveyors, and floor lifts are not likely to be outmoded by changes in cultural methods or crops. They are multipurpose equipment pieces and are usually better initial investments than are specialized machines.

Machines to plant and care for crops

The potting area is usually the focus point of activity at a greenhouse or nursery. And because so much work is done there, it is a good place to begin looking for labor savings through mechanization.

A soil mixing and handling system is perhaps the most necessary piece of equipment in a container plant operation. Any plant growing business which progresses beyond the hobby stage will use large amounts of blended soil. Even if prepackaged soil mixes are used, for best results they will generally require some type of mixing or conditioning before planting.

Movable benches in this greenhouse can be easily rolled from side to side in order to eliminate the need for lateral aisles. These benches can also serve as an efficient trough watering system.

Soil mixing is accomplished satisfactorily and economically by several means. Tree and shrub nurseries often find that the huge amounts of soil they need are best mixed outdoors by using a front end loader or by using a tractor having both a loader and rototiller. Greenhouses normally use a good deal less soil than do nurseries (relative to the number of containers planted) and find that mixing soil is best accomplished indoors with a specialized mixing machine.

After the soil is mixed, some means of moving it to and depositing it in the proper area for potting to take place is essential. A good soil mixer is of little value unless the soil transport equipment finishes the job by getting soil to the point where it can be most efficiently used. Soil mixing and moving is a rough, dirty job unless it is mechanized. This can be done easily without undue expense.

The equipment necessary for efficient potting of container plants can run the spectrum from only a potting table of the proper height to very complex machines which perform almost every task associated with filling containers and moving plants into the growing area. Small greenhouses and nurseries can seldom justify a great deal of expensive potting machinery because the large number of container sizes and varieties they utilize are not potted in sufficient volume at any one time to warrant the use of high production methods.

Larger growing operations can lower potting costs considerably by making full use of mechanized systems. An efficiently designed system will not only reduce the actual amount of manual labor necessary but will also help keep workers productive by requiring them to keep pace with the speed at which equipment is operating.

The potting area is often crowded with materials and people. Since it is usually a busy centralized operation over which good supervision can be provided, many new employees are given their first duty there. The equipment in this area must be especially simple to operate and safety oriented since inexperienced personnel cannot be expected to master complicated controls quickly. The dependability of potting area equipment is also of prime importance. Breakdowns and irregular operational patterns will often cause an entire crew to be idled.

After plants are placed in the greenhouse or moved to outside growing areas, the sometimes long process of development into a saleable product is begun. During this considerable timespan, all the water and nutrients necessary for good growth must be supplied in the proper quantities and with religious care.

This is a big job and consumes a good deal of labor in the average container plant operation. It is another area which is ripe with opportunities for employing labor saving equipment. Mechanization also relieves the tedium associated with hand watering thousands of plants, sometimes every day.

Many nurseries and greenhouses supply in the irrigation water at least a part of the numerous nutrients necessary for plant growth. And various insect and disease control agents which are easily transported in water are often applied as irrigation takes place. Other special jobs, such as applying plant growth regulants or modifying soil chemistry may also be accomplished in the same manner.

Considering the frequency with which it is used and the number of important purposes it serves, the irrigation system in a container plant operation should be carefully designed and constructed. After all, if we were to compare it with the human anatomy, the irrigation system serves as the circulatory, nutritional, and regulatory systems all combined as one. The nursery or greenhouse often cannot survive even one day if the watering system is totally nonfunctional. And, in the event of less than optimum irrigation system operation, crops will not grow and develop as profitably as possible.

The basic necessities for an irrigation system are: an adequate supply of high quality water, a means of transporting it with the proper pressure and volume to the point of use, a means of applying it to the plants, and an accurate and efficient method of mixing necessary additives into it.

Not all greenhouses or nurseries are suited to what is called automatic irrigation but all of them can employ at least some simple labor saving devices. Easy on and easy off water controls, quick couple connections, full flow valves, float valve shut offs, and hose guides can all add to labor efficiency yet cost little in terms of money or time to install.

Conditions must be appropriate in order to water crops efficiently by automatic or semiautomatic methods; the exact number and type of necessary conditions will vary under different circumstances. But, in general, larger crops of a single growth pattern, grown in similar containers and soil, and in a comparable stage of growth are especially suitable to this means of irrigation. The actual physical layout of the facility must also must be compatible to automatic watering. Several methods are available to accomplish the desired result and a detailed analysis is often necessary to determine which means is most practical and economical.

Whenever an irrigation system is installed, some attention must be focused upon the flexibility it possesses. Changes in markets and cultural procedures may dictate that crops be watered somewhat differently. It is always desirable if the initial irrigation system can easily be adapted to a new method of application. Unfortunately, this is not always the case and growers must make trade offs between efficiency and flexibility when design decisions are made.

Compatibility with environmental laws is now a major consideration when irrigation systems are designed. Some emphasis must be placed upon lessening contamination of ground and surrounding surface waters.

A modern potting system which includes a raw material conveyor, mixing bin, and automatic pot filling station.

Many chemicals which are presently a part of crop cultural methods and cannot be carried through the irrigation system must be applied by specialized methods. For many years the usual equipment used for this purpose was the sprayer, but several newer means of chemical application are now available. The method chosen will depend upon several factors, not the least of which is safety to personnel, plants, and the surrounding environment.

Application of chemicals is a very technical operation and often is quite expensive due to the need for supervision, preparation, and the cost of specialized chemicals. The successful realization of the intended result often hinges upon how easily and how precisely the equipment being used operates. The safety of crops and employees is also dependent upon reliable and accurate operation. These factors dictate that chemical application equipment be of initial high quality and be closely maintained on a regular basis.

Miscellaneous nursery and greenhouse equipment

Numerous specialized devices have been developed to cut down the amount of hand labor required in greenhouses and nurseries. Oftentimes a by-product or even a prime objective of using such equipment is a uniformity in performance which was unobtainable with hand action alone. Some machines even accomplish tasks which cannot be done manually.

Although some specialized devices are readily applicable to widely varying types of nursery or greenhouse operational methods, many are very job specific or condition specific.

A larger container plant business may be easily able to justify expenses for automatic seeders, plug dislodgers, instruments to test for various chemical compounds, carbon dioxide injectors, special rooting and seed germination facilities, and other even more specialized equipment. But a small operation cannot often expect to profit by trying to take advantage of every available device. Only a serious analysis of alternative means of accomplishing the objective will allow growers to make intelligent decisions.

Purchasing services or products from other suppliers is often a viable alternative to buying seldom used special equipment. Seedling plugs of difficult to germinate varieties, chemical tests, and rooted cuttings of slow to root plants are only a few of the many services and products which may be easily purchased to eliminate the need for all but the more common equipment.

Computers in the greenhouse or nursery

With so much information about computers being directed towards business managers nowadays, it is natural to conclude that running a profitable business without one is impossible. Although computers are certainly a godsend to productivity in many applications there are actually cases where attempts to employ computers might cause productivity declines.

Computer technology is most useful under conditions where repetitious tasks are involved. This is why computerization is often so satisfying, it enables humans to free themselves of monotonous details and concentrate upon more stimulating objectives which require creative thought.

No one can properly make decisions about whether or not to computerize particular tasks unless he or she possesses basic knowledge of computer applications. Even if experts are hired to determine the feasibility of employing computers, the ultimate evaluation of these experts' recommendations depends upon the manager responsible for approving implementation. A reasonable evaluation can be made with careful common sense logic most of the time but there are situations where some basic technical knowledge is indispensable.

If a grower is unwilling to critically evaluate the applicability of computer systems and if even the most basic understanding of computer technology is neglected, an attempt at computerization would most likely be unwise.

Complete and unmonitored control of basic business operations should not be turned over to people who are unqualified to integrate these operations into the total business plan. A few weeks spent becoming familiar with exactly what computers can and cannot do efficiently will allow individuals to form reasonably accurate assessments of whether or not such technology will benefit their business.

On the other hand, nursery and greenhouse managers might unwittingly neglect their principal job of providing overall management to the operation if they become overly involved in day-to-day computer system design, implementation, and operation. Managers must walk a thin line between being ignorant about what is going on and between excessive involvement in details.

In general terms, most nurseries and greenhouses would benefit to some degree from a simple computer installation. Any business which relies upon a large number of machines that require frequent checking will find some form of computer control of these machines helpful. Inventories, payrolls, accounts receivable, planting schedules, and equipment control are some types of repetitious tasks which computers handle well.

As computers and the satellite devices used with them continue to drop in price, not much justification is necessary to purchase at least a basic system. The Internet and e-mail provide growers a means of gathering information quickly, and this capability allows individuals to be much better managers. For example, if a problem turns up concerning crop nutrition, a live video conference with experts would allow them to visually assess the situation and perhaps prescribe immediate remedies. This process might have taken weeks to accomplish only a few years ago.

The economical availibility of handheld computer and communication devices is increasing at a rapid pace. These machines are particularly suited to nursery and greenhouse operations since they offer almost unlimited contact over large production areas and encourage easy entry of inventory and cultural data.

Numerous horticulturally related companies now maintain a website and the number is growing quickly. These sites will likely become the chief source of up-to-date information available for growers, to some extent replacing trade shows, catalogs, and trade magazines.

Large nurseries and greenhouses would certainly benefit a good deal by installing fairly sophisticated computer systems while many part time operations which produce only a small number of plants may not yet find the use of computers economical. The owners of these smaller businesses need not feel apprehensive about deciding to forgo the use of a computer if a realistic appraisal shows no tangible benefit can be expected.

Although computers are one of the most useful tools we have to help increase production in commercial enterprises, they have no justification unless a true need for their services exists. An informed assessment of computer capability and how it relates to the tasks at hand is the only credible means of determining whether or not to computerize and how much emphasis to place upon it.

Chapter 3

GREENHOUSE AND NURSERY MANAGEMENT

Creative, hard working people start their own businesses to achieve goals such as financial success, possession of power, or independence from others. These individuals are the entrepreneurs, the innovators of the business world. Quite often these entrepreneurs lack the aptitude for efficient management which is necessary to carry a project any distance beyond the starting line. Entrepreneurs may also have little time to be concerned with management. Numerous studies show that more businesses fail due to poor management than from any other cause. This fact should illustrate to every business person just how critical it is to develop well planned management strategy right from the start.

Entrepreneurs must force themselves to find time for management or allow someone else to fulfill this aspect of business. The founder of a small or mid-sized container plant business would seldom have the resources to hire full time managers nor would the founder normally be comfortable with other people taking over the idea and ushering it to completion. The business also benefits when the "idea" person who conceived of it participates in planning the strategies and techniques which ultimately lead to success. Most people starting a plant business enjoy playing an active role in management if adequate time is set aside to prevent an overly stressful situation from arising. A good basic understanding of what management involves and the methods of practicing it will make the duties easier to accomplish and more enjoyable.

WHAT IS MANAGEMENT?

Some form of management is practiced in every business whether the operator knows it or not, but a well conceived and successful management program does not just happen. It takes many hours of careful thought to delineate objectives and efficient means of reaching these objectives. Many more hours will also be spent in making sure all the different goals become integrated into a workable master plan.

It is difficult to define just where management duties begin or end. There will always be some overlap with the province of the entrepreneur and also with labor. Equally difficult is the task of stating hard and fast rules as to what constitutes a good management plan. Managers are paid well because of their individualistic approach toward devising a method of organizing and controlling a company successfully. If the process of devising a management plan for the thousands of unique business situations possible could be codified and set in stone, ordinary workers could look up the formula and apply it as well as anyone. Each business has a unique environment and requires an individualized management program. Only a person who has special capabilities, either as an innate gift or through training and experience, can organize an excellent management program.

Since management requires an individual approach, it is not surprising that several well planned programs for the same business may differ in some respects. The question of right or wrong is answered by the smooth operation and success of the business.

Management can be interpreted as falling into two broad categories: strategic management, which may only be practiced at crucial turning points in the life of a business; and tactical management, which includes the more concrete problems of organizing systems to accomplish stated objectives. The following discussions will point out the main components of a management plan. Examples of strategic and tactical management decisions are presented under each topic to familiarize the reader with the concepts. It must be remembered that each individual component should integrate with others when a management program is complete.

Since management is such a large and varied subject and because a thorough explanation of the many competing theories and methods in use would require at least a separate book, the author will relate only brief comments and examples as they pertain to horticultural businesses.

Business objectives

Businesses are started by people for different reasons or combinations of reasons. For many the chief objective is financial success, but a significant number of people begin in business mainly for a sense of personal satisfaction. Possession of power or recognition may also be important motivations. Most often the founder has several objectives in mind for the new business to satisfy. Business objectives should be enumerated and arranged in order of the importance they will assume in the new business; these objectives must not be in opposition to one another.

The development of a formal hierarchy of business objectives is one example of strategic management. These goals should be altered only when the needs of company principals or basic business conditions undergo fundamental changes. Decisions of this nature may be made only once in the lifetime of a business or they may be made several times over a period of many years.

Tactical management in the area of business objectives is concerned chiefly with the methods and organization used to accomplish the strategic goals set forth. If a person's main goal is financial gain, container plant crops and markets would be scrutinized to determine the most profitable combination with little regard for the personal satisfaction derived from working with them. When the primary goal is recognition within the community, tactical management decisions to donate plant material for community beautification may be made without undue concern for possible ill effects on company profits.

Tactical management decisions made to accomplish the major goals of a business must not be allowed to endanger the actual survival of the enterprise. Emphasis on goals other than profitability are valid as long as the business continues to remain in healthy financial shape. The enterprise must maintain at least minimal economic solvency or other goals will have little hope of being realized.

Production objectives

One example of a strategic crop production objective would be a decision to provide wholesale container plants for all retail garden shops in a prescribed area. An alternate decision might be to supply all plant material for a single retail outlet which is a joint venture with the grower's greenhouse or nursery. In another example, one firm may specialize in a single crop for regional or national distribution while other producers are committed to a wide variety of crops for local use.

Tactical production management is often altered considerably by the strategic production objectives one has in mind. Structures and machinery installed for a large wholesale operation may not be the most economical choices for a small retail firm. In addition, the tactical management of particular programs, such as pest control, are considerably complicated by the presence of retail customers and by location in a heavily populated area suitable for retail sales. Changing the strategic objectives of crop production usually necessitates adjustments in a much larger number of lower level management programs.

Labor objectives

Instituting broad goals to minimize labor costs through capital investment is an example of high level management. In order to realize this strategic goal one might employ tactical steps organizing crop production schedules which lend themselves to mechanization. In a further example, if maintaining a skilled year round work force is a strategic objective, then reasonably constant sales and production schedules are necessary to keep workers busy.

When labor resources are managed intelligently, half the battle towards a profitable greenhouse or nursery is already won. Labor is perhaps the most difficult area of management since one is dealing with individual people who have a variety of rather unpredictable emotions and needs. Understanding how to deal with people is more difficult than organizing production schedules or devising a financial records system.

Marketing and pricing objectives

The interrelatedness of objectives is demonstrated by the obvious effects different production goals would exert on marketing and pricing objectives. An objective of maximum possible production is seldom compatible with a goal of maximum price per unit sold. Businesses often develop a strategy of marketing to particular segments of the population based on such attributes as economic class, sex, and age. The theory is that one cannot be all things to all people. Management decisions made as a consequence of such a strategy must organize tactical marketing efforts to appeal to the group selected.

Marketing strategies, once conceived and implemented for a length of time, may be very difficult to change since the perception the public has of a business is influenced in great part by marketing efforts and vice versa. When an image is sufficiently implanted in the public mind, it may be impossible to successfully change the marketing strategy unless it coincides with this image. Changes in production, labor and investment strategies can normally be made reasonably easily if one is willing to exert the effort and incur additional expenses sometimes associated with radical change. A change in the nebulous area of public perception is, however, sometimes elusive no matter how much effort and money is spent.

Financial objectives

The idea of financial objectives seldom concerns inexperienced business persons. Most people entering business for the first time would think the goal of making a profit is enough. This is perhaps a valid approach when the business is young and not making much money. After a reasonable degree of success has been attained and the business is generating good profits, financial objectives generally need to be more sophisticated. When funds are accumulated in excess of what it takes to operate the present business, a decision must be made as to how this extra money will be utilized. It could be reinvested for expansion of the business, invested in other business interests, used for personal enjoyment, or set aside for children or for charitable purposes. The choices must be carefully weighed to prevent expensive mistakes which arise through improper money management.

Financial objectives will usually change as a person matures, with more emphasis being placed on providing for retirement through conservative investment while less money is allocated for business expansion (a sale of the operation may be expected when the owner retires). Older owners sometimes wish to set aside much of the business profits as gifts for children and grandchildren. The continued existence of the business after the owner's retirement or death must be carefully planned to avoid costly consequences and disruptions in management.

Tactical financial management must be tuned to the main objectives. Taxes, for example, will vary greatly with the uses to which business income is allocated. Money reinvested in the business is generally taxed differently than dividends or salaries distributed to the owner or shareholders. Careful watch must be kept on the everyday financial workings of the company to make sure there will be adequate resources available to accomplish the selected goals.

The hard won gains of a lifetime of successful business operation can be lost in a few months if financial objectives and management methods are not properly planned out.

Integration of management decisions

In the previous discussion of management objectives, only a few examples were presented to acquaint readers with the general types of problems which may be encountered. It should be apparent that a great number of management decisions will be made in even a small container plant business. An essential feature of management duties is the integration of separate objectives and decisions into a compatible whole. All parts of a management plan must function harmoniously together. Much effort and expense can be saved by designing a management program before commencing operations. The specifics of management will vary with (among other considerations) the business's geographic location, but the need for a basic management plan remains constant worldwide.

ECONOMICS OF GREENHOUSE AND NURSERY OPERATION

The following discussion is aimed primarily at presenting methods which enable the reader to calculate the costs of crop production and then determine what prices to charge for each product. Certain related topics are included to show how prices and costs may change with different modes of production. A section concerned mainly with sales and marketing will follow and expand more fully on pricing.

Production costs

The first step in determining production costs is to gather up all the expenses of the greenhouse or nursery and arrange them into logical categories for later reference. If one has not operated a container growing business previously, it will be necessary to estimate all costs as accurately as possible. Costs can be estimated with a reasonable degree of precision if care is taken to be thorough in locating all potential outlays and current prices are used in calculating the actual cost of these outlays. Outlays or expenses are normally split into fixed and variable categories. If an economic model is constructed which has compartments for each possible expense, all that needs to be done to arrive at an up to date growing cost is to feed in current prices for each outlay. Table 3 illustrates a hypothetical model for both fixed and variable production costs. It should be pointed out that no two businesses will have the same costs and some managers may wish to interchange certain fixed and variable costs depending on their operation and inclination.

Readers should study the categories of fixed and variable costs quite carefully so that they understand the relationship of these costs to their own particular operation. The importance of certain categories changes with the type of buildings, interest rates, local labor costs, etc. Production costs vary considerably with the location and type of operation. Some experts prefer to assign labor, fuel, fertilizers, and insecticides to variable costs since the cost of these items changes considerably with different crops and methods of operation. Larger companies which specialize in a few crops and sell in a highly competitive market may wish to detail the cost of each crop more carefully and put more costs in the variable category. Placing more items in the fixed cost category generally simplifies cost accounting but tends to de-emphasize legitimate cost differences which may occur between crops. When deciding how to arrange a cost accounting system, some consideration should be given to the fact that the more complicated an analysis becomes there is less likelihood of it being employed on a regular basis.

Several items in Table 3 warrant further emphasis since some people tend to forget them entirely or do not adequately address their importance. All financial contributions to the business by the owner should be charged as an expense. This means that the owner is compensated for any land, vehicles, buildings, cash, or other items which he or she owns and which are utilized by the business. A fair means of accomplishing this is to figure the value of the item and then charge at least prime rate interest for its use.

Owners should also make sure that any labor (including management time) they or their family contribute to the business is included under labor expenses. Making out actual paychecks to the party involved is the easiest way to assure this situation is taken care of properly. Since the two cost

Table 3
Cost analysis categories and totals for container plant crops.

Fixed production costs	$ Per Year
Interest on land, machinery, vehicles, and buildings which are financed....................	
Depreciation of applicable assests.......................	
Cost of renting or leasing business items.............	
Property tax, if any...	
Insurance, property and liability........................	
Electricity...	
Greenhouse fuel, if applicable.............................	
Vehicle fuel..	
Labor, includes management and sales................	
Fertilizer, insecticides, water, cultural supplies...	
Repair and maintenance..	
Bad accounts...	
Telephone, postage, office supplies.....................	
Miscellaneous..	

Total fixed costs per year....................................

Variable production costs	$ Per Unit
Plant material—cuttings, seedlings, seeds.............	
Containers...	
Soil..	
Labor—above normal use for special labor intensive crops...	
Special expenses for crop......................................	

Total variable cost per unit.................................

Note: Freight should be included in purchase price of all items. Certain fixed costs could be treated as variable costs if the situation warrants.

areas mentioned above often account for over one half of total fixed costs, failure to fairly compensate the owner for his or her contribution in these areas will result in grossly underestimated cost projections.

"Depreciation" is a term used to signify the reduction in value which occurs to certain items that possess a limited lifetime of use. If a vehicle has an anticipated lifetime of 10 years, it is obvious that it will lose some value each year. Most people readily understand that the most rapid loss of value for vehicles occurs in the first few years (accelerated depreciation). Other assets are sometimes accounted for by "straight line depreciation", in which an equal loss of value theoretically occurs each year. Depreciation, whichever way it is handled, must be allocated as a cost for the producer.

Inexperienced business persons sometimes fail to anticipate such things as bad accounts and all the small items which form the category of miscellaneous expenses. These types of miscalculations are often at the root of business failures. A business, particularly a new one, simply cannot succeed unless the manager has a reasonably accurate idea of how much it is costing to run the business.

The expense percentages shown in Figure 1 are not typical for all container growing businesses. As examples: Larger wholesale greenhouses may have considerably lower labor costs (due to mechanization) but larger marketing costs, while an outdoor tree nursery would likely have higher costs for soil and containers than the greenhouse pictured but less repair costs (assuming the outdoor nursery had less buildings). Each business will possess its own expense pattern, but we may assume that it would appear relatively similar to Figure 1. With a few educated assumptions, a predicted expense pattern for a different container growing business could be estimated.

After fixed and variable cost totals are established, the per plant cost of production can be figured out. The best way to accomplish this task is to establish a simple formula which best approximates the actual production methods being used. Two commonly employed formulas are explained below. Variations of these formulas may be devised to serve particular circumstances.

The reduction of total yearly fixed costs to an expression of weekly fixed cost per square foot of growing space is widely practiced by analysts in the greenhouse and nursery industry when crops require less than a year to mature and when several varieties of crops are grown which occupy different amounts of space.

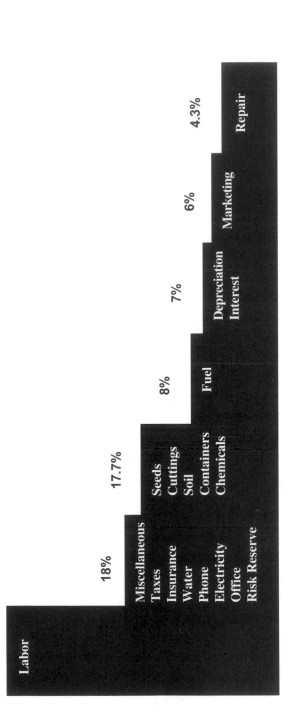

Fig. 1

Relative greenhouse production expenses. Compiled from a typical year from a small wholesale facility in the northern United States. Sells product primarily to own retail outlet; marketing costs are low as a result. See text for further discussion. Total expenses equal 100%.

Total fixed costs	÷ 52 =	Weekly fixed cost for greenhouse or nursery	÷	Square feet of growing space in greenhouse or nursery	=	Weekly fixed production cost per square foot of growing area

The end product of this equation can be used to quickly calculate the cost of producing a plant unit.

Weekly fixed production cost per sq. ft. of growing area	x	Number of sq. ft. of growing area occupied per plant unit	x	Number of weeks occupying growing area	+	Per unit variable costs	=	Production cost per plant unit

An even simpler method of deriving production cost per plant unit can be employed when the entire crop is composed of plants which occupy the same amount of space or when the amount of space occupied is felt to be an inconsequential cost (the latter case might arise when a grower was not producing to full capacity).

Total fixed costs per year	x	Proportionate part of year required for production of crop	=	Total fixed costs per crop

The product of the above equation is then reduced to an expression of production cost per plant unit by using the following steps.

Total fixed costs per crop	÷	Total number of container plants produced	+	Variable cost per plant unit	=	Production costs per plant unit

People who are new to the container plant business will have need to utilize formulas like these quite often until they become familiar with the cost and pricing schedules of each crop. Growers should carefully analyze the production costs of each variety and size not only to have a basis for pricing decisions but also to see what crops have the most favorable production costs in relation to the selling price which can be obtained. It is not unusual to find that more money can be made by emphasizing one variety or container size over another.

It is apparent from the formulas that, when operating at full capacity, the amount of time it takes to grow a crop and the amount of space each plant occupies are generally the prime factors which cause variation in production prices per plant unit. Only in rare cases can either one of these factors be ignored. When efficiency in either of these factors can be improved, the result will be reduced production costs.

Growers must recognize that some production area is empty at times but fixed costs for this vacant space continue to mount. If 3 crops are normally realized during the year, each crop would be charged for 17.3 weeks of growing space (if we assume each crop required equal growing time). Or we could say that each crop required 0.33 years growing time if the second formula for computation was employed. Of course every crop does not require the same length of time to grow but vacant space must be assigned to each crop in an equitable manner.

If only 1 crop of trees and shrubs were realized per year then the entire year's fixed costs would have to be charged against this crop even if only 3 months were required for actual production. Readers can easily recognize that where total fixed costs are high, a strenuous effort must be made to keep growing space productive at all times but when total fixed costs are low, there is less incentive to insure continuous usage of growing space. Outdoor nursery grounds are usually much less expensive to operate than is a comparable area of greenhouse space. The greenhouse manager is, therefore, required to account for space utilization more completely than is the outdoor grower.

Pricing

There are several means of determining selling prices but, realistically, prices are usually arrived at by a combination of methods. Setting prices is a difficult task and may involve considering a number of factors to arrive at what is thought to be a composite price which reflects production and market realities in the best possible fashion.

In retail situations a standard markup over production or purchase costs is often employed. These retail markups are usually fairly well established through conventional use in the industry. Many growers and retailers also arrive at prices, partially at least, by responding to competition and some managers simply charge whatever they feel the market will bear.

A detailed analysis to arrive at retail prices which yield a fair profit is rather difficult since a large array of items are usually sold. This is why standard markups are common in the retail trade. Wholesalers who market a limited number of plant varieties and sizes can quite easily determine reasonably exact production costs for each item and then establish a selling price which reflects an assured and desirable profit. The computer is a wonderful analytical tool which now allows growers and retailers to routinely plug in new figures once model formulas for operation have been constructed. No clear definition exists of what constitutes desirable profit; this depends a good deal upon the expectations of the owner. It is certain, however, that profits for all capital invested in the business should at least equal the monetary return possible from equal risk investments available elsewhere.

Any profits over and above the level where an owner is adequately compensated for all work done and for all capital invested in the operation should be considered as a premium. Some business people consider this premium as a necessary reward for being in business while others do not feel they deserve any excess profits. This is why two companies selling similar plants which cost an equal amount to produce can both feel comfortable even though the price they charge per plant is different. If interest at prevailing rates is charged as an expense for all money the owner has invested in buildings, land, machinery, and operating costs, a return on investment need not be added to the cost of production since the interest recovered acts as a return on the investment. This assumes that the owner is satisfied with a return equal to the interest rate, and that he or she is being adequately compensated for any labor contributed; if not, additional markup would be added to the selling price. Prices should reflect a profit at the production level and at the retail level if both operations are combined in the same business. The cost of retail activity must be included as an additional expense.

Inexperienced people should always rely on a cost analysis and check the return on investments when setting prices for crops. As they become more familiar with the cost of raising different crops and the prices necessary to make a decent profit, adjustments in price can be made without a detailed analysis. When major price moves are necessary every

1 or 2 years, costs and returns on all crops should be analyzed.

In reality, it is not always possible to establish rigid prices according to the return on investment expected. It may be necessary to meet competitors' prices in certain instances, or to lower prices if customers exhibit a great deal of resistance. On the other hand, it may be possible to obtain higher prices than necessary on selected crops. Growers should be on the lookout for and concentrate efforts on those crops which exhibit strong demand and a high rate of return while reducing those crops which show a low rate of return due to strong competition, high production costs, or consumer resistance.

If greenhouse and nursery owners concentrate upon intelligent marketing and pricing and upon those crops which are highly profitable, they will likely be successful. It is not unethical to receive returns on investments of 3 or 4 times that which would satisfy most people. If a person has the capability and does the work necessary to identify and take advantage of rewarding situations, he or she should be compensated accordingly. Most owners would be happy to receive a 10-15% return on all money invested in the business in addition to drawing a suitable salary for their own work in the company. It is possible to increase this rate of return markedly through careful growing practices, cost control, effective marketing, and wise business management.

The prices a business charges will generally have a marked effect on the volume of merchandise sold. Other factors will affect volume but price is a major consideration in most cases. Greenhouse and nursery owners must sometimes alter pricing to achieve a certain level of production. An example might be where the minimum order for bare root nursery stock purchased for potting is considerably more than could be sold at desired prices. The grower must decide whether to lower prices to the point where minimum shipments can be sold without loss or if it is better to omit this crop. Another example might be where a grower wishes to fill an entire greenhouse with a single crop which requires a particular temperature and cultural practices. It is possible that the selling price may have to be lowered in order to move a full greenhouse of one variety instead of a mixture, but the savings in ease of culture may also lower growing costs. There are many cases where the price versus volume dilemma will need to be addressed. Growers must weigh the advantages and disadvantages carefully so that the most profitable overall course is taken.

Many business people become overly cost conscious, trying to save a few pennies when their time could be better spent in an effort to realize top prices and increased yield. A simple example will demonstrate the tremendous effect a small rise in prices or yield will have on profits:

10% Price Rise

1 plant sold at $5.00 - $4.50 production cost = $0.50 profit

1 plant sold at $5.50 - $4.50 production cost = $1.00 profit or 100% increase in profits

---

10% Increase in Yield

10 plants sold at $5 = $50 - $45 production cost = $5 profit

11 plants sold at $5 = $55 - $45 production cost = $10 profit or 100% increase in profits

It may often be easier to institute price rises or increase yield than to save a like amount on costs. All growers buy supplies at about the same price as long as they are reasonably careful to compare prices and purchase in larger quantities, but not everyone sells at the same price or obtains the same yield. Yield and sales price are in large degree determined by the capabilities of the manager and grower.

Record keeping

It should be evident by now that profitable management of a greenhouse or nursery depends on knowing how different aspects of the business will affect each other. A capable manager must be able to predict the eventual outcome of actions taken. Good records not only document what took place in the past but they also allow one to prepare models which can predict the future with some degree of success. Even in a very small business no one can hope to accurately remember all that needs to be recalled.

Growers and managers should analyze carefully what data needs to be recorded and the most useful system of recording it. Collecting unnecessary data and organizing records in a fashion which prevents easy access is a waste of time and often discourages personnel from performing these tasks. People are more likely to collect information and use record systems frequently if they can see a well organized plan behind their actions.

Cutting or sowing Date		Open Flat	Direct Sow		Plug Flat		Crop #, Initial Pot Later Pot Size	# Finished Flats or Plants to Plant			Xtra Crops		Comments
Sched	Act		Plate Size	# Times to Seed	406	200		Sched	Act	+ -	Date Sown	# Flats	
11/8	Sow							Small					
	Date							Crop					
							1-10" Pot	25					
							2	30					
							3	30					
							4	25					
								Total:	Total:	Total:		Total:	

Comments: Dracenas, Vinca, try some with Baucopa   Variety: 10" Pot, Begonia Non-Stop   Year:00

A simple notebook system for recording essential crop data in a small greenhouse operation. As crops are planted and marketed, the blanks will be filled in.

In a small greenhouse or nursery there are two relatively distinct areas about which records should be kept. Important aspects of crop culture must be faithfully registered at the time each task is performed. Inexperienced growers usually think they will remember the important aspects of crop culture. It is true they may recall 75% of the information accurately but the other 25% is rather fuzzy. Acceptable crops may be produced without good records but exceptional quality plants which are timed properly for the market and grown in quantities which will eliminate overproduction losses can only be grown by people who have a proper respect for accurately recorded information.

At the very least, crop records should include the propagation or shipping date, number and size of plants grown, ready-for-sale date, number of plants sold and price received, and any cultural procedures specific to the crop. The correct variety name must, of course, accompany each record sheet. Some growers prefer to collect more detailed data concerning weather conditions, labor costs, spacing dates, photographs of crop progress and quality, etc. There is no end to the details one can keep track of — make it brief!

Financial records must be maintained not only for business use but also for satisfying the requirements of local, state, and federal laws. The minimum amount of information required will be determined by the need to comply with these laws. Data needed for filing federal tax returns will generally be sufficient for most business purposes if records are organized so that information on pricing, sales, and profitability of different aspects of the business can be retrieved at will. Financial records should allow a reasonably capable person to appraise past performance and plan future operations intelligently.

Larger companies may need to keep files on other business areas. Labor or personnel matters become more important as a company grows, managers must then evaluate the need for beginning a formal employee file. Governmental regulations can become quite complex in this area and one should become familiar with the important laws concerning employees and working conditions. Periodic evaluation of employee performance must also be kept track of as the business grows beyond the stage where managers have close daily contact with the work force. Repair and maintenance records become necessary when the manager cannot accurately recall the necessary details to assure proper care of buildings and equipment. Many inexpensive computer programs are available which will adequately address business data and aid in tax preparation. Specific software for filing tax forms are of great assistance, but they do not eliminate the need for careful tax planning and knowledge of the law.

It should be emphasized that records are merely a business tool and must not become an end in themselves. If the owner or manager of a greenhouse or nursery firm is not capable of or inclined toward keeping business records, it is possible to have a large part of them handled by accounting or bookkeeping specialists. It should be realized that this is another expense and these specialists may often not perform their work as conscientiously as people employed directly by the business. Taxes are an extremely important aspect of running a business, especially when it becomes successful. Tax planning can greatly affect the after tax profits of a business.

Risk control

Growing and selling live plants is a risky business. It is imperative that managers fully realize this important point and take appropriate steps to avoid unpleasant consequences which are bound to arise if they fail to do so. Hailstorms, extreme heat or cold, insects and diseases, market mistiming — all of these potentially damaging factors (and more) await the unsuspecting.

Fortunately, 90% of such calamities can be avoided entirely through careful advance planning and the faithful execution of necessary precautions. The remaining 10% are unavoidable but can be managed just like other problems which arise in any business. Liability and property insurance is an important aspect of risk control but there are many situations which cannot be covered by standard policies. In these latter cases, the greenhouse or nursery owner must seek out insurance providers who will cover such special circumstances (often very expensive) or accept the risk personally by building a reserve fund which is specifically meant to cover risk factors.

Simply by recognizing the inherent risk involved in the live plant business and by taking steps of avoidance or control, greenhouse and nursery managers bring this factor into the realm of ordinary problems rather than allowing major catastrophes to develop. The author favors a program where by a small additional charge is automatically built into each product's sales price. This assures that the risk "premium" will be collected, but it is only part of the solution: The "premium must be safely segregated from normal operating funds (it must be used only for the intended purpose).

Overemphasizing the importance of risk in the live plant business is not the author's intention. However, many years as a commercial grower have convinced me that this subject warrants the specific attention of all growers (especially smaller ones).

THINK AND PLAN FOR INCREASED PROFITS

Everyone who operates a greenhouse or nursery business must realize that knowledge (not soil, water, or other physical components) is the ingredient most necessary for success. No amount of hard work or luck can compensate over the long run for good knowledge of the many and varied subject areas which comprise the science and art of ornamental horticulture.

Profits from growing container plants can be increased significantly by operating according to a well thought out plan which emphasizes cultural, marketing, and management practices conducive to high revenues while minimizing expenses. To devise such a plan, managers and growers must carefully analyze each production and marketing step and adjust them to produce maximum profit, then one must assess whether the individual steps will integrate successfully. Many of the practices which lead to higher profits have been alluded to previously; the following information will summarize some of the more important ones.

A profitable plant business is fostered by integrating many different facets of growing and selling, undue emphasis cannot be placed on isolated areas. The business should progress with the technological, marketing, and financial environment but change for the sake of change must be avoided. Profitable operations are built upon crop production and marketing activities which are reproducible from one year to the next. Sticking to established production schedules from year to year saves time in both labor and management and also reduces the risk of crop failure or unsuccessful marketing. Changes in operation should be made only after careful study and, if possible, test projects. As an example, many new poinsettia varieties have been introduced in the past few years which are vast improvements over those available 10 or 20 years ago. These new varieties, however, often have specific timing schedules and growth requirements which must be learned through practical experience before a grower could feel safe about switching to them.

Market conditions will change periodically and influence the relative proportions of crops which should be grown. Growers must identify trends early so that new crops or changes in emphasis may be phased in gradually. Waiting until trends are full blown and then altering production schedules drastically all at one time is an invitation to disaster. Introduction of new plant varieties should follow the same cautious path. Certain new varieties will become the best sellers of the future but 90% of them will be relegated to obscurity after thorough commercial production and marketing tests. The fortunes of a well run greenhouse or nursery will not rise or fall on the basis of being the first to offer a new, highly publicized variety but rather on whether that variety has been trialed carefully enough to insure consumer satisfaction and long term profitability in production.

Optimum utilization of growing space and equipment is a major factor in increasing profits. In addition to growing plants in the most profitable manner during strong marketing seasons, managers must attempt to sell crops at those times of the year when slack market demand causes excess production capacity. More plants can also be produced by lessening the length of time a crop is growing. Some growers specialize in buying plants from other sources which will mature in a few weeks. In this manner revenues are increased greatly because of the larger number of crops which can be raised in a year. The drawbacks to this program are that purchasing larger plants increases expenses and causes the greenhouse or nursery to depend on the reliability of outside growers.

One fertile area for reducing costs lies in mechanizing the work process. Each step in the production sequence should be analyzed to see if mechanization is possible. A cost analysis of manual labor versus machines will then enable the grower to decide which avenue is most profitable. Relatively minor comparisons may be made by constructing a simple chart with side-by-side cost and productivity estimates for the annual labor versus mechanical alternatives. The two columns can then be tallied to see if there is a readily apparent difference between one or the other. In those cases where no easy decision can be made, or where very important production processes are involved, a more complex (and hopefully more accurate) analysis method will need to be employed. Test runs which yield real comparison data for the specific process are advisable if at all possible. It should be pointed out that mechanization may sometimes be desirable even though it is slightly more expensive than manual labor. If mechanization permits the grower to go through the busy spring season with only a slight increase in the amount of labor hired, much of the confusion and inefficiency inherent when large numbers of seasonal workers are employed will be eliminated.

Some growers are machine lovers and will buy all types of gadgets without subjecting the purchase to a cost and need analysis. Small operations can seldom take advantage of the numerous automated systems which are profitable for larger businesses. A small grower will generally be better off to limit the purchase of machinery to those items which can be utilized regularly. One advantage of using manual labor is that when business is slow, employees can be laid off whereas machinery, once purchased, is a continuing expense.

Certain aspects of a container plant business may be more profitable than others. Managers should evaluate the plant production and marketing records of their business and concentrate their future efforts on the most profitable crops possible. Hundreds of greenhouses in the United States have been forced out of cut flower production in the past decade by foreign competition. Those managers who detected this trend early and switched production to potted flowers, bedding plants, and foliage plants have generally prospered while their less observant counterparts are out of business. Propagating plants for other greenhouses and nurseries can be very lucrative but usually requires more skilled labor, more initial investment, and a longer time to establish reliable markets. If growers have the patience and resources to specialize in propagation it may be one means of remaining profitable in the long run. Each greenhouse or nursery manager should periodically analyze the need for changing his or her operation to fit newly arisen business conditions.

Unless management is constantly on the alert, there are several potential inefficiencies in production and marketing which can lead to serious problems. Labor is usually the largest single expense in growing plants. Greenhouses and nurseries which have an industrious and capable work force are in a strong position to be competitive and successful. The most important knowledge one can possess in building a solid core of employees is that money is seldom the prime motivation for workers to be highly productive. Within the framework of a traditional fixed pay schedule, additional wages do not result in significant increases in productivity as long as the salaries paid are reasonably competitive with similar job opportunities in the area. Incentive and profit sharing programs are probably conducive to increased productivity but require additional bookkeeping and administrative work which many managers feel is not worth the effort when applied to lower level employees. Study after study in recent years has generally shown that such benefits as flexible work schedules, pleasant working conditions, and an interesting job are more important to most employees than is extra money.

The pay schedule for horticultural employees has traditionally been on the low end. This makes it difficult for container plant growers to pay high wages and still remain competitive in the marketplace. Workers who do not have a genuine love of plants seldom last long in the greenhouse or nursery. Managers must emphasize the positive aspects of horticultural work as much as possible to makeup for generally low wages. If hours can be somewhat flexible and the working atmosphere and conditions pleasant, little trouble will be encountered in attracting suitable workers who find horticultural work preferable to other available employment.

Many people in horticulture feel that the generally unimpressive wages within the industry are something of which we should be ashamed. However, the many other rewards associated with working as a "plant person" should be stressed more often. There is nothing dramatic which can be accomplished in the short term to alter the existing economic facts, but the advantages of horticulture as a career can be brought forward at every opportunity.

In the past, businesses in ornamental horticulture could depend upon some amount of inexpensive labor from temporary migrants. However, as immigration and labor laws become more restrictive, this labor pool may prove more unavailable, thus tending to help push overall wages up in the less-skilled positions of the industry.

Managers should review labor trends which periodically appear in trade magazines. This information is not only helpful in setting wage policies, it can aid in providing unbiased data to workers when wage negotiations occur.

Industrious and intelligent workers do not guarantee high productivity. Their activities must be organized by management into a structure which leaves little room for wasteful practices. Managers who are constantly at odds with the majority of employees over a lack of productivity should look to themselves as the primary cause of the problem. Either the proper people are not being hired for the job or work is not sufficiently organized so that workers can give their best effort. Chronic problems may arise with a particular employee and occasional troubles can surface with other workers even when management is excellent.

Communicating objectives and instructions to employees is a particularly troublesome area. As a rule, carefully worded written work orders will result in increased productivity and eliminate acrimonious debate about who should have done what or who did what wrong. This type of communication procedure also frees the manager from constant interruptions during the day so that he or she may find sufficient time for productive tasks. Effective communication requires that it be planned in advance and carefully analyzed for clear presentation to employees.

As any business grows, it becomes necessary for top management to delegate tasks and authority. It then follows that a process must be instituted so that the performance of the people entrusted can be evaluated. Delegation and evaluation are vital concepts in modern business; they are often the stumbling block which prevents a small business from growing further. Some people posses a natural ability to delegate and evaluate, but for most of us these talents are gained only through extended study and experience.

Maintaining an effective work force is a never ending job. There is always a certain amount of turnover, even among longtime employees. Training replacements and temporary spring help is an ongoing task. However, if several good people are employed throughout the year, training of new people can be entrusted to them. Periodic sessions should be held with employees in private and as a group to go over operational policy, introduce new material, and discuss any problems which may have arisen since the last session. These encounters cannot be held too frequently or the degree of importance employees place on them decreases. Supervisors should be judged on their ability to organize work efficiently and motivate workers to accomplish objectives, while lower level employees must display a willingness to work and a concern for the future of the company. Anyone who does not display these qualities will fail to contribute to a successful business climate.

Many greenhouses and nurseries are operated in an inefficient manner because crops are not tailored to fit the market. The result is a high percentage of unsold plants. Successful operations should dump no more than five percent of their crops. When dumpage rates exceed this level, there is definitely a problem in the planning stages. The problem of unsold plants may be solved by constantly growing too few to meet market demand. However, this practice reduces revenue considerably and encourages customers to find their merchandise elsewhere. The objective is to satisfy market needs and have as few plants as possible left over.

After the crop is sold payment must be received. The profits from several sales can be erased by one bad account. Many experts advise that strict collection policies be enforced without fail. This type of policy can lead to the loss of some very good customers who simply do not pay attention to due dates on bills. The best insurance against bad debts is to know customers well. If there is little personal contact with customers, a strict collection policy is best. Overdue accounts constitute an additional expense to the business. This money could be used to finance operations or be put in an interest bearing account. When past due accounts are not charged interest, the cost of carrying these accounts must be reflected in the price of plants.

Periodic reviews of greenhouse and nursery costs enable managers to notice changes in the price of supplies, labor, services, and fuel before there is any serious impact on profits. Cost reviews will also uncover excessive or wasteful use of materials. Buying supplies at the right price is the first step in controlling costs; but even more important is the need to prevent wasteful use in the business operation.

Each individual business may display different sizes at which it is most profitable relative to the capital invested. A small backyard greenhouse or nursery may be extremely profitable as long as it can be operated by the owner and overhead expenses are shared with the owner's residence. If the business expands and overhead is not shared, the business then must be large enough to make full economic use of the new site. Whenever expansion is considered, it should be determined whether or not this action will contribute toward making the business more of an optimum economic unit.

Many greenhouse and nursery owners become obsessed with meeting the price of competitors. It should be understood that plant prices are relative entities and must vary with the quality and services offered. Persons who are knowledgeable about plants should market not only a product but their expertise as well. There are numerous businesses and consumers willing to pay extra for the services and convenience offered as part of the price.

Success in the container plant growing business is achieved through a combination of ingredients. Hard work, perseverance, vision, and luck all play their part but one cannot hope to rely on these qualities alone; a thorough knowledge of the economic principles inherent to the business is also necessary.

SELLING THE CROP

Brief references to selling container plants have already been made in several previous sections. There is now a need to bring these points together, to expand on them, and to present additional topics which pertain to sales and marketing.

Everyone who grows plants as a business should have a well thought out plan for selling the product. The great majority of finished trees, potted flowers, bedding plants, and tropical foliage is sold directly by the grower to either retail outlets or the end consumer. In other words, a middleman distributor is not used. These self-directed channels of distribution require that the grower become intimately familiar with sales techniques and theory. Direct sales to retail shops or consumers may seem to be an inconvenience to those growers who prefer to concentrate their skills on plant culture, but it is also a blessing in that it gives them a good measure of control over the promotion and pricing of their products. Many cut flower producers sell at auctions or to middleman distributors and consequently have little to say about how flowers are marketed or what price they will receive. They are in a passive market posture much like the rest of American agriculture. In certain locations and under special circumstances a large percentage of ornamental plants may be sold through auctions or distributors, but this is not regularly the case. The large horticultural auctions in The Netherlands are a prime example of the exception.

Fundamental marketing decisions

Each grower must make some basic decisions about the nature of his or her business before much progress can be made in the direction of developing a coherent sales program. Is the operation to be wholesale or retail or a combination of both? Will it emphasize services and convenience to customers as well as plants or will it be mainly production oriented, with customers fending for themselves in the selection and care of plants? The choices made here will affect many aspects of the business.

In the last few years, numerous plant growers who previously sold mostly to a wholesale clientele have been forced into offering at least a portion of their crop on the retail level. The intense price competition caused by mass marketers has forced these wholesalers to increase their profit margin by dealing directly with the public and by offering some revenue generating services along with the plants, trees, and flowers they sell. Most of this change has proven successful as long as the grower does not perpetuate the rock bottom price strategy of the mass market chain stores.

People who are primarily interested in the technical aspects of plant culture and who have little desire to spend a large portion of their time devising sales programs would most likely be happier as wholesalers. This is not to say that marketing skills are not important to the wholesale trade but sales are confined to one level rather than two and, generally, fewer sales contacts must be made. A person who enjoys contact with consumers and has skills as a salesperson would very likely enjoy managing a retail greenhouse or nursery. A mix of the two marketing channels might prove more satisfying to some people.

Whether one prefers a wholesale or a retail business may have little bearing on what is possible. Wholesale operations usually require more initial capital to begin and considerable risk may be present in growing the first crops in the hope that a few large accounts can be landed. Many more plants need to be raised in the wholesale business because the markup over expenses is lower than in retail sales, thus operating expenses and investment in buildings and machinery are greater. The competitive situation in a locality may dictate whether a wholesale or retail business should be set up. A mixture of the two levels of sales is very difficult to combine since other retailers are reluctant to depend on their supplies from a competitor. To a certain extent, wholesale and retail businesses have different objectives and doing a good job at one level of sales may preclude successful operation in the other.

Businesses in the United States have tended to diverge into two different categories over the past several decades: those who offer full customer service with their products and those who provide little or no services with merchandise. The owner or manager of a full service outlet is likely to be a professional in the particular product line sold while those businesses offering little service may be operated by persons whose main interest is merchandising.

The horticultural industry has reflected these national trends. At the retail level today approximately fifty percent of plant products are sold in a self service atmosphere. Forty years ago very few plants, trees, and flowers were offered outside the traditional full service store. The result of these marketing trends has been generally lower prices to the consumer but in many cases a serious drop in quality and customer satisfaction. The problem of quality in self service stores is not caused by the sales strategy but rather through most managers' insistence on emphasizing low price rather than quality at a reasonable price. The chain and grocery store personnel handling plant material often have no training at all in buying, marketing, or caring for the product. This situation is improving as experience is gained by everyone involved. Greenhouses and tree nurseries face similar problems when dealing with chain retailers, but there are specifics that differ. Trees and shrubs are generally not so perishable as are greenhouse products, but trees and shrubs generally must be more closely adapted to the local environment.

There are opportunities for plant sales in every level of service and product combination but the operator must be aware that choosing one or the other will affect many phases of the business. The battle between traditional stores and self service outlets has perhaps reached a stalemate where neither is losing or gaining a great deal of market share. Any greenhouse or nursery which doesn't focus their production and marketing upon a carefully selected portion of the industry will likely fail to remain competitive.

The great opportunities in retail horticulture for the new century will belong to those people who devise sales methods which emphasize top quality and reasonable prices along with competent services when they are requested. Customers would then have the privacy of self service shopping but with knowledgeable professionals available for further information or service.

The perishable nature of plants along with the complexities of their proper care and use will always require trained people to handle and sell them if customers are to be satisfied. Low price may entice consumers to purchase plants for the first time but only satisfactory performance of the product will encourage customers to return.

To a lesser degree, people who enter the wholesale container plant business must make a choice to concentrate upon product or upon services. Delivery to stores, decoration and pricing, care tags, and display upkeep are some of the services a wholesaler may offer to customers. Other growers may sell strictly plants for pickup at the greenhouse or nursery. Obviously a manager of a more service-oriented business would have more diverse problems to deal with.

As ornamental plant producers have faced the rise of larger and more powerful outlets, the price growers receive for their products has become dangerously low in many cases. Large growers, especially, have reached the point where plants, trees, and flowers are considered commodity items rather than semi-artistic creations. There is very little growers can do under such conditions except to continue educating the public about the true value of their product and to refuse business where the price does not sufficiently reimburse the grower for production costs and acceptable profits.

Although this lamentable state of price dictation by monster retailers is a natural phenomenon of the capitalistic marketplace (and as such, it will play itself out until equilibrium is reached), the greed (another natural phenomenon) of growers has simply fueled the intensity and pace of the process. Many larger growers sow the seeds of their own demise by begging retailers to accept product at almost any price. Some large growers are indeed making good money supplying the large volumes of plants which mega-retailers can move at extremely low prices. However, there are many more that teeter on the edge of bankruptcy or are earning less for the time they invest than could be expected working in a decent 9-5 job.

From the start of this price degrading process, there have been a large number of plant producers who refuse to play the loser's game of chasing every order regardless of whether it will yield a profit. They emphasize quality, plant artistry, and proper plant adaptability to the environmental site.

As we enter the 21st century, the ornamental plant industry in developed countries has evolved to a point where relatively few large growers are truly successful. They manage to survive on the basis of modern efficiency even though the prices they receive are low. There are numerous small growers who also enjoy good profits through carefully nurturing the artistic and service aspects of their products. Both groups of survivors are good managers, but they manage with differing strategies. The growers who failed to adapt successfully to new conditions have been lost by the wayside. This fact is borne out by USDA statistics which show a slight decrease in the number of United States growers from 1993 to 1996.

No attempt has been made to exhaust the ramifications which a choice between retail or wholesale and full service or self service may have on the operation of a plant growing business. The reader will hopefully be stimulated to reflect carefully on his or her psychological makeup before attempting to make any such decision. A common sense evaluation of the possible combinations of marketing strategy will enable potential managers to predict the varied effect such a choice will have on other aspects of the business. One must also base these fundamental marketing decisions on factual observation of the particular market needs in the chosen locality, or choose the desired marketing strategy and discover a locality suitable for implementing it.

PLANNING FOR MAXIMUM SALES

Owners and managers of plant growing operations should perform a careful self-evaluation to determine if they possess the qualities necessary to formulate and lead a sales program. It often happens that good growers are not especially competent sales persons, requiring that someone else should be placed in charge of this area. In smaller establishments, it may not be feasible to have separate sales personnel, in which case it is necessary for the manager or grower to become as proficient as possible in this field through careful study.

Some people organize and carry out good sales programs without ever knowing how they did it. Even when company sales are adequate or better, an effort should be made to identify the reasons behind the success. This is necessary so that key ingredients in a winning combination are not changed unknowingly and so that the formula becomes formalized for use by future personnel. The essential points of a good sales program should be recorded in the same manner a grower keeps records of plant culture in the greenhouse or nursery. Understanding exactly why a business is successful in its sales efforts will help in predicting how new and different lines of merchandise will be accepted. Whenever possible, business managers should rely upon factual information (numerical data is best) rather than hazy personal opinions or outright guesses. Facts are the currency of modern business.

The appearance of a business is an extremely important factor in promoting sales. Well maintained facilities and displays give customers the impression of success. People prefer to shop at stores they think are doing well. An attractive business setting need not be expensive but it must be neat, clean, and well organized. Sales of plants are generally much greater in an inviting atmosphere than in the "four walls and a roof" type building used for most retail stores. Spring garden sales are especially enhanced by cultivating a sylvan atmosphere.

Landscaping on the premises is of major importance to any business handling plants and flowers but It becomes exceptionally critical when outdoor plants are sold. Customers cannot be expected to have confidence in the plants sold for gardens if landscaping on the business grounds is not well maintained. All dead or sick plants must be removed from the landscape immediately. In addition to instilling confidence in customers' minds, a pleasing business landscape creates demand for the product through suggestion. If a garden store has certain varieties planted on the grounds, a perceptible increase in sales will be noted for those plants. A good landscaping job is probably one of the least expensive methods of enhancing the image of a business.

The sales force is the primary contact a business has with the public. Therefore, employees should be selected and trained to reflect the image a business wishes to establish. The care and use of plants is sometimes complex, especially when there are many different varieties. Much of the information needed by consumers concerning their purchase can be communicated by means of signs and tags, but selling plants and flowers will always require a high degree of personal contact to insure customer satisfaction. Signs may be adequate for many people but others shop at a particular business because it offers courteous, personal service.

All salespersons need not be experts in plant culture as long as they have been trained to answer the most common questions and to consult reference books when they do not know the answer. One person should always be available in person or by telephone to deal with complex or uncommon inquiries. People who have done a great deal of gardening or make a hobby of house plants are often ideal for plant sales since they will need little training in the technical aspects. Some of the best advertising a plant store can do is to have knowledgeable sales people. Customers like to shop for plants where competent help is available.

Salespersons should also be trained in basic sales techniques such as how to tie in one sale with another and how to spot a customer who needs help. The most basic qualification for being an excellent salesperson is a genuine enjoyment of being with and helping customers. The good will is immediately apparent to the customer and makes it much easier to make a sale. Managers should select sales personnel mainly for their personality and natural inclination and secondarily for technical knowledge.

The topic of "guarantees" for plant material elicits a varied and vocal response among owners and managers. If this problem is viewed from the standpoint of good business practices rather than who is responsible for the damage, it is best to be very liberal with guarantees and satisfy the customer except in extreme cases of flagrant abuse.

Most people are fair minded; when a knowledgeable sales person politely explains how the merchandise was damaged the customer is more likely than not happy without a refund if it is apparent the damage was not the result of poor merchandise. Those people who still feel the store is obligated to some extent will generally be satisfied with a smaller plant or a one-half refund. Full refunds or exchanges should be given when the customer demands it or if it is likely the plants were at fault. Always attempt to replace the merchandise rather than refund with money; and make certain the customer now knows how to care for the product.

A guarantee which is honored grudgingly is as bad as no guarantee. Cheerful refunds and exchanges make a customer loyal and will result in good word of mouth comment about the store. The total cost for guarantees is generally not a major expense and easily pays for itself in advertising the good will of the company. If refunds and exchanges become too common, the quality of plants should be evaluated and sales people should check to make certain proper care instructions are being given to customers. People are more particular about where they buy plants than they are about where they but catsup or dish soap. A liberal guarantee policy assures customers of your integrity and will insure a good amount of loyalty, which leads to repeat business: the backbone of any sales program.

Wholesalers need not be as liberal in their guarantee policy. Complaints can normally be handled on a case by case basis because of the limited number of clients. Most retailers are reasonably knowledgeable about the plants they handle and do not expect any type of guarantee. If the merchandise did not meet their specification, they should not have accepted it. Growers should not honor complaints unless they are made on arrival of the merchandise or if a problem which appears later can reasonably be attributed to the growing operation.

The degree of emphasis which must be placed on actively promoting sales may differ with general economic conditions and upon the stage of growth the business is in at a particular time. Some people entered the plant business in the early 1970's and had never known the need to really promote sales because a definite boom was taking place in green goods. The severe recession of the early 1980's jolted many owners into the realization that the easy ride was over. Sales dropped off and it became necessary to fight for every sale possible rather than waiting for the customers to beat a path to the door. Some people never realized the need for a different sales approach and were not heard from again. The late 1990's have led to another boom period in which service has generally become less emphasized. Similar business cycles can be expected nationally and locally over the ensuing years. In order to promote stable long term business success, managers should be careful to avoid "fads". Sticking with established programs until new ideas have been reasonably tested and proven successful helps to avoid a good deal of wasted effort.

A business just starting out must obviously advertise heavily and devise other means of obtaining sales. After a stable clientele has been established, the chief emphasis may pass from sales to internal organization or refining purchasing and pricing policies to increase profitability. The emphasis placed on each major aspect of the business will change from time to time depending on the manager's evaluation of what is most important at a certain stage. When market demand for plants becomes reasonably satisfied, it may be necessary for businesses to again stress sales promotion if they wish to expand beyond their present size. The same situation may arise not because of internal decisions to expand, but because a competitor expands or a new one arrives on the scene.

There are circumstances where maximum sales promotion and expansion are not essential business goals, in which case money spent on theses objectives is wasted. As an example, if a business has reached the limit of sales or production which can be carried on in its physical facilities, it would perhaps be better to concentrate on means of increasing net profit until the decision is made to expand those facilities. Other situations which might weigh against pursuing increased sales are a lack of qualified personnel, the desire to spend more time on personal or other business interests, and a lack of capital to finance business expansion. It should be pointed out that a constant and long term policy of down playing expansion is likely to lead to the irreversible decline of a business. The old axiom in business is that if you are not going forward, you are going backward.

Product prices almost always have an important effect on sales programs. A discussion of pricing was presented in the preceding section concerning production economics. Only a few additional comments which pertain especially to retail sales will be added here. A popular retail markup for plants is to double the purchase price, including freight and packing. This markup should enable most stores to return a profit and assumes that a fair amount of sales personnel are available to customers. Somewhat lower markups would be in order if emphasis was placed on doing a large volume business in a self service setting. Markups of three to four times the purchase price are valid if plants are artistically arranged or other comparable services rendered. Each manager must evaluate the services offered and determine what prices are suitable for the individual business. One fact seems certain as the new millennium dawns: All prices will be vigorously contested. Smaller growers, therefore, will almost certainly be wiser to focus their marketing efforts on factors other than price.

A topic which bears some discussion is that of the sales unit price. It has become popular in recent years to talk of reducing the size or number of plants offered as a sales unit so the price would appear to be more competitive. Actual prices of plants are increased but consumers are offered a smaller and smaller package so that the price per sales unit remains relatively low. The primary causes of this phenomenon are a steady march of inflation and the entry of low priced outlets as a major marketing force. The purpose of such a strategy is quite obvious; the customer is hopefully duped into believing the true price is remaining stable and that prices are just as low as those of the competition down the street.

There are some not so obvious disadvantages to shrinking the sales unit. Customers shop not only because they expect to spend an allotted amount of money or because they need a certain number of plants but also because they respond to the size of sales units offered to them. For example, if only a large sized sales unit is offered, many people will purchase it even though they would not have purchased two sales units half that size. Offering smaller and less costly sales units should be practiced only when it is deemed likely that sales lost due to people not picking up the larger unit are more than compensated for by the increased incentive to purchase because prices appear to be lower.

Decreasing sales unit sizes may also have the effect of making the product less useful for the intended purpose. Special occasion flowers in the 6 inch pot size have become the general industry standard partially because they represent a convenient size for decorating and they appear big enough to represent a gift one does not have to be ashamed of giving. Smaller flower sizes may be marketable if decorating needs change or if smaller gifts are appropriate, but sellers should be certain that size changes will provide the desired results. Decreasing the size of outdoor hanging baskets and porch planters may allow the prices and profits to remain steady in the face of inflationary pressures, but a decrease in the container volume will make it harder to keep plants watered during summer weather. If the size were decreased several times, the usability of these baskets and planters would be seriously impaired. In another case, most people who purchase trees want at least some visual effect immediately and although smaller trees may cost less, the average buyer will elect to purchase a tree which is 6-10 feet tall rather than one which is 1-3 feet tall.

The marketing year for greenhouses and nurseries exhibits several peaks and valleys of sales activity. A great majority of sales are concentrated at holidays and in the spring planting season. Devising sales programs which create demand during the summer and fall slack periods should be a prime objective of management. Most overhead expenses continue unabated at these times and any extra income adds greatly to the profit picture. Container grown trees and shrubs can easily be planted through the summer and fall if customers are persuaded to do so. Special promotions may be necessary to accomplish this objective since most people prefer to do landscaping work in the spring months. Sales of larger garden plants and container gardens in the summer and of hardy perennials, especially colorful garden mums, offer opportunities for additional income. Greenhouse managers may find that a crop of tropical foliage raised during summer months will find a ready market in fall before poinsettias must be moved to final spacing. The addition of one profitable extra crop can make a marginally successful operation into a super successful money maker.

Table 4 recaps some of the important points about selling which have been mentioned throughout this book. Once a sales program has been decided upon, it should be given adequate time to prove its worth. Deviations from the plan should be for good cause and not because of short term market gyrations.

The preceding discussion of sales has been primarily aimed at the retail level. Wholesale marketing is of course somewhat different in emphasis but the general principles are similar. A wholesaler's primary sales tool is usually the telephone. Weekly calls to retailers in the slower times and more frequent contact during rush periods will increase sales considerably. A follow up to make sure the retailer is happy with plants and flowers ordered is necessary periodically. Many times, a small misunderstanding can be cleared up before it becomes a serious problem. Fax transmissions and direct mail brochures or catalogs are also important. Tree and shrub growers may depend principally upon their annual catalogs to generate sales. Growers must resist the temptation to send out the last few reject plants in a crop; this can quickly lead to the loss of a customer. When the grower has only a few retail stores to deal with, it is extremely important to understand the personality of owners and managers if maximum sales are to be achieved. The grower must care about the retailers' businesses because if they don't sell merchandise, orders to the greenhouse or nursery will drop. If suggestions are made to retailers about how to improve business, it must be done very tactfully since they will resent anyone trying to tell them how to run their business.

Table 4
Summary of important aspects in the marketing of plants.

A. Quality will always sell. Even if inexpensive items are sold, make sure the quality is there.

B. Stand behind your merchandise. Repeat sales are the backbone of a sales program.

C. Business structures and grounds must be clean and well landscaped.

D. Service commensurate with price should be offered.

E. Cultural information is a necessity for the eventual satisfaction of customers.

F. Provide adequate merchandise for maximum sales but avoid waste.

G. A wide variety of plants and flowers attracts more customers than a limited selection.

H. Proper surroundings must be provided to display merchandise at its best.

I. Eliminate insect pests and sick plants; either one of these will completely ruin a display.

J. Let people know you are in business. Advertise conventionally and by other means. Be aware of the high costs associated with most conventional types of advertising.

K. Be ready for sales peaks. A high proportion of yearly sales in container plants is done in a relatively short time.

L. Extend the sales season as long as possible.

M. Budget for daily care of plants and flowers and of displays.

N. Weather is perhaps the most important factor which controls the sale of outdoor plants, trees, and flowers. You cannot change the weather, but plans can be made to deal with it.

Chapter 4

HOW PLANTS GROW

Anyone proposing to grow plants for profit should have a rudimentary knowledge of the principles underlying plant growth and development. In very simple terms, green plants are factories which process the physical energy of light into chemical energy stored in the millions of molecules making up various plant parts. Light is the energy source utilized in these factories but other materials and conditions are needed for the energy transfer to be completed. "Photosynthesis" is the technical term given to the chemical reaction taking place. Carbon dioxide, oxygen, water, various mineral elements, and a proper temperature are also essential for plant growth. A detailed presentation on each of these factors is beyond the scope of this chapter but brief statements concerning their functions will be given.

LIGHT-CARBON DIOXIDE-OXYGEN

Photosynthesis is a series of reactions in which light energy is used to split water (H_2O) molecules. Breaking the chemical bonds between Hydrogen (H) and Oxygen (O) releases energy which is usable in the reduction of carbon dioxide (CO_2) to sugars. Reduction means the addition of H molecules to CO_2 in the appropriate number for the formation of sugar ($C_6H_{12}O_6$). A schematic representation of the reaction is as follows:

$$6\ CO_2 \quad + \quad 6\ H_2O \quad \xrightarrow[\text{chlorophyll pigment}]{\text{light energy}} \quad C_6H_{12}O_6 \ + \ 6\ O_2$$

$$\text{carbon dioxide} \qquad \text{water} \qquad\qquad\qquad\qquad \text{sugar} \qquad \text{oxygen}$$

Readers must realize that this is merely a summary equation of the basic energy transfer; there are many chemical reactions actually taking place. Carbon dioxide enters the leaf through small openings called stomates and water is absorbed by the roots.

Numerous substances present in plants are manufactured from the basic building blocks of sugar. Proteins, fats, chlorophyll (photosynthetic pigment), hormones, and vitamins are some of the more commonly known molecules synthesized. The activity of building these various molecules requires energy which is liberated during respiration, a process whereby foods are oxidized or "burned" in a somewhat analogous fashion to the use of foods for energy in animals. The energy of respiration is also used in such processes as cell division, absorption of minerals, and translocation of foods. The schematic representation of the respiration reaction is as follows:

$$C_6H_{12}O_6 \ + \ 6\,O_2 \quad \longrightarrow \quad 6\,CO_2 \ + \ 6\,H_2O + energy$$

  sugar   oxygen   carbon dioxide   water

Again, it must be emphasized that this is a simple picture of a very complex process. Oxygen is necessary in the reaction much as it is required for a fire to burn.

The energy relationships of plants may be summarized in the following simplified statement. Light energy is used to produce a photochemical reaction (photosynthesis), involving water and carbon dioxide, which converts transitory light energy into a more stable and usable energy storage packet, sugar. Energy contained in sugar remains locked up until called for to produce other molecules such as proteins or to do some form of work such as absorbing minerals. The energy of sugar is released in a chemical reaction (respiration) which is somewhat similar to the burning of fuels and is basically the reverse process of photosynthesis except that light and chlorophyll pigments are not required.

MINERAL ELEMENTS

As mentioned, molecules other than sugars are found in plants. Carbon, hydrogen, and oxygen are the elements found in greatest abundance in these organic molecules, but many contain other elements. These additional ingredients will be called mineral elements since they are generally taken up by the roots from the soil or substrate. The number of distinct molecular configurations containing these mineral elements is in the hundreds but we will limit our discussion of each mineral to prominent examples of how it is utilized.

NITROGEN (N) – Nitrogen is utilized in fairly large quantities by plants and crop yields are closely related to an adequate supply. Nitrogen is necessary for the production of proteins, chlorophyll, amino acids, and nucleic acids. When nitrogen is deficient, chlorophyll content decreases and plants will progress from light green to yellow as the deficiency becomes more severe. Symptoms appear first on older leaves. Large supplies of nitrogen result in plants that are very lush and may cause delays in flowering and weak stems.

PHOSPHORUS (P) – Phosphorus needs of plants are not large in comparison to nitrogen and potassium but this element is very important in plant growth. High energy phosphate compounds are basic to energy transformation within plant cells. Phosphorus promotes flowering and stiffer stems, and helps balance large nitrogen applications. It is found in particularly high concentrations in seeds. Deficiencies of phosphorus translate first into stunted growth, and plant parts often eventually take on a purplish hue.

POTASSIUM (K) – Potassium is not known to be a part of any molecules in plant cells but it is extremely important in many of the metabolic processes taking place. Potassium is necessary for protein and carbohydrate synthesis and carbohydrate movement. A prominent symptom of deficiency is the presence of necrotic (dead) spots on the edges of older leaves.

CALCIUM (Ca) – Calcium is especially important in the compounds forming cell walls and is necessary for proper development of the growing tip and roots.

SULFUR (S) – Sulfur is needed for the formation of some enzymes and vitamins in the plant.

MAGNESIUM (Mg) – Magnesium is at the center of chlorophyll molecules and, therefore, is obviously indispensable to green plants.

Several mineral elements are required by plants in minute quantities and, as such, are termed trace minerals. Iron (Fe), manganese (Mn), boron (B), copper (Cu), zinc (Zn), molybdenum (Mo), nickel (Ni), and chlorine (Cl) are the known trace elements. They are all essential for normal plant growth. The small quantities required for growth may be illustrated by chlorine which, despite years of investigation into plant nutrition, was found to be essential for plant growth only in 1954. Iron is required in the largest amounts, and the young leaves near the growing tip will exhibit a chlorotic yellowing between the veins if it is deficient.

WATER

Water has been shown previously to be essential for plants as a source of hydrogen and oxygen and also as a source of energy when the molecule is split. The importance of water for plants does not end here. Water serves as a universal solvent for chemical compounds, as a reagent for chemical reactions, and to maintain the turgor pressure of plant cells (which prevents wilting). Water comprises 80-90% of the fresh weight of most plants. The predominance of water in plant tissue certainly indicates the central role it plays in influencing many aspects of plant growth.

TEMPERATURE

A fundamental characteristic of chemical reactions is that they accelerate as temperatures rise. Within certain life threatening extremes of temperature, plants will normally make more rapid growth as temperatures increase. The upper and lower temperature limits beyond which plants cannot survive will vary with the species and with the particular stage of life. Winter dormant plants can survive temperatures well below the freezing point but if the same plants were subjected to frost while actively growing in summer they would quickly die. Most plant species make optimum growth at temperatures below 100^0 F, but certain algae (primitive photosynthetic plants) are quite at home in hot springs where temperatures may reach 200^0 F. Providing optimum temperatures for growth is a primary responsibility of the grower.

INTEGRATION OF PLANT REQUIREMENTS

All the various factors which have been mentioned as essential for plant growth must be present in the proper proportions. Each factor is interrelated with all other factors and the absence of only one will render the remaining ones impotent. If all factors are present within an acceptable range, the required chemical reactions take place and a multitude of different molecules are manufactured. These molecules arrange themselves in an orderly fashion into the tissues which make up various plant parts and these parts will be integrated into what we know as a complete plant.

Plant growth factors serve not only in building and maintaining body tissue but also help control the developmental stages and processes which occur in the plant's life cycle. Activities such as flowering, reproduction, and dormancy are strongly influenced by such factors as light and temperature. Many chemical compounds, which we might term secondary growth and development factors, are present in plants. These secondary factors are derived initially from the primary chemical elements and serve not so much in structural and energy related roles but more as regulators which control and integrate the entire life process.

The importance of growth and development processes within plants must not be neglected. These subjects are often not emphasized both in scientific and practical literature sources simply because the subject material is unusually complex and does not lend itself to easily understood statements of proven fact. As readers digest the remainder of this book, it will become apparent that numerous aspects of commercial plant production are influenced by factors which relate only indirectly to the obvious building up, maintenance, and degeneration of plant tissue. The purpose of *The Greenhouse and Nursery Handbook* is to point out important commercial aspects of plant science, not to unnecessarily engage in speculation concerning the underlying processes. However, readers should maintain a healthy respect for the inherent complexities of plant life.

GENETIC INFLUENCE AND REPRODUCTIVE CYCLES

The method by which predetermined reactions are completed and molecules and plant parts are arranged in a harmonious fashion is governed by the particular genetic makeup of the species and individual. Tiny bits of nucleoproteins known as "genes" are the means by which the information necessary to program all the life processes of plants is transmitted from one generation to the next. These genes are information particles which direct the growth and development of plants. It is very important to recognize the central role genetic inheritance plays in the production of high quality plants and flowers. Careful provision for all the required factors by a greenhouse or nursery owner cannot turn a thistle into a rose. One must select the proper variety for the intended purpose in order to attain peak production.

Manipulation of the essential requirements of plants may not only speed up or slow down growth but can also dramatically alter the normal development pattern prescribed by the genes. It is thus apparent that neither environmental factors nor inheritance is predominant, but that the quality of plants will depend upon each factor being given proper consideration.

The majority of green plants reproduce sexually in much the same manner as higher animals. There are minor differences, especially in structural form, but the essential process is comparable. Plants also reproduce asexually, which is something higher animals are incapable of doing. The genetic makeup of offspring is affected dramatically depending on whether they were produced sexually or asexually, even though they may all come from the same mother plant. Progeny resulting from sexual reproduction have 50% of their genetic heritage from the father and 50% from the mother. Asexually reproduced offspring obtain 100% of their genetic makeup from the mother. Sexually reproduced populations are variable in their characteristics while asexually reproduced individuals of a population are exactly alike genetically. The method of reproduction is extremely important to plant growers from a practical standpoint. It should be noted that under certain breeding conditions, such as controlled hybridization, self-pollinating plants or inbreeding populations, sexually reproduced plants can approximate the uniformity found in asexually reproduced populations. Fig. 2 is a simple diagram of a higher plant life cycle.

PLANT INTERACTION WITH OTHER SPECIES

Although scientists have known for many years that the healthy growth and development of one plant species may depend to some extent upon interaction with other plant and animal species, practical ornamental horticulturists have only recently placed emphasis upon discovering how these interorganism relationships affect the growth and development of their specific crops.

Many types of microorganisms are known to affect soil structure and chemistry, and, therefore, the life process of plants. These microorganisms often act as single species or they may work in various degrees of physical combination with one or more other species. In either case, they are often referred to as "mycorrhizae," this term being more commonly used when the microorganisms, either as a single species or in combination, form a distinct and sometimes visually perceptible structural network of "tissue". Further information will be presented concerning this topic in later chapters dealing with soils and tree growth.

The preceding discussion has dealt only with some of the major concepts which are essential for a basic understanding of how plants grow. Reference to a college level botany text will satisfy the more inquisitive reader. Our purpose in this book is to concentrate on the more practical aspects of plant growth and development. A sound theoretical knowledge of plants cannot but help a greenhouse or nursery operator but is certainly not essential for success.

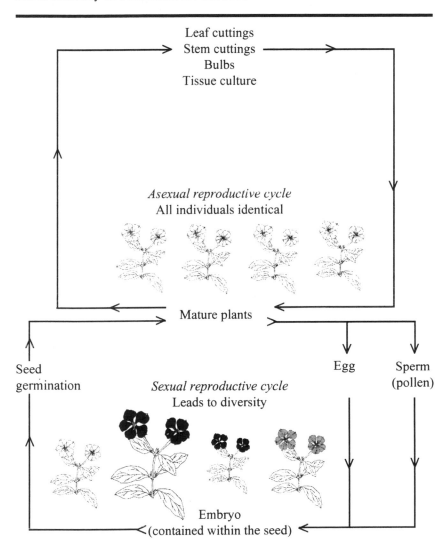

Leaf cuttings
Stem cuttings
Bulbs
Tissue culture

Asexual reproductive cycle
All individuals identical

Mature plants

Seed
germination

Egg   Sperm
(pollen)

Sexual reproductive cycle
Leads to diversity

Embryo
(contained within the seed)

Figure 2
Sexual and asexual life cycles of plants

Chapter 5

PLANT PROPAGATION

The success of every crop depends upon a grower's proficiency at producing a new population of plants from the previous generation. Propagation of new plants is generally more difficult than finishing a crop once it is well established. Because of this, a great deal of propagation is left to firms which specialize in this particular aspect of horticulture. Young plant production requires skilled labor and carefully controlled environmental conditions. However, with a little effort everyone can become an acceptable propagator of all but the most difficult plants. The initial stages of plant growth are often the most profitable, and, as a consequence, growers who can provide the required conditions should propagate all their own plants possible. The purchase of too many seedlings and cuttings can erode potential profits. If your greenhouse or nursery location is not near major transportation arteries it may be necessary to learn propagation since minimum shipments required by suppliers of young plants may be too large for your needs or there may not be adequate transport to ship plants safely.

As mentioned previously, plants possess two very different means of propagating themselves: sexual and asexual reproduction. Both of these methods require basically the same environmental conditions and careful handling to be successful. Propagating beds or structures should normally be heated to 70-80^0 F, preferably with the heat source located underneath the surface on which cuttings or seeds will be placed, thus allowing heat to rise upward through the rooting mixture. Each plant species has its own temperature preferences and a few will not do well under this temperature regime. Inexpensive propagation areas may be made by laying thermostatically controlled electric heating cable in a bench or groundbed at 3 to 4 inch centers and covering 2 inches deep with clean sand. Ready made rubberized heating mats are available for the same purpose and require no sand layer. Another method is to heat a small reservoir of water with either a standard home water heater or a portable tank heater and then pump warm water through plastic tubing underneath a sand bed. The pump can be controlled by a thermostat in the sand bed. The sand beds mentioned will require frequent sterilization to prevent disease outbreaks. Locating the heat sources in a false box below a metal or heavy plastic top surface will facilitate cleanup since a sand layer is then not necessary. Several other means of supplying heat to propagation beds are available.

Rodent populations near propagation areas must be controlled for two reasons: they cause electrical shorts by chewing cables and they can destroy much valuable seed in a short time.

If a propagating area is located in a shaded and humid tropical foliage greenhouse, there may be no additional work to do on it other than providing bottom heat. If it is in a well ventilated, sunny house or cold frame the area will need to be covered with a shade cloth and provided with a water mist system to maintain the almost 100% humidity necessary for good propagation. Shade is provided to prevent the sun from drying out the area, but there must be enough light for photosynthesis to take place normally. A propagation structure may be erected quickly by constructing a plastic covered hut containing a portable electric heater. The cost for heating these huts is high and temperatures may rise to unacceptable levels speedily on a sunny spring day. Opening the sides to prevent high temperatures allows drying out unless a mist system is installed. These huts are particularly useful for winter and early spring seed germination and when located within a house which is already shaded. Much propagation of woody plants is done outdoors in the warmer months without benefit of bottom heat.

Any of the different means of maintaining proper temperature and humidity can be employed in enclosed areas other than a greenhouse, but sufficient light must be provided artificially. Most people fail to provide enough light intensity under these conditions and young plants turn out tall and spindly. Light fixtures must be those of a quality manufactured for growing plants, otherwise the proper wavelengths of light energy are not present for good growth. An advantage of this type of set up is that growth can be speeded by providing a 24 hour day. It is also easier to maintain a constant temperature than it is in a greenhouse. Numerous horticultural supply firms can provide propagating structures. However, they are often expensive and should be checked out carefully prior to purchase. A homemade structure is usually just as effective if adequate thought is put into construction.

Oftentimes, inexperienced growers, in an attempt to provide the warm, moist conditions necessary for propagation, tend to neglect the need for fresh air entry and circulation of it through propagation areas. Oxygen is absolutely essential in the rooting medium to allow seed germination or promote rooting. It must be emphasized that an airtight propagation area with a stagnant atmosphere will not allow seed germination or rooting and invites invasion of disease organisms. It is the worst possible environment. This is why amateur horticulturists so often experience failure in the propagation process: They have been advised by supposed experts to enclose their propagation material in a plastic bag. This is not a good situation for air movement even if instructions to open the bag periodically have been given.

The medium or substrate which young plants are propagated in must be loose and porous. A porous medium allows sufficient oxygen exchange to promote plant growth. Seed germination and root growth depend upon energy from respiration, which requires the presence of oxygen. Seedlings and cuttings can also be removed from the medium with less damage if it is loose and fluffy. The container in which a propagation mixture is placed must be well drained to avoid standing water which will prevent oxygen from reaching the root zone. Propagation media should be only lightly fertilized. Two formulas which can be used to prepare propagation media are presented in Table 5; the author has found these to be adequate. Extensive testing during the development of these formulas has demonstrated the extremely deleterious effects which poor propagation media can have on rooting and seed germination. Every grower should carefully evaluate the selection of the propagation medium being utilized to make certain it does the job effectively. Of course there are numerous other ingredients which could be successfully employed.

When mixing either of these formulas, the potassium nitrate is dissolved in 5 gallons of water and distributed evenly throughout the mix. Sufficient water is added to moisten the media thoroughly but not enough to cause large lumps to appear when wet particles start sticking together. The media can be stored in black, heavy duty trash bags in a cool shaded area for

Table 5
Typical media used for propagation

Formula #1	2 bales (3.8 cubic foot each) compressed sphagnum peat
	8 cubic feet perlite coarse grind (coarser than 6 mesh)
For cuttings and	5 ounces potassium nitrate (KNO_3)
coarse seed	4 pounds ground limestone ($CaCO_3$)
	15 ounces triple superphosphate or 30
	ounces single superphosphate
Formula #2	Same ingredients as formula #1 except 6 cubic feet
	of fine vermiculite is substituted for the perlite.
For fine seed (petunias,	Peat should be finely ground.
begonias, portulaca,	
gloxinia, etc.)	

Note: If a faster draining mix is desired for rooting crops such as geraniums, the amount of perlite in formula #1 can be doubled.

extended periods without appreciable chemical change. No additional fertilizer is needed unless plants are in the medium for extended periods or if the variety of plant is a conspicuous fertilizer lover (such as chrysanthemums).

Successful propagation depends, to a large degree, upon constant cleanliness. Young plants, like human infants, are susceptible to numerous diseases and pests. Completely sterile conditions are impossible to maintain but one can make sure strict housekeeping rules are enforced. Sphagnum peat and the other ingredients in these mixtures are almost disease free and, if handled carefully to prevent contamination, will allow good success without sterilization. Most operations which specialize in propagation find that media sterilization is economical if it can be done in large quantities through the application of superheated steam, chemical gases or solutions, or by extreme dry heat.

Several commercially prepared solutions are available to aid in sterilizing tools, surfaces, containers, and plant material. Most of these do a fine job on inanimate material if used properly, but they all must be used with caution on plant material to avoid phytotoxicity. Needless to say, personnel should also be careful to avoid contact with these materials, especially in the concentrated forms. Workers should wear rubber gloves and also protective eyewear when recommended by the label.

Even when every recommended procedure and environmental factor are included in the propagation plan, failure can quickly materialize due to a lack of cleanliness in any phase of the operation. Even the water source for misting must be treated unless it is certified as acceptable for human consumption.

Numerous commercially prepared propagating mediums on the market are clean and will do a nice job. The cost is generally much higher than

---

Table 6
Basics of successful propagation.

A. Every detail must be accomplished in the proper sequence.	F. Adequate skilled help to carry out sufficiently.
B. Speed is often essential to prevent dessication of plant materials, especially when vegetative cuttings are involved.	G. Control mice and pests.
	H. Seeds and cuttings not planted too deep. Air is essential for germination and root development.
C. Porous, disease free, lightly fertilized medium.	
D. Sufficient moisture in the atmosphere and medium at all times but never in excess.	I. Adequate light for photosynthesis.
	J. After establishment, move cuttings or seedlings to normal growing area for hardening period.
E. Temperature 70-80° F. Some plants may like it cooler or warmer; check requirements.	

Above all – have a definite plan. Propagation should be scheduled months in advance.

The emerging black "nipples" in the center of this photo are actually potential roots on the leaf petiole of "piggy back plant". They will develop into vigorous roots within a few days after being put in contact with moist soil.

that of homemade formulas. Many companies sell mixes similar to the ones just detailed. Another popular medium for starting new plants is a compressed peat pellet which swells when moistened; cuttings or seeds are then inserted. These pellets grow very nice plants but are expensive in comparison to loose mix. Many propagators use foam blocks for rooting cuttings. These blocks do a good job of rooting but plants must be handled carefully after transplanting to avoid plant damage. Additional materials such as rock wool, rubbery sponges, and bark materials can serve alone or in mixtures as rooting and germinating media. Table 6 sums up the basic requirements for successful propagation. Additional details concerning propagation by sexual and asexual means follows.

ASEXUAL OR VEGETATIVE REPRODUCTION

Asexual plant reproduction is accomplished by means of cuttings, bulbs, corms, tubers, and tissue culture. Some species are vegetatively propagated because plants do not come from true seed or, in some cases, because the seed is too expensive. Normally, marketable adult plants can be reproduced more quickly by vegetative means than from seed. Each plant reproduced vegetatively has the same genetic make up as the mother plant and very uniform crops are the result.

Cuttings are usually taken from stem tissue but occasionally, some plants—such as certain begonias, peperomias, African violets, and others will root more economically by means of leaf cuttings. Stem tip cuttings are commonly used for a number of reasons. In rapidly growing plants, the stem tip may outrun viral and bacterial diseases present in older tissue. Stem tips often root faster and more uniformly, resulting in faster, more evenly developed crops. When tip cuttings are not plentiful enough, cuttings from older tissue down the stem may be taken. Because of the difference in rooting speed, tip cuttings should not be mixed in the rooting container with cuttings from more mature tissue. Cuttings must be taken only from healthy, pest free plants, failure to select only the most desirable and healthy plants will doom a propagation program right from the start. Never select mother plants from discards which did not sell in the previous season. Attention should be focused on obtaining groups of mother plants which possess the greatest combination of desirable characteristics. Each species is quite variable and certain plants within it will exhibit traits which are valuable to the grower.

Plants grown under the highest light intensities desirable for that species produce the best cuttings because the tissue contains more food than that taken from plants grown under lower light levels. The process of taking cuttings is analogous to major surgery in humans and any extra food reserves improve the chances of success. Sanitation is especially important with cuttings because of the wound produced. Moisture loss from cuttings should be minimized by taking them in early morning or late evening, then sticking (placing the part to be rooted in the medium) and watering in as soon as possible. In general, it is not important whether the cut is made at or between leaf nodes. Some plants root from the wounded cut, some on the sides of the stem, and some at the leaf node. In the

Spider or airplane plants develop numerous "babies" on long, modified stems which arise from the main plant. These "babies" then develop considerable roots while suspended in midair.

latter case the cutting must be inserted so that the leaf node is in firm contact with the medium. Crowding cuttings too closely in the rooting tray restricts air movement, thus encouraging fungal growth. Close spacing will also require cuttings to be transplanted on a more rigid schedule than if they are spaced further apart. Most modern growers root cuttings either directly to finishing pots or into sheets of pre-spaced small containers; this practice is more effective in controlling the spread of root diseases and relieves workers from deciding how much space should be given. Cuttings should be stuck at the normal growth orientation, in other words, upside up. The upside is not so easy to ascertain in some cases unless the growth orientation is observed on the mother plant before cutting.

Leaf cuttings can be made by slicing the leaf into several pieces and inserting them into the medium or by placing the whole leaf on the medium underside down, and then cutting slits in several places. Roots will then form at leaf veins in the wounds if they are in contact with the medium. Only a small proportion of species will root successfully from leaves (such as Begonias and African violets) under normal nursery conditions. Many plants exhibit rather unusual morphological forms and it may be difficult to distinguish between the different plant parts. Normally, if rudimentary roots have formed on a structure, closer inspection would classify it as stem tissue.

Pothos or devil's ivy often begins to root at the leaf nodes before cuttings are removed from the mother plant.

Easily rooted plants are often propagated directly in the growing container; this eliminates transplanting and reduces the total production cost. Some growers provide extensive propagation areas so that even harder-to-root varieties can be treated this way. The determining factor as to which method is used is whether one has more labor than money since these large propagation areas are expensive to construct and heat.

Seasonal growth rhythms may affect rooting capabilities in plants, especially trees and shrubs. Flower and fruit production usually lengthens rooting time. Tissue which has been growing rapidly but is not yet fully mature generally seems to root quickly. Some trees may be almost impossible to root unless cuttings are taken at a specific stage of growth. Woody plants normally root less easily than herbaceous ones and take more time. Unless easy to root species such as cottonwoods and willows are being done, it is often more economical to purchase woody cuttings from a specialist.

Since most woody mother plants are grown outdoors, the availability of ready to root tissue occurs within limited time frames (a much larger number of herbaceous species are cultured in greenhouses, allowing almost year-round availability of cuttings) thereby requiring a large amount of propagation space at the season of harvest for cuttings. Fortunately, propagation of these woody species occurs mostly in the warmer months so that rooting can successfully take place outdoors without additional heat if a suitable media bed and appropriate mist and shade are provided. When the species is particularly slow rooting or slow growing, the rooted cuttings may be left in the rooting bed for a full year before transplanting to growing beds or pots. Some winter protection may be needed for rooting beds in this case.

The use of rooting hormones is widespread with hard to root plants and even some propagators of easily rooted varieties use these treatments to speed rooting. Of course the cost of chemicals employed and the cost of applying them must be weighed against potential benefits. Some growers even question the effectiveness of these treatments. A simple test project will quickly let individual propagators know the best course of action under their own specific circumstances.

Specialized methods of taking cuttings are sometimes utilized. Plants which produce extensive runners are often propagated by placing moist soil on top of the runners in several places. Roots form at these spots and the young plants can then be separated from the mother. Air layering is accomplished by severely wounding the stem, then surrounding the wound with moist moss which is held in place and wrapped with ventilated plastic film. After roots form at the wound the stem is severed below them and the new plant potted. Rapid propagation of desirable woody varieties is often accomplished by grafting portions of stems to more common root stock. Sometimes a root stock is used not because of being readily available but because it is more suitable for particular environmental conditions than the original root stock. Most roses and many trees are commonly reproduced in this manner. Thus, when roses and trees are killed back to ground level for one reason or another, the plants which often generate from the root stock are generally unsuitable for serious cultivation as ornamentals.

A more detailed knowledge of propagation by cuttings can be obtained through studying books which are devoted entirely to this subject, but nothing can substitute for acute observation of actual conditions which lead to success. First attempts at cutting propagation often lead to failure. Even experienced growers will occasionally find new varieties difficult to root until they discover the particular methods and conditions which work best with that variety. Success often hinges upon minute changes in method or conditions. Unsatisfactory moisture conditions in the plant tissue or in the immediate environment are probably the chief causes of failure. Most varieties prefer a medium amount of moisture while a minority like it either extremely moist or dry.

Diseases are potentially a major problem whenever cuttings are taken. Every effort must be made to reduce the incidence of infection. The chief methods of doing so are to utilize disease free stock plants, maintain extremely clean conditions, prevent sources of infection, and provide environmental conditions which minimize microorganism reproduction and spread. Unfortunately, the conditions which promote rapid rooting are often the exact conditions which favor disease organisms. Excess moisture usually leads to disease outbreaks. Only the amount of moisture necessary to encourage rooting should be applied to cuttings. Good air circulation around cuttings and a porous rooting medium minimizes the possibility of excess moisture buildup. Of course, insects, mites, nematodes, slugs and snails, and other animal pests must be eliminated from mother plants and from the propagation area. More information about reducing pest and disease problems during propagation will be provided in a later chapter dealing with these subjects.

Many growers routinely utilize chemical disease control in propagation areas. This means of controlling diseases is effective but may constantly expose workers to unhealthy conditions. Every effort should be made to control diseases through environmental manipulation in order to minimize chemical use. Only a slight change in methods and conditions can sometimes eliminate the need for chemical controls after the initial sterilization of tools, surfaces, containers, and cuttings has been accomplished.

Many crops are grown from bulbs, corms, or tubers but most growers purchase these from specialists. Proper treatment during shipment and after receipt is necessary. Tulips and many other bulbs contain a small fully organized plant inside the bulb so that exposure to extreme conditions such as heat can prevent the small plant from developing properly. Freezing is a common occurrence when bulbs are shipped in winter. Excess moisture in the packing containers and infection with diseases from adhering soil particles leads quickly to rot during shipment or storage. Bulbs and tubers should be stored in cool, dry conditions. Certain bulbs must be subjected to specific environmental conditions before successful flowering will take place; this process can be done by the specialist or grower, but it is imperative that the grower knows whether or not the bulbs have been preconditioned.

Tissue culture has been used by experimental propagators for many years, but widespread commercial application of the technique has come only recently. New plants are started in sterile nutrient media from single cells or groups of cells. The big advantage of tissue culture is that a large number of plants can be obtained from a single mother plant, eliminating the cost of maintaining a large inventory of mother plants. Tissue culture is normally economical when practiced by specialists who can use or wholesale large numbers of small plants.

There are some drawbacks to tissue culture, the chief one being that the mother stock can mutate (change genetically) and cause variation in future generations. Due to the large number of baby plants produced and the speed of the multiplication process, many generations can become contaminated with undesirable genetic material before the mother stock mutation is discovered. Another factor which limits the wider employment of tissue culture is the need for well trained personnel and proper equipment to effectively practice this method of propagation. Several reasonably priced "off the shelf" tissue culture kits are now available for growers who wish to experiment with the process or who plan on propagating a limited number of species which are well-adapted to this technique.

A final word of caution before leaving the subject of vegetative propagation. Many plant varieties are protected by federal patent laws. Propagating these varieties without a license from the patent holder is unlawful. Patented varieties are usually well marked by labels or tags when they are sold by the original propagator and it is now standard practice to require all succeeding propagators to continue marking plants. Some patent holders even insist that the plants be properly marked when sold to the retail consumer.

Some further comments concerning asexual reproduction will appear, as appropriate, in the following discussion of sexual reproduction.

SEXUAL REPRODUCTION

Seeds contain a fully developed embryo and are the result of sexual reproduction by plants. When seeds are used for propagation, the progeny are generally more variable than if they had been propagated vegetatively. Large numbers of plants can usually be started much faster and more economically by seed than vegetatively. Introduction of diseases and pests into the greenhouse or nursery is less likely with one's own seedlings than if cuttings or seedlings are shipped in.

The starting point for obtaining superior seedlings is to purchase seed from a reputable seed house. Growers cannot afford to have plans upset at the last minute by poor quality seed which does not germinate or yields stunted seedlings. Numerous very good wholesale seed companies exist but there are often large differences in price due to the specific services offered. Some seed companies specialize in annuals, perennials, trees and shrubs, or other specialty areas. Seed packets should be labeled with the date of packing, germination percentage, and any special conditions necessary for germination. Conscientious seed companies will welcome any complaints you may have about failures. Same day shipping after order placement is important to greenhouse growers during the busy season. Seed houses usually offer large discounts for quantity purchases; this practice often makes it more favorable for a grower to order almost all seed from a single source. Discount schedules are published in seed catalogs but additional rebates may be available upon inquiry, depending upon seasonal promotions and other such factors. Seed should be ordered only for use in the immediate season; there is no sense in tying up money with a large inventory; this, after all, is the function of seedhouses. Most seeds gradually lose their viability and there is always the chance of an accident causing their destruction. A cool, dry, mouseproof location is necessary for seed storage.

The selection of seed varieties for greenhouse or nursery operation is of primary importance. New growers will have little to base their choices upon other than the recommendation of salesmen or seed house catalogs. Careful personal observation of the crops resulting from different seed varieties is the only sure means of developing an accurate appraisal of the benefits each one offers.

Hybrid seed is normally more expensive but in general, more desirable since the resulting plants possess a vigor and uniformity lacking in those plants derived from seed produced by other methods. As a grower's knowledge of varieties progresses, it will become apparent that in some cases the extra cost of hybrid seed is not justified by its performance.

Visits to the trial grounds maintained by some seed companies are a good means of observing new varieties in actual use. Seed companies

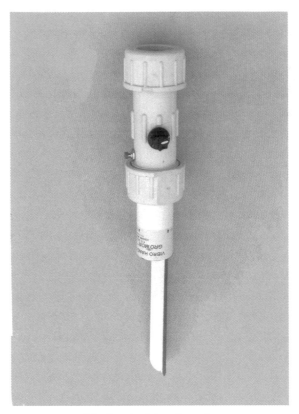

Mechanical hand seeder.

usually have a promotional event each summer to allow customers the chance to tour the trial grounds with informed company personnel who can provide on the spot information. The All-America seed selection organization also maintains trial grounds but these are not as accessible to widely scattered growers as the seed company facilities. Growers should study the All-America selections of both seed and vegetatively propagated plants for inclusion in their programs. Each of these varieties receives widespread publicity in all types of garden news sources. This creates a good deal of public demand.

   Seed is available for an almost limitless number of plant varieties. The grower's dilemma is to limit the number of varieties employed to a manageable figure while providing a reasonable selection of high performance plants. A selection containing too many varieties results in uneconomical production and confusion while one of too few does not allow customers a choice.

Seed production, storage, and marketing is a highly specialized business. In almost every case, growers will be well ahead to purchase seed from specialists instead of attempting to produce it themselves.

The seed of each species requires a particular set of environmental conditions for optimum germination but if a grower provides adequate moisture and 70-80^0 F temperature, very few varieties will fail to germinate acceptably. In some varieties the presence or absence of light will affect germination a great deal. The only practical way of determining if light is essential is to learn through packet labels, seed company brochures, or in the literature. Table 7 contains the main points of a germination regimen which can be used in the average greenhouse. Optimum germination of each variety may not be achieved but much time is saved by providing

---

Table 7
Practical guide for acceptable manual seed germination in most species of annuals. Assume direct transplant of seedlings to approximately 72 cell bedding plant flat. Propagation media formulas given previously in Table 5.

A. Temperature 70-80^{0}F.

B. Provide adequate moisture.

C. Depth of medium not less than 1 1/2 inches.

D. Sow to achieve approximately the following number of usable seedlings from a standard flat (11 1/2 X 21 1/4 inches). Heavier sowing produces crowded, weak seedlings. Lighter sowing is a waste of space and medium.

     Petunias 700

     Impatiens, marigolds 400

     Tomato, pepper 500

     Alyssum, portulaca, sow for 2200 and use as clumps of 2 to 3 seedlings.

E. If seeds are large, cover with 1/8 -1/4 inch medium unless packet says light is required. Use #1 formula propagation mix.

F. If seeds are small (raw petunia or smaller) leave uncovered. Spread seed on #2 formula propagation mix. Seed bed should be pressed firm with smooth board for extremely small seed (raw begonia).

G. Water in well with fine spray. Do not puddle water or seeds will float and concentrate together. Large water droplets will splatter seed from one flat to another.

H. Remove seedlings to normal growing area as soon as sufficient germination has occurred – before they begin to stretch.

only one germination environment. If particular trouble is encountered with some varieties, their requirements may be investigated more closely. The light requirements of seed are met by covering or not covering with medium.

Some seed is relatively inexpensive and some is worth more than its weight in gold; how carefully a particular variety is handled will depend chiefly on the cost. With inexpensive seed it is often more economical to sow quickly rather than taking the time to be exact. Certain varieties require special treatment to break seed dormancy; depending on the species, seed may be subjected to freezing temperatures or acid baths, it may be soaked in boiling water, or the seed coat may be nicked or cracked. Tree, shrub, and perennial plant seed often requires dormancy treatments. Often, dormancy in these varieties can be broken by approximately 4 weeks of chilling in the vegetable bin of a refrigerator. Extreme care must be taken to prevent moisture in the refrigerator atmosphere from reaching the seeds. Alternating day-night temperatures may increase germination in some plant varieties, but, normally it is not economical to worry about providing this regimen unless one is germinating very expensive seed.

The foregoing discussion of seed germination requirements has been brief and slanted towards practicality. The factors influencing germination and the various combinations of them is, in reality, more complicated. Our purpose, however, is to achieve practical results rather than dwell on the possible permutations of factors. Most parts of the presentation relate primarily to the requirements necessary for adequate germination in annual plants. Tree and shrub seedlings are seldom raised by the smaller nurseries for which this book is intended. If these small nurseries require juvenile plants, they are usually purchased from a specialist propagator.

During the past few years a virtual revolution has occurred in the annual plant seed industry. In general, seed houses now offer raw seed, seed selected as superior by weight or size, seed modified to germinate more quickly and uniformly, and seed which is pregerminated and then suspended in a state ready to resume growth once placed in the proper environmental conditions. In addition, many varieties are available in a pelleted form in which the seed is enclosed in an inert material (usually clay) which increases the size and uniformity of seed batches. Sometimes multiple seeds are enclosed in a single pellet. Pelleted seed is usually easier to sow by hand and by mechanical devices. Various means are used to pelletize, coat, detail, or defuzz seed in order to increase sowing efficiency. Previously, almost every greenhouse produced its own seedlings from the raw seed which was offered for sale. A great many growers now purchase seed which has been modified in special ways to enhance germination or to make the whole process easier to accomplish. And a significant number of greenhouses germinate very little seed, preferring rather to purchase seedling plugs in various stages of maturation.

Plant plugs

Plugs (seedlings of various sizes with a soil root ball) are becoming the normal method of raising both annual and perennial bedding plants, rather than being the exception. Actually, no basic changes have taken place in the way plants are grown but significant changes have occurred in the mechanization of seedling production and marketing channels.

Plugs are sown with mechanical seeders possessing varying degrees of automation. Most plug growers are large greenhouses that either utilize millions of plugs themselves or raise plugs for sale to other greenhouses. These plug operations have become so efficient and reliable that it often makes no economic sense for small growers to worry about the details of germination; they simply buy small plugs for transplanting.

The speed with which plugs can be transplanted also promotes their use. And they generally survive better than bare root seedlings. Many smaller growers can realize an extra crop of annuals during the busiest spring months by using half grown plugs; those plugs can make a flowering crop of bedding packs in two weeks if fast maturing varieties are used and environmental conditions are excellent.

Although many growers continue to germinate their own seed for a variety of good reasons, the trend in annual plant production is clearly towards greater utilization of specialist plugs. Every grower should realize that plugs do not come cheap. In almost every case, it is less expensive for greenhouses to produce their own seedlings if the expertise and conditions are adequate on premises. Plugs can enhance productive capacity and profits under the proper conditions but their added expense must be thoroughly considered before a decision is made to use them extensively.

Perhaps the chief reason why many growers still produce their own seedlings is because a wide variety of seedlings can be grown on a reliable and individual need basis. Plug production has not yet become so well refined as to provide the wide selection of varieties which some growers demand. And receiving greenhouses must often modify their cultural plans somewhat to fit production, marketing, and shipping programs of the plug producers. Problems related to reliable receipt of plugs and quality of merchandise sometimes surface and must be considered as a risk factor by anyone planning to purchase plugs.

The overall picture concerning plugs at the present time might be summarized by saying they are definitely a profitable and useful tool for greenhouse managers but they must be used properly and under the right circumstances to be fully effective.

Direct sowing

In certain cases growers may find that sowing seed directly to bedding plant cell pack containers is advantageous. Obviously, this route saves the time necessary to plant bare root seedlings or plugs to the final selling flat. Full spacing is required, however, as soon as the seed is sown. Another disadvantage of direct sowing is that a greater amount of carefully climate controlled germination space is necessary.

Not all varieties of annuals and perennials are suitable for direct sowing. Several conditions must generally be met: 1) seed for the variety must be inexpensive; 2) it must germinate easily; 3) germination climate must be relatively easy to provide; 4) plants must be fast growing to establish easily in the relatively large initial container; 5) the seed must be easy to handle in the direct seeding process.

Since relatively few trees and shrubs meet the above criteria, this method is seldom used for them. Many perennials are suitable since a good number of popular varieties are easy to germinate and their seed is cheap (contrary to the fact that many perennials are hard to germinate). Annuals such as Alyssum, Portulaca, and Lobelia are very adaptable to direct seeding, especially since pelleted products containing several seeds are easy to obtain.

Easy to germinate varieties such as Petunias and Marigolds are also sometimes sown direct, but the drawback here is that these plants grow so vigorously that many growers prefer not to have more than one plant per cell (at least 2 seeds must be placed in each cell to allow for the fact that a certain percentage will not germinate. If only 1 seed were put in each cell, there would be several empty cells per flat).

Each grower must evaluate whether direct sowing has a place in their operation. It can be a valuable time saver at critically busy times, thus eliminating some need for inexperienced temporary help. This is a big consideration for bedding plant growers where the success of an entire season may rest upon a few days of all out activity. Direct sowing requires more expertise and more expensive space, but it saves sometimes unobtainable labor.

Tree, shrub, and perennial seed propagation

Most of our detailed discussion concerning sexual reproduction focuses upon the methods and materials required for sowing annual plants (simply because this category is more frequently sown, by far). There are, however, some special considerations which should be mentioned in addition to those given elsewhere for trees, shrubs, and perennials. No attempt at an exhaustive presentation is made, simply enough to allow readers to realize that differences do exist and should be researched before extensive commercial production is begun.

Tree and shrub seed (when sold by reputable dealers) is often identified with the geographic location from which it originated. Perennial seed is sometimes identified in the same manner, but the practice is not so frequent. This notation method is important because the survival of trees, shrubs, and perennials is partially determined by the genetic makeup of parent populations from which the seed was collected. Obviously, a geographically widespread species such as Colorado Blue Spruce (*Picea pungeus glauca*) has many more or less ecologically stabilized wild genotypes represented by specific geographic populations. Thus, the suitability of such trees and shrubs for a particular ornamental landscape can depend to a large degree upon where the seed used to produce the plants originated, even though the plants are considered to be in the same species as are plants from another location.

Tree, shrub, and perennial seed may also be labeled with a short description of plant characteristics (such as exceptionally highly colored fall leaves) which the seller regards as important and distinguishing from other populations of the species.

Growers interested in collecting their own tree, shrub, and perennial seed should realize that collection of seed for certain species or of any species' seed in specific protected areas may be regulated by governments of the country, state, or political entity in which the plants are located. Serious fines or other punishment may be leveled against persons who break the law. Since numerous collectors travel world wide, they should realize that not only highly developed or populated countries impose such sanctions. The territory may indeed appear wild and uninhabited, but such countries as Chile, Argentina, and Australia are very serious about prosecution for poachers of plant species which are considered akin to national treasures. These are certainly not the only countries to follow such a practice. In the United States, a person is relatively free to collect most seed from plants on private land if the owner consents. However, collectors should not assume this to be the case in foreign countries (many of which do not have a strongly developed concept of private property rights).

Oftentimes, several other characteristics of the seed or plant plugs can be ascertained from a dealer's catalog. If tree, shrub, or perennial plugs or liners are offered, the descriptive literature will usually mention whether the plants are derived from seed, cuttings, grafts, or budding. In the latter two cases, the root stock used for grafting or budding onto may be mentioned. Whether or not the plants are self-fruitful may also be noted.

Some suppliers offer further data about seedlings, cuttings, or plugs. Look for information about virus certification, plant bed density, fertilization methods, transplanting, and root pruning practices.

Of course, not all the various data mentioned here will be available for every batch of seed, cuttings, or plugs. In fact, the majority will have only the most basic notations, if any. Every purchaser should, however, look carefully in catalogs since the information may be inconspicuous or in a code form used within the wholesale trade. Figure 3 explains some commonly used nursery notations as they appear in catalogs.

As readers can see, a good deal of abbreviated information may be available upon which to base cultural decisions. Catalogs offering annual seed or cuttings are often similarly profuse with specific data, but the conventions for notation in this case are not nearly so widely accepted, with individual companies choosing to provide their own version of seed types, etc.

One final aspect of tree, shrub, and perennial propagation should be touched upon. These classes of plants (as opposed to annuals) need to be monitored more carefully for root congestion and root circling in the

Acer platanoides (Norway Maple)
Description and seed origin location.

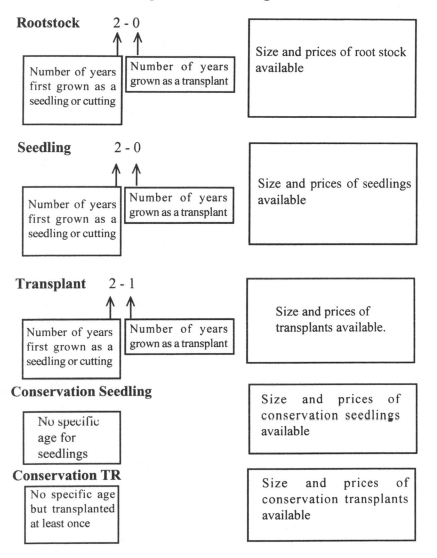

Rootstock 2 - 0

Number of years first grown as a seedling or cutting

Number of years grown as a transplant

Size and prices of root stock available

Seedling 2 - 0

Number of years first grown as a seedling or cutting

Number of years grown as a transplant

Size and prices of seedlings available

Transplant 2 - 1

Number of years first grown as a seedling or cutting

Number of years grown as a transplant

Size and prices of transplants available.

Conservation Seedling

No specific age for seedlings

Size and prices of conservation seedlings available

Conservation TR

No specific age but transplanted at least once

Size and prices of conservation transplants available

Figure 3

Standard notation for tree and shrub seedlings or rooted cuttings – above is for seedlings but rooted cuttings are treated similar. Other determinations which might be seen are : P-1 (1 year plug with media ball or pot; 3+ cane (shrub with 3 or more canes); budded tree 1 year (budded on rootstock for 1 year); CVI (Certified Virus Indexed stock). Other notations may also occasionally be seen, including multiple seed origins and elevation of origin above sea level.

propagation container. Annuals also develop deleterious root congestion, but since they are in use for only one season, the long term effects are not so detrimental or noticeable in the permanent landscape.

Improper treatment of trees, shrubs, and perennials in the propagation phase can negatively effect future growth for years to come. Poor treatment arises most often not as a result of ignorance but because growers are unable to find space or labor resources to transplant and root prune plants on the proper schedule. As a result, they concentrate upon more pressing needs at that time until many tree, shrub, and perennial seedlings or cuttings are almost worthless for future use. Further discussion of this topic will be presented as trees and shrubs are treated in detail in a later chapter.

THE PROPAGATION PLAN

Precision growing requires a grower to formulate definite plans long before the first cutting is taken or the first seed is sown. The details of crop planning will be dealt with in a later section but some mention should be made now of the major factors which will affect propagation schedules. Other than environmental influences, the propagation date will affect crop timing more than any factor and great care should be taken when determining it. Whenever possible, most growers prefer to have a sequence of crops within the same variety so that all plants do not mature at the same time. Too many propagation dates for the same variety will lower efficiency but too few will result in a glut of plants at one time and not enough at other times. Only experience enables growers to determine a near perfect crop sequence. However, with careful planning even the neophyte can produce acceptable timing.

After a propagation and growing plan has been completed for every crop in the greenhouse or nursery, the individual data should be gathered into a central data bank or notebook. This "cookbook" will enable employees to determine a daily activity schedule throughout the busy season without having to consciously evaluate each step.

An added benefit of time sequencing crops is that the labor required to transplant and care for plants is spread out. Employees get tired of working on the same thing every day; they stay happier if a crop can be transplanted in a reasonable length of time. The same variety may have to be worked on in a week but there has been a break in the monotony. The total amount of work to be accomplished at a particular time must be reflected in the propagation plan. It makes no sense to germinate more seed than the labor force can handle; seedlings and cuttings are highly perishable and will decline in value quickly if not transplanted at the proper time. Available production space will also influence the propagation plan. Projected available space at transplanting time may force the delay of germination dates a few days; if the delay lengthens to more than a week the entire crop plan should be reevaluated to avoid missing the expected market. Growers should label all propagation containers with waterproof markers. The variety name, date, crop number, number of finished plants to be made, pot size, and the number of propagation flats the crop includes should be clearly visible. A well documented, neat label enables employees to work independently once they have been carefully instructed on how to interpret the labels.

Even if growers do not propagate their own material some type of modified production plan, based partly upon the expected maturity of starter plants they purchase, is necessary. Bare root or container grown starts of woody plants must be of a size which will produce the desired size crop in the proper time frame. And it is of prime importance to correlate the size of annual seedling plugs and cuttings with the predicted crop marketing date. Buying starter plant material does not relieve the grower of responsibility for devising a propagation plan, it simply shifts the emphasis to shipping times and size characteristics rather than cutting or sowing dates.

To aid growers in timing crops, a list of germination and marketing dates is presented in Table 8. The comments about greenhouse temperatures or other significant factors should be noted carefully since they will alter maturation. This list is complied from data collected at a latitude of 43^0 N and under normally high light conditions. It must be emphasized that this information is only a guide and actual results can vary considerably when any environmental factor is changed. Even if all factors appeared to be similar, no two crops ever seem to progress exactly the same from year to year. A grower should always plan to deal with some variation in timing.

Since propagation is such an important phase of nursery and greenhouse production, it makes sense to allow only the most dependable, fastidious, and capable employees to engage in this work. They should also have extensive experience with plants in general because they will need to recognize the importance of properly naming each variety as well as having some conception of the critical role they play in the success of the overall operation.

Table 8
Approximate germination and marketing dates for some major greenhouse crops. Latitude 43⁰ North. Unless otherwise noted crops are grown 72 plants in 11 1/2 inch x 21 1/4 inch flats.

Variety	Germination date	Growing temp F^0	Market date	Flowers present	No. plants per pot and pot size
Ageratum Royal Hawaii	3/22	55	5/20	yes	1
Alyssum New Carpet of Snow	4/22	55	5/30	yes	several
Alyssum Saxatile	3/21	50	5/20	no	several
Alyssum Rose Wonderland	4/12	55	5/30	yes	several
Aster Ball Florist Mix	4/25	55	5/30	no	1
Asparagus Sprengeri	9/1	55	5/20	no	1 per 2 1/2 in
Begonia Scarlandra	2/1	62	5/30	yes	1 per 3 1/2in
Begonia Non-Stop	12/20	62	5/30	yes	1 per 4 1/2 in
Broccoli Early Dividend	4/10	50	5/25	no	1
Cabbage Golden Cross	4/10	50	5/25	no	1
Canteloupe Burpee Hybrid	5/1	60	5/30	no	3 per 3 1/2 in
Carnation Grenadin	3/11	50	5/10	no	several
Cauliflower Snow King	4/10	50	5/25	no	1
Chrysanthemum White Snowland	4/1	55	5/30	yes	1
Coleus Wizard	3/20	62	5/25	no	1
Cucumber Sweet Slice	5/7	55	5/25	no	3 per 3 1/2 in
Dahlia Figaro	3/4	55	5/20	yes	1 per 2 1/2 in
Daisy Shasta Alaska	4/1	50	5/25	no	several
Dianthus Prize Mix	3/15	50	5/30	yes	1
Dianthus Indian Carpet Mix	4/1	50	5/25	no	several
Dracena Indivisa Spike	6/1	50	5/1	no	3 1/2 in
Dusty Miller Silver Dust	3/7	50	5/25	no	1
Eggplant Dusky	4/3	60	5/25	no	1 per 3 1/2 in

Table 8 (cont.)

Variety	Germination date	Growing temp F^0	Market date	Flowers present	No. plants per pot and pot size
English Daisy Bellis	4/15	50	5/20	no	several
Fuchsia (cuttings)	2/1	55	5/25 pinched	yes	1 per 3 1/2 in
Geranium (cuttings)	2/15	55	5/20 no pinch	yes	1 per 4 1/2 in
Geranium Ringo 2000(seed)	2/15	60	5/25	yes	1 per 3 1/2 in
Impatiens New Guinea (cuttings)	3/1	62	5/30	yes	1 per 3 1/2 in
Impatiens Super Elfins (Imp. Germ.)	3/25	62	5/25	yes	1
Ivy Geranium (cuttings)	2/15	55	5/30 no pinch	yes	1 per 3 1/2 in
Lobelia Riviera Midnight Blue	3/10	50	5/25	yes	several
Lupine Russell Mix	4/1	50	5/25	no	1
Marigold Inca	3/1	50	5/25	yes	1
Marigold Bonanza Series	3/20	50	5/25	yes	1
Marigold Boy Series	4/1	50	5/25	yes	1
Marigold Crackerjack	4/25	50	5/25	no	1
Marigold French Vanilla	3/1	50	5/25	yes	1
Mums Garden (cutting)	2/20	55	5/1-5/25 pinched	yes	1
Nicotiana Starship	3/20	55	5/30	yes	1
Pansy Bingo Mix (Imp. Germ.)	2/1	50	5/20	yes	1
Pepper Better Belle	3/21	60	5/25	no	1 per 3 1/2 in
Petunia Single Grandiflora	2/26	50	5/25	yes	1
Petunia Double Grandiflora	2/1	50	5/25	yes	1
Poppy Oriental	3/5	50	5/25	no	1
Portulaca Sundial Mix	3/18	55	5/30	yes	several
Primrose Pacific Giants	2/7	50	5/25	no	1
Pumpkin	5/1	55	5/25	no	3 per 3 1/2 in
Pyrethrum Robinson's Single	3/1	50	5/25	no	1
Ranunculus Bloomingdale	9/10	50	4/15	yes	1 per 4 in

Table 8 (cont.)

Variety	Germination date	Growing temp F^0	Market date	Flowers present	No. plants per pot and pot size
Salvia Fuegeo (Imp. Germ.)	3/15	60	5/25	yes	1
Snapdragon Floral Carpet	3/20	50	5/25	no	1
Snapdragon Rocket	3/20	50	5/25	no	1
Squash Zucchini	5/8	55	5/25	no	3 per 3 1/2 in
Strawberries Fresca	1/10	50	5/10	no	1
Thunbergia Alata	3/1	60 pinched	5/25	yes	1 per 3 1/2 in
Tomato	3/20	55	5/20	no	1 per 3 1/2 in
Tomato	3/1	55	5/25	yes	1 per 6 in
Tomato	3/30	55	5/20	no	1 per 2 1/4 in
Viola	3/2	50	5/20	yes	1
Verbena Quartz	3/15	55	5/30	yes	1
Vinca Vine (cuttings)	2/1	50 pinched	5/25	no	1 per 2 1/2 in
Zinnia Thumbelina	5/8	60	5/30	no	1
Zinnia State Fair	5/7	60	5/25	no	1
Zinnia Peter Pan	3/25	60	5/25	yes	1 per 3 1/2 in
Begonia Non-Stop	12/20	60 no pinch	5/30	yes	4 per 6 in
Calceolaria Brite and Early	8/22	60 early 50 late	2/1	yes	1 per 6 in
Carnation Lillipot	11/7	50	6/10	yes	6 per 6 in
Cineraria Improved Festival	8/22	60 early 50 late	2/10	yes	1 per 6 in
Cineraria Improved Festival	11/7	60 early 50 late	4/1	yes	1 per 6 in
Cyclamen Hybrid (fast crop)	3/3	60	11/15	yes	1 per 6 in
Cyclamen Hybrid (fast crop)	4/7	60 early 50 late	3/1	yes	1 per 6 in
Gloxinia Ultra Scarlet	10/15	65	5/10	yes	2 per 6 in
Gloxinia Ultra Scarlet	7/1	65	12/1	yes	2 per 6 in

Table 8 (cont.)

Variety	Germination date	Growing temp F^0	Market date	Flowers present	No. plants per pot and pot size
Kalanchoe (cuttings)	7/7	62	12/20 no shade no lights	yes	4 per 6 in
Martha Washington					
Geranium (cuttings)	11/15	50	5/1	yes	1 per 6 in
Christmas Pepper					
Holiday Cheer	5/31	60	10/20	yes	1 per 6 in

Note: Successive crops will require less time during higher light seasons or more time in lower light seasons. To time hanging baskets or larger pots when plants are pinched, add four to five weeks crop time. Seed is unmodified in germination characterisitics unless noted.

MANUAL AND MECHANICAL SEED SOWING

As readers may have deduced from the previous discussion, there are several methods by which seed is placed in the sowing medium. These different techniques all require the same basic environmental conditions but certain differences in handling allow the grower to produce seedlings which are better suited for specific needs.

Most of the information presented so far has referred to the manual sowing of raw seed for the production of more or less bareroot seedlings. This is the older method of sowing and it is still used in many instances, particularly in small operations and in cases where a restricted number of plants are needed for numerous varieties. Manual sowing is entirely satisfactory to use in those instances where it still makes economic sense.

Mechanical sowing can be accomplished with numerous types of machines which exhibit various levels of efficiency, cost, and adaptability to the task. Since the machines are so variable, growers should develop some set of criteria which must be met by the seeder to be used, then a specific design is sought out to fulfill these predetermined criteria. Once a seeder is chosen, it should be tested under actual conditions before it is put into daily use. Of course, one must also evaluate the cost of seeders to be certain a positive economic return can be achieved by their use. There is little doubt that a seeder meeting necessary specifications can be found. The question is: Would it be economical?

Mechanical seeder models are available from the very simplest hand vibrators which can be homemade from electric shavers up to extremely complex machines costing perhaps $100,000. The latter will perform the entire sowing process for plant plugs at a high rate of speed. Choosing the appropriate model for your needs at an economical price is the tricky part.

Most smaller growers can purchase an adequate seeder with basic accessories for under $1500. These models usually require a considerable amount of handwork, but most are quite reliable and seldom break down. They are generally of rather simple construction so that repairs can be accomplished on site by a competent handyman.

The larger, more sophisticated seeders are available in many configurations. A grower must have enough volume of seeding to justify the cost and to warrant the sometimes skilled operators necessary for efficient operation. Repair of complex seeders may require a manufacturer's representative to do the job. These machines usually must be fine-tuned or adjusted to handle particular types of seed so that changing between varieties often requires extra time.

Numerous ancillary apparatus are commercially available to aid growers in the basic seed germination process and to complement mechanical seeders. Many of the simpler devices are easy to construct a similar product from locally available parts at the nursery or greenhouse.

Various seed germination chambers, watering stations, misting lines, and heat sources can be easily set up to serve the same purpose as expensive commercial substitutes. If the device is particularly complicated or proper operation depends upon another "sister" machine, it is often best to purchase the expertise which the manufacturer invested in the system.

Visits to industry trade shows or studying catalogs are perhaps the easiest ways to become familiar with the numerous products available to aid in seed germination. The same companies may also offer a web site address. After a particular device or system is chosen on a preliminary basis, it is often prudent to visit another greenhouse or nursery to see the product in actual operation before a purchase is made. The first step of producing "baby" plants is, afterall, the most crucial phase in growing ornamentals. It must be consummated without serious problems. This stage of the operation is no place for casual experimentation, everything must be well-tested.

NEW PLANT VARIETIES

Readers will notice reference to new or improved plant varieties throughout this book. However, due to the extreme importance of this subject, some specific emphasis is in order before leaving the topic of plant propagation.

Permanent outwardly expressed variations in plant material are due to the underlying genetic diversity which all plant populations possess in a greater or lesser degree. The abundance or rarity of genetic diversity within populations is caused by several factors, not the least of which is the specific evolutionary history of a population. Some species possess natural genetic, mutational, and breeding patterns which lead to greater variation, while other species are naturally less diverse in this regard.

Natural evolutionary diversity has been enhanced within the last few thousand years by human manipulation of plant populations. This fact is most evident in the numerous food crops which early man artificially selected and developed from wild populations. Some of these crops are almost unrecognizable In many characteristics when compared with the wild plants which gave rise to them (several important crops have been genetically traced beyond reasonable doubt to their parent species). Even a child can recognize the validity of these processes when they are applied to the myriad breeds of familiar animals such as the dog, cat, pigeon, cattle, and others.

Our purpose in the present discussion is not to dwell upon the origination of plant variation but to celebrate it and point out the great benefits which can be realized by enthusiastically seeking out, manipulating, and utilizing the immense pool of genetic variation available. There is literally almost no limit to possible plant variations which could serve as ornamental subjects.

During the greater part of recorded human history, and before, our ancestors simply selected (unconsciously or with premeditation) those plant variations which were desirable. Some of the plant variations likely were produced by natural interbreeding or interbreeding caused indirectly or directly by man. In this manner, numerous useful plant crops which we now utilize were developed and stabilized. Later, man developed a keener understanding of how to crossbreed both plants and animals. This led to an even larger number useful domesticated varieties. In the last few hundred years, these primitive means of selection and crossbreeding have been improved through the use of scientific methods so that we can now produce predictable (often precise) results.

Although numerous new ornamental plant varieties have already been developed, the bonanza for ornamental horticulture resulting from selection and hybridization of plant varieties is just beginning due to the fact that most of the earlier effort was focused upon important food and fiber crops (everyone is familiar with the Green Revolution brought about by genetic research in corn, cotton, rice, wheat, etc.).

The first part of the 21st century will see a much greater expansion of ornamental plant varieties than has previously been witnessed. All this background is provided in order to emphasize the great opportunities which will continue to arise in the industry. We can expect no less than the revolution which occurred in field crops due to exactly the same basic factors. The commercial benefits to nursery and greenhouse operators will be nothing short of miraculous.

However, only those growers who recognize the immense benefits to be realized from consistently seeking, testing, and marketing new varieties will reap the full profits. Poisettias are a perfect example of the near total change which has been brought about through breeding and selection. This crop was unimportant to the greenhouse industry less than 100 years ago. Due to the efforts of a few pioneers, the genetics of the crop were improved somewhat through the years until more or less acceptable plants could be produced for Christmas. They were not, however, easy or cheap to grow, nor did they satisfy customers greatly since there were several important problems such as poor leaf retention and excess plant height.

During the 1990's an explosion of breeding and selection produced 100's of new poinsettia varieties, many of which possessed extremely valuable traits: good leaf and bract retention, desirable height characteristics, unusual leaf and bract colors, ease of culture, a variety of maturity dates, predictable branching, and lower production temperatures.

Now the Poinsettia is easily the most important potted flower in North America, and most of the credit is due to the introduction of improved varieties. Marketing has been important, but everyone must realize that it is tough to consistently expand sales of an inherently poor product.

In addition to the rosy prospects just described, there is a second beneficial bombshell which is starting to impact the ornamental plant industry; it also relates to the introduction of new and better plant material. Genetic engineering via several technological pathways is becoming a commonplace event, starting with food crops and now entering the ornamental area. The exceptional potential value of genetic engineering is that it is an even more precise means of altering plant characterisitics than are selection and breeding programs. It also has the advantage of often proving to yield valuable changes much more quickly. It is more precise because scientists can often alter a simple gene rather than the usual case in breeding and selection where at least several genes are affected. Thus, a gene for pest resistance or perhaps more rapid growth can be inserted without changing other desirable characteristics of the variety. This process will prove to be of immense value to horticulturists in the near future.

Of course, it is up to the knowledgable horticulturist to take advantage of these powerful technologies. Growers must realize how greatly these important developments are now affecting and will affect the industry in the future. They will be every bit as important as were the marketing changes which have occurred over the past 20-30 years.

One final point should be made in regard to new plant material: The ability to take profitable advantage of this phenomenon depends almost entirely upon a grower's knowledge base and willingness to assess and trial new varieties. They will be easily available to anyone, not just the bigger growers or ones with more money to invest. Therefore, a smaller grower can easily possess the most powerful tool in the industry simply by choosing and growing the proper plant material for a particular environment or market. This situation, if properly utilized, will allow smaller growers to regain some competitiveness which has been lost. Smaller establishments, by their very nature, can react to varietal changes much more quickly than can large growers.

A DETAILED SAMPLE PLAN FOR SOWING SEED

Novice commercial growers and interested amateurs may benefit by referring to the Appendix for a detailed account of seed sowing and transplanting which the author has prepared previously for a particular set of conditions. This account is very elementary but it is useful in that each single step is covered in extreme detail for beginners. It "walks" the participant through the complete process and emphasizes all the details which, when followed religiously, will almost certainly yield favorable results.

Chapter 6

SOILS AND GROWING MEDIA

In the not too distant past, most container plants were grown in true soils. Because these true soils are a wonderfully adapted natural plant growing system, growers needed little more than a passing knowledge of their properties in order to produce acceptable crops.

Today greenhouses and nurseries utilize growing media composed of highly amended soil or of totally artificial components. This change requires successful growers to become acquainted with the elementary physical and chemical properties of different media ingredients and with the properties resulting from mixtures of ingredients. Many substances are utilized as media ingredients in an almost endless variety of proportions and combinations.

Since the substrate in which plants are grown affects crop production greatly, it is imperative that growers select the appropriate mix for their operation carefully and with some knowledge of the technical factors involved. Slight changes in media makeup can vastly affect crop quality.

The question might be asked; "if true soils are so wonderfully adapted to grow plants, why have we found it necessary to either alter them substantially or replace them altogether"? The answer is that only a small proportion of true soils are well adapted to growing a wide variety of container plants under a wide variety of conditions. And these more universally adapted natural soils are not now easy to find or procure in most locations. Plant growers have sought to improve upon the properties of natural soil for use in container culture and to provide media alternatives which can be readily obtained.

In the following discussion, the term "soil" will be used as a general name for the substrate plants are grown in (whether natural or artificial). More specific terms will be applied when necessary.

SOIL FUNCTIONS

The functions of soil are plant support, storing mineral elements and moisture, and providing an oxygen transfer route from the atmosphere to roots. Most modern scientists would agree that soil also serves as a background in which microorganisms carry out various processes which are very important to plants. A good soil should combine the various physical and chemical properties of ingredients in such a way as to carry out each function properly. Secondarily, it must be economical, readily available, uniform from batch to batch, free of diseases, insects and weed seed, and contain no harmful chemicals.

PHYSICAL AND CHEMICAL PROPERTIES OF SOIL

The suitability of a particular soil for use in container plant production depends chiefly upon its ability to hold adequate moisture for plant growth while maintaining sufficient root aeration and upon its having enough mineral element storage capacity to satisfy plant requirements. Soils may be superbly productive when field crops are grown and yet be only marginally useful for container crops. This change in productive capacity is brought about by the destruction of soil structure when it is lifted for use and by the shallowness of container soil masses as compared to the natural depth in the field. Both of these changes in field soil cause it to retain more water when irrigated in containers. As a consequence, it does not allow enough oxygen to reach the root zone. This general unsuitability of field soil for optimum container production forces growers to modify it with various amendments or to make artificial mixes containing no true soil.

The water holding capacity of soils is dependent upon the size of pore spaces between particles and upon total porosity. Large pore spaces decrease the water holding capacity. Sandy soils with big soil particles have large pore spaces and retain little water, aeration is good because water drains quickly and leaves pore spaces open for oxygen movement. Clay soils with small soil particles have small pore spaces and retain more water; aeration in them is poor. Total porosity by volume is greater in clay soils but pore size is greater in sandy soils. Soils with fine particle size, such as clay, are able to store more mineral elements than sandy soils which possess larger particle sizes. It should be apparent by now that the important attributes of soils as they relate to plant growth in containers are, to a large extent, determined by particle size. Water and most critical mineral elements are held more strongly in soils with small particle size because they both exhibit residual positive electrical charges while soil particles exhibit residual negative charges on their surface. Thus water and the important mineral elements are attracted to the negatively charged soil surface. Smaller soil particles increase the quantity of negative charges exposed on the particle surface because small particles have more surface area per volume than do large particles.

An understanding of the relationship between soil particle size and moisture and mineral element retention enables a grower to postulate the effects on plant growth which may occur if certain ingredients are added to or deleted from soil mixes. Table 9 may help in visualizing the effect particle size has on various soil properties. The ideal soil mix is one in which there are enough large particles to ensure proper movement of oxygen to the root zone and sufficient numbers of small particles to retain water and mineral elements in quantities suitable for plant growth. There are many different combinations of ingredients which will approach this ideal mix; the particular combination chosen will depend on the grower's estimation of which one fits the particular situation best. All varieties of plants do not grow equally well in the same soil conditions. It is incumbent upon the grower to choose a soil mix which will meet the need of the greatest number of plants. Any varieties of plants which will not grow well in the soil mix settled upon should be candidates for exclusion from the greenhouse or nursery program. It is, of course, possible to select several soil mixes for different crops but this lowers efficiency, especially in small to medium size operations.

While particle size is the major determinant of soil mix characteristics, soil texture or structure may also have some effect. Field soils normally have a well defined structure; that is, the individual particles are arranged or aggregated into definite patterns with one another. The process of lifting these soils and mixing for use in containers tends to destroy their structure. Artificial structure may be given to soils by adding such amendments as coarse peat or chopped coir chunks which are aggregates of finer peat and coir particles. Soil structure is also a reflection of the degree of packing or porosity of the soil. Generally, soils which have larger aggregates will pack less tightly and consequently have more macropore space. An

Table 9

Characteristics of natural field soils. Total porosity is greater in clay even though pore size is smaller because there are many more pores in clay than in sand.

Natural soil types	Average particle size	Average pore size	Total porosity	Water retention	Mineral element retention	Oxygen movement to roots
Clay Loam Sandy loam Sand	Small ↓ Large	Small ↓ Large	Large ↑ Small	High ↑ Low	High ↑ Low	Poor ↓ Good

example of how the geometry of soil amendments will affect structure is illustrated by the fact that sharp sand particles will pack more tightly than dune sand particles whose edges have been rounded by wind action. This relationship is pictured in Figure 4. Soils having a structure which tends to promote larger pore spaces will drain well and provide better oxygen exchange to the root zone. Soil structure can be modified somewhat by the mineral elements present. Calcium tends to promote formation of structural aggregates while sodium disperses soil particles and destroys structure. Compounds containing sodium should be eliminated as much as possible from fertilizer programs.

Soil fertility is determined mainly by the extra fine particles present which possess a diameter of less than one micron. This portion of the soil is known as the colloidal fraction and is composed of clay and decayed organic matter. Mention has already been made of the negative charges present on the surface of soil particles; these charges attract positively charged ions of mineral elements (cations). The capacity of a soil or soil fraction to hold mineral elements is known as the cation exchange capacity. Higher figures indicate more fertility. Sandy soils have a cation exchange capacity of perhaps 5, while clay may approach 100. Organic colloidal material is in the neighborhood of 300 but this figure does not mean that

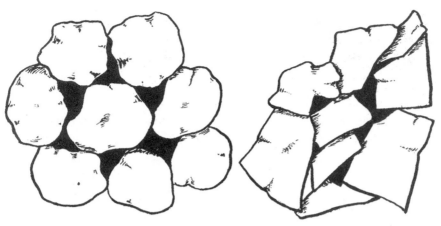

Dune or windscoured sand.   *Fractured or sharp sand.*

Figure 4

Soil structure is affected by the shape of individual particles. Pore space is greater and more regularly spaced in dune sand than in fractured sand. Pore space in black.

all organic matter (such as peat moss) which is added to soil increases the cation exchange capacity so greatly since only the very finest particles are classed as colloidal material. These figures are very approximate and would change considerably with the particular soil or material measured; they are given solely to show the reader comparative extreme values.

A special situation may arise where the water present in soil pore spaces becomes highly saturated with mineral compounds. The level of mineral saturation is commonly known as the soluble salts concentration (although the two are not always strictly comparable). High concentrations result from a high level of mineral salts in the soil initially or from an excess applied as fertilizer. These salts may be leached away by applying an excess of water, which drains through the pores and flushes the substrate. Soils with large pore spaces (which drain more easily) are obviously easier to clear of high salt levels. Other factors which may secondarily affect soluble salt concentrations are: water purity, mineral element types, soil species, types of organic matter, frequency and amount of irrigation, and irrigation methods. Any one of these factors may, at times, assume primary importance.

The pH is a measure of the acidic or basic nature of soils; it varies with the chemical makeup of soil particles. Lower figures indicate more acid conditions and higher figures a more basic situation. A pH of 7 is neutral. Many people use the terms basic and alkaline interchangeably; this is satisfactory for general purposes but is not true in the strict scientific application. Most plants will grow in a fairly wide pH range, those soils with values of 5.4 to 6.8 would be suitable for the majority of crops. Wider variations in pH can be tolerated under certain fertilizer programs but normally the soil pH is adjusted at the time of mixing by the addition of limestone to raise values and addition of sulfur compounds to lower values. Since special soil fertility problems can arise due to improper pH levels, more detail of these situations will be presented in the discussion of fertilizer programs.

PROPERTIES OF SOIL MEDIA INGREDIENTS

Let us now turn our attention to presenting basic information concerning the more common ingredients used in preparing greenhouse and nursery soils. Growers can then formulate specific mixes which fit their particular situation. Information presented in Table 10 summarizes some of the important attributes of commonly used ingredients.

Field soil

Field soils are variable but may average approximately 50% pore space with perhaps 5% solid organic particles by weight, the remaining content being mineral. As mentioned previously, particle size is a prime determinant of a soil's suitability for container plant production. Mineral soil particles are classified according to size into gravel, sand, silt, and clay. Particles from 0.05 to 2.0 millimeters in diameter are classified as sand, while gravel is anything larger than 2.0 millimeters. Silt particle diameter is 0.002 to 0.05 millimeters. Clays have a diameter of less than 0.002 millimeters.

Sandy soils, dominated by large particles, are well drained and aerated. The small surface area of large particles makes sandy soils retain little water and nutrients. Because of the small particle size with a subsequent increase in surface area and negative electrical charge, the clay fraction of field soils is responsible for holding the majority of nutrient minerals. Water holding capacity is large and aeration poor in clay. The plasticity and stickiness of clays make handling difficult. Silt particles, being

Table 10

Characteristics of commonly available materials used in greenhouse and nursery soil mixes.

	Loam	Sand	Perlite	Vermiculite	Sawdust	Ground bark	Coir	Peat Moss
Uniform from batch to batch	-	+	+	+	+ -	+	+	+
Stable under pasteurization	+-	+	+	+	+	+	+	+
Aeration good	+-	+	+	+-	+	+	+	+
Fertility low	+-	+	+	+-	+	+	+	+
Moisture retention good	+	-	-	+-	+	+	+	+
Nutrient retention good	+	-	-	+-	+	+	+	+
Free of weeds	-	+	+	+	+	+	+	+
Disease and pest free	-	+-	+	+	+-	+-	+	+
Inexpensive	+	+	-	-	+	+-	+-	+-

note: + denotes the material possesses the characteristic.
　　　　- denotes the material does not possesses the characteristic.
　　　　+ - denotes the material possess the characteristic in
　　　　　intermediate form.

intermediate in size, have properties lying between those of sand and clay. Loam type soils are mixtures of sand, clay, and silt in varying proportions with the prefix denoting which soil particles dominate the mixture; for example, "sandyloam".

In modern greenhouse and nursery production, field soils are seldom used without addition of amendments. Sandy loams or loams are the only classes which approach any degree of usability by themselves. Sandy soils can be used but require large, frequent, and precise application of fertilizer elements. Usually, field soils are mixed with appropriate amounts of organic matter and inorganic aggregates to satisfy plant requirements. The chief benefits of incorporating field soil into media mixes are that it is inexpensive if suitable local sources are available and the inherent fertility and buffering capacity of soils containing some clay reduces the need for growers to precisely control fertilizer application to avoid serious deficiencies. Drawbacks are the unavoidable lack of uniformity, possibility of herbicide contamination, and abundance of weed seed, soil pests, and microbes. Novice growers may find the presence of some fertility in soils a blessing because there will be less chance of crop failure due to mineral deficiencies. Experienced growers with an adequate knowledge of fertilizer needs may prefer a mix with little or no fertility so they can adjust applications to the precise needs of crops.

Organic matter

Organic matter in various forms has been and still is the most common amendment to container plant soils; it is derived from dead plant tissue and, as such, will vary considerably in quality depending on what species it comes from and the state of decay. Although many types of organic matter may be appropriate as soil additives, some alteration of basic properties is often necessary before use. Organic matter has the beneficial attributes of adding to water and nutrient retention in sandy soils and aiding aeration in clay soils. Possession of qualities particular to both small and large soil particles makes organic matter the universal additive in container plant mixes. Several physical and chemical properties of organic matter should be kept in mind by the grower. A) Organic matter generally has a good water holding capacity and good aeration. B) Organic matter generally has a high cation exchange capacity (holds nutrients well). C) Certain types of organic matter can cause what is known as ammonium toxicity after being pasteurized for diseases and pests. D) Certain types of organic matter cause rapid removal of nitrogen from the substrate. An evaluation of different organic sources follows.

PEAT MOSS — Several very different materials are commonly called peat moss. Humus, reed, and sedge peats are usually almost black in color and, because of an advanced state of decay, have a large proportion of fine particles; high soluble salt contents may sometimes be encountered, depending upon the site of origin. These peats are generally unsuitable for greenhouse and nursery soils, unless a medium containing a greater number of fine particles is desired. There is a much lower organic fiber content in these peats. Sphagnum and hypnum peat mosses are less decomposed and, unless ground, contain fewer fine particles. Color is from dark brown to brownish-gray. Plant cellular and tissue structure may be apparent in the higher grades if the peat has not been ground. Hypnum moss is available in some local areas and can be obtained from distributors but it is not as widely encountered and economical as sphagnum moss.

Because of its beneficial properties, wide availability, and reasonably low cost, sphagnum peat moss is the most widely used organic constituent for greenhouse soils. Growers should take care that the material purchased is labeled sphagnum peat moss and that the quality is in line with price. A very dark brown color with numerous sticks and possibly some soil contamination indicates poor quality. Lighter grayish color with plant tissue structure apparent and no sticks or soil contamination are indications of high quality. Economical sources of sphagnum will usually lie somewhere in the middle quality grades. Texture may vary from fist size chunks down to very fine material if the peat has been mechanically ground. Small chunks are very suitable if one is growing in larger containers but finely ground peat is desirable for soil used with small pots or propagation media.

Sphagnum peat normally is low in soluble salts and adds no appreciable quantities of nutrients to soils. The pH is quite acidic but may be raised easily with the addition of limestone at the time of mixing. Sphagnum soil mixtures may sometimes be used without initial elevation of the pH when acid loving plant varieties are being grown or when the fertilizer used to grow plants on has a mild basic reaction (the basic properties of the fertilizer gradually counteract the acidic properties of sphagnum). A water source which possessed basic properties would cause similar changes as would fertilizers with a basic reaction.

The uniformity of peat varies considerably from brand to brand; one should investigate the quality and availability of a particular source carefully and then purchase only from that source to avoid variations in crop growth.

SAWDUST — Sawdust is often available in small quantities from lumber yards and cabinet shops; lumber processing areas have unlimited supplies. Cost is minimal. Walnut and incense cedar sawdust are toxic to plants, making cabinet shop sources undesirable. Redwood sawdust can be toxic if not weathered or leached thoroughly. Sawdust compares favorably with peat moss in most instances as a soil amendment if it is readily available. The pH depends upon the species of wood utilized but it is normally less acidic than peat.

A rapid depletion of nitrogen in soils is the chief drawback of using sawdust. Adding supplemental nitrogen will ameliorate this problem but the added cost incurred by doing so should be calculated into the soil cost. The amount of extra nitrogen needed will vary with source and species but it has been suggested that 2% nitrogen by weight of the sawdust is adequate. A lookout must be kept for toxic soluble salt levels when this much nitrogen is added. Hardwood sawdust from deciduous trees (oak, hickory, maple, poplar) depletes soil nitrogen more heavily than does softwood sawdust from evergreen needle trees (fir, redwood, pine). Nitrogen depletion may be lowered by using old sawdust which has decayed somewhat; the degree of decomposition is hard to assess and usually takes many years to progress appreciably. Sawdust can be treated by chemical processes to eliminate the nitrogen depletion problem but this treated sawdust is not widely available and the costs become uncompetitive with peat as an organic matter source.

Under some rare conditions (especially when the microorganism activity in soils is practically nonexistent) the use of sawdust in soil mixtures may not appreciably alter the nitrogen balance. Only a careful chemical and biological assessment of the soil will determine whether or not this situation exists. The typical biologic assessment would be made by observing growth characteristics of plants being cultured in soils with and without sawdust. Secondarily, one could also infer microorganism activity by recording their population density in the soil. Sawdust should not be used in soil mixes without a complete test of actual effects it will have on plant growth.

COIR (coconut hull fiber) — This type of organic matter has only recently become available as a widely distributed commercial product. Initial laboratory tests and on-site plant growth tests indicate that coir is economically competitive and physically comparable to peat moss in most respects. This statement assumes that the coir has been processed and composted properly. It is available as tightly compressed bricks (inexpensive to transport in this form) or in various particle and chunk forms.

Since coir has not been field tested for many decades (as has peat moss), growers would be well-advised to continue using peat moss as their chief organic media constituent until all of the properties of coir have become well known through actual use with many crops. Of course, there are instances where a quick change to coir may be justified. Nurseries or greenhouses located in tropical coir producing locations or at important depots in temperate regions may realize a significant cost savings through using coir as an organic amendment.

Coir can vary significantly in quality and composition, depending upon the source, but this is also a problem with any other ingredient. The chief potential problems with coir are: insufficient composting, poor processing, possible high soluble salts in some sources, somewhat different water holding properties than peat, reportedly erratic concentrations of mineral elements in some sources, and a higher pH (almost 7) than most growers normally expect in an organic amendment.

It appears that coir will eventually become a widespread and dependable source of organic matter for growers (especially in the tropics), but its use must be tempered by practical experience and test runs. Coir does have a feel, color, and consistency which is likely to make it appeal to both growers and customers.

BARK — Tree bark is similar to sawdust as a soil additive except that available particle size is not as restricted and the problem of soil nitrogen depletion is not so severe. A partial solution to this latter problem is to use softwood bark which is partially decomposed. In the past few years, horticultural grade bark has become reasonably available nationwide at prices competitive with those for peat moss. In locations where there is a transport savings over peat moss, bark may be the more economical choice if it is of suitable quality and particle size.

There is perhaps more variability in bark quality than in peat moss, simply because there is great variability in the species of tree available for obtaining the raw material. Additionally, sources of bark may offer a product which is in varying degrees of decomposition. Purchasing barks from a reliable horticultural source which specializes in providing material to plant growers will help eliminate some of the potential problems. These sources are knowledgable about the need to provide a consistent grade of product which is uniformly composted and meets the particle size needs of growers.

One favorable characteristic of bark is that the particle size remains relatively stable once it has been established. In other words, if bark pellets are mixed lightly with other ingredients, the pellets will remain reasonably intact through the mixing process. They also do not break down quickly in the soil mix as plants are being grown in it. Thus, bark base mixes will tend to retain their original water retaining properties for considerable periods. Bark products are often used widely in tree potting operations if there is a local source of supply which provides the proper grade. Local availability reduces the cost of the huge amounts of soil required for large pots.

MISCELLANEOUS ORGANIC MATTER SOURCES-Manure causes a buildup of toxic ammonia when pasteurized and is not uniform from batch to batch. Pasteurization is essential because of diseases and weed seed present. It should not be used in greenhouse or nursery soils.

Wood chips cause less nitrogen depletion than does sawdust but, because of their large particle size, do not offer the same water holding properties.

Ground corncobs are not readily available and cause severe nitrogen depletion of soil.

Peanut hulls may be very economical in certain areas as a source of organic matter. Nitrogen depletion of soil does occur with their use but it is much less of a problem than with sawdust. Rice hulls are comparable in quality and availability to peanut hulls.

Many other organic matter sources have been used to amend greenhouse and nursery soils but their use is limited in modern production methods by more economical, widely available, and uniform sources having more desirable characteristics.

ASSESSMENT OF ORGANIC MATTER

As a practical matter, it would seem that most growers who mix their own soil (unless local supplies dictate otherwise) have a choice of utilizing three primary organic material sources (based upon wide availability, consistent quality, economy, suitability). Peat moss is the most proven source in almost all respects, while bark products follow in second place, with coir being an up-and-coming third. These products can be used as the only source of organic matter or mixed together if the grower so decides.

Inorganic soil ingredients

Inorganic materials are usually added with the purpose of increasing the proportion of large particles in soil mixes, leading to better drainage and aeration. Only the more commonly used components will be discussed individually.

SAND-Sand is the most inexpensive and readily available source of larger particled material. Weight is sometimes a drawback if one is shipping wholesale, but, for local growers, the extra weight may be an advantage in that it prevents pots from tipping over easily when the soil is dried out. Some sand in organic mixes also anchors plants more securely. Pure sand is more or less inert chemically but most common sand will contain small amounts of clay and silt which lend some nutrient and water holding capacity. Clay should represent less than 10% by weight of the sand used. Too much clay in soil mixes containing sand can lead to compaction because of clay particles occupying the pore spaces between sand particles. If "washed" sand is used there will be very little clay or silt present.

There seems to be some disagreement in the literature about the size and shape of sand particles which are most useful in soil mixes. Some sources recommend sharp sand with relatively large particle size, only a small portion being less than 0.50 millimeters in diameter. Other authors are adamant that particles be no larger than 0.50 millimeters and with rounded edges to avoid compaction. On a practical level, many growers have found that both the fine dune sand and coarser "washed" sand will produce good crops when blended with the proper amount of organic material. Washed sand is readily available from local sand and gravel companies; it may also be called "mortar sand". Dune sand and shore sand is not always available and deliveries of small quantities are not often possible; locating a reliable source of these sand types may be difficult. When purchasing sand, growers must make it very clear that no chemicals should be added. This can sometimes be the case if sand companies are making batches for special mortar or concrete orders. It is sometimes possible to obtain heat treated sand to eliminate the possibility of microorganisms, but the availability and cost are quite variable.

PERLITE — Perlite is a light, rather fluffy, white mineral product which is chemically inert and holds very little water; cost is moderately high. Many growers who ship plants long distances prefer perlite over sand because it weighs very little. It is especially suitable for propagation mixes. Perlite is sterile and highly desirable as an ingredient. It may be obtained in several particle sizes for different uses. Over mixing when moist will cause rapid degradation of particle size. Perlite dust is a serious health hazard if measures to both reduce its presence and personnel exposure to it are not taken. Fluoride sensitive plants may do poorly in perlite mixes.

VERMICULITE — Vermiculite is a clay mineral which is physically expanded through a heating process. Being a clay, it retains the ability to hold moisture and nutrients. Vermiculite contains large amounts of potassium and magnesium so that soils mixed with it can usually function with reduced applications of these elements. When wetted, vermiculite breaks down easily with excessive mixing. Finer grades of vermiculite are especially suitable in mixes for germinating small seed. Vermiculite should be obtained from reputable horticultural dealers because construction grades do not absorb water well and are not handled to maintain a sterile product.

CALCINED CLAY — These are clay particles which have been heated to form small, hardened aggregates which do not break down easily in growing media. Calcined clay has good nutrient retention (because it is clay), and yet it provides coarse particle structure in media so that drainage is good.

A major drawback to this otherwise excellent material is the variability of product due to the sources of raw clay from which it is obtained. Another problem is that it is not locally available in most areas, thereby requiring growers to ship by the truckload to obtain reasonable transport costs.

CINDERS AND SCORIA —Cinders cost very little in coal burning regions but quality may be quite variable depending on the coal grade used and how it is burned. Large quantities of sulfates may be present in cinders and these compounds must be leached out prior to use. In high rainfall areas cinders may be leached naturally if left outdoors a minimum of one year. Cinders of proper size with good porous structure are excellent additives to peat moss if careful attention is paid to possible deleterious effects due to the chemical make up of the raw material.

ROCKWOOL — Rockwool is a cottony or woolly substance which is manufactured by subjecting mineral rocks to very high temperatures. It is sterile, uniform, and free of secondary materials. Rockwool is modified in several ways to enhance and broaden its use as a horticultural plant medium.

The raw, undifferentiated material can be used alone in blocks or containers, or it may be mixed with other soil components. In many applications as a soil additive, rockwool is conditioned to form small, cottony ball-like particles which tend to retain their individual nature when added to soil mixes. When rockwool is intended as a soil additive product, it is offered in the natural hydrophilic (water attracting) state or it is conditioned to be hydrophobic (water repelling). Thus it can be used to either increase or decrease the water holding capacity of soils, depending upon whether the hydrophilic or hydrophobic material is used.

The use of rockwool as a soil additive is not especially widespread at the present time and some evidence seems to be accumulating that the expected properties when mixed with other ingredients are not fulfilled as well as when using more traditional additives. Although it is rather expensive the cost is competitive with perlite which it is sometimes used to replace.

SOIL MIXTURES

The preceding discussion of soil components should enable a grower to devise plant growing media which fit a particular circumstance. For those readers who do not wish to make a detailed study of soil mixes, some recipes which can be utilized in many general applications are presented below.

Peat-sand general production or growing mix

This mixture is presented because it is applicable under a wide range of plant growth conditions and because the materials are economically available in almost every locality. It is moderately well drained but can tend to become waterlogged if plants are irrigated too heavily during periods of light water use.

- 2 3.8 cubic foot each bales sphagnum peat
- 11 cubic feet washed sand
- 18 ounces triple superphosphate
- 5 ounces potassium nitrate
  (dissolve in 5 gallons of water and distribute evenly)

Note: When peat is taken from the compressed bales it expands to nearly double the volume to yield approximately one cubic yard of total mix. This is a ratio of 55% peat: 45% sand by volume. Single superphosphate can be substituted for triple superphosphate but the amount should be approximately doubled.

The peat should be finely ground if there are small bedding plant containers to fill. A coarse grind peat with fingertip size chunks is preferable if only 3 inch pots and larger are being used. Peat chunks in the mix improve drainage. Triple superphosphate (some prefer to call it double superphosphate) is less expensive to ship than single superphosphate.

Superphosphate is supplied in luxury amounts to all mixtures described in this book because phosphorous can become deficient under certain long term growing circumstances. This condition is correctable through liquid application of phosphorous but phosphorous tends to precipitate out of irrigation waters in the presence of other mineral fertilizers, unless special precautions are observed by choosing appropriate ingredients. It is easier to provide phosphorous in the slowly available superphosphate form at the time of soil mixing.

The peat-sand mix as described above will have a decidedly acid reaction initially. When fertilizer solutions with a basic reaction are used for growing on, it may not be necessary to adjust the pH upwards. The fertilizer solution will gradually accomplish this objective.

If the fertilizer solution is neutral or acid in reaction, the soil mix pH may be elevated at mixing by the addition of approximately 5 pounds of calcium carbonate (ground limestone) and 2 1/2 pounds of ground dolomitic limestone (the latter will provide extra magnesium). Precise adjustment of the soil mix pH with differing amounts of ground limestone or dolomitic limestone may be accomplished by testing with a pH meter or by submitting samples to a laboratory. A soil pH of 5.2 - 6.2 is optimum for most crops and should be brought about approximately by the quantity of limestones listed above.

Pasteurization of the peat-sand mix is desirable but seldom absolutely essential. The ingredients are clean initially, although not sterile, and no serious outbreaks of soil borne diseases should be noted except under conditions especially favorable for their transmission and growth.

Additional fertilization must be programmed to start soon after potting with this mix; the potassium nitrate added to the medium is only a starter solution.

The peat-sand soil mix is best if moistened slightly as it is mixed to avoid the need for immediate watering later as plants are potted and to make handling the mix more pleasant. This mix can be stored for approximately 3-6 months.

Peat-perlite mix

See chapter 5 for this formula. This mix is much lighter than the peat-sand mix just described. It serves well for rooting cuttings, germinating large seed, and as an alternative potting mix for those plants which prefer a fast draining, light soil. If shipping weights of plants are a concern, the peat-perlite mix reduces them to a minimum. Many foliage plant growers use a similar recipe for general production. If the peat-perlite mix is used for growing on, the amounts of superphosphate recommended in Chapter 5 can be increased to the same levels as in the peat-sand mix. Both peat and perlite are essentially sterile if they have been handled carefully and no sterilization should be necessary. Plants potted in this lightweight mix tend to fall over easily when the soil medium dries out, this can be a problem in the production greenhouse but it causes even more irritation in the retail store. The cost of perlite generally prevents this mix from being widely used with larger containers.

Making retail potting soil at the greenhouse or nursery can often be more profitable than growing plants if a good marketing program is developed.

Peat-vermiculite mix

See Chapter 5 for the formula of this mix. Everything which was said about peat perlite mixes applies to peat-vermiculite mixes except that they are not as well drained. They are most frequently used for germinating fine seed and in plug plant production.

Retail potting soil

Making up a retail potting mix and marketing it in either zip-lock type bags or in custom made bags is often a lucrative sideline for greenhouses and nurseries. The formula suggested below is intended mainly as a potting mix for house plants and African violets but can be used to germinate most seed which consumers are likely to buy in packets. The resulting seedlings can also be grown in it until they are planted in the garden.

   2 3.8 cubic foot each bales sphagnum peat

    (approx. 15 feet loose peat)

   5 cubic feet washed sand

   4 cubic feet perlite

   5 pounds calcium carbonate lime

  15 ounces triple superphosphate

Note: As in other mixes single superphosphate can be substituted at double the rate. Water should be added to the point where the mix feels only slightly moist. Too much water will make the bag sweat. Unless the soil is sterilized, filled bags must be in the dark when stored for prolonged periods to prevent algae growth.

A less expensive retail potting soil for general garden work can be made from the peat-sand mix described previously. Stronger bags are necessary for this mix if it is sold in larger sized quantities. Normally, the consumer will be able to add about 50% regular garden soil to this mix at the time it is used outdoors. Most states occasionally monitor the weight and volume stated on bags of retail potting mix; you may perhaps avoid this inconvenience by not claiming a specific measure. At least one state (Georgia) requires a complete ingredient analysis label to be applied to containers.

Mixes containing field soil

In cases where sandy loam or loam field soils of good quality are available at reasonable prices, the grower may wish to utilize them in container plant mixes. Sandy loams should be mixed in approximately a 1:1:1 ratio of loam, peat moss, and coarse sand or other aggregate. When field soil is incorporated in media, it is difficult to recommend specific fertilizer additives because some fertility will already be present. A rule of thumb might be that if a mix is 50% soil, fertilizer additives could be cut by 25% from that recommended in the peat-sand production mix. Field soil should not be considered for use unless it is uniform and can be certified to be free of herbicide residues. Pasteurization of field soils is often necessary because of the large number of soil organisms and weed seed present. Media containing field soil generally do not require microelement application and are less sensitive to small variations in the micronutrient supply.

Mixes containing ground bark

Ground bark can be substituted in part or totally for peat moss in most soil media. A total substitution is generally not made because bark which has a fairly large proportion of particles recognizable by the naked eye does not possess the water holding or colloidal nutrient holding properties to as great a degree as does peat moss.

Alterations in the nutrient supply both initially and for later growing on may be necessary when bark is used as the chief source of organic matter. Generally speaking, the nutrient supplies will need to be increased somewhat as more bark is substituted for peat moss and as the size of bark chunks increases.

Well decomposed or decayed bark does not contribute significantly to nitrogen depletion of container soils but non-decomposed material can be a problem. Growers using bark as a major additive to soil must be certain about the quality and state of decomposition.

Bark soils with a high proportion of large particles present will drain well.

Some literature sources imply that bark based media often possess the characteristic of reducing the activity of harmful soil microorganisms. The author is unaware of any specific studies showing this to be a proven fact.

COMMENTS ON SOIL MIXES

Perhaps in no other major plant culture area is there more inherent uncertainty than in soils. Natural soil is a tremendously complex biological system and when one aspect of the system is altered, there will be changes in all other parts. No listing of soil components or recipes for blending these components can hope to mention all the possible combinations which might be utilized and there is even less possibility of determining the effects which these variations might have on plant growth.

The complexity of this problem is magnified by the unavoidable variations in quality which typify soil ingredients.

Every recommended soil recipe must be viewed only as a starting point for further alteration and testing by the grower, until a suitable combination is determined for the particular circumstances existing. Any soil mix which is to be used for plant production should be carefully trialed by actual plant growth tests! A detailed explanation of how to conduct a simple biologic test will be presented in the following chapter.

Several important points should be summarized concerning the soil mixes just described.

All of them are based on the assumption that further fertilization with major and minor plant nutrients will be necessary, excepting that phosphorous has been added in initial amounts adequate for the entire crop cycle. In fact phosphorous has been included in overabundance. Growers who anticipate only short term use of these soils (for production of fast growing annuals) could likely decrease the phosphorous recommendations by 1/3 or even 1/2.

When calcium is not supplied as part of the ongoing fertilizer regimen, it may be necessary to make certain it is adequately supplied by using some gypsum, ground limestone, or dolomitic limestone (all of which contain large amounts of calcium) in the soil mixing process. If calcium nitrate is used as a liquid fertilizer component, plenty of calcium is available from this source as it is applied during crop growth. Calcium is also often present in fairly high concentration in some irrigation water sources.

In areas where irrigation waters are low in magnesium and sulfur the inclusion of these elements into the soil mix or fertilizer program should be investigated. Dolomitic lime (containing magnesium) and gypsum (containing sulfur) are often used as soil amendments to supply these elements at the time of mixing. Epsom salts (containing both sulfur and magnesium) is often supplied through periodic injection into irrigation water, or it can be mixed into the soil. Epsom salts may precipitate out of solution when mixed with other fertilizers, therefore it is often injected by itself.

No provision has been made in these soils for the possible inclusion of slow release fertilizers at mixing. Any addition of slow release fertilizers must be reflected in an alteration of the fertilizers listed for that soil mix.

Growers of outdoor nursery stock which is not irrigated with fertilizer solutions will often find that inclusion of at least some slow release fertilizer in mixes is desirable, this will necessitate a revaluation of the fertilizer amounts listed in the recipes. These growers will also find that the large amounts of soil needed for bigger pots require that inexpensive, locally available ingredients such as bark or field soil must form the base for their soil mixes.

Minor elements or micronutrients are not supplied in these mixes except as they may be supplied incidentally by the ingredients. In some cases there is no need to actively supply micronutrients since an adequate amount may become available incidentally through soil mix components, irrigation water, and major fertilizers and amendments added. But a close eye should be kept for minor nutrient deficiencies whenever soil mixes composed of mostly artificial ingredients are used, the safest course of action for inexperienced growers might be to add slow release minor elements to the soil mix or to begin a fertilization program which includes them shortly after planting.

Some mention has already been made concerning the pH of peat-sand mixes. Attention must be paid to this factor in all soils used since it greatly influences plant growth. Soil pH is quite easy to determine and there is no reason why growers should remain in the dark about this important soil characteristic if they have any suspicion that it is not in a desirable range.

The use of artificial soil mixes places a large responsibility upon the grower to ascertain if the proper conditions are being met for economical plant growth. With some alteration of cultural methods, good quality plants can be grown in almost any root medium. However, when all facets of an individual container growing operation are taken into account, there usually remain only a limited choice of soil media suitable for practical use on an everyday basis.

Choosing the proper soil mix is one of the most important decisions facing growers. Large quantities will be used and even small differences in price can be very significant over a period of years. Even more important, however, is the influence soil choice will have on crop production. Careful study must precede selection and once a medium has been chosen, changes in the formula should not be made lightly.

A basic knowledge of soil characteristics and how they affect plant growth will enable growers to make some educated guesses as to how a particular soil will perform in the greenhouse or nursery, but it should be stressed again that testing plant growth in any unknown soil is the only sure method of determining its suitability.

SOIL PASTEURIZATION

Most large container plant operations regularly pasteurize soil media to eliminate diseases, soil pests, and weeds. Pasteurization is economical when large batches of soil are processed. In smaller greenhouses and nurseries it may be more realistic to choose soil ingredients which are reasonably clean and dispense with the pasteurization process. More plants will be lost to diseases this way but omitting the cost of treating small batches of soil may make up for these losses. When plants are being propagated, even more attention must be paid to the cleanliness of the medium used.

A detailed discussion of soil pasteurization will not be given. Soil is pasteurized by exposing it to heat sources which kill microorganisms and weed seed present. Small electric heating units are available which will heat treat limited amounts of soil but steam pasteurization is by far the most commonly used and practical method of treating large quantities. The details of steam treatment can become quite technical, growers who intend to pasteurize soil should consult a reliable and thorough information source.

Microorganisms and weed seed in soils may also be killed by various chemical treatments prior to planting. This method is becoming less practical as additional restrictions are placed upon chemical use in greenhouses and nurseries. Proper use of the chemicals is mandatory since they can be extremely dangerous to both humans and plants.

There has recently been some focus upon the possible deleterious effects of sterilizing planting soils. It has been suggested that beneficial microorganisms as well as harmful ones are destroyed in the process. This undoubtedly is the case, but the question still remains as to whether the benefits of sterilization outweigh the liabilities. On balance, the author suggests that in the majority of cases where sterilization has been found to be economical, the benefits are in the majority. However, soil sterilization should not be carried on blindly; it may not be economical in some cases, and, in certain instances, the elimination of beneficial microorganisms may cause more loss of plant quality and production volume than did the presence of harmful microorganism species. Most people have assumed that the beneficial microorganisms soon recolonize the planting medium so that no permanent damage is done, but there is no agreement upon this subject.

New biological products are now available which claim to (through the action of beneficial microorganisms) control some of the most harmful soil microorganisms. If these products eventually prove successful and economical, there would be less incentive to automatically sterilize potting soils (and there would be less need to apply chemical control measures after plants are containerized).

Tree growers are more interested in the role of beneficial soil micro-microorganisms (meaning mycorrhizae as discussed here) since their crops are meant for long term use in the landscape. Some experts suggest that a lack of mycorrhizal activity in modern potting media leads to poor survival and poor overall performance in numerous trees and shrubs. Inoculants which are supposed to assure the presence of beneficial microorganisms (mycorrhizae) in soils have been developed to overcome this problem.

COMMERCIALLY AVAILABLE MEDIA

Some growers will naturally ask why so much effort has been expended In thls book on detalling the characterlstlcs of various soil components and mixtures when ready made mixtures can be easily purchased from a large number of horticultural suppliers.

Mixing soil on the greenhouse or nursery premises is often a great deal less expensive than buying it ready-made. Additionally, a blend may be devised which fits individual growing needs more closely than does any commercially available mix.

Commercial mixes can be the wisest choice for many growers but a thorough evaluation should be made before deciding to follow this route. A cost analysis is the first step, followed by a careful determination of whether the commercial mixes which are readily available will perform adequately in the situation under consideration. Part of this determination will consist of actually growing plants in the intended mix to observe their performance (refer to biologic tests in the next chapter).

Using commercial mixes does pose some risk to the grower. The companies formulating and mixing these soils are subject to mistakes just as is every other business. There is the possibility of receiving mixes which do not conform to the established formula standards. And supplying companies can and do change the formulas, sometimes requiring growers to make alterations in their carefully crafted cultural programs.

The soil mix used by container growers is a central part of their cultural program and every effort should be made to minimize the chance of unnecessary soil mix changes upsetting the smooth operation of this program. This objective is most reliably achieved through a diligent in-house control of the soil source.

There is no easy way to determine whether or not growers should mix soil on site or buy ready-made media, only a detailed analysis of each specific operation can provide a reasonable answer. The author is inclined to favor on-site mixing in most cases but numerous large scale growers (who should be able to economically mix their own media) have switched to commercial mixes. They presumably have good reason to do so.

Table 11
Per bag cost estimates of media mixes in year 2000.

Typical Commercial Mix 3.8 cubic feet compressed	$25.00 Freight included Catalog price
Sand/Peat Media Formula mixed on site, equivalent to 3.8 cubic feet compressed bale above	$14.40 Freight included

---

Note: The sand/peat mix has all costs of mixing, labor, and fertilizer included. The comparison of costs is based upon small batches of less than 10 bales. Larger media batches would probably favor onsite mixing even more.

A simple cost analysis is provided below to help readers evaluate which alternative might best suit their needs. Please be aware that this is only one model of a complex situation. Prices are based upon late 1999 estimates at a specific location in the United States of America.

EVOLUTION OF ARTIFICIAL MEDIA

The artificial soil mixes discussed in this chapter generally evolved in the United States from concepts proposed by investigators at The University of California and Cornell University. Additional work has been done and is ongoing at several other universities, soil companies, and through individual efforts. Similar projects in the United Kingdom were conducted at the John Innes Horticultural Research Facility.

Readers who wish to evaluate the critical decision concerning growing media more thoroughly are advised to at least review the original works from The University of California and Cornell in detail. Additional literature sources concerning this general topic are also listed in the back of the book. When one considers the impact which a soil system has upon a nursery or greenhouse, this is one area which growers cannot afford to neglect.

Chapter 7

FERTILIZERS

The term "fertilizer" in the following discussion shall mean those mineral elements (either free or in compound form) which were listed as essential for plant growth. Although here they are called mineral elements because their ultimate source is from the soil, they may also be provided in organic form from the remains of dead plants or animals. It has become common to speak of two different classes of fertilizers: organic and inorganic. Many people believe organic fertilizers are more effective and more natural but plant and animal remains are no more natural than are "naturally" occurring deposits of mineral fertilizer in the earth's crust. Plants absorb fertilizers in the elemental ionic (electrically charged) form; they do not absorb minerals as parts of more complex organic compounds. All mineral elements present in different fertilizers (whether inorganic or organic) must be reduced to simple ionic forms before they are in a chemical state which the plant can take up.

FERTILIZER AVAILABILITY

It is true that a mineral element from one material source may be more or less available to plants at a particular time than the same element from another source, but this phenomenon is not directly related with whether the source is organic or inorganic.

As a general rule, chemical fertilizers (another name often applied to inorganic forms) are more quickly available than are organic fertilizers. The plant and animal tissue from which organic fertilizers are derived is composed of highly complex molecules while many chemical fertilizers are very simple compounds. This means that most organic compounds will require considerable modification before the mineral elements in them can be absorbed by plant roots while many chemical fertilizers will require a lesser amount of modification. In simple terms, more modification usually takes more time.

The total amount of an element present in soils has no direct relationship to the amount available for plant requirements at a specific time. It may be that an element is present in abundance but with only a small amount being available at any one time; this is often the case when the element is derived from organic sources. Or an element may be present in only minimal quantities but with the entire amount being available immediately, as is the case with many chemical fertilizers.

Some elements are present in soils in forms which we would not normally classify as fertilizers. This is because the chemical form in which the element is constituted is very stable and becomes available to plants so slowly that, in a practical sense, it cannot be relied upon to play any role in the nutrition of plants. Rock gravel would be a case in point, it obviously contains some elements which could be used in plant nutrition but the elements are so tightly locked in the molecular make up of the gravel that they are only very slightly available to plants.

The above points might be summarized by saying that the chemical elements used by plants are available from different sources and that the availability of these elements, both totally and within a specific timeframe, can vary tremendously depending upon the exact chemical configuration in which they are present.

Availability of nutrient elements is determined by many factors; the following are some of the more important: soil pH, soil organisms, compound stability and complexity, concentrations of other elements, and soil composition. Factors may be interrelated; as in cases where soil pH affects microorganism populations, which in turn determine nitrogen availability to a large extent.

Soil pH affects the availability of several elements other than nitrogen. High pH decreases the solubility of iron compounds and can induce iron chlorosis; the reverse occurs at a low pH with iron levels occasionally becoming toxic below a pH of 5.0. A similar situation arises in the case of manganese. The concentration of one element in relation to another often affects plant growth simply because large supplies of one element will limit the physical opportunity of another element to be present near the root zone. Another effect of element concentration may be seen in the case where large overdoses of phosphorous will precipitate iron from the soil solution and cause iron deficiency. In some instances, growers may wish to increase the calcium level of soil mixes without the increase in pH which additional limestones would cause. In this case, one could add $CaSO_4$ (gypsum); this compound also provides sulphur, and it does not affect the pH appreciably.

The effect soil composition has on mineral element availability should be obvious since composition will affect pH, element concentration, soil organisms, and water holding capacity (remember, water is necessary for elements to enter into solution). Some mention has already been made concerning molecule complexity as it relates to element availability. Stability of compounds is another chemical attribute which vitally alters element uptake. The iron present in nails is not an especially complex form but it is very stable and is not nearly so available as is the iron in iron sulfate or in blood meal.

Numerous crops can often be grown to a reasonable degree of commercial quality by applying the same fertilizer regime. Many crops, however, will show improved quality with a slightly altered fertilizer formula. There are a relatively few ornamental crops which actually require a rather specific fertilizer regime in order to produce a commercially acceptable grade. Azaleas, for instance, require a high acid, high iron fertilizer which is rather low in total soluble salt potential.

Discussion of fertilizer availability and all the interrelationships it involves could be the subject of an entire book. For present purposes, it is enough if the reader realizes how complex the situation can become and that minor changes in soil mixes and fertilizer application programs can have unexpected and sometimes disastrous results. The purpose in presenting the following material is to elaborate practical information a grower may need to raise crops. The information is not a complete presentation of this complex field and readers should have a thorough understanding of the ramifications before they attempt to devise personal fertilizer formulas or modify existing ones.

FERTILIZER APPLICATION

Basically, fertilizer may be applied to plants in three different forms: dry, liquid, and coated with a polymeric resin membrane. Dry application is seldom made to smaller containers except when mixed into the soil at potting time. It is time consuming and difficult to apply a proper dosage by this method after plants are already potted.

Phosphorus is almost always incorporated dry into soil mixes in the single or triple superphosphate form rather than being applied as a liquid.

A portable fertilizer injector.

Reasons for this are that readily soluble forms of phosphorus are expensive and phosphorus is very tightly bound to soil particles, making it difficult to leach out. Since phosphorus is needed in relatively small quantities by plants and it doesn't leach appreciably, the amount initially incorporated into soil usually suffices for the crop cycle.

Other dry fertilizers are sometimes mixed into the soil either in the dry form or after being dissolved in water, the objective usually being to provide plants with some initial available nutrients until liquid feeding or coated slow release fertilizers begin building up in sufficient concentrations for normal plant growth. Sometimes slowly available forms of dry fertilizer are incorporated into the soil with the idea of providing most of the nutritional needs of plants through the entire crop cycle.

Liquid application of fertilizer is accomplished normally by providing nutrient solutions to the root zone but foliage feeding is occasionally used, especially in the case of iron. Fertilizer injectors or proportioners are commonly used to inject concentrated stock solutions into the irrigation water. These injectors are available in many different price and performance ranges. Some are very expensive and reliable. Others, which can be hooked directly to a garden hose and which operate strictly as siphon devices, cost only a few dollars but understandably, do not proportion solutions in a very exact manner.

Durability, accuracy, and the volume capacity of fertilizer injectors are the chief factors which must be related to the price of different models. Generally, if the purchase price is low, one or another of these performance factors will suffer. Growers must decide which fertilizer injector is most suitable for their operation in terms of price and performance. Several brands of inexpensive but reliable fertilizer injectors are now available so that it makes little sense not to take advantage of their labor saving potential.

Liquid fertilizers may also be applied by simply mixing them in a tank with the proper amount of water and then pumping the resultant solution to plants. This method is very accurate when the mixing procedure is carried out carefully, and the volume which can be delivered is limited only by the capacity of the tanks, pumps, and distribution lines. One obvious drawback of using tanks to mix and hold diluted fertilizer solutions is the large size and cost of tanks to handle the great amounts of water generally needed.

Fertilizers used in proportioners or tanks must be easily and completely soluble and attention must be given to choosing ingredients which are compatible with one another. Many forms of phosphorous cannot be included in liquid fertilizer formulas because they cause other elements to become precipitated out of the solution. A practical method of determining if precipitation is occurring in mixtures is to observe the complete solubility of ingredients separately and then mix them together. If a residue becomes apparent at the bottom of the mixing container, precipitation has occurred. Precipitation may sometimes be overcome by using less concentrated stock solutions, dilute solutions often being less susceptible to precipitation than more concentrated ones.

Fertilizer application in irrigation water will correlate roughly with the nutrient needs of plants if the proper concentration of fertilizers is constant in the irrigation solution applied. When plants are growing rapidly in high light and temperature conditions, the need for water is greater and consequently more fertilizer is applied. The reverse is true during the darker, colder days of winter. When applied with the irrigation water, fertilizers are usually diluted to extremely low ranges. This method of lightly fertilizing at every watering seems more satisfactory than less frequent but stronger applications. With stronger concentrations one runs the risk of burning tender new leaves and plants may become "hungry" between feedings.

Constant liquid feeding programs usually include nitrogen and potassium in the range of 100-200 ppm (parts per million) each. The term "parts per million" designates the number of parts (molecules) of a fertilizer element present in one million parts (molecules) of water. To obtain ppm, multiply the percentage of an element present in a fertilizer by 75. This results in the ppm when 1 ounce of fertilizer is dissolved in 100 gallons of water. The decimal representation of percentage should be used; in other words 44% equals 0.44. This formula is not exact but can be used for most horticultural purposes.

A few final words of caution before leaving liquid fertilizers. Concentrated stock solutions should not be made up in advance and stored. Chemical reactions can slowly take place which may significantly alter the original solutions. Concentrated fertilizer solutions are often quite caustic and can severely burn tissue, especially eyes!

Fertilizers coated with polymeric resins are usually referred to as slow release fertilizers. The use of these terms in this way is misleading. Coated fertilizers may indeed be slow release but not all slow release fertilizers are coated with polymeric resin. Most slow release fertilizers are simply quite stable elemental compounds which break down slowly in the soil. Coated slow release fertilizers are those in which individual granules of fertilizers are coated with a resinous polymer membrane. This membrane acts in much the same manner as cell membranes in plant or animal tissue. When water is present outside the membrane, it diffuses across the membrane and dissolves the fertilizers, thus making the coated particle turgid or full of water. Dissolved fertilizer elements then diffuse through the membrane into the soil. The rate of fertilizer diffusion into the soil is governed by several factors: membrane composition and thickness, the fertilizer composition, temperature, amount and quality of water in the soil.

Coated slow release fertilizers can serve some very useful purposes in container plant nutritional programs but these products must be used properly to achieve the desired results. They are merely another tool which

A small, rather inexpensive fertilizer injector.

is available to meet the nutritional needs of crops, not a magic formula which guarantees success regardless of how wisely it is employed.

Coated slow release fertilizers are, generally speaking, an expensive means of providing mineral nutrition. But when used under the proper circumstances, they can eliminate a good deal of labor and therefore result in an overall savings. These fertilizers must be handled just as carefully as any other fertilizer product to avoid crop damage. The slow release name given them does not indicate that an excess can be applied with impunity. It is a good idea to determine, through testing with actual plants, how coated slow release fertilizers will affect crops before any major applications are made.

Since higher temperatures promote the release of minerals from coated fertilizers into moist soil, it is evident that soils cannot be steamed after these fertilizers have been incorporated. Toxic amounts of mineral

GUARANTEED ANALYSIS

TOTAL NITROGEN (N) . . . . %
AVAILABLE PHOSPHORIC ACID (P_2O_5) 4.6 %
SOLUBLE POTASH (K_2O) . . . . %
SULFUR (S) . . . . %
IRON (Fe) . . . . %

The labels of fertilizer containers must be examined carefully. Many have no element names on them, only numbers. The first number denotes nitrogen (N), the second phosphorus (P), and the third potassium (K). This is a general label which can be affixed to any bag. The fertilizer percentage must be written in.

elements can accumulate in moist soil treated with coated fertilizers after prolonged storage or steaming.

Coated slow release fertilizers are offered in many different formulations to accomplish varying cultural objectives. Some are even formulated for specific crops and for specific periods of activity.

Top dressings of coated fertilizers may be made to containers but this method of application does not offer the opportunity for the best mineral release action to occur nor does it take advantage of the labor saving which soil incorporation offers. Some growers place small amounts of coated fertilizers into the soil mix and then supply additional nutrition as needed by liquid feeding techniques. This program assures that an oversupply of coated fertilizer is never introduced into the root zone. Some evidence suggests that this combination method produces better crops than either method when used alone.

Coated fertilizers are especially useful when trees and shrubs are produced under sprinkler irrigation outdoors. With the wide plant spacing often used under these conditions, the majority of fertilizer applied through

Table 12
Fertilizer application pointers

A. Stronger concentrations should be applied only to moist soil.

B. Do not store stock (concentrated) solutions.

C. Check injector calibration frequently.

D. Fertilizers are corrosive to common steel; line tanks with fiberglass or plastic coating.

E. Allow only reliable employees to mix solutions.

F. Some fertilizers absorb water from the atmosphere if left exposed and will consequently weigh more.

G. Do not store weed killers near fertilizer containers.

H. Check compatibility of fertilizers before mixing.

I. Any change of fertilizer practices should be tried on a trial basis first.

J. Avoid body contact with fertilizer salts or concentrated solutions, especially on sensitive tissue.

K. Double check all calculations.

L. Check labels carefully to determine the exact contents and recommended application rates.

M. Some fertilizers are strong oxidizers (potentially explosive or flammable), handle with caution.

sprinkler systems is lost as runoff. The latter situation results in either a need to recycle runoff or unacceptable fertilizer waste and environmental pollution. Fertilizer runoff is greatly reduced under sprinklers when coated fertilizer is mixed into the container soil and pure water is used for irrigation.

If liquid feeding of crops is possible, the most logical fertilizer program would appear to be a combination of soil incorporation (either with dry or coated slow release fertilizers) and subsequent liquid application. This program allows growers to utilize the ease of soil incorporation but assures that different crops can receive different fertilizer levels if the need arises. If too much fertilizer is incorporated in the soil at mixing it is sometimes difficult to remove, but lower levels can always be increased by liquid applications.

Inexperienced growers will be wiser to slightly under fertilize rather than risk the possibility of crop failure due to over fertilization. "Burning" plants from over fertilization is generally a much more serious mistake than is allowing a slight fertilizer deficiency to occur. The later can usually be corrected within a few weeks through increasing fertilizer application rates but "burned" tissue seldom recovers completely.

FERTILIZER PROGRAMS

Recommending specific fertilization directions for the hundreds of circumstances a grower might encounter is clearly an impossibility. The goal of this book shall be to present elementary information which will enable growers to devise their own basic formulas. A number of simple formulas will be presented which might be used if they appear to coincide with the need at hand. These formulas should be applicable for a wide variety of common cultural objectives.

Readers should review the mineral elements which were listed as being essential to plant growth in Chapter 4. In the following discussion, primary importance will be placed upon furnishing suitable levels of nitrogen, phosphorous, potassium, and occasionally iron. If a grower is lucky, these will be the only elements it is necessary to supply; the others being present as contaminants or as an integral part of the major fertilizer ingredients, occurring naturally in the substrate, or present in the water supply.

PHOSPHOROUS – Since phosphorous is usually added during soil mixing, specific recommendations have already been made under that heading. If single superphosphate is added it also supplies sulfur and calcium in considerable quantities. Triple superphosphate supplies calcium but not sulfur. Additional calcium is present in ground limestone if one alters soil pH with this compound. Dolomitic limestone can be substituted for altering soil pH and will supply both calcium and magnesium. When irrigation water has a very low degree of mineralization, the necessity of adding a magnesium source and perhaps sources of other elements required in lesser amounts should be investigated. This is why it is important to have a complete water analysis for each specific growing operation. When the recommendations for providing phosphorous which have been given earlier are followed, it is unlikely that additional amounts would be necessary during the plant growth cycle. However, this can be accomplished by applying di-ammonium phosphate at the rate of 1 ounce per 5 gallons of water.

IRON – Iron may become deficient, especially in alkaline soils or in media which contain no field soil. Iron uptake is often inadequate when soil aeration is poor. Deficiencies should be treated as they occur rather than applying iron as a matter of course. Chelated iron is normally used because it does not become immobilized by attaching to soil particles. This form of iron is quite expensive. Recommendations for soil application vary considerably, ranging from 1 ounce per 10 gallons of water to 1 ounce per 25 gallons. For mild cases of iron chlorosis, 1 ounce of 10% chelated iron per 50 gallons of water will sometimes be sufficient. This low dosage can also be used as a preventive application every 6-8 weeks if growers find that occasional slight deficiencies occur.

Iron sulphate is a less expensive fertilizer but may become quickly unavailable in the soil; soil application is commonly at a rate of 1 ounce per 2 gallons of water but using 1/2 this rate initially is safer. Using iron sulphate in strongly acid soils is not recommended because the additional amount needed (when compared to chelated iron) and its extreme acidity will only magnify the problem. Iron is often applied as a foliage spray. Inexperienced growers should be careful with this method because it is much easier to burn a crop if a mistake is made or conditions are not just right.

MICRONUTRIENTS – Micronutrient deficiencies were seldom a problem until the advent of completely artificial soil mixes. Even in media with no field soil content, micronutrient problems are not especially common but growers should be aware that deficiencies can arise under certain

SOLUBLE TRACE ELEMENT MIX
S. T. E. M.
565-791

GUARANTEED ANALYSIS:
    SULFUR . . . . as S — 14.00%
    BORON . . . . as B — 1.35%
    COPPER . . . . as Cu — 3.20%
    IRON . . . . as Fe — 7.50%
    MANGANESE . . . . as Mn — 8.00%
    MOLYBDENUM . . . . as Mo — 0.04%
    ZINC . . . . as Zn — 4.50%
    DERIVED FROM: COPPER, IRON, MANGANESE AND ZINC SULFATES, BORAX, SODIUM MOLYBDATE.
WARNING: CONTAINS MOLYBDENUM AND SHOULD NOT BE USED ON FORAGE GRASS FOR LIVESTOCK.
         Soil Must Be Wet Before Applying or Plant Injury Can Occur.
         USUAL DOSAGE—CONSTANT FEEDING WITH EVERY WATERING
         8 ounces of S.T.E.M. for every 100 pounds of fertilizer material.

                EXPERIMENTAL—1 TIME ONLY DOSAGE
BENCH CROPS: 2 ounces per 100 sq. ft. Do not repeat unless deficiency has definitely been established.
POT OR FLAT CROPS: 2 ounces in 25 gallons equal 1¼ level teaspoons in 5 gallons or ¼ teaspoon in 1 gallon.
    Applied as a normal saturation of root area. No repeat should be necessary.

WARNING! • CAUSES IRRITATION.
          • IN CASE OF CONTACT, FLUSH EYES WITH PLENTY OF WATER FOR AT
            LEAST 15 MINUTES. CONTACT A PHYSICIAN.
          • WASH SKIN WITH SOAP AND WATER. IF IRRITATION PERSISTS, CALL
            A PHYSICIAN.

The label for a full spectrum micronutrient fertilizer formulation. Follow the directions carefully. Improper application can result in costly crop damage.

circumstances. The use of very pure fertilizers, deionized water, plastic piping, or especially clean sand could lead to micronutrient deficiencies. Most micronutrient fertilizer blends are very expensive and it makes no sense to apply them as a matter of course until definite problems have been encountered. Several micronutrients are toxic to plants at very low concentrations; indiscriminate use of them to cure imagined deficiencies can lead to injury from overdoses. Fritted (slow release) trace elements can be incorporated in the soil, or liquid applications may be made with soluble forms. Coated controlled release fertilizers are also available which supply micronutrients along with the major elements. Growers should realize that plant culture in modern soilless mixes is very close to being a hydroponic-type system. A good deal can be learned about nutrient requirements by studying a good book on hydroponics.

In order to avoid overdoses, growers would be well advised to begin applications of micronutrients (if they are deemed necessary) at the lowest rate recommended by the manufacturer. Testing groups of plants grown with and without additional micronutrients will allow growers to decide if the extra expense of application is necessary. Generally, the total spectrum of micronutrients is supplied to a crop as a blend, but larger growers may wish to determine exactly which elements are necessary and supply only those found in short supply. Certain micronutrients can be supplied quite inexpensively while the full spectrum blends cost much more.

NITROGEN AND POTASSIUM – Most liquid feed programs mixed on-site from primary fertilizer salts supply only nitrogen and potassium on a regular basis. If fertilizer is applied at every watering, a solution containing approximately 100-200 ppm each of nitrogen (N) and potassium (K) is commonly used. The actual solution could vary from 50 to 300 ppm of each, depending upon the crop and time of year. Each grower must decide on the exact proportion of N and K suitable for the particular circumstance. When using the peat-sand soil mix formula given previously, the following fertilizer programs work quite well under most circumstances.

A. Six ounces potassium nitrate (KNO_3)/100 gallons of water. This formula is especially useful with bedding plants, tending to keep them from becoming overly lush. Do not use on chrysanthemums, Christmas peppers, gloxinias, or foliage plants. There are other varieties requiring high nitrogen for which this formula is unsuitable. Soluble salt buildup is very low with this formula because the entire molecule is usable by plants. There are 198 ppm potassium (K) and 63 ppm nitrogen (N) present in solution.

Calculation:

Potassium nitrate contains 14% nitrogen and 44% potassium.

75 x 0.14 x 6 = 63 ppm nitrogen
75 x 0.44 x 6 = 198 ppm potassium

B. Six ounces calcium nitrate ($CaNO_3$) and 3 ounces potassium nitrate (KNO_3)/100 gallons water. This formula can be used on all plants; but bedding plants, especially petunias, may become more leafy than desired. Poinsettias may develop potassium deficiencies unless more of this element is supplied after establishment. Soluble salt buildup is moderate with this formula because the entire molecule is usable by plants; it is doubtful, however, if the large amount of calcium supplied is totally absorbed. There are 101.25 ppm nitrogen and 99 ppm potassium in solution.

Calculation:

Potassium nitrate contains 14% nitrogen and 44% potassium.
Calcium nitrate contains 15.5% nitrogen.
75 x 0.155 x 6 = 69.75 ppm nitrogen (from calcium nitrate)
75 x 0.14 x 3 = 31.50 ppm nitrogen (from potassium nitrate)
101.25 ppm total nitrogen

75 x 0.44 x 3 = 99 ppm potassium

Both formulas A and B have a basic pH reaction. This is desirable when the soil media is highly acid from the addition of peat. Another favorable trait of these fertilizer programs is that all the nitrogen is supplied in the nitrate form. Many plants, especially if planted in artificial media, display a disorder known as ammonium toxicity when fertilizers containing nitrogen in the ammonium form are used. Basically, nitrogen can be supplied in either the ammonium (NH_4^+) form or the nitrate form (NO_3^-). The exact reason for ammonium toxicity is debatable; certain authors contend that (NH_4^+) is unavailable for plant use and builds up to toxic levels in the soil unless converted to (NO_3^-) by soil microorganisms. Other experts believe that (NH_4^+) is absorbable by plants and, in certain cases, utilized so fast as to disrupt normal plant functions. Whatever the case, it makes sense to use nitrate forms of nitrogen and avoid the problem altogether. In addition to being a problem with artificial media, ammonium toxicity is common when organic matter or fertilizers high in organic nitrogen are added to the soil before pasteurization. Nitrate nitrogen is easily leached from the soil while the ammonium form is more difficult to remove. Ammonium toxicity is typified by a burned appearance of the leaves. One might confuse this condition with an excess of fertilizer or soluble salts in the soil but it arises even in cases where soluble salts have been measured in a low range. Many growers became exposed to this problem when poinsettia crops were first planted in artificial mixes.

Another nitrogen related problem which can affect fertilizer programs is encountered when organic matter with a high carbon content and low nitrogen content is incorporated in soils. Mention was made of this situation when sawdust and bark were considered as organic matter sources. The problem arises because microorganisms in the soil utilize the high carbon fraction as an energy source for growth and reproduction, their number then quickly multiplies. If nitrogen is in limited supply, these organisms utilize all the available nitrogen and leave plants with none. Additional nitrogen must be supplied in soil mixes with a high carbon-to-nitrogen ratio, enough to supply both plants and microorganisms.

Soils containing large amounts of clay or vermiculite may require less potassium because these minerals already contain large quantities of this element. Certain crops such as poinsettias and chrysanthemums seem to thrive with high potassium levels and show deficiencies quickly.

Poinsettia growers sometimes encounter magnesium deficiencies in the crop. This can be solved with periodic injection of Epsom salts ($MgSO_4$) into the irrigation water at a rate of 8 ounces per 100 gallons of diluted water output.

The fertilizer formulas outlined above should not be followed blindly. They should work reasonably well with most highly organic artificial media but each grower must decide on particular fertilizer mixes according to soil and water chemistry and crop conditions. Observant readers may have noticed that formulas A and B are generally at the low end of the scale in ppm recommended for nitrogen and potassium. Other authors usually recommend higher ppm of these two elements. Formulas A and B may be too weak if the soil medium is extremely well drained and leaching occurs at each irrigation or when the irrigation water itself is very low in these mineral elements. Growers can easily devise fertilizer recipes if the percentage of the particular element present in a fertilizer is known and the ppm formula is then used. Table 13 lists the percentage of nitrogen and potassium in some commonly used fertilizers. Blended commercial fertilizers will have the percentage of nitrogen, phosphorous, and potassium prominently displayed on the container in that order. To arrive at the ppm of a 20-10-25 fertilizer in solution the following calculations are used:

nitrogen	75 x 0.20 = 15 ppm	present with 1 ounce
phosphorous	75 x 0.10 = 7.5 ppm	of fertilizer in
potassium	75 x 0.25 = 18.75 ppm	100 gallons of water

Table 13

Important characteristics of some commonly used fertilizer materials. Composition percentages may vary slightly between sources. Higher salt indexes result in more soluble salts in solution (assume equal weights of fertilizer material).

Fertilizer material	Percent nitrogen	Percent potassium	pH reaction	Salt index
Ammonium sulphate	20	0	Acid	69
Ammonium nitrate	33.5	0	Acid	105
Sodium nitrate	16	0	Basic	100
Calcium nitrate	15.5	0	Basic	68
Potassium nitrate	14	44	Basic	74
Potassium chloride	0	62	Acid	115
Potassium sulphate	0	48	Acid	48

If 10 ounces of this 20-10-25 fertilizer were dissolved in 100 gallons of water, the resulting solution would contain 150 ppm nitrogen, 75 ppm phosphorous, and 187.5 ppm potassium.

COMMERCIAL BLENDED FERTILIZERS

Blended fertilizers to be used in the irrigation water are readily available for different soil mixes and crops. There is nothing wrong with using these ready made mixes except that the cost is much greater than for the separate ingredients. In those few cases which the author has checked prices, the separate ingredients can be purchased for approximately 1/2 of the commercially blended fertilizer cost. Many blended fertilizers also contain soluble phosphorus which is expensive and is not needed if phosphorous has been incorporated in the soil. Growers should make it a point to know exactly what compounds are included in premixed fertilizers; ammonium nitrogen is sometimes the dominant form of this element included in premixes and, as noted, this formula could result in ammonium toxicity. Readers who spend an hour reviewing the previous discussion on fertilizers will have little need for premixes and can save many dollars over the years. Growers should not be intimidated by the apparent complexity of devising fertilizer recipes; with a little study they can usually come up with more economical materials than those contained in premixes. Using a commercial premix does not excuse the grower from evaluating the exact characteristic of the fertilizer. Growers should also be aware that switching from one premix to another can produce significant alterations in plant growth.

SOLUBLE SALTS

Various chemical compounds are known generically as salts. Any chemical salt which is soluble in water adds to the soluble salt level of a solution. Salts in the irrigation solution are derived from fertilizer compounds and naturally occurring minerals present in the water source. Salts in soil come from those added in irrigation water, those minerals present naturally in the soil, and from inorganic and organic fertilizer added during soil mixing. Soluble salts in solution are determined by measuring the electrical conductivity with special instruments. Results can be specified in ppm, micromhos, or other appropriate units of measurement. Multiplying micromhos by 0.666 will convert results to ppm; multiplying ppm by 1.5 will convert results to micromhos. Multiplying millimhos by 666 will also result in ppm. A micromho is 1000 times smaller than a millimho. A new term of measurement (millisiemen) may sometimes be encountered; it equals a millimho; therefore, the two units are interchangeable.

Soluble salts are commonly measured both in the irrigation water and soil extract solutions. Different means of preparing soil extracts for soluble salts measurement are available and interpretation of the data obtained must be related to the extraction procedure. Irrigation water solutions are measured directly without any special preparations or procedures. Table 14 provides data for interpreting general water quality as based upon soluble salt content. The term ppm is not exactly related to the other terms mentioned here which are used to express the electrical conductivity of solutions, but the relationship is close enough to a 1:1 proportion (after conversion) for most ordinary circumstances.

High soluble salts in the soil water fraction around plant roots subject the tissue to drought conditions even though adequate water is present. A graphic example of what takes place may be observed if a slug is

One of the many styles of conductivity meters which can be used to quickly determine the soluble salt content of solutions.

immersed in a saturated salt solution. Water from the slug's body will move across the cell membranes into the saturated salt solution, leaving the slug dehydrated. If the salt concentration in surrounding solutions is higher than in living tissue, water will move from the tissue to the salt solution and vice versa. Even if the salt concentration in solution is not higher than in tissue, higher levels of salt will slow down the rate of water flow from the solution to living tissue. Thus all gradations of physiological drought may be observed, from complete desiccation to almost unobservable effects.

High soluble salt problems may never occur in containers if the water supply is good, excess fertilizers are not applied, and excess water is allowed to drain out the bottom of pots if it is deemed necessary. The later process of allowing water to drain through the soil and out the drain holes

Table 14

Water quality rating of irrigation water prior to addition of fertilizer compounds. Note: growers should consider alternative water sources if readings are over 1000 ppm of soluble salts.

Water quality rating	Relative salt content	Reading in micromhos	Reading in ppm
Excellent	low	0-250	167
Good to fair	medium	250-750	167-500
Fair to poor	medium-high	750-2250	500-1500
Poor to unsatisfactory	excessive	2250+	1500+

is known as "leaching". Salts are carried out of the pot with the excess water and, as a consequence, the salt level in the soil is reduced. A grower's choice of fertilizer materials can significantly alter the salt condition of soils, even when the same quantities of nitrogen and potassium are applied. Table 13 illustrates the relative "saltiness" of common nitrogen and potassium fertilizers. It can readily be seen that ammonium nitrate contributes more than twice the nitrogen as does sodium nitrate with only a slight increase in the amount of soluble salts added to a solution. One must also pay attention to how many essential elements are added by the fertilizer material. Potassium nitrate is a popular fertilizer because it is a source of both nitrogen and potassium while possessing a medium salt index. An added benefit is that the nitrogen is in the nitrate form.

All forms of salts do not appear to be equally damaging to plants. It is generally accepted that sulfate compounds are not so toxic in high concentrations as are other salts. Plant species will also differ in their response to soluble salts. Azaleas and gardenias do not tolerate high salts while carnations grow well under relatively saline conditions. Some wild plant species which have evolved in the western United States seem to flourish under soluble salt conditions which would quickly kill the majority of species.

Table 15 lists some cultural practices which will help growers avoid salt buildup. People involved in merchandising plants to the public should convey these practices to consumers since excess soluble salts are one of the most common reasons for poor performance of plants in the home. Advanced symptoms of soluble salt injury are similar to ammonium toxicity in that marginal burning of the leaves is exhibited. Stunted growth and iron chlorosis may also indicate a soluble salt problem.

DIAGNOSING FERTILIZER DISORDERS

When crops are not growing properly, it is generally very difficult to pinpoint the cause, especially if one does not have years of growing experience. Fertilizer and soluble salt problems should be considered as prime suspects in any plant disorders. The difficulty with diagnosing plant disorders is that plants can't tell the grower where it hurts. Growers must develop an acute sense of observation to detect unusual growth patterns early enough to remedy them before major damage is done. Unless a particular fertilizer deficiency has been observed previously, it is very difficult to read textbook descriptions of the visual symptoms and then be reasonably sure of a diagnosis. There are simply too many plant "illnesses" which have similar symptoms. Accurate visual diagnosis comes only with long years of experience.

Fertilizer deficiencies do not exhibit the same symptoms in all species, so growers must keep in mind that the same disorder may look somewhat different in different species. Deficiencies are not the only problems which occur. Soluble salt buildup and, occasionally, toxic concentrations of specific elements cause concern.

Tissue analysis can present the grower with more tangible evidence of fertilizer deficiencies and excesses. The trouble with tissue analysis is that the state university or private laboratories capable of performing accurate work are seldom handy to the grower. Analysis of leaf tissue can quickly confirm a grower's suspicion of particular nutrient problems. Standard tables are available for major crops which show the desired content of various mineral elements in leaf tissue. Of course, sampling of plant tissue must be done carefully and according to the directions of the participating laboratory.

Visual symptoms are often the only practical warning a grower receives of plant disorders before irreparable damage is done. Therefore, frequent careful inspection of crops is the best means of detecting problems. Diligent study concerning the requirements of different crops and of the soils,

Table 15
Cultural practices which will help avoid soluble salt problems.

A. Allow 20% of irrigation water to flow out the bottom of pots whenever plant growth or laboratory tests indicate it is necessary. Leach heavily on a regular but intermittent schedule.

B. Choose fertilizer materials with a lower salt index when possible.

C. Choose fertilizers which contribute more than one essential element.

D. Do not apply more fertilizer than is needed for good growth.

E. Soil with a high proportion of large particles will leach more rapidly and thereby reduce salt content.

F. Maintaining a soil in a moist condition will cause less salt damage than a dry soil.

G. Choose a water supply which does not contain excessive salts.

H. Avoid sprinkling plants often; water less frequently but more heavily.

fertilizers, and water sources being used will often allow growers to pinpoint potential problem areas which require special vigilance.

Certain specific situations that arise may be indicative of more generalized problems for which the grower should be on the lookout. For example, water sources which test high in soluble salts will serve as an alert signal to search for plant symptoms caused by this condition. And when azaleas and their close relatives develop iron deficiencies, it may be logical to assume this element is in short, although not critical, supply to other less susceptible plant species. If fast growing species are being cropped, it can be expected that the potassium and nitrogen supplies will need to be increased since they are utilized in large amounts. Some species such as salvia and impatiens are especially intolerant of high soluble salts in the soil, they can serve as biological indicators of this condition for other plants in the greenhouse or nursery.

These examples are but a few of the hundreds of circumstances where some fore knowledge will put the grower on alert. Although some mention has already been made of specific essential element deficiencies and excesses, a recap of the more commonly occurring problems follows.

A poinsettia leaf showing the early symptoms of potassium deficiency (areas of dark brown tissue on the upper left portion of the leaf) and advanced deficiency signs (the dead tissue at the tip of each leaf "finger").

Nitrogen disorders

Nitrogen deficient plants fail to grow as quickly as they should and, as the shortage progresses, plants lack a healthy dark green color. Even further deficits first cause older leaves to become yellowish, eventually spreading to younger tissue if remedy is not given. Nitrogen deficiencies are easily cured by increasing the application rate if the problem is diagnosed early. Excess nitrogen leads to lush, weak, dark green growth; this condition is often of more concern than is a slight deficiency since the weak plants are easily damaged in shipping or through exposure to extreme environmental conditions. Buildups of the ammonium forms of nitrogen may occur even when total nitrogen quantities are fairly low. This condition results in a burning of leaf edges and tips and eventually the entire leaf; roots may be severly damaged. Ammonium toxicity results in symptoms similar to those shown when soluble salts are high in the soil solution.

Potassium disorders

Potassium deficiencies become evident eventually as necrotic (dead) spots on the edges and tips of older leaves. The initial stages of this disorder will appear simply as slightly darker areas on the leaf but soon turning decidedly dark; usually a brownish green color, then dark brown. The problem is easily cured by increasing applications of potassium if diagnosed in the early stages. Potassium deficiencies may be transitory in nature, showing up quickly as plants attain their maximum growth rate and then becoming less evident as the growth rate slows down towards maturity, or as environmental conditions become less favorable for rapid growth. Moderate excesses of potassium do not cause growth problems but extreme abundance may limit the uptake of other essential elements and add unnecessarily to soluble salts in the soil. .

Phosphorous disorders

Phosphorous deficiencies are first evidenced by stunted growth and eventually by a purplish color on leaves and stems. In early stages the plants may look quite healthy but miniature in size. The problem is easily solved by applying a liquid phosphorous fertilizer solution. Slowly available phosphorous compounds applied to the soil surface may allow the disorder to progress to the critical stage before any phosphorous becomes available

An azalea plant displaying a deficiency of available iron, resulting in "chlorosis".

Close up of leaves from the plant in the preceding photograph. Dark green veins with lighter yellow tissue between them are classic signs of iron deficiency.

in the root zone. Phosphorous is needed by plants in fairly small quantities; if a reasonable effort to provide this element is made, there should be no deficiencies. Phosphorous excesses are not generally a problem unless large oversupplies are made available.

Iron disorders

Iron deficiencies are visually apparent first in the young leaves near the growing tip. The leaf veins remain a darker green color while the areas between veins become a yellowish color. This disorder can be quickly cured in the earlier stages by application of iron to the root zone. Even quicker recovery is possible by spray applications to the leaves. Certain plant groups, such as azaleas and gardenias, are especially prone to iron deficiencies. Iron deficiencies are more prevalent when soil is cold and soggy. If these conditions persist, even luxury amounts of iron may not cure the problem; which is caused mainly by a lack of uptake rather than availability.

General nutrient disorders

As mentioned previously, nutrient disorders are sometimes extremely difficult to diagnose properly and even more difficult to remedy effectively.

A general deficiency of both nitrogen and potassium in geranium seedlings caused by excessive water dripping from the ceiling (drip area is immediately to the right of the photo centerline). Light color of tissue in this area is due mainly to a lack of nitrogen while dead tissue at leaf edges is primarily caused by a potassium deficiency.

Specific nutrient disorders can be interrelated with other cultural factors and with other nutrient problems. The best defense against nutrient problems is to study mineral nutrition, soil composition, and crop needs with an eye towards providing suitable conditions right from the start.

Uninformed manipulation of fertilizer applications can often lead to more severe problems than were initially experienced, especially when micronutrients are concerned; several of them become toxic at low concentrations. Ideally, every significant change in nutrient application should be trialed on a test crop.

Experienced plant growers know that crops will exhibit differences in appearance from time to time and amongst plants in the crop. Small imperfections should be noticed but not blown out of proportion; if fertilizer applications are altered wildly to cure imagined disorders, availability of essential elements can become so out of balance as to cause uncorrectable damage.

Diagnosing micronutrient deficiencies through visual analysis can become so confusing that even the most experienced grower seldom solves the mystery adequately. A few hours of thoughtful analysis

---

Table 16
Checklist of factors to be considered when devising a fertilizer program.

A. pH characteristics of fertilizers should be compatible with desired pH ranges of soils.

B. Essential fertilizer elements must be present in balanced proportions.

C. Low salt index fertilizers should be chosen whenever possible.

D. Fertilizers which supply more than one essential element are generally more desirable.

E. Nitrate forms of nitrogen are usually safer, especially in artificial soil mixes.

F. Be sure precipitation is not occurring in fertilizer solutions.

G. Double check all calculations.

H. It is safer to under fertilize slightly than to over fertilize.

I.   Relatively small amounts of trace elements can be toxic to plants.

J. Ammonium toxicity and the carbon-to-nitrogen ratio of soils must be considered when deciding upon types and amounts of nitrogen to fertilize with.

K. Soil pH and other factors can alter the availability of nutrients.

L. Availability of essential elements is more important than physical concentrations.

M. The types and proportions of soil mix ingredients may affect the type and amount of fertilizers used.

N. Different species of plants may require different forms and concentrations of fertilizers.

O. The concentration of essential elements in water sources may alter the amounts of fertilizer needed.

---

concerning micronutrient needs should allow growers to prevent any disorders from arising by judicious applications during soil mixing or as plant growth occurs. Micronutrient deficiencies are not very common even when no attention is paid to the situation. Plants most frequently manifest micronutrient deficiencies in newer leaves because these elements are decidedly immobile in the plant; they cannot be transported from older growth to newer growth.

Various fungicide, insecticide, and miscellaneous treatments can affect the micronutrient balance of plants. For example, the use of copper sprays to treat mildew and other fungal diseases often supplies all of the copper necessary for growth. Excessive treatments may result in harmful oversupplies. Growers should be aware of the chemical compositions of the various sprays and drenches which they apply.

Most nutrient type disorders are caused by improper balances in the 3 major elements, excess soluble salts, pH balance, or ammonium toxicity. These are the first areas which should be investigated. Table 16 presents a checklist of factors which should be kept in mind when devising a fertilizer program .

SUMMATION OF A PARTICULAR FERTILIZER PROGRAM

Although all growers should attempt to understand the background and implications of any soil and fertilizer programs they utilize, the author realizes that this is certainly not always the case in practical application. Due to one reason or another, a large number of growers simply adopt programs recommended by other individuals or offered as packaged commercial products. Growers who employ the commercial product route must look to the manufacturers' guidelines for further clarification; however, the author will attempt, in the following summation, to simplify one basic soil and fertilizer scheme which has proven successful over many years of daily use. The individual parts of this program have been explained in detail in previous sections of this book.

The fertilizer program to be summarized has been used primarily with a soil mix composed of approximately 50% peat and 50% sand (described in detail earlier as a peat/sand mix). The basic soil components have been altered from time to time (perlite, vermiculite, composted bark being substituted partially in some cases for sand or peat) without observing the need for any appreciable change in fertilizer application. This soil mix has not generally been adjusted for pH by the addition of ground limestone (because the fertilizers normally used tend to increase the soil pH over time). If acid fertilizer use is anticipated, then the soil pH should be raised at mixing by the incorporation of limestones. There have been cases where moderate amounts of limestone (approximately 5 pounds per cubic yard) were added for special purposes without any observed need to alter fertilizer formulas. The program described below assumes that the irrigation water source is moderately to highly mineralized and that it supplies a small amount of both minor and major essential elements even before the addition of fertilizer products. If the water source is extremely low in dissolved solids (indicating low mineralization), a higher level of fertilization than is recommended below may be necessary.

A weak solution of potassium nitrate is added to the soil during mixing along with adequate triple superphosphate. Plants are then fertilized at every watering with a solution of either potassium nitrate alone (fertilizer A) or potassium nitrate plus calcium nitrate (fertilizer B). The first solution is used on all spring bedding crops after they are well established. Fertilizer B solution is used as the general fertilizer at all other times unless the grower chooses to restrict nitrogen supplies. Petunias receive fertilizer only every third watering after they are well established. Micronutrients and chelated iron are applied every 60 days after a thorough leaching (the leaching portion of this exercise is practiced only upon plants in advanced growth stages, not upon recently planted material). This program is designed to ensure that fertilizer excess will not occur. Growers who can leach somewhat at each watering or who prefer plants in a lush condition may want to increase the fertilizer concentrations at all stages. Low soluble salt water supplies may bring about the possibility of magnesium deficiencies and could call for increased applications of micronutrients and possibly nitrogen and potassium. If sulfates are low in the water supply, some source of sulfur may need to be added in the program.

Coated polymeric resin fertilizers are incorporated at a low rate into spring flowering hanging baskets and patio planters. A three month formulation containing iron and micronutrients is used. These baskets and planters are also liquid fertilized at every watering with fertilizer B.

Trees and shrubs planted bare root in the spring are watered heavily upon potting with potassium nitrate plus calcium nitrate (fertilizer B). As trees and shrubs leaf out, micronutrients and iron are appled once in conjunction with fertilizer B. Fertilizer B is then applied at every irrigation. Trees and shrubs receive micronutrients and iron at the prescribed intervals if they remain in inventory. Trees and shrubs transplanted to containers as growing plants are simply continued on fertilizer B.

Each grower should realize that the above program cannot be blindly followed; the same applies to other fertilizer recipes one might encounter. Growers must always observe results closely and make adjustments as necessary. When large quantities of a particular crop are grown, some emphasis should be placed upon researching the more exact nutritional needs of that variety. The above program is intended to meet the approximate needs of many varieties under a wide range of conditions and may not be the most appropriate for specialized production circumstances. Growers may find that fast growing varieties receiving optimum temperatures and light will require heavier fertilization than suggested here.

Tree and shrub growers face some particular problems in relation to fertilizer practices since a large number of these species are irrigated outdoors with sprinkling systems. In these cases, the best practice appears to be that of incorporating a large portion of the plants' total fertilizer need into the soil at the time of potting (either as dry slow release forms or as a coated slow release). Growers must be extremely careful to test the amount of long lasting fertilizer incorporated into the soil. An excess can be very damaging, particularly to bareroot crops. If further applications are necessary, the containers can be top dressed with appropriate formulas or fertilizer can be injected into the irrigation water which is then applied manually (both time consuming). Sprinkling with fertilizer solutions would cause a good deal of fertilizer runoff unless an effective recycling system for runoff is in place. Another effective means of watering shrubs and trees is a spaghetti tube system which brings tiny individual plastic irrigation tubes to each pot from a main line.

FERTILIZER POLLUTION

In recent years, environmental regulators have become acutely aware of the extensive pollution caused by agricultural fertilizers. While horticultural enterprises contribute only a small percentage of the total pollutants, the intensive nature of horticultural operations may often result in a more concentrated (and easily detected) point source of pollution.

Growers should, therefore, place heavy emphasis upon reducing the volume of fertilizer use and contamination which occurs on their properties.

A large portion of the problems can be eliminated simply through a knowledge of exactly how much fertilizer is necessary and how it can be best applied. In the past, growers generally applied luxury amounts of fertilizer to their crops. This situation arose mainly because there was no incentive to reduce applications (fertilizer was cheap and no regulations existed). But it also came about because experts, who should have known better, provided the recommendations which growers followed.

The sample fertilizer formulas previously provided in *The Greenhouse and Nursery Handbook* reduce total fertilizer salts use by approximately 1/2 from the amount which was traditionally recommended 20 years ago.

As a consequence of previously using high fertilizer ratios, growers were also advised to use a porous potting medium from which excess fertilizer salts could be easily leached out at every irrigation or at least every third irrigation. Needless to say, these practices led to an immense volume of fertilizer runoff per plant produced.

At our present state of knowledge, it seems best to recommend only the minimum fertilizer amounts necessary, while using a slightly less porous and, therefore, nutrient retentive medium. This regime will greatly reduce the need for and frequency of leaching.

Even with reduced fertilizer use and better application methods, there is still great potential for fertilizer runoff or percolation to groundwater tables. This problem can only be solved by introducing methods for recycling irrigation runoff in the nursery or greenhouse.

As new greenhouses or nurseries are constructed, it is relatively easy and economical to provide for recycling runoff, but installing the necessary modifications to old structures and grounds can be very expensive. Older operations should first seek to implement all runoff reduction remedies and then determine if such measures bring the facilities into regulation compliance before expensive extra steps are taken. Growers should not automatically assume they are in violation of regulations; their present operation may be well within necessary guidelines. Once fertilizer applications and leaching have been reduced, a means of collecting and channeling the remaining product to storage or recycling areas can be accomplished through common sense methods.

The runoff can be evaporated with the remaining solid waste being disposed of or, as is more commonly the case, the liquid can be cleaned up and utilized again. Several treatments or combinations of treatments are available for water clean up but all begin with some type of filtration system. Besides the particulate matter which is filtered out, recycled water must be monitored for: mineral content, pH, harmful organisms, and total dissolved solids. A plan for bringing each of these factors within acceptable limits for reuse must be devised. Local water treatment specialists can be of great technical help since they encounter these situations daily.

On a practical basis, runoff is seldom reduced to zero. A nursery or greenhouse can often attain compliance with environmental standards by reusing water once or twice without extensive clean up treatments being required. The problems associated with reducing fertilizer pollution (as with any other type of pollution) can seem overwhelming at first but become manageable if a four-pronged method of solution is employed: 1) Reduce fertilizer input and leachate output; 2) become acquainted with regulations (they may not be as rigid as imagined); 3) use common sense to see what problems exist and how they may be solved; 4) get technical help (much of it may be offered free by various government agencies, equipment dealers, and water treatment companies).

The author has been personally acquainted with environmental compliance requirements and has found that some of the necessary solutions actually serve to increase profits since less input of expensive pollutants to the operation is often the most logical route to follow. Of course, some compliance procedures cost money. Hopefully, a balance between benefits and costs is achieved over the long run.

BIOLOGICAL TESTING

The concept of testing various cultural systems (such as soil, fertilizer, and water) was mentioned in the last chapter. Now is a good time to investigate this subject more fully. Basically, growers may test systems by 2 methods: 1) In the on-site or commercial laboratory (measuring physical and chemical attributes); 2) biologically at the production site by actually growing plants in the cultural systems.

Measuring physical and chemical attributes of the cultural systems and of the plants grown in them is generally a rather technical process, and most greenhouses and nurseries lack the facilities and instruments necessary to accurately perform a full range of these tests. Physical and chemical tests can be very precise; however, they are only as reliable as the techniques and information which are used to complete them. Growers should not accept and act upon these tests without examining the results for inconsistencies, errors, or data which simply does not make good sense.

Biological tests can usually be designed and completed at the production site without access to complicated instruments for analysis and measurement. Biological tests (at least the less complicated ones) are simply "experiments" which the grower performs by using different cultural systems with crops. Of course, the conditions must be carefully controlled to yield valid results.

For example, two soil formulas may be tested to see which one yields the best crop. In this case, one soil formula might produce better tomato plants, while the second results in better maple trees or, an alternative result might show that both plant species grow better in one soil. Readers can easily observe here that only one "variable" can be measured in a single test, otherwise the results do not allow the experimenter to determine whether the soil or the plants caused the outcome. Only one plant species can be tested with the different soils at one time. More than one plant species can be tested but this must be done in a separate experiment using only one soil.

Biological tests can yield results which are easily apparent to any observer or they can require careful measurements of such attributes as plant height, weight, color, etc. Some tests may produce inconclusive results. The real value of biological tests is that they can be performed by almost anyone and the results are usually readily interpreted by using common sense.

The cardinal rules for conducting valid biological tests are: 1) Do not arrange tests conditions with prior prejudice about how the results should turn out; 2) do not try to test more than one "variable" at a time; 3) maintain constant experimental conditions from one test to another if they are to be compared with each other; 4) validate results with a reasonable number of replicates; 5) do not "stretch" the data to fit into a preconceived notion.

All of these rules are commonsense, but it is very easy to allow improper test conditions to "creep" in without notice. Even experienced research scientists occasionally allow this to happen.

Every major cultural decision in a nursery or greenhouse should be confirmed by a carefully designed and executed biological test before full-fledged production commences utilizing a particular cultural system. Laboratory tests can be used to help confirm or refute the results obtained from a biological assessment.

Chapter 8

LIGHT

No one factor required for plant growth is more important than another but the unique biological character and importance of plants is dependent upon the conversion of light energy into chemical energy. It is not surprising therefore, that the amount and quality of light impinging upon a plant regulates, to a great extent, its requirements for other essential ecological factors. The requirements for mineral elements and water can usually be regulated at will by container plant growers; and when plants are cultured in greenhouses, the temperature can also be easily modified. But the ability to manipulate light energy, other than by simple shading techniques, is not frequently available except in specialized greenhouse installations.

Since it is difficult to affect changes in light quality and intensity, most growers are content to let nature take its course. Simple operations like shading are practiced, but sophisticated manipulations of light are left to more innovative growers or those whose circumstances definitely require light alteration. As a consequence, the average grower probably spends less time worrying about how to change light conditions than pondering how to manage fertilizer or temperature factors. In future years a more economical technology will perhaps be available to alter light energy at will and greenhouse owners may take a more aggressive attitude toward management of this factor.

In a practical sense, plant growth is generally more economical and of better quality when growers choose varieties and cultural methods which do not require extensive modification of either light quality, intensity, or duration. Of course this type of program cannot be emphasized too rigidly since market considerations may require that particular crops be grown at a specified time of year, regardless of whether or not light conditions are optimal. Those growers who have greenhouse facilities will certainly be more likely to attempt modification of the light factor than will those whose operation is carried on entirely out of doors. The following discussion of light will be limited to those aspects necessary for nonspecialized growers to acquire a general knowledge of the subject and it will be slanted towards greenhouse applications since this is the most likely area of use.

LIGHT QUALITY

Light energy is composed of wavelengths which are categorized according to the distance between successive waves. These categories are what is referred to when one speaks of light "quality." Table 17 shows the wavelength relationship between light quality categories which affect plant growth. Infrared radiation, as far as is presently known, affects plants mainly because it is absorbed by tissues and is transformed into heat. The amount of infrared radiation penetrating the greenhouse skin greatly affects temperature relationships inside the greenhouse and within the plants it holds. Ultraviolet radiation is responsible for much of the degradation occurring to plastic and fiberglass coverings. Neither ultraviolet nor infrared wavelengths pass through greenhouse coverings readily although it is obvious from the heat buildup and heat loss which take place in greenhouses that infrared light constantly enters and leaves at a significant rate.

Fortunately, the visible wavelengths which affect plant growth readily pass through the greenhouse skin. Blue and red areas of the visible spectrum have been found to account for most of the photosynthetic activity in plants. Far-red and red wavelengths are responsible for many of the flowering responses controlled by daylength. A basic knowledge of plant responses to different light wavelengths can be of practical importance when greenhouse covers are chosen and if plants are grown under any type of artificial light. Obviously, greenhouse covering materials should transmit the maximum amount of light possible in the red and blue wavelengths. It would not be as important for maximum transmission to occur in the green and yellow wavelengths since they are relatively weak in photosynthetic and developmental activity. Objects are perceived to be a certain color because they reflect light of that color. It should be evident that fiberglass tinted blue or red is not the best choice for greenhouse

Table 17

Relative wavelength of different light quality categories which affect plant growth.

Light category	Effect on plant growth
Gamma X-ray	Induce genetic mutations, phytotoxic in large quantities.
Ultraviolet C Ultraviolet B	Generally phytotoxic.
Ultraviolet A	Formative effects on leaves and internodes.
Violet Blue Blue-green Green Yellow Orange Red Far-red	Visible spectrum-affects plant growth in a direct manner. Photosynthetic wavelengths.
Infrared	Affects plant growth indirectly as a source of heat.

Increasing wavelength

coverings because a significant part of important photosynthetic rays would be reflected and prevented from entering the greenhouse.

Growers in low winter light areas can sometimes profitably provide supplemental lighting from large electrical lamps. It is very important to choose lamps emitting the proper wavelengths so that growth is increased with the smallest expenditure of energy. Supplemental light is often used in the seedling or cutting stage because a large number of plants can be accelerated in growth by lighting a small area. It would obviously take more lights to accomplish the same purpose after transplanting to larger pots. Incandescent lamps emit a large proportion of red and far-red light while most fluorescent lamps are rich in blue and green wavelengths. Light strictly from incandescent sources will increase photosynthesis and growth but causes plants to become tall and spindly. Light only from fluorescent lamps does not cause extraordinary elongation of plants but neither does it result in dramatic photosynthetic increases. A combination of incandescent and fluorescent light sources provides for balanced growth because both blue and red wavelengths are present. Blue light seems to counteract the elongative effects of red light. A knowledge of how differing light wavelengths effect plants has led engineers to devise lighting sources which are specially intended for this purpose.

Lighting and shading set ups (using relatively small energy input) intended to trigger modification of physiological responses (mainly flowering) in plants are commonplace in most year round greenhouses. But large scale lighting installations which are meant to supply additional light duration and intensity (using large energy inputs) in order to promote significant additional photosynthetic activity are generally restricted to those situations where such a practice is required by: 1) Especially low winter light levels; 2) the needs of high light crops such as roses; 3) when the cultural program benefits extraordinarily from high light at a critical stage of plant growth (propagation).

The types of light sources employed vary depending upon the objectives to be realized and the conditions under which lights are installed. Very small residential or hobby greenhouse plant growing lights may be purchased in local retail stores and installed by a trial and error process until the desired effects are obtained. Larger commercial installations should be carefully researched in advance to determine the most economical and effective means of reaching the cultural goals in mind.

Most manufacturers and distributors of commercial greenhouse lighting fixtures can supply extensive data concerning the light quality and intensity emitted by the products they sell. Lighting engineers may even be available free of charge to design a complete package.

When high intensity lighting is being installed in spaces of limited area without provision for special ventilation, some consideration must be given to the amount of heat which is generated when lights are in operation.

Germination chambers and other enclosed areas may become overheated unless adequate heat exhaust features and low heat producing light fixtures are utilized.

The installation and operation of lighting intended for significant photosynthetic increases is costly initially and over the longer term. Growers should carefully examine their present objectives and future plans before investing in such a project. If a large lighting installation is planned, it might well be that a more economical long term solution would be effected by moving the greenhouse operation to a geographical area where sufficient light is available naturally. Reduced heating costs could very well be achieved also by this course of action. As was pointed out earlier, this is why numerous large greenhouse facilities have recently been constructed in geographic areas possessing favorable light and temperature regimes.

LIGHT INTENSITY

Light intensity is a much more familiar characteristic to the average person than is light quality. If light is brighter, it is more intense. Light is often measured in units called footcandles. Full sun on a clear summer day in the Midwestern United States might equal 10,000-12,000 footcandles, while the reading on a cloudy winter day in the same location would be hard pressed to reach 1,000 footcandles. Most greenhouse and nursery crops prefer full sun for maximum production but some plant species require shade; the leaves of these latter plants may be burned at light intensities of 2,000-3,000 footcandles. Individual leaves of sun plants are photosynthesizing at maximum capacity when light levels of 2,000-3,000 footcandles are reached. Higher levels are needed, however, to reach maximum production for the whole plant because many leaves are shaded from above and outside. Thus if the inside leaves of sun plants are to receive 2,000 footcandles, the outside ones must be exposed to considerably higher intensities. Individual leaves of shade plants become light saturated at 500-1,000 footcandles. Shade plant leaves will not tolerate increased light intensity above the saturation point as well as do those of sun plants. Damage of plant leaves due to high light intensities is caused by the oxidation of chlorophyll pigments.

Crop quality can be maximized with respect to light intensity in several ways: 1) Shading or supplemental lighting may be practiced; 2) crops may be grown only at suitable times of the year; 3) spacing between plants may be varied with seasonal light conditions; 4) temperature may be correlated with light intensity. Crop production is greatest at the highest light intensities possible without chlorophyll damage. When insufficient light is available for a particular variety, whether it be sun or shade, the effects are manifested in thinner, taller stems, larger, more succulent leaves, fewer flowers, less branching, and an overall reduction in dry matter weight. Too much light may damage leaf tissue quickly and be apparent as severe burns or it may show up as a gradual yellowing process as chlorophyll is destroyed.

Greenhouses are normally constructed to admit as much light as possible. Their orientation and types of coverings as they affect light were discussed previously. Rafters and roof braces can seriously impair light transmission unless they are engineered to be as small and as few in number as possible. Greenhouse interior surfaces should be planned to increase the reflective light available for plants, and summer shading must be removed promptly in the fall to avoid serious reductions in crop quality. If light intensity is to be supplemented by lamps, the design should be engineered by persons competent to determine the most economical installation. Typically, artificial light installations on a greenhouse-wide basis will not justify themselves unless a strong market exists.

Plant spacing in the greenhouse and nursery is a critical subject which every successful grower must understand completely. If plants are grown widely spaced so that no competition for light exists between them, they will achieve maximum quality. This spacing is usually not the most advantageous economically, but in a market where a strong demand for quality exists, emphasis may be placed on spacing plants to obtain maximum quality and, consequently, maximum economic return. Certain markets where quality is less of a factor than price may dictate that growers space plants closer together in order to produce more plants per square foot.

Greenhouse space (as opposed to outdoor growing areas) is particularly expensive to provide and maintain. Generally, greenhouse growers will be best off spacing plants to a point where slight competition for light begins, resulting in complete utilization of bench space and a reasonably high quality product. Market requirements and interplant competition for light should be studied very closely; the ability of a grower to squeeze 1-2% more high quality plants out of each bench can markedly increase greenhouse profits. Recommendations for spacing can be found scattered through the literature but the final decision will always rest upon the grower's evaluation of circumstances. Latitude, local light intensities, greenhouse construction, plant varieties, and market demands will interact to determine the most profitable spacing densities. As a rule of thumb, many growers in the Midwest of the United States assume a 1 square foot spacing for the common 6 inch potted flower. Especially vigorous species may require slightly more space and less robust species a little less.

During peak demand seasons it is extremely important to have plants spaced as closely as possible consistent with good quality. Employees must constantly be reminded of the important role spacing plays. The length of time a plant is in the greenhouse and the area it occupies are two critical factors in determining the price it should command.

Careful selection of plant varieties will aid growers in producing quality crops throughout the year, even though light intensity varies greatly from one season to the next. Certain plants such as cinerarias and calceolarias do well at relatively low light intensities and, as a result, are popular crops to flower in the greenhouse from December through March in the Northern hemisphere (Southern hemisphere timing for these crops would be opposite). Plant breeders have developed numerous varieties within the same general groups which perform well at different seasons of the year. Chrysanthemums and snapdragons have been especially well developed in this sense. Growers who take the time to be knowledgeable about plant varieties which do well at particular times will have an edge over their competitors.

A good knowledge of local light conditions is essential in growing quality plants. Light intensity will affect quality and maturation dates not only directly as a source of energy for photosynthesis but indirectly because average temperatures are usually warmer when light is abundant. Crop timing varies somewhat each year because of differences in solar radiation from one year to the next. Most factors except light intensity can be controlled in the greenhouse within rather narrow bounds and, as a result, variations in crop timing from year to year will be due mostly to changing light conditions if an effort is made to hold other factors constant. Growers must evaluate published crop schedules carefully to determine how local light conditions might alter marketing dates. Crop schedules without reference to latitude and local light intensity are not as useful as those which present this information.

Growers must assess various light intensity recommendations critically. Most of the recommendations given in books and literature are based upon the author's primary geographic region of expertise, and specific location is often not mentioned. Since most of the information released to growers originates from the northern United States and northern Europe, it is likely that growers with operations in sunnier climates would need to reduce light intensities in many cases to meet published parameters. Growers at high altitudes (more natural light intensity than near sea level) would face the same situation. Always interpret light data given for crops on the basis of your specific location and conditions.

In the earlier days of the container plant industry the possibility of supplying additional light intensity to crops was not a practical reality; but shading plants to lower light intensity has been used as a cultural tool since the beginning of commercial production. Many varieties benefit from reduced light intensity at some stage of the production process and a substantial number are naturally adapted to prosper under shady conditions. Growing areas in tropical regions may require shade for some varieties on a near year-round basis to reduce light intensity and heat buildup.

The light intensity reaching plants is lowered for two reasons: first, to reduce environmental stress during critical production phases such as propagation or transplanting, and secondly, to avoid damage to plant physiological systems (the chlorophyll molecules in shade loving plants) which require lower light intensities to function properly. The objective of growers should be to grow plants under the highest light conditions which will fulfill the above production and physiological objectives; reducing light further than necessary results in reduced final crop yields and increases the length of crop cycles.

Numerous means of providing shade to indoor and outdoor crops are available, some aspects of this topic were covered in an earlier chapter dealing with structures. One method of shading greenhouses is the automatic shade curtain system. In this system, ceiling curtains are drawn and opened on demand by motorized devices which can be controlled by hand but most often are regulated through the use of light measuring instruments. This type of shading system most often functions as a secondary benefit which is realized when the curtains are installed as heat saving devices for colder seasons. Most greenhouses outside of tropical areas would be hard pressed to justify the considerable expense of interior automatic shade systems if the additional benefit of heat savings was not accomplished at the same time.

Whatever means of providing shade is utilized, the grower should keep in mind that too much shade for too long a period is both an added expense and reduces crop yield. Some informed evaluation of the light intensity needs of the crop must be made rather than simply applying or removing shade haphazardly.

This evaluation may be made by a simple but careful visual estimation based upon the grower's experience or it may be accomplished with the aid of light measuring instruments (light meters). Anyone who must modify light intensity on more than an occasional basis should purchase a reliable light meter and begin to compile data about crop requirements so that reasonably precise criteria can be established as to when plants should or should not be shaded.

LIGHT QUALITY AND DURATION IN PROPAGATION ROOMS

Some growers find that a climate controlled growth room is the best answer for most of their critical propagation needs. The temperature in these rooms must obviously be carefully regulated; it is relatively easy and economical to do so.

Of course, all of the light needs of plants must be artificially supplied (assuming the room has windowless, insulated walls) when these growth rooms are used. Supplying the correct amount of light for young plants is not an easy or cheap undertaking. Generally, low heat producing lamps must be used to avoid heat buildup. This usually means that some type of fluorescent lamps are employed which supply the proper wavelengths of light (often called Gro-Lux™).

The needs of high light plants can usually be met by supplying 1500 foot candles at plant level for 16 hours per day. A highly reflective interior for the growth rooms helps spread light evenly to every section. Unless the intensity of light is actually measured, growers are likely to provide less than is needed since the amount recommended here will seem very bright to the naked eye.

FLOWERING AND OTHER PLANT RESPONSES RELATED TO LIGHT DURATION AND QUANTITY

Flowering and other processes in plants are intricately related to light. Light energy seems to affect flowering primarily in two ways: certain plants flower only when they have been exposed to predetermined cumulative amounts of light energy while another group flowers mainly in response to the length of day regardless of total cumulative light energy received. The following presentation is arranged to acquaint the reader with basic concepts rather than becoming bogged down in detailed or qualifying remarks. Every grower must realize that although a factor such as daylength may be the primary controller of a particular plant process, this controlling factor is usually modified to some degree by other factors and may, at times, be completely overridden.

Several important crops flower primarily in response to the cumulative amount of light energy they have received. As long as a reasonable time period is allowed for normal development, flowering is independent of age. Any crop which flowers naturally year round may be suspected of possessing this cumulative energy response. Geranium seedlings planted in October have been found to require almost exactly the same cumulative light energy to flower as crops planted in February. Chronological ages for the two crops were 215 days and 126 days respectively at flowering, but each was exposed to slightly over 55,000 gram calories per square centimeter of light energy. Carnations and gloxinias exhibit similar behavior. Experiments to determine behavior must be closely controlled to separate light responses from temperature responses. Since temperatures normally increase along with light intensity, it is sometimes difficult to find which is the controlling factor.

In the earlier part of the 20th century, scientists working with agricultural crops found that flowering in some species was controlled by the length of day to which plants were exposed. The term "photoperiodism" was applied to this phenomenon. Extensive research over the years has shown that flowering in many species is regulated by complex photoperiodic mechanisms. Plants were divided into three basic groups: short-day plants which initiate flowers only when days are shorter than the critical daylength, long-day plants which initiate flowers only when days are longer than the critical daylength, and day-neutral plants which initiate flowers over a wide range of day lengths. It is important to point out that no specific daylength has been mentioned; a long-day plant may have a critical daylength which is shorter than is the critical daylength of a short day plant. The direction of change in daylength after the critical daylength has been reached is actually the heart of the mechanism. As if this terminology were not confusing enough, it was later found that the length of the dark period was actually the controlling factor, not the daylength! The terms long-day, short-day, and day-neutral were so firmly fixed in the literature, however, that plants are still referred to in this manner. Conclusive proof of the importance of the dark period is shown by the fact that brief light flashes in the dark will alter the response of short-day plants while short dark periods in the middle of the light period have no effect on the response of long-day plants. This phenomenon of short light flashes interrupting flower initiation in short-day plants is of much practical importance to growers. They need not waste energy lighting artificially until the critical daylength has been reached; short flashes provided in the middle of the night will serve the same purpose. Accidental light flashes will cause the same response. Flowering schedules may be upset by brief exposure to light when personnel enter the greenhouse at night or from automobile headlights.

In addition to the three main photoperiodic classifications, there are less frequently manifested mechanisms of flowering response. Some plants will flower eventually regardless of the daylength but the flowering response may be speeded up or slowed down by the appropriate photoperiod. Low and high temperatures will sometimes cancel the effects of the photoperiod; temperature variations might also alter photoperiod requirements. Further refinements of photoperiodic responses have been described in short-long day plants which initiate flowers only when short days are followed by long days and long-short day plants which initiate flowers only when long days are followed by short days. Low light intensities may affect photoperiodic responses. Bud abortion is common after initiation in geraniums and Easter lilies when light levels are low and temperatures high. Low light levels will slow flower initiation in chrysanthemums. Specific response to photoperiod for important flower crops is given under the appropriate species listing in a later part of this book. Table 18 lists the effects of photoperiod on some common spring bedding plants.

Table 18

Effects of daylength on common bedding plants. Critical daylengths are not precisely located. This is a general appraisal of what takes place through the season.

Plant	Long-day	Short-day
Alyssum (annual)	None	None
Balsam	None	None
Begonia tuberous	Increases branching, reduces tuber formation	
Begonia fibrous	None	None
Carnation	Speeds flowering	
Centaurea	Speeds flowering	
Chrysanthemum(perennial)		Induces flowering
Coleus		Induces flowering
Cosmos		Induces flowering
Dahlia		Induces flowering
Daisy Marguerite	Speeds flowering	Prevents flowering
Daisy Shasta	Induces flowering	
Gaillardia	Induces flowering	
Gypsophila	Induces flowering	
Impatiens	None	None
Lobelia	None	None
Marigold	Delays flowering	
Petunia	Increases height, speeds flowering	
Phlox (annual)	Induces flowering	
Verbena	Induces flowering	
Zinnia		Speeds flowering

Daylength also affects germination, rooting of cuttings, tuber formation, and stem elongation. The photoperiodic requirements for seed are usually not absolute. The light and dark and temperature requirements for seed germination are extensively presented in several trade books and seed companies will often distribute complimentary copies of these requirements but, as mentioned in the section on propagation, it may be possible to pay little attention to these detailed presentations and still realize acceptable levels of seed germination.

Growers of woody plants used for landscaping purposes may have only occasional need to consider photoperiodic crop responses since the average producer of these plants has little physical ability to modify responses, even if it were deemed advantageous. Some discussion of this topic, however, is warranted to point out the possibilities which may exist.

Perhaps the chief point to be made here is that most persons unfamiliar with photoperiodic responses in plants would generally assume that the life cycle of woody landscape type plants is related primarily to temperature rather than photoperiod. In fact, many of the trigger mechanisms for seasonally related physiological processes in plants are predominantly controlled by photoperiod rather than the more obvious temperature factor.

Knowledge of this situation can aid growers in designing cultural programs for crops which exhibit these seasonal responses. Several factors such as rooting potential, leaf loss, bud formation, and dormancy are likely to be affected to a greater or lesser degree by photoperiod in many species.

Some further information regarding photoperiod, light quality, and light duration will be presented in later sections of this book as appropriate topics arise.

PRACTICAL PHOTOPERIOD MANIPULATION

Many growers have little theoretical knowledge of photoperiodic responses but succeed quite well in obtaining the desired practical results. Most major crops have their photoperiodic requirements well documented and growers may obtain reliable light and dark schedules from large wholesale propagators of the particular crop. One must remember that these schedules will be altered by latitude because daylengths vary with latitude. If photoperiodic flowering responses are not understood well, one should follow published schedules religiously because seemingly minor details can seriously affect flowering dates.

Increasing the daylength to stimulate specific photoperiodic responses is accomplished most economically by providing light periods in the middle of the night with incandescent lamps. These lamps emit energy in the far-red wavelengths which are most suitable for photoperiodic induction. Certain species such as poinsettias are extremely sensitive to photoperiodic induction and low light levels will suffice. Chrysanthemums require relatively high light levels for photoperiodic induction. Sufficient light will be provided for most species if a single row of 60 watt bulbs with reflectors is spaced every 4 feet down a 4 foot wide bench. Bulbs should be less than 5 feet above the top of plants. An 8 foot wide bench would require 100 watt bulbs spaced every 6 feet. Lights are regulated by timers; most small growers can get by very well with inexpensive appliance timers available at any hardware store. Large growers can benefit from the installation of more sophisticated cyclic timing devices which reduce the total energy requirements by providing several shorter periods of light during the night.

Daylengths are reduced by drawing some type of opaque flexible material over plants at specified times. Black sateen cloth is the preferred material but 6 mil black polyethylene will suffice on temporary installations. Light levels should be reduced to 2 to 3 foot candles so the material must be checked for small holes and tears and sides must be fully down past bench level. Growers sometimes apply shade cloth too early in the day because quitting time is 5 o'clock. Early application during summer increases the heat buildup under shadecloth to levels which can be deleterious to crops. In addition, plants do not receive maximum allowable daylengths so crop quality is reduced. Black polyethylene emphasizes the heat buildup problem more than does sateen cloth. Crops requiring short days in winter may be present in the same greenhouse with plants requiring lighting for long days. In these cases the black cloth is drawn over long day plants near sundown and removed early in the morning. Periods of light are given during the night. Applying the cloth during the night prevents light leakage to short day plants.

Light from extraneous sources can seriously affect greenhouse operations if photoperiodic flower crops are grown through the winter.

Poinsettias will remain vegetative at light levels of 1 to 2 foot candles. The only way to monitor light intensity adequately is with a light meter but some idea of permissible light levels can be gained by knowing that the maximum intensity of bright moonlight is 0.02 foot candles. This is not a photoperiodically inductive light level. Many localities now have ordinances against light pollution. If a grower has problems with extraneous light sources which cannot be solved by friendly persuasion, it may be possible to invoke these pollution laws. It must be remembered that short flashes of light can be just as disruptive to flowering as longer exposures. Growers should not become overly nervous about light pollution, streetlights and signs near the greenhouse will cause flowering schedules to be disrupted only if they are in close proximity. Many greenhouses located in very well lighted urban locations apparently have no serious problems. Using a reliable light meter will eliminate any unwarranted worry.

Plant species vary considerably in the number of prescribed 24 hour light/dark cycles needed to completely initiate flower buds. Certain plants will be initiated after only one cycle while others may take up to 25 days. Although flower induction may be completed within a relatively short period of time, most plants require a longer period of appropriate cycles after initiation to make the flowering process irreversible. In the northern United States poinsettias have set bud by mid October under natural light conditions but some cultivars must still receive short days until mid November to assure proper flowering.

Alteration of the photoperiod is an added expense and worry to greenhouse operators. Although daylength manipulation will generally be a part of any year-round greenhouse operation, growers must carefully analyze whether it is more profitable to concentrate on natural season crops or to provide a wider variety through alteration of the photoperiod. Daylength manipulation is not always a liability to growers; it can be very helpful in precisely timing large crops for particular marketing periods. Larger growers generally prefer to have crops move out entirely within a short period so that benches may be quickly refilled. Many smaller growers prefer crops to trickle out slowly as individual plants mature so that too many plants are not ready at any one time.

It is obvious that plants grown near the equator will receive essentially the same daylengths throughout the year unless some of the light modification procedures mentioned are employed. Species which naturally flower under equal daylight circumstances (such as roses and carnations) would certainly be easier to flower profitably than would photoperiodic poinsettias or chrysanthemums.

Chapter 9
TEMPERATURE

Plants require a suitable temperature range in order to carry on life processes. Most species would be killed upon exposure to temperature extremes of more than 150^0 F or less than -50^0 F, however, the temperature range for normal active growth in most plants is approximately 35^0 to 115^0 F. For most plants, internal temperatures above $95F^0$ are detrimental. Certain plant species, having evolved in very cold or very hot regions will extend these temperature ranges for survival and normal growth. Alpine and arctic species often carry on normal physiological processes even though night temperatures dip well below freezing while some desert plants will tolerate daytime soil level extremes of over 135^0 F without damage.

Temperature not only determines the limits of survival and active growth, but also speeds up or retards the rate of growth. Within a plant's normal growth range, increases in temperature speed up chemical processes in the plant and growth accelerates. Plants may exhibit damage when temperatures fluctuate widely within a short time span even though the extreme survival limits have not been reached. This phenomenon is best illustrated by the need for plants to be exposed to gradually colder temperatures before they become winter hardy. The chemical activities taking place in plants evidently function more smoothly if temperature changes are made gradually.

TEMPERATURE AND RESPIRATION

Two basic chemical processes taking place in plants are photosynthesis and respiration. Photosynthesis is an accumulating phenomenon which contributes to the production of plant matter. Respiration, although necessary for proper growth, is a consuming process whereby plant matter is decreased. Respiration releases energy which is necessary for various physiological activities in plants to be completed. Normally, photosynthesis outpaces respiration by many times so that plants are observed to grow larger. Under some circumstances, respiration and photosynthesis may be balanced; this situation is termed the "compensation point". At this point plants do not grow larger. Several factors are of major importance in determining the photosynthetic rate but temperature is the primary factor controlling respiration rates. At very low light intensities respiration can actually exceed photosynthesis and plants can decrease in mass. Respiration is a large contributing factor to the decline in quality of plants when they reach old age, or are placed in areas where photosynthesis cannot outpace respiration. Higher temperatures speed up respiration and the consumption of plant matter; if photosynthesis is not occurring at an equal or greater rate, a decline in quality results. This readily explains why flowers harvested for bouquets last longer at cooler temperatures. The relationship between respiration and photosynthesis is one of the primary factors behind many transport, storage, and marketing activities practiced in horticulture.

TEMPERATURE AND PLANT PRODUCTION

Commercial plant growers are always concerned about what the temperature is; day and night, inside and outside. This environmental factor occupies the minds of growers because it affects plant growth so profoundly and also because it is the most easily monitored factor. Not only does the temperature affect general plant growth, it can cause immediate, irreparable, and widespread crop damage within a few minutes when it is outside acceptable limits.

This drastic type of injury normally is encountered when the temperature drops too low, causing plant tissue to freeze. However, damage from temperatures which are too high is not a rare occurrence. Plants are susceptible to physical injury from unacceptable temperatures during all stages of their life cycle but certain stages are generally disposed towards more immediate and permanent injury.

Not surprisingly, traumatic tissue damage from high or low temperature occurs most readily to plants when their metabolic rate is greatest (active growth stage), although there may be significant changes in tolerance due to other modifying factors. Every experienced grower has had the opportunity to witness plant damage occurring at the same temperature which previously had caused no injury. This phenomenon may be caused at times by the interaction of various physical environmental factors but it is also likely to occur because plants were in a slightly different physiological condition at the time of exposure.

Plant species vary widely in their tolerance to temperature extremes. Tolerance at the upper or lower temperature extremes may often be inferred by knowledge of the varieties' native habitats, but this type of prediction is certainly not foolproof.

Greenhouse crops often suffer in summer from continual high daytime temperatures unless there is sufficient cooling capacity. The damage is most often a cumulative lessening of crop quality rather than a total loss.

Because of the many modifying conditions, a precise determination of the temperatures at which plants suffer traumatic damage is not possible; but we can delineate some general guidelines. Whenever the temperature is at or below the freezing point (32^0 F) the possibility of damage should be considered in any species. A 28^0 F temperature is often mentioned in the literature as a critical freezing temperature for many varieties of plants.

Immediate physiological impairment and the possibility of further complicating disruptions often takes place in more susceptible species at temperatures somewhat above freezing. These later cases may become so severe that the crop is effectively ruined for commercial purposes even though traumatic physical damage did not occur at the time of exposure. Longer term exposure (perhaps more than 1 or 2 hours) at even rather moderate temperatures in the 40^0 F area can cause significant damage to some tropical plants.

Even severe frosts do not harm a good number of varieties, particularly if they have been exposed gradually to this regime and if other preceding environmental conditions (fertilizer or water) have been conducive to moderate rather than rapid growth. Certain plants can be frozen solid each night and show no apparent damage as they unthaw during the day. It has been suggested by many informational sources that the conditions under which thawing takes place can have a significant relationship to the likelihood of frost damage occurring. Prevailing wisdom suggests that plants be allowed to thaw slowly so that sudden physical damage to the cell membrane and cell contents is minimized. If this information is correct, it would mean that immediate exposure of frozen plants to warm temperatures or the thawing effects of irrigation water are the worst things that could happen.

The measures which greenhouse growers can take to avoid frost damage are obvious: outdoor growers do not have the same ability to modify temperature at will and must rely upon techniques which offer only limited possibilities, even when freezes are light. Covering plants with some type of fabric or plastic is effective if only a small number must be protected. If this method is used, there is danger of upright shaped plants being broken if snow loads accumulate on top of the covering and the coverings are often difficult to keep in place if the wind comes up.

Most containerized landscape trees, shrubs, and perennials suffer little or none from light to moderate frost if they have been allowed to "bud out" under normal outdoor conditions. Even hardier annuals may suffer no lasting damage from light frost.

Perhaps the most widely used means of protecting containerized outside plants from frost is to spray them with water as a freeze takes place so that the plants become covered with ice. This protective covering will help minimize damage if the temperature drops even further. Of course it has little value in the case of extremely severe frost. Outdoor crops may escape damage from light frost if they occupy ground which is less prone to frost than the surrounding terrain. Generally, cool air flows towards and occupies low spots in the topography. Fruit growers have taken advantage of this fact for many years by locating their fields on hillsides where frost damage is less likely to occur.

The productive capacity of plants is affected not only by severely traumatizing extremes of temperature, there also seems to be (at least in many species) a particular temperature zone to which prolonged exposure upsets physiological processes so profoundly that growth not only slows to an imperceptible level but the actual slow death of the plant occurs. This zone may be located on the warmer or cooler end of the normal growing range. Many tropical foliage varieties seem to encounter survival problems when temperatures are in the 50^0 to 60^0 F range for extended periods while cool loving plants such as ranunculus deteriorate when night temperatures are consistently over 50^0 F.

The varied effects which temperature has upon plant growth and development are probably masked to the casual observer by the more obvious manifestations of this factor which are observed every day. Some of the less obvious expressions of plant reaction to temperature will be mentioned in the following discussion and as specific crops are discussed in Part II.

DAY/NIGHT TEMPERATURES

It is traditional in the greenhouse industry to assume that when a particular temperature is mentioned, it refers to the night temperature crops are grown under unless further qualification is specifically mentioned. This convention may or may not make sense to some people but it does have some justification in that controlling the night temperature has, in general, occupied more of a growers time and effort than has controlling day temperature.

Temperatures mentioned in the literature for outdoor crops normally do not have such a conventional designation and must either be inferred from the general meaning in which they are used or by specific clarification. The following discussion of day/night temperatures will refer mainly to greenhouse culture since outdoor growers have no practical means of significantly altering night temperatures.

Traditionally, greenhouse growers were advised to maintain day temperatures at 10^0 to 15^0 F greater than the recommended night temperatures when days were bright and at approximately 5^0 F greater than night temperatures on cloudy days. Due to inadequate cooling equipment and sometimes to the expectations of growers that warmer days are good for plants or could somehow make up for colder than desirable night temperatures, day temperatures are often allowed to elevate much higher than those mentioned above.

As long as daytime temperatures do not exceed fairly extreme upper limits (the limit being dependent upon species) gross alterations of plant physiology do not occur. There may be modification of growth rates, and plant morphology also is often altered (as will be discussed shortly) but, in general, the process of plant development is normal. With many species, lowering the night temperature to an equally extreme degree in the opposite direction often results in noticeable modification of plant development processes, if not in actual freezing of tissue.

For many years, it has been realized that the general quality of most greenhouse crops was superior when day temperatures were kept fairly close to night temperatures but the actual factors contributing to this overall quality designation were not investigated individually. Recent research has yielded significant and quite astounding information about how the interaction of day and night temperatures contributes to plant quality (through alteration of plant morphology).

Basically, the new information shows that there is a very close link between the height of plants and the temperature difference between day and night to which they are exposed. Although the details can become rather complicated and it is known this information does not apply to all species, the general rule seems to be: growing crops with day temperatures close to the night temperature results in shorter plants than when they are grown with day temperatures significantly exceeding night temperatures. This relationship appears to be one in which the height changes take place gradually in response to similar quantitative shifts in temperatures. Further lowering of day temperatures to the point where they are actually lower than night temperatures (within reasonable bounds) causes plant height to decrease even more.

This temperature related response is referred to in the literature as DIF. DIF = day temperature - night temperature. The significance of DIF to container growers is immense. One of the critical plant quality problems in potted flowers and bedding plants has traditionally been the tendency of certain varieties to become too tall for effective marketing. The use of DIF techniques promises to improve the market quality of many species already in widespread use and to allow production of numerous taller growing varieties which previously could not be grown effectively.

Significant height control is obtained employing DIF in some major crops such as: poinsettia, Easter lily, petunia, impatiens, chrysanthemum, geranium, tomato, and several others. Small or no response has been noted in some crops such as: French marigold, tulip, and hyancith. Shifts in DIF often provide quick results if provided during the active elongation stage of growth, a significant lessening of height occurring within a few days. Additional research has shown that providing lower DIF, or even negative DIF for only about two hours after sunrise (when it is easiest to achieve this relationship) is sufficient to accomplish most of the height control benefits.

DIF is not without problems of its own. Obviously, if day temperatures must be lowered closer to night temperatures, most crops will respond by requiring a longer time to mature; and if night temperatures are raised to more closely approximate day temperatures, fuel costs will go up. Either situation tends to increase production costs. DIF is a new technique and there are likely many aspects of it which we do not yet adequately understand. Only widespread commercial use will reveal the true potential of this recent discovery. DIF has already been employed with favorable result by many commercial growers but implementation of this technique is not easily accomplished in those facilities which lack adequate daytime cooling.

The traditional practice of lowering greenhouse temperatures to retard crop maturation and to produce sturdy, compact plants may need reevaluation in many cases as we gain more appreciation of how DIF works. It would appear that in a number of instances, growers who lower temperatures (at least when night temperature is lowered relatively more than day temperature) in the hopes of producing shorter plants may be promoting the opposite reaction.

The relationship and validity of the traditional and newer techniques must be carefully evaluated to determine exactly how each works and under which conditions. It is likely that both are useful under specific circumstances but that neither can be employed in as straight forward manner as previously thought.

Another significant advance in our knowledge of day/night temperature relationships has come about in recent years. It appears that in a number of species, the commonly required minimum night temperature (for normal growth) need only be supplied for approximately one half the dark period; the temperature can then be lowered a few degrees during the rest of the night. There may be applications where certain temperature controlled physiological trigger mechanisms are activated with less energy input by utilizing this technique than by keeping temperatures up all night long. The possibility of significant savings in fuel expenses using this information is obvious.

STAGE OF GROWTH AND TEMPERATURE

Many plants seem to require a higher temperature during early stages of growth than at more mature stages in order to reach maximum size and quality. This phenomenon has been documented in several species by controlled experiments. If temperatures are not lowered during later growth stages, plants fail to accumulate as much dry weight. Some authors feel that as plants mature, the preponderance of photosynthesis over respiration is lessened and since respiration is more directly controlled by temperature, a reduction in temperature reduces respiration more than it does photosynthesis. In the majority of cases, starting plants out under warm conditions gets them strongly established in less time. Not only does this practice cut down crop time but it also reduces losses due to disease in the juvenile stage. Most losses due to disease occur in the first week or two after transplanting and the sooner plants grow out of this stage the better. Certain crops such as pansies, although having a shorter crop time under this regime, do not exhibit a marked increase in quality. Annual alyssum, on the other hand, has a shorter crop time and exceptional improvement in quality if grown at warm temperatures for the first week or two. Each of these species can be finished at very low temperatures but the alyssum does not start out as well when cold.

Starting plants warm and finishing cooler may not only improve quality and production, but since young plants generally occupy less space than more mature ones, it also reduces fuel expenses. It is possible to maintain one area of the greenhouse range at a higher temperature for young plant production, then, after being transplanted to the final container, they can be moved to cooler greenhouses.

EFFECT OF TEMPERATURE ON PLANT DEVELOPMENT

The effects temperature has on plant growth may be recognized in a general sense by people who have little more than a gardening knowledge of plants. Certain developmental processes in plants are also affected by temperature, although the relationships are often less than obvious to the untrained eye.

Flower initiation in a fairly large number of species is controlled predominantly by temperature. This group of plants is not so large as those where photoperiod is the controlling factor but some important crops are included. Temperature and photoperiod may interact in a number of species; one canceling, overriding, or modifying the effect of the other under certain circumstances. The effect of temperature may be expressed in a qualitative or quantitative manner. That is, the particular temperature treatment required for flower initiation may be absolute or it may act only to speed the flowering process which would have eventually occurred anyway. Specific temperatures for a prescribed length of time may cause flowers to be initiated during that period or, in some cases certain temperature regimes may only be the beginning in a number of factor sequences which cause flower initiation at some future date.

Many biennial and perennial plants require a period of exposure to low temperatures before flowering will occur. This low temperature exposure takes place naturally in winter time with plants that are grown outdoors. If perennial alyssum is started in the fall and then subjected to light freezes in winter, it will bloom for spring sales. Plants sown in the spring will remain vegetative through the first year. There are a number of common perennials which react in a similar manner. This low temperature exposure is not universally required for blooming in perennials. Shasta daisies and cone flowers (rudbeckia) will flower a little the first summer if sown in midwinter and many perennial violas will bloom quite prolifically 12-16 weeks after sowing even if they are germinated in late spring or early summer.

Cabbage and its close relatives are an important group of biennial bedding plants which must be subjected to cold temperatures before flower production occurs. Cabbage sown in late spring and transplanted to the garden remains in the vegetative "head" stage the first summer. If left in the field it will flower the second year, as do all biennials. Flowering in cabbage is undesirable if leafy head production is the objective. Young cabbage plants which have been spring sown and then subjected to low temperatures (45^0 F) for 2 or more weeks will flower the first growing season and lead to customer complaints. If cabbages are artificially maintained at warm temperatures, they will continue producing heads for several years. Other biennials are not so sensitive to cold treatment as is cabbage; they may require considerably more exposure to commence flowering or they may need no cold treatment at all.

Several important flower crops which are not biennials or perennials require low temperature exposure for flower initiation. Flowers are initiated when temperatures fall below the critical level for a specified period of time. After initiation, some species must remain at or below the critical temperature level to complete flower development while others can be grown at higher temperatures to accelerate flower development. Cineraria, calceolaria, Martha Washington geranium, Christmas cactus, and hydrangea are some flowering crops which are reported to require low temperature exposure at some stage of development.

Several crops require that temperatures be above a critical level for specified periods; the direction of change here must be upward in relation to the critical temperature. In low temperature plants the direction of change must be downward. As it is with photoperiod, each plant has its own critical temperature. Azalea and chrysanthemum are examples of plants requiring specific high temperatures for flower initiation. Chrysanthemum temperature requirements are strongly interrelated with photoperiod and it is photoperiod which exerts the more dramatic and precise influence. This interaction phenomenon is not uncommon in other groups of plants. More details concerning temperature as it affects flower initiation and development will be given as the culture of individual species is discussed.

Most of the common bulb crops require rather complex temperature programs for optimum development. Fortunately for the smaller grower, many of the requirements have been met before receipt of the bulbs. Response to temperature exposure is often quantitative in nature; Easter lily bulbs stored for 6 weeks at 40^0 F force in approximately 110 days. Bulbs stored at higher temperatures require a longer forcing schedule. It is quite important that the final grower know what temperature regimes bulbs have been exposed to before shipment.

Temperature affects several developmental processes in plants other than flower initiation. Many growers are under the assumption that the cold treatment given to spring bulb crops prior to forcing is necessary for flower development. In reality, this storage period controls the degree of stem elongation and flower size. These attributes may of course be affected by forcing procedures but they are to a large degree, already determined by the pre-forcing storage period. Flower shape in several chrysanthemum varieties varies depending upon greenhouse temperatures. At low temperatures some varieties exhibit a trait known as "quilling," which gives the flower a ragged, uneven appearance. Flowers may also be flattened in relation to depth. Flower color is usually improved by lowering temperatures shortly before harvest. The intensity and vibrancy of colors is enhanced by this treatment. In a few cases low temperatures may cause flower color to become less desirable. White chrysanthemums often develop a pinkish or purplish tinge under cool conditions. Many florists prefer a pure white flower. Bud abortion is common in certain crops when temperatures reach high levels, especially when light intensity is low. Easter lilies and geraniums are major crops where "bud blasting" or abortion is sometimes a problem due to excessive heat.

The various developmental processes in plants are quite complex. Seldom can it be said that one particular environmental factor or another exerts complete and final control over the expression of a developmental process. Growers must be aware of the numerous factor interactions which may occur to cause deviations from predicted developmental avenues.

Photoperiod and temperature are intimately related in the natural environment and it is only common sense to expect that they will interact in controlled environments.

The temperature requirements for propagation stages of various woody and herbaceous species were covered in Chapter 5.

INFLUENCE OF TEMPERATURE ON DORMANCY

When discussing plants, the term dormancy usually refers to a state of reduced physiological activity which plants enter into in response to the approach of winter conditions. Since low temperatures are the most obvious aspect of winter, it is only logical to assume that they are the chief cause of winter dormancy. But photoperiod, although not so strikingly apparent, performs a strong supporting role in bringing on dormancy. One only need observe tree branches near a streetlight which retain their leaves into early winter to realize that light duration must have some effect upon the leaf drop of trees.

Many of the temperature and photoperiod responses which we observe in plants are likely related in some way to the natural onset of winter dormancy which occurs at least to some degree in most regions of the earth. Under greenhouse culture it is possible to manipulate these environmental conditions to "fool" plants into reacting in different ways. In the outdoor nursery growers may lack the ability to alter photoperiod or temperature but there are cases where it is advantageous to understand how these factors might affect crop production. The performance of a number of cultural techniques (such as transplanting of trees and shrubs) may be influenced by the state of plant dormancy.

Growers who are attempting to crop unfamiliar woody plants and herbaceous perennials, both outdoors and indoors, will likely find that many of these plant species react to temperature and photoperiod in a similar manner as do some more well documented species for which detailed cultural programs related to these factors have already been worked out.

The enormous influence which temperature has upon the dormancy of nursery stock is quite obvious. Large wholesale growers of trees, roses, shrubs, and perennials spend millions of dollars on cold storage facilities to ensure that proper dormancy stages are maintained prior to shipment.

TEMPERATURE AND PLANT QUALITY

Stem length and strength and the overall lushness of growth are probably the quality related characteristics which greenhouse growers try to manipulate most frequently by temperature control on a day to day basis. In general, warmer temperatures result in weaker stems and lush growth. Plants that are too tall with weak stems and an over abundance of soft growth are probably the number one quality problem of floriculture today. This type of plant is not attractive to consumers and does not hold up well when removed from the greenhouse. Of course all environmental factors can contribute to this condition, but temperature is normally the most important and easily modified greenhouse factor which controls plant quality. Light intensity is surely as important to plant quality but is not easily controlled in critical winter months.

A great deal of emphasis has been placed recently upon producing plants faster so that additional crops may be harvested during the year. This is certainly a commendable objective but it must be accomplished without serious deterioration of quality. The high temperature, fertilizer, and moisture levels called for in these fast crop methods often result in overly lush plants, especially for garden use. Some experts contend these plants are healthier because they receive optimum growing conditions but only a single experience with transplanting an extremely lush plant into the full garden sun will convince even skeptics that garden plants, especially, must be "hardened off" to provide acceptable performance on the practical level.

A compromise approach is to start plants out quickly with elevated temperatures and then condition them gradually with reduced temperatures before marketing. Considerable fuel can be saved if young plants are started in warm greenhouses and then moved to cooler houses for finishing.

Heating fuel is now a major greenhouse expense, even when oil prices are in a lower stage. At the time most older greenhouse owners received their training, fuel was relatively inexpensive and, more importantly, stable in price. As a consequence, many cropping programs and cultural recommendations probably do no reflect the most profitable growing procedures. Much research is already being carried out in this area but it will take several years before the information finds its way into books and trade publications. Investigations should determine how far temperatures can be lowered at particular times without unacceptable reductions in crop quality and what new crops can be grown which satisfy the market while using less energy. It may be that certain crops are more profitable even though quality has been reduced slightly by energy saving measures.

Improved greenhouse technology is perhaps one of the easiest and most reliable means of producing quality crops through temperature control. Several different means of ventilating greenhouses with great amounts of outside air (retractable roof greenhouses and removable curtain walls — mechanical of course) offer not only better temperature control, but usually allow the grower to provide more suitable light, humidity, and atmospheric conditions for quality growth.

These types of installations are also advantageous to the woody plant propagator/grower, allowing a gradual hardening off of young plants before they are transplanted outdoors.

Everyone who has resided in temperate climates is familiar with the concept of winter hardiness for outdoor landscape plants. Temperature is of extreme importance (often primary) in determining the survival of these outdoor plants during winter. Even if trees and shrubs do not die, their quality as garden products can be severely impaired by improper temperature regimens. In Chapter 18, some of the important temperature related problems associated with container production of woody plants will be covered.

TEMPERATURE AND CROP TIMING

The adjustment of temperatures in greenhouses or movement of plants to warmer or cooler locations is the most important tool a grower has for timing crops as the marketing date approaches. A good grower is always evaluating crop progress so that adjustments in timing may be made before a crisis has arrived. If possible, temperature changes should be made gradually. When plants are exposed to especially high temperatures to hasten flowering, bud abortion is a common occurrence. Botrytis (a mold organism) frequently appears when flowering plants are cooled to slow development. Cool air holds less water than does warm air and, as a result, high relative humidity is more of a problem in cool greenhouses.

Botrytis is more prevalent with high humidity and open flowers are especially susceptible. Any temperature adjustments made to influence flowering dates or save fuel must be made with a full knowledge of the potential damages to crop quality which might occur. Gloxinias and African violets simply will not tolerate temperatures below 62^0 F for any length of time; at lower temperatures plants become hardened, brittle, and yellowish. Impatiens and tuberous begonias are only slightly more tolerant of cold temperatures. On the other hand, many cool loving perennials will become lush and unsalable if grown at over 50^0 F.

It is often advantageous for a greenhouse operation to have several houses operating at different temperatures. Plants may be moved from one temperature to another to correct crop timing. This method of adjusting timing is not often possible with larger ranges where a crop may number in the millions of plants. But in these situations it is usually possible to adjust temperature at will since an entire house is normally filled with only one variety.

SOIL TEMPERATURE

The temperature surrounding roots is perhaps one of the least monitored factors in the greenhouse or in outdoor growing areas. It may generally be assumed that, root zone temperatures are somewhat different but at least closely related to air temperatures. However, there are conditions under which root zone temperatures differ markedly from air temperatures. This situation arises from a number of factors but is most often due to moisture content in the soil and to the incidence of light energy upon different colors and types of containers. In addition, root zone temperatures may be considerably different because containers have been insulated in some way from the effects of air temperature and from the incidence of light energy (containerized trees outdoors are often covered with a layer of sawdust or bark chips).

Outdoor container crops are sometimes significantly altered in development and survivability by the root zone temperatures which prevail. It has been found that the winter hardiness of many varieties left outdoors in containers is more closely related to root zone temperature than to air temperature. In addition, the fluctuation of root zone temperatures affects plant survival. Growers who leave container crops outdoors should make every practical attempt to protect containers from both upper and lower extremes of temperature; particularly in the winter months. Temperatures in containers are important during the growing season but unless they are especially extreme at that time, they do not exert the same crucial influence as they do in winter.

It is not likely that the average greenhouse grower will be able to alter substrate temperatures appreciably unless root zone heating is installed or heated water is used for irrigation. The effect of soil temperature on plant growth and development has not been as thoroughly researched as has the effect of air temperature. Unless definite data exists to indicate what effect lowering or increasing soil temperature will have, no general conclusion should be made. Treatments should not be begun without adequate knowledge. If a generalization must be made, it would be most appropriate to say that, within certain ranges, warmer root zone temperatures will speed up growth and development.

Bulb crops are frequently watered with warm water or placed on heated surfaces to speed development. Research has been inconclusive as to whether or not warm irrigation water has any dramatic or long lasting effects on soil temperatures. It is certain, though, that there are no advantages to irrigation with icy water from the tap or well.

Soil temperature also affects various processes such as mineral uptake, water uptake, and microorganism activity. All of these activities are very likely to be interrelated and somewhat dependent upon one another. While the solubility of chemical compounds in soil solution will likely increase at temperature levels even higher than that which plant roots can survive, microorganism activity is mostly limited to the normal growing range for plants ($32°$ to $100°F$).

Chapter 10

WATER

Plants require water in large quantities. An average plant may require approximately 1,000 ounces of water for every ounce of dry weight added. The importance of water to plants is emphasized by the fact that young, growing tissue may be composed of 95% water. Most of the water entering a plant is lost through transpiration, in which water vapor passes out openings in the leaves called stomates. Portions of water molecules become a physical part of plant molecules, but water also serves as the background reagent in which many chemical reactions take place. The turgidity of plant cells (and thus the structural integrity of plants) is maintained by water, and without it they become flaccid and the plant wilts. If plant cells are not full of water (turgid), expansion of cells by stretching of the cell wall does not take place, and cell size can become permanently smaller than normal. This is the principle behind the common practice of withholding water to produce shorter, more compact plants. Not only must great quantities of water be supplied to plants, it must be of adequate quality.

WATER QUALITY

The factors which determine water quality vary tremendously, however, the soluble salt content is usually the principal factor. A classification by soluble salt content of the usefulness of water was presented in the discussion of fertilizer materials. The meaning of soluble salts, methods of measurement, and symptoms of plant damage were also presented at that time. If water is obtained from private wells or reservoirs it should be checked carefully for soluble salt levels to determine its suitability. Water from approved domestic sources is suitable for plants because governmental regulations specify that water with a soluble salt content of

500 ppm or higher is not acceptable for domestic purposes. Irrigation water from any source should be chemically analyzed to determine the types and amounts of mineral compounds present. Mineral content may possibly affect the types and quantities of fertilizers growers will utilize.

Water quality is often difficult to change, therefore, every effort should be made to locate an alternative supply before one attempts to modify an unacceptable source. The soluble salt content of water may be lowered to almost zero by employing a process known as reverse osmosis. In practical usage, soluble salts need only be reduced to acceptable levels so that water derived from a reverse osmosis apparatus may be mixed with appropriate quantities of untreated water. Reverse osmosis machines are very expensive to purchase and maintain, but some greenhouses and nurseries have installed them after exhausting all other possibilities. Water obtained from reverse osmosis is generally used only for special purposes such as propagation, mixing insecticides, cutflower storage, or as a plant rinse after overhead irrigation with regular water. Because of the expense involved, only a few container growing operations use reverse osmosis water for general irrigation. Outdoor nurseries, especially, would find that the large quantities of water needed are prohibitive in cost.

When soluble salts are in excess of 750 ppm in unfertilized irrigation water, precautions must be highly emphasized to prevent soluble salt buildup in containers. Water having over 1000 ppm soluble salt content is seldom suitable for long term use on container crops unless the plant species grown are salt tolerant and special care is taken to irrigate in a manner which minimizes salt buildup in the soil. Water with a soluble salt reading of 1500-2000 ppm dissolved solids could possibly be used on tolerant crops if extreme precautions were taken.

Growing in a porous medium, leaching, adding only the minimum required fertilizers, and maintaining soil moisture at high levels are precautions one can take to compensate for high soluble salt levels in the irrigation water. Soluble salts may vary in water sources, especially shallow wells, from season to season. Readings should be taken at several times during the year if there is reason to suspect any wide variations. When interpreting soluble salt information, one should be careful to note the exact unit of expression being used. Remember, soluble salt concentrations are not directly equal to electrical conductivity readings. The most common units used are parts per million and micromhos.

Milliequivalents per liter (meq/l) and multiples of micromhos are less commonly employed. Micromhos times 0.666 yields ppm (refer to Chapter 5). Milliequivalents per liter equals ppm divided by 50. Crops may vary widely in their tolerance to soluble salts. Impatiens do poorly at soluble salt levels which carnation plants tolerate easily. Salt sensitive plants, such as impatiens, may serve as biological indicators of poor water quality to the grower. Plants most often show high soluble salt damage by a general dwarfish appearance, the leaves may look as if scorched by hot wind, and root tips are often dead. In general, the plants are suffering a shortage of water because there is a high salt gradient in the soil solution and because the roots have been damaged.

Water is frequently described as being "hard" or "soft". Hard water is caused by the presence of large quantities of dissolved calcium and/or magnesium carbonate but it may also have a high salt level in the absence of these carbonates. The process of removing these carbonates from water is known as softening and is accomplished by the chemical exchange of sodium for magnesium and calcium. It can be seen that softening does not reduce soluble salts since it replaces one element with another. Hard water is not deleterious to plant growth unless calcium and magnesium carbonate are present in such large amounts as to render the water high in soluble salts. The residue left on leaves by these minerals can, however, cause an objectionable film or spottiness. This residue may be reduced considerably by the addition of sodium hexametaphosphate (calgon) to the water supply. When soluble salts are high, the addition of this compound will only magnify the problem. The carbonate residue may also be removed from leaves at market time by spraying with one of the numerous leaf-shine products available. Hard water is slightly alkaline and may sometimes cause a gradual rise in the soil pH. This is normally not a problem if soil pH is low to begin with, as it would be in high peat mixes. Alkaline water can be neutralized by utilizing a fertilizer program which acidifies the soil, or by injecting small quantities of acid (sulfuric, nitric, citric, and phosphoric are the most commonly used acids) into the water supply on a continuous basis.

Chlorine and fluorine added to municipal water supplies normally cause no harmful effects to plants. In certain situations these elements may cause a slight tip burn on sensitive plants such as dracenas or chlorophytum. If the water supply comes from an open reservoir or stream, one may find that diseases such as root and stem rot (caused by fungi present in the water) will increase. Algae growth in tanks and soil surfaces may become a significant problem in these cases also. Water may be treated with ultraviolet rays and through ozonization to eliminate disease organisms; several commercial apparatus are available to treat large volumes. Chemical agents are also available which claim to sterilize recycled water, especially being effective against algae buildup. Pollution of water supplies by various industrial, domestic, and agricultural wastes is always a possibility if the water supply is from shallow wells or surface runoff. Damage due to water pollution is often very difficult to diagnose and may take some time to correctly identify. The most common cause of problems is weed killer residues on adjacent properties which either percolate down to the water table or are carried by surface runoff to streams or reservoirs.

An adequate supply of acceptable quality water is absolutely essential for any container growing operation. Too many growers compromise in this important area and commit themselves to a continuing battle of attempting to grow good quality plants without good quality water. The finished product can be no better than the ingredients which go to make it up. The economic losses which accumulate by growing plants with poor water are simply too great to ignore. If a grower is lucky enough to avoid outright crop losses, there may still be cumulative losses in production of 50% or more.

The difference in quality and quantity of crop production when growing with good water rather than poor water is astounding. A firsthand view of the differences will convince even the most skeptical grower that obtaining a source of high quality water should be a prime management objective.

WATER APPLICATION

No responsibility will concern the container grower on a day today basis more than the irrigation of crops. If irrigation is performed manually, it will comprise one of the largest labor outlays made by management. As a consequence, improving the way water is delivered to crops represents one of the most fertile areas for production cost savings. Watering is no more or less important than the regulation of other environmental factors. It is, however, less subject to a precise delineation of methods and measurements. As an example, both temperature (in the greenhouse) and fertilizer elements may be measured and controlled rather easily, but there is no reasonably accurate means of quickly measuring available soil moisture. Present methods of determining the water needs of plants through the use of instruments are still not far enough advanced as to be counted on for consistent, economical, and accurate analysis. Proper water application depends mostly upon the grower exercising careful judgment accumulated through experience. Measurement of nutrient status may sometimes be as difficult as determining available soil moisture, but nutrients are not usually monitored on a daily or even twice daily schedule as is water.

Another difficulty with irrigation is in communicating the grower's intentions to personnel actually performing the task. A grower may be an expert at watering but this means nothing if personnel are not thoroughly trained and motivated to carry out instructions. Only the best and most dependable workers should be allowed to water. Watering is, at present, more of an art than a science. If possible, a person should water the same crops regularly to acquire a "feel" for the crop's water needs.

The frequency and volume of water applied will depend on the following factors: light duration and intensity, temperature, air movement, relative humidity, soil type, pot types, plant size and stage of growth, and variety of plant. These factors will interrelate with one another to determine how much water will be used by a plant. Not only must personnel be trained to determine when and how much water is needed at a particular time, but they must also be able to project water needs into the short-term future. Inexperienced irrigators often encounter an early morning fog and decide slightly moist crops should not be watered that day; at mid-morning the fog burns off and plants begin to wilt shortly thereafter. Employees must then interrupt the work day to water a second time. Experienced personnel would be familiar with this foggy morning pattern and water plants more heavily so the work day need not be interrupted.

No hard and fast rules can be made about when plants should be watered because there are so many factors to consider. Retail customers always ask, "How often should I water this plant?" There is no easy answer. The best gauge of whether or not water is needed is to feel the soil. A caution should be emphasized here: Various insecticides and fungicides are often applied to container soil; any training given to employees about comparisons between the "feel" and "look" of soils should be conducted with soils which are known to be free of these poisons. If it is reasonably moist and one judges the moisture will last through the day, no water should be applied. After a short time a person will be able to anticipate how moist a soil will feel simply by looking at it. Surface appearance of soils is sometimes misleading. In early morning, soils are often covered with a thin dew which dries up quickly with air movement and sunlight. Plants should be watered early enough in the day to allow growing areas to dry out before nightfall but a more accurate job can be done if one waits until the early morning dew has burned off. Soil normally dries in containers from the top downward so it may be assumed that the soil at the bottom of pots will be more moist than that at the top unless frequent light irrigations have wet only the top. However, there are cases where frequent light irrigation for an extended period will cause pots to dry out from the bottom up.

Plants may be able to go for a week or more between watering during dark winter weather although everyday or even twice a day watering is often needed in summer. Plants in clay and fiber pots will dry out more quickly than those in plastic pots. Certain varieties of plants are conspicuous water users while others consume very little. There is a world of difference between the water needs of hydrangeas and those of cacti but most varieties occupy a middle ground where water use is average.

Newly transplanted plants should be watered well at the start, and then allowed to dry out somewhat. After this period they are usually established enough to begin a normal watering program. Soil types will greatly influence watering frequency. Porous soils with a large particle size require watering more often than those with a smaller particle size.

The most definite indication that a plant needs water is when it wilts (except in those cases where the roots have been damaged in some manner, such as high soluble salts or root rot disease). This stage should seldom be allowed to occur since quality and production will be severely lowered if wilting is common. Some growers wait until a few plants in a crop wilt before watering. This is not a good practice since the crop would suffer reduced quality if all plants were near the wilting stage. Another reason for not using this method is that plants on the outside edges of a growing area may be very dry while those in the center are still wet.

The quantity of water one should apply is not nearly so difficult to decide as is the timing of water application. Except when plants are very small and not yet established, they should be watered heavily each time they become dried out. It may be necessary to water some plants of a crop lightly for a few days until the entire crop is ready for a thorough irrigation, but, usually, light sprinklings are a waste of time and do not promote good growth.

New environmental regulations concerning the runoff of irrigation water onto adjacent lands, or into waterways, or into soil beneath growing areas is causing a serious rethinking of how greenhouse and nursery crops should be watered and fertilized. Traditional wisdom formerly dictated that about 10% of irrigation water at each application should be allowed to drain out the bottoms of containers as leachate. This practice prevented the buildup of fertilizer salts in the container but allowed excessive amounts of fertilized water to enter the environment.

Today, almost everyone is aware of the need to control excess leaching but some means must still be employed to insure that fertilizer salts do not build up in the container. There are alternate strategies to accomplish this objective. The most simple means is to limit fertilizer concentrations to amounts which are actually needed by plants. The fertilizer regimes mentioned earlier in this book generally fulfill this objective well since the concentrations are on the low side and because the entire fertilizer molecules are usable by plants. Many growers still fertilize much more heavily than necessary, thereby increasing the need to frequently leach containers. Some information references, even today, recommend leaching, soil composition, and fertilizing practices which are inconsistent with minimizing environmental pollution.

Another method of controlling leachate runoff is to collect and recycle all excess irrigation water. A number of growers, both in greenhouses and outdoor nurseries are already engaged in this practice. The initial investment in recycling irrigation water can be high but at least part of the cost can be recovered later by reduced usage of water and fertilizer. Water to be recycled must generally be conditioned and treated to make it suitable for future use. The amount and kind of fertilizer salts in recycled water must be determined on a regular basis so that only the type of fertilizer actually needed is added before reuse of the water. Growers should check the environmental laws existing in their state to make sure irrigation and fertilizing methods to be used will comply with the regulations.

All other means of limiting runoff to the environment basically relate to either minimizing fertilizer input or increasing the recycling capacity. The type of irrigation system which is employed can have an important impact upon how easily and effectively runoff can be managed, and some consideration should be given to this point when watering systems are designed or chosen.

People who are chosen to irrigate must be conscientious, thorough, and mentally capable of either following directions precisely or determining themselves how crops should be watered. Serious losses in crop quality and number can result from allowing poorly qualified people to irrigate.

Workers must be impressed not only with the immediate consequences which result from improper watering but also with the long term effects on operational revenues. If a crop of 100 plants will mature in 12 weeks, it takes the death of only 1 plant every week through careless watering to equal a 12% loss of gross revenue. This is a serious decline which could make the difference between a mediocre business and a highly successful business.

A greenhouse or nursery selling $100,000 of plants a year would lose $12,000. That amount would make the payments on a nice home for the owner. This example of continuous "low level" loss is less obvious than the catastrophic plant losses which can and do occur in only a few hours of hot summer weather. Even after employees have been watering for some time, the grower should make periodic inspections and suggest methods of improvement. Meticulous attention to watering is essential for good crops and it is the grower's responsibility to communicate, educate, and motivate employees to perform their very best.

WATER AND PLANT QUALITY

Watering practices greatly affect plant appearance and quality. Judicious regulation of water applications can be a valuable tool in directing plant growth to a desirable conclusion. Reductions in quality due to overwatering are usually a result of various root and stem rots (which thrive in a wet medium) and the low oxygen supply to roots caused by water occupying the majority of soil pore spaces. Underwatering subjects plants to stress which results in smaller stature and fewer flowers. Severe water stress will cause tissue to dry up in the more succulent portions and can eventually lead to death. Generally, plants should be grown at a happy medium where root aeration is adequate but moisture stress is avoided. In the practical sense, growers usually sacrifice a small amount of plant size while subjecting plants to a slight periodic water stress. This approach lessens the chance of severe losses due to root diseases and dysfunctions.

With certain crops and under some conditions growers may deem it necessary to keep plants under a moderate water stress. Petunias are one crop which, if given plenty of water in the late season, will become too tall and spindly (especially if suitable temperatures utilizing DIF techniques cannot be maintained). Shorter, tougher plants can be produced by letting the crop dry out almost to the wilting point before irrigation. Most bedding plants transplant better into the garden if they have been subjected to periodic water stress in the greenhouse; tissue is not so succulent under these conditions and will not dehydrate in the hot sun outdoors. Some growers prefer to produce the more succulent plants which have been under very little water stress because crops become saleable more quickly.

Plants which become severely water stressed because the soil in containers is allowed to dry out may suffer permanent above ground tissue damage which detracts from plant appearance. The obvious visual symptoms of injury are likely to represent only a fraction of the total harm done. The entire internal physiological system can become upset, thereby making the plant more susceptible to predation by insects and diseases or more liable to damage from unfavorable environmental factors.

When soil dries out, the soil water solution becomes more concentrated with dissolved solid; this is in direct response to a reduced volume of water available to dilute the chemical salts present. Previous discussions in the present chapter and in the chapter dealing with fertilizers have pointed out the ill effects of too high soluble salt concentration in the soil solution.

In the greenhouse there is seldom any need to allow significant plant water stress to occur during winter. At this time plants and flowers are utilized by consumers for indoor use and have no need to become toughened up for the rough conditions which garden plants face. The most severe test winter greenhouse plants undergo is the shipping and merchandising process.

Woody plants and herbaceous perennials left outdoors in containers during winter face exceptionally trying conditions, especially when the root zone is not protected from extreme variations of temperature. Roots freeze and thaw continually while the tops of plants are subjected to drying winds. Evergreen plants are particularly susceptible to damage under these conditions since the leaves continue to transpire water during winter.

Many inexperienced growers assume that container plants left outdoors in winter are dormant and need no water. The truth is that the plants require just as careful attention to water needs at this time as they do in summer. Evergreens especially will benefit from a thorough watering each time the weather thaws for a considerable period.

The best way to minimize winter damage to container plants outdoors is to provide as much protection as possible, especially to the root zone. Not only does this moderate the temperature extremes plants are subject to but it also reduces the moisture stress placed upon them. Plants should be readied for winter storage by watering them adequately. Periodic inspections must then be made throughout the winter months to insure that the soil is moist enough to prevent damage but not so moist as to encourage rotting of tissue and low soil oxygen. Improper storage procedures which allow no air exchange to plants can result in severe losses caused by diseases which flourish under high moisture and low temperature conditions. Plant tissue surfaces must be allowed to dry thoroughly before containers are placed in storage.

WATERING SYSTEMS

Before proceeding to the different methods used to apply water, it will be useful to discuss the basic delivery system. A container growing operation cannot function without a dependable and adequate supply of water. One day without water in midsummer can cause catastrophic damage in the greenhouse or nursery. Some form of alternative water supply should be planned so that at least critical operations can be performed, even if the main water source is not functional for few days.

The delivery system which brings water to plants requires just as much consideration as the actual source. If water cannot be applied in a timely manner, it might just as well be unavailable. Water delivery systems must be sized to transport the largest amount of water which may be needed at a particular time during the year. Obviously, this volume must be deliverable within an approximately six hour period which would constitute the normal watering timespan during the day.

Allowances in volume must also be made for other necessary operational functions such as cooling, cleaning, and waste disposal. It is best to make an error on the safe side when installing a delivery system and, in addition, some thought should be given to future expansion of the growing facility. Future changes of the basic delivery pipes, valves, and pumps can be very expensive since a modification in one aspect frequently requires a corresponding change in other components.

Some basic provisions for repair and service of the water delivery system should be part of the design. An adequate number of shut off valves and union joints are essential for easy repair. And the system should be as accessible as possible commensurate with protection from freezing and mechanical damage. Strainers and clean out points in the delivery lines are essential for efficient operation of water systems in the greenhouse or nursery.

Essential spare parts for the water system are usually fairly inexpensive to keep on hand and can save much anxiety when repairs are necessary in a hurry. Nothing is more aggravating than spending a busy spring day trying to locate a $1.00 pump gasket which could easily have been ordered in the dead of winter.

Some growers may wish to add modifications to the basic water delivery systems. Separate pipes are often installed for movement of water and for water which has been altered by the addition of various fertilizers and chemicals. Provisions for warming water before it is applied to plants are sometimes included in greenhouse delivery systems. Other specialized components such as disinfectant or acidifying injectors may be made a part of the water delivery design.

There are several general methods by which water may be applied to crops. Manual irrigation is still the most commonly employed method in smaller operations. In container growing operations of this size many different crops are usually raised, each often requiring a different irrigation regime. Watering by hand can be closely regulated, especially if the grower has time to perform the task personally. With this method, workers are always in close contact with the crop and should notice many cultural problems quickly. Equipment needed is minimal but labor costs are high for manual irrigation and they can double or triple if a sufficient water volume is not available for personnel to move quickly. The degree of reliance a grower must place on other people to perform a critical task is the greatest disadvantage of manual irrigation. Frequent leaching is not always possible with manual irrigation; plants must often be gone over several times before leaching occurs.

When crop conditions allow, automatic or mechanized watering systems should be installed. Machines may be irritating at times but they are more dependable than people and they perform exactly as the grower instructs if they have been installed properly. A fully mechanized watering system can save a great deal in labor costs and will lower a grower's anxiety level. When crops are in full growth on a hot day and key watering personnel do not show up for work, the grower irrigating manually is under great stress. With automated systems, the grower can easily take care of such situations. The problem of weekend watering is also lessened. Many people contend that watering by hand is superior because individual plants can be watered or not depending on the need; but, if the system is designed carefully and only suitable crops are chosen, better results are obtained with mechanized watering. Under the proper circumstances, automatic systems do a better job because the tedium and human error associated with repetitive tasks are avoided for the most part. The key advantage of mechanized watering is that either the grower or the more experienced employees can handle all irrigation. This substantially increases the level of competence associated with the irrigation program. Leaching is also easily accomplished, if necessary, with most mechanical watering systems.

Larger potted plants, both indoors and out, are often irrigated mechanically with individual tubes leading to each pot. Water is supplied to sections of the greenhouse or nursery by pipeline; at each individual growing plot a branch line is installed which runs near the plants to be watered. Small diameter plastic tubes are then inserted into the branch line after the appropriate holes have been punched. Different lengths of tube are installed to accommodate the varying distances of plants relative to the branch line. A combination weight and water breaker is attached to the free end of the tube. When this weight is placed in the pot, it diffuses the water stream and keeps the tube in position.

This system is very effective for pots of approximately 6 inch size and larger but becomes cumbersome (due to the large number of tubes needed) for smaller containers. Large pots may be served by larger diameter supply tubes or more than one can be inserted in each pot.

The weighted water breakers are often equipped with simple push-pull shut off valves. This is especially handy when hanging baskets are harvested. With newer environmental regulations concerning fertilizer runoff, the on-off valves on each tube will reduce the amount of irrigation water reaching the ground as individual plants within a section are removed.

It is obvious that the tube system is most effective when every pot in a particular watering block is the same size and when plants are uniform in growth habit. Solenoid water valves coupled to a timing device can make any mechanized irrigation system completely automatic if situations arise where the grower or other designated personnel are not available to start the water flow. Other means of starting and stopping water flow on cue are available.

Soils which drain quite easily may allow water to flow primarily straight down through the soil after leaving the end of the watering tube. Growers not familiar with this phenomenon may have a crop severely damaged from water stress before they figure out what is taking place, especially with hanging baskets where the soil surface cannot be observed. The problem may be lessened in several ways: use larger tubes to apply water faster, decrease the number of large pores in soil, never allow soil to dry out, and do not begin tube irrigation until plant roots are established and impede the flow of water downward. Various configurations of water emitters are available to help solve this problem, and they are especially useful with large tree and shrub pots. Details on installation of tube irrigation systems are available from all major horticultural supply houses.

There are several methods of sub-irrigating plants automatically. These methods were formerly used mostly on 4 inch or smaller pots which are difficult to handle with the polyethylene tube system. Recently, sub-irrigating has become popular even with larger containers. The simplest set up is to place pots on a watertight, level growing area with a short vertical lip around the edge. The area is filled with water and then allowed to drain after pots soak up sufficient moisture. Devices which look similar to inverted plastic hats are also available for sub-irrigating larger individual pots placed into them. These "hats" perform the same function as a watertight bench, the only difference being that an individual water supply is needed for each "hat," or they may be placed close together while the entire area is sprinkled.

Another means of flood irrigating plants is to place pots into elongated troughs. This method, other than the shape and size, works like the ones described just above.

One advantage of the flood irrigation methods (other than the inverted "hats") is that excess irrigation water can easily be collected to a main settling and conditioning tank or pond and then be recycled. This is an important consideration in areas which have strict environmental laws. It is no doubt a major reason why flood irrigation is gaining in popularity. Even some large outdoor trees are now watered by flood irrigation methods so that water may be recycled. Needless to say, this requires a good deal of land preparation to accomplish properly. Numerous new greenhouse installations are now provided with a precisely leveled floor and impermeable surface so that flood irrigation of the entire greenhouse can be carried out with a minimum amount of labor.

A variation on the flood irrigation methods is accomplished by setting pots on a bed of moist sand which has a polyethylene film under it. Benches in this case need not have a lip or be exactly level. The sand is kept constantly saturated with an ooze hose and the excess water flows off the side of the bench. Capillary mats composed of fibers are available to take the place of sand layers. Moisture is absorbed by soil in pots from both the sand beds and fiber mats by capillarity and drying out of either the bed or pots can break the continuity of the water transfer. Bottoms of pots must be placed in firm contact with the sand or fiber mats. Pots manufactured with small feet on the bottom may be unsuitable if good contact with the bed surface cannot be made. Clay pots cannot be used because water loss from them is greater than can be replaced through capillary pull. Pots over six inches deep do not water properly with capillary mats. The application of water to mats can be controlled by solenoid valves and timers to maintain constant wetness.

At first glance, sub-irrigation by flooding or capillarity would seem to be ideal; but there are several serious disadvantages to these methods. Leaching action is difficult with flood irrigation and impossible when capillary action is the sole means of irrigation employed. Short term crops where soluble salt buildup in the soil is negligible present no problem but some means of dissolved solids control through fertilizer management or periodic overhead watering must be used with longer term crops.

Flood irrigation facilities are generally more expensive to construct initially than are alternative overhead systems. Installation of capillary systems is perhaps a middle ground cost-wise but does not offer all the advantages of full flood irrigation. Capillary beds can become overgrown with algae and roots growing into the mats or sand; this is a decided nuisance. Plants grown on capillary mats or sand beds may exhibit poor quality because they are exposed to constantly moist root conditions and high atmospheric humidity at pot level. These circumstances often lead to overly succulent plants which may or may not be a significant problem, depending upon the species and marketing requirements.

Both flood and capillary irrigation expose entire sections of crops to any disease which is present in an individual plant of that section. This is one of the major drawbacks of these watering methods. Extreme caution must be employed to assure that all plants and materials introduced into the system are as "clean" as possible.

Various types of sprinkler systems are the most practical way of watering bedding plants, small potted shrubs, propagation beds, and large crops of newly potted plants. Sprinklers are seldom used on potted flowers when they are spaced because of the large free area between pots and the susceptibility of flowers to rot and water spotting if watered from above. The design of sprinkler systems is limited only by a grower's imagination. The critical test of effectiveness is whether complete coverage is achieved. Overlap areas of the sprinkler patterns will receive more moisture than other sections and the area directly under sprinkler heads often receives less. Irrigations should be quite heavy so that the soil of an entire crop is brought to uniform wetness. Light sprinklings will emphasize the uneven spray patterns. Sprinkler patterns should be tested under the conditions which will exist at the time of use. Greenhouse growers frequently install sprinklers and test them in winter time; when they later use the sprinklers in the spring, they find the water patterns are changed. This phenomenon is usually traced to exhaust fans that are operating in the spring causing distortions in the sprinkler patterns. In addition, spring water use in the greenhouse is much heavier than in winter causing reduction in the volume and pressure at sprinkler heads. The result is incomplete coverage.

Modified type sprinkler systems called "traveling booms" have become quite popular in recent years. These machines consist of a water pipe which delivers a coarse spray or heavy mist downward across its length as it is moved over a crop section. The boom is propelled at right angles to the water delivery pipe by a motorized apparatus. Some newer traveling booms are self contained except for a water source and are mounted on a small motorized vehicle which travels through the crop area.

"Traveling booms" can be computerized to do almost anything the grower wishes; skip portions of a crop, repeat other sections, turn themselves off, and other useful functions. The self contained vehicles are more costly per unit but can obviously be moved at will to different sections of the greenhouse or nursery and thus may actually be considerably less expensive on the basis of how many square feet a single machine can irrigate in a 6 or 8 hour day.

No attempt has been made to present an exhaustive discussion of water systems. There are simply too many possibilities available. In addition to the extensive number of commercial irrigation components and complete systems offered for sale, there are an endless array of "homemade" systems which fulfill specific needs in special circumstances. Before an irrigation method and accompanying system are settled upon, the entire production process should be carefully evaluated. Then an extensive review of possible alternatives should be conducted, with special emphasis being placed upon first hand observation of actual working installations.

The irrigation system of nurseries and greenhouses is simply too important to be left to haphazard "trial and error" development. After all, it is expected to complete the largest job in the production process without fail every single day.

PITFALLS OF AUTOMATED WATERING

Growers often become over enthusiastic about the labor savings of automated water systems and install them without adequate forethought. Every crop and every situation is not amenable to automation. Even when such systems are justified, they should be analyzed carefully to provide maximum benefit per dollar invested. Changing the method of water application affects many other cultural operations and the interrelationships should be well understood. Soil mixtures and fertilizer applications need to be adapted to the type of watering systems installed.

The ease of irrigating with mechanical systems sometimes leads one to apply too much water. Decisions about when to water must be made more carefully with automated systems than when the task is done manually because a heavier and more general irrigation is usually given. Growers must discipline themselves to think carefully before throwing the irrigation switch. Each irrigation must be carefully monitored to make sure all elements of the system are working properly. It is not uncommon to find sprinklers which have been plugged with debris. Large plant losses can be encountered if mechanical failures are not detected quickly. The best way to spot trouble before it assumes critical proportions is to have an irrigation check and evaluation process which workers are required to complete each time they finish tending a specific crop or area.

When plants are watered mechanically, the grower must institute regular inspections of crops to check on plant development, insect populations, crop timing, and other aspects of production. If the grower was previously watering by hand, these factors were usually taken care of at the same time. The essential point to remember about automatic watering systems is that they make life a little easier physically but do not lessen the need for careful observation and analysis of crop needs and progress. One cannot simply hook up a crop to automatic watering and come back two months later for harvest (at least not with the present level of commercial technology).

Chapter 11

CARBON DIOXIDE
AND OXYGEN

The importance of carbon dioxide (CO_2) and oxygen (O_2) to plant growth through the photosynthetic and respiratory processes was pointed out earlier in this book. The only viable means of manipulating oxygen supply to plants is through selecting suitable soil components and by watering properly. Growers should realize that a sufficient oxygen supply for vital plant processes is necessary to produce a healthy root system and that, without oxygen, roots cannot carry on the energy process which is necessary for the uptake of mineral nutrients and water. Most people know that too much water is bad for plant growth but fail to realize that the real problem is a lack of oxygen caused by too much water in the soil pores. A clear understanding of the problem will likely lead to better growing practices. An adequate oxygen supply is required for good seed germination and root production on cuttings because these processes also rely on energy released in respiration.

The need for adequate oxygen to support combustion in greenhouse furnaces was pointed out when greenhouse construction was discussed. Plastic covered houses should be evaluated more carefully in this respect because they have very few air leaks in the skin. Lack of sufficient oxygen eventually causes a furnace flameout, but before this point is reached, damaging carbon monoxide and ethylene gases may be produced through incomplete combustion. Recommendations have been made that 2 square inches of air intake area be supplied for every 5,000 BTU's of furnace capacity located in the greenhouse. An estimation of the intake area provided by door cracks and other leaks should be included in the above figure.

Carbon dioxide is of course a necessary ingredient in the photosynthetic process. Many growers tend to overlook the critical importance of carbon dioxide to plant growth simply because it is normally present in sufficient quantities and because a deficiency is expressed by reductions in growth rather than by easily recognizable symptoms. If a greenhouse is tightly closed on a bright winter day, photosynthesizing plants can deplete the carbon dioxide supply quickly. Normal carbon dioxide concentrations in the atmosphere are about 300 ppm. When levels reach approximately 125 ppm, growth in plants ceases because respiration is occurring as fast as photosynthesis can take place at this carbon dioxide level. Carbon dioxide depletion takes place most quickly when there is little ventilation and light conditions are favorable for photosynthesis. Yield of winter time crops in many locations can be increased dramatically by the introduction of carbon dioxide into the greenhouse atmosphere. Production increases of 50% are common under ideal circumstances.

There is obviously no practical means of increasing the level of atmospheric CO_2 available to plants grown outdoors but the CO_2 content of greenhouse air can be manipulated quite easily at a fairly reasonable cost. CO_2 gas is generated for greenhouse use by burning fossil fuels, by allowing dry ice to sublimate, or by vaporization from the liquid state. Both natural and LP gas are easily oxidized in special burners to produce CO_2 and water. High sulfur fuel must be avoided for CO_2 generation. Sufficient oxygen is necessary to allow complete oxidation of the fuel by the CO_2 generators so as to avoid production of undesirable products (such as ethylene gas) from incomplete combustion. Water vapor released from the combustion process can be a problem for growers unless provision is made to lower atmospheric humidity. Generating CO_2 from dry ice or from the liquid presents no special problems except that of requiring an accurate means to allow release into the atmosphere. Carbon dioxide generators and monitoring devices are available commercially at moderate costs.

Injecting carbon dioxide into the greenhouse atmosphere is one of the easiest, most cost effective means of increasing crop production. There are, however, many circumstances where the anticipated benefits are less than expected or where the increases in production provide little or no practical advantage. Each situation must be evaluated individually to determine if CO_2 injection will prove to be economical.

CO_2 injection generally is most beneficially employed when responsive crops are grown for a market which has fairly constant demand through most of the year. In this situation, the ability to either increase quality or quantity of production (or both) allows growers to produce more revenue on a recurring basis without an increase in facility size.

CO_2 injection is also of major benefit in cases where a crop must be ready for a particular market date which does not allow enough time for the crop to mature without some means of speeding development appreciably. This situation often arises when cutflowers are harvested for Christmas and must be in bloom again for Valentines day.

In a great many greenhouses, especially those which produce potted crops for holidays and spring bedding plants, CO_2 injection is of limited benefit since crops generally have adequate time to become market ready without special cultural practices. Bench space is filled with plants for these major selling periods and generally there is no economic advantage in hurrying the crop along or growing exceptionally large plants. It does not matter if one can grow poinsettias to mature in September because no significant market exists for them then.

Cutting or seedling producers are likely to see immediate benefits from CO_2 injection. Improved growth at the juvenile stage is perhaps the most easily achieved. Young plants seem to be more receptive to the effects of increased CO_2.

Certain species of plants and even varieties within species show remarkably varying response to CO_2 injection. Growers must determine if the crops they wish to treat are responsive before making any major commitment to this cultural program.

Growers must also realize that increased production from CO_2 injection cannot be achieved unless all other cultural factors are provided in sufficient quantity and balance to allow maximum CO_2 uptake by the plant. It makes no sense to attempt production increases by elevating CO_2 levels while allowing fertilizer applications to remain at levels which are only sufficient for lesser degrees of plant growth. If CO_2 levels are increased plants will generally need more of all other factors essential for growth.

Increasing production through CO_2 injection is most easily achieved in the winter months. This is the season when restricted ventilation frequently causes CO_2 deficits. It is also the season when daylight CO_2 levels can be most easily raised artificially since the need to dissipate heat buildup through ventilation is not so necessary as at other seasons. Ventilating to bring greenhouse temperatures down obviously makes it difficult to maintain high levels of CO_2 in the atmosphere.

At first glance it would appear that raising CO_2 levels in the greenhouse atmosphere is an easy means of increasing production and profits. This is certainly the case under proper circumstances but growers must be careful to evaluate both cultural and market conditions adequately to determine if CO_2 injection will help their particular operation.

When the beneficial effects of CO_2 injection were discovered, there was a stampede to install generators in North American cutflower greenhouses because they offered the ideal situation for exploitation of this technique. As the importance of cutflower production decreased relative to potted and bedding plants and as imports of cutflowers increased, the use of CO_2 was discontinued by many operations. In the late 1990's it is again expanding because cutting and seedling production is being concentrated on in large greenhouses capable of economically taking advantage of increased CO_2 levels.

There is no evidence that the maximum levels of carbon dioxide (1,500-2,000 ppm) normally introduced into the greenhouses have any deleterious effects on human beings. It has been reported that 5,000 ppm of carbon dioxide can be tolerated by people for normal work day periods.

Chapter 12

PLANT PESTS, DISEASES, AND POLLUTION DISORDERS

A market for ornamental trees, plants, and flowers exists because people are drawn to the pleasure and aesthetic beauty which is inherent in culturing and viewing these organisms. Any factors which detract from this enjoyment must be brought under control to ensure the continued existence of the market. Pests and diseases have traditionally been one of the major obstacles which growers must overcome to produce plant products which are acceptable to consumers.

Every plant buyer has an immediately and totally adverse reaction when they see an army of creepy bugs crawling through a bunch of flowers. There is no greater discouragement to gardeners than watching all their labors succumb to the ravages of disease. Growers must be certain that adequate steps are taken to deliver appealing and healthy products to the people who use them, any lesser objective surely means the offending grower will suffer reduced sales over the long term. The ornamental plant industry faces a seemingly insurmountable task – on the one hand, consumers will not accept bug infested or diseased stock, while on the other hand, society in general frowns upon the chemical treatments which are sometimes the most efficient and economical means of acceptably controlling pests and diseases.

This paradoxical situation, however, is not so hopeless as it might initially appear because most undesirable effects to plants due to pests, diseases, and pollution disorders can be avoided without extraordinary measures if growers simply learn to reduce problems through anticipatory action or at least to detect them in early stages where remedial action is possible without resorting to extraordinary measures.

Good housekeeping and attention to the details of sanitation around the greenhouse or nursery are the first line of defense (and often the only defense needed) against plant damage from pests and diseases. Of course one must begin with healthy stock if precautionary measures are to be effective.

MODERN PHILOSOPHY OF PEST AND DISEASE CONTROL

The earliest growers of ornamental plants had few effective options to control pests and diseases other than practicing good preventive techniques. There were only a very few natural chemicals and biologically occurring substances (discovered through experience) which possessed curative or preventive properties with regards to pests and diseases. After the grower performed whatever sanitation, housekeeping, and primitive prevention technology which was then known, nature was allowed to simply take its course.

In the 19th century, several new synthetic and natural chemicals were found to be effective in controlling pests and diseases. This process of discovery continued into the early 20th century until a small arsenal of chemical products was available to treat many plant disorders. These chemicals were, in the main, not extremely effective but did offer some relief. In the 1930's much new work was done, especially on synthetically derived pesticides. World War II provided the impetus to utilize these chemicals in a widespread manner and it also encouraged much further activity in the area of disease control.

When the war ended, there was both a deadly array of chemical agents ready for use and a need to employ them as a means of boosting world food production. During the next 30-40 years, the terms "pest and disease control" became more or less synonymous with the use of chemical agents. In the 1980's a large number of people realized that the flagrant use of chemicals was dangerous to the planetary ecosystem while it was simultaneously failing to accomplish the task of satisfactorily controlling pests and diseases.

At the present time most agriculturalists are aware that a new strategy of pest and disease control is necessary, but there is no widespread consensus as to exactly what methods will provide the practical fulfillment of strategy. There seems to be some agreement that it will be necessary to utilize several control techniques together in order to achieve the desired results. The term "integrated pest management (IPM)" has evolved in the industry to describe this new control strategy.

IPM simply gathers all the previously effective means of pest and disease control under one umbrella and focuses upon utilizing them synergistically rather than placing undue emphasis upon any particular method. Certainly this approach is not news to many growers who have instinctively used it throughout their careers but it does help to have suppliers, research institutions, and other growers placing emphasis on IPM. In this way more effective techniques and products become available for use and growers who practiced IPM before it became widely recognized have an easier time accomplishing their goals because the entire industry is making a concerted effort to diminish the causes and sources of infection.

IPM does not mean that chemical control has no important role to contribute. Indeed, chemicals will likely remain an important, if not the most important line of defense against pests and diseases. Chemical control is not inherently unsatisfactory but it must be used with more caution and judgment than before.

Earlier pest and disease control strategies were aimed at complete elimination of the offending organisms. Under IPM philosophy it is often suggested that this objective is unrealistic and results in the use of much larger quantities of chemical control agents than would be necessary under a program of control which prevents severe economic damage but tolerates low level infestations which result in only nuisance damage. It is not clear at this time if this later philosophy is acceptable to the consumers who purchase ornamental plants. The author is in basic agreement that the idea of complete elimination is not possible but feels that periodic "total war" programs where pest detection by normal daily methods yields zero positive observations is more suitable to long term goals of preventing genetic resistance than are programs where a constant mid-level control program consistently leaves a viable breeding population which can moderately re-infect plants within a relatively short period of time (perhaps 6 weeks). The distinction between constant (weekly) and periodic (not more than monthly) control efforts is certainly one of degree, but the author feels it is a critical distinction which prevents overuse of chemical agents and reduces the ability of target organisms to gradually evolve new genetic defense systems.

The following treatment of pests and diseases will concentrate less upon chemical information than has been the habit of the author; and, as a result, it may seem that the discussion is rather generalized instead of recommending specific treatments or specific formulations. This approach is used partly because it is the nature of IPM to shun all or nothing treatment recommendations and partly because new methods, chemical formulations, etc. are being developed so quickly that the detailed information necessary for such presentations is almost certain to be outdated in a short time.

Every reader should immediately realize that the material in this chapter is presented from a limited North American perspective (as are other portions of this book). It is important to keep this in mind as we are dealing with a group of pest organisms (insects, mites, nematodes, fungi, bacteria, and other lesser groups) which, by a large margin, account for the majority of organic species occupying the earth. Each region of the world undoubtedly possesses its own specific pests which are of primary interest. No single book (much less a chapter) could deal adequately with this huge subject matter.

Two considerations must also be kept in mind: 1) different ornamental crops are grown throughout the globe – even those of Europe and North America often differ in species and emphasis; 2) environmental emphasis and objectives are diverse in every country, each has specific regulatory and enforcement policies.

Before proceeding further, it may prove beneficial for readers to again reflect upon and systemize their thoughts and emotions concerning pest and disease control. As was stated above, the author believes a particular mode of action is most effective in providing sufficient pest and disease control without using an overabundance of chemicals, but there are other experts who apparently differ considerably in outlook. Who is correct? Or is there simply a disagreement over the fine points of degree and terminology? Is it possible that the earlier method of treatment with extremely potent chemicals provided better long term control and less chemical use? Each of us will eventually have to answer these questions through individual study.

The issues surrounding pest and disease control must be managed carefully – in the author's long personal experience with ornamental plant buyers, no plant quality problem is more important in their minds than "bugs" and no greater potential financial risk faces the industry than being labeled as a chemical hazard to the environment.

MAIN ASPECTS OF INTEGRATED PEST AND DISEASE CONTROL

Although the concept of IPM is relatively new to the horticultural industry as a whole, the individual working components of the system have generally been in practical application for many years. Basically, the IPM strategy makes use of three broad avenues of pest and disease control: environmental manipulation, direct disruption of target organism life processes, and utilization of plant stock for propagation which is pest and disease free.

There is no underlying distinction in efficiency or desirability between the three avenues of approach. It will become apparent that implementation of these broad categories often overlaps. Discussion of the control of specific pest species is presented later in the chapter.

Environmental manipulation

When discussing control of pests and diseases through manipulation of the environment, we generally mean to consider only those factors which are recognized as essential to the everyday functioning of the target organism's life processes and life cycle. That is: air, water, mineral nutrients, food supplies, light, proper temperature, or whatever other ingredient may be necessary for daily sustenance and reproduction.

Although pesticide application may certainly be thought of as manipulating the environment, we normally prefer to deal with this topic as an altogether different category of environmental alteration (that of radical, active treatments which result in traumatic modification of pest and disease organism life processes and life cycles). Environmental manipulative practices to control pests and diseases may range from such generalized endeavors as good housekeeping and sanitation, to control of specific necessities in target organism metabolism (an example might be the restriction of specific food materials known to promote target organism growth).

Control of pests and diseases through environmental manipulations is not necessarily synonymous with those practices which some people call "natural pest control". Neither is IPM synonymous with "natural pest control". Both the wider term (IPM) and environmental manipulation do, however, have a strong relationship to "natural pest control" in that much of the philosophical basis for IPM and environmental manipulation are drawn from a desire to accomplish the objective of pest and disease control in as environmentally tolerable and natural way as possible.

A treatment of environmental manipulation could be the subject matter for a lengthy book in which specific techniques for use with numerous target organisms on individual plant species were investigated. More will be gained, however, in this introductory text by presenting a broad summary of what environmental manipulation encompasses and how it is accomplished. Table 19 lists the general features of pest and disease control through environmental manipulation.

The worth of good housekeeping and sanitation techniques as major preventive tools in pest and disease control should be obvious to any modern person. In order to minimize the damage done by human diseases and disorders we receive a great deal of early training about personal and environmental hygiene. The very same rules we practice for human health are applicable to plants in the greenhouse and nursery.

The basic health rule is to limit plant exposure to pest and disease organisms. This is accomplished first by making sure all passive sources of contamination (such as dirt, extraneous organic matter, dirty water) are cleaned up and sanitized. Second by preventing contact with active infection sources (other organisms affected by the pest or disease). The greenhouse or nursery need not resemble a hospital in order to eliminate the majority of pest and disease problems. Only normal household sanitation is necessary unless special precautions are warranted (propagation).

Washing and sterilizing all tools and containers which come into contact with plants must be a part of the sanitation regime, especially during the process of propagation. Weeds are a major habitat for most diseases and pests; careful control of weeds is essential to preventing reinfestation. Organic wastes in or near the growing area are prime sources of infection, they may harbor active diseases and pests or, more often, the quiescent reproductive phases of the offending organisms.

Table 19
Major aspects of pest and disease control practiced through environmental manipulation.

1. Housekeeping and sanitation — generally includes several aspects of environmental modification and may also entail the use of chemical agents (disinfectants or similar acting compounds) to kill target organisms. Restrictive procedures (barriers for example) to prevent access of pests and diseases to crop areas are commonly employed.

2. Removal or restriction of food supply — certain pests and diseases are very specific as to preferred diet. It is sometimes practical to remove their food source from crop areas and thereby reduce infestation greatly.

3. Modification of temperature — most pests and diseases have specific temperatures at which they grow and reproduce most readily. Modifying temperature to reduce pest and disease population is sometimes highly successful.

4. Modification of moisture requirements — most pests and diseases flourish more readily under particular moisture conditions. Reproductive processes especially may be highly contingent upon moisture relations in the pest or disease organism's immediate vicinity and can often be controlled through this means.

5. Removal or restriction from the environment of specific requirements necessary for target organism growth and development (example, nest area for mice) — occasionally a very effective and easily accomplished means of reducing pest and disease population. Differs only in degree from other routes of action such as temperature, moisture, and food supply manipulation or restriction.

6. Removal of required host organisms from the crop environment — many target organisms require alternate hosts (two different plant species) to complete their life cycle. Removal of non-crop hosts from the vicinity causes interruption of reproduction.

7. Elimination of unnecessary conditions which favor transmission of pests and diseases — certain cultural practices may allow pests and diseases to be present or move from one plant to another more easily.

8. Providing optimum environmental conditions for crop growth — healthy crops are less susceptible to colonization and damage by pests and diseases.

The water used to irrigate plants is another potential source of contamination, especially if it is taken raw from ponds or streams. Some treatment may be necessary to eliminate pests and diseases if water is found to contain deleterious organisms or if it is used for critical production phases such as propagation.

There are many cases where removal, restriction, or modification of various environmental factors can significantly reduce the incidence of pests or diseases. Obviously one must be aware of the particular needs of major pests and diseases in order to practice this type of control strategy but, in some cases, it is possible to predict with a fair degree of accuracy what effect modifying certain environmental factors will have on large groups of organisms. For example: disease causing fungi normally require either high atmospheric humidity or free standing water on plant surfaces to complete their reproductive cycles; it is standard practice with most plant crops to irrigate at times of day or under circumstances which will prevent these conditions from arising.

Environmental modification to reduce pest and disease occurrence must of course be consistent with proper crop growth. There is little benefit to controlling pests and diseases if the methods used to accomplish this end result in unsatisfactory plant growth.

Some growers may not be aware that certain pest and disease organisms have complex life cycles which require more than one species of host plant to be present. Specific fungi disease organisms are particularly susceptible to control through removal of one of the host plant species from the greenhouse or nursery vicinity. The required host species are known for a great many organisms and can often be identified by agricultural extension agents who specialize in disease control.

Transmission of diseases and pests is favored by certain cultural practices which can easily be modified in some cases without being detrimental to the crop. Sprinkler irrigation causes splashing which promotes disease transmission from plant to plant and from contaminated soil and bench surfaces to crop plants. Various sub-irrigation practices also favor disease transmission. A common sense evaluation of each plant production phase will bring to light those obvious practices which it may be necessary to alter in order to reduce pest and disease transmission.

Healthy plants are less susceptible to permanent damage from attacks from pests and diseases. Growers who provide optimum conditions for crop growth will not generally find that keeping pests and diseases under control is any less demanding but they will find that the more robust plants resulting from such conditions are easier to maintain in acceptable market condition.

Disease organisms, unlike most insect pests, are not generally visible to the naked eye; consumers usually are not aware of the presence of specific diseases but only of the actual damage and general reductions in plant quality which they cause. Many disease problems (especially in shrubs and trees) become evident only over a long period of time. Reduced survival in the landscape, however, soon manifests itself in a reduction in sales volume.

Direct disruption of target organism life processes

As mentioned earlier, pest and disease control methods discussed under the present heading could certainly be thought of as forms of environmental manipulation but it is perhaps more helpful to consider these more direct and traumatic methods separately. Generally, what we intend with this form of action is the death of a significant portion of the pest or disease population immediately or within a reasonably short time period.

This objective was previously accomplished mainly through the application of chemicals which caused a direct poisoning of the target organism. But now, although chemicals are still the main means of action, several other methods are gaining in favor. The impetus towards alternatives to direct poisons is caused primarily by the popular perception that these methods will prove less environmentally intrusive. Although it appears this may be likely, some caution should be exercised to make sure alternative pest and disease control methods do not cause different but generally equally as serious environmental problems.

Another reason for interest in alternatives is the ability of pests and diseases to often develop a resistance to various direct poisons, thus either requiring the use or development of another poison or a need for higher dosages of the original formulation.

There are several means of directly and traumatically altering the viability of either individual pest and disease organisms or the viability of populations made up of these individuals. See Table 20 for a summary of these methods. Whenever chemical agents are involved it is apparent that the chemicals

Table 20
Summary of pest and disease control methods which generally cause a traumatic alteration of viability in either individual target organisms or the populations of which they are members.

1. Direct chemical poisons — generally thought of as those chemical agents which act quickly and cause traumatic damage to the life systems of individual target organisms, resulting in death or occasionally only in impairment which prevents future population growth.

2. Chemical growth regulators — compounds which normally act more slowly and have a more subtle effect than direct poisons upon the life processes of target organisms. Often causing no direct harm to certain life cycle stages of target organisms but impairing the ability to progress from one stage to the next, thereby preventing future population growth.

3. Biological controls — usually refers to the destruction of target organisms or the interruption of their life cycle through the introduction of predatory organisms into the greenhouse or nursery environment.

4. Alteration of population characteristics — modification of essential population survival characteristics through alteration of individual target organism behavioral or physical characteristics. Does not normally rely upon the death of treated individuals (example, sex modification).

5. Repellents and mechanical traps — in addition to actual control functions, trapping procedures may be used as a means of monitoring and identifying target organism populations.

may be obtained from naturally occurring sources or synthesized through manufacturing processes. Neither synthesized or natural chemicals are inherently more environmentally safe. The safety to man, plants, and the environment is dependent upon the characteristics and action of the specific chemical involved.

The spectrum of pest and disease control methods outlined in Table 21 encompasses a field of knowledge which is not generally familiar to persons who lack specific technical training. Even most experts will admit to being knowledgeable only about a portion of this field. Growers should therefore not expect nor attempt to appreciate even a small part of the scientific detail which abounds. Their time will be better spent accumulating a sound understanding of the overall perspectives and thus being aware of the general options available for use.

Table 21
Selection guidelines for specific chemicals used to supplement a total Integrated Pest Management program.

Chemical formulations used should:

1. Be the least toxic effective treatment available (to both humans and other non-target organisms.)

2. Be tested and documented onsite as effective against the target organism.

3. Be economical after consideration is given to other selection criteria.

4. Provide decided cost effectiveness or other benefits over substitute chemicals or other methods which are less environmentally intrusive.

5. Exhibit no significant phytotoxic or long term developmental problems to crops being cultured.

6. Exhibit no properties which require long re-entry periods (over 12 hours) or which cause other work flow problems.

7. Cause no objectional residues or odors to be present on plants when marketed.

8. Cause no long term accumulation of objectionable materials onsite (biodegradable within acceptable time limit).

9. Be reasonably easy to apply without extraordinary measures.

10. Be lawful for specific crops, pests, and locality.

11. Present no undue disposal problems or expenses for empty containers, leftovers, etc.

12. Present no undue storage or shipping problems.

13. Act in a systematic manner (enter and translocate through plant tissue) if at all possible. This guideline does not apply to edibles or other situations where the poison entering cells would effect humans.

The grower must act as a manager, selecting those options which appear to offer the most promise and then seeking technical advice from competent sources. This advice is available from university extension services, private pest control services, publications, professional seminars, and companies which market and distribute associated products and services.

The following discussion will be aimed towards providing the overall background which is necessary to help growers evaluate which general pest and disease control methods might be applicable under particular circumstances. No concerted effort is made to recommend specific chemicals or treatments since these number in the thousands and are often outdated by new developments. Mention of specific chemicals or brand names will be made only as it is felt an example is necessary to facilitate the general discussion of topics.

Another complicating factor in recommending specific treatments is the well known fact that, in practical usage, these recommendations seldom work in a straightforward manner. The expected results may be totally lacking due to variations in circumstances surrounding the usage of products and methods, or as is often the case, further modification and evaluation is necessary to bring only minimally encouraging results into agreement with what is expected. And in more than a small number of cases, recommendations result in a total lack of beneficial effect; even when circumstances are modified in the hope of a better result.

The author has repeatedly considered whether or not it would be appropriate in a book of this nature to provide readers with concrete brand recommendations for chemical pest, disease, and weed control. After all, many years of valuable experience have been necessary to arrive at the generally excellent and predictable control methods which result from the author's personal methods. Such a presentation has been decided against for the following reasons: 1) the availability of pesticides, fungicides and herbicides changes frequently, often making specific recommendations outdated and even unlawful within a short time; 2) most chemicals are licensed for use only in particular states or countries – thus limiting the geographic validity of specific recommendations; 3) environmental conditions at the application site may render specific treatments unsuitable and even ineffective; 4) each facility has particular circumstances which dictate the choice of one treatment over another; 5) recommending a particular formulation prejudices the reader to reduce the independent evaluation which might result in an even better program.

Table 21 provides the essential criteria which should be employed when choosing any chemical control treatment. Readers should realize that any chemical selected will likely represent a compromise of the listed criteria.

Growers seldom find that a single chemical formulation controls one pest or one disease adequately much less the numerous species which are likely to be encountered. Therefore, most growers will eventually select a number of chemicals which are used for different pests and situations. The universe of possible circumstances for selection is too large to cover within a single chapter, but the following examples for pest control application are presented to familiarize readers with several concepts: 1) a quick knockdown and widely effective adulticide such as pyrethrum or resmethrin may be followed by the application of a slower acting and equally widely effective treatment such as Azadirachtin which interferes with the development of eggs or larvae; 2) or, a relatively slow acting systematic adulticide such as Abamectin may be combined in the same application with a slower acting developmental poison (Azadirachtin); 3) another scenario might involve the use of either or both of the above plus Imidacloprid as a systematic soil treatment to guard long term against whitefly, which neither 1 or 2 above control adequately in most cases; 4) Other widely effective chemicals (such as Acephate, a systemic organophosphate available as a spray or granule formulation) might be substituted or rotated into the program to help prevent pesticide resistance by target organisms.

Various brand name formulations are available for each of the above generic chemicals. Consult a detailed product reference guide for selection of specific brands. All are available in a signal word "caution" formulation.

All of these examples might be used at different times in the same pest control program. They were chosen to illustrate that more than one chemical is usually necessary for: 1) effective treatment of all life stages of the target; 2) control of different target species; 3) control of difficult target species (whitefly); 4) providing long term or immediate control; 5) providing systemic control; 6) providing different entry points into the plant (soil vs. leaf surface spray); 7) helping to prevent genetic resistance of the target organisms.

Incidentally, the basic program outlined above has proven quite successful for most circumstances in the author's commercial nursery and greenhouses. A similar plan of attack for plant diseases is necessary utilizing appropriate fungicides and bactericides.

Growers must follow a process of education about and selection of general methods, then proceed to acquire technical information from appropriate sources, and finally, to evaluate results in actual practice. The latter goal is normally dependent upon a good deal of trial and error.

It is apparent that the development of an effective, safe, and economical treatment program for pests and diseases of container crops is not an easy or inexpensive endeavor. Therefore, it should be planned with a good deal of care so that major investments in time and money are not wasted. The best way to accomplish this objective is to develop an overall strategy which can be used as a guide in making day to day decisions.

The treatment program strategy must be consistent with other major management and operational programs of the greenhouse or nursery and it should conform to environmental and safety laws. The program will be more useful if it can be applied consistently over the longer term.

Although smaller growers cannot be expected to invest major money and time in developing a treatment program, they must progress beyond the stage where a bottle of "Old Reliable" disease and pest elixir is sprayed unthinkingly on crops each time a problem arises.

A major step towards developing a responsible and effective treatment strategy can be made by writing down the essential components in an organized form and requiring a detailed effectiveness report and overall evaluation of each specific method employed. No treatment program is likely to be so simple in action as to display all its benefits and drawbacks in obvious form. Only a follow up analysis which makes use of carefully observed and recorded facts will allow growers to make intelligent decisions.

Chemical poisons which directly affect the survival of disease and pest organisms are still generally the first treatment methods which come to mind when an infestation gets out of control. In fact, many growers practice a preventive chemical program rather than waiting for signs of an epidemic. This reliance upon chemical methods has not developed by accident. With proper usage, chemicals are effective and economical; and sometimes the only practical means of dealing with a situation.

In addition to effectiveness and economy, a primary concern of any chemical disease or pest control technique is safety; to humans, to the crop, and to the environment. Some specific information regarding safety is presented later in this chapter under application methods. In modern times every grower must assess the risk factor associated with chemical usage at the business site. Not only the possibility of injury or damage must be considered but also the likelihood of various legal actions.

It is possible in most cases to greatly increase the safety aspects of a chemical control program by employing only those agents which combine both safety and effectiveness while ruling out the use of compounds which exhibit a high degree of hazard. Achieving this goal will require the grower to develop criteria for chemical selection. The data necessary for assessing safety are usually readily available from the manufacturer, literature sources, or extension services. Data concerning effectiveness and economy for a particular operation can only be secured through careful testing under actual production circumstances.

Some chemical pest and disease controls act in a less direct manner than the types which we usually consider as poisons but still result in a disruption of the normal growth and development of the target organisms. This interference in normal functioning often requires a longer timespan than do typical poisons and it often affects only a particular aspect of the pest or disease organism's existence. Interruption of the life cycle is a common means of action for these compounds which are frequently called "growth regulators".

In general there are no easily defined differences between growth regulators and what we normally call poisons or between the natural and synthetic compounds from which they are manufactured. The decision to use one name or another often rests only upon interpretation and the conventions of language.

The many modes of action which poisons or growth regulators may exhibit mean that it is essential for the grower to know under what circumstances and at what times treatments will prove to be effective. Hit or miss treatments may show some benefit but precise usage under the proper circumstances often improves the results manyfold.

A good deal of emphasis has been placed recently upon "biological" control of pests and diseases. Generally, this control technique is taken to mean the destruction of target organisms or the interruption of their life cycle through the introduction of predatory organisms into the greenhouse or nursery environment.

Although the validity and economy of biological control has been proven many times under commercial growing conditions, this control technique has not achieved widespread effective use as yet in the ornamental greenhouse and nursery industry.

Predatory organisms are available commercially for most common insect and mite pests but generally must be utilized under rather specific conditions in order to achieve reasonable success. Operations where a single crop species is grown can usually employ biological controls more easily than can businesses which grow a large number of varieties.

This situation results because one dominant pest is more likely to emerge when single species crops are grown. Since the use of predatory organisms often requires a rather complex manipulation of environmental conditions and careful timing, it is much easier to provide the proper circumstances for a single predatory species than when two or more are involved. Growers must realize that successful biological control almost always involves much more planning and effort than simply releasing a bottle of lady bugs.

Biological control is not a risk free technique. Predatory organisms, although useful under proper circumstances can become a nuisance or even dangerous under others. Probably everyone is aware that some biological control plants and animals have expanded beyond the scope of their intended usage to cause major economic and environmental problems.

It should be remembered that one of the primary consumer objections to insects is not the actual plant damage caused by them but simply a psychological distaste of their presence. Any predatory organism employed is likely to elicit a similar response if it is allowed to remain on plants during marketing.

Predatory organisms often cannot be utilized at the same time chemical or other disruptive control techniques are being employed. The latter methods are sometimes effective not only against the target organisms but also other species, including predators.

Commercial availability of predatory pest and disease control organisms in ornamental plant greenhouses and nurseries has only recently become a practical reality. Although this control technique has seen limited practical agricultural use for many years, only of late have a significant number of tree and flower growers begun to experiment with it. Recently, several biologically based means of destroying or preventing diseases in the soil medium have been introduced. This was an area where attention was severely lacking. Although these new methods appear to be economically effective, only widespread use will prove their long term applicability. It is likely that at least several additional years will be necessary in order to more completely commercialize the competing technologies for effective use in greenhouses and nurseries on an everyday basis.

Most pest and disease control programs are aimed towards control of individual organisms and only as a cumulative result of achieving this objective is the entire population reined in. There are some control techniques which, although modifying the behavior or physiology of individual organisms, do not rely upon their actual death but rather upon rendering them incapable of performing essential functions necessary for the survival of the population.

Many of these latter type techniques are based upon sexual modification of the individual organism, thereby causing general reproductive failure in the population. A common means of effecting sexual modification is by sterilization of individuals through the use of radiation. Other techniques and agents of modification are available. Both individuals and populations of pests and diseases are susceptible to genetic manipulation by man. This "genetic engineering" is carried out in order to make pests and diseases either less predisposed to attack plants or less able to survive and, hence, less destructive.

Pest and disease organisms are frequently present in mind boggling numbers (especially as they become perceptible as a definite problem). This characteristic usually dictates that some means of controlling them in mass be utilized. Mechanical means of control are seldom effective against the vast numbers of organisms involved but there area few cases where this means is practiced. Wider application for more or less mechanical techniques is often restricted to situations where they serve to monitor target organism populations. Various types of traps are used to ascertain the presence and population density of some pest species, thereby allowing growers to determine if other control measures are necessary or if the use of particular methods has been successful. Sticky strips are the most common means of trapping insects in the greenhouse while other types of traps are often necessary outdoors.

Some larger pests such as rodents and deer can be managed with mechanical traps or repellents. These types of animals are not often given high priority in pest control research programs but can occasionally cause very serious crop damage. When the organism targeted for control is considered desirable by many people (deer, for example) it is especially difficult to implement a control method unless it is non-injurious to the animal.

All of the pest and disease control techniques mentioned previously deserve consideration when an overall strategy is designed. Environmental manipulation, good housekeeping, and sanitation should form the base of any control program; the techniques which disrupt target organism life processes are most sensibly employed only when actually proven necessary. The use of chemicals is still often the most practical means of providing control in severe cases of infestation but technology is developing rapidly which will allow growers more choice of effective methods.

Propagation of disease and pest free plants

No amount of preventive housekeeping or other control techniques can be acceptably successful unless stock which is free of pests and diseases is utilized to start the crop. If young stock is produced at the greenhouse or nursery site, extreme precautions must be enforced in this production phase to assure disease and pest free propagation conditions. In addition, all plant material used in propagation must be initially clean. A minimal amount of time and expense spent religiously practicing intense control in the propagation phase can save untold effort and cost in later production phases.

It has been the trend in recent years for propagation specialists to provide much of the young stock for ordinary greenhouses and nurseries to finish off into marketable crops. At the beginning of this trend there were severe disease and pest control problems throughout the industry because propagators had not yet developed suitable control programs; the plant material they were shipping all over the country was providing excellent transportation for pests and diseases.

Fortunately, there have been great strides made in both control methods and the vigor and responsibility with which they are employed; most shipments of juvenile plants are now remarkably clean. Although technical advances have made this "clean up" possible, the basic impetus was derived from the refusal of growers to tolerate the continual importation of pests and diseases into their production facilities. Even today, every grower must clearly inform suppliers that pest and disease ridden plant material will not be accepted. The pocketbook is the ultimate means of forcing propagators to provide clean stock.

Disease and pest free propagation is accomplished by several means. Naturally, the previously discussed methods of reducing or eliminating target organisms must be employed to clean up small plants, but a concerted effort is also necessary to assure a minimum of contamination originating from their parent plants.

From earliest times growers have realized the necessity of "rouging" plants to eliminate disease and pest ridden parent stock. They understood (perhaps without knowledge of the actual causal factors) that "rouging" tended to provide better stock for reproduction as well as to reduce the actual presence of pests and diseases. This form of parent selection is still widely employed in horticulture and the basic reasoning behind it has led to refinements in technique which are so distinctive as to be given totally new names.

"Indexing" is a specific technical program which is used to systematically eliminate particular plant diseases (most of which are caused by viruses or bacteria rather than fungi). The end result of indexing is a parent stock clone which can be certified through various tests to be free of specific diseases. The process of indexing does not usually rely simply on removal of diseased plants but also upon different active means of eliminating the disease.

Most plant species are certified as free only from one or a very limited number of major diseases. The process of indexing and maintaining parent stock free of particular diseases is very expensive and cannot be economically justified for only nuisance or minor diseases. Reproduction can take place from indexed parent stock through normal propagative techniques.

Tissue culture (in which only one or several plant cells are used for propagation) is a favored means of reproducing indexed parent stock since it is possible to obtain a great number of offspring from a single parent. And reproduction can occur under rigidly maintained sterile laboratory conditions.

Only the first generation of plants produced from indexed parent stock can be expected to be virtually free of the specified disease. Contamination creeps in at various rates (depending upon environmental conditions and the presence of the disease in the surroundings). Under some conditions, offspring will maintain at least part of the beneficial effects from indexing for several years.

Reproducing plants strictly from seed will help growers reduce the amount and incidence of pests and diseases in crop populations. Only very rarely are pests transmitted through seed propagation; although diseases are more often carried in or upon the seed, it is still not a common occurrence.

Genetic engineering of plant varieties (modification of the plant genome) is a new and fertile means of producing both parent and stock plants which possess the ability to resist attack by pests and diseases. This methodology has been successfully utilized with a number of major agricultural crops but has not been widely practiced on ornamental species as of yet. Once the theory and technology of genetic engineering become more mature, the everyday practice of it on horticultural plants will become an economic reality. Hopefully, when this happens, a good deal of the money and effort previously spent upon pest and disease control will be unnecessary.

A continual effort is necessary in greenhouses and nurseries to assure that disease and pest ridden young plants are not allowed into the production sequence. These plants seldom make a profitable crop and merely take up expensive space until such time as it is finally realized that they are a "lost cause". It is better to reject infected stock before materials, fuel, and time are wasted. Dumping a large block of young stock for disease and pest control preventive purposes is not an easy thing to do but is usually the wise choice in the long run. A regular program of "scouting" for pests and diseases must begin and be most frequently practiced during the propagation phase. No treatment program can be started until the presence, extent, and nature of infestations is documented.

PLANT PESTS

Insects, mites, nematodes, slugs, and rodents are the common pests which attack plants in temperate regions. The seemingly unlimited reproductive capacity of these pests has perhaps led to more grower frustration than any other cultural problem. One faces a never ending battle with these animal competitors. Infestations are cleared up only to reappear in a different location a few days later. Much of the frustration caused by plant pests can be overcome if growers assume an aggressive posture against them rather than a defensive reaction to their destructive capabilities. Obtaining a knowledge of how to control pests is the first step in gaining the upper hand; a religious implementation of this knowledge is the second step. Insects and mites are initially irritating to customers mainly because of their visual presence but the long term effects of their activity may result in permanent disfiguration or death for the plant. Entire crops can be made worthless in a short time if pests are allowed to multiply without hazard. Once a critical population level is attained, it is useless to attempt control and the crop should be discarded. Retail sales experience is helpful in convincing growers of the need never to allow infested plants into marketing channels. No other plant defect will turn customers away faster than the presence of pests.

Many types of rodents may occasionally cause damage to container plants but mice are the chief offenders. Seeds and seedlings are the main target of mice, and crop schedules can be badly upset when a seed sowing is destroyed by their activities. Only one or two mice can play havoc with a large number of seed flats in one night. Mice are especially fond of the following seeds: pepper, marigold, pansy, cucumber, squash, melon, zinnia, tomato, asparagus sprengeri, dahila, eggplant, and aster, but they will devour almost any seed species if given a chance. Having cats on the premises will eliminate much of the mouse population but cats may cause more damage than mice unless they are trained to stay off the benches in greenhouses. Poison baits are quite effective in controlling mice but foul odors may result if the mice die and decay in the greenhouse. Traps will do an effective job without the drawbacks of cats or poison baits. Once the traps have served their purpose they must be removed from the greenhouse to avoid being ruined by rusting in the humid atmosphere.

Several larger animal pests may cause damage to outdoor crops. Deer, squirrels, and rabbits are usually the main offenders. They are distributed over a large part of North America and Eurasia and are often plentiful in the city fringes where many horticultural crops are grown. Dealing with these offenders can prove difficult in that many neighbors (and game departments) object to control measures which involve the death of the animals. If crops are to be grown outdoors, serious investigation of potential damage which can be expected to occur from these pests should be made before locating a nursery. Deer damage can be especially extensive and difficult to control. A deer tight fence is perhaps the only truly effective and acceptable method of control. This measure can require extensive investment.

Mites and insects often seem to appear in the greenhouse or nursery as products of spontaneous generation. Entry to the greenhouse by insects is usually gained through their own locomotion or by being carried in on plants. Very few insects are introduced on personnel and supplies. The suction created by ventilating fans can sweep in any insects close to air entries. Simple precautions will eliminate the entry of most insects. Plant life outside the greenhouse should be eliminated for a distance of at least 20 feet. Screens should be installed on all air entries; mites and very small insects will not be denied entry by ordinary screens but many of the larger species will be kept out. Special screen which will prevent the entry of small pests such as mites and thrips can be purchased from horticultural suppliers. Evaporative cooling pads not only help in bringing down greenhouse temperatures but also make entry more difficult for insects. Plants brought into the greenhouse must be carefully inspected for insects and mites. If infestations are found, they should be treated by appropriate means at the earliest possible date.

Weeds on the floors are probably the largest contributor to insect populations in most greenhouses. Crops may develop infestations of insects but within a short time the crop matures and is sold or removed as dumpage. Unless growers allow old, worthless crops to occupy greenhouse space indefinitely, the insect population growing on these plants will be removed with the crop. If weeds are not removed on a regular schedule, a carry over insect population resident on the weeds remains on them even when crops have been harvested. Plants kept from one crop to the next should be inspected very carefully to prevent a carry over of insects. Many growers are reluctant to dump crops which have passed their prime and have no reasonable prospect of being marketed. Such a crop not only occupies valuable greenhouse space but also enhances the possibilities of insect outbreaks. A well planned marketing strategy is a positive step in the control of insect transmission to succeeding crops.

Plant pests have free access to outdoor crops. Here again, weeds are the primary source of infestation. One bright spot in outdoor insect control is that many geographical regions experience a winter cold spell which naturally reduces insect and mite populations to minimal levels. If every effort is made at this time to eliminate old plants and debris which might cause reinfestation, it is often possible to get through a considerable part of the next growing season without serious problems. Since entry is no problem to insects and mites, outdoor crops often suffer attack from a greater natural variety of these pests.

A program of early detection of insect and mite pests is essential to their eventual control. No amount of remedial measures can be effective once a full blown epidemic is allowed to develop. Growers should check crops at least every two weeks for possible outbreaks, more frequent inspection is necessary when environmental conditions for pest development are optimal or during major cropping periods.

Growers soon learn that certain plant species are prone to infestation by particular pests; knowing this fact will allow for more efficient monitoring. Time can be more profitably spent if one knows the most likely places to look for pests. Once a localized outbreak of pests has been discovered, fast action is necessary to minimize the population. The quickest means of accomplishing this is often through discarding all infected plants and then treating the specific area with a pesticide which is known to be effective against the particular pest.

Several hundred dollars in subsequent control measures can often be saved if growers have enough courage to throw away infected plants rather than attempting to salvage them. Most major outbreaks of pests get their start through insufficient crop monitoring and failure to act swiftly and decisively once a problem is discovered.

Preventive treatment with various chemical agents must be carefully monitored to eliminate undue costs, to reduce environmental contamination, and to avoid the possibility of pest populations building up a genetic resistance to these measures. Many authorities recommend preventive chemical treatments on a rather frequent and regular basis. The wisdom of this action is perhaps more often questioned now than in the past. Frequent chemical treatments not only cause more environmental pollution but they often do not make economic sense.

Alternation of chemical families in treatments is often practiced with the hope of reducing a buildup of genetic resistance in pest populations. This strategy seems sound at first glance but further analysis sometimes indicates that control programs might be more logical if emphasis was placed upon applying the most useful chemical compound under ideal conditions at the proper times rather than alternating with those which perhaps exhibit less efficient action. It seems illogical, at least to the author, to routinely alternate with pesticides which are not proven at least as effective in control as was the original formulation.

If a particular pest becomes a consistent problem in the greenhouse or nursery, a longer range control strategy which is specifically tailored to fit that target organism must be devised. Hit or miss tactics which are aimed at a variety of pests are seldom effective against persistent problems.

The control strategy adopted for specific pests will vary with circumstances but, hopefully, would take full advantage of non-disruptive techniques before resorting to those which pose a high risk to the environment or personal safety. The full range of IPM methods should be considered whenever pest control programs are designed.

Only a well thought out overall plan for pest and disease control which addresses each specific problem will have a chance for success. Not only must the plan be knowledgably constructed, it must also be religiously implemented as regards to timing and detail. Pests and diseases did not become the consistent problem they are to all horticulturists by being "push overs". If you expect to at least minimize their damage within acceptable limits, it will require a good deal of ongoing effort and research into effective methods. No grower has yet solved this problem completely and none is likely to do so in the near future.

A basic knowledge of how to detect and identify pests is essential for every grower to possess. Once this initial step is accomplished, some understanding of the target organism's reproductive processes and basic life requirements is helpful in devising appropriate control methods. Information about specific common pests is presented shortly which will aid growers in this respect; but care should be taken not to become so immersed in the details as to lose track of developing an overall concept of how to deal with broader issues. Memorizing details is useless if they can be readily accessed from literature sources when needed.

Insects and mites reproduce sexually in much the same manner as higher animals. But some can also reproduce asexually, without fertilization of the egg. This latter capacity adds some degree of flexibility to their reproductive capabilities and does influence the genetic recombination which takes place.

Some insect species emerge from the egg more or less resembling the adult stages but lacking the ability to fly and being sexually immature. This stage is referred to as a "nymph". Other insect species emerge from the egg in a relatively undeveloped stage (larvae) and often must pass through an intermediate "pupal" stage before developing into adults. Those species which emerge as nymphs usually have no pupal stage. Insects possess a relatively unexpandable exterior skeleton which must be shed as the interior body mass grows. Each shedding is termed a "moult" and the stages between moults are referred to as "instars" in more scientific descriptions.

Depending on the species, life stages may possess anatomical or physiological characteristics which make them more or less susceptible to particular methods of control. Control programs are often less effective when aimed at the relatively inactive egg or pupal stages but this is not always the case. The ability to recognize target organisms in all their life stages is sometimes critical to detecting and successfully containing an outbreak.

The presentations given in this book concerning various pests and diseases are simplified in many respects to avoid unnecessary confusion, it should be recognized that much more detailed information is available in other specialized literature sources should the need arise. In addition, there are often considerable numbers of different species and races of target organisms than are mentioned herein. These variants may differ somewhat from the descriptions given. Readers only need reflect upon the fact that pest groups restricted to tropical and subtropical climates have not been mentioned in the discussion, and yet they certainly far out number those of temperate regions. Figures 5-9 depict some common pests which attack container crops in North America.

Aphids

Perhaps the most common and widespread greenhouse insect pest, which is also ubiquitous outdoors. Several species can become established on container crops but the green peach aphid is by far the most frequently encountered. It is rather fat and sluggish in the wingless stage which can attain a length of 1/8 inch but is usually smaller. Their color may range from the usual yellowish-green or very light green to less common shades of greenish-tan or reddish-tan, depending on the season and environment.

The wingless nymphs develop from unfertilized eggs. When colonies become crowded there is apparently a stimulus for the production of winged female forms which then migrate to infect other plants. The winged brownish-black females are very weak flyers and can be distinguished from other small fly-like insects by this characteristic. Even the rather lazy

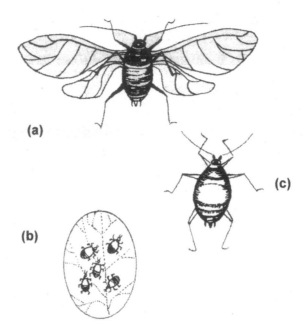

Fig. 5 Green peach aphid prevalent in greenhouses. (a) adult winged female; (b) group of wingless adults on a leaf surface magnified approximately 10 times; (c) wingless adult detailed.

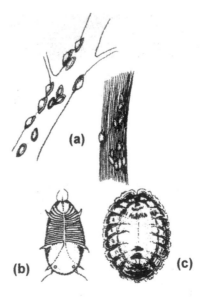

Fig. 6 Common greenhouse brown scale with rough shell. (a) armored stage attached to plant stems; (b) crawler stage before forming a shell, magnified several times in relation to the shell, (c) close up of armored shell.

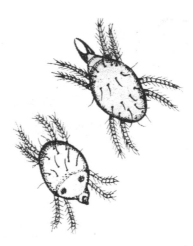

Fig. 7 Red spider, spider mite, or two spotted mite. Spots may not be evident under some conditions. Certain immature stages have less than eight legs. Some observers report pronounced mouth parts while others do not; this may be due to observing different stages of maturity or variation in populations.

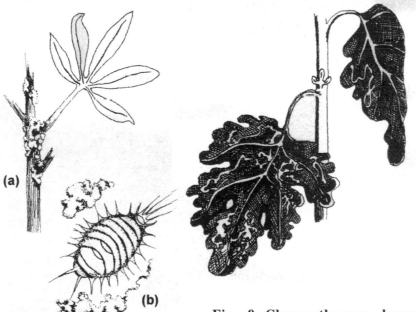

Fig. 8 (a) Cottony egg sacs deposited by mealybugs; (b) common greenhouse mealybug adult.

Fig. 9 Chrysanthemum leaves showing characteristic serpentine tunneling between the upper and lower epidermal layers by leaf miner larvae. Tunnels seldom cross the harder tissue at main veins.

Wingless aphid nymphs on gynura (purple passion plant) flower buds. Aphids love gynura, this plant species should therefore be inspected frequently since it is one of the first palaces the pests will show up if present in greenhouses.

fungus gnat adults will fly when touched while winged aphids will not usually fly even when prodded. Male aphids are normally produced only in the fall and in cooler regions. In continually warm environments, such as greenhouses, male forms may never appear. The absence of sexual reproduction in such cases would seem to prevent population variability and the resultant capacity to acquire immunity to pesticides. Alternate methods of recombining genetic material are present in aphids, however, and account for population variability without sexual union.

In cold areas the peach aphid can overwinter as adults or nymphs in protected areas outdoors or in unheated greenhouses. Mating, egg laying, and hatching resume quickly when temperatures become warmer and populations can increase quickly. When aphids moult or shed their skins it is sometimes easier to detect infestations by looking for the whitish cast off skins on leaves or flowers than it is to find living specimens. Large colonies often leave a sugary glaze of excrement on plant parts below them. A blackish, sooty mold may then begin to grow on this waste material. The sugary glaze and sooty growth are not specific to aphid colonies and may also result from mealybugs, scale, and whitefly. All of which are related.

Aphids can be found on any plant part but young stem tips, flower buds, and delicate new leaves are their favorite locations. These immature plant parts may be permanently disfigured when aphids insert their sucking mouth parts into the young tissue. Direct damage caused by aphids is only part of the story, many disease viruses are transmitted in the feeding process.

Female nymphs begin producing offspring in about 7 days (depending upon environmental conditions). The frequency of pest control treatments should be timed to break the reproductive cycle.

Most aphid strains are not difficult to keep under control with a variety of contact chemical insecticides, but it is nearly impossible to eliminate them completely unless a suitable long lasting systemic poison is introduced into plant tissue. This type of treatment eventually kills all the adults as they emerge from resistant stages.

Beetles

This group of insects is very large. The adults are generally easily recognized as a class by even inexperienced gardeners and the immature larval stages are commonly known as "grubs". Adult beetles normally feed upon above ground plant parts (leaves and flowers) while grubs attack roots, bulbs, and germinating seeds. This feeding scenario is not always adhered to and it is possible to discover either life stage feeding over the entire plant; depending upon the circumstance and the species of beetle.

When beetle larvae attack the stems of plants and bore into the tissue they are given the broad name of "borers". These pests are extremely damaging to outdoor woody plants and can seriously affect the quality of crops for landscape use even if the infestation is not discovered during nursery culture. Borers are readily detected by the holes they make in woody tissue and by the seepage of plant juices out of these openings.

Sawdust from borer activity may accumulate at the entrance to the bore hole or on the soil directly below.

The Japanese beetle is one of the most damaging, widespread, and numerous of beetle species. It can be recognized by the iridescent bluish-green body and grey-brown streaked wing cases. Japanese beetles are most fond of floral parts but will readily consume leaf tissue if no flowers are present. Roses are particularly susceptible to attack but many other flowers and trees serve as a food source, including the elm and linden.

Great numbers of these beetles may appear in midsummer as the eggs which were laid in lawn sod hatch to produce larvae and then adults. The grubs will destroy lawns if present in large enough quantities. Obviously, chemical treatment of nearby grassy areas or elimination of these hatcheries by weed control techniques or plowing will greatly aid in beetle control. A bacterial spore which paralyzes and destroys Japanese beetle grubs is widely available but control by this means usually takes several years.

Caterpillars

This name is not specific for a particular group of insects but refers to the wingless, wormlike larval stage characteristic of many species. Many commonly encountered caterpillars are the larvae of moths.

Caterpillars are easily recognized and everyone is familiar with the extreme damage which they can inflict to outdoor plants. Fortunately, outbreaks of caterpillars are often short lived and the larvae are very susceptible to spray treatments. Even greenhouse plants may become seriously damaged when caterpillars migrate indoors from outside vegetation or when adult moths actually lay eggs in the greenhouse. The main source of infestation normally occurs outside though and must be primarily controlled at that point.

Cutworms are also moth larvae although they may sometimes be called grubs. Cutworms can become serious pests indoors or outdoors although the latter is more often the case. All plant parts can be attacked by cutworms although they receive their name from their practice of severing the plant stem at ground level. This action assures the destruction of many more plants than the worms can actually eat.

Cutworms are nocturnal feeders and may remain undetected unless growers are familiar with the characteristic damage they inflict. These pests may crawl up the stem and sever small immature branches on

Hornworms and the typical damage they have inflicted upon fuchsia leaves. Note fecal droppings on the smaller leaf. Hornworms are the larvae of large moths and can cause considerable damage indoors or outdoors.

shrubs and trees. The damage often appears as though deer or rabbits had been feeding on the plants; but unlike deer or rabbits, the cutworm will leave the stem tip unconsumed on the ground below as evidence.

Cutworms burrow into the soil to avoid cold weather. No control treatment can be successful which does not include a means of eliminating these larvae from the soil on a continuing basis.

Fungus gnats

This insect and other look-a-likes have assumed the status of major greenhouse pests in recent years. At first, most people thought of the problem as only involving fungus gnats but now it is known that shore flies and perhaps other small black flying insects contribute to the irritating swarms often found in greenhouses. Physical, above ground damage to plants due to this poorly defined group of insects is usually small unless large populations are present but consumers are irritated when infested plants serve as breeding grounds in the home, office, or hospital.

Fungus gnat larvae which inhabit the soil can feed on plant roots and cause poor growth. There is some question as to how much damage they cause unless infestations are very heavy since it is thought that the larvae generally feed mainly on dead soil organic matter. Shorefly larvae are believed to feed mainly on algae but, here again, they readily attack plant roots when available. In addition to the irritation caused by adult shore flies, they often leave black fly specks on leaves and have been observed to destroy leaf tissue. This problem is quite severe with heavy infestations. Recent research has shown that both fungus gnats and shore flies are a major vector in the transmission of soil borne root diseases. It is also likely that the leaf damaging shore flies also spread various above ground diseases. Both of these insect pests are much more of a problem than was originally thought.

Shore fly and fungus gnat adults are generally less than 1/8 inch long and are greyish-black in color. Both fly readily upon stimulation but when in the air, the shore fly flies strongly while the fungus gnat is much slower. The shore fly adult is rather husky and has several poorly visible light dots on the upper surface of the wings while fungus gnat adults have a much more fragile body and legs and do not have any spots on the wings.

The larvae of shore flies and fungus gnats are easily visible with the naked eye once a specimen has been isolated but locating them amongst soil particles or algae slime is not always easy. They are generally a little longer than 1/8 inch, thin, and twitch actively. Fungus gnat larvae are reportedly translucent and relatively colorless while shore fly larvae are supposedly brownish.

In some cases, other similar looking flies or gnats may become pests. Although the poorly identified third group may be controlled to some extent by the same methods, each group of organisms undoubtedly possesses characteristics which would make individualized control techniques more effective against it. The author suggests that shore fly and fungus gnat taxonomy is still in an uncertain state and that it is likely this situation leads to the confusion which surrounds every aspect of their appearance, activity, treatment, and effect upon plants.

The widespread adoption of growing media high in organic matter has created an ideal situation for population explosions of fungus gnats since an almost unlimited food source is available. Switching to inert mineral media ingredients may only trade the problem of fungus gnats for that of shore flies since heavy infestations of them can become established in media such as rock wool, perlite, scoria, and gravel if algae are available as a food source on particle surfaces. Conditions which lead to excess greenhouse moisture are conducive to large populations of both fungus gnats and shore flies. Shore flies in particular reproduce rapidly when algae colonies are allowed to establish on wet media surfaces or in standing pools of water.

Control of these blackflies is difficult by normal chemical means unless a long lasting pesticide is introduced into the soil to kill larvae. Some success has been reported using disinfectants and water treatments to eradicate algae in the greenhouse, thus removing a major food source and breeding ground. Beneficial nematodes are also reported to help control fly larvae in the soil. Diatomaceous earth is also effective against larvae, as it is with other crawling, soft-bodied pests.

Leaf miners

Adult leaf miners are small, blackish flies which vary in appearance depending upon the species. Eggs are deposited under the leaf epidermis by these flies. When hatched, the larvae bore between the upper and lower leaf epidermis and consume the soft tissue between veins. These tunnels are serpentine or blotchy and become tan or brown as tissue dies. The serpentine nature of many tunnels and their abrupt termination at hardened major veins distinguishes leaf miner damage from dead tissue caused by other means. Tissue damage is generally the earliest warning one receives concerning the presence of these insects, unless adults have been trapped. Adult flies of leaf miners may go undetected if more numerous fungus gnats and other small flies are present. The larval stage is difficult to observe unless one peels back the upper epidermal layer and observes carefully with a hand lens. Control is much easier when systemic insecticides are applied since larvae are protected from surface sprays by the leaf epidermis.

Outdoors, leaf miner damage usually appears in late summer and may become epidemic on certain preferred species before remedial measures can be taken. Since infection is almost certain to occur each year on outdoor plants, preventive action is necessary on known problem species before obvious visual symptoms appear. Cottonwoods, poplars, and aspen are all notoriously susceptible to leaf miner and should be sprayed with systemic insecticides before the known season of larval activity.

In the greenhouse, leaf miners may be seldom encountered until a shipment of contaminated plants is received. The insects can then build up to epidemic proportions before the problem is identified. Chrysanthemums are a prime target of leaf miners and infestations are sometimes imported with the cuttings.

Mites

Mites are not technically insects but belong to the spider family. At maturity they have 4 pairs of legs while insects have only 3 pairs. Two types of mites are particularly common: a broad group generally referred to as two spotted spider mites or red spider mites, and another less common pest, the cyclamen mite.

Spider mites may be represented by more than one species which partially accounts for their variability in color from rather transparent light greenish shades to definite reddish specimens. The individuals in many populations display two rather prominent black spots on their backside. Spider mites are quite small but can be seen easily with the naked eye if your eyesight and light conditions are good. Small, immature individuals are almost invisible to the naked eye. Red spiders are found most frequently on the undersides of leaves but will migrate to other areas of the plant. They move only infrequently unless prodded. A fine, whitish web is spun by spider mites on the undersides of leaves and, when sufficient numbers are present, this web becomes easily visible. In advanced outbreaks, the web may extend from branch to branch and mites may be seen crawling through the web.

Spider mites damage plants by inserting their sucking mouthparts into cells and feeding on the contents. Very tiny yellow puncture wounds then become apparent from the top side on thinner leaved varieties. As the mite population increases, the puncture wounds maybe so close together that the entire area becomes yellow. Eventually, affected leaf portions turn brownish-yellow and die. Severely infested plants may take on the appearance of having been dried out or windburned. Spider mites flourish under warm conditions. The speed of reaching maturity and producing young doubles between 70⁰ and 80⁰ F.

A complex life cycle which includes several resting stages and an egg stage make control difficult since only the active stage may be affected by common insecticides. In addition, spider mites have shown an amazing ability to develop acquired immunity to many chemicals.

Plants infested with spider mites may display a dwarfishness inconsistent with the actual physical damage which the pests have inflicted. This is thought to be due to a growth regulating chemical which mites inject into plants as they feed.

Cyclamen mites are very small. A 10x hand lens is necessary to observe their physical presence. Their appearance under this magnification is most often a semitransparent dirty glass color. Individual body parts may be difficult to observe but movement can be discerned. The presence of cyclamen mites is usually detected by characteristic deformations of leaves and flowers rather than by observation of the mite itself.

Cyclamen mites infest very young leaf and bud tissue at the stem tip and inflict many puncture wounds with their sucking mouth parts. These wounds cause further growth of the leaf to be distorted in various ways, depending on the plant species. Sometimes growth of new leaves almost ceases and they appear hardened and dwarfed. African violets and gloxinia exhibit this type of leaf growth when affected and the crown or center of the plant becomes whitish and pubescent because leaf growth has stopped but hair growth continues. Some plants, such as ivies, exhibit hardened leaves, some of which are distorted as if they were made of rubber and stretched out of shape. Infested flowers characteristically fail to open. Whenever growers begin to observe a consistent pattern of leaf or flower distortion, they should suspect cyclamen mites.

Begonias, impatiens, ivies, cyclamen, silver lace vine, African violets, and gloxinias are particularly susceptible, but other species can surely be infested. The damage caused by this pest may sometimes be attributed to chemical gaseous pollutants because of the growth distortions caused without any apparent agent visible to the naked eye.

Although some longer lasting contact pesticides are effective in controlling different mite species, appropriate systemic poisons offer a much easier means of treating plants. Contact poisons must be applied so as to cover the undersides of leaves and to penetrate into the nooks

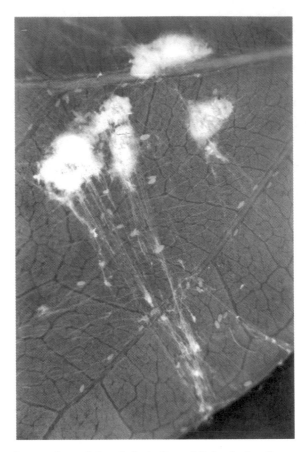

An advanced case of mealybug infestation with typical cottony web holding eggs. The mobile nymph stage is just hatching here on the underside of a leaf. Cottony sacs are more often found in the crotches of stems.

and crannies of flower and leaf buds if they are to be effective against mites. This is a difficult task to accomplish thoroughly. Systemic poisons are effective without such a painstaking application procedure.

Mealybugs

Mealybugs are oval shaped insects which are normally 1/8 to 1/4 inch long with discernible transverse lines across the back. Long tailed varieties have hairlike projections of up to 1/2 inch at the rear while some varieties have no easily observed tail. The body color of white to whitish-grey is imparted by a waxy powder that covers the soft body. Mealybugs are much like aphids in their feeding mechanism and the honey-like substance which they excrete. Mobility is not swift but is easily observed once the pests decide to move. Very young mealybug nymphs tend to be slightly

A more developed mealybug "crawler" with numerous new nymphs near the leaf mid-vein and leaf edges.

flesh colored because the waxy powder covering their back is thinner. Most mealybug species deposit eggs in a cottony sac which they usually leave in a leaf axis or the forks of branches. This cottony sac is often the most immediately recognizable indication that an infestation has begun. Long tailed mealybugs give birth to living nymphs and leave no egg sac. Mealybugs are easiest to kill when they are young and lack the protective powdery coat.

Some types of mealybugs can occasionally become serious pests on plant roots. Outbreaks may be far advanced before the small cottony egg sacs are discovered on roots. Slow plant growth and foliar chlorosis, while also indicative of many other disorders, should alert growers to suspect root mealybugs.

While mealybugs are related to aphids and feed in a similar manner, their control is generally more difficult. Most applications of contact insecticides will have little effect because of the covering which protects the various stages. Appropriate systemics are much more effective. Oil sprays which cover the egg sacks and cause suffocation of the contents are also effective but must be applied carefully to achieve full coverage. The active nymph stage is when mealybugs seem to be both most susceptible to the effects of chemical treatment and most accessible to physical contact by the agent utilized.

Nematodes

Plant nematodes probably are a greater pest than is commonly realized. They often go undetected in the soil or plant tissue which they inhabit and thus the effects of their parasitic action are either not realized or are ascribed to other factors. Nematodes are generally microscopic to slightly visible to the naked eye; a lack of pigmentation in their wormlike body further reduces visibility. Adults in some species lose their wormlike appearance and develop a saclike or spherical shape.

Nematodes which feed on roots are more common but foliar nematodes can sometimes become a problem. Those species which invade plant tissue lay eggs in the tissue or retain the eggs within the body. In either case, plant tissue can become a major cause of nematode transmission.

The salivary secretions produced as nematodes feed may cause abnormal cellular growths or distorted tissue on plants. If soil nematodes are known to be a significant problem they can be eliminated by a preplanting soil sterilization or fumigation. Various chemical pesticides applied as soil drenches may be used after planting to clear up infestations. If the nematode species is known to invade plant tissue, it will be necessary to use a systemic poison; preferably one which enters through the root system. Nematodes can be eliminated from indoor or outdoor production areas through chemical or heat treatment of soils prior to planting crops.

Obvious visual symptoms of nematode infestation are often lacking, especially when roots are the object of attack. Most often plants will exhibit poor growth, yellowing of foliage, and leaf drop. Wilting of plants even when sufficient moisture is available may occur. All these symptoms can be easily confused with those caused by root rot or soil fertilizer and soluble salt imbalances. On the roots, nematodes may cause various galls and lesions which can be easily confused with damage caused by other pathogens or even with the nodules produced by nitrogen fixing bacteria.

Snails and slugs

Snails and slugs are related to common aquatic animals such as oysters and clams. Eradication programs aimed at insects have little effect on snails and slugs because the metabolism of the 2 groups of animals is considerably different. Everyone is familiar with the physical appearance of snails. Slugs exhibit much the same soft, slimy body shape but have no shell; their length is usually 1/2-1 1/2 inches but large ones up to 4 inches are sometimes found. The eggs of snails and slugs are roundish, more or less colorless, and gelatinous. They are often found as clusters in moist areas, especially underneath pots or even in the soil (sometimes being mistaken for the moisture filled capsules of long lasting fertilizers). Slugs and snails damage plants by chewing. They prefer dark, moist areas and are active mainly at night and early morning. Slugs may be detected by shiny trails of slime they leave behind when crawling over benches and plant tissue. Maintaining dry floors and benches in greenhouses will inhibit slug and snail populations greatly, as will eliminating vegetation from the outside perimeter of structures. Watering early in the day outdoors will help to eliminate the moist conditions these pests prefer. Old flats and stacked pots are a major source of infestation. They should all be carefully cleaned before reuse. Slugs and snails, particularly in moist climates, may become major pests, mainly because of the cosmetic damage which their slime trails and chewing cause on adult plants and because of the extremely severe damage even a single individual can cause by devouring and disfiguring hundreds of seedlings in a single night. Significant lasting damage to plants is unusual unless large infestations occur.

Scale

Scale insects are represented by several groups which vary somewhat in their color, life cycle, and type of shell. All groups are distinguishable, however, by the turtle-like shell which covers the immobile female as she lays eggs or gives birth to living young. Scale insects are often divided into hard-shelled and soft-shelled groups. Depending on the species, shells may be round, oval, or oyster shell shaped and the outer texture may be smooth or rough. Shell color varies but brown and gray are common. The size of shells is commonly in the range of 1/8 inch but may be up to 1/4 inch.

The nymph (crawler stage) is produced through live birth or eggs and is sluggishly mobile and naked; as with mealybugs, this is the stage most

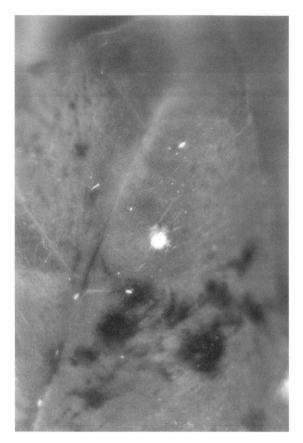

The black, sooty mold which often starts growing on excrement left on plant tissue by aphids, whiteflies, mealybugs, and scale insects. Here the offending insect was mealybug.

susceptible to control through pesticide use. Crawlers move about until they insert their sucking mouth parts and then begin to form a shell. Many scale insects excrete honey-like substances in the same manner as aphids and mealybugs but some do not. Shells are commonly found attached to mature plant stems but are also present on leaves. The number of shells may be few but in advanced infestations shells can cover the stem completely. The adherence of old shells to the plant even after elimination of the insects makes it imperative to control scale early. Customers will not accept plants with shells attached even if there are no live insects present. Control of scale is difficult because only the short lived crawler stage is susceptible to contact insecticides.

Dormant plants outdoors are often treated successfully with oil sprays before leafing out occurs. This treatment causes suffocation of the scale insects. Some newer oil spray formulations allow spraying to be done while plants are in leaf. The latter formulations may also be utilized on greenhouse plants if the label allows.

Thrips

These small (about 1/16 inch or less), slender insects were once only a significant problem outdoors.

In the last several years they have become the major greenhouse pest in many areas of the United States. There are several species but the Western flower thrips seems to be the predominant offender at the present time. It has migrated from its initial home in California to cover the country and along the way has developed a good deal of resistance to some of the insecticides which offered good control previously. Some species of thrips prefer succulent leaf tissue while others primarily affect flowers.

Thrips are highly mobile in both the larval and adult stage. In addition to running and jumping, adult thrips can fly weakly. Their wings are fringed at the edges and may be lacking altogether at times. Thrips are not easy to detect with the naked eye but, once located, their characteristic mobility makes a hand lens unnecessary in most cases. Color varies from more or less colorless to yellowish to dark brown.

The tissue where thrips have been feeding on flowers begins to appear colorless while areas of affected leaf tissue will display a silvery gray color. Dark fecal deposits may be noticed when infestations are heavy. Distortions of buds, flowers, and leaves are frequent in later stages of attacks by thrips as the young plant tissue which was injured fails to develop properly. Although thrips cause considerable direct damage to greenhouse crops, their most objectionable attribute is the fact they are a major transmission agent for impatiens necrotic spot virus and tomato spotted wilt virus. These viruses (despite their rather specific names) infect a large number of greenhouse crops, and they have no definitive cure other than the disposal of infected plants along with elimination of thrips in the greenhouse.

Thrips larvae may burrow under the soil surface to pupate or pupation can take place on the host plant. Good control of thrips is difficult unless stages in soil, or other locations such as moss on greenhouse floors or walls are killed. Thrips may even overwinter in cracks and crevices. Once control is achieved, it is important to prevent entry from outdoor plants since thrips are common agricultural and grassland pests. Special fine mesh greenhouse screens are available to cover all entry points by which thrips might gain access to the greenhouse. The range of crops which thrips attack is very wide and infestations can spread rapidly from one plant species to another.

Even when precautions are taken to deny entry, reinfection of the greenhouse most often gradually occurs because survivors in soil and greenhouse floors can seldom be completely eliminated. During colder winter weather, when thrips are quiescent, growers may feel that these pests have been eliminated, only to find that the hot, dry conditions of summer (which thrips prefer) produce a population explosion. Once thrips have been detected in the greenhouse, control programs for the overwintering populations must be continued for at least one year after the last summer infestation has been noted.

Whiteflies

Whiteflies are probably the most easily recognized insect pest because of their pure white color which distinguishes them immediately. Adults are approximately 1/16 inch long and will fly vigorously for short distances when disturbed from their usual resting place on the undersides of leaves. Tomatoes, lantanas, fuchsias, and poinsettias are particularly susceptible to whitefly infestation. Although many other species are troubled by whitefly, the above 4 should be inspected exceptionally carefully when new plants are being introduced into the greenhouse. Many growers ship in large numbers of poinsettia cuttings each fall for Christmas marketing. Whiteflies may be introduced on a broad scale with this crop unless suppliers are warned that no infested plants will be tolerated.

Whiteflies damage plants with their sucking mouth parts in much the same manner as do aphids, mealybugs, and scale insects. Excretion of a honey-like substance with the resultant growth of a black sooty mold is also similar. Evidence of whiteflies may be gained by the presence of whitish, round egg chambers attached to the undersides of leaves. These chambers are no larger than a pinhead and may contain eggs or be merely the remains left after crawlers have hatched and moved on. Extreme infestations will be characterized by the black mold mentioned previously. Crawlers are small, greenish, and flattened and are seldom observed unless one pays particular attention. They resemble scale crawlers to a large degree. Adults are easily killed by a number of insecticides but younger stages are difficult to eliminate without resort to specific formulations which kill all stages. The egg chambers are especially difficult to penetrate with conventional pesticides.

Effective control of whiteflies has been difficult for many growers. Prevention is the most successful course since whiteflies can normally be easily spotted on incoming plant material. Ruthless rejection of infested plants will usually prevent any major outbreaks. Leftover plants of susceptible species such as poinsettias and tomatoes should be discarded at the end of a crop cycle so little possibility of whitefly carry over to the next crop is likely.

Whiteflies may become major agricultural pests. Since many propagators of ornamental material are located near extensive fields of cotton, melons, and other susceptible species, control in the greenhouse or outdoor nurseries becomes very difficult.

The appearance of the sweetpotato whitefly as a major horticultural pest has magnified the difficulty of control. These pests are often difficult to distinguish from regular whiteflies and some races show little response to traditional whitefly control methods.

Miscellaneous pests

The insect order includes over one million species. This fact illustrates the variety of pests which a container grower might encounter. Fortunately only a tiny fraction of this vast host are ever found in a specific growing area and even a lesser number are considered damaging to plants or objectionable to consumers. The fore going descriptions have dealt with the major troublemakers found on ornamentals in North America. Brief mention is now made of some minor or infrequently troublesome pests.

Grasshoppers - May inflict major damage to outdoor crops during years when grasshopper plagues occur, at other times they are only a nuisance. Adults are easily controlled with common pesticides but treatment must include a considerable area around the growing ground to prevent immediate reinfestation.

Spittle bug - Recognized by a frothy spit-like secretion on stems or in leaf axils. Seldom dangerous to plants but objectionable to customers.

Leafhoppers - Easily recognized by the hopping method of movement.

Ants - May destroy small seedlings but the major damage is caused by helping to transmit both diseases and other pests from plant to plant.

Sow bugs and pill bugs - These rolly-pollies do not generally cause serious damage to plants since they feed mainly on dead organic matter. However, major infestations may lead to destruction of roots. The major objection to sow bugs and pill bugs is their habit of tunneling into soil at the bottom holes of containers and hiding under containers. Consumers dislike finding these pests each time a pot is moved.

Earwigs - Will damage any plant tissue but are especially fond of buds and fruit. Troublesome in summer, most invasions occur from old weed or debris piles. Excessive numbers can even lead to painful bites on employees.

Leaf rollers - Moth larvae which roll themselves up in leaves to pupate. Generally serious only outdoors in the summer. Large populations can damage the appearance of trees and shrubs.

PLANT DISEASES

The term "plant disease" has traditionally included those disorders which are caused by organisms known as viruses, bacteria, and fungi. Chemical control programs for plant diseases are not generally so well developed and not so numerous or effective as are those available for control of insect pests. The lack of control measures is due in part to the extreme resistance of certain life stages of these diseases and in part to the microscopic size of most organisms causing disease. Even though plant losses due to diseases may outstrip those caused by insects, the lack of a visible agent tends to cut down on the research applied to develop control techniques.

The following discussion concentrates upon providing a general view of disease organism classes rather than descriptions of specific organisms. Their extremely small size and the large number of species which are indistinguishable to observers who lack special equipment, information, and training makes detailed description of the organisms pointless for the average grower.

Viruses

Viruses are the smallest of disease causing agents (submicroscopic) and are chemically similar in composition to the genetic material contained in plant cells. The diseases caused by viruses may occur because their similarity to plant genetic material creates confusing signals for the direction of cell processes. No effective chemical means of controlling viral diseases exist and once plants are infected they should be removed from the growing area. The spread of viral diseases is predominantly through the feeding of juice sucking insects which insert their contaminated mouth parts into plant cells. Some viruses can be spread by the contact afforded when plants are pinched, disbudded, and propagated.

Plants seldom outgrow or overcome a viral infection but the effects may become masked for periods of time, thus giving the appearance of a cure. This apparent cure or "sleeping" of the virus in many plant varieties leads the grower to propagate vegetatively from infected plants and eventually spread the disease more widely. Virus indexing is a method devised to uncover the presence of specific viruses in plants which show no external symptoms. After special cultural and propagation techniques are performed upon the plant to be tested, it is exposed to special indicator varieties which are known to display prominent visual symptoms of the disease in question. Since the virus itself is microscopically undetectable, the gross, visually apparent symptoms which appear on indicator plants are indispensable for diagnosis. If no symptoms appear in the indicator varieties, the plant tested is declared free of the particular virus to which the Indicator variety is susceptible.

The use of virus indexed plants for vegetative reproduction is an important method of preventing the spread of viral diseases. Specialist propagators offer these indexed plants at very reasonable cost for growers to either use as mother plants or to actually finish as a crop. Most plants distributed for crop finishing are not the actual plant tested to be virus free but are offspring taken from the mother plant under stringent conditions to prevent reinfection.

Growers should take advantage of virus indexed stock whenever it is available. For a cost of only a few cents per plant, these costly diseases can be virtually eliminated as a risk factor. One of the main reasons why vegetatively propagated geraniums are making great strides in popularity at the present time is the near universal use of virus indexed cuttings. It is extremely important to utilize CVI (certified virus index) stock for trees, shrubs, and perennials since consumers will lavish considerable care and expense over long periods of time on these plants. Not all species are available as CVI stock but most of the important ones have been indexed.

Although there are exceptions, viral diseases are seldom transmitted from one generation to the next through seeds. Growers should take this advantage into consideration when deciding whether to propagate by seed or cuttings when a choice exists.

The symptoms of viral infection are varied. Stunting or dwarfing of the plant is one of the most common manifestations. Changes in leaf shape and color are striking evidence of virus activity. Leaves are usually affected in localized areas of mosaics, streaks, or blotches with light green, yellow, or white colors replacing the normal green color. Leaf shape may be puckered or stretched in appearance. Flowers may show many similar symptoms and sometimes revert to a semi-leafy structure. Every horticulturist who has grown roses has undoubtedly seen the characteristic puckering and distinct yellow blotching or streaking in leaves caused by mosaic virus of roses. Although this disease is aggressively combated by propagators, it has not been possible to completely eradicate it from even the most conscientious growing programs.

Bacteria

Bacteria are larger than viruses but still very small. Control by chemical means is difficult for most bacteria but some bactericides are available. Bacteria are often spread by water and can be present in soil. Proper sanitation and selection of disease free plants are the keys to preventing bacterial blights. Important diseases caused by bacteria are bacterial wilt of carnations; bacterial stem rot of various crops, especially geraniums; soft rot of cuttings and bulbs; crown gall, especially on geraniums, roses, and chrysanthemums; bacterial leaf spots of geranium and English ivy; and fasciation of chrysanthemum, geranium, and carnations stems. Numerous bacterial leaf spots affect various foliage plant crops. Plant stock free from bacterial infections may be obtained by purchasing culture indexed material. In this program, cuttings or mother plants treated and declared to be free of particular bacterial or fungal diseases have been carefully evaluated by removing sections of tissue from various portions of the parent plant and then culturing these sections in a sterile nutrient agar medium. Any sign of target bacterial or fungal species growth in the agar disqualifies the plant that the tissue was taken from for culture indexing.

Fungi

Fungi are lower plant forms which range in size from only a few cells to very large mushrooms. They are devoid of chlorophyll and must obtain their nourishment from dead or living organic matter. Those forms which derive their nourishment from living plants are the subject of present discussion. Fungi produce threadlike filaments called "hyphae" which when grouped together form a "mycelium". More developed fungi, such as mushrooms, may develop several distinct tissues, but lower forms, characterized by bread mold and powdery mildew, are little more than a collection of hyphae. Fungi reproduce vegetatively sometimes when the mycelium breaks into pieces, but the sexual production of spores (analogous to seeds in higher plants) is more common. Transmission of fungal diseases is by wind-borne spores or by water and contact transport of spores and mycelia. Mycelia and some forms of spores die readily if environmental conditions are not favorable but certain types of spores are extremely resistant to adverse conditions and can cause reinfection after it appears an outbreak of disease has been cleared up.

Chemical control of fungi is more advanced than for viruses and bacteria but not so well developed as for insects. Much chemical disease control is aimed at prevention, particularly with regard to soil borne fungi. Post infection treatment is often futile because early stages of diseases go unnoticed and plants are severely damaged when visual symptoms appear. Preventive soil drenches composed of two or more compatible fungicides are often used since one formulation rarely controls the full range of harmful soil fungi.

Powdery mildew, which is caused by several varieties of fungi attacks numerous commercial plants. Almost everyone has observed the familiar white to slightly grey mycelia of powdery mildew on the upper or lower leaf surface of garden roses. Stems and flowers may become affected in serious outbreaks of the disease. Infected leaves and growing tips can become severely distorted in addition to being covered with mildew. Chemical control of powdery mildew is impossible if greenhouse conditions are maintained which promote rapid growth of disease organisms. Powdery mildew flourishes when relative humidity is high.

In the greenhouse, lowering humidity through ventilation and the application of night heat is the best way to bring this disease within possibility of control by chemical means. Repeated trouble with serious

The white areas on these rose leaves are the vegetative phase of powdery mildew. Advanced cases quickly lead to permanent disfigurement and injury of the affected parts and reduced vigor of the entire plant.

infections of powdery mildew should cause growers to carefully evaluate their ventilation and heating practices.

A combination of warm days and cool nights is perfect for mildew growth on outdoor plants. Little can be done to alter humidity in the open air except to irrigate early in the day so that excess moisture is burned off before the temperature drops at night. Relative humidity increases as air temperature decreases because cool air holds more moisture than warm air, thus a film of moisture forms on plant surfaces. This moisture allows rapid growth of powdery mildew.

Roses are a major crop which is particularly susceptible to mildew. If a close watch for this disease is not practiced, the entire crop can be ruined in a few days. Preventive sprays with a triforine based or copper based fungicide every week will normally provide adequate control.

Botrytis or grey mold is a serious greenhouse and nursery disease particularly in those areas where high humidity prevails. The disease most often attacks leaves and flowers but can affect stems. Botrytis outbreaks on flowers are particularly disheartening because a crop has been nurtured along patiently only to be destroyed at the last minute. The course of the disease may proceed with amazing speed when conditions are favorable. Growers unfamiliar with visual symptoms may suffer severe crop losses before the problem is diagnosed and remedial action can be taken. The practice of bringing poinsettias into bloom for early sales and then lowering temperatures to retard development and save on fuel has led to more than a few serious losses from botrytis. The increased humidity brought about by lower temperatures provides ideal conditions for botrytis development.

Botrytis is recognized usually by a brownish or greyish, water soaked appearance of affected tissue. Flowers, petals in particular, may appear transparent when held to the light. Grey mold eventually covers the rotted areas if high humidity persists. Evidence of botrytis on red poinsettia bracts appears as sunken tissue which has a purplish-black color. Similar symptoms may appear on red poinsettias if soluble salts are high or if plants suffer from lack of water; in these cases, damage is usually confined more to the edges and tips of bracts.

Environmental control of humidity as practiced for mildew is also the chief means of preventing outbreaks of botrytis.

Several fungal diseases attack the roots and lower stems of plants. Control of these diseases is primarily a matter of managing the soil environment and of practicing good soil and plant sanitation. Soils which allow good drainage and air circulation will help prevent extensive damage from these organisms. The spread of these diseases is primarily through contaminated soil particles, water droplets, plant tissue, or utensils.

Damping off disease and stem rot are both caused primarily by fungi in the genus *Rhizoctonia*. Damping off causes young seedlings to fall over because stem tissue at the soil line has rotted. Stem rot due to *Rhizoctonia* has a dry, brown appearance while stem rots caused by *Thielaviopsis* are dry and black. Root rot is primarily caused by *Pythium* which also is responsible for blackleg of geraniums. *Fusarium* and *Phytophthora* are other genera of fungi which often cause rots.

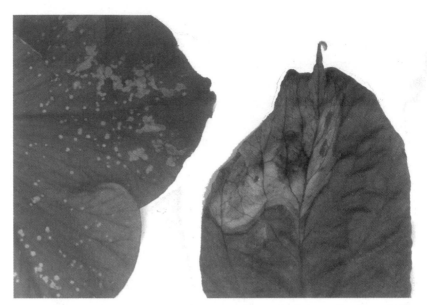

Damage caused by botrytis fungi on petunia petals (left) and poinsettia bracts (right). The "gray mold" from which the disease takes its common name is not evident here and is most often not noticed except under specific circumstances.

Plants affected by root rots show varying degrees of root loss. Severely infected plants, even if mature, will have a very weak or practically nonexistent root system. Healthy white roots are few in number or absent. This condition can mirror similar symptoms produced by high soluble salts in the soil or by ammonium toxicity.

Since root and stem rots may be caused by several different organisms, it is generally best to administer soil drenches composed of compatible chemicals which will control all important fungi likely to be involved. The layman would generally lack the background and instruments necessary to definitely identify the fungus responsible for damage. Lately, easy to use kits have become available for use in detecting and distinguishing some major fungi. These kits can aid the grower in choosing a particular curative treatment. Certain plant varieties may exhibit a sudden severe wilting condition when root or stem rots have progressed to a critical stage. Poinsettias are particularly prone to this phenomenon. Since transmission of damping off and root and stem rots depends heavily on contaminated soil particles and water droplets, it is very important to remove infected plants immediately.

Although soft stemmed plants are generally more susceptible to the ravages of bacteria and fungi, numerous diseases of woody plants are

Wilting of the poinsettia on the left is caused by rot of either the roots or main stem. Rapid collapse is most probably caused by stem disease while a slower progression of symptoms over the entire plant is likely due to root rot.

also caused by these agents. Everyone has heard of "Dutch Elm Disease" and the "Vinifera" disease of grapes.

The fungal diseases just described are the more important and widespread but growers should be alert to possible damage from less common diseases. Various other leaf spots, mildews, wilts, rusts, stunts, and cankers can at times become a problem. Broad spectrum chemical control programs aimed at the major offenders will often also reduce damage due to the more exotic diseases.

PREVENTIVE CONTROL OF DISEASES

Since effective post infection treatments are often lacking, control of plant diseases is primarily aimed towards preventive measures. Visual detection of the actual disease organisms or early stage symptoms of disease in plants is usually difficult. Thus plants are often severely infected before a problem is evident. This fact also limits the effectiveness of remedial measures.

Virus and culture indexing of mother plants and good housekeeping measures will greatly reduce the need for future chemical disease control measures. A clean, organized operation without plant debris lying about or weeds growing inside or out is an absolute necessity for the success of any disease control program.

Old pots and containers are major sources of disease. If containers are used again, they must be sterilized. Growers should analyze whether pot recycling is economical; it is questionable if the labor required to sterilize small plastic pots can be justified on an economic basis alone. Potting tables and greenhouse benches should be periodically sterilized. All tools and containers used in propagation must be sterilized. Cleanliness is more important than ever in the propagation process. Common household bleach (5.25% sodium hypochlorite) in a1-to-10 dilution with water can be used as a sterilant. Other commercially available sterilants labeled for horticultural use are preferred since household bleach is not cleared for this application by environmental agencies.

People working in the greenhouse or nursery must be alerted to common sense rules of cleanliness which can reduce the incidence of disease considerably. Soil from the floor or outdoors is almost certainly contaminated with disease organisms, and it should never be allowed on benches or growing areas. Hose ends and shoe soles are obvious means of transport for infected soil to plant areas. Whenever plant cleanup work, pruning, or disbudding and pinching are done, all plant tissue should be gathered up rather than left in the greenhouse or nursery area. Crop residues and unsalable plants must be removed immediately after the last good plant is gone. Reject plants are the ones most likely to be disease carriers since they are often smaller or have other objectionable characteristics associated with disorders caused by disease organisms.

Some aspects of chemical disease control have already been discussed. Treatment is almost always done on a preventive basis since plants which exhibit obvious visual symptoms are often beyond saving from an economic point of view.

In light of recent regulations concerning pesticide runoff from horticultural operations, growers may wish to reevaluate their use of fungicide drenches on plants. This is a prime source of heavy volume contamination which will often prove difficult to recycle in an effective manner. Less reliance upon these chemical means of control would be necessary if one is to reduce the risk of environmental contamination. Newer biologically active formulations for soil disease prevention are slowly appearing on the market.

They will be a welcome addition to the grower's arsenal if they prove consistently effective on a commercial basis.

Some mention has been made previously concerning controlling disease by manipulating environmental factors. The most frequent strategy is to eliminate excessive relative humidity, condensation, and standing water on growing areas, floors, or benches. Many diseases grow and reproduce more quickly in moist situations. Ventilation and adequate night heat with constant air circulation are the chief means of reducing humidity. When greenhouses are being closed for the night, humidity can be reduced by allowing ventilation to continue for a few minutes after the heat comes on. Constant air circulation at night removes high humidity from the microenvironment around leaves and stems. Watering should always be done before afternoon so that growing areas are dry by evening. Certain disease organisms flourish at particular temperatures. However, no universal temperature regime is effective against the majority of diseases. Soil pH can sometimes be used to control particular pathogens. *Thielaviopsis* is seldom a problem when soil pH is lower than approximately 4.5 to 5.0. Good soil aeration brought about by soils with large particle sizes and by proper watering practices reduces disease damage which is due to water logged soils.

Other than good housekeeping measures, media sterilization is the most practical means of assuring diseases are controlled in the root zone. This objective can be realized without the use of environmentally hazardous chemicals although, in certain cases, chemicals are sometimes also used for this purpose.

Soil pasteurization and fumigation provide a disease free medium for plants to grow in. In certain cases the media or media ingredients chosen will be clean enough so that pasteurization or fumigation are not considered economically necessary. Clean sphagnum peat, vermiculite, perlite, rock wool, and other materials sometimes are so nearly free of disease organisms that crops grown in mixes made from these ingredients show no appreciable adverse disease symptoms. However, no media or media ingredient should be automatically considered disease free until it has been proven so by careful analysis and testing.

Those growers whose operations are small or lack appropriate equipment for media sterilization may find that this process simply is not economical for them. In this case the cleanest ingredients available should be chosen to reduce soil diseases to the lowest point possible under the circumstances.

If one finds that the soil mix being used results in negligible losses due to stem and root rots, there would be little incentive to pasteurize or fumigate. Each grower must balance the losses suffered from disease organisms with the considerable cost of treating soils. Any grower using natural field soils in the planting mix should certainly consider treating it.

Steam is the preferred method for treating soils if there is an available source but many smaller establishments must rely on chemical fumigants since they lack the equipment for steam generation. Soil treated with chemical fumigants must be allowed to air out prior to planting. Because fumigants are dangerous to both humans and plants, soil treatment should not take place in greenhouses. Chloropicrin (tear gas), formaldehyde, methyl bromide, and "Vapam" (sodium methyldithiocarbamate) are common chemicals used for soil fumigation. Methyl bromide is perhaps the handiest to use since it has the shortest aeration period and can be used in greenhouses containing plants but it is extremely hazardous to humans and, at the present time, its use is very likely to be banned in the near future. Aeration periods of soil fumigants can vary with soil characteristics, temperature, and moisture content. The recommendations of the chemical manufacturer should be carefully followed concerning the length of aeration periods.

Steam sterilization of media is a rather involved process if it is to be done in the most effective manner. Appropriate literature sources should be consulted if design and operation of a steam sterilization process is intended. Steam sterilization can lead to certain changes in media chemistry which should be thoroughly understood before crops are grown in such media.

Small electric oven type devices are sold in which media can be heat treated. This type of heat treatment is not the same as steam treatment and the manufacturer's directions should be followed closely.

The extreme importance of utilizing disease free planting stock has already been alluded to in several earlier sections of this chapter. Preventive control measures will prove useless if growers fail to take appropriate action on this matter. Along with good housekeeping, it is the least expensive means available for reducing the incidence of diseases and neither carries any possible environmental liability.

SAFE USE OF PESTICIDES, FUNGICIDES, AND HERBICIDES

Growers must realize that pesticides, fungicides, and herbicides are chemicals designed to interfere with the life processes of various organisms and many of the chemicals are also poisonous to mammalian metabolic systems. Careless use of these chemicals can result in tragic consequences which could have easily been avoided. Toxicity to humans may be immediate or evidenced only after a long period of accumulated exposure. All pesticides should be handled as potentially life threatening substances; this action will instill a habit of caution in the individual even though some compounds are relatively harmless to humans. Although contact with pesticides does carry some risk, the degree of that risk is relatively low in comparison to numerous other everyday activities. In 1987, actual studies showed that the level of accidental death associated with bicycling, swimming, power mowers, skiing, hunting, home appliances, and general aviation was greater than with pesticides. In fact, pesticides ranked number 28 in a list of 30 risk categories. Chemical application should be delegated only to responsible personnel who have been adequately trained to do the job safely. Failure of employees to follow the common sense safety rules should result in an immediate reprimand with further infractions being followed by suspension. Misuse of poisons is simply too serious a matter to let slide.

Pesticides should be stored in a well ventilated, locked storage area where extremes of temperature do not prevail. Excluding sunlight from windows will result in a longer shelf life for some compounds. The contents of the room or cabinet must be prominently advertised with warning signs. Periodic inspections of the storage area will insure that all labels are intact and no spills have occurred. Labels are very important to safe, effective pesticide use. The words "Danger-Poison" and the skull and cross bones symbol are required on the labels of all highly toxic compounds. The word "Warning" is required on the labels of all moderately toxic compounds. The word "Caution" is required on labels of slightly toxic compounds. Containers with no label should be discarded. In most cases it is against the law to store pesticides in any container other than the original one. Pesticides stored in familiar looking household containers may be ingested by children or handled carelessly by nursery and greenhouse personnel. Chemicals may corrode containers not specifically intended for them. Table

---

Table 22
General pesticide safety rules.

---

1. Know and follow Environmental Protection Agency procedures for general application and for the pesticide you are using.
2. Read the label thoroughly and follow instructions.
3. From the label or from other sources, try to determine how toxic the poison is to man.
4. Store in a securely locked location which is prominently and correctly marked with signs.
5. Handle carefully, clean up spills immediately.
6. Do not mix pesticides where food stuffs or drinks may be prepared. Do not smoke while handling.
7. Always store pesticides in the original container with a readable label.
8. Always wear protective clothing and other necessary devices.
9. Check all equipment to make sure it is in safe operating condition.
10. Do not use more or less pesticide than necessary (as instructed on the label).
11. Dispose of containers, leftover pesticide, and rinse water in a responsible manner. The label, local health authorities, and Environmental Protection Agency will advise you of specific procedures.
12. Observe the recommended reentry and ventilation restrictions.
13. Rinse all application equipment three times and store in a safe place.
14. Wash yourself and clothing thoroughly after handling any pesticide.
15. Know the appropriate persons and institutions to contact in the event of an emergency.
16. Watch for any symptoms of illness or abnormal body functions during or shortly after pesticide use.
17. Be aware of possible environmental hazards associated with specific pesticides.
18. Do not mix pesticides together or with other substances unless specified.

---

22 lists some general rules for handling pesticides safely.

Although the toxicity of various pest control substances to humans is our main concern, growers should evaluate each product they use in relation to its effect on the total environment. Certain substances may possess little human toxicity but be particularly deadly to other life forms. Provisions must be made to limit unintentional environmental side effects which may occur when pesticides are employed. Repeated or careless usage of toxic substances can result in contamination of surrounding soils, plant life, and water supplies. Only the more dramatic side effects will usually be immediately apparent. Gradual long term deterioration of the environment is the more common scenario.

Common sense and caution are the most important ingredients in pesticide safety. Pointing nozzles away from the body at all times, not blowing out clogged nozzles or hoses with the mouth, and dispensing concentrated pesticides carefully without spilling would seem self-evident precautions, but they are routinely violated by careless personnel unless training programs are constantly repeated. Any employees who lack common sense and a proper regard for pesticides should never be allowed to handle them. Goggles and a respirator covering the mouth and nose are sufficient for applying low toxicity chemicals. With more toxic compounds a full face gas mask is recommended. Both respirators and gas masks are equipped with cartridges to filter fumes and particles from the air. Gas masks have a more complete filtering capacity than do respirators. Replacement of cartridges must be observed according to the manufacturers' recommendations if they are to be effective.

Application of pesticides should be accompanied by warning signs, when work is in progress and afterwards if warranted. If the property is left unattended, it should be locked. Pesticides and empty containers must be disposed of properly when they are no longer useful. Labels will contain disposal information but the local health service or county agent will have more detailed instructions concerning disposal sites.

Although the author and publisher have attempted to present responsible information concerning the control of various unwanted organisms, they will in no way be liable for the application or use of any chemical mentioned in this book. The accuracy and adequacy of information is not guaranteed and the author and publisher specifically recommends confirmation from other sources before chemicals are used. The information contained upon lawfully approved product labels and material data sheets (MDS) issued by the manufacturer should supercede all other sources of information concerning products. Environmental conditions may alter the activity of many chemicals and the susceptibility of organisms to them. To avoid plant damage, one should initiate experimental treatments before widespread use. In the event of suspected poisonings of humans by pesticides, a physician should be contacted immediately and remedial measures on the label followed. The container may be needed by the physician or treatment center. The local phone book will contain a number listed under "Poison Control Center" which can be called for emergency treatment information.

The application and handling of pesticides is controlled by national and state laws which are enforced by appropriate regulatory agencies. At the present time there is a good deal of activity and change taking place in both the lawmaking and regulatory areas. Growers would be well advised to consult periodically with local representatives of the Environmental Protection Agency (EPA) and state agricultural and environmental agencies in order to keep up with the latest developments in requirements. Growers are required by law to observe specific pesticide use procedures and to keep adequate records of their activities. Ignorance of the law concerning pesticide application is no defense. Every responsible person in a horticultural operation must be aware of the statutory requirements or face severe financial and personal risk of being held in violation of the various environmental laws which are in effect. Summaries of these laws can be obtained from the Environmental Protection Agency or from several suppliers of safety material. Understanding and meeting the requirements of all the regulations is not an easy job, but it is necessary in order to avoid running afoul of the law.

Several information sources in the greenhouse and nursery trades present growers with a list of chemical agents and the pests which they control. But detailed information concerning the human toxicity of these substances rarely accompanies the list. Our primary consideration when employing potentially dangerous chemical agents should be the safety of all persons who work in or visit the growing operation. Knowing something about the relative human toxicities of different chemicals can go a long way towards making a pest and disease control program safe for all concerned and it can considerably reduce the possibility of lawsuits arising from accidental poisonings.

The first thing to realize is that different insecticides and fungicides demonstrate a very wide range of human toxicity, from super toxic (where only slight exposure may result in death) to essentially nontoxic (no more dangerous than some common household food additives or personal hygiene products).

Although we normally consider the moderate use of common table salt to be safe, it is reported that oral ingestion of only 400 mg/kg of body weight can make some persons violently ill. If certain everyday substances are abused they can be as dangerous as some lower toxicity insecticides. The only way to assess the relative toxicity of different substances is to have reliable data at hand.

Scientists have conducted tests over the years concerning the inferred human toxicity of numerous substances. Of course, they have not administered these substances to humans in order to determine fatal doses; the amount necessary to cause death is estimated by testing actual populations of laboratory animals. The results are represented with the notation LD 50 (the lethal dosage for 50% of test animals expressed as milligrams of toxicant per kilogram of body weight). LD 50 for humans is then inferred from the animal LD 50. Although it is hard to picture exactly the relationship of absolute quantities involved in this expression, it does give us a good representation of the differences in relative toxicity between substances. Table 23 is a crude attempt to show the relationship between various ranges of LD 50 and the actual lethal quantities of orally ingested substance adjusted to a human body weight of 170 pounds.

Several important points should be made as we discuss the toxicity of various substances to human beings. Poisons can enter the human system through ingestion and inhalation or they can be absorbed through the skin. Oral ingestion generally requires less substance to produce fatal effects than does dermal absorption. But the reverse is occasionally true. Oxamyl is a good example of the first extreme (5-110 oral LD 50 as opposed to 2960 dermal LD 50) while tetradifon illustrates the latter case (5000 oral LD 50 as opposed to 1000 dermal LD 50).

The concept of LD 50 as we have been using it refers to single doses at a specific time. With certain toxic substances we may need to alter our conception of lethal dose because although the human body is able to

Table 23

Probable lethal quantities of orally ingested substances related to various human LD 50 ranges.*

EPA Category Meaning	LD 50 Range	EPA pesticide Label "Signal" Word	Quantity of Substance Ingested Orally
I. Highly Hazardous	0 to 50 mg.	Danger/Poison	A taste or a few drops to 1 teaspoon
II. Moderately Hazardous	50 to 500 mg.	Warning	1 teaspoon to 2 tablespoons
III. Slightly Hazardous	500 to 5000 mg.	Caution	1 ounce to 1 pint
IV. Relatively nonhazardous	5000 mg. or over	Caution	1 pint or more

* **Adjusted to human body weight of 170 lbs.**

   Refer to text for explanation of LD 50.

** **If category I products are assigned on the basis of oral, dermal, or inhalation toxicities, the word "Poison" (in red) and a skull and crossbones must appear.**

eliminate, or detoxify (over a period of time) most substances which enter it, some substances resist these processes and accumulate in the body through a number of exposures over time. Thus persons may be exposed to several nonlethal doses of a cumulative toxic substance and show no pronounced symptoms of illness until a critical amount of the substance accumulates in the body. With repeated exposure the LD 50 may be reached.

   The accumulation of toxic substances in the body should concern every person who works with them. If people are subject to regular long term exposure to toxic substances, they should be advised to request medical tests which monitor accumulation levels at their regular physical examinations. Many medical doctors may be unaware of the specific tests used but should be able to research the subject and prescribe a detection program. Doctors will not normally test for these types of accumulated substances unless they are advised of the patient's particular occupational hazards.

Anyone who handles potentially dangerous substances should be aware of the great variability in toxicity which can result from changes in the specific chemical formulation used. For example, regular diazinon has a reported oral LD 50 of 66 while an encapsulated form of diazinon (PT 65 Knox Out 2 FM) is reported to have an oral LD50 of 21000. Toxicity may vary not only with intentional alteration of the formulation but also as an unintentional side affect when different agricultural pesticides are mixed together to accomplish 2 or more jobs at once.

Pesticides are often formulated with various substances which act as carriers of the active ingredient. Petroleum solvents are commonly employed for this purpose. Exposure to these solvents can prove as dangerous as exposure to some of the lower toxicity active ingredients. Of the common organic solvents, toluene and xylene are generally considered as offering the greatest threat.

Table 24 presents the LD 50 toxicity classes for a number of frequently used chemicals. No attempt has been made at an exhaustive compilation; this is better left to reference texts dealing with the toxicology of agricultural chemicals.

These figures are collected from a number of sources and different authorities are not always in agreement concerning the exact LD 50 for a particular substance. When there is disagreement of substantial nature, a range of values is given. There may be many technical reasons for this variation. The fact that substantial variation exists should put a red flag out to growers. Even reportedly low toxicity substances must be handled with care since significant alteration of the LD 50 might be expected under certain circumstances.

Each grower should become aware of the reported human toxicity of substances used in pest control programs. This is an integral part of pesticide safety.

The term "pesticide hazard" is often used to describe the concept of pesticide accumulation, but it also refers to the quantitative potential for exposure due to any circumstance. For example, a highly toxic and

Table 24
Toxicity of common horticultural chemicals.

Trade or common name	EPA Toxicity Class	Relative toxicity	EPA signal word
Avid, abamectin	III	Slightly	Caution
chlordane	II	Moderately	Warning
diazinon	II, III	Moderately-	Warning-
(depends on formulation)		Slightly	Caution
DDT	III	Slightly	Caution
dieldrin	II	Moderately	Warning
Di Syston	I	Highly	Danger-Poison
Dursban, chlorpyrifos	II	Moderately	Warning
Guthion	I	Highly	Danger-Poison
Kelthane, dicofol	II, III	Moderately-	Warning-
(depends on formulation)		Slightly	Caution
Lannate, methomyl	I	Highly	Danger-Poison
lindane	II	Moderately	Warning
malathion	III	Slightly	Caution
Meta Systox-R oxydemethon-methyl	III	Slightly	Caution
naled	I	Highly	Danger-Poison
nicotine	I	Highly	Danger-Poison
Omite, propargite	I	Highly	Danger-Poison
Orthene, acephate	III	Slightly	Caution
oxamyl	I	Highly	Danger-Poison
parathion	I	Highly	Danger-Poison
Pentac, dienochlor	II	Moderately	Warning
Phosdrin	I	Highly	Danger-Poison
pyrethrin	III	Slightly	Caution
resmethrin	III	Slightly	Caution
rotenone	I, III	Highly	Danger-Poison
(depends on formulation)		Slightly	Caution
Sevin, carbaryl	II	Moderately	Warning

Table 24 (cont.)

Caution

Systox, demeton	I	Highly	Danger-Poison
Talstar	II	Moderately	Warning
Temik, aldicarb	I	Highly	Danger-Poison
Thimet	I	Highly	Danger-Posion
toxaphene	II	Moderately	Warning
Vapona, dichlorvos	I	Highly	Danger-Poison

Growth retardants

B-9, daminozide	III	Slightly	Caution
Cycocel, chlormequat	II	Moderately	Warning
A-Rest, ancymidol	III	Slightly	Caution
Bonzi	III	Slightly	Caution

Soil fumigants

Chloropicrin	I	Highly	Danger-Poison
methyl bromide	I	Highly	Danger-Poison
Vapam, metam-sodium,	II	Moderately	Warning

Herbicides

diquat	II	Moderately	Warning
paraquat	I	Highly	Danger-Poison
Roundup,glyphosate	II	Moderately	Warning
2, 4, 5-T	III	Slightly	Caution
2, 4 D	III	Slightly	Caution
simazine	III	Slightly	Caution

Rodenticide

coumafuryl	III	Slightly	Caution
warfarin	I, II, III	Highly,	Danger-Poison,
	(depends on formulation)	Moderately,	Warning,
		Slightly	Caution

Fungicides

Benlate, benomyl	III	Slightly	Caution
captan	II	Moderately	Warning
Terraclor, PCNB	III	Slightly	Caution
triforine	I	Highly toxic	Danger-Posion

Highly toxic 0-50 mg/kg oral
Moderately toxic 50-500 mg/kg oral
Slightly toxic 500-5000 mg/kg or more oral

} Classification may vary somewhat since data is compiled from several sources.

Table 24 (cont.)

LD 50- The lethal dosage for 50% of the test organisms expressed as mg/ kg (milligrams of toxicant per kilograms of body weight). Human toxicity is inferred from tests with rats. Exact parameters may vary with the data source.

Some of these chemicals, although cancelled for use in the United States, are still used in other parts of the world.

cumulative pesticide might be described as a negligible "pesticide hazard" if workers are carefully protected from exposure in addition to rarely having the opportunity for exposure (pesticide seldom applied).

PESTICIDE AND FUNGICIDE APPLICATION

Pesticides may be applied in several ways. The method will be dictated by many different criteria, most important of which are effectiveness, economy of labor and materials, possibility of crop damage, and safety to personnel. The criteria mentioned above may change dramatically for the same pesticide, depending on the method of application. As an example, many pesticides are available as either emulsifiable concentrates (EC) in a petroleum carrier or as wettable powders (WP) dispersible in water. Spraying with EC rather than WP formulations usually increases the risk of plant damage due mainly to the petroleum carrier but EC sprays are easier to apply because WP dispersions may clog sprayers and must be constantly agitated to maintain the dispersion.

High pressure sprays have been the most common means of pesticide application for many years. They are economical and effective. Good results hinge primarily upon achieving complete coverage of plant surfaces by having adequate pressure and proper nozzles to produce small droplet size and upon directing spray from several different angles. To prevent spray droplets from beading up on the often waxy surface of leaves, a spreader or surfactant is sometimes added to mixtures. Spreaders may cause plant damage with some pesticides, check the label. The pH of water used to mix pesticides can also have a significant effect upon results. Generally, a pH of 6.0-6.8 is a good range, although slightly higher or lower is suitable for most applications. Equipment should be checked regularly to make sure hoses have no weak spots and that on-off valves shut tightly automatically whenever positive hand pressure is not being applied. Motor or engine driven pumps should always be regulated by a pressure gauge. Tanks and lines must be cleaned immediately after use. Leftover spray must be safely disposed of to prevent accidents; in no case should it be saved for later.

Mist blowers are much the same as sprayers except that the pesticide is delivered to plant surfaces by dilution in a high speed airstream rather than by pressurized liquids. Droplet size is usually smaller in mist blowers than with sprays. Directing the mist to undersides of leaves may be difficult on crowded greenhouse benches because pesticides are often many times more concentrated than in spray mixtures; close misting between plants may cause damage due to the pesticide strength. Some mist-blower type application nozzles now possess a charging device which places an electrical charge upon the pesticide particles as they leave the orifice. This charge allows pesticide to be attracted to leaf surfaces (including the underside). Mist blowers can be used for applying insecticidal dusts.

Pesticide dusts are available for some formulations but use in the greenhouse is not widespread because of the visually objectionable residue left on ornamental plants. Dusts are usually a very safe application method from the standpoint of plant damage. Coverage is good on the top sides of leaves but dust is difficult to apply on the underside.

Pesticides are sometimes applied to the soil surface as granules or to the entire soil mass as liquid drenches. This type of application is particularly useful in the eradication of insects, such as fungus gnats, which reproduce primarily in the soil. Systemic soil insecticides not only kill susceptible insects in the soil but are absorbed by the roots and translocated to above ground tissue where chewing or sucking insects are poisoned. Application of pesticides to soil should not be made prior to pasteurization or handling by workers unless the label specifically recommends such treatment.

Certain methods of pesticide application are obviously more useful, cost effective, and safe when used in enclosed areas such as greenhouses. The exposure of large outside air masses to the effects of pesticide fogging seems almost ridiculous at our present state of awareness, but it has been practiced on a significant scale, especially by public health agencies.

Pesticide applicators must now take into account (much more so than in the past) the sensibilities of close neighbors and even those who reside at some distance from the application site. Application methods which allow chemical drift off the site are not acceptable.

Recent years have seen a large increase in the greenhouse application of pesticides as vaporized fogs. Ready made formulations are often quite expensive, but growers who take the trouble to mix their own concentrates can cut costs considerably. Pesticides diluted with petroleum carriers are injected into hot exhaust pipes or air streams to cause vaporization and, subsequently, a fog with exceedingly small droplet sizes. The fog penetrates to every nook and cranny in the greenhouse, but little effective pesticide residue is left once ventilation has taken place. Wind and leaks in the greenhouse covering will lessen the effectiveness of fogs. The great advantage of using fogging equipment is that it covers a large area in a few minutes.

Aerosol pesticide bombs function in much the same manner as fogging machines except that small pesticide droplets are carried by gases formed when pressurized liquid propellants are released. Aerosol bombs are expensive because of the packaging and carriers used. It is seldom that a medium or large sized operation would make use of aerosols for greenhouse wide application, less expensive methods would be available. The real benefit of aerosols lies in their handy use for localized infestations. Growers can grab an aerosol canister as they close up at night and treat small areas without time consuming mixing and cleaning. Very small greenhouses may find aerosols the most economical means of pest control because no elaborate preparations need be made before application and the convenient size will permit frequent purchase of fresh pesticide.

Smoke application of pesticides is very similar to that of fogs and aerosols but the carrier is a combustible material, which when ignited, distributes the pesticide with the resulting smoke. Smoke bombs are expensive but convenient for smaller growers. Canisters of material are placed at predetermined locations in the greenhouse and then ignited. Caution should be exercised to prevent accidental fires and to determine if the smoke bomb burned completely. Malfunctions sometimes cause the bomb to go out before combustion is complete and pest control is therefore limited. Application precautions and conditions are similar as for fogs and aerosols. The range of pesticides which can withstand the combustion process is limited. Plant damage is usually minimal because petroleum carriers are not used.

Methods of application for fungicides are comparable to those for pesticides. Soil drenches are the most commonly used methods since several major fungal diseases are soil borne. Complete production areas, especially indoors, are often sterilized before a new crop is moved in. This is a very effective means of reducing the amount of treatment necessary during later crop stages. Pesticides and fungicides must be compatible with one another if two or more are applied at the same time and they must be compatible with other cultural chemicals which may be in use. Check the container label for compatibility; if specific recommendations are not made, the material should not be applied at the same time or immediately before or after use of another chemical. Pesticides and fungicides should be purchased in quantities which will ensure usage within one year. Any material kept after this period should be inspected for signs of deterioration, especially if the container has been opened. Emulsifiable concentrates may show a tendency for separation of the components or may fail to produce a milky color when added to water if the material is too old. Container labels will sometimes indicate how long the pesticide can be stored. Diluted material often loses its effectiveness quickly.

Various diseases are often transmitted through recycling water and by the use of untreated pond or stream water. In addition to filtration, which was mentioned previously when discussing fertilizer runoff, these waters can be treated through ozonization or by ultra violet source exposure to virtually eliminate disease causing organisms and algae. Various chemical means of water treatment are available (chlorination for example). The precise method to be used will depend mainly upon cost and how it fits into cultural and physical aspects of the facility.

Fewer application mistakes will occur if a complete notebook is constructed which details the types and amounts of material to be used along with all other essential data needed for routine applications. This notebook also saves time which would be spent looking up data frequently.

PESTICIDE LAW AND COMPLIANCE

Every commercial or institutional horticulturist is now required by law in the United States to comply with numerous and often complex regulations if they use any of the products which are administered by the Environmental Protection Agency (EPA). Other countries of the world have similar agencies which serve the same purpose (some are more restrictive and encompassing, while others are less so).

Every state in the United States must uphold certain levels of environmental stewardship which meet or exceed the standards adopted by the EPA. There are certain states which have adopted more stringent regulations regarding specific environmental issues than has the EPA. As each state provides complete documentation of compliance with national standards, their individual environmental departments are basically allowed

---

Table 25
Summary of Worker Protection Standard requirements. This list is not complete. Refer to the full WPS document issued by the EPA.

1. **Posting of information:** EPA safety poster, nearest medical facility, facts concerning pesticide applications within 30 days.
2. **Pesticide safety training:** A certified applicator or WPS designated trainer must provide training for all employees within the first 5 days of employment and every 5 years thereafter. This training is to provide such information as pesticide toxicity categories, exposure methods, bodily entry routes, signs and symptoms of poisoning, emergency procedures, hazards from residues, clothing requirements, cleaning, eating and smoking rules, label interpretation, container disposal, and accidental spills.
3. **Notice of applications:** Workers must be notified of each application and the areas to be treated.
4. **Decontamination sites:** Where to find and how to use.
5. **Emergency assistance:** Who to contact, what to do, and transportation.
6. **Restrictions necessary:** During application and after, especially Restricted Entry Intervals (REI).
7. **Equipment safety:** Inspection, repair, cleaning, adjustment.
8. **Personal Protective Equipment (PPE):** Location, repair, cleaning, proper use.
9. **Workers rights:** Inform of right to know, where to obtain, and freedom from disciplinary action.
10. **Approved pesticide storage area:** Special dangers, restricted entry.

to oversee regular compliance programs in their state. The EPA still monitors the adequacy of such programs and may be called in to provide expertise, investigatory services, training services, and occasionally enforcement procedures in cases of extreme importance. Every state (at the time of publication) is now in charge of its own environmental program, but this status could change if the EPA finds, upon regular checkups, that a particular state is in violation of independent regulatory status.

Growers in each state should first contact their own state environmental agency for guidelines concerning how to comply with general regulations and to find which laws apply in specific instances. These state agencies can then inform growers as to whether there is any need to contact the EPA directly. Each state environmental agency may have a slightly different name, but they can all easily be found in a local phone book under state government listings.

Every state will provide copies of the basic environmental rules which apply, and they can supply educational and testing material to help growers meet the necessary standards. EPA also has numerous information packets in this regard, as do many horticultural safety firms.

It is the horticultural grower who has the responsibility of being aware of and of complying with all the laws which exist. Although you may receive periodic notices concerning particular aspects of environmental programs, the EPA and state agencies are under no obligation to provide notification of your need to set up and administer environmental compliance programs. You cannot use ignorance of the law to avoid penalties.

Although some of the specific environmental regulations may seem unnecessary or even ridiculous to growers, there is no doubt that some type of national environmental coordination is necessary. As population density in the United States increases, the potential hazards of pesticide use has increased manyfold. Almost no one would doubt the necessity of using pesticides wisely, but debate arises around issues concerning how much regulation is enough, who should administer the programs, how penalties and citations should be issued, and so on.

The author (as a practicing commercial grower) has suffered much inconvenience under the new environmental rules but can truthfully say that the changes in operation which have been faced are basically positive, and, for the most part, economically advantageous over the long run.

Growers will find that further emphasis upon environmental policies requires an increased level of knowledge concerning the subject. With this added information, growers often notice that pesticide usage declines while pest control is enhanced. Increased safety for nursery and greenhouse personnel (along with persons and other organisms in the neighborhood) are simply an added benefit, reducing financial risk of law suits and penalties.

Compliance procedures

It is not the purpose of this book to provide a detailed point-by-point rehash of all environmental laws (which, no doubt, run into thousands of pages). Our objective is to show growers how to deal with compliance in a practical manner which will drastically reduce (but not eliminate) the possibility of citation for violations. The author and publisher present the following summary as a helpful (but incomplete) guide so that growers may bring their premises into compliance with the main features of environmental law quickly (thereby lessening the possibility of costly violations). The author and publisher specifically make no claims as to the completeness or factual accuracy of the material presented; growers are obligated to check all features with individual research to confirm or reject each aspect of compliance procedure.

The first step growers must take is to become familiar with the laws and regulations by contacting their state environmental departments for all pertinent information. After becoming thoroughly knowledgeable about their obligations, the next required step will likely be to obtain the necessary licences required for applying (or supervising application of) pesticide, fungicide, and weed control substances. This process can consume a good deal of time, depending upon the educational and training program offered in your state and upon the complexity of certification procedures and testing. It is best to start early with this licensing process since the validity of further compliance programs depends upon the fact that the person responsible for implementation is legally qualified.

In the process of obtaining an application license, growers will become familiar with all the requirements necessary to comply with the EPA Worker Protection Standard (WPS). In addition, they will be exposed to a wide variety of books, posters, bulletins, videos, and other information which is available to aid growers. Perhaps the main problem a pesticide application and worker protection trainer will encounter is how to select

Cover of *Worker Protection Standard for Agricultural Pesticides* **issued by the Environmental Protection Agency.**

the most practical, economical, and effective information for presentation to greenhouse and nursery staff. It is important to provide thorough training to be sure each aspect of the Worker Protection Standard is fulfilled, but it is equally important to present material in a manner which does not confuse workers with needless detail. This can easily become the case unless the trainer limits presentations to essential material which can be easily remembered or accessed with little effort.

The WPS rules cover all workers (although self-employed owners and their families may face less stringent requirements under certain circumstances) who work with the cultivation and handling of crops. It also covers a second group of workers called "pesticide handlers" (anyone who takes part in pesticide application procedures).

The inspection process

Every grower dreads the inspection process which is an inevitability under current environmental law. If you haven't been inspected at least once previously, the future certainly holds one in store. Compliance with pesticide law cannot simply be left up to the good will of growers; there must be an enforcement process; it begins with an inspection by state or federal agents.

In almost every case, the agents who visit your property are trying to make the law work for everyone in society. They have not targeted your operation for harsh punishment action unless serious complaints have been lodged by third parties. In general, the inspection process is a routine affair to ascertain whether or not a growing operation is complying with the WPS or is making sufficient and speedy progress toward compliance. A detailed investigation of the entire facility is not normally conducted unless serious violations are uncovered, or if there have been complaints. Although most growers who have made a serious effort towards complete compliance with the WPS will find they have no immediately punishable violations to worry about, even a routine inspection will often cite specific details of your program which should be improved — you may even be officially warned of possible future punitive action unless certain recommendations are promptly followed.

Environmental inspections are perhaps best compared with audits by the Internal Revenue Service. Most are routine checkups intended to make sure important laws are being upheld. And most are conducted in a businesslike and unbiased manner by personnel who have "no axe to grind". Occasionally, however, either the inspector or the party being inspected allows personal prejudices and animosities to govern the process.

Growers should make sure they are not the party who poisons an otherwise routine inspection by displaying a hostile and uncooperative attitude. If it is the inspector who displays such behavior, the grower should remain calm and resolve all questions through designated appeal processes rather than through personal confrontation. Be sure you do not interpret a reserved, businesslike manner by the inspector to prejudice your behavior. The inspector is trained to be fair, concise, and businesslike; after all, they are in the serious business of law enforcement.

Once an inspection begins (the inspector is required to show identification and ask permission to enter), you should be cooperative in all aspects of the processes which you believe are covered under the law. Do not be overly friendly or suggestive; simply let the inspector do his or her job by requesting specific information. As in an IRS audit, it seldom pays to "volunteer" information before it is definitely requested. This type of "eager beaver" attitude can lead down paths which may bring to light violations which neither you or the inspector would have been aware of if you had kept quiet. When the inspection is over, make sure you understand all aspects of the completed report. If not, ask for explanations. Then, make sure you receive a signed copy.

There are some preparatory measures which can be taken to make an inspection proceed more quickly, smoothly, and with less chance of a citation being issued. First, be sure your facility meets WPS to the best of your understanding; every item in Table 26 should be fully addressed. Second, use Table 26 to anticipate other items which may be requested. You should always be able to produce each within a reasonable time interval, but it is much easier for all concerned if you have a complete file organized specifically for inspection purposes.

In addition to the suggestions in Table 26, there are a few common sense actions which can be taken to reduce the chances of a facility encountering environmental problems. They are: 1) Use no restricted use pesticides; 2) require all workers to use latex gloves while on duty; 3) fully inform all potential employees before hiring that pesticides are being used on the property and explain the safety precautions; 4) perform all pesticide-related tasks on the weekend when a minimum number of employees are present; 5) allow all pesticide odors to dissipate completely, if possible, before workers or customers re-enter the facility (even if this requires more time than the legal re-entry period; 6) be aware that pesticides are not the only substances covered by the WPS regulations; various solvents, fertilizers, cleaning compounds, herbicides, growth regulating chemicals, paints, etc., are also regulated.

COMMERCIAL PEST CONTROL SERVICES

After studying this chapter, many growers might ask, "Wouldn't it be easier to hire an expert to plan and execute a pest control program?" This is certainly a natural reaction to the complexity and uncertainty which accompanies this subject. In addition, hiring an expert might reduce the amount of time necessary for regualtory compliance.

Some larger growers do in fact contract pest control experts to service their facility. Often, they serve only in an advisory capacity, but, in a lesser

---

Table 26
Worker Protection Standard (WPS) inspection file information which will facilitate the inspection process.

---

1. Copy of valid pesticide application license or training certification.
2. List of general workers on premises, along with pesticide handlers. Include first date of employment.
3. Signed documentation by all workers concerning the date and details of training.
4. Outline and samples of all materials and information used in training.
5. List of applicators, trainers, or administrative personnel who are authorized to speak and act for the facility in regards to the inspection process.
6. List of all types and quantities of materials present in facility which fall under WPS regulation. Make special notice of restricted use pesticides.
7. Permanent records of all pesticide applications, crops covered, dates, rates, etc.
8. Written outline of pesticide preparation, application, and clean up procedures.
9. List of all common application rates for specific crops and conditions.
10. Material safety data sheets and product labels for all products on hand. They should be stored near labeled containers.
11. Written outline of disposal procedures.
12. Quantities, dates, and means of disposal.
13. Written outline of accidental spill procedures.
14. Dated records for inspection, clean up, and maintenance of personal protective gear and application equipment.

---

number of instances, they provide full service.

The main reason more greenhouses and nurseries do not hire out this task is cost. Finding a reputable firm which can *guarantee* at least an acceptable level of economical control is an even greater barrier. In addition, even though the experts might perform most of the WPS compliance functions, the owners of the facility are still the responsible party regarding violations, citations, and risk control.

Smaller nurseries and greenhouses are in an even more untenable situation. The value of their crops would seldom warrant the costs involved for regular help from pest control services.

As the situation rests at present, smaller growers generally must educate themselves through information available from books, articles, pesticide company literature, and government advisors, and then devise their own pesticide programs as carefully and effectively as possible.

COSTS OF PEST AND DISEASE CONTROL

Once a grower decides a definite pest or disease problem exists and begins formulating methods of solving it, he or she should become aware of the costs which will be involved. There are alternative choices which can be made and each one of them carries a different price tag. The objective is to devise a program which safely accomplishes the desired degree of control at the most economical price. Table 27 lists the cost factors which should be evaluated before choosing a particular combination of control measures.

Table 27

Factors which must be considered when determining the cost of particular pest control programs.

A. Actual implementation expenses of equipment, labor, materials, research.

B. The possibility of crop damage resulting from control measures.

C. Liability and environmental damage expenses which may result from control measures.

D. Proper training for employees.

E. Protective devices and facilities for employees.

F. Production time sacrificed when control programs are in use. New laws will probably increase this significantly.

G. Time spent evaluating effectiveness.

H. Related expenses necessary to maintain effectiveness—weed control in and around production facilities, general sanitary measures, plant quarantine precautions, purchase of indexed plant material, dumpage of infected material, etc.

I. Record keeping for regualtory agencies.

J. Disposal costs for containers, leftovers, spills.

Some of the factors listed are fairly obvious although a complete evaluation of them is performed by only a minority of growers. Several of the cost factors often receive little or no attention; liability risks, training costs, loss of production time, and evaluation of program effectiveness are the less obvious expenses which can easily be overlooked. If a careful analysis of all expenses which relate directly or indirectly to implementing an effective pest control program were instituted, the high cost would shock most managers.

The possibility of expensive liability claims should always be a prime economic consideration when analyzing control methods. Even a small settlement for injury or environmental cleanup could put many growers out of business. Does the nursery or greenhouse have insurance for this possibility? Pest control expenses should always be adequately represented in production cost models.

One factor which deserves special attention is that of evaluating program effectiveness. No matter what type of program is utilized, each specific step in the process should be carefully evaluated to make sure it is actually accomplishing the intended goals (and at what cost). Effectiveness will hopefully be recorded in numerical terms so that various components can be directly compared.

PLANT DISORDERS FROM POLLUTION

Strictly speaking, any of the environmental factors treated previously in this book could be considered pollutants if their presence were of a degree or nature to cause harm to plants. Topics which the general public would normally consider pollutants will now be discussed briefly. Dramatic plant losses due to pollution are not encountered frequently except in certain problem areas, but almost every grower has experienced at least one crop failure from this cause. Subtle reductions in crop yield are, however, all too common in many urbanized and industrial areas where smoggy conditions limit light intensity at certain times during the year.

Pollution generated by the operation of the greenhouse or nursery itself is more frequently the cause of plant damage than is pollution from outside sources. Natural gas leaks, inadequate venting of furnace burners, plant tissue respiration, weed killer residues, soil fumigant vapors, wood preservative and paint fumes, and equipment exhaust are all sources of potentially harmful materials to plants. Oxidation of carbon compounds, whether occurring naturally in the respiration of plant tissue or as combustion of fuels, produces ethylene and carbon monoxide, both of which can damage plants. Plants are sensitive to ethylene at much lower concentrations than they are to carbon monoxide. Ethylene can be produced in sufficient quantities by respiration in plant tissues to cause plant damage, if dissipation of the gas is restricted, as is the case when plants are shipped in closed boxes. Carbon monoxide liberated by respiration is not sufficient to cause problems. Fuel combustion in furnaces and gasoline motors generates large amounts of ethylene and carbon monoxide. All furnaces should be vented properly and vehicle engines turned off as they enter greenhouse buildings. Ethylene may be detected in the greenhouse by introducing young, vigorous tomato plants to suspected areas. If ethylene is present, it will cause leaves to grow downward as if they were wilted even though the tissue is still turgid. African marigolds are even more sensitive indicators.

The dangers of herbicide residues and fumes to plants have been discussed previously. If the growing operation has a shallow irrigation well, the possibility of water contamination with herbicides from adjacent properties should be considered. Growers must always keep alert to potential crop damaging chemical fumes or combustion by-products. The best policy is to keep all chemicals, paints, and fuels in an area separated from the growing area. All natural gas pipes, furnace vent pipes, and heat exchangers should be checked for leaks before the winter season. Tomato plants will also show leaf distortion in the presence of natural gas. The soil fumigants chloropicrin, formaldehyde, methyl bromide, and Vapam are all harmful to plants until complete dissipation has occurred.

Air pollution at great distances from the growing area can sometimes cause plant injury. Industrial and urban areas produce ozone, PAN (peroxyacetyl nitrate), sulfur dioxide, ethylene, and other less well known pollutants that damage plants. Air need not always appear smoggy to contain enough of these chemical compounds to cause injury. The toxicity of some common pollutants is listed in Table 28. Information concerning concentrations of various pollutants in particular geographic areas may be obtained by contacting local air and water quality agencies. Constructing greenhouses or nurseries in a different location would be advisable if pollution injury could be expected to occur frequently. The prevailing wind pattern might be studied if site construction is planned near major urban or industrial sites. Upwind locations would be more desirable.

Table 28

Concentrations at which common pollutants can cause plant injury. Caution must be exercised because numerous plants which have not been tested could suffer damage at lower concentrations.

Pollutant	Concentration (ppm) at which damage occurs	Plants tested
Ozone	0.05	Most plants
	0.02	Petunias
PAN (peroxyacetyl nitrate)	Less than 1.0 physical damage, 0.15 growth slowed 5%	Petunia, tobacco
Ethylene	1.0 or less	Most plants
	0.1	Tomato
	0.017	African marigold
Sulfur dioxide	0.1-0.3	Reduces photosynthesis
	1.0	Most plants
	1.0 and below	Roses, salvia buckwheat, tomato
Mercury vapor	0.0083	Rose
Hydrogen fluoride	0.05	Gladiolus
Hydrogen sulfide	40-400	Many plants
	40.0 and below	Aster, salvia, cosmos, tomato; very slight damage.

Table 28 (cont.)

Chlorine	50.0 or less in water, no damage. Chlorine in domestic water is approximately 0.5-1.5.	
Fluorine	1.0 usual amount in water supply. 0.25 may injure some Liliaceae.	
Nitrogen dioxide	10.0-200.0 May be cumulative.	Many plants.
Natural gas	10.0	Most plants
	1.0	Tomato, marigold.

Chapter 13

PLANTING THE CROP INTO CONTAINERS

A great deal of the labor and material costs involved in running a greenhouse or nursery are incurred when transplanting young plants into growing on containers. The job must be done with speed and efficiency, but these goals can be met only when proper facilities and direction are provided. Plenty of space and a proper work layout increase workers' transplanting productivity greatly. The grower should analyze the entire potting process and devise a plan and layout which best fit the circumstances. Adequate room is needed for movement in the potting area because it is likely to be the most heavily utilized space of the entire operation.

WORKFLOW

Most container growing operations are equipped with a structure called the potting shed or head house where the majority of soil mixing and transplanting are done. A production line sequence for planting tasks should be set up in the following manner (See Figure 10). Plenty of room is the key to eliminating bottlenecks and slow work flow from one stage to the next. Work bench height should be determined carefully so that employees do not suffer undue back or arm fatigue. Since workers are on their feet constantly, bare cement floors should be avoided in the immediate area surrounding potting benches.

Unless the process is mechanized, moving transplanted pots to the growing areas is time consuming. Some growers feel it is more efficient to do much of their planting at the growing area, especially when large numbers of plants are involved. Soil is moved to the area planting station by means of tractors or large carts because moving soil is generally easier than moving pots filled with plants. One drawback to this scheme is that

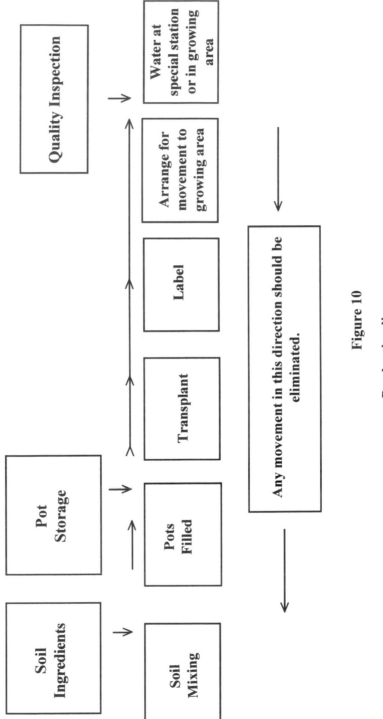

Figure 10

Production line sequence.

all pots, labels, and other work needs must also be transported to the location and if something extra is needed, more trips back to the storage area are necessary. Another disadvantage is the constantly changing climate in the greenhouse or outdoors; it is much easier to maintain pleasant working temperatures and light conditions in a conventional building.

Major advances in machinery have reduced the larger grower's transplanting labor. Almost every stage in the process can now be partially automated to the point where only occasional hand labor is necessary. Since these machines are quite expensive, larger growers are generally able to take more advantage of labor saving devices than are smaller ones. However, even tiny neighborhood growing operations must utilize every practical means of getting the job done as quickly and efficiently as possible. Each machine purchased must save enough labor so that the initial investment plus continuing upkeep are more than made up by the increased efficiency of the greenhouse or nursery. Increased efficiency may not always be directly measurable in dollars and cents; it may show up in the improved attitude and creativity of employees when they are no longer required to perform boring repetitive tasks which the machine now handles.

Major equipment purchases should always be subjected to a cost and benefit analysis to see if the machine will prove as effective as appears at first sight. If the machine cannot be utilized regularly, it is often questionable if it will pay for itself unless it performs a critical task which cannot be done in a practical manner by any other means. Nursery and greenhouse owners sometimes become fascinated by machines and buy them without careful consideration of whether extra seasonal employees could do the job just as well at less expense.

Mixing soil adequately is a tough job, even in a small container growing operation. Since it is of such obvious benefit, a mixing system is often the first piece of machinery purchased. If the purchase is made wisely, it is usually one of the most justifiable expenses a grower will ever make. Moving soil to the potting area also requires a good deal of effort; this job can usually be accomplished easily through a reasonably inexpensive conveyor system. Many other machines such as pot and flat fillers, plug poppers, transplanters, taggers, watering stations, and movable conveyor benches are available, but these more specialized devices will not likely be a boon to every grower. Each must be chosen to fill a specific need at a cost effective price.

Transplanting often comes in surges so that seasonal employees are almost always needed to get the work done on time. Larger establishments must rely upon a general labor pool but smaller neighborhood greenhouses and nurseries can often find adequate help from teenagers and other job seekers living nearby. This latter labor source often results in generally more capable and enthusiastic workers whose backgrounds can easily be checked for serious problems which might interfere at the workplace.

These people are often happy to be on "vacation" during the summer and winter holiday season when there is little planting to do, then returning in early spring for another season. In addition, many plant lovers would rather work in a greenhouse or nursery than anywhere else. This fact often translates into a happy productive work force. Neighborhood growers can usually obtain a highly capable and reliable seasonal work force at reasonable wages by making the work atmosphere pleasant and informal and by tailoring much of the production work to the schedules of teenagers, retirees, and housewives.

Transplant workers must be trained carefully in the fundamentals of their job. If the grower instructs them properly and has a good system of information tags in each batch of plants to be done, work will progress smoothly and efficiently with only occasional need for supervision. Each detail in the transplanting process must be accomplished thoroughly if significant plant losses are to be avoided. The job is repetitive and can be taught to anyone but seemingly minor alterations in planting procedure can lead to the death or much reduced vigor of plants. Each new worker should be carefully observed for a period of time to assure that all instructions are being carried out.

PLANTING PROCEDURES

Seedlings sown into open flats should be transplanted when the first true leaves appear, or when they are large enough to handle. Cuttings are easiest to remove from the propagating medium when roots have begun to form but have not spread appreciably. Leaving either in the propagating trays too long arrests growth and increases planting labor because the larger root system is more difficult to arrange in the new soil. Many crops are ruined because growers fail to provide adequate transplanting labor, thereby allowing plants to become stunted and flower prematurely. Seedlings which have not been planted on time should be discarded if they are overgrown or show significant evidence of growth disorders.

Most workers tend to be overly cautious when removing plants from the propagating tray and placing them in the growing container. If the transplanter runs a hand under the seedlings or cuttings and loosens the soil somewhat, most plants can be pulled quickly out of the tray with little lasting damage. Many roots will be broken off but the ones remaining will generate new tissue within a few days if the soil is kept well moistened. Constant availability of water until new roots are formed contributes greatly to success. Young plants, however, should not be waterlogged; this leads to inadequate soil oxygen for root growth.

The availability of high quality seedling plugs has diminished somewhat the need for experienced and carefully trained transplanters in greenhouses. But growers can't expect that purchasing plugs automatically assures success in this critical production phase. Only a few steps in the middle of the process have been modified, every other rule for successful transplanting must still be observed.

Using plugs can speed up the transplanting process 2-3 times. In this respect, it is even more important that all instructions be carefully communicated since mistakes made on the production line will be magnified by the increase in speed. Tree and shrub seedlings or actively growing cuttings can be treated in much the same way as greenhouse annuals.

Woody landscape plants and roses which are received in the dormant state must be carefully handled during the transplanting stage. Improper treatment here is the major reason why dormant plants fail to bud out properly. This statement of course assumes that all of the previous production, harvesting, and storage steps have been completed properly.

A constantly humid atmosphere is necessary for bare rooted nursery stock before, during, and after transplanting. Some species may adapt well to reduced humidity after plants are watered in well but most will perform better if high humidity is maintained around the canes or stems until buds have developed the first few leaves. After leaves have appeared, it is important to make sure the humidity is reduced gradually so that tender tissue is not dried out too quickly before it has a chance to harden off. If high humidity is maintained too long, diseases may become more prevalent.

Transplanting areas and benches must be kept clean. Old soil, plant debris, and used containers should never be allowed to contaminate new soil and plants. Another way of reducing disease losses is to plant seedlings and cuttings as shallow as possible coincident with proper anchorage. Shallow planting increases the oxygen available to roots and reduces exposure of tender stem tissue to disease organisms in the soil. Crop uniformity and ease of watering will be increased if the transplanting crew is instructed to fill containers with soil in a standardized manner. Differences in the degree of soil compaction and soil volume in pots lead to irrigation difficulties later.

The number of seedlings or cuttings placed in a container will be determined by the grower's evaluation of needs. Fewer plants may be used and then cut back or "pinched" to induce branching; this method increases growing time and charges against the crop for greenhouse space will be greater. More plants in the containers reduces crop time but increases propagation costs. Multiple planting is not often used with woody landscape material because the cost is usually prohibitive and because the final landscape form of many shrubs and most trees is not enhanced by this practice.

If mixed color seed formulas are used, seedlings should be taken from the seed flat at random. Choosing the larger or healthiest looking seedlings may result in a finished crop which is predominantly one color. When the seedling or cutting is placed in containers, soil is gently but firmly pressed around the base of the plant. This brings soil particles into close contact with roots, thus eliminating air pockets and anchoring the plant. Enough empty space left at the top of pots is necessary to provide an adequate water reservoir. It often helps to use a stick with rounded ends to "poke" soil into the air pockets which may form under the main crown present on roses, shrubs, and trees.

When plants are moved to growing areas, it is often possible to stack containers one on top of another without plant damage. This is much more efficient for transport and is especially useful with bedding plant flats. Of course certain varieties must be left in a single tier or stems will be broken.

Newly transplanted plants can be killed in a few minutes if left unwatered on a sunny greenhouse bench or outdoor growing area. It is critical to begin proper watering practices immediately. Many plants, such as bare root nursery stock or herbaceous plants placed in very porous soil will benefit from immediate heavy irrigation while others which are placed in shadier areas or are planted with an existing root ball in heavier soils may do best with somewhat restricted irrigation to start.

The exact amount and frequency of watering necessary after transplanting will vary with the species and condition of plants and with the environmental conditions into which they are placed; but, in general, if a mistake is to be made at this time it will prove less serious if made on the side of a little excess water.

Some growers prefer to shade plants for a time after transplanting; this is normally not necessary if good attention is paid to proper watering. Shade is an added step which increases costs and, if plants are in a growing condition, shade will inhibit photosynthesis.

Plants which have been growing for some time in containers and are ready to move up in pot size should be moistened thoroughly prior to transplanting. This eliminates the need to water the new soil mass heavily for a few days until roots are beginning to penetrate it. Roughing up the roots on older plants being transplanted stimulates new root growth and rejuvenates the plant. Extremely root bound plants will have to have the roots torn apart and some cut off to satisfactorily stimulate new growth. When roots are cut off severely it may be necessary to prune back top growth to bring the plant into balance. Whenever plants are pruned heavily, watering should be reduced until new growth becomes evident.

Dormant woody plants normally require some root pruning so that roots will fit into pots without bending or circling the roots around. Even when woody plants need no sizing down, some pruning of main roots will be necessary if the tips are broken or ragged.

As mentioned, transplanting tends to become a rather repetitive process once one has been doing it for a few days. New workers can observe the process for a few minutes and assume wrongly that "any old method will do". In truth, however, transplanting is an extremely critical step in the production process. If one realizes that the plants being handled are either juvenile (babies) or severely traumatized (injured by removal from the ground or excised from the mother plant recently), it becomes easier to understand that although healthy plants will usually survive transplanting remarkably easily, they must be treated properly and given optimum conditions immediately. Someone who is well-trained and very detail oriented should supervise the entire process carefully from beginning to end.

Extensive training for the supervisor is also necessary because different species of plants and plants in different stages of growth or conditions of dormancy may require alternative treatments. Only a summary of transplanting has been provided here. In reality, each group of plants will likely need some small alteration of planting requirements in order to realize the full economic potential at harvest. Only someone who has extensive experience in all phases of nursery and greenhouse production can fully appreciate the huge difference in quality, quantity, and speed of growth which ultimately results from modifications of the planting process.

PLANTING CONTAINERS

Many greenhouse and nursery owners begin business using all shapes and sizes of containers which can be obtained free or at little cost. These pots are normally not sterile and do not present a professional image to customers. Disease and loss of sales due to dirty, unattractive pots are the price one pays for trying to save a few dollars. Old pots are seldom a bargain when a person's time collecting them is taken into account. This is time that could be better spent managing the growing operation.

The main criteria one should use in choosing growing containers are economy, consumer appeal, ease of handling, freedom from disease organisms, and quality of plant growth in them. Red clay pots in the greenhouse and wooden containers in outdoor nurseries were the industry standard for many years. Both of these types of containers grow a quality plant and are esthetically pleasing to customers. But they are relatively high in cost and hard to handle in quantity; most growers use them only in special situations nowadays, they are especially appropriate if plants are to be sold in an upscale market.

Plastic containers have mainly replaced clay and wooden containers in greenhouse production and both plastic and wood fiber containers have replaced wooden ones in outdoor tree and shrub nurseries. Growers should remember that the consumer's decision to purchase a particular plant can be significantly affected by the color, shape, and base material of containers in which the plant is grown.

Choosing lines of containers for a growing program should be done with careful thought about the unique circumstances surrounding each

Common configurations of small plastic pots, packs, and flats used in bedding plant production.

crop. Spring plants for outdoors are not usually chosen by consumers with so critical an eye as are gift plants; consequently, square pots may be preferred for spring because they hold more soil and are more amenable to handling easily in standard rectangular flats. Drain holes in all containers must be adequate. Drainage is less impeded if a portion of the drain holes are located on the extreme lower sides of containers instead of entirely on the bottom.

Containers must have enough material strength for the purpose served. Hanging baskets especially should be tested for weaknesses at the juncture of hangers and container and again at the hook by which they are hung. Square pots and those with ribbed sides are preferred for long term crops such as trees; theses shapes lessen the tendency of roots to circle the outside edge and supposedly stimulate roots to grow downward. Whether or not containers separate from one another readily is important to transplanting efficiency. There is nothing more aggravating to employees than struggling with pots that won't come apart when the boss is expecting top speed.

Color and physical composition of containers can affect soil temperatures, especially out of doors. Black pots absorb more heat from the sun than lighter colors and plastic pots are less efficient insulators than are wood fiber pots. Containers which fit easily and tightly into trays are much more easily transported; this is one of the big benefits of square pots. Clay and wood-fiber pots are often considered easier to grow quality plants in than plastic because root aeration is better. No one type of container will satisfy every growing and merchandising need. A balance must be struck between the need to standardize and the necessity of accommodating peculiarities in plant growth and sales.

The environmental movement is having some impact upon horticultural container production and usage. Container manufacturers are now offering a wider line of biodegradable containers and plastic pots are often produced in grades made from recycled material. The latter types of pots can sometimes be more prone to cracking and breaking under stress so that they may not be appropriate for use under all conditions, especially if the growing medium is heavy or the weather is cold.

Growers should be aware of customer preferences concerning the recycling of plant containers. Certain market areas may demand containers which can be recycled while other areas attach little importance to this quality. The trend seems to indicate that recycling or use of biodegradable containers will assume more importance in the future. Short discussions of containers made from different materials follow.

Container costs can vary greatly depending upon economic conditions (price of plastic base materials), transport, grade, style, and many other factors. A large savings in cost may be realized by estimating production needs for 6 months or a year and submitting the order for bids to several manufacturers or distributors.

Plastic

Pros and cons of plastic pots have already been discussed. A porous soil mix is necessary to compensate for the impermeability of plastic pot walls to air flow. Growers will have a tendency to over water in plastic containers, more so than with containers having air-porous walls. Plastic flats filled with removable inserts having small individual cells are the standard container of the bedding plant industry at present. The common size of these rectangular flats is approximately 11 inches by 21 inches, but new, slimmer sizes have been introduced to accommodate the demand for cheaper per-unit prices. Prices for different grades and weights of plastics will vary considerably and growers must choose the most economical combination which fits the need.

The price of plastic parent material gyrates considerably with that of oil, from which it is derived. Developments in the oil market can quickly make plastic containers less desirable from a price standpoint. This fact, along with the undesirable environmental effects of plastic garbage, make it imperative that growers experiment with containers made from other materials so that switching container types, if necessary, would not involve unknown crop reactions.

Tree growers use a substantial number of heavy plastic bags as growing containers. These bags are sometimes utilized in conjunction with individual outside wire mesh retaining supports. Bags are less expensive than rigid containers and some evidence has accumulated to show that under certain cultural techniques, the bags help prevent root circling. Plantable plastic fiber bags are also used so that trees and shrubs may be placed directly in a ground hole for later easy removal of a concentrated root mass. Tree and shrub growers are also using "pot in pot" systems to make the harvesting process easier and faster. In these systems, a more or less permanent pot is placed in the ground to various depths, then a slightly smaller growing pot is slipped into this "sleeve". The growing pot is simply pulled out at harvest.

Clay

Clay pots are still used to some extent in localities where a manufacturing plant for them is located. Most consumers regard plants in clay pots as a mark of quality and would be willing to pay a slightly higher price. If the grower feels there is a market for high quality plant material with a distinctive container, clay pots may help distinguish the product clearly. It is doubtful that growers will ever return to clay pots in great numbers because they

Most consumers regard plants in clay pots as a mark of quality.

are difficult and heavy to ship, store, and handle. In addition, modern potting machines are not set up to handle clay pots efficiently. Clay pots are a popular retail item.

Wood fiber

Fiber containers are manufactured from lumber industry by-products. The walls are somewhat air-porous so that growing in fiber pots is similar to growing in clay. Purchase price is normally reasonable but shipping is expensive due to their bulk, which also complicates storage. Pots are often difficult to separate because rough outside surfaces stick to the next pot. Flats and bedding plant containers are also available in fiber. Tree growers use the majority of fiber pots because trees planted in these pots can be transferred to the ground in a final landscape application without removing the tree or shrub from the container. This allows growers to use bareroot trees and shrubs and sell them before they are heavily rooted in the pot.

The fiber pots, if not treated with preservative, do not prevent (although they may restrict) roots from growing through the container walls into the natural earth of the final planting site. In addition to allowing root penetration, fiber pots decompose rather quickly in moist warm soil. The rate of decay varies from a month or two under ideal conditions to fairly long periods in extremely dry or cold climates.

Nursery pots manufactured from wood-fiber. Commonly used for trees and shrubs but finding more acceptance recently as a flower pot which is biodegradable.

Fiber pots offer an ecologically acceptable solution to the problem of waste disposal for greenhouses and nurseries. Most gardeners accept this type of pot readily as an obviously biodegradable product. It is questionable if the final environmental consequences of fiber pot use are a good deal different from plastic pot use. The transport of fiber pots is especially energy consuming since they are bulky; it may be that this energy use cancels out some of the favorable biodegradable aspects of these containers.

Peat

Peat pots are similar to wood fiber pots but because of the weaker and more porous nature of the construction material, they are used only in small sizes and root aeration is even better. Peat is also used in

Wooden baskets which are often used as plantable containers for trees and shrubs. Treated baskets also make a rustic and inexpensive planter pot for flowers.

manufacturing pellets enclosed by a light reinforcing net. Roots of herbaceous plants will grow through the walls of these peat materials quickly. This phenomenon has led to their extensive use by propagators. Many spring bedding plants are offered in peat pots or pellets. Less damage to surrounding plants is encountered if individual peat pots are grouped in small plastic sales unit containers rather than in an open flat. Peat pots and pellets are easy to grow quality plants in but purchase cost is generally quite high when compared to similar sizes in plastic, especially if the peat products are grouped in sales unit containers.

Styrofoam

Both pots and bedding plant packs are sometimes made from styrofoam. There is little to distinguish them from plastic containers except they are bulkier and, depending on construction methods, could possibly lead to better aeration of the root zone. Styrofoam containers offer much greater protection from extreme soil temperatures because the thick walls provide good insulation.

Wooden

Wooden bedding plant packs and flats were once quite common but are now seldom encountered. In lumber country, tree boxes are used extensively but bulkiness prevents their transport in volume to other regions. Wooden baskets are an excellent container in which to plant trees. Numerous small holes in the walls and bottom allow roots to penetrate quickly into surrounding soil. Basket cost is usually somewhat higher than that of equivalent sized fiber pots. Treatment with wood preservatives increases basket life above ground but decreases usefulness as a planting container in the ground. Wooden baskets make excellent one season patio planters for annuals. They offer a rustic appearance at very reasonable cost and they are biodegradable.

Metal

Metal containers were once extensively used by tree and shrub growers but plastic and fiber have almost completely supplanted their usage. Cost and safety are the main reasons metal containers are seldom used now. The sharp edges exposed when cans are cut for use by consumers have resulted in numerous serious accidents.

Miscellaneous materials

Almost every material conceivable has been used for plant containers. Only a few have stood the test of time to become accepted for long periods in general crop production.

Many small containers are made in some way from paper products. Accordion-like paper cell units are fairly commonly used in short term propagation of some plants. These small containers are very inexpensive and package well for economical shipping.

Tar paper is often used in tree nurseries for lining wire mesh baskets. This material, if thin enough, allows roots to grow through and into the ground when planted. It is quite inexpensive. Burlap cloth can be used for the same purpose and is even more permeable to root growth.

Containers manufactured from seldom used or encountered materials should be checked out thoroughly before being employed in extensive crop production . Plants may exhibit different growth patterns in alternative materials and certain materials may even prove to be toxic under some conditions.

Containers for retail

Today's gardener and landscaper are often willing to spend considerable sums to create special effects with plants. Container manufacturers have recognized this trend and offer a wide variety of specialty containers which are not meant for general production use. These containers often cost more than the plants in them. Every plant retailer should investigate taking advantage of selling decorative pots; it can lead to a significant income stream.

SPECIAL CONTAINER CONSIDERATIONS

Several topics which relate to containers merit some attention: 1) Root spiraling, especially in trees, shrubs, and perennials; 2) water retention in containers as related to container depth; 3) water retention in containers as related to media filling methods.

Root spiraling and congestion in containers has only recently been given proper attention. Perhaps this situation arose because the containerization of nursery stock is only a relatively recent development in itself. The roots of trees, shrubs, and many perennials tend to circle the walls of round pots, eventually becoming extremely spiraled, with strangulation of some roots often occurring. Plants within this type of root system seldom perform well in the landscape. Experienced nursery workers have all seen root spiralled plants that retain this deformed shape many years later when the plants are dug up to be replaced because of poor performance.

Root spiralled plants can sometimes be reinvigorated by undoing the spirals and then pruning them back severely. It is better, however, to eliminate this situation before it develops. The best method of preventing root spiral is to sell plants and put them in the landscape before spiralling sets in.

Nurserymen often prefer square containers or those with corrugations in the side in the belief that these shapes prevent some degree of root spiralling. Recently, container manufactures have offered pots which are either coated on the inside or impregnated with substances (mostly copper compounds) which arrest the growth of root tips as they reach the container wall, thus preventing spiralling and, hopefully, providing a more dense accumulation of branched roots in the center of the container.

Special pot configurations which allow for air pruning of roots at the base and on the sides of the pots have also been developed to help prevent spiralling and to produce more dense root systems.

Experimental evidence shows conclusively that deeper containers retain a smaller percentage of water after draining (more air space) than do shallow containers, even as the percentage of solid material in the medium remains constant. This phenomenon is additionally affected by the type of materials in the medium and by the filling methods used.

Readers can easily see that the height of containers chosen can have serious implications for irrigation methods. One can also imagine the way in which containers are filled with soil as being a major factor in watering frequency and uniformity. This is why all transplanting employees should be trained to fill pots in as uniform a manner as possible.

Chapter 14

REGULATING GROWTH BY NATURAL AND CHEMICAL MEANS

Growers must often regulate plant growth and development in different ways to produce a visually pleasing crop and to promote certain processes which make production more economical. Regulating plant growth may be approached through several avenues: selecting genetic cultivars, managing environmental factors, physically altering the plant, and applying chemicals are the basic methods available. The greater part of this book has been devoted to explaining the interrelationships between plants and environmental factors. Readers should refer to the appropriate sections for detail in assessing the impact environmental management may have on plant growth. Several specific methods of growth regulation will now be presented.

SELECTING GENETIC CULTIVARS

Ever since the advent of agriculture, man has actively practiced the selection of plants and animals possessing desirable characteristics in order to increase the quality and quantity of crops. This process of human directed evolution has led to thousands of varieties which, for the particular purposes of the user, are superior to wild species. Every grower should take an active interest in selecting only the most suitable varieties available for production schedules. It is generally much more economical to select appropriate varieties than it is to alter the growth of unsuitable ones to achieve the same purpose. Plant breeding has become a fast moving science in recent years and one must continually evaluate new varieties in order to stay current. Looking over the catalogs of major seed companies and nursery stock suppliers should convince neophytes of the importance which must be placed upon selecting a proper variety. There are literally thousands of varieties offered and each one has its individual good and bad points.

A grower should list all the proposed crops and then study the varieties available for each one, eventually selecting one or several varieties which seem to fit the particular production and marketing circumstances most closely. Descriptions of varietal performance in seed catalogs tend to be loaded with superlatives which make it difficult for the uninitiated grower to choose with any degree of confidence. This is why a well-tested list of suitable varieties for local market preference is a valuable tool for the grower. Observing field trials and other growers' results and listening to recommendations from experienced nursery stock and seed salesmen are the best methods of choosing which varieties to grow initially. Careful observation of growth patterns in succeeding seasons will provide information which enables the grower to personally evaluate performance. Newly introduced varieties should be grown the first season only on a trial basis if they are an important crop.

Certain crops such as crabapples, lilacs, maples, petunias, and chrysanthemums have been extensively selected and bred so that the choice of varieties is bewildering. Seed houses, nurseries, and salesmen will be happy to recommend what varieties to use, but there can be no substitute for careful evaluation and selection by the grower. Many people who are primarily growers and have little contact with the ultimate consumers tend to overestimate the value of certain cultivars simply because they grow well and are economical to produce. They forget that plants have little value if they are not appealing to the public and do not fulfill the purpose for which they were purchased. Growers who also retail should listen carefully to customers' reports of plant performance; those growers who sell wholesale only must devise some means of obtaining data on customer satisfaction. Perhaps the best method of evaluating varieties is to use them one's self in the home and garden. Selecting proper varieties for the market and for the growing facilities is of prime importance to success and should be given adequate consideration.

PHYSICALLY ALTERING PLANTS

Every gardener is familiar with the process of pruning and pinching plants to obtain more desirable shapes or promote vigorous growth. Many greenhouse and nursery crops require some type of physical alteration to realize their full potential as ornamentals. These alterations are usually performed by hand and can add considerably to crop expenses. As a consequence, there are numerous efforts toward using chemical applications to accomplish the same purpose. The efficacy of these chemical methods will be discussed in later sections of this chapter.

Physical alteration of plants most often falls into two broad categories: pruning or pinching and disbudding. The words pruning and pinching are not well defined and should be used carefully to make the meaning clear. The word "pruning" is normally used to denote the removal of unwanted growth. Pinching primarily means removal of the growing tip from stems to promote branching. One can readily see how the two words may overlap in meaning but the essential difference should be clear. Some plants develop too many stems to allow vigorous growth of them all. Quality is improved if the weaker shoots are removed. This allows more nutrients, water, and light for development of the remaining branches. The purpose of pruning may be to promote larger, more prolific flowers or ensure stronger, thicker stems. Occasionally one prunes to improve flower visibility or to train plants in a certain direction or form.

Many plants are not full enough naturally to have a pleasing shape unless pinched to increase the number of branches. Employees should be trained to administer pinches in a precise fashion. The growing point may be missed if the pinch is too far up the stem and few branches result if a pinch is made too far down the stem. The terms "soft" and "hard" pinch are qualitative terms meaning those pinches made higher or lower on the stem respectively. When workers fail to excise the growing point, the main stem will continue growing upward and lateral branches are not induced. An entire crop can be ruined by improper pinching because the flowering schedule is thrown off and plants may be irregular in height. Pinching to alter plant shape must be correlated with the desired plant height and bloom date because these attributes are often also affected. Poinsettias initiate flowers naturally in late September or early October in the northern United States and delaying the pinch closer to the flower initiation date will decrease the final height of plants as compared to plants pinched earlier. In those groups of plants where flowering occurs irrespective of day length and temperature induction, the pinch date may be the primary method of regulating bloom date. Geraniums, carnations, and roses are examples of such crops.

A knowledge of the individual crop's response to pinching is essential if one is to predict the outcome accurately. Certain chrysanthemum varieties

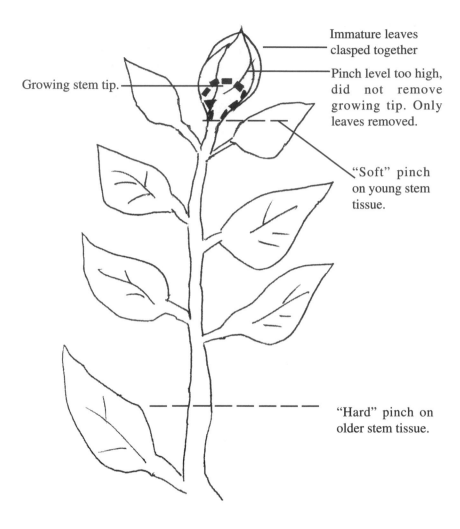

Immature leaves clasped together

Pinch level too high, did not remove growing tip. Only leaves removed.

Growing stem tip.

"Soft" pinch on young stem tissue.

"Hard" pinch on older stem tissue.

Figure 11

Diagram of relative meaning usually given to "soft" and "hard" pinch. Meaning can vary somewhat between species.

"break" or produce lateral branches quite readily and must be pinched relatively hard while other varieties must be soft pinched because lateral branches do not form easily on older tissue. Some newer poinsettia cultivars reliably produce a lateral branch at each leaf axil when pinched. If the pinch is too soft on these varieties (leaving too many leaves) there will be too many branches, resulting in weak stems with small flowers. Geraniums will bloom earlier with a soft pinch than with a hard pinch. The need for pinching may be overcome in some crops by increasing the number of cuttings put into a pot. This method eliminates one step requiring skilled labor and generally reduces crop time. A reduction in crop time not only makes room for additional crops but, more importantly, shortens the response time necessary for needed alterations in inventory due to increased or decreased demand.

It should be emphasized that roots are often cut to induce branching and restore vigor to newly re-potted plants. It is common practice to prune tree roots the year prior to moving the trees to new locations. This induces lateral branching and a compact root system next to the trunk.

Disbudding is the practice of removing all flower buds except the ones selected to remain on the stem. When every bud but the terminal one is removed, the purpose is generally to direct nutrients to that flower alone and thereby increase the size. This method is practiced extensively with potted chrysanthemums. Many chrysanthemums are raised as sprays for filler in flower arrangements and only the terminal bud on these sprays is removed. If allowed to remain, the terminal bud blooms earlier than the lateral buds and will reduce their size. The shape of the spray may be influenced by how early or late the terminal bud is removed.

Flower buds of chrysanthemums are usually removed whenever their size permits easy handling by workers. Buds should be rolled off to the side rather than being picked like fruit. This procedure results in less damage to the plant and will break the flower stem off closer to the main stem. When the flower stem breaks too far up, there is the possibility for new bud development. Disbudding should begin with the lowest buds and progress up the stem. In this way, if the terminal bud is inadvertently removed it can be replaced by leaving the bud directly below it on the plant. When workers start disbudding at the top, the terminal bud, if broken, might have to be replaced with a bud further down the stem which would bloom at a later date than the terminal buds left on other stems. The discussion of disbudding has referred mainly to chrysanthemums since they are the main flower crop which requires extensive disbudding. More detailed explanations of the effects pinching and disbudding may have are given in the references pertaining to individual crops.

Tree pruning is an art which, when practiced in an accomplished manner, requires a good deal of knowledge concerning the growth and physiology of the species being treated. And it requires an appreciation of the various effects which one wishes to produce. Improper pruning of fruit and ornamental trees and shrubs may have disastrous effects upon the plants for many years to come. In some cases, mistakes can never be adequately corrected.

The flowering of many shrubs and trees can be totally upset by pruning at the wrong time of year. Lilacs, for example, cannot be pruned in early spring like some other flowering shrubs because flower buds are already formed and will be cut off in the pruning process.

Some mention of tree and shrub pruning has already been made in previous chapters, but certainly not enough to equip nursery growers with the knowledge they need for properly directing the growth of numerous species to the most desirable end. Growers must consult texts which refer to the specific topics and species before attempting any permanent pruning projects.

In addition to the complexity of accepted pruning practices, there is also the fact that not all "experts" agree about how pruning of trees and shrubs should be accomplished, and there is little easily available factual data to show exactly how different pruning techniques will affect landscape plants many years after the fact. Perhaps the best advice the present author can give is for growers to thoroughly understand that pruning certainly involves more than turning a half-baked "expert" loose with a saw and a pair of shears. The topic should be studied carefully to avoid serious mistakes.

REGULATION OF PLANT GROWTH THROUGH ENVIRONMENTAL MANIPULATION

Details concerning how environmental factors such as light and temperature can be used to influence plant growth have been presented in previous chapters. All that needs to be emphasized now is the very specific purposes which certain plant responses can be directed towards.

Daylength and temperature are two factors which are easily controlled under certain circumstances and much work has been done towards understanding how these factors can be used in rather precise fashion to control plant development.

The control of flowering by management of both photoperiod and temperature and control of plant height and shape by day/night temperature relations (the DIF technique; chapter 9) are but some of the more obvious examples of managing specific crop characteristics through environmental manipulation. Mention was also made concerning the manipulation of water and fertilizer resources in order to accomplish particular growth objectives. Other equally effective means will undoubtedly be found useful as our knowledge of plants increases.

Growers should review all aspects of their cultural programs to evaluate whether the total physical environment they are providing to crops is consistent with the specific plant characteristics which are desired.

ALTERING GROWTH BY CHEMICAL MEANS

Chemical means of altering plant growth have been devised mainly to lessen the cost associated with manual alteration and to produce effects which are not available by physical means or genetic selection. Much of the impetus given to chemical growth alteration was supplied in the 1920's by plant scientists who discovered that chemical compounds occurring naturally in plants were responsible for determining or regulating plant growth and development. These compounds were not used for building plant tissue or as essential ingredients for chemical reactions but as control mechanisms regulating the occurrence and speed of growth and development. Synthetic or natural regulators in use today may function in the manner just described or they may alter growth by physical alteration or destruction of the tissue organization in various plant structures.

Many natural growth regulators have been identified in plants since the initial discoveries. Their history of discovery, classification into groups, and modes of action are interesting but not especially relevant to the present discussion. The action of growth regulators depends on their concentration, their interaction with other regulators, and the tissue in which they are present.

Growth regulators affect cell enlargement and division, initiation of roots, lateral bud development, fruit and leaf abscission, tropic movements, fruit set and enlargement, flower initiation, dormancy, germination, aging, growth, fruit ripening, and dwarfism. One can readily see from this list that numerous opportunities to manage the growth and development of plants exist through the judicious use of growth regulators. Synthetic compounds have been found that can be substituted for most natural growth regulators. No distinction will be made in the following presentation between natural and synthetic growth regulators.

MANAGING CROPS WITH GROWTH REGULATORS

Growers should be aware that growth regulators cannot take the place of proper culture in the production of quality plants. Growth regulators are a technical aid and cannot magically correct the errors of poor judgment and inattention to the details of crop culture. If the desired plant characteristics can be obtained by another management technique more economically, growers should use that method. Preference should be given to minimizing the use of chemicals in greenhouses and nurseries even if it costs slightly more to do so. Not only does this choice lessen the danger of chemical contamination to employees but it also lessens the chance of crop damage from improper application. Application concentrations and interactions with other chemicals may be of extreme importance in the proper use of growth regulators. Labels should be studied carefully to avoid crop damage and harmful effects to personnel. Brand names for growth regulators will be mentioned only when doing so aids the reader.

Stimulating root growth

The initiation of roots is enhanced by several compounds. Indole-3-acetic acid (IAA), indole-3-butyric acid (IBA), and alpha-naphthalene-acetic acid are the most commonly encountered. The rooting compound applied is only one factor determining the success of propagation by cuttings. Environmental factors and the quality of cuttings are of prime importance. Many cuttings root so quickly that there is little benefit from treatment with growth regulators while other varieties are almost impossible to propagate without this artificial stimulation. The majority of plants fall somewhere in between. Rooting compounds are applied in most cases to speed up and increase the quality of rooting. Rooting compounds may be applied as dusts or by immersing the base of the stem in a dilute solution. An effort should be made to standardize application so that cuttings root as uniformly as possible within a batch. Contamination of the rooting compound with diseased cuttings is a major problem and only healthy, clean cuttings should be used. Some commercial rooting compounds may contain fungicides to retard the spread of diseases. Active strength of compounds is generally increased for harder to root cuttings. Growers should always question whether the increased speed and quality of rooting is balanced by the added labor for application of growth regulators and the possibility of spreading diseases.

Retarding plant growth

The use of growth retardants to produce shorter, more desirably shaped plants has become a standard practice for many varieties. Until relatively recent times, growers could do little more than withhold water and fertilizer, lower the temperature, and prune plants to control height. Growth retardants have provided one of the most economical improvements in plant quality to be introduced in quite some time. Prior to their introduction, managing environmental factors to control plant height usually resulted in rather small, light green plants. Retarding stem elongation by chemical means has allowed growers to continue irrigating and fertilizing adequately to produce large dark green plants of a desirable height. The rise of chrysanthemums and poinsettias to preeminent positions in sales of flowering plants is due in no small measure to the introduction of growth retardants.

Most varieties which respond to growth retardants show no major morphological changes other than the reduction in stem length. When additional characteristics are modified, the change is evidenced often by smaller flowers, greener, thicker leaves, and a small delay in flowering. Retardants can be used as a foliar spray or as a soil drench; the application method is sometimes limited by the type of chemical used. The most common brands of growth retardants available to the industry are A-Rest (ancymidol), B-Nine-SP (daminozide), Cycocel (chlormequat), Atrimmec (dikegulac sodium), and Bonzi (paclobutrazol). Additional formulations have been used widely in the past and new ones will undoubtedly be introduced. Recommendations concerning which retardant to use will be found under the cultural information for specific varieties later in this book. Growth retardant activity may be modified by many factors and growers should treat experimental groups of plants before exposing an entire crop to an unfamiliar product.

Weed control

Weed control is discussed under growth regulation because many of the common weed killers are synthetic growth regulating substances. The familiar 2,4-D (2,4-dichlorophenoxyacetic acid) herbicide is a growth regulator which acts by causing plants literally to grow themselves to death. Weeds must be eradicated from greenhouses and nurseries mainly because they provide a haven for insects and diseases. Good insect control is impossible if numerous weeds are growing under the benches, along roadways, or in the growing areas. When weeds are allowed to get out of control, they can spread into containers and cause a reduction in quality. Weed infestations throw a poor light on the capabilities of managers when customers or business associates tour the premises. Weed control is often done by hand, which is very expensive, or sometimes by flame throwers, which is very dangerous.

The most effective and economical means of controlling weeds is by using herbicides; it is also very hazardous if not done properly. Many growers are reluctant to use herbicides because of personal or second hand knowledge about severe crop damage caused by weedkillers. Herbicides, especially 2,4-D, should never be stored on the growing grounds; many should never be used on weeds in close proximity to crop plants. Even the slightest presence of certain herbicide vapors can damage a crop beyond use. Generally, herbicide damage manifests itself in abnormal growth patterns; the most prominent symptoms are twisted and curled leaves and stem tips. Little remedial action can be taken. Sprayers and utensils used for herbicide application must never be used for any other purpose. No herbicide should ever be used without recommendation from reliable experts and even then a trial application should be made safely away from major crops.

Herbicides can be classified as pre-emergence types which prevent seeds from germinating or post-emergence types which actually kill the plant. Each type is useful under certain circumstances. Many pre-

Common greenhouse and nursery weeds. Oxalis lower left, annual bluegrass lower middle, dandelion lower right, chickweed top of photo. All easily controlled by Roundup herbicide but several applications are usually necessary to exhaust the seed supply in the ground.

emergence herbicides are nonvolatile and will not harm established plants. They do, however, remain active for quite some time and can be spread to unwanted locations by dirt particles and water movement on top of or in the soil. Contamination of seed germination areas with preemergent herbicides is serious. Growers should always make sure preemergent herbicides are nonvolatile and that contamination of desirable areas is not possible.

Several post-emergence herbicides are suitable for use in greenhouses and nurseries but most of them remain active in the soil and can cause contamination problems. Roundup (glyphosate) is very useful in greenhouses and nurseries. It is effective, nonvolatile, and deactivates upon contact with the soil, thus preventing contamination. Seeds are not affected so control must continue until the seed crop is exhausted. Roundup has been used in greenhouses without damage from vapor or contamination when careful application procedures are employed but each grower should thoroughly test the product to make sure damage to crops does not occur under the particular application circumstances existing at the time. Roundup is nonselective; it will kill any plant it contacts (crops are just as susceptible as are "weeds").

Care should always be taken to prevent spray from drifting onto desirable plants when herbicides are used. When weed growth is relatively continuous, a wick applicator may be used more effectively than sprays. Rock salt applied to greenhouse floors is a safe and reasonably effective method of killing weeds. The labor cost of spreading is high and salt may cause pollution and is corrosive to metal posts. Applying herbicides to growing containers is not common in the greenhouse and the number of herbicides which can be used in this manner is very limited. Tree nurseries are often forced to apply herbicides to pots and several formulations have been marketed for this purpose. Whenever herbicide is applied directly to growing pots, the dosage must be measured accurately to prevent damage, and trial applications to test for possible crop damage should be thoroughly conducted beforehand. Recommendations for specific herbicide use have been omitted because, in most cases, their use is limited to fairly specific circumstances and newly improved formulations are introduced quite often to render old ones out of date. County agricultural agents are often the best source of up to date information concerning herbicides.

Evaporative cooling pads may become overgrown with algae in summer months. Algae can be controlled in the cooling system by adding EPA approved disinfectants containing benzyl ammonium chlorides to the water tanks on a weekly basis. These compounds may also be used for sanitizing tools and benches in the greenhouse, and for controlling algae on clay pots. Some damage to plants is possible when clay pots are treated since chemical residues may infiltrate into the clay unless rinsed heavily.

Pinching, pruning, and disbudding

Much industry effort has been directed toward developing chemical agents which will efficiently and reliably perform some of the time consuming tasks of pinching, pruning, and disbudding flower and nursery crops. Although many compounds show some promise, the results so far have been satisfactory on only a few major crops. Azaleas are often pinched chemically when larger crops of appropriate varieties are being grown.

Some chrysanthemum varieties have been successfully disbudded chemically but this process is not so well established and is not so consistently successful as is chemical pinching of azaleas.

Chemical agents which are used to simulate the manual pinching process are also used occasionally under specific circumstances to reduce the need for manual trimming of hedges, ground covers, and even some trees. As was mentioned in the previous chapter, certain types of chemically treated containers are used to help root prune trees and shrubs.

Prolonging cut flower life

Although cut flowers are not the subject of this book, it is useful for anyone in the floral industry to have a passing acquaintance with their care. Cut flower life can be improved dramatically (up to 3-4 times) with proper handling. Flower preservatives are very economical. They perform their function by preventing stem plugging, providing respirable food sources, enabling tight buds to open, and preventing undesirable changes in flower color. The main ingredient in flower preservatives is sucrose sugar, which provides a substrate for respiration. Numerous preservative formulations which perform well are available commercially. Additional chemicals are usually added to the sucrose base to prevent stem plugging and color change.

Controlling leaf abscission

There are circumstances when it is beneficial to promote leaf abscission on horticultural plants. Nurserymen often use synthetic defoliants to speed up tree leaf abscission in the fall so that trees may be harvested before winter sets in. Hydrangeas must be subjected to cold temperatures after flowers are initiated to break dormancy, the plants are placed in dark coolers where diseases can cause severe damage unless leaves are removed before storage. Various chemicals are used to promote leaf drop. Ethylene gas is a natural product of plant respiration which will cause leaf abscission when critical levels are reached. Hydrangeas are commonly placed in a closed space with apples (which produce ethylene). Leaf drop occurs after a few days of this treatment.

Undesirable accidental leaf drop may be induced under certain circumstances. Greenhouse plants should never be placed in close proximity to ripening fruit unless adequate ventilation is provided to avoid ethylene buildup. All plants give off some ethylene gas but it is only under certain conditions that concentrations build up enough to cause damage. Large amounts of rotting plant tissue on floors or in trash bins can also cause ethylene buildup. Shipping fruited decorative orange trees with other plants can lead to defoliation if ventilation is not provided. Many growers use a chemical formulation under the brand name of Vapam as a soil fumigant. Unless treated soil is properly aired out before introduction to the greenhouse, Vapam fumes may cause severe defoliation. Improperly vented or defective furnaces are often the cause of plant defoliation due to an accumulation of combustion gases.

Some chemical compounds have been found to retard abscission. This phenomenon can be useful in the growing and marketing of certain crops. Geraniums propagated from seed have become a major crop in recent years but their flowers suffer from a tendency of blooms to "shatter" (petals fall off quickly). Since flower petals are actually specialized types of leaves the same processes which prevent or increase leaf abscission will apply to them. Silver nitrate sprays are often administered to seed geraniums to prevent bloom shatter.

Promoting flowering and fruiting

Considerable effort has been expended towards overcoming or replacing the natural flowering responses of plants with various chemical applications. It would be very advantageous, for example, if chrysanthemum growers could simply spray crops with a chemical rather than invest in the costly shading and lighting set ups now required. Although it has become apparent that many growth regulating substances can induce, promote, or inhibit flowering under certain conditions, few widespread commercial applications have arisen. Ethylene gas has been found to induce flowering in the bromeliad (pineapple) family. Commercial pineapple farms spray field plants with alpha-naphthalene-acetic acid which induces plants to produce the flower initiating ethylene in their tissues. Many ornamental bromeliads are also brought into flower by treatment with ethylene.

Some use of growth retardants and gibberllic acid has been made in azalea culture to enhance flower production. Gibberllic acid applications have been useful in stimulating cyclamen plants to produce large numbers of flowers at one time, thus increasing their eye appeal. The applications also cause the flower stalks to elongate so that flowers are held well above the foliage with a subsequent increase in visibility. Some chemicals have shown the capability of inhibiting flower initiation in plants. Chrysanthemum and kalanchoe are two major crops which respond in this manner to certain chemicals. Preventing flowering could, of course, be advantageous where plants are kept for purposes of vegetative propagation.

Producing fruit without pollination is termed "parthenocarpy". Chemical treatment of flowers to induce fruit set has become widespread. Most readers will no doubt be familiar with various blossom set and berry set formulations they have seen at garden stores. Chemically induced fruit development can be advantageous for commercial growers since fruits will mature evenly, thus facilitating the harvest. Greater numbers of fruits may also be set by this means. Parthenocarpic fruits usually lack some of the juiciness of pollinated fruits because seeds are not formed and the reproductive fluids surrounding them are absent.

Chapter 15

HOW TO GROW PLANTS THAT SELL

Anyone who has read the preceding chapters of this book should be able to produce attractive plants which please the end consumers. It will be advantageous, however, if the essential factors which lead to production of beautiful plants are outlined in a concise discussion. Readers may come away with a better overall understanding if the necessary but sometimes confusing details of previous chapters are forgotten for the moment. All greenhouse and nursery managers should periodically evaluate production methods to be certain that the product is attaining the necessary standards and that the standards reflect market demand. Growers can sell many more plants if they know what type of plant is wanted and how to produce it reliably.

PLANNING AND FACILITIES

The first step in producing beautiful plants is planning the crop carefully. If a complete knowledge of crop requirements is lacking, the grower should consult reliable references well in advance. Supplies and suitable growing space can be reserved more accurately if the details of crop culture are known adequately. Scheduling has a direct bearing on plant quality. If crops are propagated without regard to greenhouse or nursery space, possible markets, labor available, and seasonal weather factors, one cannot expect to achieve success.

Space and labor must be available to transplant crops at the proper time so that plants grow vigorously without check. When seasonal weather will not permit quality growth of particular crops, growers should try to find suitable substitutes which will naturally grow well at that time of year. Even well grown crops deteriorate quickly in appearance and quality if markets are not available at harvest time. Every successful grower must have one eye on the market and one eye on the greenhouse or nursery if plants are to be harvested at their peak value.

Growers can increase the quality and accuracy of their planning and timing by keeping adequate crop records. It is much easier to produce good plants if well documented data from previous personal experience are available. Cultural and scheduling recommendations from books and articles can never anticipate the exact growing conditions in a particular location. Buyer satisfaction is also improved by being sensitive to the keeping quality and other desirable attributes of particular varieties. It is sometimes the case that certain flower colors in the same variety last much better, thereby providing better value to the customer. Everyone is familiar with the necessity of providing vegetable transplants which are suitable for local climatic conditions; the same care is also required for selecting fruit trees and landscape nursery stock.

Sales records by variety and colors will aid growers in planning future crops. Consumer color preferences are very important and as much thought should be put into growing the right colors as is expended in selecting crops and varieties. If men are selecting, red is the most popular choice; if women are choosing, pink or salmon may replace red. The various shapes and size of flowers can also be a large factor in customer preference. Novelty shapes such as spider or anemone mums and smaller flowers are popular at the present time. Tropical foliage plants may exhibit subtle variations of color and form within a variety which will greatly affect sales. Highly variegated golden pothos sells much better than the greener leaved types. Different colors, shapes, and sizes of shrubs and trees are necessary to pleasing landscape designs. Every nursery must have an adequate variety to meet these needs.

Top notch plants that sell quickly cannot be produced in a facility which is not suited to the crop. Short, bushy chrysanthemums are impossible to grow in a structure which has low light transmission but tropical foliage would prosper under the same light conditions. If the facilities are not adequate to produce the crop in a reasonable manner, it is better to search for an alternate crop which can be grown to high standards. Structures and grounds need not always be fancy to produce good crops but they must be suitable for the task at hand. Labor is necessary in sufficient quantity and quality to care for crops in a timely manner. A crop may be of particularly high quality until a labor bottleneck occurs, but then quality falls rapidly because an essential task is left undone. Growers can increase quality simply by employing workers who display a genuine interest in plants. These people will always produce better merchandise than those who work only for money.

The requirements enumerated above for producing appealing plants do not depend on a high degree of technical knowledge but rely mainly on the good sense of managers. These nontechnical aspects of growing are probably the most neglected ingredients in profitable production. It is amazing how many growing operations are run in a haphazard manner, with crops being grown and sold primarily on the day to day whims of the owner or manager.

HEIGHT AND SHAPE CONTROL

Perhaps the physical features which most often affect the saleability of plants is overall height and shape. Many plants grown in crowded greenhouse and nursery conditions are too tall and lack a pleasing, full body of growth which is necessary for best acceptance by consumers. While crowding of plants is responsible for a good part of this condition, several other factors such as high moisture levels, improper pruning and pinching, high fertilizer levels, and use of the wrong genetic varieties can often add to the problem.

The relatively recent introduction of effective chemical height control compounds has greatly increased the ease with which growers can produce a short, compact plant possessing a pleasing shape. Growers should become familiar with the attributes of major growth retardants and the degree of effect they may have on different varieties. Only by having a reasonable appreciation of their action and applications can one use growth retardants in a knowledgeable manner. Chemical height suppressants should be used as supplementary cultural tools rather than as cure alls for excess height. Plant height can be controlled by proper manipulation of environmental factors in most varieties. Growth retardants cannot take the place of intelligent growing practices. When chemical means of height control are absolutely necessary or prove to be the most economical avenue, their use is justified.

Most greenhouse conditions which promote stiffer, shorter stems also produce a tougher, less succulent plant. When environmental factors are modified to limit stem length, one must make sure plants maintain a fresh, robust appearance rather than becoming so toughened as to look overly dwarfed and dried out. A certain amount of toughening or "toning" will prevent damage during the process of shipping and retail selling. Table 29 outlines those conditions which will lead to shorter, more shapely plants if properly manipulated. Readers should refer to previous chapters for more detailed discussions of these environmental factors.

GENERAL PLANT APPEARANCE

The combination of stem length and shape of plants was discussed separately because it is so often a major detriment to sales. There are numerous other attributes which must be properly attended to before a plant exhibits that near perfect healthy appearance which makes it irresistible to consumers. No physical characteristic can be said to be more important than another in contributing to plant sales because any factor which makes a plant unattractive takes away the buyer's incentive. One negative attribute can nullify all the positive qualities a plant may possess. Growers must realize they are in the business of selling beauty and not that of producing a certain number of units regardless of appeal.

Yellow leaves may be present on plants for a number of reasons. Too much water, too little water, too hot, too cold, too much fertilizer, too little fertilizer—all these extremes will produce yellow leaves. Yellow leaves are a universal symptom of sick or weak plants and the causative agent is often difficult to determine since so many factors can be responsible. Close spacing results in yellow lower leaves due to shading while, at the other extreme, intense summer sun may cause upper leaves to yellow when chlorophyll is destroyed. Leaves may turn yellow, especially around the edges, when soluble salts are high in the soil or ammonium toxicity is a problem. Attacks by disease organisms or insects also cause leaves to yellow in certain cases. A few leaves turning yellow on plants is a natural occurrence as each leaf reaches old age, and growers should not become over anxious at the first sight of this happening. Only when the number of yellow leaves is significant should one begin to worry about diagnosing the problem. A diagnosis to determine the cause of yellow leaves must follow a methodical process of elimination in which the grower considers each factor which might be responsible for the problem. High soluble salts are quite often the culprit when soils are tight and the grower is unaware of the need for leaching.

A well-balanced fertilizer program with adequate iron and micro nutrients will keep plants dark green and healthy looking. Feeding slightly less than

Table 29
Cultural conditions which will result in shorter, more compact plants.

A. Light	Provide adequate spacing and clean, high quality greenhouse covering.
B. Temperature	Grow at the low end of acceptable crop temperatures but try to maintain day temperatures as close as possible to night temperatures.
C. Ventilation	Provide adequate air exchange whenever temperature or humidity becomes excessive.
D. Water	Grow at the low end of acceptable crop requirements.
E. Flower induction	Induce flower initiation before stems elongate excessively.
F. Fertilizer	Grow at the low end of acceptable nitrogen requirements.
G. Containers	Use porous walled containers which will maintain average soil moisture at lower levels.
H. Plant Material	Choose varieties which naturally grow short and are suitable for the particular season of the year.

the optimum concentrations reduces the chances of soluble salt damage and keeps plants from becoming overly lush. Very succulent tissue is damaged easily during the marketing and shipping process. Using growth retardants may result in leaves which exhibit a deep green color without the excessive succulence associated with heavy nitrogen applications. Nitrogen is the most frequently oversupplied element and leads to lush growth more so than other elements. An over abundance of fertilizer can often result in plants growing larger than planned and becoming crowded, causing yellow leaves at the base from shading. Fertilizer must contain adequate amounts of potassium and especially phosphorous in proportion to nitrogen if flowering is to be profuse. A well designed feeding program can result in significantly more and larger flowers which will in turn increase the sales appeal of plants.

Many plants develop flowers under a wide range of conditions but much improvement may be noted if growers are knowledgeable concerning the optimum requirements for flower initiation. Once flowers are developed, employees must take care to avoid getting water or dirt in them since this generally leads to an attack of botrytis. Watering should be done from below the foliage level whenever possible, not only for the above reason but also because minerals in the water leave an unsightly white residue on the leaves and flowers of many varieties.

As the crop matures and is ready for market, a cosmetic clean up of plants is necessary as they leave the greenhouse or nursery. A small percentage of plants will always have a few minor blemishes which would never be noticed if attended to before merchandise reaches the buyer. Proper maintenance before and at harvest will result in crops being sold to the last plant rather than having a 5-10%, or even higher, dumpage rate. Many growers make it a practice to lower the temperature a few degrees on flower crops a week or two before harvest. This usually results in brighter, more vividly colored flowers. Caution must be exercised since lower temperatures can lead to botrytis and certain warm crops such as gloxinias do not benefit from this practice. White flowers may tend to "pink" at lower temperatures and render them unsuitable for some uses.

PREPARATION OF CROPS FOR GARDEN AND HOME ENVIRONMENTS

It is not uncommon for consumers to purchase apparently healthy plants only to have them develop problems within a week or two. This situation arises partly because of neglect or lack of knowledge on the part of the purchaser and partly because growers failed to condition plants properly for the environment to be found in the garden and home. Movement to a new environment is always a shock to any living organism. This trauma can be reduced by preparing plants in advance of harvest for the move to a new home.

The conditions found inside the new indoor environment are normally less humid and bright than that of a greenhouse. Most foliage or green plants destined for interior decoration will adapt quite readily if they make it through the first two or three weeks. The principal cause of unsatisfactory initial performance is the inability of plants to function properly under suddenly reduced light levels. This problem is significantly reduced if growers acclimatize foliage to lower light levels at least two weeks before sale. Many growers are unwilling to provide heavy shade before sale because plants grow slower and because of the extra expense involved. One must realize that dissatisfied customers will not purchase plants in the future and eventually there is a lowering of greenhouse production and profits.

Greenhouse plants destined for use in the garden will be subjected to generally drier, windier, and sunnier conditions. Temperature extremes in the garden are likely to be more pronounced. Growers can improve garden performance by adjusting greenhouse conditions at least ten days before harvest. Night temperatures should be turned down, watering and fertilizing reduced, and maximum ventilation afforded. Care must be taken to adjust these factors only to the point of toughening plants somewhat, not subjecting them to a starvation diet and arctic temperatures. Excessively lush, pampered plants do not perform well in the garden but neither do ones weakened from unsuitable conditions. Maximum sunlight compatible with specific varieties should have been provided throughout the growing period but it is even more important directly before harvest so that plants can withstand outdoor sunlight. New greenhouses which allow plants to be moved outdoors on suitable days or which allow the roof to open widely are an excellent means of preparing bedding plants for the eventual rigors of garden life.

Trees and shrubs which have been containerized for extended periods are sometimes in poor condition to transplant well. It is not uncommon for these plants to be neglected if they are the last of a crop or have been outdoors all winter after being kept over from the previous year. Fertilizer levels are often very low, even to the point of severe imbalances in existing plant tissue. And roots are commonly crowded and circling the inside walls and bottom of the container.

Trees and shrubs in this condition should be leached, then fertilized well, and eventually transplanted to new soil after root pruning and thinning has been performed. If trees are in an actively growing state, root pruning must be done carefully and it may be necessary to selectively remove some top growth to compensate for the temporarily disturbed root system. A little cosmetic pruning of trees or shrubs just prior to sale can often work wonders for their appearance. Of course, pruning should be performed by a knowledgable person who understands future implications of the actions taken.

HIDDEN FACTORS AFFECT QUALITY

Several factors which affect consumer satisfaction after the sale should be attended to by growers. Extremes of temperature and moisture just before and during harvest often result in poor plant performance. This type of treatment may cause disorders such as flower drop, die back of stem tips, and defoliation. Excessive exhaust fumes in shipping areas during busy periods may cause delayed damage due to ethylene gas. Plants should be inspected carefully for unnoticed insects and diseases prior to sale, this is a high priority item because customers are almost certain to return plants when they discover an infestation. No other plant defect irritates people so much and causes future ill will.

Excess soluble salts in the soil is perhaps the number one cause of the long term decline of plant health in the home. Growers can alleviate this problem for at least the first several months by making sure that plants are thoroughly leached periodically so they do not enter the consumer's home with soluble salts at a high level. A responsibility many growers fail to fulfill is disseminating information concerning the care of their product. Whether plants are sold wholesale or retail, sales personnel should be trained to offer well prepared advice whenever questions about plant culture are asked. The people who actually grow plants are the ones best qualified to begin a flow of information to consumers. Certain factors such as the importance of mycorrhizae to tree growth, vernalization as it affects flowering in perennials, and hardening off bedding plants to ensure good garden performance can only become widely known to customers if the "experts" who grow plants commercially provide a means of including this information along with the products.

A SUMMARY

Growing beautiful plants and flowers which insure loyal repeat business cannot be accomplished by haphazard methods or by personnel who feel their only responsibility is to provide for the day to day needs of plants. Successful growers must realize the need for careful crop planning and marketing efforts. One can no longer be competitive if the needs of the marketplace and consumer satisfaction are not thoroughly integrated into crop plans. If consumers are not pleased with their purchases of plants and flowers, overall demand will fall. Special effort must be exerted toward insuring that when plants leave the growing area, they are in a physiological state which will maximize their chances of survival in a new environment.

Cultural practices, which are the traditional province of the grower, must be refined and methodically analyzed so that a generally excellent program is not nullified by one or two mistakes or omissions. Growers today must be knowledgeable in many disciplines to compete in the fast changing horticultural field.

Part II

Introduction

Cultural notes for specific crops are presented in the following chapters. The information given results mostly from the author's experience as a practical commercial grower and represents mainly a distillation of actual cultural programs. Other growers will have different crop objectives and cannot hope to use the author's programs on a word for word basis. They should be employed only as a guide.

It is assumed the reader has thoroughly studied Part I of this book so that a detailed explanation of terms and environmental relationships is unnecessary when discussing each crop. Most cultural details are premised upon the use of more or less artificial soil mixes of the major types described earlier and the use of full complement fertilizers which are necessary with these low fertility mixes.

Schedules represent what can be expected at a high altitude, northern latitude of approximately 43^0 with abundant winter light conditions. Temperatures recommended for greenhouse crops refer to night time at container level unless otherwise stated. Each grower must adjust published schedules, no matter what the source, to the geographical location, market situation, and environmental circumstances prevailing at individual greenhouses and nurseries.

It is obvious that the global location of a nursery or greenhouse has far reaching effects upon the cultural methods which will apply to crops. Not only are the seasons of the year reversed in the Southern Hemisphere, the angle of winter sunlight comes from the opposite direction. Near the equator, daylengths and the angle of the sun are more or less equal throughout the year. These factors have a great effect on the manner in which plants grow and develop. For example, long day or short day blooming plants might never bloom naturally at the equator unless provisions were made to provide the proper daylength artificially.

Other climate modifying factors must also be considered. Altitude, large bodies of water, wind patterns, sea currents, and all of the phenomena which determine overall climate must be considered when a grower attempts to predict how particular ornamental crops will grow in a specific area. This is one reason why horticulture is still more or less an inexact science and relies so greatly upon the practical experience of those who are involved.

Growing the crop is, of course, only the first step – it must then be marketed. Everyone is aware that the outdoor landscaping plants utilized in the different climatic zones of the world are very diverse; they represent not only the constraint of climate but also the history of plant evolution and cultural traditions. Every grower must not only be proficient in the physical culture of plants but is obligated to also understand how the immediate marketing environment will modify production strategy and details.

One would assume that the flowering plants popular in northern Europe might also be of prime importance in North America – and this is true to a large extent. But there are significant differences in preference by consumers between the two areas, both in species and season.

For those who would like to consult a more cosmopolitan presentation of the world's ornamental plants, please see the Appendix.

Certain crops will be omitted; mainly to allow expansion on more important crops but also on occasion, because the author has no actual knowledge of them or because they do not fall logically into the general subject outline of this book.

Recommendations of specific varieties are not given for a crop unless it seems justified. New and better varieties are introduced at such a fast pace that much of this information would be quickly out of date. Details on size of containers to grow in and how many plants to use per pot will be given only when it is deemed necessary. Different markets require different container plant sizes.

Chapter 16

BEDDING PLANTS

No segment of the horticultural industry has shown such sustained market strength in the past thirty years as have flowering and vegetable plants used for outdoor gardening. Growers sometimes have trouble producing enough plants for the peak demand periods. Although the strong market demand has generally provided growers with excellent to adequate financial returns, there are a few operations that have either failed or do not consistently have positive cash flow. Some smaller growers, either through inefficient production or through ineffective marketing strategies, have lost completely in the struggle to survive against the massive movement of chain stores into spring bedding sales. Other larger growers (generally supplying the mass market) continue to grow ever larger volumes of bedding plants but cannot realize a profit because they fail to receive an adequate price for their merchandise. This industry is in a considerable state of flux as everyone involved tries to identify their proper and profitable position in the new market scene. More upheaval is likely until the pace of evolution gradually reaches a state of relative equilibrium. In general, most operations are doing quite well after having positioned themselves in a production and marketing niche which fits well with their special conditions.

The down side to bedding plant production is that it is a highly seasonal business. Growers who do not meticulously plan ahead may find themselves in the main planting season and out before they have a chance to adjust for unanticipated problems. A good deal of total crop volume is often marketed in a one to two week period. Product which is not ready to sell or which is not marketed effectively during the peak demand season is often irretrievably lost.

Success in the spring season hinges upon detailed advance planning which creates the background for staff and management to work quickly and efficiently during the short growing and marketing season. Each task must be performed on schedule so that delays do not cause the overall plan to become hopelessly tangled by critical bottlenecks.

The most successful operators in the bedding plant market are those who recognize three key facts: 1) Every precaution must be taken to plan production and marketing so that maximum advantage is taken of the natural spring demand; 2) long range efforts must be made to increase demand (especially in those periods preceding and following the natural season of peak demand), extending the season, as in the latter corollary, is the single easiest way to increase operating profits; 3) consumers demand new products, and those growers who supply new or simply revive and recondition old ideas for plant use are the ones who will prosper. Extensive new selection and breeding programs are providing growers with a wealth of exceptional new varieties, and every grower must have an effective and consistent strategy for integrating these new ideas and material into their program.

Two major new developments in the bedding plant industry can significantly help growers to extend the selling season. The first is the rise in popularity of larger, profusely flowering containers of pre-planted garden plants. Whether this development was brought about by consumer demand or grower promotion is not certain; both factors were likely important causes. Large containers obviously help growers sell plants well past the dates when customers stop putting small plants in traditional gardens.

The bedding plant market no longer is completely dominated by sales of small plants in packs. In some areas the larger instant color crops such as 4 and 5 inch pots, hanging baskets, and patio planters have outrun the volume of smaller plants sold. This situation puts more of a premium upon creative means of packaging and promoting plants rather than strictly upon growing a standard line of small plants.

The second major factor helping to prolong the bedding season is the development and promotion by major seed companies of partially grown plant "plugs". These plugs, whether purchased or home grown, enable growers to sell their first spring crop and replace it with half grown plug crops which will be ready for market while reasonably good garden demand still exists. Thus growers and consumers alike are not forced into a one shot approach to spring gardening, the season can easily extend a week to ten days further because plenty of product is available at the tail end of the season. To the grower, this extended selling period can easily add 10% to total revenues and even more to the final profit picture.

Bedding plant culture must reflect the fact that plants are to be used in the outdoors environment. Crops grown with too much shade, heat, water, and fertilizer are likely to suffer severe damage when exposed suddenly to the more demanding surroundings outside the greenhouse. Growers should plan cultural programs which will condition plants for effective use in the garden or landscaping area. This conditioning will also help prepare plants for the sometimes rough journey through wholesale and retail marketing channels.

Different marketing objectives may require that the same varieties be treated differently under particular circumstances. Moderate restrictions on growth must often be practiced with plants intended for sale in flowering packs. The same variety when sold as younger packs of green plants or as flowering plants in larger containers may be most effectively cultured by providing growing conditions which place very little restrictions on growth.

Schedules mentioned under the varietal descriptions assume that bedding plants will be in bloom unless they are varieties traditionally sold green. Some plants such as tall snapdragons and zinnias would be too unwieldy if sold in flower. Propagation is by raw, unmodified seed unless otherwise noted in the description. Please refer to the earlier chapter on propagation for the basics of seed germination. A low rate of fertilizer application after establishment (especially nitrogen) is recommended on annuals grown in packs except for those varieties such as marigolds, which develop better with reasonably high fertilizer levels. Since seed companies are now offering a wide variety of seed modified for special purposes, readers should take note of how specific seed treatments (such as partial germination) might effect culture and timing.

Although the following presentation reflects mainly a northern United States aspect, readers will easily notice that the southern or other milder climate regions of the United States, and other countries of similar climate, may have significant fall or midwinter bedding plant activity. While some mention of this fact is occasionally made, persons interested in these climatic regions must generally adjust their schedules to fit the appropriate circumstances.

Ageratum (Floss flower)

Customers in need of short border plants will appreciate ageratum. Newer varieties seldom reach a height of more than 8 inches. Blue is the most predominant color but pinkish-purple and white are also available. Ageratum is especially popular when blue is popular in the garden while demand decreases if that color is not in vogue.

Ageratum presents a very neat appearance in packs because of its short stature but plants which are past their prime tend to retain old flowers and can become unsightly unless cleaned up.

Seed is fairly small but germinates easily in about 1 week. Pelleted seed is helpful, especially is one wishes to sow direct to the pack, using 2-4 seeds per cell. After transplanting, a temperature of 60^0 F until plants are well established will help avoid stem and root rot. These diseases can become very serious in young plants if they are overwatered or kept on the cool side. Growing on temperatures of 50^0 F will help keep plants bushy and short, heat can be lowered even more to delay crops. Older plants are not especially susceptible to rotting out at lower temperatures.

Full sun is preferred but very light shade can be tolerated without harm. Ageratum becomes grassy easily if too much fertilizer is applied, especially in the early stages of growth.

Packs sown March 1 will bloom near Mother's Day at an average temperature of 55^0 F.

Alyssum (Lobularia)

Alyssum is the most widely used border plant. Height seldom exceeds 6 inches and blooms are very fragrant, especially the white varieties. Well grown packs of alyssum are attractive but quickly become overgrown in hot weather.

Alyssum performs best if a cool 50^0 F is maintained after 1 or 2 weeks of establishment in the packs at 60^0 F. Pink and purple varieties especially need an initial warm period to start well, they are not as fast growing as the white varieties. Full sun is a must to assure profuse blooming. Over application of water, nitrogen, or heat results in grassy plants with fewer blooms. Diseases and pests are seldom a problem after establishment but damping off disease occurs quite readily in the seedling stage.

The medium sized seeds germinate readily within 3 or 4 days and should be left uncovered by soil. Plants are often transplanted as small clumps since the seed of most varieties is very economical. This practice results in higher quality packs which are ready for sale quickly. Easy germination and inexpensive seed allow growers to make plugs of alyssum on the premises, even if they must be sown by hand. Seedlings left in germination chambers too long are ruined quickly by the heat and high humidity.

Direct sowing to packs is easy with alyssum. Use 4-6 seeds per cell. Over crowding with excess seed often leads to damping off disease.

Alyssum is a very profitable crop due to the short bench time and low priced seed but it must be scheduled carefully to prevent excess dumpage due to overgrowth. White varieties are much more vigorous with purple making the slowest growth.

Sow April 1 for Mother's Day flowering. Pink and purple varieties will require 1-2 weeks longer growing periods.

Asparagus (Sprengeri)

Asparagus sprengeri is useful in outdoor plantings mainly as a feathery green foliage mixed with flowering plants in patio planters and hanging baskets. The varieties meyeri and plumosous are cultivated as indoor foliage plants and floral arrangement greens, as is sprengeri.

Growth is slow below 60⁰ F. Plants are more compact if full sun Is given during winter but in those areas where light intensities are very high, some shade must be given in summer to prevent yellowish growth. Too little soil moisture will cause lower leaves to dry up and quickly become yellow; excess water for short periods is seldom harmful when plants are well established.

Asparagus is easy to grow under less than perfect conditions and does not suffer greatly from disease. Aphids love the tender tips of new shoots. Although other pests are not especially troublesome they are difficult to eradicate when established because the plants produce very dense growth.

Higher fertilizer and temperature levels will produce longer branches on asparagus. This is often useful when the plants are being used as a foliage filler. Lower fertilizer and temperatures lead to more compact plants, this cultural scheme is often best for foliage plant specimens.

Seed of asparagus sprengeri sown August 1 will yield heavy 3 inch plants by May 1 in the North. Seeds germinate irregularly over a 4-6 week period and must be covered completely to prevent drying out during the hot weather in which they are usually sown. The seed is reported to lose viability relatively soon and should not be stored for long periods.

Aster (Callistephus)

Gardeners looking for an exceptionally nice color range in cut flowers or tall background plantings will enjoy asters. Dwarf varieties are available in addition to the popular long stemmed plants. Few cut flowers last as long in the home.

Asters can be grown straight through at 50^0 or 55^0 F and should receive full sunlight. Excessive water may bring about outbreaks of stem rot on young plants but when foliage covers the pack, copious amounts of water are used on bright days. Asters are quite profitable because of their rapid growth to saleable size in the green stage. Customers should be warned to move aster beds at least every 2 years to prevent outbreaks of stem rot resulting from contaminated soil. Most varieties do not bloom until midsummer in the garden because plants are photoperiodic.

Seed sown April 1 germinates in 5-6 days and will produce heavy packs of green plants for Mother's Day. Summer potted flowers can be obtained using dwarf strains sown in the late spring. Stem rot in these pots is a difficult problem unless soil is sterilized.

Common aster varieties are easy to sow directly to packs. Two of the large seeds are usually sufficient for each cell. This crop is quite profitable due to inexpensive seed and ease of growth.

Bacopa (Sutera)

This is a relatively new plant on the bedding scene, but it is already important. White is the most popular color, although pinkish and reddish varieties are available.

Bacopa makes a wonderful filler in hanging baskets and combination planters. The small white or pink flowers completely cover a crawling, small-leaved plant. It can also be used for small 5-6 inch gift items in the spring. Bacopa is not perennial in northern areas but can serve admirably as a seasonal ground cover in cooler seasons or localities.

Perhaps the only real drawback for this new hit is the lack of a good name. The newest white variety is appropriately called "Snowstorm". This might serve as an adequate name for all the white varieties, but it is unfortunately attached to a patented variety. Other common names which have been applied are "Montana White" and "Snowdrift" but neither has become predominant.

Bacopa is produced from cuttings which root within 2 weeks if misted for the first 4-5 days. Keeping under mist for too long or later overwatering will quickly cause stem rot. This disease, along with whitefly are the two main cultural problems.

Early growth is quick at 60-65^0 F but 50-60^0 F is a better finishing temperature to produce bushy plants. At least 1 pinch is necessary before transferring small plants to combination plantings. For 3 inch pots, 2 pinches are required, while 5-6 inch containers will need frequent light shearing to make exceptional specimens.

Larger plants or those which are intended to trail in hanging baskets or planters should be propagated before New Years if fully developed specimens are needed at Mothers Day. Pinched 3 inch pots can be taken shortly after New Years while smaller filler material for late spring work can be propagated 6-8 weeks before use.

Bacopa does not thrive under the hot, dry conditions of midsummer. At this time it must receive adequate cooling, and, in high light areas, some light shade. Excessive fertilizer at any time produces lush green growth but few flowers. The plants must be adequately watered during warm periods but, as mentioned, will develop stem rot quickly with overwatering in cooler seasons.

Bacopa has quickly become one of the most popular filler plants because it presents a dainty but extremely floriferous character. It can, however, quickly degenerate into a tangled mess of non-blooming stems if plants are not spaced and trimmed as necessary. If plants are propagated too early for the intended use, a good deal of expensive labor is necessary to continue shearing and spacing until market time.

Begonia

Ever-flowering or waxed leaved begonias have achieved outstanding acceptance as garden plants in recent years. Extensive breeding has resulted in a wide range of varieties to please the consumer. These plants perform well in sun or shade if they are not exposed to excessive sunlight without being conditioned to it. Certain climates where summer sun is extremely brilliant are not suitable for these begonias unless planted in shadier areas. Growers shifting plants from moist, shaded houses to full sun must choose a period of cloudy weather to avoid severe damage to succulent

Tuberous Non-Stop begonias produce unequaled specimen flowers.

leaves. Fibrous rooted or wax begonias make an excellent show in pots or packs. Small, inexpensive blooming pots are very popular for gifts and table decorations on Mother's Day at church and nursing home celebrations. Three or 4 inch pots are also useful in combination work for planters and baskets.

Begonia seeds are very fine and take extra care for proper germination. The seed bed should be pressed firm and seeds left uncovered. Water is applied as a fine spray to avoid puddling and consequent clumping of seeds. High moisture levels must be maintained since the seed is lying exposed on the surface. A plastic covering over the germination flat to maintain moisture levels is essential unless conditions in the germination chamber are perfect. Germination is poor in the dark. Seeds are up within 2 weeks although the tiny plants may be difficult to see. Rough watering practices soon after germination will cause the seedlings to be covered up and result in poor survival. Pelleted seeds are much easier to use and will result in better stands of seedlings with less work and risk.

Growing temperatures should be no lower than 60^0 F until plants are well established, at which time they can be lowered to 50-55^0 F if necessary. Growth is slower at these temperatures but flower color is enhanced. If plants become overgrown, they can be sheared back and will return to flower in 3 or 4 weeks. Dwarf strains are by far the most popular and are essential in pack production. Packs with larger compartments should be used when growing fibrous rooted begonias if they are to be sold in flower.

January 1 sowings grown at 60^0 F will make heavy 3 1/2 inch pots in the North for Mother's Day. Packs require approximately 3 weeks less time. Good demand also exists for large specimen plants in the spring. A monthly sowing schedule will provide growers with nice 4 to 6 inch material through the winter when there is a need for inexpensive window plants.

Several tuberous rooted double flowered begonias are available for garden usage. Some are good for pots and hanging baskets, while others are suitable only for hanging baskets. They generally must be grown under some shade in higher light areas. The flowers of these tuberous begonias are impressive both in color and form. Gardeners can hardly resist at least 1 plant.

Large patio tubs and hanging baskets of tuberous begonias are very popular. Starter plants for home use are usually sold in 3-4 inch pots because of the large leaves present on plants. Six inch pots make excellent gift plants for the floral trade from early spring through the summer months.

Early December sowings will yield good 4 inch plants on Mother's Day. Hanging baskets and 6 inch pots should be started 4 or 5 weeks earlier. A $62-65^0$ F temperature is necessary through mid winter but established plants may be carried at 55^0 F in March and April. Four hours or more of additional light is needed for tuberous begonias until March 15 to encourage vegetative growth and branching. Young plants must be transplanted to a porous soil mix for mid winter growing in small pots but the final shift to larger containers can be made with a heavier soil mix if necessary. Growers should consider planting 6 inch pots and hanging baskets with several smaller plants to produce heavy flowering in very short order. Single plants in large containers can tend to be somewhat skimpy if basal branches have not been heavily produced.

Tuberous begonias are difficult to produce because of the exacting germination requirements, slow winter growth, and extended lighting necessary to prevent growth stall. Pelleted seed is helpful but cannot substitute for poor grower technique. The final flowering requirements in spring are not nearly so troublesome. Bedding growers may wish to purchase well started plugs to avoid the problems associated with winter culture. In this case, it is essential that well lighted, vigorously vegetative plants be received for final planting in March. Earlier planting of plugs can result in a return to a stalled growth stage if no extended lighting is provided. Southern growers will find tuberous begonia culture to be somewhat easier in the earlier winter stages.

Both fibrous and tuberous begonias require only light fertilizing. Heavy applications result in extremely succulent growth with fewer flowers. Crowding or constantly wet conditions lead quickly to severe stem and leaf rot.

Browallia

Browallia loves warm temperatures and grows well in semi-shade. Northern growers will have some trouble with early growth stages unless they can maintain temperatures of 65^0 F. Once plants are started, they become very vigorous and make excellent hanging baskets or tubs. Large plants may be difficult to keep watered if exposed to direct sun or windy conditions.

Blue is the most popular color but lavender and white are also available. The bell shaped flowers will almost totally cover mounded masses of deep green leaves if fertilizer is not excessive. Leafy growth results from high nitrogen levels.

The small seed germinates in about 2 weeks and should not be covered. Early growth may be slow in the North but several small plants in a hanging basket will quickly fill out during early June. Sow March 1 for late June baskets in the North.

Aphids and spider mites can become serious pests if they are allowed to become established. Early pest control must be practiced because the dense vigorous growth of plants makes later efforts difficult.

Calendula

These cold tolerant plants are popular where summers are cool. They may be used for winter and early spring gardens in warmer climates. Colors are limited to yellow and orange shades, normally with a black or brown eye. Recent variety introductions are compact in the garden and make excellent bushy plants which are normally 10-18 inches tall.

Seed germinates easily in approximately 1 week. Plants are not especially attractive in packs and become ungainly before flowers are produced. Sow April 1 for green packs at Mother's Day. Plants not sold early as green plants can be sheared off and allowed to flower in the pack.

Carnation (Dianthus)

Several dwarf annual carnations have been introduced in recent years. They may be used as garden plants or as florist pots. Plants outdoors are beautiful in spring but do not tolerate the burning sun and hot days of summer. A full range of colors is available, except blue.

The seed germinates easily in about 10 days and must be removed to cooler temperatures as soon as it breaks the soil.

Flowering plants must be grown under full sun at cool temperatures and moderate to low fertility. Heat and high nitrogen will cause plants to become grassy. Packs are seldom offered because the seed of varieties now produced is extremely expensive.

Aphids are troublesome on carnations, and the buds should be inspected regularly for signs of infestation.

Flowering pots for Mother's Day are possible in the North from a November 1 sowing if plants are grown at 50^0 F after establishment. Four plants will fill a 6 inch gift pot nicely while 1 plant is sufficient for 3 inch garden specimens.

Celosia (Cocks Comb)

Bright colors in the red, orange, and yellow shades and easy growth make celosia a favorite garden plant. Celosia is easy to grow if it receives plenty of heat (65^0 F) and light. Under these conditions it will use copious amounts of fertilizer and water when established. Lower temperatures lead to slow growth and danger of stem and root rot. Aphids can be troublesome if allowed to get a start.

Restricting growth in small containers causes premature flowering from which the plants may never recover full vigor after being placed in the garden.

A full range of plant heights from 8 inches to 3 feet is available. Flowers are produced in either a cock's comb shape or in feathery plumes.

Seed germinates easily in about 1 week under warm conditions and most varieties will produce saleable green plants within 8 weeks of the sow date. More vigorous varieties can be sown 2 weeks later.

Chrysanthemum (Dendranthema)

Both the annual and perennial varieties will be discussed in this bedding plant section.

Celosia perform well in hot, dry climates.

Perennial chrysanthemums from cuttings are perhaps one of the more popular bedding plants because they are easy to grow and can be sold in bloom from early spring through late fall. Spring and fall crops are especially easy to grow while summer crops require artificial manipulation of the daylength to bloom at precise dates. Chrysanthemums provide late summer and fall color in the garden when other flowers have spent themselves or succumbed to frost. Light frosts only serve to intensify color in chrysanthemums. Many varieties are available in a complete range of height, flower color and shape, and bloom dates. Growers in areas where severe frosts come early should offer 7 or 8 week cushion varieties that bloom in August and September. Chrysanthemums are classified by the number of weeks needed for plants to flower from the onset of short days. Chrysanthemums have become a premier floricultural species because of their unequaled lasting quality and vigor of growth. Mass displays of chrysanthemums in bloom are a sure sale.

Manipulating daylength for flowering garden chrysanthemums in summer becomes quite detailed and no precise schedule will be presented here. Readers may refer to manuals published by cutting suppliers for excellent timetables. Daylength control at this time of year means a short period of long days to encourage vegetative growth and establishment and then a long period of short days provided by shading to induce flowering. Unless a definite market exists for a good volume of summer plants, it is usually best to omit crops at that time and concentrate on no light-no shade crops for spring and fall when the great majority of sales are made.

Mums generally require a temperature of 62^0 F to set buds evenly. After buds set, temperatures may be dropped to 55-60^0 F for growing on and even to the freezing point for conditioning or storage when flowers are opening. Garden varieties will generally form suitable buds at 55^0 F but better crops are obtained with a 62^0 F initial temperature. Full sun is essential to avoid tall, skimpy plants. Two applications of B-9 growth retardant at 0.25% are necessary to control height on taller varieties. When plants become established they will use large amounts of water on sunny days. No disbudding is practiced on garden mums.

Mums are prone to aphid attacks and if the pests are not eradicated before flower buds open, it is almost impossible to obtain control of them. Leafminers may also become a problem, especially if cuttings are not obtained from reliable propagators who are aware of and practice stringent preventive measures for this pest. As plants begin to flower, especially in late summer, a good eye should be kept for thrips infestations in the flowers. Preventative measures are usually best if problems with this pest are common. Diseases are seldom a problem if clean soil and pots are used along with cuttings which have been carefully selected from mother plants free of the many wilts and stunts which affect chrysanthemums.

Spring garden mums in the North are usually planted 1 cutting per 3 or 4 inch pot about March 1, pinched 1 week later and grown under a no light-no shade schedule. Seven week varieties will flower at the end of April while 8 week plants bloom the first part of May. The schedule varies slightly with latitude. No light-no shade programs are not reliable after a planting date of approximately March 10 although some growers plant 2 weeks later with good results on selected varieties. If cuttings are already showing buds, the pinch should be very hard so vegetative growth is forced from the base. Three and 4 inch pots grown pot to pot will become crowded

Garden mums show impressive color on display and in the garden. Very easy culture and extremely profitable.

and weak if soft tip pinches are given which allow too many breaks to appear. The first B-9 application should be made when new breaks are 1/2 - 3/4 inches long.

The cuttings which result from pinching can be stuck and rooted easily if they have not set bud and if they are large enough. No lighting is needed. Patented varieties cannot be propagated in this manner without a license agreement. Cuttings rooted from the original plants will bloom well in 2 1/4 inch pots with no pinch.

Spring mums are usually grown in flats with no spacing so control of height with B-9 applications is essential. Fertilization predominately with potassium nitrate as recommended in this book for most other bedding plants will also check lush growth. After buds have appeared, crops can be split into 2 or 3 temperature regimes so that a succession of bloom dates occurs. Choosing an assortment of varieties and including some 6 week, 7 week, and 8 week varieties will also insure that the crop does not bloom all at the same time. Customers should be warned that spring is not the normal blooming time for mums. Inexperienced gardeners may become upset if plants do not flower the next spring.

Fall mums are grown on a 1 or 2 pinch schedule for heavy 6 or 7 inch pots and as a no pinch fast crop in 5 and 6 inch pots. Pinched crops are planted in May and June and allowance must be made for about 3 weeks between pinches for new growth to elongate. No pinch should be made after July 25. Published schedules recommend planting the no pinch fast crop about July 23; some growers realize better production with an earlier June or July plant date when early flowering varieties are grown. Unless exceptional quality is desired, the fast crop is more economical since less time is spent caring for the crop and an inexpensive plant may be offered to gardeners. A B-9 application is made when breaks are 1/2 to 3/4 inches long after the final pinch or about 10 days after no pinch cuttings are planted. A second application should follow in 10 to 15 days if the varieties are especially vigorous. Plenty of space is usually available in the fall for wide spacing so that heavy fertilizer can be used to promote maximum growth.

In areas where hard frosts come early, growers must choose varieties with the earliest natural flowering date. Certain varieties are more reliable in no light-no shade spring schedules and some varieties produce a better plant under fall fast crop conditions. Propagators will supply this information on request for their current offerings. Growers must evaluate performance under their particular conditions since propagators' recommendations do not always work out under all circumstances. Cuttings are normally ordered from specialists since it is uneconomical for most greenhouses to maintain stock plants of the many varieties needed. Some growers finish their fall crop outdoors. This allows for plenty of space and tones plants well for garden planting but often leads to additional need for pest control.

Annual chrysanthemum seed is offered in white (otherwise known as Leucanthemum multicale) and yellow (otherwise known as Gleostephus myconis) flower colors. The plants are 6-12 inches tall and can be used effectively in borders. Some afternoon shade may be necessary outdoors in areas of high light.

Seed germinates easily in about 1 week and the resulting seedlings are quite vigorous. White flowered plants bloom in approximately 13 weeks while yellow flowered plants take 2-3 weeks longer. A temperature of 50^0 F is suitable after plants are established well in the packs.

These annual chrysanthemums make cheery additions to combination pots. The seed is inexpensive, growth is fast and easy, and customers readily purchase a good quantity of plants once they have tried them. A very profitable crop.

Coleus

Bright colored foliage and a tolerance of shade and warm temperatures make coleus a favorite for garden and indoor use. There are numerous colors, sizes, and leaf shapes available. The market for coleus includes packs, pots, hanging baskets, and planters. Plants grown for the garden are usually from seed while hanging baskets and indoor pots are often propagated from cuttings as well as seed. Spring packs remain neat and saleable for extended periods if compact varieties are used and temperatures are lowered to 60^0 F. Hanging baskets sell very well even through the winter months. Several asparagus sprengeri plants at the edges of coleus baskets make a particularly nice combination.

Vigorous growth of coleus takes place only above 60^0 F but plants may be lowered to 55^0 F in order to keep crops from becoming overgrown. Although coleus is classified as a shade plant, the nicest greenhouse crops are obtained with light shade only in summer. Coleus wilts quickly when water is deficient and a slight wilt between waterings will discourage stem rot and excessive succulence. The appearance of flowers from early fall through late winter in the North is somewhat of a nuisance and can be overcome to a certain degree by careful selection of those varieties which have the weakest and shortest flowering response. Soft pinches of terminal shoots at 3 to 4 week intervals will eliminate the remaining flowers.

Fertilizer can be restricted on packs for garden use but larger pots and hanging baskets of coleus should receive adequate concentrations to develop their full growth potential.

With year-round schedules it is best to take the majority of cuttings before and after heavy flowering occurs because both cutting production and rooting will be slow at this time. Five hours of additional light starting 4 weeks before flowers normally appear will keep stock plants in a vegetative stage if cuttings must be taken during winter. Seedlings can be

Large coleus hanging baskets sell steadily throughout the year. Used indoors and in the shade outdoors.

treated in a similar manner to prevent flowering. Cuttings root very easily and many growers stick them directly to the finishing pot.

Seeds germinate readily in 8-10 days if the medium is kept warm. Mid-March sowings in the North will be ready for sale in packs by mid May at 60^0 F. Four inch pots are saleable in 6 weeks in summer and 9 weeks in fall or spring when 3 cuttings are stuck directly to the pot and pinched once when established. Heavy 10 inch baskets take approximately 6 weeks longer with 8 cuttings per basket and 2 pinches. Varieties for hanging baskets should be selected so that growth is spreading and compact rather than straight up. A good supply of 4 inch pots in the taller varieties is valuable for centerpieces in spring shade planters with begonias and impatiens around the edges.

In recent years, some varieties of coleus have been developed which will tolerate full sun in all but the most sun-drenched areas of the United States.

Dahlia

Dwarf dahlias are the main concern of bedding plant growers, the taller, giant flowered varieties being generally unsuitable for pack and small pot production. Bedding varieties range from 10 to 24 inches in height and display a wide assortment of colors with either single or double flowers. Three or 4 inch pots of dahlias can be used for inexpensive Mother's Day gifts or for use in planters. Six inch pots sell well in some markets; they can be produced in the same time frame as smaller flowering plants simply by combining 4-6 plants per pot just before buds form. If packs are to be sold in bloom, a maximum of 48 cells per 11 1/2 inch x 21 inch flat should be grown to avoid spindly plants. The large seed germinates easily in 4-5 days.

Dwarf dahlias are one of the most suitable varieties available for 6 inch pots (here 5 plants per pot).

Dahlias prefer warm temperatures of 60° F to start out but excellent plants will result from temperatures as low as 45° F for finishing. Full sun is required to prevent stretching and promote flowering. Aphids are particularly fond of dahlias.

A mid-February sowing in the North will produce flowering plants in mid-May. Direct sowing to packs is very successful since the seed germinates easily and quickly. Coated seed is best for direct seeding if a mechanical seeder is used. 2 seeds per cell is sufficient. Dahlias germinate and grow very fast and extra late season crops can be turned by selling them green in 72 cell flats approximately 4 weeks after sowing at 60° F. Flowering is inhibited somewhat by high summer temperatures.

Dahlias are a high profit crop which sell well if the better varieties are grown properly. Most growers could probably move more if some emphasis were given towards marketing a variety of container sizes. Dahlias from cuttings are available, but the extra cost is hardly justified since customers readily accept the very good seed varieties.

Daisy, marguerite (Argyranthemum)

These plants have been a favorite of cut flower producers for many years but they are also attractive in outdoor plantings, especially when used in larger patio containers. White and yellow flowers are most common but pink strains are available. Plants in the garden or big containers grow vigorously and may reach a height of 2 feet.

Marguerite daisies are sensitive to photoperiod and bloom profusely only during the longer days of spring and summer although a few flowers may be seen in winter. Propagation is by cuttings which root easily when in the vegetative state. Propagation of large specimen plants for spring sales should take place in early winter or as soon as stock plants begin to produce vegetative branches. Cuttings for 3 and 4 inch pots should not be taken before March 1 in Northern states since earlier propagated plants will become too tall before flower buds are initiated; this schedule assumes no pinching and no growth retardants. Cuttings propagated after early spring will bloom as soon as they are rooted.

Specimen plants intended for large containers can be sheared during March to allow for 6-8 inches of new growth before flowering begins. Several early March cuttings planted to a 6 inch pot make a nice gift item in May.

The marguerite daisies filling the upper portion of this planter really cheer things up.

White varieties usually exhibit the best form and yield the most cuttings. They also bloom more predictably. Marguerites love the sun but do not tolerate excessive high temperatures in summer. Aphids are the main pest.

Several new varieties have been introduced in recent years, but it is questionable if the extra cost of obtaining cuttings is justified when compared to the traditional strains.

Dianthus (Pinks, Sweet William)

Dianthus includes a large group of useful garden flowers. Carnations, treated previously, are a member of this genus as are annual dianthus, annual sweet william, and their perennial counterparts. Varieties are quite variable as to height, ranging between 6 and 18 inches. Colors heavily

Dianthus breeding is progressing quickly. Many new varieties make the garden dianthus popular not only in areas with cool summers but also in warm climates where it is used as a winter annual.

favor the pink and red shades (hence the common name "pinks") mixed with white.

Garden emphasis in the past has been upon the perennial forms of dianthus and gardeners still associate the name with them. Improved strains of annual dianthus have been introduced recently and are rapidly displacing the perennial forms in popularity because of the increased color they produce. Annual dianthus are best used in areas where the summers are cool or as winter annuals in sunbelt states. If given some winter protection, most annual varieties will persist in the northern garden for several years; gardeners can often treat them as tender perennials.

Dianthus like cool temperatures. They should be fertilized lightly and grown at less than 50^0 F after establishment. Lush growing conditions cause plants to become grassy. Full sun is necessary for compact plants.

Dracena spikes are often very profitable for the independent garden store since they are seldom available in chain outlets.

The seed of most varieties, including perennials, usually germinates easily in about 2 weeks. If the germination chamber is warm, seedlings must be quickly moved to cooler temperatures to avoid stretching.

A March 1 sowing of annual varieties in the North will produce flowering packs in late May. The dwarf annual sweet williams will bloom several weeks earlier. Perennial varieties can be sown in mid March for sale as green pack plants in May.

Dracena spikes

These plants which look like a large, coarse grass are indispensable as a central focal point and for height in patio planters. Smaller specimens serve the same purpose in hanging baskets.

Once acclimatized outdoors, dracenas will tolerate a wide variety of growing conditions from just above freezing to summer heat and from heavy shade to full sun. The most balanced and economical growing temperature in the greenhouse is about 60⁰ F with full sun. In this cultural framework, seed sown in the North July 1 will make heavy 4 inch pots for mid May. Fall sowings will provide smaller plants for spring hanging baskets.

Seed germinates slowly and may require 6-8 weeks even in the heat of summer. Since seed is usually sown in the drier months, precautions should be taken by covering well with soil to prevent desiccation during the long wait until seedlings become apparent.

Dracena spikes are a long term crop and several insect pests may become established, especially spider mites.

After consumers see dracena being used in larger containers, a healthy market in 3 and 4 inch pots will usually develop as people begin to create their own patio gardens. Although dracena is easy to grow and can be spaced closely, growers must remain aware of the nearly 1 year crop cycle for 4 inch plants; prices charged should reflect the long growth period. Crop time can be reduced somewhat by sowing a clump of 4-5 seeds for each final plant needed. It is reported that dracena seed loses viability quickly; therefore, it should be purchased fresh each year.

Dusty miller (Senecio, Cineraria)

This silver leaved foliage plant for the garden is an old favorite whose popularity is increasing because of its usefulness in patio planters and hanging baskets. Dusty miller is a medium height to low, mounding plant which is easy to grow both in the greenhouse and outdoors. It comes in several leaf shapes and eventually develops small yellow flowers which are inconspicuous and are usually pruned off.

Once dusty miller is well established, it will survive extremely low temperatures. Plants left in the garden often suffer little damage from milder northern winters and can be used in planters to brighten home entry ways until the Christmas season.

The seed is fairly small and germinates in 10-14 days when left uncovered. Some varieties may be difficult to germinate easily and it is necessary to pay attention to details and to make sure seed packets have the germination percentage of the seed lot recorded. This information will

Dusty miller is an old favorite whose popularity is increasing because of its usefulness in patio planters and hanging baskets.

allow growers to determine if poor success is due to improper conditions or low viability seed. Pelleted seed is easier to use and should definitely be used if one is planting plugs or direct to the cell pack. Three to 4 seeds per cell should be plenty if it is left uncovered in good moisture conditions.

Dusty miller seedlings are subject to rotting out unless a 60° F initial temperature is maintained and some care is taken to avoid overwatering. Established plants may be grown at near the freezing point if necessary but crowding and overwatering under these conditions will result in leaf rot. Low temperatures and good sun intensify the silver color in leaves.

Dwarf varieties to be used in Mother's Day combination planters and hanging baskets should be sown December 15 in the North and 3-4 weeks later in warmer regions if plants are to be grown at 50° F after establishment. Leaving the plants crowded in packs will help stretch them so that they are tall enough to be easily visible in combination work. Taller varieties may be chosen and the sowing date delayed.

February 15 sowings will provide shorter pack plants which are more suitable in the garden proper. Dusty miller is easy to grow under good conditions and makes a very neat appearing flat of plants. It is one of the most durable bedding plants in the marketing process and in the garden.

Several related genera are often included as dusty miller. The nomenclature is confusing to say the least. Also see chrysanthemum and centaurea.

Flowering kale and cabbage (Brassica)

These unusual bedding plants are becoming more popular as consumers look for something to provide color during fall and early winter. Flowering kale and cabbage perform much like traditional cabbage plants in the garden but become highly colored as nights cool down in the fall.

Gardeners will be best advised not to plant seedlings in early spring since temperatures lower than 40^0 F will cause flowering to be initiated and plants will not develop properly for best fall performance. Plants should be started in the warmer months and allowed to gain size without flowering until fall. Pink, white, and red varieties are available.

Seed germinates easily in 4-5 days and saleable green plants can be ready in as little as 4 weeks during warm weather. Temperatures should be kept as cool as possible, preferably at 50^0 F or lower (but above 45^0) after establishment.

Flowering kale and cabbage are edible, often being used as a garnish in food presentation. Keep this fact in mind as pesticides or other regulators are employed on nearby crops.

Fuchsia

Well grown fuchsia pots or hanging baskets always draw more than their share of attention. People are taken by the unfamiliar bell shaped flowers and rich colors. When they discover fuchsias do well in shade, a solid repeat business will develop from year to year. Six inch pots of the more compact varieties are sometimes produced as spring and summer flowering plants but acceptance as an indoor decorative has been limited because flowers drop off quickly. Both trailing and moderately upright varieties are used in hanging baskets.

Fuchsias are normally propagated from tip cuttings. Extremely succulent or overly mature tissue should be avoided. Cuttings must be kept moist and turgid until they are stuck and placed in a shady location. Propagation during hot dry weather is often difficult unless mist is used. The cuttings root rapidly with bottom heat of 75^0 F.

Fuchsias prefer cool temperatures of about 55^0 F but where compactness is not a critical factor (hanging baskets) $60\text{-}62^0$ F will produce acceptable plants in a shorter time. Full sun should be given in northern greenhouses at all times except summer to prevent weak stems. One cutting is usually placed in 3 or 4 inch pots and pinched when established. Six inch pots will require at least 2 pinches and 10 inch baskets will need 2 or 3 pinches if 5 cuttings are used.

Stock plants of fuchsias must be meticulously inspected for the presence of spider mites and especially white flies. Either one of these pests can render an entire crop worthless in short order.

Cuttings taken in mid January in the North will yield good 4 inch pots in early and mid May with 1 pinch. Baskets for early April sales can be propagated around Thanksgiving. Plants should receive the last pinch approximately 8 weeks before sale in early spring and 6 weeks before sale at later dates.

Fuchsias require daylengths of more than 12 hours to flower profusely. Cuttings rooted in April and May will flower too quickly so that plants do not attain an appropriate size. Cuttings taken in late fall must be constantly pinched to keep plants in bounds because plants remain primarily vegetative until mid March.

Cuttings are difficult to obtain in summer and early fall when plants are in the flowering mode. The best time for fuchsia propagation is from early January through mid March; temperatures are cool at this time and plants are in the vegetative state. Numerous excellent traditional varieties are available. Recently, some cultivars which tolerate more heat have been introduced. Fuchsias are extremely popular in cool coastal climates but have limited demand in hot arid areas.

Gazania

This plant with daisy-like flowers is especially useful in hot, dry climates. Many different flower colors are available but yellow and orange shades predominate. Flowers close up at night or in deep shade.

New varieties of geranium are making this old favorite even more popular. Larger 6 inch pots like the one above can be an important part of the market.

Aphids are a particular problem on gazania and preventive measures are necessary. Plants not treated for aphids early are almost certain to be overrun with this pest.

Seed is hairy and difficult to handle unless the fuzz is removed. A relatively heavy covering of germination medium is necessary to exclude light from the seeds. Overwatering should be avoided. Seedlings emerge in 7-10 days if the soil is kept warm. Northern grown plants will flower in May from a February 1 sowing.

Since gazanias are relatively unknown, they will usually need to be offered in flower in 3 inch or larger pots. If they are well known in your climate, green packs may be good sellers as well.

Geranium (Pelargonium)

Geraniums are one of the most important crops in floriculture today and their popularity increases yearly. Many greenhouses rely on them as the number one spring crop. Well grown geraniums can generate a great deal of traffic in plant stores since it is often difficult for customers to locate high quality plants. The widespread use of geraniums has come about because of their free flowering habit and ability to tolerate adverse conditions. In addition to being excellent performers outdoors, geraniums are present in the window sills of millions of homes, schoolrooms, and businesses. They are truly the All American plant.

Geraniums are sold in all sizes up to large planters and hanging baskets. The standard size for garden use is the 4 inch pot. Introduction of improved seed propagated varieties has led to sales in packs. Growers have perhaps neglected important sales which can be made in the 6 or 7 inch pot price range. Well branched plants of this size with several large flowers are valuable merchandise for retail flower shops in the spring and particularly at Mother's Day and Memorial Day for garden centers. A large stock of geraniums is necessary to fill the need for them in planter and basket combination work. Even geraniums in 10 inch and larger pots are now popular because people want instant color on the patio.

The recent renaissance in geranium production is the result of improved varieties from plant breeding programs, disease free stock plants and cuttings produced by specialist propagators, and improved cultural programs made possible by the 2 previous advancements. Thirty years ago the typical 4 inch geranium might have been started in November and was sold at Memorial Day. Today it is possible to begin with disease free rooted cuttings and market a well done plant in 8 weeks. The development of acceptable seedling varieties has led to more widespread use of geraniums in the garden. Consumers could previously seldom afford to make mass plantings with 4 inch pots but this practice is now feasible with seed geraniums in packs.

Vegetatively propagated geranium varieties are numerous and there is considerable variation in their resistance to diseases, growth, habit, flowering performance, rate of growth, and adaptability to garden conditions. It is necessary for growers to carefully select varieties suitable for the particular production and market conditions prevailing. Certain varieties have flowers which shatter or fall apart easily; these are especially unsuitable for shipping long distances. Geranium varieties should be evaluated for their performance under crowded spring greenhouse conditions. Some may do well at other times but will not produce profitable crops under

These 4 inch seed geraniums provide an effective mass display.

the close spacing necessary when greenhouses are completely full.

Some geraniums are bred for particular types of use, such as shady areas. If substantial geranium production is planned the grower should develop a check list of desired characteristics and evaluate each prospective variety with reference to the standards required. Some of the more universally important characteristics would be : resistance to diseases and pests, fast growth and rooting, tolerance of crowded conditions, good blooming capability with long lasting blooms, easy to grow, good outdoor performance, pleasing plant form, and durability in the harvesting and marketing process. Flower color is, of course, one of the most important varietal properties.

Much production has been shifted to seedling varieties, especially in larger, more mechanized operations. Seed geraniums lend themselves to automated production more so than do cutting varieties. This economy in production has made seed geraniums popular at chain stores and supermarkets. Some trials indicate that seed geraniums will, in general, out perform vegetatively propagated plants in the garden, but this is far from a proven fact. Cutting derived varieties unquestionably are more desirable at the time of sale from the standpoint of beauty. Growers must evaluate their own market conditions to determine what proportions of the 2 types to grow. Low price-low service outlets will likely move a large proportion of seed geraniums while full service garden centers may sell mostly plants from cuttings since they cannot compete with prices at low service stores. The latest market trends suggest that seed geranium sales might be down in proportion to cutting types.

The greatly expanded development of varieties and cultural techniques in vegetatively produced geraniums during the recent past could not have taken place were it not for progress in the ability of commercial breeders and propagators to control several very serious fungal, bacterial, and viral diseases.

Fungal and bacterial diseases such as blackleg and bacterial blight can ruin entire crops in short order if contaminated stock is used for propagation. Viral diseases usually work in less spectacular ways by reducing overall crop productivity but their end effect is just as costly. All these dangerous diseases can largely be ignored as threats today if good hygiene is practiced throughout production and cuttings are derived from plants recently indexed for viral, fungal, and bacterial diseases (stock plants should be discarded after 1 year).

Reinfection of certified plants can take place quickly if old geraniums are allowed to remain in the same greenhouse with new stock plants. All old leaves and soil should be removed from the benches and surface sterilants applied before clean stock is planted. Needless to say, growers should have adequate assurances that geranium plants they buy for finishing or as stock are propagated by reliable sources which use only disease free mother plants. No modern vegetative geranium program can produce profitable crops over the long term without taking advantage of disease free plant stock.

If stock plants must be saved for more than 1 year, a rigorous selection of only the best plants should be practiced rather than starting next year's crop from leftovers. Plants left at the end of the season are often late bloomers or have hidden diseases which delayed their development.

Selection of stock plants like this year after year can lead to a large percentage of slow growing, late flowering plants in a crop. Most growers nowadays purchase disease free stock plants from specialists each year to assure good crop performance. These plants are grown in larger pots through late summer and fall, with tip cuttings being taken periodically to shape the original plant and to accumulate additional stock. Depending on market dates, cuttings for 4 inch material are usually taken January through March for the spring season. Southern growers may begin propagating sooner to meet earlier marketing needs.

Either stem or tip cuttings may be used. Cuttings from older woody tissue are more likely to contain disease organisms and should not be used in the early phases of building up a stock of mother plants. Stem cuttings will require an additional 2 weeks to bloom. A large crop of stem cuttings may be taken on the last cut when stock plants are cut completely up or trimmed severely to stimulate new growth. If stock plants are to be sold and have been in the same pot for an extended period, they should be removed from it after trimming the tops and planted in new soil. Roots may be cut back at this time and watering must be reduced greatly until new growth is evident. This method of treating stock plants ensures that new growth will be vigorous and plants will produce large flowers rather than being hardened, woody plants with few and undersized blooms.

Geranium cuttings must be handled with care to prevent contamination by diseases. Several commercial sterilizing agents can be used to dip cuttings thoroughly. Clean knives and containers are necessary. Any plant which appears odd or malformed should be culled immediately. When cuttings are taken, stock plants should be cleaned of all old leaves to prevent conditions conducive to disease growth. Cuttings are stuck with enough space to assure air movement; crowded cuttings inevitably lead to mold. Geraniums root with less loss to disease if the medium is kept a little on the dry side, with just enough moisture to allow rooting. Different varieties must be rooted in separate trays since rooting time may vary considerably between them. Rooting hormones may be used to increase rooting speed and uniformity but are not necessary.

Several different rooting media are suitable for geraniums; but whatever type is used, it must provide good aeration and be free of diseases. The lower leaves along with their petioles should be removed from cuttings before sticking. Large leaves which restrict air movement near the surface of the rooting medium will cause cuttings to rot.

Most varieties root in 2 weeks without hormones. Certain fast rooting ones may show roots in 1 week. Bottom heat of 75^0 F is necessary. Cuttings which are rooted in open flats of media should be planted to growing on containers before roots develop too far, this reduces the amount of breakage during transplanting.

Geraniums root easily with or without misting. A few days time may be gained through misting since full sun can be allowed under this regime. Cuttings propagated without mist must be shaded and therefore will not carry on photosynthesis as rapidly as those in full sun.

When mist is used, extreme caution is necessary to prevent undue buildup of moisture in the medium or upon plant tissue. This will lead to serious rot problems quickly unless absolutely sterile conditions exist. Too heavy misting can also leach nutrients from the leaves.

Cuttings planted to the final containers when roots are less than 1/2 inch long will suffer fewer broken roots and lessen the chance for entry of diseases into wounds.

If the soil was moist at planting, irrigation should be done sparingly until plants are established. Overwatering is the nemesis of young geraniums. Directions advising growers to water young geraniums in heavily after transplanting often accompany the plants in shipping containers. This procedure can result in heavy losses if the potting medium does not drain quickly and if full sun and warm temperatures are not provided immediately.

Admittedly, heavy irrigation from the start will produce crops more quickly under ideal conditions but some risk is inherent in this cultural avenue.

Temperatures of $62\text{-}65^0$ F help newly potted cuttings off to a fast start after which $55\text{-}60^0$ F will suffice for growing on. The growing on temperature may vary with the needs of the grower. Closely spaced plants are more compact at lower temperatures while plants that are given adequate space will be saleable even at temperatures of 65^0F. At times it is necessary to grow at 65^0 F to meet a particular time schedule for markets. Some growers who have plenty of propagation space prefer to stick cuttings directly to the finishing pot.

Vegetatively produced geraniums must normally be spaced to at least 6x6 inches to allow pinched 4 1/2 inch pot plants enough room for proper development. No pinch 4 1/2 inch pots can be produced pot to pot but results are much better if they are spaced to at least 5x5 inches. Many growers prefer wider spacing but this crop can quickly become unprofitable unless a close eye is kept on the amount of space allowed per plant. Specific varieties are available which flower well with restricted spacing.

Well rooted cuttings can be finished as 4 1/2 inch flowering pots for Memorial day from an April 1 transplant date if conditions are ideal. This schedule allows no pinching. A soft pinch will delay flowering 3-4 weeks while hard pinches cause delays of 6 weeks or more. Severe root pruning and removal of cuttings from stock plants must take place at least 8 weeks before the mother plants are to be sold in bloom. Even more time is required if temperatures are below 60^0 F or if light is low.

Geraniums benefit from full sun at all times in most sections of North America. Some shade may be necessary in the greenhouse during midsummer if sunlight is especially intense in certain geographical areas.

Fertilizer programs for geraniums must be designed to produce healthy plants which reach their full flower potential but excess fertilizer causes plants to become leafy and soft. In this condition plants will not be suitable for sale unless large amounts of space are allowed; thereby leading to unprofitable production economics.

Pests seldom become a great problem with geraniums unless control programs are poorly handled. Insects and mites will usually show up on other species long before they become numerous enough to attack geraniums. Some care must be exercised with pesticides since several common formulations cause severe damage to open blooms. Fungal diseases must be constantly guarded against to prevent excessive losses. Blackleg or stem rot is the main disease contributing to losses. Blackleg is recognized by black, rotted areas appearing on the stem, usually at the soil line but lesions higher up the stem are not uncommon. Roots may also be affected but are less often diagnosed. Pythium and fusarium fungi are usually the agents of root diseases. Botrytis on leaves and flowers is also common when proper control of humidity in the greenhouse is not exercised.

Virus diseases of geraniums such as crookneck, crinkled leaves, and mottled leaves are not controlled by any chemical means. Plants showing evidence of viral diseases must be culled immediately. Using culture indexed stock plants and practicing careful sanitation will eliminate serious losses due to diseases. Fungicides are necessary as a preventive measure on young plants. A condition known a oedema sometimes occurs on geraniums under conditions of high soil moisture and excessive humidity. Cork-like eruptions occur on the undersides of leaves and sometimes on the petioles. Less frequent but heavier waterings and good ventilation help in controlling this physiological condition. Certain varieties seem to be more prone to damage than others.

The tremendous increase in breeding work with vegetatively reproduced geraniums has led to so many good varieties that it is impossible to present a condensed list of the better selections. Even 15 years ago this could be done with some assurance that a service had been done for the grower; but now a short listing of varieties might actually discourage investigation into other fine selections which could prove to be even more suitable under specific circumstances. The grower must evaluate each prospective selection and determine if it fits the overall greenhouse and marketing program.

Different markets require adjustments in the crop percentage which is grown in each color of geranium. Only experience will allow growers to accurately predict their needs. Geraniums now come in a wide array of bloom colors, some of which were unavailable only a few years ago.

Since geraniums are now used in many more situations than a Memorial day urn, red is declining in relative popularity. Pinks, salmon, magenta, and orange are increasing. The following percentages of colors to grow represent only the general experience of the author in a single full-service retail market and could vary considerably with other applications; red 51%, pink 15%, salmon 15%, magenta 12%, white 3%, and orange 4%.

Of course there are cases where it is difficult to class a particular flower as belonging to one color or another since it is intermediate or even so unusual as to defy easy placement. Only experience will help in this case.

Similar temperatures and light conditions are applicable to seed geraniums. Diseases are usually of much less concern since a carry over from generation to generation is not likely. Seed geraniums are often given a Cycocel spray or drench at 1500 ppm when plants are about the size of a 50 cent piece. This produces a well branched, compact plant. Some leaves may discolor to yellow after treatment but plants will soon grow out of this condition. Seed geraniums should be timed carefully to prevent flower shatter from becoming a problem. It is best if plants can be sold before flowers are more than 1/4 open.

Larger growers who must ship seed geraniums in bloom may find that applications of silver thiosulfate sprays which have been developed at several major universities are helpful in preventing flower shatter.

Seed geraniums are seldom offered in pots larger than 4 inch. Green plants in packs are suitable for garden use in mass plantings and offer the consumer a good value. Many varieties are available, some being better for certain applications (such as pack production) than others.

Seed germinates easily in 4-5 days and small green pack plants can be ready for sale without Cycocel application within 8 weeks from sowing when grown at 62° F. Packs with larger cells (approximately 21/4 inch square) require at least 12 weeks. Flowering 4 1/2 inch plants take 16 weeks from sowing. These schedules are based on high light northern locations.

Seed geranium varieties are often classed by the length of time required before flowering occurs. The above plants would be classed as a 15-16 week variety while others may flower in as little as 13 weeks. Some growers prefer to apply Cycocel a second time in order to grow more compact plants. This practice must be balanced with the possibility of reducing garden performance through indiscriminate dwarfing of plants.

Geraniums from seed are easy to grow and produce very nice plants with proper culture. Some progress is being made in making the flowers more acceptable to the majority of customers. Further improvement in this vein is likely to greatly increase seed geranium popularity in comparison to the vegetatively reproduced varieties. For the smaller grower seed reproduction is a distinct advantage, allowing disease and pest free crops to be grown without the expense involved in obtaining similarly clean vegetative stock.

Gerbera (Transvaal daisy)

Gerberas are slowly gaining acceptance for outdoor use in the garden and in patio pots. The striking daisy-like flowers with a multiplicity of beautiful colors can not be easily substituted for by other species. Both tall and short varieties of gerbera are available although the taller strains are normally derived from vegetatively propagated starter plants. Tissue culture is often employed by propagation specialists.

Several compact varieties for pots are now available but the seed is generally very expensive. It germinates easily in 10-14 days but seedlings must be monitored carefully to assure healthy growth to the transplant stage. Warm temperatures of 65° F and careful regulation of watering to avoid soggy soil are important at this time.

More mature gerberas prefer full sun in the northern greenhouse except during midsummer. Plants are best grown at about 60⁰ F but well started pots will withstand both higher and lower production temperatures.

Aphid and white fly are both serious pests on gerbera and will undoubtedly become established if contamination is present in the greenhouse. Losses due to diseases are sometimes serious unless stringent sanitary practices are followed. Gerberas are somewhat the same as geraniums in this respect, growers can produce beautiful crops if sanitation is good but poor housekeeping often leads to unsalable material.

A January 1 sowing will produce 4 inch flowering pots in late May for northern growers. Southern growers may deduct 3-5 weeks from this schedule.

Herbs

The use of home grown herbs has increased greatly as a result of the numerous articles about them in magazines devoted to ecology and natural foods. The recent popularity may be enduring but the wise grower will stay alert to signs of declining demand if publicity does not continue. Unless one intends to promote herb sales extensively, it would be best to grow only those varieties which have wide public recognition and may be counted on to generate an adequate volume of business. Herbs are usually offered as 2 1/4 to 4 inch pots with informational name tags attached.

Both perennial and annual herbs are available but perennials are in more demand. A growing temperature of 50-60⁰ F and full sun will suffice for the more common varieties. Most varieties of perennial herbs grown in 2 1/4 inch pots at 55⁰ F will be saleable in early May from a March 1 sowing. Annual varieties generally require 2 to 3 weeks less crop time.

The number of herb varieties is very extensive and growers can easily begin to produce an unwieldy number of them. The garden market for herbs must be viewed in perspective; herbs constitute only a small portion of total sales. If numerous varieties are offered, the price charged must be adequate to compensate for the extra time required to handle small quantities.

The following is a list of some top selling herbs: parsley, basil, rosemary, thyme, tarragon, cilantro, mints, oregeno, dill, chives, echinacea, comfrey, valerian, anise, hyssop, bay, chamomile, lavender, marjoram, sage, catnip, caraway, St. John's wort, and tansy. Almost all of these are easy to grow from inexpensive seed, thus leading to good profits if a market exists.

There are markets for large quantities of harvested herb products (as opposed to living plants), but this is not the focus of this book. Restaurants, food stores, and specialty shops have greatly increased the business in fresh and dried herbs.

The growers who appear to flourish producing herbs are those who are definitely interested in this particular subject and who develop an expertise and knowledge of beneficial use which the average grower cannot match.

Impatiens

Growers have been increasing impatiens crops faster than any other bedding plant in recent years. Reports now indicate that more impatiens plants are grown for market than any other species. It is certainly the gardener's number one choice for shady spots. Sales may not be so spectacular in areas of the country where summer sun is extremely intense or in newly built up neighborhoods where shade from large trees is negligible. Every house, however, has a shady north side. Newer varieties of impatiens are often tolerant of somewhat higher light levels. Impatiens is particularly useful in hanging baskets and planters which are used in covered patios. Indoor use in sunny windows, atriums, and home greenhouses ensures steady demand for plants through the winter.

Few plants exhibit more color to entice customers than properly grown impatiens. Hanging baskets and large pots are particularly showy. Plant breeders have contributed to the impatiens success story by introducing many fine varieties in the past 30 years. Taller types reaching 14 inches in height are available as well as varieties only 8 inches tall. A wide range of colors from soft pastels to intense reds and purples is offered. Specialization has reached the point where varieties are created to fill particular needs, such as plants for hanging baskets.

Germination of impatiens seed can be difficult because it is very sensitive to moisture stress. Since light is required, seed will not germinate if covered heavily with medium to retain moisture, but a very fine covering will help to keep seed from drying out. Germination problems are particularly acute in late spring and summer when temperatures become warmer. Impatiens seed is expensive and if germination problems persist, it may be best to order seedlings from specialists or to start with a form of enhanced or pre-germinated seed. All of the enhanced stage seed is easier to germinate than raw seed but, as the stage of pre-germination is increased, the ability of seed to survive long storage periods goes down. Careful environmental control is still necessary for enhanced stages of seed to germinate, but the process is reduced in time from about 10 days to 4 or 5 days, depending upon the stage of seed purchased. Raw seed takes at least 2 weeks for germination. Seed purchased in the later stages of pre-germination is susceptible to freezing; growers should be aware of this danger in shipment and storage. Damping off is frequently encountered in the seed flat and shortly after transplanting. Impatiens is sensitive to many fungicides so applications should be made at 1/2 strength if used. Removing the seed flat after germination to a slightly shaded area with plenty of air circulation will reduce the possibility of damping off. Seedlings must be handled carefully when transplanted; their succulent nature renders them easily damaged.

Domes are useful over germination flats to assure adequate humidity for seeds but the domes must be removed quickly as soon as germination occurs. Failure to do so will almost certainly lead to damping off. If dome covered flats are subject to strong sunlight, they must be covered with newspaper to prevent undue heat buildup.

Impatiens is quickly damaged by excess soluble salts and soggy soil. A porous soil mix is essential to prevent salt buildup and to insure adequate drainage. Once plants are well established, they will tolerate somewhat tighter soils as long as heavy fertilizer applications are not made and leaching occurs periodically. Ammonium forms of nitrogen are reported to damage impatiens. Nitrogen in any form should be applied cautiously because excesses will result in lush vegetative growth and few flowers. Over fertilization is harmful both from the standpoint of poor quality and the possibility of increasing soluble salts in the soil.

Temperatures of 65^0 F will help plants establish quickly after transplanting but $55\text{-}60^0$ F is more acceptable for growing on. Temperatures lower than 55^0 F for extended periods will result in yellowish, constricted growth. In plastic or older fiberglass houses, impatiens should be grown in full sun to promote flowering. Glasshouses may need to be shaded lightly for best results. Watering should be heavy but infrequent to reduce the possibility of soluble salts damage. Wilting is not desirable but more compact plants are obtained if the soil is allowed to dry before irrigation. Impatiens is not difficult to grow but attractive plants are obtained only if growing procedures are followed carefully. These plants react wonderfully to proper care but will not tolerate abuse as well as some other species. If

New Guinea impatiens is gaining quickly in popularity. Extremely useful in larger containers.

packs or pots become overgrown, they can be sheared back to re-bloom in about 3-4 weeks at 55⁰ F. For the smaller grower, this may be a more satisfactory alternative than treatment of the entire crop with earlier growth retardant application. Impatiens bloom under any daylength regime, but the extremely limited light conditions of northern winters may delay flowering and cause excessive stem length before blooms appear.

Impatiens is not especially susceptible to pests unless problems already exist in the greenhouse. Growers who operate year round may find that spider mites and cyclamen mites become established on plants if sources of infestation are not cleared up before spring crops are put in. Particular care must be exercised since these 2 pests may escape notice until populations are beyond control. Crops are often completely ruined before visual confirmation of cyclamen mites occurs. Tomato spotted wilt virus (TSWV) and impatiens necrotic spot virus (INSV) are both potentially dangerous diseases which are often spread chiefly by thrips populations in the greenhouse.

Packs sown in late March will flower in late May at 60^0 F. Three inch pots which have been pinched require an additional 3 weeks. Three pinched plants per 6 inch pot will be ready at the same time as 3 inch pots. Seed for 10 inch Mother's Day hanging baskets must be started in early January. Six plants are planted per basket and sheared heavily when foliage covers the surface. If the season is warm and bright, these baskets may be up to 3 weeks early but plant quality will not suffer appreciably. Time schedules are for the variety Super Elfins Mix. Southern growers may be able to deduct a week or 2 from this specific time schedule but if plants are started sooner to market in early May, the total production time should be roughly equal. The sowing date may also be shortened a few days through the use of pre-germinated seed. If the latter is employed, growers may wish to direct seed impatiens to the packs, using 1 seed per cell.

New Guinea impatiens are an altogether different group of impatiens than the bedding types discussed above. Much of the culture is similar with the important exception being that New Guineas will tolerate somewhat more light. Blooms do not develop properly in heavy shade.

Well grown New Guinea impatiens can be truly spectacular. The blooms often reach 2 or 3 inches in diameter and there are many varieties with interesting variegations and colors in the leaves. Several seed propagated varieties are now available but at the present cost of seed, it is questionable if the reduction of choice in varieties represents a true savings over the numerous excellent cutting propagated strains.

Cuttings root quickly and easily if they are not allowed to wilt and bottom heat is provided. Most new varieties are patented and cannot be propagated without license agreements.

Several well rooted cuttings transplanted to 10 inch baskets or patio pots in mid February will bloom well by Mother's Day if only 1 soft pinch is administered. This schedule assumes a $60\text{-}62^0$ F growing temperature in the North. Six inch pots are also popular for this holiday.

Spider mites will predictably ruin crops of New Guinea impatiens unless extreme caution is used to prevent entry of the pests on purchased cuttings.

A physiological disorder known as "oedema" on the underside of an ivy geranium leaf. This disorder may also less commonly affect regular geraniums.

The greenhouse must be free of mite infestations at the time of planting. Even with clean stock and a clean greenhouse, preventive measures are still a wise course of action. Due to the possibility of virus infection, growers should order new stock plants each year from a reputable virus free supplier.

Ivy Geranium (Pelargonium)

The increased popularity of hanging baskets in recent years has led to more interest in ivy geraniums. They are also useful as trailing plants on the edges of planters. Garden use is limited to varieties which exhibit a more compact habit. Light purple, pink, red, rose, white, and variegated colors are available. Most ivy geraniums are decidedly trailing and have flowers which tend to shatter. Sybil Holmes is the most widely grown variety because it is compact and has full, double pink flowers which do not shatter. Well grown hanging baskets on display ensure a brisk demand for 3 and 4 inch pots. Ivy geraniums are often not offered at chain stores and supermarkets so a premium price can sometimes be realized.

Development of new ivy geranium varieties is beginning to take place rapidly, although lagging somewhat behind the common geranium.

Growers should keep abreast of these new developments since some exceptionally nice flower colors are resulting. Recently introduced varieties also tend to have more compact growth habits.

Care of stock plants, cutting production, and cutting establishment should be guided by the same considerations as were mentioned previously for geraniums. A temperature of 55-60⁰ F is ideal for growing on. Higher temperatures will contribute to the legginess of plants and nullify the good done by pinching. All varieties must generally be pinched but acceptable pots and baskets of compact strains may sometimes be produced without a pinch in high light periods. If flowers are desired for Mother's Day, no pinch should be given after April 1. Ivy geraniums are basically sun lovers but Sybil Holmes will continue to bloom under slight shade. Most varieties are more or less susceptible to heat stall in midsummer and should be located near coolers at that time.

Fungal diseases are not a special problem with ivy geraniums when reasonable care is taken with sanitation. Spider mites can sometimes cause extensive damage if the pests are not completely eradicated from stock plants prior to cutting production. Oedema, a physiological disorder, is the chief production problem. The petioles and undersides of leaves may be seriously disfigured by the cork-like eruptions which characterize oedema. Excessive soil moisture and humidity are thought to be the chief causes of this disorder. Experience shows that if extremes of temperature and soil moisture are avoided and good ventilation is practiced, oedema will be relegated to the status of a minor inconvenience. Oedema is not transmitted from one plant to another.

Cuttings taken in mid January make flowering 3 1/2 inch pots for early May at 55⁰ F. One hard pinch will be necessary. If 6 or 7 cuttings are planted to a 10 inch basket, the same schedule will be appropriate for Mother's Day. Baskets pinched more than once should have 3 to 4 weeks added to the schedule. Southern growers can begin propagation 2-4 weeks later.

Lantana

These free flowering plants are from the mint family and have a distinctively minty aroma when leaves are crushed. Culture in the greenhouse and outdoors is easy if warm conditions prevail. Plants are quite vigorous if plenty of sun, water, fertilizer, and heat are provided.

Lantana can be seeded but the majority of production takes place from cuttings. More uniform and desirable plants are obtained from vegetative reproduction. The cuttings root easily with bottom heat.

Plants tend to become large and woody with continued growth. Stock plants should be periodically replaced by young cuttings so that the vigor of plants is maintained. Whitefly is especially troublesome on lantana. All stock plants must be completely free of this pest if any hope of profitable production is entertained. The practice of bringing outdoor plants into the greenhouse in fall as stock plants is a good way of helping to maintain whitefly infestations.

Varieties are available both for upright growth in the garden and as trailing hanging basket material. Cuttings taken in the South February 1 will produce hanging baskets in flower for Mother's Day if 6 or 7 rooted plants are planted per basket. Plants should be pinched no later than early April. Northern growers must add 3 or 4 weeks to this schedule. Lantana can be treated as a perennial in mild climates but is grown as an annual bedding plant in northern locations.

Lisianthus (Eustoma)

The potential for lisianthus (Texas blue bell) as a bedding plant in hot dry climates is considerable. It has been used as a cut flower for several years but practical use in the garden and as a potted plant was not possible until dwarf, self branching varieties were recently developed.

Blue is the predominant flower color although white and pink are available. Most varieties have single flowers but some are double. The most useful strains will bloom at only 6-10 inches of height. Tall varieties for background planting must be offered as green plants because they become ungainly if allowed to bloom in the pack or pot.

A January 1 sowing is necessary to have blooming plants in the North for June. Considering the long growing time, lisianthus is best offered in 4 inch or larger pots as an upscale item. Northern growers will find winter and early spring culture difficult unless 65^0 F can be maintained until plants are well established. After large seedlings are transplanted to 4 inch pots, a 60^0 F temperature with plenty of light is sufficient.

Southern growers can deduct 3-4 weeks from the above timetable and will likely have more success with this early crop. A late crop of lisianthus for summer bloom is often more practical for growers in the North.

Seed germinates readily in about 2 weeks but is extremely small and much care must be taken to avoid too deep a soil covering or drying out if left uncovered. Pelleted seed is much easier to use. Seedlings develop very slowly and must be kept warm and relatively dry. Overwatering causes considerable harm to lisianthus in any stage of growth. Lisianthus is relatively easy to grow if the 3 factors of good heat, limited water, and high light are provided. Difficulty is quickly encountered if any of these environmental factors is not properly supplied. Seedlings which are stressed by too much heat, cold, or drought in early stages often form a rosette which it is difficult to bring plants out of.

Aphids are a constant menace and should be guarded against. The hot dry conditions which lisianthus prefer are also conducive to spider mite growth and reproduction. If these pests are present in the greenhouse, preventive treatment is necessary.

Lisianthus is a long day plant, therefore, if sufficient vegetative growth has occured, 4 hours of additional light (as used for many plants) will speed up the production of flowers during late winter or early spring.

Lobelia

Low growing varieties of lobelia are used extensively as edging in gardens while the trailing varieties are often used in planters and hanging baskets. Blue is the color most in demand but white and reddish varieties are also available. Packs grown very cool will bloom at a height of 3 to 5 inches with a dense mass of foliage. Crops sold in mid and late spring should be sown in progression since lobelia becomes overgrown quickly in the greenhouse as warm weather approaches.

Lobelia is best if grown at 35-45^0 F because it will remain short in the packs. At higher temperatures plants often become overgrown before they reach the flowering stage. Temperatures of 50-55^0 F will produce acceptable green plants if they are sold quickly. It is important not only to keep night temperatures cool but also to reduce day temperatures as much as is practical. Good hanging baskets can be grown at the higher temperatures but plants are not so compact. Lobelia will tolerate light shade in the garden but greenhouse plants do best in full sun except at mid summer. Small clumps of seedlings are usually transplanted to packs since seed is inexpensive.

Plants sown January 1 in the North will bloom May 1 if grown at 40-45^0 F. Heavy green plants in packs may be sold June 1 from an April 1 sowing if grown at 50-55^0 F. Hanging baskets grown at 50^0 F for mid May must be sown in early December. Six plants per basket are sufficient and no pinch is necessary. If hanging baskets are offered, some trailing varieties should be grown in packs for those customers who prefer to plant their own baskets. Heavy fertilization, especially with nitrogen, should be avoided in packs to prevent lush growth.

Lobelia is a bedding crop which can assume major market status in areas with cool summers. It is useful in so many ways. As an edging in the garden it is unsurpassed and it is one of the most satisfactory and economical fillers available for combination pots and hanging baskets. Many growers are likely to have seen striking hanging baskets of lobelia but few people have as yet discovered that it is even more beautiful when viewed from the top as a patio planter.

Lobelia seed germinates easily within 7-10 days and should not be covered with medium. Since the seed is very small, pelleted seed is easier to use. Some growers may wish to direct seed into packs using multi-seeded pellets. A total of 6-10 seeds should be sown in every cell since the seedlings are small and grow slowly at first. Extreme care must be taken to provide direct seeded packs with optimum conditions during the first week or so after germination.

Several new varieties have been developed for both bedding use and hanging baskets. In general, these varieties are superior to older ones only in that they produce flowers about 1-2 weeks earlier on shorter stems. The old standby Crystal Palace is still one of the best garden performers even though it was introduced in the late 19th century. It is one of the oldest popular bedding plant varieties.

Growers who specialize in lobelia will find it highly profitable. It grows easily, is inexpensive to produce, and really satisfies the customer.

Lotus vine (Parrot's beak)

Not a widely known spring item but very useful and adaptable as a trailing filler in hanging baskets and patio planters. These plants are somewhat similar to asparagus sprengeri in habit but have a more branching character with striking silver foliage and stems. Lotus vine is quite vigorous once established and overgrows containers unless planted sparingly and pinched back as needed.

Brilliant reddish-orange flowers appear on the plants at times but are not the chief attraction of this vine. Most literature sources list lotus vine as a perennial and flowering is thus related to low temperature exposure in the winter. Plants grown under warm temperatures through winter remain primarily in the vegetative state. A yellow-flowered variety is also available.

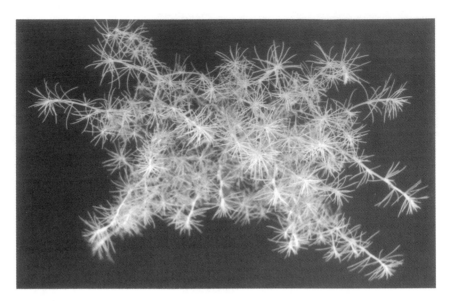

The silvery foliage of lotus vine contrasts nicely with other varieties in combination work.

Propagation is from cuttings which must not be allowed to wilt before sticking. Mist or a plastic covering over the propagation tray will insure that cuttings do not dry out. Coverings and mist must be discontinued quickly as soon as rooting begins or serious losses can result from mold which starts easily among the delicate and densely crowded needlelike leaves.

Lotus vine tolerates a wide variety of temperature, light, and soil water conditions but produces the most attractive foliage and habit at approximately 60⁰ F with reasonably high light and moderate moisture. Under extreme moisture stress, the lower branches will drop numerous leaves and turn yellowish. The silver color of plants is not so pronounced when grown in the shade and branches are less compact.

Compact plants in 3 inch pots require 16 weeks from cutting in the North. At least 1 pinch is necessary to induce sufficient lateral branching. Plants must not be allowed to become greatly elongated before the first pinch.

Marigold (Tagetes)

A continual growth in marigold sales has taken place because they are one of the most easily grown and floriferous annuals. All heights are available from 6 inch dwarfs to 3 foot background varieties. Yellow, orange, and deep reddish-bronze are the prevalent colors in marigolds but the patterns these colors are arranged in are numerous. Even a creamy white called "French Vanilla" is now available in a medium height carnation flowered type. Flower form and size also has a wide range. Large flowered carnation through medium size doubles to single pinwheel types are common. The number of varieties in marigolds is large and increasing every year. Some attempt must be made by the grower to limit offerings to 2 or 3 basic colors in each height and flower form class.

The tallest background marigolds are always sold green at about 2 to 5 inches of height. Crackerjack is an example of this extremely fast growing class with fully double carnation-like blooms. A medium height group of marigolds (14 inches) with fully double, carnation-like blooms is represented by such varieties as the Incas. This latter group may be sold green or grown on to flower. Flowering plants are most often sold as 3 to 4 inch pots. The smaller edging and bed type marigolds such as the Boy (8 to 10 inches) and Bonanza (10-12 inches) series are generally sold as packs in bloom. Properly grown marigolds in flower can seldom be matched for consumer appeal. Large displays of them are very effective in producing good sales of this profitable crop and providing a bright spring atmosphere for the shopping area. Information should be available to customers so that the correct use of each variety is clear.

Marigolds are a grower's dream. They are quick to germinate, fast to reach saleable size, easy to grow, and they have a sizable market demand. They are one of the most profitable spring crops available and every effort should be made to maximize their sales. Marigolds are especially useful in sun planters and patio pots. Garden performance is as superb as it is in the greenhouse.

No problems are normally encountered in germination but mice are especially fond of marigold seed and 1 mouse can destroy an entire sowing overnight. Seedlings must be transplanted from the seed flat quickly or plants become stunted and flower in the packs before sufficient vegetative growth has occurred to make them appealing. Seedlings develop excessively long stems if they are subjected to the warm, shady conditions of germination chambers only a few hours too long.

Since marigold seed germinates quickly and easily, many growers seed direct to the packs. When seeding directly or to plugs, coated seed is most often used — it is absolutely essential for mechanical seeders. The seed is elongate in shape and not all seeders will handle it easily. When sowing directly to packs, 2 seeds per cell are used. A larger number will cause crowding of plants and often results in small blooms on plants which flower prematurely.

Marigolds grow reasonably well at temperatures from 45-65^0 F but 50-60^0 F is the most acceptable range. Lower temperatures may be used to slow crops. When summer temperatures become excessive, growth and flower production are lessened. Full sun should always be given to develop adequate flowers and compact plants. Flowering of marigolds is enhanced by short days so that crops grown into mid summer may tend to be less floriferous and require extra time to bloom. No daylength manipulation is absolutely necessary. A few growers have used shadecloth to flower African marigold varieties at earlier dates than would be possible with the normal daylengths of late spring and early summer. Some newer varieties of the latter group flower especially well under longer days.

Proper fertilization is the key to exceptional marigold crops. Many growers become accustomed to restricting nutrients to prevent petunias and cool temperature bedding plants from becoming lush and overgrowing the container. This is a mistake with marigolds, they must receive adequate fertilizer in order to develop appealing green foliage to go along with the flowers. Hungry marigolds produce smaller blooms and have little foliage. The faster growing midsize and tall varieties are very susceptible to nutrient deficiencies if adequate fertilizer is not applied. The above suggestions do not mean excessive amounts of nutrients can be applied without harm. Too much nitrogen especially will cause foliage overgrowth and crowding in the pack.

Marigolds use copious amounts of water when they become larger and weather is warm and dry. Slight wilting on occasion is not harmful, but, if it occurs too often, plants will be more restricted in growth than necessary for their best appearance. Pests and diseases are seldom a problem with marigolds when reasonable care is given. Despite the old wives' tale that marigolds repel aphids, serious infestations of these pests can occur if left unchecked.

The schedule related here refers to specific popular varieties. Growers must realize that a change in varieties may require timing adjustments. For mid May sales in the North the following seeding dates are applicable at growing temperatures of 50-55⁰ F: March 15 for packs of the Boy series in bloom; March 7 for packs of Bonanza types in bloom; March 25 for packs of Incas as green plants or February 20 for 3 1/2 inch pots in bloom; April 15 for packs of Crackerjack as green plants. An additional week of growing time could be added if plants are desired in full bloom rather than just breaking color. Since most of these sowing dates are late, southern growers may not need to adjust greatly to account for faster growth.

Raw marigold seed is difficult to sow because of the tails (chaff) attached to it. Seeds adhere to one another and drop to the soil medium in clumps. This problem can be solved by ordering detailed seed which is available for most varieties. Detailed seed is especially useful when sowing varieties which are expensive. Other coating or cleaning treatments are given to marigold seed to make it more amenable for mechanical sowing.

Mimulus (Monkey flower)

This is a fast growing bedding plant with snapdragon-like flowers. Its use is limited to those areas with cool summers. Mimulus grows naturally along cool, bright stream banks and rocky mountain meadows. The flowers are strikingly different and very brightly colored in shades of yellow, red, orange, and ivory. Plants reach a height of about 1 foot in the garden.

Mimulus packs will flower in mid-May from a March 15 sowing. The seed germinates easily in 1 week but is very small and must be handled carefully. It is also quite expensive. Plants are succulent and easily overgrow the pack if not sold quickly or are exposed to hot conditions during the vegetative stage.

After establishment in the pack, a temperature of 45-50⁰ F with full sun is ideal for mimulus. Days longer than 13 hours are required for blooming. Moderate fertilizer is best to prevent overly succulent growth.

When aphids are prevalent in the greenhouse they can become a problem on mimulus. Mold in the seed flat or in densely foliaged packs is the major disease concern and overwatering or overcrowding must be avoided.

Plants started in the long days and heat of summer generally flower quickly on very small plants.

Nicotiana (Flowering tobacco)

Several good varieties of this flowering tobacco have been introduced in recent years. The dwarf types now available will grow 10-12 inches high in the garden and have a wide range of flower colors, excepting blue. Taller varieties can easily reach 2 feet and are quite vigorous.

One of the best selling points of nicotiana is the pleasant scent of the flowers; it attracts hummingbirds from far and wide. These plants grow easily and will tolerate a wide range of conditions. Their flower display is equivalent to that produced by most of the more popular bedding species. Considering the extremely positive attributes of nicotiana, it should be more widely promoted by the floral industry. One factor limiting its popularity at the moment is the small number of varieties available.

In the early stages of growth, nicotiana looks and grows like petunias (to which it is related), but it is much more vigorous. Similar growing conditions will suffice for both. As flowering approaches, however, nicotiana develops (in contrast to petunias) a prominent central stalk which produces numerous star-shaped 1-2 inch flowers. Nicotiana requires long days to bloom and plants started too early will continue growing taller before flowers are produced.

Packs of dwarf varieties sown April 15 in the North will be saleable as green plants in late May. Since nicotiana is quite vigorous, bringing plants to flower in the packs must be done carefully to prevent overgrowth. An additional 4 weeks is necessary for flower production. Southern growers can deduct 1 week from the schedule for green plants. Dwarf varieties flower nicely in 4 inch pots or as multiple plants in 6 inch pots. Aphids are fond of nicotiana flowers and buds. Nicotiana is amenable to height control using B-9 or DIF techniques.

If plugs or direct sowing to packs are employed, pelleted seed should be used. Since 2 seeds must be used per cell when direct sowing, the plants often become overcrowded in the pack unless they are sold green.

Osteospermum (African daisy)

These cool season plants are relative new comers but show very good consumer acceptance. Early spring is the best time to offer small pots and larger containers of Osteospermum. They are excellent for combination work also. A good deal of recent selection and breeding work has provided numerous varieties which exhibit a good color range and different habits of growth and bloom. Most varieties are patented and must be propagated vegetatively under license agreement.

Nicotiana is one of the most colorful and easily grown annuals but, unfortunately, not widely utilized as of yet. Used here as the central focus of a porch planter.

Plants propagated at New Year's should be grown at 65^0 F until March 1, giving a pinch soon after they are well-established. The temperature is then lowered to $45\text{-}55^0$ F in order to stimulate production of buds. Flowering will occur from late April through May in 3 1/2 in pots. Two plants will fill a 4 1/2 inch pot or several may be combined for progressively larger containers. Shorter growing varieties may be used to control height. B-9 is effective on taller varieties. Full sun is necessary at all times.

Osteopermum do not flourish under hot summer weather but will bloom well again as temperatures cool down in fall. Plants should be cleaned up and trimmed in midsummer.

A new variety of seed Osteopermum has just been released which offers good potential for bedding pack sales. If it performs well, this could lead to major usage by gardeners in cool areas and for winter gardening in the South.

An older group of plants in the genus *Dimorphothecae* (also called African daisy) has previously been cultivated, but only a limited number of new varieties has been released. They exhibit characteristics similar to *Osteospermum*.

Both groups are easy to grow as long as the temperature requirements for bud set are provided and sun is available. Neither will tolerate soggy soil.

Aphids can become a major pest if they are not controlled from the start.

Pansy (Viola wittrockiana)

Gardeners can seldom resist purchasing at least one pack of blooming pansies. Their flower colors are some of the most interesting and beautiful encountered in the plant world. Early blooming habits and cold hardiness make pansies a natural for heavy promotion when frost first leaves the ground and gardeners are looking for something to plant which tolerates late snows and frosts. The color provided by pansies in early spring and late fall is especially welcome since most other plants are out of bloom at these times. Many gardeners still believe that pansies should be planted in shaded areas but this notion has been outdated by the introduction of new varieties which will tolerate summer heat. Although pansies are annuals, they will overwinter in mild climates and also in northern areas if some protection is afforded by a loose mulch cover.

It is becoming common practice to offer pansies in bloom for fall gardeners. With a little care, these fall planted pansies provide good color into the early winter and again in early spring. Sunbelt gardeners are beginning also to see the benefits of winter pansy culture.

Numerous new pansy varieties are being offered each year, this will undoubtedly spur additional growth in the use and production of this versatile group of plants.

The traditional method of producing pansies was to start seed in the late summer and carry well established plants through the winter in cold frames insulated with straw or similar materials. Frost protection was removed at winter's end and plants were in bloom after the first week or so of moderate temperatures. During the past 30 years a shift to sowing seed in winter and marketing plants without overwintering has occurred. This method greatly decreases production cost. Although the best pansies are those from late winter seedings, growers in very cold climates may

Recent breeding advances and a push towards additional fall marketing have increased the volume of pansies grown and sold.

sow seed into mid April for summer gardeners. These late crops must be sold quickly or plants become overgrown.

Pansies develop an undesirable lush growth whenever temperature, fertilizer, or water is excessive. After establishment, temperatures between 35^0 and 45^0 F with full sun will result in excellent plants. If no heat is available, plants can be allowed to freeze lightly when they have had 1 or 2 weeks of cold temperatures to become adjusted. Greenhouse flowering when nights exceed 50^0 F is impractical because plants tend to become weak and spindly. Fertilizer, particularly nitrogen, should be held to a minimum as long as plants maintain a healthy green color. Slight wilting between irrigations is permissible to check excessive growth. Plenty of ventilation to prevent high daytime temperatures and reduce humidity is necessary. Night time ventilation is also advisable when the danger of heavy frost damage is past.

Many growers move pansy crops outside after the harsh weather of early spring is over. These plants must be carefully monitored for water each day and protected from wind damage to maintain quality. The full sun, good ventilation, and generally cooler nights afforded by outdoor conditions can result in a longer selling season. Aphids must be kept in check or they can become a serious problem. Infestations are easily apparent to customers since the pests congregate on flower stems and flowers. Control of aphids should be taken care of early since many insecticides will damage open flowers and, as plants become grown together, it is almost impossible to achieve a satisfactory kill.

Pansy seed germinates easily within 2 weeks as long as temperatures do not become excessive (over 75^0 F). The considerable cost of seed for most newer hybrid varieties dictates that a good deal of care be exercised in planning for germination and the use of seedlings which emerge. Young plants must be moved to cooler temperatures as soon as the majority of them have broken the soil covering.

Pansy seed is also offered in pre-germinated stages. This is a distinct advantage for those growers who sow direct to the pack (2 seeds per cell) or those who sow summer crops (pre-germinated seed does better than raw seed under warmer temperatures). The use of pre-germinated seed will, of course, speed up schedules a few days.

As pansies which tolerate a wider range of environmental conditions and which offer unusual flower colors and patterns become more common, growers should look for new uses on a regular basis. If you offer only the standard flat of mixed color pansies in early spring, you are missing a large part of the market.

Most new pansy varieties sown January 1 in the North will bloom in mid April if growing temperatures are maintained at $45\text{-}50^0$ F. Two or 3 weeks may be deducted from southern schedules. Fall grown plants will usually require somewhat less time since most of the growing period takes place when conditions are warm and sunny. Fall sowing should be done after temperatures have moderated to some degree.

Hanging baskets and patio planters are very economical for the grower and allow consumers to begin enjoying flowers early in the season. Another crop can be planned for fall sales. Generally, the seed for larger containers should be started 2 weeks earlier than for packs. This extra time allows plants to be in full bloom for maximum appeal. A 10 inch hanging basket with 9 plants or a 12 inch patio pot with 16 plants will be ready shortly after transplanting from green packs. Since pansies are well known, they can be sold in reasonable volume as green plants during the summer months for fall flowering gardens.

Petunia

Petunias are synonymous with flower gardening in many people's minds; every garden shop must maintain an adequate supply to meet demand. The dominance of petunias in sunny gardens has perhaps been brought about more by chance than any other factor. There are certainly other flowers which demonstrate equal beauty and performance in the garden but flower breeding technology was first focused in a concentrated and successful manner on petunias. Consumers and growers alike recognized the value of the improved varieties and began planting petunias in increasing numbers. Petunias soon became the number one garden flower. Their relative popularity has been slipping the past few years as plant breeding efforts have been concentrated on other groups of flowers. Impatiens are now the number one annual used for gardening although petunias still reign supreme in sunnier areas.

Modern petunias are available in 7 basic types: floribunda singles, floribunda doubles, multiflora singles (small flowered), grandiflora singles (large flowered), multiflora doubles, grandiflora doubles, and California giants. Multiflora singles were the first truly popular petunias and are contrasted with the grandiflora singles by having smaller flowers, smaller leaves, more branches, and earlier and more numerous blooms. Grandiflora singles replaced the multiflora singles in popularity not because they are better plants (in fact many authorities rate the multiflora as superior overall), but because the flowers are much larger and attract consumer attention. Grandiflora singles comprise a large percentage of petunia production today. The difference between the multiflora and grandiflora double flowered petunias is much the same as for single petunias but in this case no real predominance in popularity is evident. California giants were a class of extremely large flowered plants with a coarse habit. They enjoyed a brief period of success but, because of inherent weaknesses, were replaced by the multiflora and grandiflora singles.

The floribunda single type (Madness type) petunia was first offered commercially only a few years ago and has, in that short time, replaced the grandiflora singles and multiflora singles to some extent in bedding sales. The floribundas produce masses of weather tolerant blooms, as do the multiflora singles, but with nearly the same size flowers of the grandifloras. The floribundas appear to combine the best characteristics of both earlier classes. Some seed houses maintain that the floribundas also exhibit greater disease resistance. Double floribundas have recently been introduced.

Some valuable cutting type petunias have been available for several years. Most of these are basically very spreading in nature and serve mostly as flowering ground cover or hanging basket material. The flower size of cutting types is quite variable and only a limited color selection is available. Some excellent seed derived petunias mimicing these basic characteristics have been developed, but the seed is extremely expensive. The latter also contain a few varieties which are bushier and can be used for more upright pots or as traditional clumps in the garden. Both groups produce superb hanging baskets which perform much better over a long period than do traditional seed varieties. Certain of these are also very fragrant. As more varieties and color become available, these new seed produced sprawling varieties are likely to become very important.

A few very small flowered seed petunia varieties have been recently developed. They grow easily like other petunias but do not overgrow so quickly. Thus, they are useful in small patio containers or as filler in combination work.

Growers must determine the relative cultural and marketing benefits which each class of petunia offers in particular localities. Normally, the great majority of petunias offered at present will be of the single floribunda or grandiflora types.

The number and diversity of petunia varieties is large and no specific recommendations will be made here. Neophyte growers will generally do well to start with the most popular varieties a seed company offers and build upon this base as they gain experience. A cropping program of approximately 18-25 varieties will allow 2 varieties each for red, white, true pink, purple, and a good selection of more exotic colors. This variety range may be too much for the small grower and perhaps too few for extremely large operations. Grandiflora doubles are in good demand for pots and special locations but are ineffective in massed beds because they are not as floriferous as the single flowered varieties. Growing more varieties than warranted by market conditions decreases productivity.

Color preferences will certainly vary from market to market but red is

Petunias are unequaled in flower power when good sun is available. And they are versatile – in hanging baskets, 6 inch pots, patio planters, and garden beds.

far and away the most popular color, followed by white and the many shades of pink available. Deep burgundy, red and white bicolors, purple, yellow, wine with veins, lilac, and rose are also colors in good demand. So many possibilities in petunia flowers are available that it is difficult to arrive at a manageable variety list for production.

Distinguishing varieties according to their adaptability to greenhouse culture is fraught with uncertainties since conditions from one greenhouse to another will differ considerably. However, some colors and types exhibit fairly definite characteristics. True red colors are often much more susceptible to botrytis damage during rainy, humid weather. Pinks and purples usually bloom earlier than most other colors and sky blue colors tend to grow tall. Summer Sun (a popular single flowered yellow variety) and grandiflora double types often require additional nutrient applications when compared to other petunias in order to develop their full potential. Growers should observe the special growth attributes of different varieties and, if practical, grow each under the ideal conditions which it requires.

Petunia seed is quite small but germinates more quickly and easily than many other types of flower seed if reasonable care is given. The seed should never be covered and must not be allowed to dry out. Because petunia seed is round and small and rolls out of the packages easily, it is often sown too heavily. After the seedlings are visible, petunias are happy at a 55-60^0 F location in full sun. Excessive stem elongation and damping off will occur if seedlings are left in warm, moist germination chambers.

Petunia plugs are readily available from specialists or they can easily be grown on the premesis using pelleted seed placed in plug flats 1 seed per cell. If more than 1 seed is used, the plugs in which 2 plants result (the majority) are usually overcrowded, thus resulting in lower quality. This overcrowding by multiple plants is the main reason why direct seeding to the packs is not often practiced.

The debate over methods of petunia culture waxes hotter than for most other bedding plant groups. One faction advocates higher temperatures and plenty of food and water to produce a softer, actively growing plant at the time of sale. A central tenet to this philosophy is that the plant should go into the garden without any check in growth. The opposite faction believes in withholding water and fertilizer and lowering temperatures to produce a short, tough plant which will hold up under rough harvesting, sales, and transplanting treatment. The perfect petunia for marketing and gardening probably lies somewhere in between.

Overall, the best petunias seem to result by maintaining approximately 50-55^0 F temperatures after plants are well established. Full sun is required. Although petunias become very lush when fertilizer and water are plentiful, these growth factors should not be withheld to an extreme degree in order to keep plants short, as severe reductions of flower size and yellow foliage may result. Excessive daytime heat can also greatly reduce flower size. To a large extent, pack petunias may be kept short by practicing DIF techniques or through B-9 applications (other growth retardants may also be effective). B-9 delays flowering slightly.

Fast growth undoubtedly increases the profitability of petunias but anyone who has visited a garden center full of tall, lush plants falling over in the packs after being handled a few times will understand the need for a cultural program which toughens up plants. On the other side of the coin, customers will not buy dwarfed, starved plants either. Growers who monitor growth carefully, follow a middle course, and refrain from cultural extremes will have excellent crops. An ability to anticipate the needs of plants is essential to a good petunia crop.

Aside from botrytis, which can severely affect flowers and foliage; petunias in northern greenhouses are relatively disease free. Southern humid areas may be plagued to varying degrees with various stem rots. Growing on raised benches with plenty of air flow and at least some night heat will reduce these problems.

The following is a recap of cultural conditions which result in shorter, tougher plants: Keep temperatures cool, down to 50-55⁰ F; go easy on the fertilizer, especially nitrogen; irrigate heavily but only when plants definitely need water; never allow any shade on plants; grow on raised benches, if possible, and provide plenty of air circulation. Application of B-9 growth retardant at concentrations of 2,500 ppm are recommended by some authorities for height control but this is an added expense and should not be necessary if proper cultural and marketing procedures are followed.

Single grandiflora petunias sown in the North on March 1 and grown at 55⁰ F will begin to flower in packs in mid May. Single multifloras and floribundas should be sown a week later and double grandifloras 2 weeks earlier. Double multifloras will respond with double grandifloras. Two weeks can be added to this schedule for production of 3 1/2 inch pots without a pinch. Later sowings will require less time to flower as daylength and temperatures increase. Extra fertilizer and water should be applied to the double petunias if full realization of their flower form and size is to be reached. Southern growers can reduce growing time by about 2 weeks.

Hanging basket petunias are very popular and easy to produce. Most seed houses now have specific varieties which they recommend for this purpose (as mentioned previously) but any good floribunda or single grandiflora petunia is usually suitable. Seed for Mother's Day baskets grown at 55-60⁰ F should be planted January 15. Six plants are transplanted from packs to baskets and pinched shortly after establishment. A second pinch about 5 weeks before Mother's Day should bring a fresh bloom for the holiday. This schedule produces very heavy baskets which are not yet cascading. Large baskets of the newer cutting varieties mentioned earlier can be produced by rooting cuttings before January 1 and pinching several times after planting 6 plants per basket.

Polka dot plant (hypoestes) is a highly profitable crop which does well in semi-shaded gardens or as a high light foliage plant in the home. Versatile and popular.

Phlox

Several varieties of annual phlox are available. Each is very colorful but somewhat harder to germinate and grow acceptably in the greenhouse than most other annuals. Plants tend to become grassy when fertilizer is abundant or if they are shaded to any degree. Phlox do best under cool conditions in both the garden and greenhouse.

Newer varieties are helping to overcome some of the traditional problems, such as poor germination. Growers will want to trial new varieties as they become available in order to find those which perform well for them since this group of plants possesses good habit and flower characteristics and could become very popular.

Polka dot plant (Hypoestes)

This plant is grown mostly for its colorful foliage. It is a comparatively recent seed introduction and appears well adapted to limited bedding use in somewhat shaded areas. It is extremely attractive when used as a foliage accent in combination patio planters and hanging baskets which are intended for shade. It is also a good short term foliage plant indoors; mostly offered in smaller pots of 2 1/4 to 4 inches.

Polka dot plants are available in pink, white, and red leaf colors which are mottled with varying degrees of green. Flowers are inconspicuous and generally detract from the plant's appearance. When flowering occurs under short winter days, vegetative growth becomes insignificant. Constantly germinating a new crop of seed and providing 4 hours of extra light seems to avoid the undesirable flowering for those growers who wish to use hypoestes as winter foliage plants.

Packs for bedding will require about 10 weeks from sowing at 60^0 F. Several of these pack plants transplanted to 4 inch pots will be saleable as soon as they are rooted in (about 2 weeks). Plants raised in packs for combination planting require 3-4 weeks extra time to develop enough stem length to show up properly in hanging baskets and patio planters.

Hypoestes is easy to germinate and grows without difficulty, although damping off disease is common in early stages. Considering the many uses it has and the ease of culture, this plant definitely has high profit potential and should be investigated by every grower.

Aphids love polka dot plants and become a problem if preventive measures are neglected. Hypoestes can be easily propagated from cuttings but seed is cheaper, cleaner, and avoids the problem of low cutting production under short days.

Portulaca (Moss rose)

Sunny hot spots are ideal for portulaca. It is a short, creeping plant with succulent leaves. Portulaca is becoming a more important bedding plant as population shifts to the hotter and drier regions of the United States. Flower colors are very bright and predominantly of red, rose, orange, and yellow. The double flowered varieties are selected most frequently for pack production but there is some use of the single flowered varieties in hanging baskets. Packs of portulaca are attractive and remain short for a long period. Sales displays must be in a sunny area because sunlight triggers the blooms to open each day. One of the breeding objectives in portulaca is to produce plants in which the blooms remain open when not in full sun.

Portulaca can be grown as low as 55^0 F after it has been well established. Better crops are produced, however, if temperatures can be maintained at 60^0 F for the entire period. Soil should be kept moist after transplanting but once plants have rooted it is advisable to lean toward the dry side so that serious problems with rot are avoided. Dry soils delay the crop a bit but excessively moist conditions can result in crop failures. Portulaca is relatively pest and disease free except for the rot problem mentioned above. High relative humidity in the greenhouse can be as destructive as excessive soil moisture because it encourages the growth and reproduction of stem and leaf diseases.

Varieties with less expensive raw seed can be sown heavily in the seed flats and the seedlings transplanted as small clumps to packs. Or the seed can be hand sown to plug flats for transplanting without root disturbance. Direct sowing is also practiced. Portulaca seed germinates quickly (3-4 days) but the new seedlings are difficult to see. Inexperienced growers may fail to notice germination has occurred and leave the seed flat in the shade and high humidity a few extra days. This mistake quickly leads to excessively long stems and serious cases of damping off disease.

Improved portulaca bedding varieties generally produce double flowers more reliably and stay open longer. This seed is expensive. Pelleted seed is therefore recommended since the number used can be carefully regulated by using a mechanical seeder. Pellets are usually multi-seeded, so it is wise to ask the seed company exactly how many are included in each pellet. If sowing plugs, 4-6 seeds per plug cell should be sufficient. For direct sowing to packs, 10-15 seeds per cell may be necessary if less than ideal conditions cannot be maintained.

Several varieties of vegetatively propagated portulaca are available. These are sometimes used in special purpose situations but have not achieved great popularity. Aphids are more commonly a problem on these plants than with seed varieties.

Low light intensities and excess fertilizer will encourage plants to produce very few flowers. Portulaca is a very important crop in dry, high light areas but is seldom grown by gardeners where these conditions do not prevail.

Pack plants grown in the North at 60⁰ F from a March 1 sowing will flower at the end of May. Portulaca freezes easily in the garden and should not be offered for sale too early. Packs sold green will be ready 3-4 weeks earlier if several seedlings are transplanted to each cell. Schedules in the South can be shortened by 2-3 weeks.

Primula (Primrose)

A discussion of primula culture could as well be presented in later sections dealing with potted flowers or with perennials. The majority of primula varieties in common use today are tender perennials in the Acaulis and Polyanthus variety groupings. Perhaps the greatest volume of use is found as small mass market cool season pot plants, mostly from Acaulis varieties.

Even the hardier perennial primulas are, however, cultured primarily in a similar fashion as cool season annuals. Perennial primroses are an old favorite with gardeners and considerable sales can be made of flowering or green plants. A wide range of extremely vibrant flower colors make primula a close second to pansies in consumer appeal when plants are in bloom for early spring. Numerous florets in clusters are borne at the tip of a naked stalk with a neat rosette of leaves at the base. Flower stalks are seldom more than 10 inches high so that primula makes a nice perennial border. The Acaulis varieties generally possess a shorter stem than the old favorite perennial Pacific Giant Polyanthus strain.

The high cost of seed and the need for cold exposure to initiate flowers has led to most garden primula being sold in 2 1/4 inch pots or larger celled packs when in bloom. Green plants in packs can be profitable if less expensive seed strains are used. Many growers offer primula in 3 or 4 inch pots from late winter until Mother's Day for small gift or impulse sales in supermarkets. The plants do not hold up well under the 70⁰ F temperatures of home or store but are attractive for a few days.

Primulas to be sold as small flowering pots in the early spring or late winter should be sown in the fall and allowed to cool off to 40-50⁰ F during early winter. Those which are to be sold as 2 1/4 inch pots or flowering packs for the garden can be sown in the North in late December and January for blooms beginning in mid April. The later schedule requires a 60⁰ F establishment period before rooted plants are grown on at 40-50⁰ F. Higher growing temperatures may result in poor flower formation and flower stems which do not elongate above the foliage. Plants to be sold green can be sown 10 weeks before sale if grown at 55⁰ F.

Watering and fertilizing of primula should be somewhat on the lean side if plants are to be sold in bloom. A combination of high fertilizer and temperatures can lead to grassy growth with few flowers. Plants to be sold as soon as they are large enough in the green stage do not require the same restrictions of temperature, fertilizer, and water. Spring crops of primrose require no shade in the greenhouse but if plants are grown in summer, they will benefit from a light sunscreen. Excessive daytime temperatures will limit the ability of growers to produce good crops of primula. Aphids may infest flowers and stalks if precautions are not taken but primula is seldom bothered by other pests and diseases.

Malacoides varieties are sometimes used as small pot plants but do not find great acceptance as a garden flower. They require the same cool temperatures as the perennial types. Obconica annual primulas are also used for small pots and can be grown at approximately 10⁰ F warmer temperatures. There is some question whether to class the latter 2 groups as tender perennials or annuals (as is also the case with Acaulis types). The Obconicas sometimes provoke severe skin rashes on people who are allergic to them.

Primula germination requires about 3-4 weeks and can be irregular. The seed should not be covered with media. Germination temperatures must not become excessive and the seed sprouts poorly if allowed to dry out. Domes or plastic coverings placed over seed flats to raise the humidity should be removed quickly when seed comes up to prevent damping off disease.

Ranunculus

The flowers of ranunculus are among the most beautiful to be found. All basic colors except blue shades are available in the double camellia-like flowers. This plant would certainly be more popular if it were not for its rather exacting production requirements and relatively limited usefulness in the garden.

The common Bloomingdale variety grows 8-12 inches high and can be used as a colorful early spring pot or as a half hardy perennial in the northern garden. High temperatures are the nemesis of ranunculus and plants should be grown cool (45-50⁰ F) at all times after germination. Full winter sun is necessary to avoid stretching of plants. Extraneous light, which causes extended daylength, will interfere with bud formation and development.

Temperatures over 50^0 F are actively deleterious to early growth. Blooming plants can withstand somewhat higher temperatures but the keeping quality of plants is seriously impaired. High day temperatures in the blooming stage cause rapid deterioration of flowers and plants alike. Ranunculus is a rather impractical (although beautiful) crop for most situations.

Seed is germinated in September for flowering 3-4 inch pot plants in late March. Seedlings emerge in 2-3 weeks without much difficulty if seed is not exposed to excessive temperatures. Ranunculus can also be grown by purchasing treated roots which flower shortly after planting in January or February.

Regal geranium (Pelargonium)

Perhaps better known to past generations as Martha Washington geraniums, these spectacular bloomers are now coming into their own as a substantial crop; both as outdoor plants for patio or garden and as potted flowers for gifts or indoor decoration. Although the Martha Washington geranium has been around for many years, it is only with recent breeding, propagation, and disease control efforts that the crop has become practical and predictable on a larger scale. It was formerly grown mainly as a specialty item by those growers who wanted to offer something a bit different.

The dual role which regals can serve as indoor or outdoor plants makes them an ideal plant from the marketing standpoint during the gardening season. Substantial numbers can be raised for gift sales at Mother's Day or other high demand periods; if plants are not all sold for premium prices at those times, they can be marketed as garden merchandise.

Even more regal geraniums could be sold than are at present if they possessed better keeping quality as gift plants and if their flowering activity outdoors was more suited to warm summer weather. Regals initiate flowers only at lower night temperatures (most authorities specify approximately 55^0 F as the upper temperature limit for flower initiation). These plants see limited outdoor use in areas of the country where gardening season temperatures regularly exceed those required for flowering. Some progress has been made on plant form and keeping quality but regals are still a crop which must receive cool temperatures.

Marginal leaf burn appears quickly on regal geranium leaves when plants are allowed to approach the wilting point on hot, sunny days.

An exact flower initiation program is not universally agreed upon within the industry but growers can safely count on good blooming plants if the temperature is lowered to 50^0 F for 8 weeks.

Full winter light is required in the greenhouse for development of compact plants. Some shade may be necessary in the greenhouse and outdoors during summer in extremely high light areas. Regals will make excessive vegetative growth when fertilizer, water, and heat are supplied in luxury amounts. The best plant form is produced by finishing temperatures of approximately 55^0 F with the minimum of fertilizer necessary to maintain a healthy green color. Regals can be forced in the later stages at $60\text{-}63^0$ F to meet holiday schedules but plants will become less compact under this program.

Young plants can be irrigated sparingly to maintain compactness but large plants in the flowering stage will quickly show marginal leaf burn if they are allowed to approach the wilting point on a sunny day.

Regal geranium flowers are extremely susceptible to botrytis disease; this problem is one of their major faults. It can be almost entirely avoided by finishing plants with sufficient night heat to prevent humidity buildups in the greenhouse. Some newer varieties are reported to possess greater botrytis resistance. Whitefly is also a major problem during production if these pests are on the plants or in the greenhouse to begin with. Whitefly control in the later stages of growth is almost impossible due to the dense foliage present on plants.

Regal geranium production is concentrated in the 4-7 inch pot range but overgrown plants can be transplanted to larger pots and sold as soon as they are sufficiently rooted in. These older plants grow quickly and will often double their size within 3 weeks in late spring.

Most growers purchase disease free regal cuttings from specialists, they are sold as non-precooled and precooled plants. Precooled ones can be forced immediately since flower buds are already initiated. Non-precooled ones must be treated as described above. A 1 shoot cutting is usually grown to 4 or 4 1/2 inch pot size without pinching. One pinch as soon as plants are rooted in will yield a good 6 1/2 inch flowering pot at flowering.

When very small buds are visible in the stem tips, early spring plants can be forced into flower in approximately 6 weeks at 60^0 F. Late season crops will force more quickly.

Rudbeckia (Black-eyed Susan)

These sunflower-like plants have long been used in the perennial garden, but the recent introduction of several varieties classed as hardy annuals has broadened their garden usage. Most have yellow or orangish blooms 2-4 inches in diameter with a black center.

Rudbeckias can be used in the garden or as inexpensive summer patio plants. They are tolerant of both heat and cold, thus making their culture rather simple. Blooming is controlled by daylength, they will not bloom naturally in the North until approximately mid-June (depending upon the variety) unless days are artificially lengthened after vegetative growth has become vigorous.

The seed germinates easily in about one week. A light covering of media will help maintain moisture.

Toto is an excellent variety to use in small pots and even packs. It blooms reliably on short, stiff stems which continue to produce new flowers. Taller growing varieties are responsive to B-9.

Rudbeckia is a charming and easily grown plant which can provide beautiful plants in midsummer when many others have passed their prime.

Red salvia is a brilliant addition to pack, pot, or patio planter production programs. Growers in cooler and extremely high sunlight areas may find salvia less popular than in the midwest portions of the United States.

It is doubtful that lighting artificially for earlier sales would be widely practical since numerous excellent plants with a broader color range are available at that time.

Goldstrum is a standard long-lived perennial variety which does not bloom as reliably the first year from seed.

Salvia

The brilliant red spikes of scarlet sage put on perhaps the showiest display of any garden flower. Other colors are available but do not compare in importance or display with red varieties. Salvias range in height from about 10 inches to 2 1/2 feet, depending upon the variety grown.

In some sections of the U.S. salvias rank near the top in volume of plants grown for garden use. Warm areas of the East and Midwest which do not have brilliant sun are favorable for salvia. Most cultural guides recommend full sun but in extremely high light locations salvia may do better with some mid day shade.

Salvia grows well in the greenhouse at 55^0 F with full sun, but temperatures below this result in poor performance. Seedlings recently transplanted fare better at 60⁰ F until well established. Unless steady temperatures in this range can be maintained, growers should postpone sowing until warmer weather arrives.

Salvia is sensitive to high soluble salt damage. A porous soil and heavy irrigation will prevent salt buildup while allowing adequate fertilizer concentrations to be used. The plants are heavy feeders when growing well but will not tolerate excessive build ups of fertilizer in the soil.

Seed must be kept uniformly warm and moist for good germination. Since salvia seed requires light for germination, a dome or cover can be placed over the flat to maintain humidity. Alternatively, seed may be covered very lightly with soil media to aid moisture retention. The latter method often results in more predictable, although perhaps not optimum, germination. Plastic coverings often encourage damping off disease to get started unless the cover is removed immediately upon germination. Salvia is very sensitive to methyl bromide and media treated with this chemical should not be used for germination or growing on. Since the germination of salvia seed is sometimes difficult, growers should seek varieties in which improved germination grades of seed are available.

The combination of warmer temperatures, disease control, and low salt soil and water are essential to salvia culture. Neglect in any one of these areas can lead to severe problems. Salvia is a magnificent plant when given good growing conditions but rather unforgiving of less than ideal circumstances.

Whitefly is a constant danger with salvia and should be completely eliminated prior to planting.

Salvia is popular both in packs and small pots. It is very useful in combination work with patio planters and hanging baskets. Scarcely any other plant can provide such brilliant red colors in these mixed plantings.

The earlier dwarf salvias should flower in the North by late May if sown in mid March. Growers in the South should be able to sow salvia by March 1 to take advantage of naturally warmer days, these plants will be ready in late April. Taller salvia must be sold green.

The blue or white flowered Farinacea type salvias are an attractive bedding plant which are perhaps, for the average grower, more easily grown under less than perfect conditions. They generally have a more dense growth of smaller leaves than the red salvias and thus do not tend to appear so spindly in crowded packs. Height in the garden is 1-2 feet.

Shorter growing snapdragon varieties make excellent 6 inch pots but require careful growing procedures to develop the proper vigor and form.

Snapdragons (Antirrhinum)

Improvements in snapdragon varieties has been the major impetus in making them an important spring crop. A full range of heights and colors is now available in these delightfully fragrant flowers. Since the introduction of the dwarf (6-8 inch) varieties and medium height plants, snapdragons are more popular for edging and bed use than they are for background and cut flower purposes. The snapdragon lasts well as a cut flower in homes and offers an unusual form for incorporation in arrangements. Plants which have been preconditioned may be set out in early spring and will tolerate light frost.

Snapdragons are much like pansies in their tolerance of low temperatures and can be used in a similar manner as winter annuals. Snaps do not perhaps make as attractive a plant for this purpose since the flowers take longer to bounce back and develop after prolonged heat than do pansies.

The key to appealing, husky snapdragons is cool temperatures. Plants may be subjected to light frost if heat is lacking but the most economical crops are produced at 45-50^0 F. Full sun and plenty of ventilation will help keep stems strong. The height of plants in packs will remain under control better if water and fertilizer are applied somewhat sparingly. Aphids are the most common pest to afflict snapdragons while several fungal stem and root rots may become problems if plants are overwatered frequently.

Snapdragon seed is rather small but germinates easily in about 10 days if care is taken to provide proper conditions. Some authorities recommend chilling the seed for a few days before sowing to improve germination. Since the seed is generally quite expensive, this extra step may prove economical but is not necessary to obtain a good stand of seedlings. No covering is recommended but a light dusting of germination media evenly over the flat will help keep seed moist. Transplanted seedlings establish more easily if 60^0 F is maintained for 2 weeks before reducing the temperature for growing on. Pelleted seed is available for use with mechanical seeders when sowing to plugs or direct sowing to the pack. The seedlings are small and do not grow quickly, thus requiring at least 3 seeds per cell when direct sowing. Direct sowing requires careful control of environmental conditions.

Tall snapdragons of the Rocket series will be ready for sale as green plants in packs by mid April from a February 15 sowing if grown at 45^0 F. Many authorities recommend pinching tall snaps to 3 or 4 leaves to produce a bushy habit, but plants are quite acceptable if left single stem. The cost of pinching in terms of labor and extra bench time is prohibitive in most markets.

Packs of edging varieties such as Floral Carpet will bloom in mid April from January 15 sowings when grown at 45^0 F. Green plants are ready 3 to 4 weeks earlier. The dwarf varieties make very nice 3 or 4 inch pots. Crops of snapdragons for late May and June sales must be planted in weekly progression to avoid having too many ready at one time. The plants become weak stemmed easily as warm weather arrives.

Garden performance of snapdragons is better in southern areas in the cooler seasons and growers must adjust their schedules accordingly. Marketing and growing snaps for May or June sales is not practical in the South.

Black-eyed Susans respond wonderfully to warm temperatures when adequate nutrient levels are present.

Thunbergia

Thunbergia or black-eyed Susan is especially useful in hanging baskets and as a climbing vine which quickly provides shade or acts as a screen if given support to climb on. The variety having orange flowers with a black eye is most popular but white and yellow flowered varieties are also available. Black-eyed Susans will vine to a considerable height in the course of a season and bloom freely without interruption until frost. Many consumers are unfamiliar with these plants since they are not commonly offered at garden stores. Displaying a large number of hanging baskets in bloom will lead to a good demand for green plants in 2 1/4 or 3 inch pots.

Thunbergia seeds germinate and grow quickly so plants must be transplanted from the sowing flat before growth is restricted. If a suitably warm environment is available, seed may be planted directly to the pot (approximately 2 per 3 inch pot). Since the seed is large, it can be covered with about 1/2 inch of media. A minimum temperature of 60^0 F should be maintained until plants are well established. Temperatures of 55^0 F will suffice for further growing on but the speed of growth is much less satisfactory than that obtained at 60⁰ F or above. Black-eyed Susans require full sun to remain compact and flower profusely. The plants are heavy feeders and must be given supplemental fertilizer if only minimum nutrient levels are being maintained for other bedding and spring plants.

A light application of slow release fertilizer (reinforced with iron) incorporated into the soil for thunbergia will help boost nutrient levels if increasing the concentrations of liquid irrigations is not practical. Iron chlorosis is common in thunbergia and an application of this element is essential to maintain a dark green color. Warm temperatures also reduce the occurrence of iron chlorosis. Stem and root rots plague the young plants if they are overwatered but more mature containers use copious amounts of water.

Spider mites can cause serious damage to thunbergia if sources of infection are not eliminated. Control of these pests is very difficult when the plants become densely twined together. Spider mite damage should not be confused with dark brown specks or blotches which may appear on leaves when potassium is deficient.

Early January sowings grown at 60⁰ F will result in heavy 10 inch baskets for Mother's Day. Plants to be used in hanging baskets are normally grown in 2 1/4 inch pots and pinched once before transplanting 4 or 5 of them to baskets. Two more pinches are needed to produce good quality, the last one 5 weeks before sale. Green plants in 3 inch pots for mid May are obtained from a March 1 sowing with 2 soft pinches. Plants may be flowered on a small trellis with the same schedule for hanging baskets.

Torenia

The "wishbone" flower resembles snapdragon blooms to some extent. Torenia is a minor bedding plant but is surprisingly easy to grow into good looking market packs or pots. It is also quite useful in the garden; mostly preferring cool, moderately shady places but performing reasonably well in sun also. Perhaps more of this low (8-12 inches) mounding plant will find its way into the garden as both growers and consumers become familiar with it.

Torenia was originally offered with blue flowers but recent introduction of the Clown mixture has made several other colors available. The new variety is also more compact.

Torenia is a relatively unknown plant which offers good potential for pack and pot production. Does best with some shade in the garden.

The small seed germinates easily in about 10 days but should not be covered with media. A growing on temperature of 50-60° F encourages good growth and compact plants but the temperature can be above or below this range slightly if necessary to meet market schedules.

Aphids easily become established beyond control in the dense growth of torenia. Control should be practiced from the beginning if there is reason to suspect the possibility of infestation.

A March 1 sowing in the North will produce blooming packs for late May. Southern growers can deduct 2-3 weeks from this schedule. The hottest summer months may prove too much for torenia in southern regions.

Torenia is also available from cuttings, but these are not a great advantage over the seed types.

Verbena

This colorful minor bedding plant could become a popular garden flower in moderately dry, sunny regions if production problems in the greenhouse can be overcome. Basically, there are 2 factors which limit success: the seed of many varieties does not germinate well, and plants rot out easily if moist conditions prevail.

The first problem is being solved as new varieties have just been released. The second factor depends upon each grower paying strict attention to watering practices.

Growers should select several of the varieties recommended by seed houses for germination trials before choosing one for production.

After an experimental crop is grown at approximately 55°F, production can be increased from year to year as demand rises.

Well started plugs and cuttings are generally very easy to grow on to flower, however, most varieties are susceptible to mildew if conditions are favorable for the spread of this disease.

Several cutting varieties which make excellent hanging baskets have been released recently. Some are better than others as regards mildew resistance.

The better seed varieties take about 12 weeks to flower from sowing if grown at 55-60°F.

Vegetables

Many customers who view flowers as a luxury item will readily purchase vegetable plants because some economic value can be realized from them. Plant stores stocking a full line of healthy vegetable transplants will attract an added segment of the gardening public. There has been a nationwide trend for people to grow more of their own vegetables. Gardens are even springing up in the centers of large cities. The growing popularity of vegetable gardening seems assured since more young people are being introduced to the delights of fresh home products.

Growers should concentrate on this strong demand for vegetable plants because these crops often command a premium price while being less expensive to produce. Production costs are generally lower for vegetables than for flowers because less time is spent on the bench and culture is often easier. Vegetable seed is large and easy to germinate and the plants grow rapidly. The selling season for vegetable plants is lengthening because larger plants are more popular than before and varieties suitable for growing in patio planters have been developed. Developing a thriving business in vegetable plants is based upon selecting the proper varieties for the local climate and providing adequate cultural information to consumers. Healthy, strong plants are, of course, the beginning of any sales program.

A discussion on the greenhouse culture of vegetable transplants may be conveniently divided into 2 sections based upon the temperatures required for production of quality plants. Broccoli, brussels sprouts, cabbage, cauliflower, kohlrabi, celery, chives, onions, lettuce, and strawberries all thrive with rather cool night temperatures while cucumbers, eggplant, melons, okra, peppers, pumpkins, squash, and tomatoes prosper under somewhat warmer temperatures. Vegetable plants will generally be better products if subjected to the same slower than maximum growth and final hardening process as was recommended for floral bedding plants. A middle course should be followed, with neither lush growth nor excessive hardening being allowed to take place.

Chemical applications to control pests and diseases on vegetable plants must be more carefully monitored since the products are intended for human consumption. More and more consumers may be expected to demand plants which have not been treated chemically.

The selection of varieties to grow will revolve mainly about the expected maturity date. It is especially important to offer early maturing plants in areas where the growing season is short. The number of days until harvest quoted in seed catalogs is the growing time required from setting out small plants in the garden.

Certain varieties exhibit characteristics such as resistance to specific diseases which make them more suitable for growing in one geographic area than in another. Active breeding programs have provided disease resistance in some varieties of major vegetables. For example, the "VFN" notation which accompanies the name of certain tomatoes means "verticillium, fusarium, nematode resistant". Growers and gardeners alike should certainly pay close attention to such beneficial characteristics.

Many new specialty vegetables have been recently introduced; such as brociflower, miniature fruited vegetables, and highly or differently colored vegetables. Although these oddities are not usually important to the average grower, they may have significance in specialized markets.

Garden stores located in ethnic neighborhoods may need more of some plants than others. People of Italian descent will favor eggplant while German and Polish cooks make heavy use of cabbage. Greenhouses in areas where Hispanic culture is strong should raise adequate quantities of jalapeno, chili, and other hot peppers. Catering to ethnic tastes will ensure that these customers return when other plants or flowers are purchased. There are numerous varieties of vegetables. Growers must be aware of the predominant uses which their customers favor. Cucumbers may be picklers or slicers, tomatoes for juices or salads, cabbages for sauerkraut or fresh use, squash for winter or summer. The choices are almost endless.

Vegetables which prosper under cool greenhouse conditions are usually grown at 45-50^0 F. Lower temperatures for prolonged periods will cause premature flowering or "bolting" in cabbage, broccoli, brussels sprouts, cauliflower, and celery. Higher temperatures lead to weak grassy growth. Most cool vegetables grow to market size quickly and are good profit makers. Strawberries, onions, and chives from seed require longer growing periods but still produce adequate returns.

In regions where autumn weather is mild, customers will sometimes plant a second crop of cool season plants. Except for strawberries, cool vegetables are most often sold exclusively in packs.

Full sun is recommended for all cool vegetables. Fertilizer should be on the lean side to guard against weak grassy growth. The cabbage family can become infested with aphids unless precautions are taken but other pests and diseases are not normally a problem. Seed of most cool vegetables germinates quickly and seedlings must soon be moved to cooler temperatures to avoid spindly growth. If plants must be held back severely by restricting water and fertilizer, small heads or other unwanted side effects may be evident in the garden. Careful scheduling will eliminate the need to hold back plants in this manner. At 50^0 F most cool vegetables are saleable 6 to 7 weeks after sowing or, in the case of strawberries, planting the dormant roots. Lettuce will be ready 1 to 2 weeks earlier and onions, chives, and strawberries from seed require several extra weeks of growth.

A temperature of 55-65^0 F is used to grow warm vegetables. The lower range is employed only when plants are to be hardened for market or held back for a short period. Temperatures below 55^0 F will halt growth in most varieties and cause leaves to become yellowish. Tomatoes are by far the largest selling vegetable and special attention should be given to selecting the proper varieties and growing an adequate mix of fruit types

The tomato is king in most vegetable gardens. An extremely profitable crop for those growers who schedule carefully and offer a wide selection of sizes and varieties.

and container sizes. Peppers and cucumbers are the next most important warm vegetables. Larger pots are becoming more and more popular with this group of plants as pack sales have declined. Most crops are now produced in 3-5 inch containers but tomatoes especially are in good demand even in 8 inch pots with blossoms and green fruit. Five gallon pots with ripe tomatoes are profitable in summer if greenhouse space is not being used for other purposes. Larger tomato plants will usually need a sturdy stake for support. Do not tie the stems too tightly to stakes or stems will be injured as they grow larger.

Tomatoes are a good crop because they sell in volume and return a high profit. Growth is quick and easy. Greenhouses that make a special effort to grow excellent tomato plants will draw additional customers for other products. Preparations must be made to move large volumes of plants in a short period of time. Significant tomato plant sales can be made past the main gardening season by offering 6-8 inch plants in quantity. These larger plants can be ready in 2 to 4 weeks from 2 1/4 inch material if water and fertilizer are at high levels.

Scheduling for tomato plants must be precise to take advantage of optimum sales yet prevent overgrowth. The main marketing season is short and furious with no mercy for the grower whose crop is late. Crops should be sown to be saleable every 5 to 6 days during the main season and timed 1 week early. If growth is normal and plants are ahead of schedule, the greenhouse can be cooled and water restricted somewhat to slow development.

Eggplant and peppers grow best a few degrees warmer than tomatoes and can be placed in the warmer areas of a vegetable house. Neither of these plants is usually grown in larger than a 4 inch pot. Eggplant will grow at approximately the same speed as tomatoes while peppers require 2 additional weeks to reach marketable size in 4 inch pots.

Cucumbers, squash, canteloupe, watermelon, and pumpkins are all sown directly into the finishing pot. Typically, 3 seeds are planted in a 3 1/2 inch pot, covered with soil, then watered in. Multiple seeding also provides a pollination source in those varieties which require a pollinator plant. At 70^0 F seed will germinate in 4 to 7 days with squash and pumpkin being the earliest. If space is at a premium, the flats of pots may be stacked until germination occurs. These direct seeded plants are undoubtedly the most profitable greenhouse crop available. Marketable size is reached in 3 to 5 weeks from sowing. Cucumbers and squash are quite popular while canteloupe, pumpkins, and watermelon are minor crops in most areas. Watermelon and canteloupe are very sensitive to cool temperatures but the other varieties may be held back by lowering the temperature to 50-55^0 F. Squash and vine plants must be handled carefully when transplanting to the garden. They will not tolerate root damage. All 3 plants in the pot should be planted together.

Warm vegetables thrive in full sunlight. Water and fertilizer can be restricted somewhat to maintain sturdy growth but not to the point where plants lose good green color and lower leaves become yellow. Peppers and eggplant are especially vulnerable to aphids with peppers also being subject to heavy damage by slugs. The most bothersome pests to tomatoes are whiteflies. Cutworms can damage all 3 crops when plants are grown on the floor. Clean pea gravel or plastic on the floor will usually eliminate trouble from cutworms. Allowing weeds to grow on floors during the summer off season is sure to cause cutworm problems. Melons and vine plants are seldom in the greenhouse long enough to be infested by pests. All warm vegetable seeds are favorite foods of mice and only one mouse can cause several hundred dollars damage overnight. Peppers, canteloupe, and watermelon are susceptible to stem rots if greenhouse temperatures are low and excess water is applied.

A schedule for warm vegetables is presented in Table 30. Crop time lessens as the season progresses toward longer days.

Southern growers might expect crops to require approximately an equal amount of time since crops would be sown several weeks earlier when temperatures and light are comparable.

Table 30
Schedules for marketing on May 20 with a growing temperature of 60° F. Latitude 43° North.

Crop	Sowing date	Pot size (inches)
Tomato	4/4	2 1/4
Tomato	3/20	3 1/2
Tomato	3/5	6
Tomato	2/20	8
Pepper bell	3/21	2 1/4
Pepper bell	3/10	3 1/2
Eggplant	3/22	3 1/2
Cucumber	4/20	3 1/2
Squash Zucchini	4/29	3 1/2
Pumpkin	4/29	3 1/2
Cantaloupe	4/20	3 1/2
Watermelon	4/20	3 1/2

Vinca vine is extremely useful in many situations and will tolerate almost any amount of abuse.

Most vegetables (other than the ones specified) are not direct seeded since customers prefer only 1 plant per garden space. Tomatoes and most cole crops also make better garden plants if they are transplanted once before going to the garden.

Vinca (Periwinkle)

This botanical group contains several horticulturally useful types of plants. The bedding type (vinca rosea) which have green waxy leaves, a creeping or mounded upright habit, and numerous small to medium sized 5-petaled flowers are becoming quite popular in hot dry regions. Then there is vinca major which has been the traditional variegated trailing vine used in hanging baskets and patio planter combination work, and finally, vinca minor (myrtle) a more or less green smaller leaved creeping groundcover vine which is fully winter hardy and develops numerous blue flowers in season.

All vincas are tolerant of heat and drought once established but only the bedding types actually require especially warm temperatures from propagation to maturity. Growers who cannot supply 65^0 F for establishment and 60^0 F for growing on will find the flowering rosea vinca a difficult crop.

The vine types (vinca major and vinca minor) will flourish at 60-65^0 F at the start but require lower temperatures to finish as compact, well branched plants. Once they are well established, vinca major and vinca minor can be routinely grown at 50^0 F and will even tolerate near freezing conditions for short periods without a loss of quality. Once adequately conditioned, vinca minor will easily withstand frost and vinca major is only slightly less cold tolerant. Both are evergreen perennials even in many northern areas. Several selections of each are available, mostly differing in the pattern of leaf color.

Full sun is generally recommended for the flowering vincas (rosea) although they may thrive in slight shade in extremely high light areas. The vinca vines grow most luxuriantly in full sun but will perform adequately even in fairly heavy shade.

Vinca rosea will not tolerate soggy conditions and is reportedly sensitive to high soluble salts in the soil. Vinca minor and major, while not fond of either of these conditions, are decidedly more tolerant once they are established.

Spider mites seem to proliferate on vincas, undoubtedly because the plants are often grown in dry, hot situations which also are the favorite habitat of these pests.

Vinca rosea seed germinates well in about 2 weeks in the dark if warm temperatures are maintained (up to 80^0 F for the first few days and then a reduction to 75^0 F is permissible). Seedlings thrive at 65^0 F.

Vinca major and minor are propagated by tip or stem cuttings or through division of heavy clumps. In order to develop enough tip cuttings in winter, stock plants in large pots are sheared back frequently. Allowing stems to elongate unchecked produces skinny, weak cuttings. Although vinca vines elongate rapidly, they do not form heavy branched growth unless pinched repeatedly. Cuttings for spring 3 1/2 inch pots should be taken in the fall and pinched through the winter as cuttings are needed for smaller sizes. These smaller plants propagated later are very useful as filler and vines for the hanging baskets and combination pots which most greenhouses produce.

Vinca minor (myrtle) will find some use in the larger sizes (3-4 inch pots) but normally is needed in reasonably small plants to economically plant the larger areas over which it will serve as ground cover. Cuttings for small packs can be taken as late as March 1 for sales in late May as 1 pinch plants. Tip cuttings of either major or minor vinca root quickly if they are not allowed to wilt. Mist or a plastic tent over the propagation tray will accomplish this purpose.

About 15-16 weeks at 60^0 F is necessary to flower most vinca rosea varieties for pack sales in the North. Flowering will occur 2-3 weeks earlier in the South. Some growers may wish to grow flowering vinca only after warmer weather has arrived; specialist plugs are useful for this purpose. *Vinca rosea* has recently been transferred to the genus *Catharanthus* by some experts.

Viola

These cheery "baby pansies" have been a favorite perennial through the years. They will be discussed in this section on bedding plants because most violas are grown as annuals in the greenhouse. Violas prefer full sun but will tolerate light shade in the garden. A good selection of colors is present, with apricot being one of the more exotic and popular. Most varieties have flowers about 1/4 the size of pansies but there is one group, called Johnny jump ups, with flowers much smaller than this and possessing a more compact vegetative habit. Jump ups are one of the first harbingers of spring in the greenhouse and few customers can resist choosing a pack or two to plant out on the first fine days. Violas look very nice in the packs if heat is kept to a minimum; late season displays may become tall and ragged quickly as the nights warm up. Jump ups bloom profusely.

Viola culture is the same as for pansies except flowering occurs sooner and plants will generally overwinter in cold frames more easily than pansies when seed is sown in the fall. The majority of crops are now handled as conventional bedding plants without an overwinter stage. January 1 sowings of the larger flowered violas will bloom in early April and plantings of the jump ups must be delayed 2 weeks to flower at the same time. No cold treatment is necessary for flowering to occur but the quality of plants declines as temperatures rise with plants becoming very grassy and having only a few blooms.

If growers prefer, violas can easily be sown directly to the pack using 3-4 seeds per cell.

Violas are generally more profitable than pansies because seed is less expensive and less time is required in the greenhouse. Several excellent groups of naturally dwarf viola have been developed recently. These new varieties make it much easier for growers to produce top notch crops of this particular plant.

Zinnia

Although zinnias are easy to plant from seed, gardeners increasingly prefer to buy started plants. Zinnias come in all sizes and colors and have been a favorite flower for many years. No other flowers seem to love the hot days of summer more. The taller, larger flowered types are still the most popular but short varieties with small flowers are being used increasingly for foreground planting. Zinnias are quite nice as cut flowers in the home. Short varieties such as Thumbelina can be flowered in packs but taller varieties must be sold green unless offered in 3 or 4 inch pots.

The increasing popularity of zinnias as bedding plants results from their remarkable garden performance and a good deal of variety improvement through plant breeding. Zinnias are certainly one of our "All American" flowers.

Zinnias prefer temperatures of 60-65^0 F with full sun. Plants grow extremely fast and must be transplanted out of the seed flat quickly. Seeds can be sown directly to packs if a warm spot is available for germination. Overwatering will certainly lead to losses from stem rot; plants should be allowed to dry out well before the next irrigation. The major portion of zinnia crops can be transplanted after Mother's Day and still be saleable by June 1. They are one of the most profitable crops because of the short time necessary to reach marketable size.

Tall varieties for packs should be sown May 1 in the North for late May sales as green plants. Short varieties will benefit from an extra week of growth if they are to be sold green and will require 4 more weeks from the green stage to flowering. State Fair is a popular tall variety with inexpensive seed. Dwarf varieties with larger flowers sell well in 3 and 4 inch flowering pots; an April 1 sowing will provide 4 inch flowering pots in early June.

Total crop time in the South will not differ appreciably but seed sowing should be done a few weeks earlier to accommodate an earlier gardening season.

The newer hybrid zinnias are usually quite expensive so seed must be carefully handled. Pack production is often not profitable unless less expensive seed is used. Several stem. leaf, and root rot diseases attack zinnias severely unless moisture is applied carefully and adequate temperatures are maintained. The seed is large and does not lend itself easily to mechanical sowing.

BEDDING PLANT SCHEDULES DIFFER WITH PLUGS

In chapter 5 of this book, it was pointed out that a great change in cultural technique for bedding plants had been brought about by the widespread usage of plant plugs (small plants in various stages of growth to be transplanted into the final containers). The benefits and drawbacks of using plugs were discussed at that time but no specific directions were given about how to use them in practical production situations. A brief summary of this topic will now be related.

No exact predictions can be made about how the use of plugs will affect schedules presented earlier for bedding plants. The reason for this uncertainty is that no uniform grades for plug maturity or size are established in the greenhouse industry. Each grower must evaluate the plug sizes available from reliable suppliers and predict maturity dates based upon the information provided. Most suppliers will provide helpful data and a few will even provide sample batches of plants for inspection and testing.

Growers can expect reliable data for plug planting dates to flower dates only by growing the plugs under actual production conditions. No large scale move to plug usage should be made without practical experience involving the actual size and grade of plug to utilize. If possible, the specific grower's plugs to be used should be trialed rather than simply generic products offered by large distributors. The more exact information available, the more accurately crops can be scheduled.

Plugs may be offered in many stages but 2 frequently encountered sizes are approximately 400 or 800 seedlings per 11x21 inch flat. The author is going out on a limb to provide maturity information here but it is felt some attempt is better than none. With early variety petunias of the floribunda single type, plugs grown 400 to the flat and transplanted to 72 cell pack flats in late season will generally bloom well in 4 weeks at 60^0 F. Petunia plugs grown 800 to the flat and transplanted in late season to 72 cell pack flats will generally bloom well in 8 weeks at 60^0 F.

Dwarf impatiens can be relied upon to produce results in the same time frame as petunias but temperatures may need to be held $2\text{-}3^0$ F higher.

In order to achieve the optimum economic benefits from plug usage, growth of plants after transplanting must not be allowed to slow down appreciably. This means the transplanted flats are irrigated heavily with dilute fertilizer solution and immediately placed in the greenhouse at satisfactory levels of light and heat.

Many growers have found that receiving large numbers of plugs at one shipment time results in significant losses due to a poor understanding by greenhouse workers in the essentials of handling these small plants. The problem results chiefly from not realizing that the extremely limited soil volume of plugs leads to quick drying and nutrient depletion. Plugs must be inspected much more frequently than normal bedding plant crops until they are well rooted in the final container.

When too many plugs are received to transplant within 2 or 3 days, it is often advisable to store them in conditions of slightly reduced light and temperature than would be provided for growing on. This environment lessens the possibility of damage due to insufficient care but does not lead to "soft" plants which will damage easily in the transplanting and establishment process.

The cardinal rule of plug usage is to get them unpacked and into proper conditions immediately upon arrival. Delays of a day or two in unpacking can be very damaging to eventual plant quality and scheduling.

Growers should also realize that when producing their own plugs or direct sown flats, the use of pre-germinated seed products will slightly reduce the time needed to finish a crop.

LARGE CONTAINERS OF SPRING FLOWERS

Large containers of spring flowers have been produced and marketed throughout the history of the bedding plant industry. No especially new concepts or technical information are necessary to introduce this topic.

Cultural recommendations for the major varieties which might be used have already been discussed under their individual headings. Readers must, however, become aware of the tremendous increase in importance which this group of products has assumed in the past few years. And they must investigate the details of efficient production and marketing for these large containers.

A consumer trend towards purchasing large pots of spring flowers seems undeniable but the trend is taking place at different speeds and directions in various markets. In one market locale hanging baskets may be the popular item, while in another the emphasis is on 6 inch pots. The volume of sales in larger containers may be well-established but increasing only slowly in some markets while in other locales the sales volume may be smaller but growing rapidly. The general trend is unmistakable however!

The growers's task is to identify the needs and desires of the market and to fulfill them in the most efficient and profitable manner possible. A secondary objective must be to help give impetus and direction to the trend by introducing new products or emphasizing new uses for old products. Growers must function as both followers and leaders, too much emphasis on either end can prove costly.

One mistake which growers often make when producing larger containers is to approach each individual pot as a new task. Repeatable programs must be designed which yield a quality product within an assembly line production process. Special orders "for one of a kind" creations simply run costs up too high to move a good volume of merchandise.

Offering a variety of plant combinations in larger pots may be one of the most important means a grower has of differentiating his or her operation from "run of the mill" establishments which also sell spring plants.

The following discussions of different types of larger containers will stress general principles. If emphasis were placed upon the details of each possible product type or upon possible combinations of varieties the topic would soon require a book in itself.

Single variety large pots

No exact limits can easily be placed upon the size of pots to be included here. In general, the pot size will range between 4 and 10 inches in diameter. It is arguable that 4 inch pots are not much different than bedding plants of the same variety which are sold in up to 3 inch pot size. The cut off point is certainly in question.

We might define the single plant variety large container product group by some rather loose criteria: 1) plants are often transplanted, usually in multiples, to the larger pot shortly before blooming stage rather than as smaller seedlings; 2) plant varieties must possess specific traits, such as an upright but not excessively tall growth habit; 3) plants must bloom well in the container to be accepted by the market; 4) pots normally must be spaced to develop full potential as specimen plants; 5) plant varieties must perform well outdoors; 6) consumers must perceive the particular variety as possessing characteristics which warrant the increased price necessary for a larger pot.

Obviously every plant variety grown by itself in a large container will not possess each of these characteristics in full measure, in fact it may lack particular traits altogether and still be a reasonable success in this product group. Petunias and impatiens certainly are border line in several of these criteria but due to their tremendous general popularity, a fairly large volume of these varieties can be sold as large pots.

The particular sizes and varieties of large pots which are most popular will vary from market to market. Only trial offerings in quantity will allow growers to accurately determine how much to grow of each specific kind. A good deal of what consumers will purchase depends upon what they are exposed to. In many cases growers will be surprised at the extra price consumers are willing to pay for high quality larger pots which provide instant color.

Since larger pots must often be spaced in the greenhouse to achieve full development of plants, a very cautious eye must be kept upon the amount of space occupied by each pot. Too little space fails to allow quality growth while too much runs the cost of each pot up to an unacceptable level. An accurate assessment of the proper price to charge for larger pots must be based, in large degree, upon the greenhouse space occupied.

If growers charge too high a price without adequate justification, it will almost certainly decrease the sales volume and perhaps lead to unnecessary failure of a program which might have been successful with correct pricing. Prices which are too low create an even worse situation.

Culture of single variety large pots is not significantly different from that practiced with smaller sizes of the same varieties. The main difference being that slightly more ideal growing conditions must generally be supplied for the plants to develop as showy specimens. A little more heat, fertilizer, water, and space make the larger specimens stand out from common bedding plants.

A cardinal point in producing larger pots is to get the smaller plants transplanted while they still have adequate time to fill out before flowering and before they have suffered significant restriction of growth in the smaller containers. Transplanting too early is of course a waste of space and often makes it harder to get plants established easily. Timing is critical!

Hanging baskets

Hanging baskets have become increasingly popular with consumers and show no sign of market weakness. They offer a significant opportunity for local greenhouses to increase sales since long distance shipping is especially impractical for larger specimen plants. A well done display of heavily blooming hanging baskets will generate impulse sales and set a plant store apart from competitors.

It is important to have a large number of hanging baskets ready for Mother's Day, but the majority will be sold at other times during the spring and early summer, especially after gardeners have completed their main bed plantings. Baskets must be shaped and allowed enough growing time to develop into heavy floriferous specimens. Skimpy plants with few blooms simply will not move. Having an adequate supply of baskets which are striking enough to sell well but not overbloomed takes careful scheduling. Enough labor must be available to care for the plants in a timely manner. Hanging baskets, like any other specialty crop, should be planned in detail to develop a good cultural and marketing program.

Many growers, in order to have an inexpensive line, offer hanging baskets in container sizes too small for plants to grow and bloom in without constant watering by the consumer. This practice may result in good sales for a few years but the ultimate outcome is customer dissatisfaction and a declining market. Plants for sunny areas should be in at least 10 inch baskets and those for shady spots in at least 8 inch baskets. Containers with porous sidewalls, such as moss lined types, will require extra watering in dry climates. Cultural instructions should accompany each basket since customers will often fail to realize that these plants must be cared for on a more timely basis than similar varieties in the garden.

Hanging baskets warrant special emphasis by the grower since they

Large flowered marigolds like this Inca Yellow plant are especially suited to production in 6 inch pots but can easily occupy too much space to be profitable unless careful attention is given to scheduling and pricing.

can be grown in the ceiling where potted crops are impractical. The extra revenue afforded by this opportunity to utilize space more effectively cannot be ignored if the greenhouse is to be successful. Judgement must be exercised to prevent undue shading of crops underneath the baskets and excessive weight stress to structural members of the greenhouse roof. Extra production of hanging baskets is of little use when other crops are reduced in value or buildings damaged. Placement in the ceiling must also be guided by the need to water and care for the baskets on a regular basis. If the location will not permit reasonable access, it is better not to locate plants there.

Irrigating hanging baskets presents some problems. Automatic watering tubes do not allow the flexibility of mixing different sizes or varieties of baskets on a particular line, and, unless tubes deliver a sufficient water volume, water tends to drain in a straight line through the soil and out the bottom with no wetting to the sides. When the conditions of plant uniformity and large volume water delivery can be met, automatic watering is a real benefit. Hand watering of hanging baskets must be done by experienced

Several thousand dollars of increased production per greenhouse can be realized through carefully planned hanging basket culture.

and conscientious workers to prevent excessive moisture being applied to plants below the baskets. The location of baskets overhead makes it harder for personnel to determine when water is needed and also increases the chances that the task will be forgotten entirely on busy days. Growers must exercise extra vigilance to assure watering is being done properly. It is definitely recommended that baskets remain on benches where they are easily viewed until they are well established. When the plants are growing vigorously, water can be applied heavily and then withheld until the soil dries somewhat. There is less chance of overwatering if saucers are removed from baskets while they are being grown.

Hanging baskets generally benefit from a little more fertilizer than is given to the same plant variety in packs. This can be accomplished without altering fertilizer schedules by incorporating a small amount of slow release fertilizer in the soil. The danger of overgrowth is considerably less in baskets. Most plants will make better baskets if they are pinched at least once. Some varieties may require 2 or 3 pinches to produce specimens. This is assuming that 6 small plants are planted per basket. It is difficult to generalize for all varieties but flowering usually occurs about 6 weeks after a soft pinch. It is better to be a little ahead of schedule than to miss

Petunias are hard to beat as inexpensive hanging baskets intended for use in sunny areas.

the market. If flowering occurs too early, it may be necessary to clean old blooms off before putting baskets on display. Pests may be more of a problem on hanging baskets simply because they are in the greenhouse longer than pack annuals and, if grown higher than eye level, infestations can remain undetected until damage is severe. It is important to completely eradicate pests before the baskets are hung.

The choice of containers for hanging baskets is considerable but most growers choose an inexpensive plastic type. If there is a market for more expensive containers, redwood, clay, ceramic, or moss lined wire baskets may be used for at least a part of the crop. Saucers, if present, should be detachable and easy to reattach. Careful attention must be focused on the strength of hangers and the rim or lip of the basket where the hanger is attached. It is not uncommon to find that some brands under certain conditions will fall because of structural weaknesses. This is both dangerous and costly. The strength of baskets can be tested on samples before ordering large quantities. The soil should be soaked with water when tests are made.

Table 31
Flower varieties commonly planted in hanging baskets. Those suitable for shaded areas are followed by an (S).

Asparagus sprengeri (S)	Lantana
Ageratum	Lotus vine
Bacopa	Lobelia (S)
Begonia (S)	Marigold, dwarf
Brachycome	New Guinea Impatiens (S)
Browallia (S)	Osteospermum
Chrysanthemum (annual)	Pansy
Coleus (S)	Petunia (seed, cutting)
Dracena	Polka dot plant (S)
Dusty miller	Portulaca
Felecia Daisy	Salvia, dwarf
Fuchsia (S)	Scaevola
Gazania	Snapdragon, dwarf
Geranium	Strawberry
Gypsophila	Thunbergia
Helichrysum (Licorice)	Torenia (hanging)
Herbs	Verbena
Icc plant	Vinca vine
Impatiens (S)	Vinca rosea
Ivy geranium	Viola

*Many more varieties can be used; these are only representative of the better and more easily available plants.

Almost any flower can be planted in spring hanging baskets but certain varieties lend themselves better to this use than others. The decision as to which varieties should be planted must not be left in question or guided by what is in surplus. Only first quality material and suitable varieties will produce the desired result. Baskets which do not perform well result in customer dissatisfaction and an eventual decline in sales. Perennials which bloom once a season should specifically not be used in hanging baskets.

Wooden fruit baskets are an ideal low cost container for patio planters.

Blooming garden mums may make an attractive basket but when the flowers are gone in late spring no more are produced for summer color. Mixing appropriate varieties is fine but the bloom dates may not correspond exactly to produce the most striking display. Fillers of foliage such as asparagus sprengeri or vinca vine can be advantageous with flower varieties which do not display a cascading effect. Table 31 lists flower varieties most commonly used in hanging baskets.

Planters

A considerable market exists for large outdoor planters for porches, patios, and apartment balconies. These items are seldom handled by plant stores unless produced locally since they are generally unsuitable for long distance shipping. Garden centers that handle large planters may increase slow

Redwood containers are beautiful and long lasting but increase the selling cost of patio planters considerably.

summer sales and tap a market in which little competition exists.

Planters must have a large enough soil volume for plants to grow vigorously and not require constant watering. In drier climates, containers less than 12 inches in diameter are generally too small for customer satisfaction. Containers must be chosen carefully to compliment the plants yet be economical enough to attract customers.

Wooden fruit baskets often fill this need admirably. These baskets are inexpensive yet have a rustic look which most gardeners favor; when treated with green tinted wood preservative, they easily last a full season and are quite attractive. Plastic containers are fine but must be chosen carefully to look distinctive at an economical price. Clay containers are ideal for planter work but may not be economical unless a manufacturing facility is close by.

The main objective of a planter program is to sell plants at a good profit. Every effort should be made to ensure that the most inexpensive containers suitable for the job are used. This allows the grower to keep the total product cost down and increase volume. Since the greenhouse manufactures plants, both the consumer and grower will profit more from using plants to arrive at a desired level of beauty rather than doing so by the use of expensive decorative containers.

In order to develop significant sales volume, growers must schedule planters like any other crop and present them to the public as a pick up item rather then relying on customers to special order. Individually prepared planters require too much sales time for taking the order and too much production time in the greenhouse. A special order planter takes 4 or 5 times longer to produce than ones scheduled as a crop and planted in quantity. If some care is taken in the production process to vary the plant combinations and colors, most every customer will be able to find a pre-planted container to their taste.

Sufficient plant material of the proper size, variety, and maturity must be available to meet planter schedules. The quickest way to make a failure of this program is to fill planters with left over or sick plants. A certain amount of fill in work with excess plants may be possible but only first class material which will add to the appeal of the product should be used. If the material being used is in the bud stage, planters generally look their best for market 2 to 4 weeks after planting.

Planters for shady areas will require large supplies of impatiens, coleus, and begonias. Taller coleus varieties or dracena spikes can be placed in the center to add height. Lobelia and balsam are two other plants which will stand some shade. Some growers even add inexpensive foliage items such as purple wandering Jew or Swedish ivy to shade planters. Some imagination is necessary since the number of flowering varieties suitable for use in the shade is fairly limited.

The range of flowers which can be grown in sun planters is large so that many interesting combinations are possible. A showy geranium is the preference of most customers for a center plant. Dracena spike, dahlias, marigolds, or other appropriately tall plants can also be used for height. Lobelia and alyssum are especially good at the edges of sun planters. The different combinations of plants are endless and growers will discover by experience what sells in a particular locality.

Plastic containers are moderately priced and offer many varied designs to make displays interesting.

Workers who create planters must be instructed in the proper use of different plants and given a good idea of colors which will compliment one another. Depending upon what the selling price is to be, some guidelines should be outlined concerning the number and value of plants to be used. A thorough soaking of all plants prior to transplanting allows them to become established somewhat before watering of the larger containers is necessary. A real danger of overwatering exists if planters are irrigated heavily too soon. Greenhouse personnel generally do very nice work on planters if sufficient time is spent teaching them how to go about the job.

Planter soil should be fortified with a small charge of slow release fertilizer and customers must be instructed in the proper methods of fertilizing and watering. The development of a good business in planters, hanging baskets, perennials, or any other specialty item takes time and will only come about if care is taken to provide a quality product which satisfies consumers. Happy customers spread the word quickly.

─────────────────────────────────

Table 32

Miscellaneous minor spring plants. Some are utilized by themselves, but many are combined with other varieties.

Name	Description	Use	Temperature	Light	Propagation
Anagallis	Small, intense blue flowers	Combination	Med	High	Cuttings
Brachycome	Mid-blue daisy flowers	Combination	Med	High	Cuttings, Seed
Calandrinia	Ruby-red flowers	Low growing bedder	Warm	High	Seed
Cleome	Masses of small flowers	Tall bedder	Med	High	Seed
Centradenia	Small violet flowers	Semi-trailing	Med	High	Cuttings
Convolvulus	Small morning glory flowers	Semi-trailing	Med	High	Seed
Cosmos	Daisy flowers, many colors	Upright bedder or combos	Med	High	Seed
Cuphea	Small, violet or white flowers	Upright pots and combos	Med	High	Cuttings
Felecia	Blue mostly, some other colors	Upright, combination	Cool	High	Cuttings, Seed
Godetia	Many colors on long stems	Tall bedder or cutflower	Cool	High	Seed
Gypsophila	Several varieties pink or white small flowers	Filler in comb	Med	High	Seed
Heliotrope	Intense blue flower head	Combos for high fragrance	Med	High	Cuttings, Seed
Helichrysum	Mostly white or yellow straw flowers	Combos and dried	Med	High	Cuttings, Seed
Ipomea	Sweet potato leaves	Combo foliage accent	Warm	High	Divisions

Ivy gernaium.

Table 32 (cont.)

Name	Description	Use	Temperature	Light	Propagation
Lysimachia	Yellow globes of small flowers	Combos trailing	Med	High	Cuttings
Malva	Hollyhocks, most bloom 1st year	Tall bedder	Warm	High	Seed
Nierembergia	Cup shaped flowers blue and white	Spreading bedder	Med	Med	Seed
Nasturtium	Mostly red and yellow flowers	Bedder, combo	Cool	High	Seed
Nemesia	Small snapdragon-like flowers	Bedder	Cool	High	Seed
Plectranthus	Variegated trailer	Combo pots and baskets	Med	Med	Cuttings
Scaevola	Small blue flowered creeper	Hanging baskets, combos	Warm	High	Cuttings
Statice	Small flowers many colors	Combos or dried upright	Med	High	Seed
Sunflower	Generally large single flower	Pots, accent bedder	Warm	High	Seed

Chapter 17

HERBACEOUS PERENNIALS

A discussion of herbaceous perennials necessarily straddles the area between greenhouse and outdoor nursery culture. Some herbaceous perennials are better suited to outdoor growing in fields or containers while some are more easily cultured in the greenhouse. And most can be grown just as logically outdoors or indoors, depending upon the specific cultural scheme which best suits the circumstances at hand.

The number of herbaceous perennial varieties currently used by gardeners in North America numbers in the thousands. Obviously we cannot discuss even a small portion of these in detail, but a general overview of some effective cultural and marketing programs can be developed. And some cultural techniques which apply to most all perennials can be pointed out.

If a greenhouse or nursery grows perennials only in a casual manner to help fill a few empty spaces or to offer a somewhat more rounded plant line, it may be best to purchase all but the most easily propagated starter plants. The large number of possible varieties, the rather small volume of sales usually associated with each particular variety, and the widely varying cultural needs of different varieties make it difficult to offer an extensive line of perennials if each is propagated on the premises by seed or vegetative means.

The nature of the perennial business tends toward promoting a division into growers who simply finish pre-started material and specialist perennial growers who supply the starter plants. Of course this division is seldom absolute. The discussion of herbaceous perennials in this book is not aimed at specialists, they will need to consult more complete sources.

Recent publicity about perennials in trade magazines and gatherings (particularly in the greenhouse field) might lead one to expect that this area of horticulture is entering into an explosive growth stage. The market

This flat of perennial Coreopsis could be sold for planting to the garden at this stage, or it can be transplanted to larger containers for growing on.

is indeed growing but possibly not as vigorously as the publicity might indicate. Woody ornamentals and annual bedding plants still account for the vast majority of horticultural plants sold at local garden stores. Perennials form a more important aspect of the mail order market.

Growers who wish to enter the perennial market will do well to begin conservatively and gradually become familiar with the approximate volume of business which can be expected; along with which varieties are in most demand. The majority of perennial growers who serve a local market must often rely upon a good volume of wholesale business to other growers and retailers in order to develop a viable specialized growing operation. They generally cannot sell enough perennials from a single retail outlet to remain in business, unless it is only a part-time endeavor.

SPECIAL CHARACTERISTICS OF PERENNIAL MARKETING

The fact that perennials do not normally bloom the first growing season has important effects upon their marketing. Perennials to be offered for sale in flower must generally be carried into the second growing season; this greatly increases the cost of production and selling price. Selling prices can be reduced by offering perennials as green plants the first growing season. Either of these alternatives, high selling price or green plants, tends to limit the volume of sales which can be achieved.

Satisfactory volume is possible only if consumers are educated about the benefits of perennials. Thus, selling most perennials is a tougher job than marketing showy annuals which are moderately priced. Information about perennials can be provided through sales people, signs, or tags which accompany each sales unit. Tags are by far the most economical and effective way of accomplishing the educational task. Perennials sold as green plants not only need a tag but they need one which accurately shows the consumer what the plants will look like in flower. Growers who wish to specialize in retail perennial sales will benefit greatly by developing an extensive display garden containing all the varieties they expect to market. The costs of this marketing tool should of course be reflected in prices.

Since herbaceous perennials often require more production time or are sold in smaller volume than annual plants, growers must expect a higher selling price per unit to compensate for these factors. The production and marketing of this crop must be evaluated carefully so that realistic prices are determined. If prices are set too low to account for the extra services and production outlays provided, the program will be unprofitable; and if the prices charged are higher than necessary, a much reduced volume may also contribute to failure.

Many perennials will withstand considerable cold after being transplanted to the garden. Properly conditioned ones may often be exposed to frost without harm. This characteristic allows growers to get an early start on the spring selling season. And in summer, when many consumers have quit planting blooming plants, they are receptive to planting perennials because they know their investment in time and money will not be lost at the end of the growing season. Thus, perennials offer a good means of prolonging the spring busy season. This is very profitable

Informative tags are especially essential to profitable perennial programs since plants may not be in bloom at the time of sale. The 100's of varieties available also promote confusion unless every container is labeled.

business since the extra sales volume generated is often added onto profits because operational overhead costs have already been covered.

Perennial growers are faced with the task of merchandising their product in a viable manner. The nature of the product does not make that task easily accomplished. Each grower must develop an integrated marketing plan which coincides with the specific production program utilized.

THE LIFE CYCLE OF PERENNIALS

The name of perennials indicates their chief characteristic. They live on past the immediate season. And another important trait has already been mentioned, they generally do not bloom the first growing season.

Perennial retail displays may often be located outdoors since most perennials will withstand light frost if they have been properly conditioned.

In most cases, a perennial is defined as a plant which lives more than 2 growing seasons while biennials are described as existing for only 2 seasons; growing vegetatively the first and flowering in the second growing season, then dying. In actual practice, both perennials and biennials are often grown and cultured in much the same manner and for the same general market.

The factors which determine whether a plant species is perennial, biennial, or annual are primarily associated with the inherited genetic material present in the cells of individual plants. But it is not unusual to find plants scientifically classified as annuals which behave under some circumstances as perennials; and vice versa.

The 2 environmental factors which appear to influence the inherent biologic tendencies concerned with lifespan and reproduction 1 way or the other are temperature and photoperiod. That is to say, whether or not a plant species is annual or perennial is predetermined by genetic factors but this genetic predisposition can sometimes be altered significantly by different conditions of temperature and photoperiod.

Thus plants belonging to a perennial species often fail to bloom during the second growing season if they have not been exposed to the proper conditions of temperature and photoperiod; usually a cold period of some extent coupled with shorter daylengths. And annuals may behave as perennials (at least in respect to living more than 1 year) if they are not exposed to cold sufficient to kill the entire plant or if photoperiods are artificially extended to keep plants growing vegetatively under long days.

The exact conditions of temperature and photoperiod which promote or inhibit particular annual or perennial tendencies in plant species are not well understood in most cases and may well interact in different ways in different circumstances. But we may be generally correct in the majority of situations by assuming that if perennial plants are subjected to colder conditions for extended periods, along with shorter daylengths; they will bloom as expected the second growing season.

Knowing the general aspects of perennial plant life cycles and how environmental conditions can alter the life cycle is important in providing cultural conditions which insure a profitable crop.

A good deal of recent university research gas been focused upon determining the exact conditions necessary to promote flowering in specific perennials. As this research continues, it may prove possible to flower many popular perennials on a routine basis.

THE PERENNIAL LIFE CYCLE RELATED TO GROWING PROGRAMS

Several perennial growing programs have been developed over the years. Each of these programs is useful under particular circumstances; there is no all inclusive cultural scheme which adequately satisfies every different market and production scenario.

Growers must assess exactly what it is they wish to accomplish and relate these goals to the resources at their disposal. They may then choose a production program which functions most efficiently to realize the objective.

Four basic methods of perennial culture are widely used. They may often intergrade with one another and a single growing operation normally will utilize more than 1 method. The choice of methods is often determined by several marketing and production factors and may sometimes be dictated in part by the inherent characteristics possessed by plant varieties. A simplified discussion of each major method follows.

Traditional one year or longer culture

This method of perennial growing results in large plants which normally flower for the consumer the first season they are placed in the garden. Depending upon the species, the commercial grower propagates by seed or vegetative means in the spring or early summer and young plants are then transplanted to the field or to large pots for the rest of the growing season.

If plants are transplanted to the field they may be left to overwinter there and then be dug in the spring or they may be dug in late fall after the first growing season and placed in bareroot storage. In either case, the plants can be sold bareroot to consumers or placed in pots to begin active growth before the sale takes place.

Young plants which are containerized shortly after propagation (as opposed to being left in the field) are allowed to grow through the first season and are then generally given some protection by mulching or in rudimentary structures for the winter. The following spring, they are removed from protection and sold when growth begins.

Plants produced by these traditional methods are normally quite vigorous and result in good customer satisfaction but the high cost of production causes the final product to be out of the price range many consumers are willing to pay.

This traditional perennial growing program may be carried out entirely upon the premises or the grower may depend upon obtaining partially finished plants, either bareroot or containerized from perennial specialists.

Almost all perennial plants can be handled by the traditional methods although there are a good proportion of varieties which can be satisfactorily produced and marketed by more economical means. Certain plant types such as peonies and bleeding hearts are commonly handled by the traditional method because they cannot be easily done otherwise and because consumers are willing to pay the extra price for these exceptional plants. Rhubarb and asparagus are examples of vegetable plants handled in this manner. Some of these plants just mentioned may require a propagation to market cycle of more than 1 year.

Traditional culture requiring less than one year

This method of producing perennials also results in large vigorous plants which normally flower for the consumer the first season they are placed in the garden. Most perennial plant species can be handled in this manner but a few which require longer growth periods cannot.

Starter plants are propagated from seed or by vegetative means in late summer or early fall to allow significant growth in containers before winter arrives. As temperatures cool down the plants are subjected to degrees of cold which promote full dormancy or to temperatures which are not low enough to cause full dormancy but which do cause plants to enter a flower formation process. The exact temperature necessary to induce flowering varies with the species but normally is lower than 40^0 F for several weeks duration. Some varieties may require considerably lower temperatures while a few may begin floral induction at above 40^0 F. The photoperiod may alter the exact temperature required.

Plants may be carried through the winter in small containers and then transplanted to the finishing container as active growth begins in spring, or they can be transplanted before being cooled down. The winter cooling process can be accomplished in a cold greenhouse or plants may be placed outside under protected conditions.

Many growers propagate and condition their own plants under this method but a growing number are now purchasing precooled plants from specialists in late winter for immediate transplanting and forcing.

Although this means of perennial production eliminates the need to grow plants through the summer months, the production cycle of over 6 months is still costly and results in a relatively high priced product which does not fit the budget of many consumers.

Winter propagation for spring or summer sales

Several species of perennials will flower readily the first season if they are propagated during the immediately preceding winter. Violas, Primula Polyanthus, Shasta daisy, and Iceland poppy are some of the more popular groups to react in this manner. Many species will flower erratically or only slightly with such treatment, while others will not flower at all.

Reproduction by seed or cuttings takes place in December or January and plants are established under normal greenhouse temperatures of $55\text{-}60^0$ F for a short time. The temperature is then dropped to approximately $35\text{-}45^0$ F for further growing and eventual flowering of the crop.

Plants grown under this program are normally sold in packs or small pots but several plugs can be transplanted to larger pots if there is a need for these sizes. Certain varieties such as Shasta daisies can be grown as single plants into larger pots since they do not bloom until later and have sufficient time to develop some size.

Some species such as the Johnny Jump Up violas do not require any period of cold night temperatures to flower well and they can be sown all the way into April for summer sales in packs. Other species, such as Shasta daisies require early winter sowing and must receive the cold spell to flower well. Only experience will allow growers to feel confident in predicting the response of different species.

This winter propagation technique of growing perennials is especially attractive because relatively inexpensive plants which flower the first season in the greenhouse or in the customer's garden are available. Unfortunately only a few species flower well under this method.

Propagation shortly before sale to customer

The chief value of this production method is that it results in low cost plants for consumers. Reproduction takes place by seed or cuttings under the same general schedule as is used for annuals and plants are grown right along with other crops. No specific attempt is made to subject perennial varieties to colder temperatures except as it is required to benefit growth and maintain plant form.

Plants grown under this method are often put in packs and production is usually limited to those varieties in which seed is inexpensive and germinates readily. Certain varieties which propagate easily from cuttings can also be treated in this manner; various sedums, hens and chicks, vinca minor, silver lace vine (in the mint family), and moon vine (also a mint) are examples of cutting propagated varieties. Table 33 shows some perennial varieties which grow quickly from seed and are easily incorporated into an annual type program.

The plants which result from this short term perennial growing method are every bit as vigorous as any other method and, in some cases, may be superior. In some of the longer term growing methods, plants are allowed to stay in containers too long and the heavy roots of certain varieties become hopelessly spiraled and tangled. It has been the author's experience that plants put in the garden in this condition may still exhibit a deformed, dwarfed, and tangled root system even after several years of growth outdoors.

Table 33

Some popular perennials which germinate from seed easily. At an average temperature of 50-55⁰ F varieties designated by * will produce nonblooming pack (72 cells) plants within 10 weeks of sowing, ** 12 weeks, and * 14 weeks.**

Alyssum basket of gold	**	Anacylus mat daisy	**
Achillea	*	Anaphalis pearly everlasting	**
Anthemis kelway daisy	*	Aquileja columbine	***
Armeria sea pinks	**	Aster alpine	***
Campanula blue clips	***	Campanula Persian bell flower	**
Carnation grenadin	**	Cerastium snow in summer	**
Coreopsis early sunrise	**	Daisy English	*
Daisy Shasta	**	Delphinium Pacific Giant	***
Dianthus Sweet William single	**	Digitalis foxglove	**
Dianthus brilliant	**	Erigeron speciosous	**
Gaillardia	**	Geum	**
Gypsophila pink creeping baby	***	Gypsophila double snowflake	**
Heuchera coral bells	**	Liatris	***
Linum blue flax	***	Lupine	*
Myosotis blue	**	Poppy oriental	**
Poppy Iceland	**	Pyrethrum painted daisy	**
Primula Pacific giants	***	Salvia blue	**
Rudbeckia	**	Veronica repens creeping	**
Stachys lambs ear	*	Viola	**

Note: Many of the faster growing varieties may be sown directly to the pack.

A recap of perennial production methods

It is obvious that the 4 basic methods of perennial production just described grade into one another at several points and many species can equally well be treated in more than 1 way. There are also some species which do not fit exactly into any of the methods presented; most chrysanthemums, for example.

The methods described apply more closely to northern conditions than to those found in the South. Growers should interpret the presentations in light of their own local conditions. It can easily be seen that late fall propagation in the South corresponds closely to the winter propagation scheme which was described. Intermediate climatic conditions will result in other cases where clear cut distinctions between methods are not possible.

It is the author's opinion that the quicker methods of production offer the most likelihood of increasing perennial sales significantly over the market which has traditionally existed. Late propagation with generous use of color labels seems to be the most inexpensive way of offering most perennials to the consumer, and it results in perhaps even better overall garden performance if the customer is willing to wait for blooms until the next season. With appropriate varieties, this method is also more profitable to the grower since the amount of time required for production is greatly lessened.

Of course, certain varieties are not amenable to the quicker methods of production and there are many customers who will feel more comfortable purchasing larger, more established plants.

Another point which should be made is the possibility of producing perennials for fall markets. This is nothing more than carrying the market prolongation scheme a bit further into a new season. In many areas of the country, it is even easier to establish perennials in the garden in autumn than in late spring or early summer.

Garden chrysanthemums have been handled this way for many years and provide significant volume for many growers at this traditionally slow time of year. There are no doubt a good many species which could be handled the same way. That is, to bloom in fall from a spring propagation date. The bloom date of many species (such as chrysanthemums and perennial asters) is governed more by photoperiod than by exposure to cold winter temperatures.

BASIC CULTURAL REQUIREMENTS OF PERENNIALS

In most respects, herbaceous perennials are handled in the greenhouse or nursery in much the same manner as any other plant. The great majority of perennials require full sun to develop properly but there are some which prefer shade. Most tend to like cooler temperatures and grow better with fairly moderate fertility levels in container culture. High temperatures and fertilizer encourage grassiness.

The various perennial species react differently to low winter temperatures. Some will withstand exposure to minus 30-40° F below zero without undue damage while other species suffer greatly at only 0° F unless they are heavily protected.

The author knows of no species which actually require temperatures much below 32° F for proper conditioning to induce flowering, thus the most prudent course of action is to protect all perennials left outdoors from extreme cold by providing a good cover of mulch. They may also be held in unheated buildings.

When perennials are held in unheated greenhouses or cold frames it is important to avoid alternate freezing and thawing. This phenomenon is generally considered to be more harmful than continuous hard freezing. It can be avoided by shading the greenhouse heavily and ventilating well during warm or sunny days. Plants can also be covered with a heavy shade cloth or insulation material. When perennials are allowed to go dormant for the winter, whether outside or inside, rodent damage should always be prevented by a control program.

As perennials are cooled down or put into full dormancy, watering requirements are greatly reduced. Continuing to water as if plants were in active growth will surely result in rotting of the crowns and roots.

PERENNIAL PROPAGATION

Perennials are propagated by the same means as are used for other types of plants but there are some specific techniques associated with perennials more frequently than with other groups. Division of dormant crowns and rhizomes is one such method which is often practiced when larger sizes of perennials are required.

Perennial seed often requires a chilling treatment to break dormancy. Without this cold exposure, some species simply will not germinate while the seed of others will germinate only fitfully. There are also a good many species in which seed chilling seems to offer no advantage.

The average seed germination temperature for perennials is lower than for most common annuals. Perennials generally germinate well from 60-70° F; some at even lower temperatures. When the germination temperature rises above 75⁰ F, severe emergence problems begin to occur with many species.

THE BLOOMING SEASON OF PERENNIALS

The blooming habits of perennials, particularly as they relate to cold exposure and length of daylight periods, has been mentioned earlier. Considerable emphasis was placed upon temperature requirements at that time, but readers will perhaps benefit from further reference to how daylength may affect cultural and marketing activities.

It is obvious that among perennial species which are sown on the same date, those with a later natural bloom date will generally have longer to grow vegetatively and will be larger plants at the time of bloom. This fact must not only be considered when setting prices for plants but also when choosing the size of containers into which they will be transplanted.

Various plant characteristics other than simply final size may be affected by the length of day during crop culture. If a species blooms naturally in response to short days, it is unlikely that good vegetative growth can be expected under the natural daylength occurring from late fall through late winter; this happens because these plants quickly enter the reproductive mode whenever days are short. Similar but reverse phenomena occur with plants which flower in response to long days. And there are day-neutral species which flower mainly in relation to the total cumulative light intensity which has been received.

Readers can easily see that there are many practical benefits in knowing the blooming responses of the perennial species they wish to grow. The blooming response of plants is seldom so simple as to be controlled entirely by one environmental factor alone, usually there is a dominant initiating cause with several modifying factors of lesser importance.

A simplified list of blooming periods for some common perennials follows as Table 34. Bear in mind that this grouping is for a latitude approximating that of Chicago with a more-or-less interior United States location. This listing is not entirely satisfactory because some varieties simply will not fit into such a rudimentary scheme and there is much overlap. For example, Violas are among the earliest to bloom in spring and the last to stop blooming in fall because their flowering and growth is more dependent upon cool temperatures than upon day length. As another example, Artemisia (Sage) blooms in the fall, but most species are useful all season because the foliage is generally the most desirable aspect of these plants.

Another characteristic of perennial plants which is often of interest to the grower and purchaser as well is the finished height. Plants that naturally grow tall and skinny do not present a flattering appearance in containers and often are difficult to sell although they are indispensable in the landscape. Very short mat-forming plants may be easy to flower in pots but do not grow to sufficient size to look worthy of the purchase price.

Perhaps the perfect perennial plant from a commercial grower's standpoint is one that begins flowering relatively early (but not extremely early) and develops a nice bushy size that looks well-worth the purchase price but isn't so big as to be floppy or top heavy. It is also helpful if the bloom period is relatively long. This ideal plant allows the grower to start selling a good value specimen as soon as people begin shopping during the early spring season, and yet it blooms long enough to catch late comers. Very early and very late sales can be important in some parts of the country, but for most growers the traditional spring rush is when most sales are made.

The commercial grower must take many aspects of plant growth and development into consideration when planning crop culture and marketing. A species must not only be beautiful, it must be profitable to grow and market.

The roots of container grown plants should be inspected at transplanting; if they are spiraled at the edges of the container and heavily tangled together, loosen them slightly and snip off the most severely tangled portions. This pruning operation will stimulate new root growth. If roots are left in a spiraled condition, they may fail in the landscape or in new containers. Of course, you must take care not to remove more roots than necessary.

Growers who leave plants in too small of containers for prolonged periods are doing their customers a disservice. Plants may look big and of good value, but the root system is generally crowded and tangled. Depending upon the variety, these plants may never recover after transplanting.

Table 34

Blooming times of popular perennials.

Very Early	Early		Late
Ajuga	Achillea	Feverfew	Artemesia
Allium	Alpine Aster	Forget-Me-Not	Aster
Alyssum	Anaphalis	Foxglove	Chrysanthemum
Anacyclus	Antennaria	Gaillardia	Erigeron
Anemone	Aquileja	Gypsophila	Hen & Chicks
Beacon Silver	Armeria	Heuchera	Liatris
Bleeding Heart	Avens	Iris	Physostegia
Cerastium	Bishops Weed	Jacobs Ladder	Sedum
Dianthus	Blue Salvia	Lotus Vine	Viola
English Daisy	Campanula	Lupine	
Phlox, Creeping	Carnation	Myrtle	
Poppy, Iceland	Chamomile	Penstemon	
Primrose	Clematis	Peony	
Strawberry	Coral Bells	Poppy, Oriental	
Viola	Coreopsis	Pussy Toes	
	Corn Flower	Pyrethrum	
	Day Lily	Rudbeckia	
	Delphinium	Shasta Daisy	
	Dianthus	Sweet Pea	
	Evening Primrose	Veronica	
	Festuca	Viola	
	Flax, Blue		

Note: A new research emphasis at universities has determined the exact methods necessary to bring certain perennial species into bloom artificially. Much more of this information can be expected to surface in the next few years.

POPULAR PERENNIAL VARIETIES

The plants described below are arranged alphabetically according to the name which the author believes is most commonly employed. Only the most convenient means of reproduction is mentioned unless more than 1 is equally satisfactory for small growers.

Achillea (Yarrow) – An excellent, rugged perennial. The foliage of Yarrow is fernlike and lacy, often being somewhat gray. Although there are dwarf varieties which are good rock garden subjects, most selections are 18-36 inches tall when blooming. Older varieties were predominantly yellow or sometimes white. Newer seed offerings have a good flower color range and are one of the finest perennials for summer long color. Achillea must have full sun and good drainage to prosper. It is one of the best perennials for arid climates.

Yarrow seed germinates easily and grows into small garden transplants within approximately 10 weeks. Cheaper varieties may be planted as clumps of seedlings in cell paks, thereby reducing the crop time somewhat.

Aegopodium (Bishop's Weed) – This is a moderately vigorous ground cover which spreads by means of underground stolons. It has attractive green and white variegated leaves which grow on weak stems to a height of 6-12 inches. The small white flowers are inconspicuous. *Aegopodium* (Snow on the Mountain or Gout Weed) seems to prefer a shaded or semi-shaded location but will tolerate full sun. When planted in the latter situation, the foliage often develops edge burn in mid- summer, especially if water is deficient. Spider mites can also become epidemic in hot, dry conditions.

Bishop's Weed is easily reproduced by detaching rooted runners from established plants and either transferring the small plants to the desired landscape situation or to small pots. Although propagation is easily accomplished, it often takes a good deal of time to produce numerous baby plants unless a large area of mother stock is available. Although there are likely to be slight variations in the vegetatively reproduced material, only a single variety is commonly recognized. About 12-16 weeks is required to produce a heavily rooted 3 inch pot after a small rooted cutting is planted to it.

Ajuga (Bugleweed) – A low growing ground cover that spreads by means of short stem runners which quickly root as they contact moist soil. Several distinct varieties are available, differing mainly in the color patterns present in the leaves. Plants with solid bronze-green leaves are

Achillea

Aquileja

most common but there are many variations with silver, green, and white leaves.

The flowers of Bugleweed are most often blue but can be white and are borne only slightly elevated above the low growing foliage. Due to the compact nature of this plant, it makes an excellent early blooming potted specimen which retains a neat appearance with only minimal care. Larger flowered varieties with relatively big leaves are available.

Ajuga is very hardy and will thrive under considerable drought. Although it tolerates both extreme sun and fairly heavy shade, it does best when the sun is good but not excessive. The leaves remain evergreen in all but the most severe winter conditions.

Bugleweed can easily become weedy unless it is planted where excessive spread is limited by natural or man-made barriers. This is a plant which even the least experienced gardener can grow easily.

Ajuga is most often reproduced by lifting established clumplets or by taking stem cuttings which already have small roots beginning. Cuttings which have no roots forming as yet can also be used but additional care is necessary.

Seed for the more common bronzy-green leaf variety is available and germinates relatively easily although it is not inexpensive. Considering the ease with which vegetative reproduction is accomplished, this would seem the most preferable method of propagation when a limited number of plants are required. Reproduction by cuttings yields usable plants quickly (as little as 4 weeks for small ones), while seedlings are rather slow (requiring perhaps 20 weeks for small plants).

Allium (Ornamental Onions) – Easy to grow and very hardy but possess a rather short blooming season. Larger varieties vegetatively resemble domesticated Onions although they have a more tufted habit. Smaller varieties look like common tufted chives (which are in this group) and make good rock garden plants.

Alliums display globes of small blooms which are held well above the slender grasslike leaves; the flowers are generally of a rosy color but can be lilac, white, or blue. These plants tolerate dry conditions as long as a reasonable amount of moisture is available during their more active growth and flowering period. Smaller varieties make a very neat and compact plant in packs or larger containers if they are grown in full sun. Too much shade, fertilizer, or water tends to make plants very grassy and weak.

Allium seed germinates easily within about 2 weeks and requires another 6-8 weeks to establish small plants. Some larger varieties are also propagated from bulbs.

Aquileja (Columbine) – Aquileja does best if given good garden conditions, but it will tolerate a good deal of drought and can be used in rock gardens. Cool, sunny locations are preferred. Columbine blooms from midspring through early summer. Most varieties are 1-2 feet tall, but dwarf strains are becoming available more often.

Seed germinates rather slowly (2-4 weeks) but dependably and plant growth follows a similar pattern. Garden transplants are not hard to grow but require adequate time; they take 16-17 weeks from sowing. Two or three seedlings per-pot will produce a saleable small plant in less time, and there is little danger that they will crowd each other out. A winter cold treatment for plants is necessary to obtain blooms the following season.

Although Aquileja does not flower prolifically or grow especially vigorously, it is quite popular because it is dainty and somewhat unusual. It is adaptable to culture in larger pots and remains in bloom for a considerable time.

Armeria (Sea Thrift) – Several Armerias can be easily propagated from seed in about 10-21 days. The foliage forms basal rosettes of grasslike tufts with ball shaped groups of small flowers elevated above on naked stalks. Flower color can range from reddish-pink through white.

The taller varieties of Thrift or Sea Pinks make excellent cut flowers. Compact strains grow easily into fine bedding plants or small containers. These smaller varieties resemble Chives or dwarf ornamental Onion plants.

Armeria is one of the easier perennial species for inexperienced growers. It germinates reliably and can be set out as small plants about 14 weeks after sowing. It is best to use groups of 4-5 seedlings when transplanting to cell paks or small pots. Divisions can be made from mother plants if large plants are desired more quickly.

Artemesia (Sage) – There are many common names for specific varieties: Wormwood, Mugwort, Tarragon, Silvermound, Dusty Miller, Sagebrush. The defining characteristics of the entire group are a pungent smell, silvery white and silky textured foliage, and small flowers which are inconspicuous.

Sages are not commonly used in the landscape but probably should be planted more often (especially in drier Western country).

Silvermound is a beautiful, low-mounded plant with delicately divided leaves – it makes a good container specimen. Silver King is a tall (2-3 feet) several stemmed, upright, semi-shrub which is good for a contrasting background in the garden.

There are domesticated and native varieties that can be well-employed as creeping, dry land ground covers. Several varieties are used for herbal purposes (Tarragon, Wormwood).

Sages are in the Sunflower family and produce small flowers in later summer. Most varieties can be propagated by seed (if it is available commercially) or through self-collections. Some plants such as Silvermound and the creeping types are perhaps more easily propagated through cuttings.

Most Sages are extremely hardy, especially in relation to drought tolerance, and will tolerate poor soils. Full sun is recommended.

Some fast rooting creeping varieties will be rooted and ready for sale as small ground cover plugs in as little as 4 weeks if larger cuttings are taken from a mother block. Other groups such as Western Big Sage develop slowly from seedlings.

Perhaps the reason perennial Sages are not used more in the landscape is that several very fine annual Dusty Millers are available which produce a similar color scheme at less initial cost.

Aster – There are many varieties of perennial Asters from which to choose. They vary in plant height from about 8 inches to 3 or 4 feet tall.

Dwarf alpine asters germinate reliably in 2-3 weeks and grow quite easily into nice bedding plants in about 12 weeks if propagation takes place in late winter. Fall germinated seedlings do poorly during midwinter, even under greenhouse conditions. The alpine asters will bloom reasonably well in late spring of the first year if they are grown under cold conditions. Because of their dwarf habit, the Alpine asters make fine potted perennials if 3 or 4 small plants are used in a 1 gallon pot. These plants are nice to use in rock gardens and can be obtained in mixtures of blue, pink, and white or in single color seed selections.

Most people are probably more familiar with the taller Asters which produce a profusion of fall color. These plants are usually propagated by dividing existing clumps or by rooting vegetative cuttings. Although blue is probably the most common flower color, fall Asters also come in reddish, pink, and white.

Fall blooming Asters are more reliably hardy in areas with severe winters than are most Chrysanthemums. Asters are a good alternative for brilliant color displays at this time of year. They are excellent as cut flowers. One of the major Chrysanthemum propagators has recently introduced several good Aster varieties available as spring cuttings for fall crops. This will probably lead to more frequent availability of this fine flower for home gardeners.

All Asters prefer full sun and well-drained soils.

Astilbe (Feather Flower) – A very popular plant in shady, moist areas of the country which have plenty of rainfall and good soil.

The small seed germinates rather erratically in 3-5 weeks. Although it is quite expensive with a large proportion never breaking ground, enough plants are obtained to profitably produce small pots. Due to the cost of making seedlings and their subsequent slow growth, Astilbe is not usually cost effective when sold as small bedding plants in cell paks.

As might be surmised from the common names, Astilbe produces elongated, feathery flowering stems which hold thousands of tiny flowers. Although most varieties are pink or white, there are some which are red and purplish.

Ground cover varieties which grow less than 1 foot tall are available but most Astilbes are 2-3 feet in height; these latter make fine plants for cut flowers. A much wider selection of varieties is available if growers purchase or make their own vegetatively reproduced starter plants.

Avens (Geum) – Perhaps one of the most overlooked perennials. The large seed germinates easily within 2-4 weeks and quickly grows into small, compact bedding plants within 12-14 weeks. If Geum is sown in the fall, it blooms reliably late the following spring. When plants are grown cold, even those started in late winter will bloom fitfully the first season.

The flowers are displayed conspicuously about 1-2 feet above dense mounds of compact foliage.

Although the foliage grows vigorously, Avens will tolerate fairly dry conditions and prefers full sun. They make fine cell paks quickly, or can be grown into compact larger plants for sale in the flowering stage. Avens is one of the best perennials for commercial production because it is so easy to grow in all stages. Geum can be propagated by divisions if only a few plants are needed.

Beacon Silver (Lamium) – There are several variations of this vigorous member of the Mint family which is grown mainly for the showy foliage rather than the small rose or white flowers. It makes an excellent low ground cover for shaded and semi-shaded areas. Most varieties have a predominantly bright silver leaf color with various green markings. The variety Aureum is less vigorous and has golden foliage rather than silver.

Beacon Silver (Moon Vine) is easy to root from cuttings of older stems which already have small roots started on them. Tip cuttings without roots already showing may also be used but take more care and time to develop into usable plants. If a large stock plant or outside beds of parent stock are available, the numerous cuttings produced will make this plant profitable even in cell paks which can be sold 3-4 weeks after sticking. Larger pots can be planted with several cuttings so that plants obtain good size quickly. Plants can also be divided.

The beautiful, dense foliage and shade tolerance of Beacon Silver allow it to be used as a cheap indoor foliage plant in cool, bright situations. It is especially attractive in small hanging baskets.

Beacon Silver can be reproduced and grown easily, but it suffers the disadvantage of being prone to attack by spider mites which are difficult to eradicate from the dense foliage. The best insurance against these tiny pests is to maintain stock plants in perfectly clean conditions and to avoid the hot, dry environment which promotes mite reproduction.

Bleeding Heart (Dicentra) – Old fashioned Bleeding Heart (*Dicentra spectabilis*) is one of the most popular perennials. It sells quickly on sight

Avens

Blue Flax

when tubers are forced into flowering. Unfortunately, the heart shaped blooms produced on arching stems do not last long because they are more-or- less produced all at once. Then the foliage usually deteriorates quickly as plants endure summer heat.

Bleeding Hearts are very easy to produce from purchased tubers when planted in large pots. They sprout and flower quickly on rather large plants (1-3 feet tall and as wide). Depending upon the temperature, tubers can be forced to flower in as little as 3-4 weeks.

Dark pink flowers are most common but a white variety is available. The flowering period can be extended by keeping plants out of direct afternoon sun. Seed is available but for the few plants needed by most growers it is usually better to purchase tubers.

Dicentra eximia (Fernleaf or Fringed Bleeding Heart) is a smaller plant (about 1 foot tall) which has a longer blooming period. It is not, however, as well known or as spectacular a bloomer as the common variety. It is fairly often produced from seed or it can be divided from rapidly spreading underground stems.

Blue Flax – The sky blue color of Flax flowers is not easily found in other perennials; this fact, along with ease of culture, makes Flax a popular garden plant. Although Blue Flax grows well under proper conditions, it does not develop quickly. Avoid trying to force growth too quickly with excessive water and nutrients.

The plants are rather delicate in appearance with small, narrow leaves but are actually quite easy to grow if overwatering is avoided. Most varieties are about 1 1/2 feet tall with rather small flowers born in open sprays at the top. Blooms appear in late spring and are produced throughout the summer.

Flax is a good rock garden plant and will tolerate other dry conditions quite well.

The seed germinates readily, but seedlings develop slowly. It is usually advantageous to transplant several seedlings together in order to develop a respectable looking clump of plants at maturity. Single plants will look skinny and won't develop enough flower mass to show up well.

Blue Salvia – A vigorous grower, the seed germinates easily and quickly. Masses of small blue flowers appear on the stalk during the first

Blue Salvia

Carnation

growing season if seed is sown by early winter. Blue Sage grows from 1-3 feet tall, depending on the variety chosen. These plants are very useful when large masses of blue are required in the landscape.

Salvia do not like excessive moisture and will grow in less fertile sandy areas where many other plants are unhappy. Blooms appear in late spring and continue through the summer. Blue Queen is a good variety to start with although several new ones have become available, including some from cuttings.

Cactus – These prickly plants are probably overlooked by most people who discuss perennials. They are especially adaptable to container culture and therefore make beautiful patio and indoor specimens.

Cacti come in many shapes and sizes. They generally grow slowly with their worst enemy being excess water and poor drainage. The numerous varieties almost uniformly produce exquisite blooms for a short period each year. The display is often stunning – even small Cacti sometimes produce flowers nearly the size of the plant.

Cacti can be reproduced by seed (slowly), but quicker specimens are made from cuttings or divisions. Cuttings must be placed in a very well-drained medium and may often root without watering or only very occasional irrigation.

Gardeners in many Northern regions which have reasonably moderate winters could likely use some Cacti as patio plants if they are protected from excess natural moisture. A few Cacti will tolerate extreme dry cold, but they are not normally the varieties of more interesting form.

Although Cacti are rightly pictured as being able to survive hot, dry, infertile situations, they will make much faster growth when slightly shaded from full summer sun with judicious use of extra water and fertilizer.

There are numerous varieties of succulent plants that make great planting companions with Cacti. *Portulaca, Yucca, Agave, Aloe, Crassula* and *Sedum* are only a few of the genera which make fine plants in dry rock gardens and containers. Everything that was mentioned about Cacti generally applies to succulents except that they do not often bloom spectacularly but generally root and grow more quickly.

Campanula (Bellflower) – Most of the frequently planted varieties are available from seed. Although the seed germinates easily, it is generally extremely small so that a good deal of care must be exercised in preparing the seed bed and watering in.

Campanulas range in habit from short (6 inches tall), clumpy varieties to those which grow upright to 3 or 4 feet. The most common flower color is blue or violet, but white selections are generally available in most varieties.

Campanula carpatica is the most popular low growing (8 inches) species in use today. It makes a compact clump for offering as small bedding plants but takes considerably longer than most perennials to reach adequate size (perhaps 16 weeks or more from seed sowing). During the early stages of growth, the tiny plants are rather delicate to care for, but as they reach garden-size they are no more difficult to handle than any other plant. *Campanula carpatica* is compact and neat if grown cool but can quickly become a tangled mat if given heat or excess water and fertilizer. It is a good rock garden plant with a long blooming period.

Cup and Saucer (*Campanula calycanthema*–actually a biennial) and Persian Bellflower (*Campanula persicifolia*) are popular tall Campanulas which make good cut flowers as well as being useful in the garden. They are both easily grown from seed.

Carnation (Dianthus) – These old favorites are easy to germinate and grow but do require an extended time to form large clumps. Most Carnation varieties are annuals – you must choose seed carefully to make sure perennial plants will result. Grenadin is the most popular variety.

Carnations tolerate a wide variety of growing conditions, but they will not do well in wet soil. Flowers cut from plants last very well in arrangements.

Since blooming Carnations are tall (1 1/2-2 feet) and have but a few slender leaves, they are not especially attractive in large pots. Most plants are sold in the green stage 14-16 weeks after sowing as non-blooming bedding plants.

Centaurea (Cornflower) – Also known as Mountain Blue or Perennial Bachelor Button. These are tall perennials which grow on long, sparsely leaved stems, usually 2-3 feet tall. Blue and pink are the common flower colors but yellow is also available. They make fine cut flowers and can be dried.

The very large seeds of Centaurea sprout quickly within 10 days, and transplants can be sold within 10 weeks of sowing. Since Cornflowers grow rather tall without dense foliage, they are not the best subjects for growing on in larger containers.

Although Cornflowers are easy to grow, the seed is quite expensive on a per-plant basis when compared to many other common perennials. Centaureas prefer plenty of sun and well-drained conditions. They bloom in late spring and early summer.

Cerastium (Snow in Summer) – A short (3-9 inches), silver- leaved creeper that does well in the rock garden or the foreground of perennial beds. It must be kept in check or it will become invasive. The latter characteristic is a blessing if one desires a ground cover over areas where less hardy plants succumb to drought and cold.

Cerastium blooms profusely from midspring through early summer. The silver leaves are attractive even when summer heat has caused plants to go out of flower. Although the masses of small white flowers are the main attraction, the foliage is beautiful as ground cover in late fall and early winter.

Seed is fairly small but germinates easily within 2 weeks if it is not covered heavily with soil. Seedlings will make garden transplants within 12 weeks of sowing if several in a clump are put to small pots. Large, cold-treated pots will bloom profusely.

Cerastium quickly becomes an overgrown and tangled mat if too much heat, fertilizer, and water are applied, but, fortunately, a quick haircut with shears brings the plant back into shape, and it will be better looking upon 2nd growth.

Coreopsis (Tickseed) – Coreopsis seed germinates easily within 2-3 weeks. Small garden transplants are ready about 10-12 weeks after sowing.

Flowers can be either single or double. Yellow and orange are the predominant colors, but some varieties have dark maroon centers. Most grow from 8-24 inches tall, although some selections used for cut flowers grow up to 3 feet tall.

These perennials resemble marigolds and most will bloom the first season from seed. They prefer full sun.

Cerastium

English Daisy

Daylily (Hemerocallis) – Probably the most heavily planted perennial in American gardens. As might be expected with such a popular group, there are thousands of cultivars which vary in characteristics. Several traits are common to all:

- The lily-like flower.
- Bunchy growth with grasslike leaves.
- Relatively long blooming season.
- Easy to grow and propagate by division.

During the past 50 years Daylilies have been hybridized to the point that flowers in almost every color are available along with several variations in flower form. Some are fragrant while others are not. Even night bloomers can be found. There are very robust tall varieties and also dwarfs.

Hemerocallis likes full sun but will tolerate some afternoon shade. Daylilies range from ones that enter dormancy during winter to those which remain evergreen. Dormant varieties are usually hardy in northern regions, but those which are semi and fully evergreen must be tested for local survival.

Daylilies can be propagated by seed, but the usual means for commercial growers is through root divisions or by rooting the slips which develop on flower stalks. If large divisions are made before plants sprout in the spring, they can be planted into good size pots which will bloom at the normal time for the variety. Smaller divisions will generally bloom somewhat but do not flower well until additional vegetative growth has been made. For early sales, choose varieties that flower naturally at that time.

Growers may choose to propagate their own Daylilies from mother beds or purchase divisions from specialists. Buying small starts allows a choice of many varieties, and the cost can be quite reasonable at wholesale prices. Varietal characteristics must be evaluated to fit market needs.

Delphinium (Larkspurs) – Perhaps the most regal of all widely-planted perennials. Although the seed is generally rather expensive on a per-plant basis, the production of small garden transplants can be economical if all the details of germination are carefully attended.

Germination is often reasonably easy during the cool seasons but becomes difficult when summer heat approaches.

Most Delphinium varieties are predominantly dark or light blue, but extensive selection has allowed violet, lavender, rose, lilac, and white colors to be easily available.

Delphiniums are commonly tall plants (2-6 feet) with a large tuft of broad, deeply clefted leaves at the base. There are dwarf varieties which grow to about 10 inches, these latter are suitable for rock garden use.

The larger Delphinium varieties require a rich, deep soil for best growth and do not react well to extreme heat or drought. Those which are smaller and more akin to prairie wildflowers will perform well in poorer soil and moisture conditions. Full sun to partial shade is suitable.

Common large Delphiniums are often treated as biennials, being planted one year to flower the second year and then being removed for fresh plants. This often results in a more spectacular blooming display.

Production of Delphiniums for garden use is not difficult but neither is it carefree. The seed is generally a little difficult to sprout adequately, and plants can easily become overgrown if not sold on schedule.

Dianthus (Pinks) – A highly diverse group represented by annual and true perennial varieties. Even in extremely harsh winter climates, many annual Pinks survive from year-to-year quite nicely.

The true perennial Pinks are represented by numerous varieties which are generally low growing (4-12 inches), although there are some which may reach 18 inches. Flowers are mostly pink or red but there is at least one yellow selection (Dianthus Knappii, "Yellow Harmony"). Most perennial Pinks make excellent rock garden subjects since they will withstand drought conditions when flowering is completed.

Dianthus seed sprouts easily within approximately 2 weeks. In most cases, small garden transplants are ready within 12 weeks after sowing – some smaller types may require 3-4 seedlings per-transplant.

Most perennial varieties flower reasonably without overwintering if they are started in later winter and grown cold. Warm temperatures, excess fertilizer and water, and shady conditions are deleterious to Dianthus. Poor flowering and weak, grassy growth result when plants are grown under any of these conditions. Dianthus is difficult to flower properly in containers unless careful attention is given towards managing these factors. Dianthus flowers best in cool spring weather. They often go out of bloom during midsummer and begin to flower again as temperatures cool down in the fall. Most perennial Dianthus are easy to propagate from cuttings and divisions when fewer plants are desired.

English Daisy (Bellis) – Although these plants look something like multicolored Dandelions, they are pleasing to consumers because they grow quickly and reliably. Most varieties possess a ball-shaped flower head with numerous small florets sticking out in all directions from the central axis. Thus, they do not look like a traditional daisy flower but more like a pom-pom.

English Daisies grow in a short clump (4-8 inches) with tightly bunched leaves. Numerous flower stalks project from the clump and bear a single flower head at the top. These plants are regarded as rather tender and may need to be replaced in the landscape after severe winters.

The common multicolor flower seed mixes produce blooms reliably the first growing season if they are sown in late winter and are allowed to grow in cool conditions. Although the seed is small, it germinates very easily and quickly if it is not covered too heavily with soil. This little plant is amazing in that it comes from such a small seed but can produce a vigorous flowering plant within 12 weeks under ideal conditions. Undoubtedly, this is the reason inexperienced gardeners like it so much.

Growers who wish to offer English Daisy for sale as small, nonflowering transplants must be careful not to allow too much growing time from seed to sale. If a small clump of seedlings is placed in each pot, good transplants may be ready in as little as 4 weeks from sowing.

Erigeron (Fleabane Daisy) – Blue is the most common flower color, but there are white and pink flowered selections available.

The inexpensive seed germinates in 1-2 weeks with young plants being ready to sell in paks about 10-12 weeks after sowing if several seeds are sown per cell. Larger pots are easily made, but they tend to be tall, loose, and skimpy.

Erigeron prefers full sun and will flourish on rather poor soil and drier conditions.

Festuca – There are several perennial ornamental grasses which can be easily grown but Silver or Blue Fescue is perhaps the most widely used one which is suitable for a beginning program. It is compact and makes a very attractive bedding plant or larger pot. Fescue can be grown easily from inexpensive seed by sowing multiple seeds directly to cell paks. Several of these multiple plant clumps can then be used to quickly make up large pots if desired.

Bedding plants of Fescue take approximately 14 weeks from sowing. If plants become overgrown, they can be brought back to a good shape by shearing. These grasses seldom grow over 1 foot tall and make good rock garden plants or edging. They are not especially invasive or weedy and generally remain in the original clump unless allowed to frequently go to seed in a disturbed bare area.

The blue or silver color in Fescue is enhanced by running plants a little dry and providing plenty of sun. Although it tolerates some shade easily, the clumps may become somewhat "weepy" in heavier shade and require shearing at regular intervals.

Many other perennial grasses are available which require similar care. Some are much taller, however, and are not suitable for small pots except in the juvenile stage.

Foxglove (Digitalis) – Although the seed is small, it germinates easily, and plants grow very quickly into vigorous specimens with long flowering spikes. The flowers are tubular and most commonly purplish or purplish-pink with cream- colored highlights. There are white-flowered strains. Plants are generally 2-5 feet tall, depending upon the variety and growing conditions.

Foxglove is so vigorous and tall that it must be planted to the garden quickly as soon as it has reached sufficient size as a bedding plant. Although it blooms easily the first season in larger containers, these are not practical because plants become very tall and unwieldy.

There is some confusion as to whether Digitalis is a biennial or perennial – most sources list it as perennial. It can be planted in full sun or partial shade

Gaillardia (Blanket flower) – A vigorous grower with daisy type flowers, usually of orange and red shades. Gaillardia blooms in early summer and continues through to early fall. The long flowering period and tough constitution of this relatively little known plant make it a valuable addition to any perennial program. It will withstand drought and summer heat surprisingly well.

Gaillardia grows into a large clump (8-12 inches tall) rather quickly; a few flower stalks can usually be expected the first growing season if seed is sown in early winter. Winter cold treatment is necessary to produce numerous blooms. It grows easily if overwatering is avoided. The seed is large and germinates easily within about 7-10 days. Since the plants grow quickly and attain a good clumpy shape, there is no need to use more than 1 plant per pot when transplanting.

This plant satisfies the beginning gardener and should be used more whenever moderately dry or arid conditions exist. It does well in rock gardens and as a semi-wild flower on dry slopes and meadows. Large pots of Gaillardia flower very well for growers when started in early winter.

Gypsophila (Baby's breath) – Both the larger, more vigorous white flowered (12-24 inches tall) and the creeping (2-6 inches tall) pink flowered types of Baby's Breath are available. The seed of both varieties germinates and grows quite easily, but the Creeping Gypsophila develops slowly– a clump of several seedlings should be used when it is transplanted to small pots.

Both varieties generally bloom moderately the first season from an early winter sowing. The larger white flowered variety must be sold as small transplants since larger plants of it are rather sparse and open and do not have a pleasing shape when grown in larger pots. It is, however, a good garden plant when mature – producing clouds of small blooms on numerous flower stalks.

Creeping Baby's Breath is best sold as small garden transplants, but it will make reasonably nice larger pots if given sufficient time to grow (the pots, however, are not very showy since both the flowers and plant habit are diminutive). This is an excellent low growing rock garden plant which will withstand drought. Although the flowers are tiny, they are numerous.

Gaillardia

Gypsophila

Hens and Chicks (Sempervivum) – These interesting semi-succulents are some of the most easily grown perennials and can be used for a variety of purposes. Although Hens and Chicks are primarily grown for their vegetative qualities, they do bloom at specific periods. The star shaped flowers can be quite charming, as they are elevated above the foliage on more-or-less leafless stalks.

A wide variety of Hens and Chicks are available. All of these varieties prefer good sun and rather dry, well-drained conditions, but there is a good deal of difference in their growth rates, appearance, and hardiness. *Sempervivums* can be propagated easily by division of mother colonies or by seed; the latter method takes a good deal longer crop time. Seed is generally quite inexpensive.

Hens and Chicks are perhaps most useful as rock garden plants, but they are sometimes used extensively in drier climates as evergreen ground cover. They can also be valuable as inexpensive small indoor plants and especially as filler plants in indoor or outdoor cactus container gardens.

Propagation is easily accomplished by removing "chicks" from the mother plant and allowing them to root in a well-drained soil medium which is only slightly moist. The "chicks" should generally root in about 2-4 weeks without bottom heat being necessary. Small starts of more vigorous varieties may be sold in as little as 6 weeks. One gallon containers having numerous "chicks" require about 4-5 months in good growing weather. Miniature varieties could take 2 years to make a full 1 gallon pot.

Heuchera (Coral Bells) – One of the lesser known perennials, but it can be easily produced and grown if caution is exercised when germinating the extremely fine seed. Divisions may also be used when only a few plants are needed.

Once the seedlings are a few weeks old, they are relatively carefree and grow into a dense mounding plant which can be transplanted to the garden 15-20 weeks after sowing. Long naked flower stems grow out of the dense foliage and can reach up to 2 feet in some varieties. Although the common name is Coral Bells, the small bell shaped flowers which

Hens and Chicks

Lamb's Ear

Heuchera

Perennial cold frame tunnels used to protect plants from extreme cold. White plastic is used to cover the tunnels so that the sun does not overheat the plants inside. The ends of the tunnels are open to reduce daytime temperatures. Excessive heat in winter can quickly kill plants.

are arranged along the upper 1/3 of the stem can also be white, red, purple, or sometimes yellow, depending upon the variety.

Heuchera is a neat bedding plant in cell paks or larger containers because it does not easily develop wild vegetative growth.

Hosta (Plantain Lily) – Hostas are long-lived in the garden and easy to maintain once they have gone through a lengthy establishment period. They range from large varieties to dwarfs, and, although the flowers are very attractive in many varieties, Hostas are grown primarily for their foliage display. The hundreds of new varieties offer an incredible amount of variation in color, shape and texture of leaves so that any attempt to describe them is fruitless.

The leaves grow in a large clump at the base of plants with each more-or-less distinctly separate daughter plant being called a crown. New crowns are slowly developed, and there is generally no need to separate them except as new plants are desired. Seed is available for a few varieties but most are available only from specialists as divisions or tissue culture starts.

Hostas are shade lovers with only a few varieties grudgingly tolerating full sun if they are not allowed to dry out. The leaves develop full ornamental potential only when plenty of moisture is available in a deep organic soil.

Cold and heat tolerance must be tested if large scale production is planned, but most varieties are fairly adaptable in relation to temperature. If the temperatures are high, then plants must be given plenty of water.

Considerable time is often involved in producing good specimens. Since plants are slow growing and do not show their full potential until a larger clump forms, small divisions can be sold but generally appeal only to knowledgable gardeners who can imagine the finished product several years away. This lengthy production schedule causes the price of well-grown Hostas to be high.

Iceland Poppy (Papaver) – Readers can refer to later cultural information presented for Oriental Poppies for general growing guidelines. The Iceland Poppies are even more susceptible to transplanting damage and, if at all possible, should be sown directly to small plug trays or even to larger pots if germination space is available. When transplanted as small seedlings, extreme care must be exercised in the process and immediately afterwards until they are rooted in well.

Iceland Poppies come in many bright colors and possess a flower shape which resembles smaller single type Orientals. The foliage is less coarse than Orientals and generally more congregated at the base.

Some authorities classify Iceland Poppies as biennials while others say they are perennials. They bloom well early the first season from seed if sown in midwinter.

Iris – Everyone is familiar with common ornamental Iris or Flags. This is a very large and useful group of plants which can scarcely be described adequately here. Bearded Iris are the most commonly used plants, but Japanese Beardless and Siberian Iris have gained some popularity as gardeners look for new items. Iris tend to bloom from midspring through early summer, but earlier and later blooms can be enjoyed through selection of proper varieties. A wide range of flower color is available. Two characteristics shared by all Iris are the linear strap shaped leaves and irregularly shaped flowers.

Propagation is normally accomplished through division of the vigorous rhizomes (underground stems). A few species are bulbous. Since there are thousands of Iris varieties, there is a plant which will grow in almost any North American environment. Growers must employ selections which are proper to their climate and intended use. Although most Iris prefer full sun and normal garden conditions of good drainage, there are some which can be grown in rather moist soils or even where water stands for brief periods in the growing season.

Very common Iris varieties may have little retail demand since customers can reproduce their own plants or obtain divisions from neighbors or abandoned homesteads. Unusual varieties which offer something new will provide increased interest from consumers. These new plants may be obtained easily through wholesale specialists.

The small native variety *Versicolor* can be propagated from commercially available seed. It is a good rock garden plant for spring bloom, or it can be planted in moist open areas. It will also bloom well in moist meadows composed of short grasses.

The seed does not germinate quickly or especially easy, but, since it is relatively inexpensive, a good number of seedlings can be obtained within about 6 weeks for only small cost. The seedlings grow slowly–for 4 inch spring pots, seeds must be sown in fall. A better looking specimen is obtained more quickly if 3 or 4 seedlings are used in each pot.

Kniphofia (Red Hot Poker) – Also called Tritoma. The mature flower spike is red, orange, and yellow and resembles an elongated glowing ember which has been removed from a fire. Kniphofia is mentioned because it is relatively easy to produce from inexpensive seed and has an interesting flower shape. Even smaller varieties possess a spike which approaches 1 foot in length while larger varieties can be up to 3 feet tall.

Young plants are not especially attractive since the leaves are coarsely grasslike and somewhat sparse in number. As plants mature in the garden, the leaves increase in number and become bunched in a clump. Seed takes 3-4 weeks to sprout. Small transplants will look more attractive if 3-4 plants are put in each pot. Tritoma loves the sun.

Lamb's Ear (Stachys) – Grown primarily for the decorative foliage which has a soft wooly covering of hairs. The shape of leaves more-or-less approximates that of a sheep's ear.

The flowers are numerous and small (about 1/2 inch diameter). They are an added benefit of the plant but, as mentioned, not the main attraction. Flower color is either purplish-pink or white, depending upon the specific variety.

Stachys seed is large and germinates easily in 2-4 weeks. It is fairly inexpensive although not cheap. The seedlings grow quickly so that small garden transplants can be ready within 10 weeks of sowing if 2 or 3 plants are placed in each cell of a pak.

Lamb's Ear generally does not grow more than 16 inches tall in the garden if it is given full sun. Plants grown in partial shade or with too much fertilizer or water often grow more vigorously than desired, causing weak, gangly stems and poor color on the leaves. Stachys makes a nice larger pot easily and quickly.

Liatris (Gayfeather) – Until a few years ago, Liatris was seldom featured by florists, but it is now emerging as a major cut flower crop in some locations. It offers the qualities of reasonably easy and economical production with long lasting flowers which ship easily over long distances.

Persons wishing to grow Liatris in the garden will often prefer shorter 18 to 24 inch tall plants rather than the taller varieties which are used for cut flowers. These smaller plants also make more compact specimens for sale in containers.

Gayfeather seed is generally inexpensive and germinates easily in 2-3 weeks. Small garden transplants can be ready in 10-12 weeks from sowing if several seedlings are transplanted to cell pak compartments. As plants become larger, they develop a somewhat grassy looking clump from which the long narrow spikes of flowers emerge. Most varieties are rose or violet-colored, but some are available with white flowers.

Liatris prefers full sun and generally endures drought and daytime heat very well. .

Lobelia (Cardinal Flower) – A common woodland native in Eastern North America from the milder regions of Canada to Florida and Texas. It can be naturalized in the garden. The abundant seed can be collected for reproduction. *Lobelia cardinalis* has red flowers, but white and rose cultivars are available. These plants must receive some shade in sunnier climates.

Queen Victoria is a red-flowered hybrid developed from crosses of native Cardinal Flower with other species. It is readily available from seed houses at an economical price. This variety grows 1 1/2-3 feet tall and has beautiful bronzy-green foliage.

The "Fan" hybrids are very new. Seed is expensive but well-worth the price because of the intense neon-scarlet color of the long lasting flowers.

Perennial Lobelias are generally considered rather tender so that a winter mulch is often recommended. Lobelia seed is small but not difficult to germinate if handled carefully. Plants started in late December will generally bloom reasonably the first season if they are grown cool after transplanting. Color begins to show in midsummer and lasts quite well into the colder days of fall.

Perennial Lobelia differ considerably in plant shape from the popular low growing annual varieties. Perennials often have a larger bunch of leaves at the base, from which long, sparsely-leaved flower stems emerge. The flowers appear on short secondary stalks along the upper stem or even primarily at the tip.

Lotus Vine (Parrot's beak) – Discussed previously with bedding plants.

Lupine (Bluebonnet) – These members of the Pea family are exceptional in that almost every flower color is readily available. The flower spikes are displayed well above the leafy vegetation which is characterized by fingerlike leaflets originating from a central area. In other words, the leaf looks somewhat like an open palm of the hand.

There are some rather small (1-2 feet) varieties of Lupine while most grow in a range of 2-3 feet. A few may reach 3-4 feet in height.

The seed of Lupines is a small bean. It sprouts reliably in 2-3 weeks and quickly makes a saleable garden transplant. Although seed is inexpensive by the ounce, it is quite expensive when considered on a per-plant basis. This is why it is important to provide good conditions for complete germination. Place the seed singly by hand into separate compartments of a small size cell pak and then transplant the successful cells to larger paks or small pots after seedlings have become well-rooted.

Lupines are easy to grow, but they become quickly injured if drought conditions occur in containers. They are less susceptible to severe wilting after being well-established in the garden.

Some Lupines provide exceptionally beautiful spikes of cut flowers which last quite well if they are cut in bud. Full sun develops the best plants, but some shade can be tolerated. Since Lupines are vigorous plants, they generally prefer a reasonably rich but well-drained soil which is not allowed to dry out severely.

Lythrum (Loosestrife) – A very showy, fast growing perennial which prefers moist or wet sites. When the environment is suitable, Lythrum can quickly become invasive along waterways. For this reason, shipment to certain states is prohibited.

Lupine

Oriental Poppy

Some dwarf varieties may only reach a height of 18 inches, but 2-3 feet is a more common size for most selections.

Flowers are generally of a rose or red color and are arranged on an elongated spike which stands above the willow-like foliage.

The seed of Lythrum germinates quickly, and small garden transplants are ready in about 9 weeks from sowing. Plants in cell paks can soon become overgrown – they wilt quickly when in this root bound condition. Therefore, only enough plants should be started as can reasonably be sold before excessive growth occurs.

Loosestrife is a useful garden perennial if it is planted in areas where there is no chance of escape to nearby waterways. Certain varieties are advertised as being non-invasive, but caution should be exercised until these claims are well-proven.

Mat Daisy (Anacyclus) – A little known small white daisy which grows in low (2-5 inches) clumps. The underside of flower petals is rosy-red, thus the unopened buds appear reddish. The ground-hugging, finely-cut leaves are grayish-green.

Mat Daisy is easy to germinate and grow and blooms well the first season from seed if it is sown in midwinter. Cell paks of garden transplants are generally ready about 10 weeks after sowing, but heavy 3 inch blooming plants will take approximately 4-6 weeks longer.

Anacyclus is especially well-suited to rock or alpine gardens and blooms in early spring. This perennial is a reliable grower but does not make a big show of flowers.

Myosotis (Forget-Me-Not) – An excellent early blooming container plant the first year if seed is planted in midwinter and grown cool. Seed germinates easily in about 2 weeks and large blooming containers can be ready within an additional 12 weeks growing time if several clumps of seedlings are transplanted to the pot.

Some seed sources list Myosotis as a short-lived perennial while others call it a biennial. Dwarf blue flowered varieties are most common, but Myosotis is also available in pink and white flowered selections. This plant can be utilized as a spring bedder (much like Pansies) if it is planted early and grown cold enough to develop flowers after being set out. The tiny but numerous bright blue flowers are a welcome substitute for annual Ageratum or Lobelia in the foreground, but they do not last as well through the season as does Lobelia. It may reseed in the garden.

Myrtle (Vinca) – Discussed previously with bedding plants.

Oriental Poppy (Papaver) – A showy and reliable perennial. Flowers appear in midspring and last only a few weeks, but they are spectacular. Mostly in brilliant red and orange colors with whites and pinks less frequent. The plants are rather tall (1 1/2-3 feet), and the coarse foliage is not especially attractive after blooming has occurred.

Oriental Poppies do not transplant easily as seedlings or as mature plants, but they are fully hardy when well-established. The tall stalk and foliage can be cut to within 2 or 3 inches of ground level a few weeks after blooming when plants have had a chance to accumulate food reserves in the roots. A basal clump of leaves will remain and keep plants nourished through the summer.

Seeds of Oriental Poppies are rather small but germinate quickly and easily if they are not covered too heavily with soil. The seedlings survive transplanting without undue loss if a little special care is given during and after the process. Iceland Poppies are more difficult.

Since the plants are tall and do not bloom for extended periods, Oriental Poppies are not the best perennial for show in large containers. They are sold mostly as small garden transplants.

Although Oriental Poppies do have some drawbacks, overall they are one of our most popular perennials because they are showy, reliable, and will stand rough treatment when established. Since they bloom rather early, Poppies provide good color even in areas where summer drought is common.

Pearly Everlasting (Anaphalis) – A little known perennial which serves especially well as a rock garden plant and for unusual cut or dried flowers.

The foliage is silver and serves as a secondary attraction to the small, whitish flowers which have yellow centers. These plants usually form a basal mat of evergreen leaves in addition to the more conspicuous flowering stalk which generally does not exceed 2 feet.

Anaphalis requires full sun and good drainage. Severe drought can be tolerated, but, if plants are to be utilized for cut or dried flowers, it is best to provide adequate moisture in order to develop good size flowering stalks.

The inexpensive seed is quite small but germinates easily in 2-3 weeks. Small garden transplants are ready within about 9 weeks from sowing if a clump of seedlings is placed in each compartment of cell paks. Larger pots which flower from late spring through the summer are easy to grow.

Penstemon (Beardstongue) – Varieties grow from about 8 inches tall to those which reach 3-4 feet. Although there are uses for each size, the commercial grower is likely to be more satisfied producing dwarf varieties since these make a more compact plant for cell paks and small pots.

Penstemon seed germinates easily within about 3 weeks, after which another 10 weeks is usually required to produce small bedding plants. The flowers are tubular in shape and arranged along the length of long stems, thus making an excellent spikelike flower for cutting–especially if the larger varieties are planted. Most Beardstongue flowers are blue or violet in color but pink, purple, red, and white selections can be found.

The wild relatives of *Penstemon* are common in dry prairie and foothill regions of the American West, thus the genus has developed a reputation of drought resistance. Dwarf varieties are especially useful for rock garden landscapes. All Beardstongues prefer a sunny location but will tolerate slight shade. The blooming period of *Penstemons* usually begins in late spring and runs through midsummer.

Peony (Paeonia) – Few flowers are more spectacular in bloom or more useful in the landscape. Perhaps the greatest benefit of Peonies to commercial producers is the near universal appeal of these plants, almost guaranteeing that good quality will sell.

It is not easy to offer vigorously growing Peonies in containers, much less ones which are blooming. This is why most Peonies are started by gardeners from dormant roots or tubers. Even good roots are difficult to find since those which are offered at discount stores and garden centers have often been subjected to poor conditions while on display.

Growers who specialize in learning how to produce healthy Peonies in containers should have a ready market. Most roots started in spring containers remain quite sparse and seldom bloom much, if at all, during the first season. Those started the previous fall may make better plants the next season, but rotting of roots in the container over winter is then a danger. Even one period of excess moisture may prove fatal.

These problems, along with the high cost of quality roots at wholesale, make it difficult to offer well-grown container plants at a reasonable price. Continuous attention to cultural essentials is the basis for a profitable crop.

The following basics must be practiced:

- Obtain roots of good size from reliable suppliers.
- Store roots in a cool, dry spot before planting.
- Disinfect root surfaces with a dip in horticultural disinfectant.
- Use clean, well-drained soil which is very lightly fertilized.
- Plant the dormant eyes only slightly under the soil level, not over 2 inches deep.
- Irrigate sparingly until vigorous growth begins.
- Cool nights (about 45° F) and cool days (45°-65° F) allow slow, strong growth. Some shade may be necessary in afternoon until containers are well-established.

Numerous classes and varieties of Peonies exist. The double-flowered or rose types are most popular. Flowers are red, white, and pink. Fickle customers may ask for exotic cultivars with special characteristics, but 99% will accept the doubles. Blooming time varies from early spring for a few to early summer for others. It is important to grow varieties which will be in bloom for the main gardening season if a program where plants bloom reasonably well in containers can be developed.

Peonies are at their best where cold winters occur but growing season moisture is not so abundant as to cause rotting of buds and crowns. Flowers will fail to form in warm Southern regions where ground temperatures fail to reach 40° F for an extended period.

Contrary to popular opinion, ant activity is not necessary for flowers to appear or open; this probably is most often caused by the following:

No buds appear–
- Plants too young.
- Planted too deep.
- Clumps too old (not likely in container culture).
- Too much nitrogen.
- Roots moved and divided too often (a possibility with commercially produced roots).
- Too much shade.

Buds appear but fail to open–
- Buds killed by late frost.
- Buds killed by disease.
- Buds killed by insect attack, likely thrips.
- Buds receiving too much overhead moisture.
- Under-nourished plants.
- Weather too hot.

If roots are grown from mother stock, they can be divided in fall after the leaves frost or in very early spring. Seed is not often available commercially.

Perennial Alyssum – Also called Gold Dust or Basket of Gold because of the profusion of small yellow flowers produced in early spring. This plant is very striking in bloom and is one of the earliest common perennials to produce color. The blooming period is rather short so that it does not make a good plant for display in larger containers. Small plants sell very well when customers actively seek out the beautiful flowers they have observed in neighborhood landscapes. After blooming, the Perennial Alyssum is a rather drab, low growing (6-9 inches) plant with grayish-green leaves.

Alyssum is very hardy and will tolerate a good deal of abuse and summer drought after it is established. Since it is especially active and floriferous only in early spring, moisture conditions at that time are usually favorable for a reliable color display. It is a good rock garden or semi-wild area flower.

The seed is large and germinates readily. Seedlings grow at a moderately fast rate and can usually be sold as young transplants 12-14 weeks after sowing if several seedlings are placed in each small container.

Do not over water small plants, as they are susceptible to rotting out.

Perennial Alyssum will sometimes bloom slightly the first growing season after sowing from seed, but winter cold treatment is necessary to develop acceptable flowering.

Physostegia (False dragonhead) – Obedience Plant is another common name given to this group. Plant height ranges from 2 feet for smaller varieties with taller ones reaching 3-4 feet.

Obedience Plant is a relative of the Mints and has the characteristic irregular-shaped tubular flowers and vigorous growth of this family. Some people consider it invasive.

Seed germinates reasonably easy and is not especially expensive. Small garden transplants are ready approximately 12 weeks after sowing. When smaller numbers are needed, the plants can be divided.

Physostegia is a good plant wherever the large white or pink flower spikes fit into the landscape readily, and where its rapid spread can be continued. It will tolerate some shade and can be used as a cut flower.

Polemonium (Jacob's Ladder) – The common name of Jacob's Ladder is apparently derived from the long ladder-like leaves which have an appearance similar to those of ferns, and it prefers a rather moist and rich soil.

Jacob's ladder is easy and fast to grow from rather inexpensive seed. Small bedding plants are ready within about 10 weeks after sowing and can quickly become overgrown in cell paks if they are not sold or transplanted to larger containers soon. This bushy, densely foliaged plant grows to approximately 18 inches maximum and easily makes a nice large pot. The flowers are blue, as are most Polemoniums, but white selections are also available.

Potentilla (Cinquefoil) – The herbaceous varieties are common wild plants with predominantly yellow flowers, although some cultivars are red or white. Most herbaceous Potentillas resemble Strawberries in both leaf and flower shape since the two groups are closely related.

Potentilla Nana, sometimes called Verna (Spring Cinquefoil) is an excellent variety for beginners to work with because it is easy to root divisions from mature clumps and it maintains a very neat, low mounding

Perennial Alyssum

Pyrethrum

habit in small containers. Spring Cinquefoil blooms profusely, the small yellow flowers usually lasting from early spring to early summer. It is very useful in rock gardens and as a low edging in perennial displays. This plant is a good substitute for miniature Strawberries since it out performs them in all ways except possessing a well-known name.

Spring Cinquefoil may be reproduced from seed, but it is difficult to find and offers little benefit over the numerous "babies" which can be started from even a medium-sized clump or pot. Large potted specimens must be started 6-12 months in advance because the growth rate is slow. Cool winter temperatures must be provided to promote heavy blooming.

Spring Cinquefoil blooms extremely early and must be held very cold so that it is not past its prime before gardeners begin buying.

Several other more vigorous herbaceous Potentillas are available from seed. The woody Potentillas are a popular small flowering shrub in many sections of the country; their best attribute being that they bloom more-or-less continuously. These plants can be propagated by cuttings or obtained through wholesale nursery suppliers.

Primula (Primrose) – Discussed previously under annuals.

Pussy Toes (Antennaria) – Resembles Pearly Everlasting (described earlier) somewhat, but the small flowers are pinkish at times and do not have a yellow center. The foliage is also more intensely silvery and ground hugging, only a few leaves being present on the slender flower stalks. Pussy Toes foliage seldom rises more than 3-4 inches off the ground and flower stalks infrequently are more than 1 foot tall.

Antennaria is an excellent rock or alpine garden plant which prefers full sun. It withstands considerable drought and makes a good dryland ground cover for limited areas.

Seed germinates easily in about 2 weeks and is reasonably inexpensive. Small garden transplants are ready within about 14 weeks if small clumps of seedlings are planted to each compartment of cell paks. Pussy Toes grows somewhat slowly and single seedlings will take 6-10 weeks longer to produce acceptable size plants for the garden. Large pots of Antennaria are easy to grow.

Antennaria is a good, rugged perennial which should be used more often if the proper spot is available. It does not like excess moisture in pots or in the garden.

Pyrethrum (Painted Daisy) – A medium size daisy which comes in several flower colors–mostly reds and pinks. It is easy to grow and makes a fine cut flower. Most varieties are 1 1/2-3 feet tall with attractive, somewhat ferny looking foliage. These plants are completely hardy in milder parts of the United States but require winter protection in most situations from Zone 4 northward.

Painted Daisy blooms in early summer and makes an attractive larger pot if plants are grown slowly and cool to maintain a good form. Many flowers can be expected from a single pot. Pyrethrum also looks good as a small nonflowering garden transplant. In this case, care must be taken not to start seed too soon since the leaves tend to yellow quickly if the pot restricts growth severely or if plants are allowed to dry out excessively.

Although a good portion of Pyrethrum seed often fails to germinate, that which proves viable comes up quickly and easily. The seed is large and should be covered with a thin layer of fine soil.

Rudbeckia (Black eyed Sususan) – Discussed previously under annuals.

Sedum (Stonecrops) – Many good varieties exist; they are characterized by rather fleshy leaves which make plants extremely drought tolerant. Sedum varieties range from the tiny creepers through taller (2-3 foot) specimens. Most Sedums prefer full sun and well-drained situations, but there are some exceptions which can be grown in moist, partially-shaded areas.

The great majority of Sedums are propagated commercially by vegetative cuttings, but there are a few specific varieties and seed mixes which are commonly available as seed. Stem cuttings root easily if they are placed in slightly moist soil for 3-4 weeks. Care must be taken to prevent excessive watering at this point but neither should the soil be allowed to completely dry out.

Rudbeckia

Viola

The seed of Sedum Acre (a low ground cover with yellow flowers) is small but comes up quickly and easily. Since it is rather inexpensive, it can be broadcast over the soil compartments of cell paks to eliminate the need for transplanting.

The garden uses for Sedums are varied, but they are most commonly employed as ground covers and rock garden plants. Some taller varieties produce colorful enough flowers to be used for cutting.

Shasta Daisy (Leucanthemum) – This is one of America's favorite perennial flowers. It blooms from late spring through the fall. The white flowers with yellow centers are truly impressive when plants are massed together.

The large seeds germinate easily and quickly, and the plants grow vigorously with little special care. Most Shasta Daisy varieties are from 1-2 feet tall with a large basal rosette of leaves. A few varieties can be obtained which are slightly shorter or taller. The variety "Alaska," which is used most frequently, is about 2 feet tall with single flowers.

Shasta Daisies are one of the most suitable perennial plants for selling in large containers; they bloom profusely and reliably if plants have received cold treatment through the winter. Plants started in early winter and subjected to hit or miss cold spells when young will usually bloom only fitfully the first growing season. Plants grown in containers must be fertilized adequately since growth is heavy and rapid; however, a large excess of nutrients will lead to "grassy" uncontrolled vegetation and few flowers.

Shasta Daisy is perhaps the best North American perennial profitwise, both from a cultural and marketing viewpoint. "Snowlady" is a better variety for pots in that it is shorter and blooms reliably and easier without cold treatment. The seed, however, is more expensive. Previously classified in the genus *Chrysanthemum*.

Silver Lace Vine (Yellow Archangel) – Also commonly known as Silver Nettle Vine. The scientific name is *Lamium galeobdolon variegatum*, but it may also be listed as *Lamiastrum* in some sources.

This creeping perennial plant with variegated silver and green leaves can be useful as a ground cover or as a trailing accent in permanent planters. It is perhaps more frequently employed as a trailing plant in

Shasta Daisy

Sweet William

annual flowering baskets and planters or as an inexpensive house plant for cool, bright conditions.

Silver Lace Vine, like other plants in the Mint family, has square stems and is a vigorous grower. It is propagated by means of stem or tip cuttings. Older stems near the plant crown often have incipient roots forming at the leaf nodes, these roots will become active within a few days if placed in moist soil.

Silver Lace Vine can be used as an alternative to Vinca Vine in many situations, but it does not tolerate extremely sunny conditions well. It is generally more vigorous than Vinca Vine and becomes coarse with age – Vinca Vine is better for most applications except as an indoor foliage plant.

The flowers of Silver Lace Vine are yellow but not particularly appealing.

Sweet William (Dianthus) – The Sweet Williams are sometimes referred to as biennials or short-lived perennials, but experience shows that there is little practical reason for not considering them a true perennial. In hardiness zone 4 they are as popular as Shasta Daisies and provide one of the most brilliant floral displays available for the garden.

The red, pink, and white flowers are truly spectacular in late spring and early summer. Flowering becomes weak in summer heat but returns on a low level when cooler fall weather arrives.

Most Sweet Williams grow less than 1 foot tall. The popular variety Indian Carpet is 6-8 inches tall, and it grows vigorously and makes a large clump quickly. The seed of this variety is large and germinates easily within 2 weeks.

Sweet William grows easily in containers but quickly becomes "grassy" and weak stemmed at the first hint of excessive nutrients. Abundant water and high temperature also lead to this problem. The Indian Carpet variety can be bloomed in containers, but strict attention must be paid to keeping nutrients, water, and temperature at the lowest levels consistent with healthy growth.

Indian Carpet will not bloom reliably without low temperature treatment the previous winter.

Many other Sweet Williams are available – both from seed and vegetative reproduction.

Veronica (Speedwell) – Creeping Speedwell is an easily grown perennial with small green leaves. It becomes covered with minute, clear blue flowers the first spring if it is sown in midwinter and grown cool. Flowers develop only slightly above the ground hugging foliage.

Creeping Speedwell (*Veronica Repens*) is not a showy plant but makes a very dense soft green mat which can be useful in some applications. The tiny seed germinates quickly and easily, producing small garden transplants in 8 weeks if multiple seedlings are placed in each cell pak compartment. This plant does not show off well in larger containers. *Veronica incana* is another easily grown Speedwell. It develops larger, silvery leaves which are close to the ground but not so completely prostrate as *Veronica repens*. *Veronica incana* has small blue flowers which develop all along a flower spike rising perhaps one foot above the foliage.

Although both Veronicas prefer good sun, the creeping variety, especially, can tolerate some shade.

Viola – Discussed previously under bedding plants.

Chapter 18

TREES, SHRUBS, AND ROSES

The nursery industry, which most people recognize as dealing primarily with woody ornamentals, is very diversified in North America. This diversity is encouraged by the numerous climatic variations which exist. Thousands of varieties are available to fill the many ecological niches presented by climatic zones which range from subtropical to arctic and from moist seacoast to parched desert.

Because of the decidedly localized need and preference for specific types and varieties of nursery stock, this discussion will be limited primarily to a presentation of general principles rather than concentrating upon specific varieties. And since the scope of this book is limited to container plant production, no attempt will be made to explore the area of open field nursery stock culture. Some passing references may be made concerning these subjects but only as is necessary to adequately cover the general topic of container nursery stock production.

An increasing human population assures a continuing demand for nursery stock in order to beautify the dwellings, business places, and public projects which a larger number of people require. Demand for nursery stock is fueled not only by population growth but also by a heightened awareness of the need to preserve the quality of life through generous use of vegetation in the modern landscape.

A diversity of geography offers the local nursery person a unique opportunity to capitalize upon his or her first hand knowledge of the specific growing conditions and market needs present in the area. Nurseries which combine both growing and marketing of the crop to the end consumer are in a particularly strong position to take advantage of a profitable situation.

Nurseries which actively grow plants will be able to supply customers not only with the most favorable varieties for the local area but will also have the practical knowledge necessary to help consumers succeed at their landscape efforts. These services provided give the local nursery grower a decided advantage (which cannot easily be overcome strictly through price) over outlets which are concerned only with the retail aspect.

The need for plant varieties adaptable to local needs is an area which every nursery stock grower should attach extreme importance. It will not only be critical in the actual production process but will ultimately be a primary factor determining the success or failure of marketing efforts. Retail customers who purchase a tree for permanent placement in the landscape are perhaps more likely to retain unpleasant memories of failure than are those who purchase items such as bedding plants or holiday flowers. The unit cost for trees is also generally several times more thus emphasizing any unpleasant experience.

Container plant nurseries may often be conveniently divided into those which grow plants only a short time (generally only for an establishment period) and those which grow plants for longer periods (generally from small starter plants into landscape size).

Essentially, there are no large scale differences in cultural techniques between the 2 methods of operation. The main variable being the initial size of plant which is containerized for growing on. Growing methods for nursery stock are governed by the same general environmental factors as were discussed earlier in this book.

Whether or not a grower decides to specialize in short term establishment of nursery stock into containers or to actively grow plants over a longer cultural cycle will depend upon many factors. But financial circumstances, marketing possibilities, and local climate are often the chief concerns which affect the decision.

Growing plants over a longer period of time necessarily means a greater monetary investment in facilities, labor, and inventory than does shorter term growing. The expected profit should adequately reflect these added expenses.

Local climatic conditions sometimes prevent profitable longer term outdoor nursery growing operations from being established in particular locations. In many situations the most profitable strategy is to purchase larger plant material from growers in more favorable climatic areas and establish this material in containers for sale in the immediate future.

Apple trees planted from dormant stock to both plastic pots (foreground) and wood fiber pots (background). Some states do not permit the sale of newly planted dormant stock in non-plantable pots such as the plastic ones seen here.

SHORT TERM NURSERY GROWING

This is the common cultural strategy employed by most smaller nursery stock growers. Marketing of plants soon after establishment in containers allows the grower to provide a wide assortment of varieties without the cost of maintaining an extensive inventory of material in all stages of growth. It also allows nurseries with a limited growing area to turn crops more frequently.

Even some larger wholesale nurseries employ a short term growing strategy because they find that certain varieties can be purchased from

Evergreens are seldom planted to containers from bareroot stock, especially in larger sizes.

specialist growers more economically than they can be grown on the premises.

Short term growing of nursery stock basically involves purchasing of plant material close to or at the size which it is normally sold, transplanting it to containers of various sizes, forcing into active growth, and selling the product when it reaches the desired size or state of growth. The time span involved in this process usually involves less than 6 months but could be interpreted to include programs which involve almost a full year. There is no precise delineation possible between short term and long term growing.

The usual scenario of short term growing involves receiving more or less dormant nursery stock in late winter or spring and transplanting to containers; then allowing the plants to become rooted in and develop top growth. In areas (some mild climate locations) where dormant stock does not play so important a role, relatively large growing plants may be transplanted to larger containers for establishment or to grow through the upcoming season.

Another commonly employed practice is to transplant balled and burlapped stock (whether dormant or in active growth) into containers for establishment and sale. In this case the objective may not be so much to increase the actual value of plants as it is to provide for easier care and display of plants at the retail site through an extended sales season.

There are certainly many minor variations to short term container nursery stock growing, depending upon the special needs each facility may experience. And often, there is a mixture of long term and short term crops at the same growing site.

The techniques utilized for short term nursery stock growing may be most easily outlined by proceeding stepwise from the receipt of starter plants to the final product as it is ready for sale.

Receipt of growing stock

The typical short term grower receives bare root dormant plants in late winter or early spring for potting. Depending upon climate, starter plant supply, and the inclination of the grower; dormant plants are instead sometimes potted in late fall. The latter timeframe is often more conducive to quality plants for the next growing season and allows much of the yearly work load to be taken care of at an otherwise slow period.

If starter plants are not in the dormant state, they are usually scheduled to arrive at a time when they can be transplanted and immediately transferred outdoors without fear of damage from severe weather.

Needless to say, when dormant plants are purchased, the grower must have extreme confidence in the supplier of such material. Most varieties of nursery stock which are properly harvested and placed in well maintained storage facilities will perform admirably for the grower after transplanting. But low quality stock which has been mistreated before arrival can mean total failure. Growers should investigate suppliers carefully; the most satisfactory evidence that quality stock will be received is the recommendations of other respected growers. In chapter 5 some introduction to grade classification of nursery stock was provided. Growers should carefully study the catalogs of any suppliers providing stock so that the appropriate grade and quality of material is ordered. Wholesale nurseries seldom guarantee their stock. Basically, the guarantee is reflected in their past reputation.

Trial orders from new suppliers should be tested before any large quantities of stock are purchased. The risk of receiving poor stock is simply too great to commit oneself to large orders from unproven sources. Some attention must also be focused upon the ability of suppliers to provide reliable, low cost transport and to deliver on schedule. Long delays or especially early deliveries can prove to be costly.

Dormant nursery stock must be transported carefully as well as handled carefully after it arrives. Growers should always look for evidence of freezing or drying out of plants during transit. Any suspected damage must be noted on the shipping documents and reported to the supplier immediately.

Inspection of arriving dormant nursery stock is especially important not only for registering complaints but also in order to plan future handling of the stock. Especially hard or prolonged freezing or drying out of stock may cause further expenditure of time and materials to be fruitless. Sometimes, if it is judged stock is too badly damaged, it is better to discard it than to attempt revival.

Light frost in dormant stock is normally not fatal if the frost is allowed to leave gradually, preferably at temperatures just above freezing. Drying out of stock in transit is a more serious problem. The degree and duration of desiccation are often difficult to assess accurately.

Once the dormant plants have arrived, high humidity levels must be constantly maintained around the roots and preferably also around stems if there will be any delay in planting. Stock should be stored at cool temperatures from about 35-45^0 F. Slightly warmer temperatures are permissible if the humidity is high and plants have not already begun to leaf out. Although sawdust and small wood chips are probably the materials most often used to "heel" in tree roots to maintain moisture around them, sand, clean straw, hay and other means may also be employed. Maintaining high humidity levels does not mean submerging plants in water for any extended period, this action can prove just as damaging as desiccation although the damage does not occur with shorter exposures.

Every effort should be made to transplant dormant stock before leaves become visible at the buds. It is very difficult to avoid damage to new growth if it is exposed suddenly to the less humid and less shaded growing environment.

Pre-planting treatment of nursery stock

Most dormant nursery stock benefits from at least some cosmetic pruning before being planted, and some individual plants or perhaps entire varieties will require pruning to prepare them for forcing properly.

There is much disagreement over how much pruning should take place on dormant nursery stock. The traditional practice was to severely trim back tops on most varieties while cutting off whatever portion of the root system which would not fit easily into a reasonable size container.

Some experimental evidence suggests that pruning of top growth does not result in improved growth or survivability of containerized nursery stock and that larger containers should be employed if one finds that anything more than minimal root pruning is required.

The author (and many other experts) tends to agree with the evidence against severe pruning. Dormant nursery stock is usually purchased by size classes; it makes no sense to pay good money for large size stock and then trim away the great majority of it. Pruning labor is also expensive, it can account for 20-25% of the labor required in transplanting.

When high quality nursery stock is handled properly at every step in the transplanting and forcing process, there seems to be no survival advantage to pruning tops any further than what is necessary to remove dead branches or those which will detract from the shape and appearance of the plant.

Roots also should not be pruned severely. Only the odd large root which sticks out from the main mass needs to be cut off (of course, all broken roots should be trimmed).

Occasionally, certain plant varieties develop a large tangle of fibrous roots; it is sometimes necessary to thin out this root mass by severe pruning so that adequate soil can be worked into the root system. Any long, trailing roots which exceed the perimeter of the main root mass should be cut off so that there is no need to wind them around in the pot. If the container is not large enough to hold a root system trimmed as above without bending and crowding roots, a larger size pot should be chosen.

Some nurserymen recommend pruning off the terminal portions of roots to stimulate new root growth. The author feels that enough trimming has

Some varieties, such as these dormant lilacs, should not normally be top pruned because the flower buds are already formed in the buds.

taken place in the harvesting and preparation stage to make this final procedure unnecessary unless the root tips are ragged and exhibit damage from the harvest.

Dormant roses are received with wide variation in the length of canes, depending upon the supplier's practices. Most rose shippers now trim plants to between 1 and 1 1/2 feet of top growth so that excessive storage, packaging, and shipping space is not required. There seems to be no benefit in trimming rose canes lower than 8-12 inches; only enough to prevent plants from appearing overly tall and to remove any rotted stem portions.

Some suppliers state that they will trim rose plants to 8 inches for the grower. But the final trim is best left until transplanting in order to prevent moist storage conditions from causing stem rot to begin in the wound.

Stem rot is prevalent in some regions and is encouraged by improper storage and unsanitary conditions. Some growers take the precaution of trimming the cane tops at transplanting and then applying an acceptable disease control spray directly over the wounds.

Correct labeling of nursery stock is of prime importance. Customers become very irritated if they plan on a particular variety in the landscape and eventually find that the plant was mislabeled. It is easy to get labels mixed up in the transplanting process and only an expert can place the correct label on dormant nursery stock if the original identification tag gets lost. Even knowledgeable persons cannot readily distinguish between dormant stock of cultivars in the same species.

Some dormant species are difficult to bring into active bud stage. A process called "sweating" is often used on these species to insure revival from dormancy. Bare root plants are enclosed in a moist atmosphere (inside a shaded plastic tent is ideal) where the temperature is raised to the range of 50-70° F. Plants can be "sweated" after planting but will require more room. Suppliers of dormant plants can supply the names of plants which will benefit from sweating.

The sweating process usually requires a week or less until buds become swollen. Leaving plants in the sweat house too long so that actual leaf development begins is perhaps worse than no treatment at all. Species which break dormancy easily require no sweating. Plants which have been potted after sweating should not be placed in a cold, dry environment. They need at least moderate humidity and temperatures.

Actively growing plants which have been propagated or purchased for growing on should be conditioned prior to planting. The first step in this process is to allow plants to become acclimatized to the general environment into which they will be placed after transplanting. Sometimes plant tissue is tender from rapid growth in more ideal climates or from being in protected transit for several days.

Plants should then be leached thoroughly and provided with a proper dosage of fertilizer which is typically being used at the nursery. It is helpful at this time if a balanced micro nutrient formula is added so that the grower need not wonder if certain elements may be lacking in plant tissue. The leaching and fertilizer applications will insure (as much as is practical) that the plants begin growth with a healthy soluble salt and mineral balance in the soil.

A dormant rose plant trimmed properly top and bottom for planting. Immediate labeling is extremely important with bareroot stock.

Prior to transplanting actively growing plants, the root ball should be roughed up on the sides and bottom. If roots are severely crowded and circling the pot, they may need to be cut and pulled apart on the outer edges. All excised roots should then be removed and any of those remaining which are long and scraggly should be further pruned.

Transplanting into containers

The size of container necessary for nursery stock has been previously mentioned. It must, in general, fit the root system. Most short term growing of nursery stock takes place in wood fiber pots, thin-walled wooden baskets, or some other "plantable" type container. More durable plastic, metal, or other types of containers may be used if plants are to be grown

A dormant rose plant at the proper depth in a container size which does not require crowding of the roots.

somewhat longer to the point where an extensive root system forms to hold the root ball together when it is removed for planting.

Plant roots must not be allowed to dry out in the transplanting process. This is one of the critical steps where plants can become injured quickly.

Most plants, whether bare root or actively growing, should be planted at the same soil level which existed previously. On grafted trees and roses this means the graft union will be above the soil line; and on trees where a cut has previously been made to train a single leader, the cut should remain above the soil.

A determined effort is sometimes required to work soil into the root system with hands or wooden sticks which have rounded ends. Working the soil in is very important so that air pockets are eliminated, it also ensures that plants are more securely anchored.

Although planting shrubs and trees exactly straight up in the pot makes little difference in how they grow, it makes them much more appealing to the ultimate customer. The most vigorous, healthy tree on the sales lot will remain unsold if it is planted crooked.

If a mechanical planter is utilized, some inspection is usually necessary to correct occasional improperly planted containers. Smaller growers can seldom justify the cost of mechanical planters which are used for a short time each year.

Trees and shrubs which are being planted from ball and burlap can have the burlap taken off carefully after being placed in the container or it can be left on. In either case, the top tie down around the trunk should be removed. Taking the majority of the burlap off is perhaps the best treatment since a better and quicker union is made between the new soil in containers and the original ball soil.

In almost all cases, the plants should be watered in heavily after transplanting. Certain species may require somewhat drier conditions to become established but they are few and far between.

The question of how much fertilizer to allow for newly planted nursery stock is very important. Some growers prefer to incorporate the entire amount of fertilizer which short term growth will require into the soil mix in a slow release form. This is a good method but must be handled carefully to avoid severe problems. *Too much fertilizer in the soil initially can result in total crop failure.* The amount to be added must be carefully tested under a variety of environmental conditions before large scale application is made.

Many growers prefer to start bare root nursery stock off with no fertilizer in the soil at all (except superphosphate) until growth becomes evident. This latter course is certainly the safest procedure for those who are inexperienced.

Numerous formulations of slow release fertilizers are available. The best method of application may be very specific as to timing, placement, and dosage. If growers choose to use these products, they should evaluate the technical directions supplied with the fertilizer very carefully.

Placing nursery stock in the growing area

Most growers of containerized nursery stock move the transplanted material from the potting shed directly to the outdoors location where it

This crop of shrubs has been started indoors and will be moved to open air only after all danger of frost is past. An expensive but safe method of operation.

will be grown on for sale. Sometimes the stock is actually planted into containers at the growing site.

Many growers modify this direct to site method to some degree. Usually this is done to give additional protection from the elements until plants have a chance to become acclimated. Every operation which grows plants outdoors is faced with the perennial problem of how to protect them during the first few critical weeks until they become rooted in.

The need to protect nursery stock is brought about by the serious harm which drying out or freezing can cause to newly planted stock. Growers who live in humid climates where the spring temperatures do not gyrate wildly may experience little need to provide protection. But the climate in other areas is not so agreeable and makes starting nursery stock outdoors a real challenge. In general, newly potted material can be seriously injured if tops or roots are exposed to 20^0 F or less. Roots in the soil will, of course, be less likely to reach this temperature.

Attempts to protect nursery stock during establishment take many forms. Sheds open on one side, shade houses, burlap coverings, and greenhouses are all ways which have been used. Sometimes early protection backfires in that plants are allowed to leaf out, only to experience a hard freeze or drying windstorm the very first day they are left unprotected.

The risks inherent with outdoor culture cannot be completely eliminated. This is why a growing proportion of nurseries are investing in starter facilities (usually polyethylene covered greenhouses) which can be used for protection until all danger of damaging frost is past. Using greenhouses to start material is expensive and can cause more harm than good if sufficient cooling and ventilation is not provided.

Every grower will be faced with somewhat different problems in the plant establishment phase of nursery operation. It is a difficult transition and one where a good deal of stock can be lost or damaged quickly. The good judgment and experience of the grower is particularly important here. Generally, if there is an error to be made, it should be made on the side of caution. A little extra effort and expense to insure proper plant establishment is better than risking catastrophic losses.

Most short term nursery growers feel a need to get stock potted as early as possible so that the work is out of the way and plants may be well on their way to rooting in before the spring sales rush begins. This early planting timetable may not be the most culturally sound method in many geographic areas.

Later planting is often preferable because temperatures are warmer at that time. This allows the plants to develop faster and reduces the chance of severe frost outdoors. Areas which experience very humid late spring and early summer conditions have the best luck with this later timetable. This method would not work so well in locations which are likely to experience dry weather or high winds in late spring.

Growers must be aware that it is necessary to handle nursery stock carefully in each stage of the growing process. Carelessness at any point can render all further efforts futile.

As soon as plants are established, they should be spaced adequately for proper development. Most varieties will benefit from full sun. As warmer weather comes on, timely irrigation becomes important. There is no sense in carefully nurturing plants to the full leaf stage and then allowing them to become stunted because one lacks the ability to apply enough water on hot days.

Insect and disease control is not usually of extreme concern. Isolated outbreaks of pests may occur but, hopefully, most of the crop will be sold before midsummer when a full range of insect attacks can be expected. If deer are prevalent at the growing site, they can cause significant damage at any season, and even more pronounced antler rubbing damage in fall plantings.

Plants which remain unsold at season's end should be given winter protection if the nursery is located in an area which requires this precaution. These plants may need repotting before the next season due to an overgrowth of roots in the original container.

Most of the previous discussion of short term nursery growing has concentrated upon the handling of bare root stock. As was mentioned, this is not the only method by which short term growers operate. Some growers, particularly in mild climates, transplant actively growing material to grow on a few months. No detailed transplanting procedures were presented for this method because they have been adequately covered in other sections of this book.

LONG TERM GROWING OF NURSERY STOCK

Smaller growers (to whom this book is primarily intended) will generally find long term growing of container nursery stock an unattractive business proposition. Most of the operations which specialize in this production method are larger and grow relatively few species which are well adapted to rapid and healthy growth under the local climatic conditions. The cash flow in a long term growth nursery obviously takes a few years to reach its maximum.

As was mentioned earlier, long term growing is generally taken to encompass those situations where nursery stock is grown for longer periods than are necessary strictly for vigorous establishment of plants after transplanting. Long term growing usually involves holding stock through the winter after it has been grown at least one season in the container.

Specific evergreen varieties are suitable for training to unusual landscape attractions.

Thus, we have difficulty classifying as short term or long term the considerable number of plants which may be grown for longer than a short establishment period but which are sold before the winter season. This is a problem of small consequence since the division is only employed as a means of facilitating discussion.

The basic cultural techniques used for growing nursery stock longer term in containers are similar to those presented earlier in several sections of this book. Only the need for and means of providing winter protection requires further clarification at this time.

Containerized nursery stock which is left to face the rigors of winter without adequate protection often suffers severe loss of quality and even death in extreme cases. The amount of loss will vary with many circumstances but the species involved and severity of climate are the

Norway Maple Cleveland

two most important factors.

The degree of winter protection necessary will vary mostly in relation to the two factors mentioned above. If a species which possesses exceptional winter hardiness is being overwintered in a rather mild climate, no protection at all may be needed. Growers must use experience as their best guide to winter protection needs; but lacking this, one would certainly be safer to protect stock about which there is any doubt.

Protection needs may vary considerably from year to year. Just because little damage is noted after one winter season does not mean these results will persist in succeeding years. Low temperatures are not the only climatic factor which affects plant viability in winter. In fact, other characteristics such as wind speed, moisture, and light intensity may be more important in certain areas.

The price of this specially trimmed juniper specimen justifies the use of a higher cost container. Since the plant may be in the container for a considerable time during production and display, a long lasting construction material must be used.

In general, it must be realized that low temperatures and temperature variation are more important in the root mass than they are for the above ground portion of nursery plants. Research has shown that roots are damaged much more easily through low temperature exposure than are tops. Excessive root temperatures in summer are not likely to kill plants (unless water is deficient) but can severely limit growth potential. Growers must determine if some protection of containers from the sun is necessary.

A variety of means is used to protect nursery stock during the winter months. Shaded greenhouses, shaded poly tunnels, straw or mulch cover, snow cover, foam insulation, sawdust cover, and unheated sheds are all

Acer platanoides – Silver variegated maple

used with some effectiveness. Shaded poly tunnels, foam insulation, and covering roots with mulch, sawdust, or straw are perhaps the most commonly employed methods.

Whichever practice is employed, common sense must be used to avoid more damage through storage than might be encountered without it. Plants must be watered adequately before storage and checked regularly for moisture needs thereafter. And attention must be paid to the possibility of disease, deer, and rodent damage during storage. Diseases may become rampant when nursery stock is laid down and covered with foam or other materials which allow humidity to build up around the plants.

Putting stock into storage too early is a constant danger when the top growth is covered. If temperatures are too warm, poly houses can heat up and cause plants considerable harm. And if plants are covered with foam or mulch too early, plants remain in low light or dark conditions longer than

Carpinus betulus – Pyramidal hornbeam

necessary. Poly tunnels must sometimes be ventilated during sunny periods.

Alternate freezing and thawing is perhaps the greatest common winter danger to nursery stock. Especially when it occurs rapidly. This is why plants left in an unshaded and unheated greenhouse will almost always exhibit more winter damage than those left unprotected outside. Overwintering methods should be designed towards preventing this phenomenon.

Southern nursery stock growers must not assume that species which are hardy in colder climates will not need some protection in winter. Occasional severe winters in the South can cause significant losses. And, as has been pointed out, low temperatures are only one of several factors which determine winter survival. Temperature variability is perhaps even more important.

The longer nursery stock is grown, it will of course require more attention to continuing needs such as fertilization, pest and disease control, and

Cedrus libani

soil chemistry balance. Over time, any one of these or other factors can easily become critical to plant survival and growth because it is outside acceptable ranges. Growing longer term crops requires a grower to continually and consistently monitor the needs of the plants and assess crop progress.

The types of containers which can be used for long term nursery culture are somewhat different than for short term establishment of plants. There is no real need to grow plants long term in "plantable" or easily decayed pots; in fact, one must be assured that the containers will remain intact long enough to easily complete the anticipated crop growth cycle. Short term growers must be concerned with state regulations which specify how long plants must be established in containers before they can be sold in non-plantable pots such as metal or plastic. Long term growers need not address this concern.

Betula pendula – European white birch

When plants are grown in containers for considerable periods of time, their root systems can become so greatly restricted and deformed as to prevent acceptable performance in the landscape after they have been transplanted (unless the roots are properly spread apart and pruned at transplanting). In severe cases, the roots and, consequently, the entire tree may be permanently damaged. The descriptive term often applied to this condition in woody nursery stock is "root spiraling".

Some companies have designed the shape of their containers with the objective of preventing root spiraling to some degree (at least in the early, less severe cases). Independent research has not always borne out the claims of manufacturers concerning the effectiveness of various container configurations in preventing this problem. There does seem to be some connection, however, between noncontinuous pot wall configuration (not smooth surfaced and not continuously round) and prevention of root spiraling, at least in early growth stages. No amount of altering the geometry of containers can prevent the simple process of root crowding when it reaches advanced stages. Every grower must realize that a tree or shrub which has reached the stage of severe root restriction and deformation is worthless. Plants in this condition will never grow out of it and often die in the landscape. Customers who purchased root deformed trees are not likely to recommend the offending nursery to friends and family. Severely root restricted material should be thrown away!

Long term growers must carefully assess the length of time plants will be in containers so that the optimum size is provided for uninterrupted growth into a quality product. Too small a pot will result in excessive root spiraling and reduced growth while too large a pot can significantly increase container, soil, and transportation costs.

Whether a nursery operates within a short term or long term growing timeframe, the question of soil and container costs must be carefully addressed. Expenses for both of these necessities, however, makes up a greater percentage of total nursery costs under a long term scenario. Soil can become not only expensive but difficult to handle and procure unless plans are made in advance.

The amounts of soil used in some nurseries is considerable. A mechanical means of mixing, treating, and handling this vast amount of material must be incorporated in the nursery plan. There are many types of soil mixing and handling systems available but most small nurseries can get by using a tractor with front loader to serve as both a general nursery utility vehicle and soil handling unit.

Weed control is an important aspect of nursery management, particularly when plants are grown long term. Although good prevention practices prior to planting can alleviate the majority of problems, some chemical weed control in pots will generally become necessary.

TYPES OF NURSERY STOCK

As with many other aspects of horticulture, it is difficult to separate different categories of nursery stock into convenient and totally exclusive compartments. However, some attempt at this task will perhaps allow

An interesting use of grafting and sculpture techniques with spruce species grown in wooden tubs.

emphasis at certain times upon particular broad groupings and permit the discussion to be more specific. Only such cultural material as relates especially to such groups will be discussed in this section, the more general information having been considered under earlier topics. The following presentations concerning trees, shrubs, and roses do not address specific varieties unless it is felt this will add appreciably to the discussion. In most cases the number of total varieties available for such a great land mass as the North American continent is so diverse as to render mention of specific varieties as meaningless unless referenced to discrete climatological zones. The latter is clearly impossible to achieve in the present book dealing with such a broad range of horticultural topics. Various plant groups which many growers would consider equally at home under nursery stock (ground covers, perennials, tropical shrubs and trees) have been covered elsewhere in this book as a matter of classification convenience.

It is difficult in a general text to adequately explore varietal adaptiveness to even broad climatological regions. Growers must realize therefore, that when planning nursery production; a detailed investigation should be made into the varieties which are suitable for both the production area and

Populus tremula – Swedish columnar poplar

potential market locales.   There is perhaps some benefit in pointing out the contrast in cultural practices and varieties which are applicable to greatly differing climatic zones; such as the mild seacoasts and more southerly semitropical locations as compared to primarily inland and northerly locations which experience harsher winters. Such an example of widely differing situations makes it evident that nurserymen must tailor their growing practices and crop varieties to specific climatological entities. Distribution of climatologically unsuitable varieties and species to mass market outlets is perhaps one of the most urgent problems in the nursery industry.

Trees

Almost everyone who purchases a new or used home, a business, or piece of land begins to dream of how it will look with a tree here and 1 or 2 over there. People who are left unmoved by the beauty of annual or

Pinus contorta (modified by pruning)

perennial flowers or who do not wish to spend hours in a rose garden are aware of the practical benefits which trees serve. Aside from beauty, they provide shade, soften noise, and reduce wind speeds.

Trees are regarded by most people as a desirable and necessary investment for their properties. Every knowledgeable home owner knows that landscaping, particularly trees, will not only pay for itself but actually grow in value.

And trees are relatively trouble free. Once planted and shaped, they normally grow for decades with only occasional care. Most trees, if it were not for the perfection desired by owners would survive and prosper with no care after they were well established. Billions of dollars of free advertising have been given to commercial tree growers through the yearly celebration of Arbor Day and more recently, Earth Day. Trees are perhaps receiving more than their fair share of attention (amongst plants) as

**Picea pungens – Colorado blue spruce, one of the most widely planted and
well adapted species in North America.**

being beneficial to the environment.

For all these reasons, there is a good and increasing demand for well
grown trees. In temperate regions this demand is concentrated mostly in
spring but, since the growth in availability of containerized stock, people
have begun to plant more into summer and fall. Containerized nursery
stock allows planting to go on year-round in mild climates although most
takes place in the cooler months.

If individuals, business, or other types of customers are landscaping a
location for the first time, their purchase of trees may amount to a significant
sum of money. In such cases the customer will be acutely interested in
the proper choice of varieties, initial planting and ongoing care instructions,
and the guarantee policy of the seller. If the tree grower also engages in
retail activity, providing these essential services will certainly allow a

The pines and spruces pictured here are commonly planted throughout the cooler regions of North America, displaying an amazing adaptability to differing soils and climates.

competitive advantage over other outlets which simply act as retailers and know little about tree culture. Providing landscaping services to install and design the material is another important source of income for some nurseries, many customers are grateful that such help is available.

When extra services are provided to customers, the grower must ensure adequate profit by increasing the selling price proportionate to the value of services rendered. In many full service situations, the value of service in the transaction will be equal to the actual wholesale price of nursery stock. Most smaller growers of nursery stock find themselves in this type of marketing situation and cannot profitably survive without charging for the services rendered.

Those nurseries which supply mass outlets will find it necessary to provide planting and care instruction on tags which accompany each tree. The success or failure of the ultimate consumers who buy trees from these outlets is felt eventually by the nurseries supplying stock, thus growers have a vested interest in providing as good information as is possible under these circumstances.

There are several more or less distinct groups of trees which can be used in the landscape. They are distinguished mainly by the functions

An extensive field of container grown Arborvitae. Golden globes in foreground and green semi-uprights in back.

which they serve.

Decorative or special purpose trees are mostly those which flower or possess specific forms, leaf color, or other characteristics which make them desirable. In many cases these trees are fairly small. Catalogs may also refer to these as ornamental trees. One of the most popular groups in this class are the flowering crabs, of which there are numerous cultivars suitable for different landscape effects, planting sites, and climates. Resistance to different diseases is also an important characteristic for which many new crab apple varieties have been developed.

A host of other ornamental groups are available. Some of the most important are: dwarf maple, hawthorn, magnolia, mountain ash, tree lilac, dogwood, and flowering fruit trees (cherry, plum, and pear). Many of the decorative trees are important sources of food for wildlife (especially birds).

Acer platanoides – Fairview, young specimen

Shade trees usually include those larger trees which form a dense canopy. They are perhaps in most demand by the general public and are the more well known varieties which can be depended upon for steady sales year after year. Perhaps the most widely planted shade trees are various maple, ash, oak, willow, elm, and linden varieties. Of course, these old standbys are not always the best choices in certain climatic areas. Cottonwood and hackberry trees are popular in some regions with a more rugged climate. Other shade trees such as buckeye, Kentucky coffee tree, ginkgo, catalpa, and aspen are seen less frequently but may assume major importance in certain locations.

Lawn trees may be of many different sizes and shapes; but if they are large, the leaf canopy normally is not so dense as to prevent some sun from reaching grass underneath. Locusts are a good lawn group because they are larger but seldom so dense as to prevent healthy lawn

Planters utilizing dwarf varieties offer additional cash and carry possibilities to the nursery trade.

underneath.Some birch such as cut leaf and weeping varieties are also excellent. Of course many flowering or decorative trees are used in lawn areas but they generally are not favored for this purpose if they produce numerous fruits which interfere with lawn use or care.

Evergreen trees are especially useful for enhancing the winter landscape. In this case the author is referring mainly to conifers rather than broad leaved evergreens. It is difficult to classify evergreens as primarily shrubby or tree types, as the same genus often contains both. The Colorado blue spruce is perhaps the most widely adapted and planted large evergreen tree in North America, but low growing shrubby cultivars of this species are available although not widely planted. Several other species of spruces show the same variation in form.

Junipers, arborvitae, and yews display the opposite tendency — most

Betula papyrifera – Paper birch

are small or medium size shrubs, but a few varieties can be large enough to serve as trees in the landscape. There is at least one variety of juniper which will grow in almost every climate of North America, although they need irrigation in arid locations. Only a knowledgeable nursery person can advise customers concerning the many varieties, shapes, and uses of this indispensable landscaping genus. The wrong choice may dramatically lower the effectiveness in the mature landscape.

The last general group of trees are those which are grown primarily for fruit. A good deal of expertise is often necessary to properly sell fruit trees so that the customer receives the variety which will fulfill the intended purpose. The customer must often be led into the correct choice since many people have only a vague understanding of what varieties will produce in the local climate and how to choose for compatible pollinating trees when they are required. The matter of choosing the proper tree is

Potentilla has been extensively selected to yield numerous excellent cultivars. Its usefulness stems mainly from an ability to flower continuously and adapt to many ecological habitats.

also complicated by specialized fruits for different uses (fresh eating apples as opposed to pie apples, etc.) and different ripening seasons. There is no end to the professional pointers which can be given to grateful gardeners who will, as a result, advertise the nursery's name far and wide. Fruit trees sell steadily to private individuals but there is little demand from professional landscapers or other larger tree users such as park departments.

Mention has been made of these several general types of trees so that growers can focus their attention upon providing particular groups of trees for the market or upon having a well rounded selection of types available. Certain wholesale growers may find there is opportunity in specialization but the great majority of growers who sell both wholesale and retail will be best off to provide customers with a complete selection of trees to fill various landscaping needs.

Depending upon the market one is planning to supply it may be advisable to stress production of different general types of trees. If landscape contractors are expected to be the major purchasers, it has already been pointed out that few fruit trees would be sold. Landscapers would, however,

Cornus alternifolia ragoda – Dogwood

make heavy use of special purpose and decorative trees. Park departments are more likely to require stock for shade or lawn purposes. The general public can be expected to utilize a wide spectrum of tree types but shade and fruit trees are perhaps safer bets to sell in a soft market.

A good deal of selection and breeding with popular groups of trees has taken place in the last quarter century. Many improved performance and disease resistant varieties are now available. As in other aspects of horticulture, these new varieties are extremely important to industry progress. Improved products insure a higher degree of satisfaction and more business in the future.

Unfortunately, many of the benefits which new varieties offer are not readily apparent when the plants are sold in smaller containers. The nurseryman must make it a practice to let retailers and customers know about the value of improved varieties, even if the initial purchase cost is considerably higher. If a new variety grows fast, and has much less chance of an early death due to disease, the average homeowner will certainly understand that it is worth $5 or $10 more initially.

Container tree growers seldom propagate their own stock except occasionally in the case of a few standard varieties which are easy to start from seed or cuttings. Efficient production of newer varieties often requires a good deal of facilities to perform tissue culture, grafting, and difficult rooting or seed germination techniques. The smaller and medium sized grower is well advised to leave all but the easiest propagation to specialists.

Container production of trees involves many different sizes. The most popular is usually termed a 5 gallon container. Trees of this size are large enough to please the majority of consumers but small enough to be handled by an individual person. They are also moderate in price.

Larger 7 and 10 gallon container trees are commonly produced to satisfy those people who want larger plants to start and are not so concerned with price. Even larger containers find a ready market but are not practical unless machinery is available to handle them during production, marketing, and planting.

The overall shape of a tree used in container production is very important. First, it must look like a tree and should have some branching; secondly, it must have a straight trunk because people seldom buy trees with crooked trunks. Even if the trunk is straight but the tree is put into the pot at an angle, it is difficult to convince consumers that this does not detract from the value.

There is a speciality market for artistic trees; those which either by genetic predisposition or through training appear unusual in some manner. But the average customer does not have an appreciation for these oddities and usually will not pay a regular price for them, much less a premium. If specialty trees are to be grown and sold, a marketing program geared to this type of use must be implemented.

If wholesale nurseries which supply dormant stock for transplanting do not provide the shape of tree necessary for making attractive containers, growers should shop around. There is a good deal of difference in the appearance and quality of plants coming from different suppliers. Tree shape is generally more important than is size, although the latter is a

---

Table 35

Simplified pollination characteristics of fruits.

Small fruits	Self-fertile.
Apples	Usually not self-fertile. Use 2 varieties. Bees are necessary for pollination since apple pollen is not dispersed by wind.
Apricots	Self-infertile, use 2 varieties.
Blueberries	Self-fertile, better with 2 varieties.
Sour cherries	Self-fertile.
Sweet cherries	Self-infertile, use 2 varieties
Peaches	Self-fertile.
Pears	Most self-infertile, better with 2 varieties.
Plums	Most self-infertile, use specific varieties recommended by nursery or American plum.

*Note: Pollinators must bloom at the same time as trees intended for fruit.

---

prime factor in the final product price.

It was mentioned in an earlier section of this chapter that there is no hard evidence to indicate that severe pruning enhances the survival rate of nursery stock. Trimming 2 or 3 feet off the top of a tree for no good reason makes poor economic sense if the average customer strongly relates plant size with value.

Other than gross negligence in planting and growing technique, perhaps no other cultural factor affects the value of containerized trees more than improper and unnecessary pruning. Only experienced persons should be allowed to prune tree stock. Not only can poor pruning reduce nursery revenues, it can greatly reduce the landscape value of trees for years to come.

As potted trees are placed at the outdoor growing location it may be necessary to devise means of preventing strong winds from toppling the containers. Some growers construct a center rail on either side of which trees are placed and loosely attached by means of twine. Another method is to place containers in a large square and then put a rope around the perimeter a few feet off the ground so that trees on the outside do not fall over. A large anchor spike can also be driven to hold the pot from tipping.

Growing containerized trees can be a profitable and rewarding business but it is seldom so simple as merely potting up a few of this and a few of that and hoping for a sale. There are many technical and business decisions to be made, not the least of which is determining what market is to be served. Whether a grower retails directly to the public or wholesales to other independent nurseries, landscapers, or mass marketers will make a tremendous difference in overall nursery operations.

Shrubs

The culture and marketing of containerized trees and of shrubs differ in only a few important points. Most nurseries which grow one also grow the other. Although a wide variety of shrub cultivars exists, there is perhaps more uniformity from one climatic area to another in the shrub varieties grown than is the case for trees.

Until recently, shrubs also have not received so much breeding and selection attention as have trees; this tends to limit the number of varieties to some extent. Since shrubs are sold in smaller sizes and at generally lower prices, the involved reproductive techniques necessary for some new varieties are not as economically practical as they are for trees.

Only a few groups of shrubs, such as lilacs, junipers, and potentillas have yielded numerous varieties to date; most other types are still offered in only one or a few basic varieties.

Because cuttings for shrubs are often more numerous when compared to trees, easier to root, require less time to reach marketable size, and are available from non-patented plant varieties; some shrub growers prefer to propagate their own stock. The availability of economically priced seed for some varieties also encourages propagation on the premises.

Some 1 gallon shrubs can be produced outdoors in less than a single northern growing season from the date of cutting or sowing while few would require more than a full season. Most 2 gallon shrubs could easily be grown outdoors in 2 growing seasons. But the vast majority of smaller growers find that purchasing shrub liners is more economical than self propagation.

Since shrubs are sold mostly in smaller sizes, many greenhouses find that shrub production fits in quite easily with the equipment and materials they have available. The limited height of most shrubs also lends to their economical production in greenhouses.

Although shrub production may not result in the same dollar return per square foot occupied as do most flowers, it is possible to root bare root species under the greenhouse benches late and bring them up onto benches as soon as some room opens in late spring. Thus most of the establishment period is spent in space which would be wasted for other purposes.

A quality container shrub is more easily produced than is a tree. This is mainly due to the fact that the shape of shrubs is not usually so important to consumers and because even most poorly shaped shrub stock can quickly be pruned to an acceptable specimen. Shrubs often grow faster and more densely than trees so that bare spots fill in sooner.

Although most shrubs do not actually require trimming at the time of planting, most growers remove ragged top growth to improve the shape and to stimulate branching. Trimming should not progress any further than is necessary to produce a pleasing shape. Certain shrubs, such as lilacs, do not bloom from new growth branches; trimming in these cases eliminates the flower buds.

Some shrubs, such as the evergreen junipers have achieved tremendous popularity over almost the entire North American continent. Most junipers are grown by large nurseries which ship regionally or nationally but some smaller growers find that they can propagate or buy small plants and economically grow larger 2 or 5 gallon material for wholesale and retail on a more or less local level. Certain other evergreens are also treated in a similar manner. These plants usually are grown at least a full season before marketing.

Vines

Perhaps the premier vine in North America is the clematis, of which there are a large number of varieties. Many plants are sold as small bare root starters, but the trend seems established toward providing clematis as a growing potted plant, even in larger sizes flowering on a trellis. Due to the high cost of starter plants and the considerable expense involved in

This rose plant has good color for Mother's Day after being planted March 1. A fast and profitable crop if essential cultural details are followed.

producing a flowering container, growers should be certain they receive a premium price for quality clematis.

Many vines (hardy kiwi, trumpetvine, American bittersweet, climbing hydrangea, wisteria, jasmine, ivy, and others) are available and seem to hold a good deal of attraction for retail customers. This is perhaps a specialty area which some nurseries could use to offer something a little different.

Roses

Roses are the most preferred flower in the United States. Scarcely any greenhouse or nursery can afford to be without at least a modest selection of rose plants for sale, either as flowering decorative pots or for use in the garden.

Roses are a profitable crop because a wide variety of good quality starter plants are easily available and because there is a well developed demand. They are also easy to grow if only a few basic procedures are followed.

Fertilizer should be restricted to low levels until active growth begins in earnest. Since the plants grow rapidly, fertilizer levels will have to be increased quickly to avoid deficiencies. Iron applications are sometimes necessary to avoid yellowing of the top leaves.

Roses must have full sun to grow properly and they must be faithfully treated to prevent being ravaged by mildew, spider mites, and aphids. The plants will grow under a wide variety of temperatures but do best between 50-63^0 F; the lower temperatures most often being used for garden roses while decorative plants are generally grown at the higher levels.

If good quality dormant plants are purchased, there is seldom any need for pinching after active growth has begun. In fact, pinching will require so much extra bench time that it is seldom a cost efficient growing technique. There are so many varieties available that predicting bloom dates is hazardous but the normal garden rose should be showing some color within 8 weeks of planting at 60^0 F.

Roses are popular not only in garden use but find a ready market for florists sales from Valentine's Day on through Mother's Day. Special varieties are often used for this purpose; but especially at Easter and Mother's Day, many predominantly garden varieties (especially miniature roses) can be adequately substituted. Those plants not sold for the holiday can be offered for garden use. This dual purpose crop is very profitable.

Although most florists will prefer a 6 or 7 inch pot be used for roses, larger pots are easier to grow in and to keep plants watered. Garden varieties are typically grown in 2 or 3 gallon pots. Small plants of miniature roses are often sold in 4 inch pots while older plants can be grown in the same size pots as regular garden roses.

Roses do not like to be continuously wet at the roots but neither will they tolerate excessively dry conditions. Excessive wetness often is signaled by iron chlorosis in the upper leaves of stem tips while plants allowed to dry out to the wilting point will quickly develop yellow leaves at the base of the plant. Choosing the proper size pot will help growers to avoid these problems. The author has seen numerous crops of once beautiful florist rose plants which were completely unmarketable because they were grown in small pots and allowed to dry excessively on occasion; thus leading to yellowing and loss of lower leaves.

The choice of varieties in roses is endless and reflects the great interest which they have received over the years. The finished quality of plants and ease of growing vary greatly between varieties. Growers should carefully document which varieties perform best for them.

Florist roses, miniatures, climbers, floribundas, grandifloras, hybrid teas, and shrub roses all have their specific uses and should be considered for inclusion in a rose growing program. Of course most gardeners will prefer to purchase standard hybrid teas but considerable sales volume can be generated by handling a good selection of other types as well. Often times these specialty roses are not available at every retail outlet. A large amount of effort and investment by major growers has led to numerous specialized rose varieties in the last few years (such as ground covers). This phenomenon helps to keep well grown roses in steady demand. Although roses are handled as a commodity item by mass merchandisers, nursery people seldom have trouble selling a high quality product at profitable prices; the demand is enormous from serious rose gardeners who insist upon the best.

Growers and retailers who specialize to some extent in roses will also want to carry many patented varieties which, although more expensive, are in good demand by rose enthusiasts (of which there are a good number).

Dormant rose plants of high quality are not difficult to force; the same procedures as described earlier under short term nursery stock treatment can be utilized. If anything, roses are perhaps more sensitive to drying out of the canes than are most other shrubs. Applying light shade and occasionally misting the canes of recently potted plants will ensure that canes remain turgid and buds emerge quickly. Excessive day temperatures should be avoided.

In mild climates container roses may be started outdoors. When outdoor temperatures and humidity fluctuate wildly, growers will generally be best off to start roses under shelter of some sort.

Chapter 19

FLOWERING POT PLANTS

The greenhouse owner who develops a good trade in flowering pot plants will enjoy a reasonably stable year around business. Potted flowers can be raised as the main crop through the year or as a fill in crop for those who specialize in bedding plants. Year around crop schedules result in a more efficient use of buildings and equipment and also permit establishment of a permanent work force. The bedding plant producer who continues to operate for holiday potted flowers is ready to go in the spring without the need for reopening greenhouses and cleaning away trash which has accumulated during the winter.

Growing potted plants through the year requires more technical and marketing knowledge than is necessary for temporary operations in the spring. More attention to detail must generally be given to individual potted flowers since people purchase them as gifts or for decorating and expect each plant to be perfect. The greenhouse environment in mid winter, when most flowering pots are grown, is not so conducive to easy growth as it is when sunlight is more abundant and temperatures higher. It is necessary for the grower to be an expert in manipulating cultural conditions to achieve good quality at this time of year. Choosing varieties which grow well at various times of the year and are the most labor efficient is an important task of the flowering plant grower. High fuel bills may cause winter operation to be unprofitable unless production is efficient and prices are maintained at levels which will compensate for increased energy use. Pest control in this season can be more difficult because weather conditions often prevent adequate ventilation for specific treatments. Some pests also decide to move indoors for the winter.

Year-round growing does not fit the objectives of all people. The responsibilities entailed in caring for crops and physical facilities will prevent a person from having any extended free time unless the business is large enough to employ a responsible and capable manager. Anyone with a little knowledge and ambition can usually turn a profit in the spring when plants grow easily and market demand is tremendous. Flowering pot plant culture is more exacting and except for holidays, demand is not overwhelming. Competition for the existing market is heavier and the individuals involved are generally more professional on both the growing and marketing levels. There are significant opportunities for profit in flowering pot plants but only people who develop a high degree of horticultural excellence will be assured of success. The year around market is for those individuals who desire to become professionals in the field and devote full time activity.

Marketing a limited number of flowering pot plants can be easy if a retail store is part of the greenhouse business. Developing a wholesale market is generally more difficult because most retail outlets will already have suppliers they are reluctant to abandon. Chain stores can be a source of business but they are often not authorized to buy from local growers and will be unlikely to pay top prices since they have the ability to buy on the national market at the lowest prices. Local florists and plant stores are excellent prospects because they are accustomed to paying normal prices. If there are no local suppliers, these smaller shops have to pay for transport and packing. There is also an advantage in having revenues dependent upon several smaller customers rather than one or two large accounts. No one customer has a great deal of bargaining leverage. The marketing plan developed for flowering pot plants may include a mixture of company owned stores, florist accounts, and chain stores or anything in between.

Company stores and florists will generally create a more even flow of daily business while chain stores are heavily oriented toward holidays. Florists may be difficult to sell to if the greenhouse maintains its own retail outlet which competes with their shop. It takes persistence and good products to overcome this understandable prejudice. The busy season for flowering pot plants begins at Thanksgiving and ends after Mother's Day. The time between these holidays becomes rather slow with the low point being reached from mid July through mid September. Thanksgiving, Christmas, Valentine's Day, Easter, and Mother's Day are the prime marketing periods but daily demand through this period is also strong. Timing crops for holidays is, needless to say, extremely critical. Secretary's

Day is becoming more important every year. Other special days may bring a small increase in sales.

Although the market for flowering pot plants has shown steady growth over the years, there is a sometimes unnoticed factor in operation which causes this growth to often be less beneficial for existing growers than might be expected. As domestic cut flower producers are edged out of their traditional markets by foreign competition, a good number of them shift all or part of their productive capacity to potted flowers. The latter are not so influenced by overseas competition since they are generally too heavy to be shipped economically and because there are restrictions against importation of soil products.

In the fiercely competitive potted flower market, growers must always be looking for ways to grow and sell at acceptable profit levels. It is necessary to evaluate every crop carefully to determine what combinations of production and marketing techniques can be successfully employed under the conditions existing for specific operations. A particular crop may be profitable and desirable for one grower while another only a few miles away finds it does not fit well into the overall production strategy of the greenhouse.

Perhaps the most often encountered comment heard from retailers and consumers of flowering pot plants is that they wish a plant was available which was beautiful and would bloom and grow continuously under ordinary home conditions. This is the miracle plant which every grower wishes he had an ironclad patent on

It may be that this plant will never be discovered and it may also be that, if it were, people would lose interest in a plant which was so permanent a fixture. At the present time, however, every grower must strive to choose available varieties for culture which approach this ideal as closely as possible. Satisfaction by consumers with the longevity and floriferous qualities of plants result in more repeat business.

Many growers find that, particularly in the spring and early summer, it makes good economic sense to aim towards growing potted flower varieties which are acceptable in both the florist gift trade and the garden market. In many cases this is not easily accomplished unless a definite long term strategy and implementation program are instituted. Normally it will be necessary to choose garden varieties satisfactory for this purpose and introduce them over a period of time to florists. Every effort in this regard will not be a success but some will.

Double begonias, regal geraniums, New Guinea impatiens, roses, combination pots, hanging baskets, and dahlias are some of the more likely candidates for this double duty. Growing varieties acceptable to either market increases the chance that crops will find a home at profitable prices.

Flowering plants for specific holidays are sometimes grown out of doors or with minimal protection in some more moderate climates. Many of these growers must depend upon shipping some of their product north to find a market.

Smaller potted plant growers may find that emphasizing certain crops for on-site culture while shipping in other varieties is a more realistic plan than trying to grow every variety in the inventory.

African violet

The African violet has been a favorite of plant lovers for many years. Although the display of flowers and plant size are small in relation to most other blooming pot plants, the African violet lends itself to good growth and flower production in the home. A discussion of African violet culture could as well be treated under foliage varieties since the plants will continue to bloom and grow for years if given proper care. Thousands of individuals have made hobbies or a part time business out of growing African violets. Many people are active in breeding new varieties and will readily purchase any new types which appear on the market. The most common market size is the 4 inch pot although 3 and 5 inch pots are not uncommon.

Miniature varieties of violets have been available for many years and are often sought out by enthusiasts. Growing these and other novelty type violets can add considerably to the volume of plants sold. A super mini-violet has been developed which can be offered for sale in pots as small as 1 inch diameter. Growers who propagate violets themselves must realize that many varieties are patented and reproduction is restricted unless a license is obtained.

Sales of greenhouse grown plants is substantial but not so large as would be expected because so many plants are propagated at home and sold or traded by individuals. An ability to flourish under the warm, low light conditions of most homes is one reason African violets are so popular.

Temperature for commercial production should be no less than 65° F. Plants grown cooler than this are subject to mildew, have an unattractive appearance, and develop slowly. Light intensities in the greenhouse should be in the range of 1,000-2,000 foot candles and shading is necessary in all but the darkest winter months. Plants that receive too little light will have elongated petioles and flower lightly or not at all. Bleaching of the foliage and overly compact growth are possible signs of excess light. Inexpensive light meters will eliminate much of the guess work about when to shade African violets. Excellent plants can be grown under artificial light at 600 foot candles for 16 hours a day. Exposure to 24 hour lighting is not harmful but there is some question as to whether the additional day length promotes further growth. Two fluorescent light fixtures 4 feet long with 2 tubes each can be hung 12 inches high over a 4 foot square bench to approximate 600 foot candles. Tubes must emit the proper wavelengths of light for best growth.

Water spots and rings will form on African violet foliage when plants are irrigated overhead with water having a temperature less than 65° F. Water should be applied thoroughly after plants have been allowed to dry out. Many growers eliminate the leaf spot problem by subirrigating pots with capillary mats or flood benches. The advantages of this system are sometimes outweighed by a lack of leaching and a greater chance of transmitting disease between plants. Fertilizer should be applied at 1/2 to 3/4 of the rates given to faster growing crops since African violets are not heavy feeders and can be damaged easily by excessive soluble salts. African violets prefer a highly organic soil with good drainage assured by the addition of granular particles such as perlite. They will not grow well in clayey, tight soils which drain poorly.

Pests and diseases are not excessive if proper culture is given to plants which are clean initially. Root rot and soil nematodes can become troublesome, particularly when water is applied from a common subirrigation system. Clean soil and planting stock will control these infestations. Mildew was mentioned as being a problem when temperatures drop below 65° F or anytime relative humidity is high. Several types of pests can affect African violets but the most devastating are the cyclamen mite and thrips. Infestations of cyclamen mites are seldom noticed until serious damage has occurred since the pests are only observable with difficulty when a 10X hand lens is used. Outward manifestations of cyclamen mites are hard, dwarfish growth of new leaves, flower buds which are malformed and fail to open, and dense whitish pubescence on dwarfed leaves. The hairiness of these leaves occurs because leaves fail to grow to normal size but hair growth is not restricted, thus increasing the amount of pubescence relative to surface area. On casual observation this pubescence is sometimes confused with mildew. Diazinon sprays are effective in controlling cyclamen mites but heavily infested plants are often beyond recovery. Thrips also cause similar leaf distortions and are generally more difficult to control since they are a common insect which often is resistant to pesticide.

Propagation of African violets is commonly done by leaf cuttings. Seed is available for some varieties but is not often used. Leaves with an inch or two of petiole are excised from the mother plant and stuck into rooting mix with the base of the leaf slightly elevated from the soil. Roots form within a few weeks and small plantlets suitable for transferring to 2 1/4 inch pots will be ready within 2 to 3 months of cutting. When these containers become restrictive, a final shift can be made to 3,4, or 5 inch pots. Multiple plantlets may have formed by this time and they can be separated if 3 inch pots are to be planted or lighter 4 inch material is desired. Some growers space cuttings more liberally and allow them to develop in the rooting flat until potting to the final container. Flowering plants are ready from cuttings in 6 to 8 months. Seed propagation requires 10 or more months until flowering.

Violets are often a very profitable crop on a square foot basis and lend themselves more readily to local production than some other flowers since they do not ship easily. Tender leaves are readily damaged and soil particles become attached to the hairy leaves when boxes are jumbled. Cold temperatures during winter shipment can affect later growth considerably. Those growers not wishing to propagate their own plants will find a large number of suppliers capable of shipping a complete range of sizes from small plantlets to budded plants.

Amaryllis

These unusual tropical bulb plants make very showy flowering pots. Unfortunately for the commercial grower, amaryllis is so easily forced under home conditions that the great majority of them are done by the consumer from bulbs purchased as preplanted kits.

The large, lily-like flowers begin to show color in about 8 weeks if forced above 65° F. Bulbs are planted in coarse, highly organic soils with about 1/3 of the crown above the soil line.

The large bulbs of amaryllis are generally expensive. The combination of high planting cost and being easily forced by consumers make amaryllis a difficult crop on which to show a profit.

Anthurium

A good deal of breeding and selection work on anthurium has been done recently to make this unusual tropical plant suitable as a potted flower. Several compact varieties now available are reasonably well suited for this purpose. The chief drawback of anthuriums as potted flowers is a fairly long term growing period until bloom (which increases the price) and a rather sparse flowering habit.

Anthuriums require warm temperatures above 65° F to prosper and will tolerate fairly low light levels. They should not be placed in full sun except in low light areas in mid winter. A well drained organic soil is necessary.

The newer pot anthuriums are patented and starter plants must be purchased from licensed specialists. The combination of sparse flowers, high fuel costs, longer growing time, and relatively expensive liner stock has contributed to price anthuriums out of the larger volume market for potted flowers; but they are becoming fairly popular as a longer lasting premium novelty plant. They may serve double duty as a foliage plant in many situations.

The colored heart shaped modified leaf which surrounds the flowers is leathery and lasts a long time. Brilliant red is the traditional and most popular color but pink varieties are available. The heart shaped leaf surrounding the flowers makes Valentine's day a good time to offer anthurium for sale.

Azaleas

High production costs have prevented the azalea from challenging for the number one sales position in flowering plants but they remain a major crop because they are exceptionally beautiful and last for long periods in the home. Customers demand them even though the retail price may be double or more that of other potted flowers. The primary colors are red, pink, and white. There are many varieties of azaleas but only a small proportion are commonly used in the floral trade, the rest being grown by nurserymen for outdoor planting. Azalea varieties should be chosen for their suitability to bloom at particular times of the year and for larger, more desirable flowers. The better varieties also have glossy, dark green leaves and a compact habit. For each season there will be only a few truly superb varieties which perform well under a grower's individual circumstances. To select azalea varieties for a greenhouse program, one should obtain descriptive literature from suppliers and then grow a limited number of each variety to evaluate performance.

The woody cuttings of azaleas are difficult to root unless conditions are naturally optimal or special rooting beds are prepared. Cuttings can be rooted at any time of year but most growers find that late winter or early spring is the best time since naturally cool, humid conditions persist and the rooted cuttings then have an entire growing season to become well established.

Some azaleas are still propagated by grafting. Propagation and the early growth stages for floral trade azaleas are usually left to specialists. The present discussion will focus on culture of dormant budded plants for immediate forcing with only an outline of the earlier steps from rooted cuttings to the budded stage. Very few greenhouses propagate their own azaleas, a somewhat larger number grow them from rooted cuttings to budded stages, and the great majority purchase dormant budded plants to force.

Azaleas are often graded or classed according to the diameter of the plant. A head size of 6/8 means the plant diameter is between 6 and 8 inches. This size is the most popular for marketing in 6 inch pots. Plants in the 6/8 range have generally been grown 2 years or more if only 1 cutting is used. Many growers have begun to use 2 cuttings per pot in an effort to shorten the crop cycle. The length of time that capital is invested in the crop and the extended period of care are the primary reasons why azaleas are high priced.

Cuttings propagated in spring are well rooted plantlets by fall. Once the plants are in vigorous growth they can be pinched every 6-9 weeks, depending on the variety and growing conditions. When a 1 cutting plant is grown predominantly under outdoor conditions, a heavy 6/8 azalea takes 2 years or more to produce in the Pacific Northwest.

Southern outdoor growers and those who keep plants continually in heated greenhouses can produce similar sized plants in less time, the exact period being dependent upon the amount of time plants are kept in a vigorously growing condition.

Pinching is practiced to shape the plant and develop numerous branches for bud formation. No pinch should be given to plants after July 1 if they are to be forced for early winter flowering. This time span is necessary to allow bud formation and conditioning. Buds are formed in azaleas when temperatures remain above 65^0 F for 8 hours a day, the bud set period usually requires about 8 weeks. This temperature requirement does not appear to be strictly necessary in all varieties and does not refer to night temperatures in particular. The author has found that under high light conditions, most azaleas subjected to the $58\text{-}65^0$ F night temperatures necessary to maintain active growth will initiate and develop buds satisfactorily.

A period of 4-6 weeks at temperatures of $40\text{-}50^0$ F is necessary after buds have set to condition plants for forcing quickly and uniformly into flower. Plants will flower without this cool temperature but require a longer forcing time and buds may open erratically rather than evenly across the top of the plant. Plants must never be exposed to freezing temperatures. The conditioning phase also induces the production of multiple buds. Every effort should be made at this time to keep temperatures uniform and prevent the greenhouse from reaching more than 60^0 F during the day.

Major azalea producers are located in areas where these autumn conditions prevail naturally. The Pacific Northwest is especially favored for growing plants to be forced in early winter. Certain southeastern states are major producers of plants for later forcing. The cooling treatment may be artificially produced by placing plants in refrigerated structures where light is supplied to prevent leaf drop. Growers invest in this equipment so that their crops will be better timed and also to produce plants which will bloom earlier in the season. Early azalea varieties grown under natural conditions in the Pacific Northwest can normally be forced by December 1 but a few growers can supply plants which have been refrigerated to force by September 1. Year around azalea forcing is possible with plants grown and conditioned under artificially controlled temperatures, but these plants become quite expensive. Natural season azaleas are forced from Christmas to Mother's Day with plants for the later dates often being supplied by southern growers.

Chemical growth retardants and pinching agents are sometimes used on azaleas to eliminate the costly process of hand pruning. The reaction of the chemicals varies considerably with the variety and application procedure; careful tests should be conducted before any large scale use of these materials is contemplated.

Pinching is a critical step in producing quality azaleas in the shortest possible time. If too much growth is removed, valuable growing time is lost, while pinching too lightly often leaves uneven growth and some flower buds which will bloom before the rest of the plant.

Each pinch should be made so that every growing tip on the plant is removed, the plant head being slightly elevated in the center. The first few pinches require little time since there are few growing tips in the early stages of growth, but these early pinches must be done with care to get the plant form established correctly and to have all branches growing in synchronized fashion. Pinching in the later growth stages, which requires considerable time, is greatly facilitated by the care taken earlier.

Chemical pinching saves considerable time if the process is applicable to the varieties being grown but it cannot be used to good effect unless the initial pinches done by hand have resulted in well formed plants with evenly developed growth. It is questionable if the considerable experimentation necessary for proper use of chemical pinching agents is justified for smaller growers.

Soils for azaleas are normally composed of at least 50% sphagnum peat; many growers use pure sphagnum as a growing medium. A grade of sphagnum with chunks the size of fingertips is best for good drainage and aeration. Perlite, sand, and wood particles are sometimes mixed with sphagnum to produce an acceptable medium. Azalea soil must be acid in nature (4.0-5.5 pH) and low in soluble salts.

An acid type fertilizer is generally recommended for azaleas but the author has achieved acceptable results using the neutral to mildly basic calcium nitrate/potassium nitrate fertilizer solutions outlined earlier in this book. The fertilizer employed should exhibit a low salt index in order to prevent soluble salts from building up in the soil ball.

Azaleas are light feeders except in those stages when active growth is being made. About 1/2 the normal fertilizer concentration allowed for vigorous species such as mums, poinsettias, and geraniums is required for azaleas. As new shoots are elongating after pinching, the fertilizer level can be increased to the normal strength required by other greenhouse species.

Azalea varieties vary considerably in the amounts of fertilizer required when in active growth. Most are satisfied with the program outlined above but some will require stronger applications at the height of growth. When buds are set and expanded, pure water is applied for most irrigations until the plants are in flower (3 water applications to 1 irrigation with fertilizer is a good approximation of frequency). Leaching is necessary throughout all phases of azalea culture to prevent soluble salt buildup in the soil medium.

Chlorotic yellowing of the upper foliage is generally indicative of iron deficiency. Immediate applications of chelated iron to the soil will usually clear up this condition within a week or two. Iron chlorosis is most frequent when the soil is kept continually soggy and temperatures are low. These conditions restrict iron uptake and even additional applications of this element will not aid until a warmer, less saturated soil environment is effected.

Not all chlorotic conditions of azaleas should be automatically attributed to lack of iron. Excess soluble salts can easily burn the delicate roots and induce leaf yellowing although the condition is usually more general over the plant in this case. Similar symptoms may occur if nitrogen is lacking or if root rot has destroyed much of the root system.

Since production of quality azaleas is intimately connected with maintenance of proper soil conditions, high volume producers will certainly benefit by devising an optimum soil/fertilizer/water regime; but occasional producers will find that the azalea is remarkably easy to grow if only the central points mentioned in this discussion are adhered to.

Water quality, especially as it relates to soluble salts, is extremely important in azalea culture. Long term growing of azaleas with water having a soluble salt content of more than 500 ppm is difficult. Forcing can be accomplished with water considerably higher in soluble salts if plants are leached at each irrigation. The content of specific minerals may also be of importance since certain of them will tend to spot the leaves of plants more so than others. Water low in soluble salts usually is not overly basic in pH but a safety check should be made to confirm this as fact. Pest and disease problems are no more acute with azaleas than other plants but the length of time they are grown until the forcing stage enhances the chance that some calamity of this nature will befall the crop if stringent precautions are not taken. Plants that are clean when received for forcing seldom experience any disease or insect problems.

Light shade is necessary for growing azaleas from late spring through early fall in high light areas of North America. Winter shade is seldom required except under the brightest of conditions.

Dormant azaleas should be checked carefully for signs of damage caused in transit. Drying of the root ball and freezing are the most common problems. Frozen plants may be thawed very slowly with no damage when frost is light but a claim should be filed with the transport company to assure compensation if damage becomes apparent after several days. Immediate planting will prevent a decline in quality which might occur if plants are left in the packing box too long. Much labor is saved if the pots are exactly the right size to slip plants into without removing a portion of the root ball or without adding extra soil around the edges. Plants should be watered in heavily after planting. Early fall crops of dormant azaleas in high light areas will benefit from light shade for several days or as long as excessive light persists.

Forcing is normally accomplished at temperatures of 60-65^0 F but plants may be subjected to temperatures of 40-70^0 F to slow down or increase the speed of forcing. Azaleas stored at 40^0 F for long periods will often develop a reddish-brown tinge to the leaves, especially on the tip. Alternating very cool night temperatures with warm day temperatures will sometimes lead to more than ordinary leaf drop. Azalea roots must never be allowed to dry out. Moisture stress, excessive soluble salts, and too high a soil pH are the leading causes of failure in the forcing process. Christmas plants are sometimes difficult to bring into flower early enough while plants for later holidays often present the problem of too rapid development. Suppliers should be asked to make certain the proper varieties are shipped for each season. Late flowering varieties simply will not force for Christmas while it is difficult to hold early flowering varieties back if they are forced for Valentine's Day and Easter.

Growers should manipulate temperatures carefully to maintain azalea crops at the proper stage for harvest. Plants are best for customers when color is showing the full length of the bud but flowers have not yet opened. Heavy shade applied to retard development will result in washed out colors when flowers are open under the shade. If soluble salt levels in irrigation water are over 500 ppm, care should be exercised to avoid spraying water on the leaves since this will result in unattractive water spots. Vegetative shoots may begin to grow around the buds of some varieties; these shoots must be removed so that flowering vigor is not reduced and flowers are not partially hidden by vegetation. Plants may force differently each year because growing conditions prior to shipment vary considerably from year to year. Growers should plan on plants flowering slowly; if development takes place too rapidly the temperature can be lowered. An experienced eye can be of help in judging the amount of time required for forcing. Early forcing may require 4 to 6 weeks while spring flowerings may be accomplished in as little as 1 week.

Azaleas are increasingly being offered in smaller sizes such as 4 inch pots. This approach allows everyone concerned to enjoy the benefits of azaleas without the generally high cost associated with the larger sizes. But the bulk of production is still aimed toward the upscale florist market where price is not the primary determinant of demand.

Azaleas are also a very popular flowering shrub in climates where winters are not overly severe. The basic cultural methods are similar to those just outlined, but many more varieties are available for outdoor use. Some are even suitable for subzero winters. Landscape azaleas are mostly offered in 1 or 2 gallon containers and generally are not subject to the same quality inspection as are florist grade plants. Most are grown under minimal outdoor protection. As with florist plants, the blooming period of different varieties varies greatly.

Begonias

The begonia family is quite large and only a few of the more popular potted flower types will be discussed. Their attraction as blooming plants in the home is due, in part, to an ability to prosper under less than full sun and at temperatures common to most homes. Fibrous rooted varieties will bloom constantly without regard to daylength or temperature while tuberous varieties generally require special cultural treatments to flower profusely. Begonias have not become a highly important potted flower crop because their succulent, brittle nature does not lend itself well to shipping long distances and both growers and consumers often consider the plants somewhat temperamental. Tuberous begonias are perhaps more demanding in their requirements and more susceptible to fungal diseases than other common flowers, but for some growers they are quite easy to grow.

Local growers may find begonias a welcome addition to their program since they can be propagated easily by seed or cuttings. A well done begonia is a very attractive plant if shipping damage can be avoided. Tuberous begonias of the Reiger (hiemalis or elatior) and Non-Stop series are quite popular, as are the Lady Frances fibrous rooted types. The culture of Non-Stop and fibrous rooted garden types has been dealt with in the bedding plant chapter of this book.

Reiger tuberous begonias are very showy plants with both single and double flowered varieties available. Manipulation of the daylength is essential for year around production of Reiger begonias. Photoperiodism is not especially strong or absolute but is used to allow small plants to grow to sufficient size before flowering. Young vegetative plants should be grown at 65-68⁰ F. To prevent flowering, one additional hour is added to the natural daylength starting September 1 and an additional half hour is added every 2 weeks until November 15, when there should be a total of 6 hours of artificial daylength until January 31. The artificial daylength is then reduced every 2 weeks in the same manner it was increased. When sufficient vegetative growth is made, plants are subjected to short days with blackcloth from 5 p.m. to 8 a.m. The critical daylength for flowers to be initiated appears to be 14 hours or less, but most growers begin a short day program in early September as is done with mums. Full sun is given in winter and light shade during summer. Flowering plants are produced 8-10 weeks after short days are begun when temperatures are maintained in the area of 63-65⁰ F.

Reiger begonias are not heavy feeders. Slightly hungry plants produce more flowers and the leaves will be more flexible so that they are damaged less during handling. Bacterial and fungal diseases are a major complication in Reiger begonia culture. There is no effective chemical treatment against bacterial oil spot sickness. Mildew and botrytis can be controlled chemically only when relative humidity is reduced through careful cultural practices. Waterings should not be done from overhead or late in the day. Common greenhouse pests may infest plants but their significance is negligible in comparison with the diseases just mentioned.

An everblooming, fibrous type of begonia known as the Lady Frances is a good year around crop for local growers. The flowers are fully double and the foliage is dark bronze. Flowering plants are produced from rooted cuttings in 12 weeks at 62⁰ F during winter. Cuttings are planted 3 or 4 to a 6 inch pot and pinched once to produce heavy material. Many growers prefer to put their main production into 4 inch pots. Full sun is beneficial at all times except mid summer. Pests and diseases are seldom troublesome. A lack of branching can sometimes be encountered if cuttings are taken from flowering stems which lack side shoots. This problem is eliminated if only cuttings with a small vegetative shoot present in the leaf axil are taken.

Various Rex begonias make excellent plants for foliage display, as does the Cleopatra. Both groups produce flowers, the Cleopatras being especially floriferous in early spring. Reproduction of Rex and Cleopatra begonias is generally accomplished by rooting smaller leaves at the petiole or by sticking sections of larger leaves perpendicular into the rooting medium.

Bulb plants

Tulips, hyacinths, crocus, and daffodils are cheery reminders that spring is not far away. They have been important pot plants for many years but their popularity is declining as longer lasting crops, such as chrysanthemums, take a greater share of the market. The main advantage of bulb plants to a greenhouse program is that they can be forced in a short period of time. If a grower can schedule successive plantings of bulb plants or has only a limited block of time available, these crops can be profitable. The initial cost of bulbs is quite high and is compensated for in the selling price by the relatively short time greenhouse space is occupied. To flower properly, bulb plants require a cool temperature regime prior to forcing. The time honored way of providing these conditions was to bury potted bulbs in ground beds outside in the fall and dig them up as needed. This method is laborious and not conducive to profitable production. Controlled temperature rooms either under or above ground now are used to provide the cool, dark conditions necessary in a more efficient manner.

Bulbs for spring flowering normally arrive in the fall with flower parts already formed inside the bulb. The cooling period is not necessary to form flowers, as many people believe, but rather to allow formation of a large root system and bring about physiological changes which will assure rapid forcing, longer stems, and larger flowers. Bulbs must be stored at 55-65° F when they arrive. Extremes of temperature in storage or transit can seriously affect bulb performance later. Large bulb forcers rely on elaborate temperature schedules and cooling rooms for precise control over their crops. The following discussion will assume that the cooling room is located underground and cools naturally to a point just above freezing during midwinter; no special temperature control is used unless the room is in danger of freezing. The conditions outlined are suitable for local bulb forcers who wish to have smaller supplies available through the late winter and early spring. Large producers will benefit from more precise schedules which ensure exact control over the forcing process.

Bulbs are planted in mid October in azalea pots or shallow bulb pans. A sufficient number should be used to give the pot a full appearance at flowering. Six inch pots of tulips will require 6 or 7 bulbs, hyacinths 3 or 4, and daffodils 3 or 4. Crocus in 4 inch pots will take 4 or 5 bulbs. Only larger bulbs should be used for forcing and varieties must be chosen carefully for their suitability to force properly as pot plants at the designated flowering date. Bulbs must be planted rather than pressed into the soil. Pressing the bulb in compacts soil underneath and when roots form they push the bulb out of the soil because they cannot grow into the compacted soil easily. Heavy soils are unsuitable for bulb plants. The nose of bulbs should be above the soil line.

Pots are watered in heavily and then placed in the cooling room. Light must not be admitted on a continuous basis or shoots will become too long. Pots should be kept moist but excessive water causes rotting of the bulbs. If mold appears on the nose of bulbs, a drench of fungicide can be applied. Cooling room temperatures should be at approximately $45-50^\circ$ F by early November. If the autumn has been particularly warm, some night air may be admitted to cool underground rooms sufficiently. Forcing begins after January 1 on early varieties. If they are ready to force, tulips will be 1 or 2 inches tall and exhibit a small bulge at the shoot base where the immature flower is located. Other varieties will exhibit at least 1 inch of growth. Mid winter temperatures in the cooling room should be low enough to hold further growth to a minimum for those plants intended for later blooming.

The following forcing temperatures are suitable: crocus 55° F, daffodil 62° F, hyacinth 65° F, and tulips 62° F. More or less heat may be applied to meet schedules but drastic lowering of temperatures to hold plants back should be practiced only after buds are visible. Shading is sometimes applied if stem length is not sufficient. Spring bulbs seldom need fertilizer since they have sufficient stored foods to flower properly. Crops of tulips and daffodils brought into the greenhouse in early January will require 3 to 4 weeks to become saleable and hyacinths and crocus about 2 weeks.

A week of extra time is often allowed for safety. Plants maturing too early can be stored slightly above freezing for several weeks.

Diseases are seldom a major problem with spring bulbs if they were not infected prior to receipt. All bulbs showing evidence of rot or being shriveled should be discarded. Botrytis is troublesome unless adequate ventilation is given and proper watering practices are followed. Aphids often attack succulent new buds if sources of infestation are present. Customers enjoy bulb plants more if they are marketed as soon as slight color is apparent in the most advanced buds. Flowers already open at the time of sale have but a short life span.

Bulbs should be purchased only from reliable suppliers to lessen the chances of crop failure due to improper handling or disease. Suppliers will also be able to advise growers concerning the proper varieties to force for particular dates. The list of varieties is enormous, especially in tulips, but relatively few are suitable for commercial forcing.

Calceolaria

Ladies' pocket book plant or Japanese lantern are the common names for these cool loving shade plants. The distinctively shaped flowers provide some relief from other more common potted flowers in mid winter and early spring. Lasting quality of calceolarias in homes and flower shops is not especially good unless room temperatures are less than 60° F at night. Mother's Day crops are often of poor quality since greenhouse temperatures in late spring are generally too high. An ability to prosper under low temperature and light conditions make calceolaria a natural for winter weather. Common flower colors are yellow, red, and orange shades. Yellow flowers are less susceptible to sun burn and hold up better under late spring conditions.

Calceolaria seed is fine and should not be covered with the medium. Seedlings are transplanted to 2 1/4 inch pots after germination and grown at 60° F until potting to 5 or 6 inch pots. Calceolarias will not initiate flowers at 60° F or higher. Heavy bud set is assured if temperatures are dropped to 50° F soon after plants are transferred to larger pots. When buds are apparent, temperatures may be raised to speed forcing if necessary. Flowering can be speeded by artificial lighting, but plants may become spindly and soft under these conditions. Full sun is given in northern greenhouses except during early fall and late spring. Some light shade should be kept on hand to prevent flower burn if abnormally clear, warm weather arrives early. Few calceolarias are grown in the South because the sun and heat are generally too intense in all but the very coldest months.

Irrigation of calceolarias must be carefully restricted to prevent stem rot, but plants should not be allowed to wilt. A porous medium reduces the incidence of overwatering and soluble salt buildup. Poor growth is frequently encountered when water sources are high in soluble salts unless plants are grown in a porous soil mix and periodic leaching is practiced. Potassium nitrate fertilizer mix should be used after plants have attained good size to prevent the luxuriant growth which occurs with high nitrogen fertilizers and to lower the amount of salts added to irrigation water. Aphids love calceolarias and careful control must be practiced from the very beginning. Early infestations are detected by looking for aphids on the undersides of leaves rather than waiting until the pests are apparent on flowers and stems. Heavily infested plants should be discarded.

Most calceolaria varieties can be flowered for Valentine's Day in 6 inch pots from a late August sowing if temperatures are returned to 60° F after buds have appeared. Growers who wish to flower in 4 inch pots should germinate seed later and subject plants to cool temperatures at an earlier stage. Crops blooming after April 15 in the North may require special provisions to keep them cool and shady.

Christmas cactus (Schlumbergera)

The literature concerning variety names and conditions necessary for floral initiation is very confusing for this group of plants. Those varieties which normally bloom before Christmas have sawtooth-like margins on the leaf with the teeth pointed slightly forward. These varieties are often called Thanksgiving cactus. Varieties which generally bloom later than Christmas have rounded points on the leaf margin and may be termed Christmas cactus. The Thanksgiving cactus is the one which is normally forced for Christmas and which is also commonly called Christmas cactus. There are also numerous hybrids. Isn't this confusing? Let's call them all Christmas cactus for purposes of the present discussion, which relates only to varieties which force easily shortly before or at Christmas in northern climates.

Both daylength and temperature seem to affect flower initiation. Some authorities cite temperature as the major inductive factor while others

Christmas cactus plants with pointed (rather than rounded) leaf margins are the type which bloom in late autumn. They can be held back for flowering at the Christmas season.

favor daylength. The 2 factors of daylength and temperature may be interrelated and possibly function differently under varying environmental conditions. A precise flowering schedule can be achieved only by observing the performance of each variety under specific conditions.

The author realizes that the data presented here does not lend to an easy understanding or to clear cut scheduling but it is felt that pointing out the discrepancies is better than simplifying the picture when such simplification is not warranted by practical experience. Many published schedules which the author has observed stress photoperiod or daylength as exclusive requirements for flowering. Some literature also stresses a drying out period as being critical to floral initiation.

Most plants are sold at the Christmas season in 3 or 4 inch pots. Hanging baskets and 6 inch pots are less common. Demand for plants in October, early November, and after Christmas is steady but not exceptional. Blooms last only a few days but a steady succession keeps plants saleable for several weeks. After buds have become visible, plants may be moved to a cooler location to hold them a short while until the Christmas season.

Christmas cactus make best vegetative growth at 60-70° F. Moderate shade is generally necessary during high light seasons. A highly organic, well drained soil is best for these plants. Excessive soil moisture promotes stem and root rots, which can cause serious losses. Christmas cactus are not heavy feeders since they grow quite slowly. Several 3 joint leaf cuttings taken in April are required to fill a 3 inch pot by late fall.

Cuttings root quite easily as warmer weather comes on and they can be stuck directly to the finishing pot if this is convenient. A single leaf joint with 2 rabbit eared joints on top makes a nice size cutting. The lower leaf joint is inserted into the rooting medium about half the length of the joint.

When grown at 60-70° F, Christmas cactus initiate flowers under short days and remain vegetative under long days. The critical day length appears to be approximately 12 1/2 to 14 hours. A simplified lighting schedule for latitude 43° N is to begin lighting an extra 2 hours in mid-August, increase to 4 on September 1, and discontinue lighting (natural daylength exposure) on October 7. This treatment yields well budded plants about November 21. The numerous varieties vary in their exact flowering response, but this schedule assures adequate daylength to prevent premature budset. By using several varieties, growers will normally have some variation of flowering response around the November 21 date.

Some Christmas cactus cultivars are patented, thus requiring a license to propagate. Many southern United States growers are able to flower plants in early to mid-December on a natural daylength schedule. In the North, natural flowering occurs from late October to mid-November.

Since plants are propagated and grown mostly in warmer months, thrips and fungus gnats can become a problem, especially since they spread and intensify the diseases mentioned above.

Christmas pepper (Capsicum)

These easy to grow plants become covered with bright colored fruits shortly before the Christmas holidays. Demand is rather limited and does not hold up after the holiday season. There are numerous varieties with different shapes of fruit but all require similar culture. Small white blossoms and deep green foliage contrast nicely with the colored fruits. Some varieties which fruit in early fall are more appropriately called ornamental peppers.

Christmas peppers grow well in the warm days of summer and fall without additional heat, but as cold weather approaches they should be maintained at a minimum of 50° F when fruits have already become visible. If fruits have not yet formed, a 60° F temperature will be necessary. Full sunlight is required at all times. Plants use large amounts of water in the summer but care must be taken to reduce irrigations as light levels decline in fall. Christmas peppers are heavy feeders when they are in active growth but their nutrient requirements decline as fruits are set and become mature. Applications of growth retardant are often necessary with the more vigorous varieties.

Aphids and whitefly can become established in epidemic proportions on Christmas peppers if preventive caution is not employed. Good air circulation will prevent stem rot from attacking mature plants as the cooler nights of autumn prevail.

Christmas peppers may be grown as 4 or 6 inch pots, depending upon the market and variety. Early June sowings of slower growing varieties in the North will result in large 6 inch pots with good color by November 1. Smaller plants can be made by delaying the sow date.

The Christmas cherry was a traditional late fall ornamental plant until the advent of faster maturing pepper plants. Now the Jerusalem cherry is seldom seen. It can be propagated by cuttings or seed and usually takes 3-4 months longer growing time than peppers, mostly because the plants must be pinched every few weeks until midsummer to develop a heavy specimen. Ornamental cherries were often grown outside during the heat of summer to avoid high greenhouse temperatures and to assure abundant fruit set by wind and insects. However, plants grown in the greenhouse with plenty of air movement seem to develop an adequate number of fruits.

Chrysanthemum (Dendranthema)

Chrysanthemums now reign supreme as the most important year around potted flower crop. The mum, like petunias in outdoor plants, has been the catalyst for a revolution in floriculture. Mum plants are vigorous growers, are predictable in flowering response, last a long time in bloom, ship well, and come in a large number of flower colors and shapes. Few other flowering pot plants can match the degree of favorable characteristics possessed by chrysanthemums. Even so, it is doubtful if such a level of popularity would have been reached if it were not for the commitment several large propagators made in making quality mum cuttings available on a year around basis.

The majority of mum plants are produced by medium to large greenhouses which have substantial wholesale business. The necessity of shipping cuttings in and providing artificial daylengths dictates that this crop is more suited to situations where a large number of pots can be grown on a regular basis. Small retail growers will find that mums, especially on a year around basis, may prove less profitable than other crops. Plantings of less than 50 pots every 2 weeks are often considered uneconomical by trade experts. Even this number is seldom considered profitable. Some alternative cultural methods exist whereby cuttings can be shipped on a less frequent basis with acceptable results. Smaller growers should deliberate carefully before beginning a mum program. Although these plants are the mainstay of the industry and are admirably suited to production line methods, they are not recommended for every operation.

Production figures may also be somewhat misleading. Supermarkets and chain stores are the premier marketers of mum plants while traditional florists and garden centers generally place less emphasis on them. Depending upon the type of market, a grower may wish to specialize in mum production or forego their culture altogether. In many cases, it is more sensible to contract with another grower to purchase mums for the limited number needed and concentrate efforts on crops more suitable for the situation at hand. Traditional retail outlets may find that their customers avoid mum plants because of their association with mass market outlets and because people simply get tired of looking at them day in and day out. Every retail florist will have a significant demand for mums but it may be much less than would be expected from national production figures.

The literature and cultural details concerning chrysanthemums is voluminous. An entire book could be written to cover their production in a thorough manner. It will be the objective of the present discussion to acquaint readers with basic cultural practices and alternatives. Growers wishing for more information on scheduling and the fine points of culture under specific programs will do well to contact the mum planning department of horticultural supply houses or request the technical bulletins available from major propagators.

Chrysanthemums are a joy to grow because they respond wonderfully when proper environmental conditions are provided. Growing facilities for mums must have high light conditions, the ability to manipulate daylengths, and a capability of maintaining 60^0 F minimum temperatures at all times in the growing season. Plants grown under good conditions with attention to detail are predictably of high quality while those suffering from poor conditions will fail to bloom altogether or be of such poor quality as to render them unmarketable. Mum growers must educate themselves about cultural details if they expect to produce high quality at minimum cost.

The number of varieties offered by propagators is bewildering and thorough study should precede selection of varieties. If salesmen or mum planning services are relied upon to recommend specific varieties, they should be given adequate information about objectives of the program and the facilities available, final responsibility for approving a selection of varieties will always rest with the grower and poor crops cannot be blamed on mistakes made by someone else.

The cultural requirement which affects the timing and occurrence of flowering in chrysanthemums most significantly is daylength. It is appropriate that mum growers have a good general understanding of this important topic. Chrysanthemums are known as short day plants; that is, they initiate flowers when day lengths are shorter than a certain critical length. The true critical daylength differs with the variety but, as a practical matter, 12 hours or less has been adopted by the trade as the effective meaning when this term is applied to chrysanthemums. Short days are needed both to initiate and develop flowers; exposure to long days before buds have begun to show color can cause serious problems with flowering. Development of crown buds is caused when short days are given to initiate flowers but not continued long enough for flowers to fully mature. Crown buds are merely buds which have differentiated to the point where the floral center is present in a semi-developed stage but petals are not.

Interrupted lighting of the type just described is sometimes used as a cultural practice to modify the shape of flower heads, mostly in cut mum programs where spray varieties are concerned. In these cases short days are used to initiate flowers, then a series of long days is given, followed by a return to short days. Interrupted lighting is not to be confused with the practice of cyclic lighting. Cyclic lighting programs have been developed which enable growers to switch lights on for brief moments during a specified period instead of leaving the lights on for the entire duration. This practice reduces the amount of energy consumed in providing artificial long days.

Mum varieties are described according to the number of weeks required for flowering after the start of short days when grown at 60° F. Rapidly flowering varieties initiate and develop flowers at longer daylengths than do slower flowering varieties. As an example, 6 week garden mums have a critical daylength of 16 hours or less while 15 week cut flower varieties have a critical daylength of 11 hours or less. Knowledge of the variance in critical daylengths may sometimes enable the grower to understand apparently abnormal flowering behavior. Blind acceptance of the widely publicized 12 hour critical daylength for mums can occasionally lead to misunderstandings, particularly when one is dealing with extremely fast or slow flowering varieties. The vast majority of pot mums are of the 9 and 10 week varieties and their critical daylength closely approximates 12 hours.

Provision for proper daylengths is made by following the lighting and shading methods described earlier in this book when light factors were discussed. The important practical consideration to remember is that mum flowers initiate and develop when the daylength, either artificial or natural, is less than 12 hours. This means shading for daylength control starts March 15 and ends September 15. The period between September 15 and March 15 has naturally short days. When shading is not to be used after March 15, the crop in progress must have flowers to the point of color or development may be arrested. Shading is normally done from quitting time at 5 or 5:30 p.m to 8 a.m, but, if at all possible, shading in hot weather should be delayed until 6:30 or 7 p.m. to prevent heat buildup under the blackcloth. Pulling the blackcloth may be omitted 1 day a week without serious consequences or delays.

Artificial lighting must be practiced if the objective is to keep plants vegetative. Recommendations vary concerning the optimum length of light periods and the time of year they must be provided. The following light schedule will be adequate: 4 hours for October through March, 3 hours for April through May and August through September, and 2 hours for June and July. Several of these months are technically long day, but lighting is recommended to prevent any possibility of premature bud set. The lighting period should occur as close to the middle of the night as possible. Lighting must not affect other crops in the same greenhouse or adjacent ones. Lighting is practiced so that plants will remain vegetative while becoming established. Especially short growing varieties can be given a longer light period to increase stem length before short days are permitted to induce flowering. Stock plants must, of course, be kept in a vegetative state at all times.

Mum propagators have made life simple for growers by compiling detailed schedules to follow during each calendar year. These schedules can be obtained by contacting the propagators or the plant broker. Caution should be exercised in relying on these timetables. Crop maturity can be altered considerably by latitude, light conditions, season of growth, and general growing practices. Informed growers will modify the schedules to fit their particular circumstances.

The temperature mums are exposed to not only affects the speed of vegetative growth but also the initiation and development of flowers. Some authors are of the opinion that adverse temperatures only delay flowering while others state that flowering can be totally prevented when temperatures depart too far from the generally accepted $60\text{-}62^\circ F$ growing range. Small variations from the optimum temperatures generally result in uneven bud set and development. Lowering of temperatures affects flowering more seriously than does an equal upward adjustment, but higher temperatures can cause spindly growth which renders plants unsaleable. The temperature the cuttings were grown at can also alter the speed of flowering.

The interaction of temperature and photoperiod is probably considerably more complicated than commonly thought but need not trouble the practical grower if suggested daylength schedules and temperature regimes are followed. An ideal temperature program is to start cuttings in the first week at $65^\circ F$ then grow on at $60^\circ F$ until a strong flower color develops. The temperature can then be dropped to as low as $50^\circ F$ to intensify and brighten colors. Certain varieties may react in an adverse manner to lowering temperatures as color develops. White flowers often tend to "pink" under cool conditions and yellow flowers may take on a bronze hue. Petal and flower shapes may also change somewhat under cool finishing temperatures.

Higher light intensities for mums translate into better quality. Shade is sometimes applied at the flowering stage in mid summer but maximum light is essential at all other times. Quality chrysanthemums simply cannot be grown in houses with poor light transmission or if plants are spaced too closely. Mums grown under low light situations will be tall and spindly and lack sufficient size. Some mum varieties perform well in winter while others do better in summer. A great deal of this difference in performance results from a particular variety's ability to prosper under the lower or higher light intensities prevalent during a season. Descriptions of mum varieties in propagators' catalogs will indicate which months of the year a particular variety may be grown with success.

Most growers put newly potted cuttings in full sunlight. Several light waterings a day for the first week will keep cuttings turgid until roots become established. Winter crops need only an initial watering to prevent wilting. Mums grow rapidly and require large amounts of water. Summer crops may need 2 or 3 irrigations a day if the soil is porous. Water must be kept out of the blooms if botrytis is to be avoided.

Mums are heavy feeders when growing actively. Nitrogen is required in good amounts but over supplies of this element lead to "soft" taller plants which are not of the best quality. Most mum fertilizers are high in potassium; plants will quickly develop necrotic spots on older leaf margins if this element is deficient. Over supplies (within reason) are not critical unless they contribute to an existing soluble salts problem.

The large amounts of water and fertilizers given to mums require that some leaching take place at each watering or that heavy leaching be done at least twice during each crop. High soluble salt damage shows up first as a yellowish scorch of lower leaf margins which quickly progresses to brown as the tissue dies. Potassium deficiency and soluble salts damage may appear similar in mums, but potassium deficiency is characterized by localized dead spots on the leaf margin rather than generalized death of the edges.

Chrysanthemum crops generally develop few disease problems if propagators ship clean cuttings. Stem blights and wilts can be troublesome when stock plants and rooting areas are not free of these diseases. Any grower having an appreciable number of wilted or stunted plants should first make sure sanitation in the greenhouse is adequate and, if the problem persists, contact the propagator so that the disease may be tracked down. High humidity at flowering time may lead to outbreaks of botrytis on the flowers.

Many common greenhouse pests attack chrysanthemums, but aphids and leaf miners are the most persistent threats. Aphids will show up in most crops if an infestation source is available. Preventive measures should be taken early when dense foliage does not interfere with control measures. Leaf miners are generally a more sporadic problem but can become devastating if the situation gets out of hand.

Aphids are easily controlled in the early stages of growth but, if present when flowers open up, they can become established in the petals and are then almost impossible to eradicate. Systemic insecticides are necessary to adequately control leaf miners since the larvae reside inside the leaf tissue. In summer, thrips are often a problem, especially in the flowers.

Cuttings must be planted and established in the proper environmental conditions immediately. The basic 6 inch pot of pinched mums is planted 4 or 5 cuttings per pot. Three cuttings may suffice if the variety is extremely vigorous and light conditions are excellent. Cuttings are pointed slightly outward and arranged in a circle at the edges of the pot. This arrangement allows plenty of light and air to enter the center so that inside branches develop well. Slanting the cuttings outward tends to broaden the plant's shape. Firming the soil more than is necessary to assure proper anchoring will result in reduced growth, particularly in the early stages. Larger growers tend to plant unrooted cuttings directly to the finish pot. This requires more precise climate control for proper rooting but considerably reduces the cutting costs and planting labor.

Most pot mums are grown as pinched plants. The date of pinching after planting is governed more by plant growth than it is by any specific date. Roots should be well established and at least 1 inch of new top growth made before pinching. A fourth to a half inch of the stem tip should be removed when a pinch is made. It is important to remember that this measurement refers to the stem tip rather than the immature leaves. Unless the actual growing tip enclosed by leaves is removed, the plant will continue growing without branching. A delayed pinch is sometimes made in an effort to reduce plant height. Plants pinched long before short days begin will be taller than those pinched closer to or after the start of short days. Delayed pinches made after the start of short days result in longer crop cycles.

Excessive height is a common cultural problem in mums. The height of many otherwise fine varieties cannot be controlled by normal greenhouse practices and chemical growth retardants must be administered. B-9 is the most commonly used growth regulant on chrysanthemums but other brands have been used successfully. Applications of B-9 are usually made on pinched plants when new growth is 1 to 2 inches long or approximately

2 weeks after pinching. Propagators may recommend delayed applications of B-9 for those varieties which are especially sensitive to its effects. The normal B-9 concentration applied is a 0.25% spray. A second treatment may be required right after disbudding on especially tall varieties. It is important that overhead watering not take place for 24 hours after application to avoid dilution or washing off of the chemical. DIF temperature control may also prove effective as a height control measure.

Disbudding of mums is a tedious process and adds considerably to the cost of production. All side buds are removed on conventional pot mums, leaving only the terminal bud on each branch. This is done so that the terminal bud develops a large exhibition bloom and is not crowded out by competition from side buds. Daisy mums and certain small flowered varieties are often treated in the opposite manner; the terminal bud is removed and the side buds are left. This practice results in a more attractive pot for these varieties and considerably reduces labor costs.

A modification of this center bud removal technique is sometimes practiced when too many flowers remain on the plant or flower stems do not elongate enough and a "club" of flowers develops at the stem tip. Removal of multiple buds reduces the number of flowers and if done early, when buds are only slightly visible, will result in an opening up of the flower head by allowing flower stems originating from the main stem to grow longer. This technique also saves labor since the tip buds may be pinched off in one movement rather than being rolled out individually. Multiple bud removal can be practiced on some varieties of larger flowered mums which do not have a pleasing appearance when only the terminal or center bud is removed.

Descriptions of mum varieties refer to plants as being adaptable to a short, medium, or tall treatment. In general, what this means is that varieties are planted and pinched at different dates in relation to the beginning of short days. Tall varieties are planted later in relation to the beginning of short days and subjected to the delayed pinching discussed earlier. Varieties listed for tall treatment will require two B-9 applications at most times and must be spaced well. It should be obvious that a continuation of long days after pinching on pinched plants or after planting on single stem plants will result in taller plants.

Many growers include a substantial number of 4 inch pots in their production program, especially if they market to chain stores. Some demand also exists for plants larger than 6 inch. Several different flower forms are grown. Large decorative type blooms are the most common and represent what most people think of as a mum. Daisy and spider flowered types are frequently grown to provide variety. Varieties with large incurved flowers (often termed football mums) are sometimes included in programs where plants are grown single stem. Yellow is the most popular flower color on a year around basis, but each holiday will require alteration of color proportions. White is popular at Christmas, but purple and lavender are preferred during the Easter season. All shades of bronze, red, and yellow are grown extensively for autumn. Selecting the proper varieties for the season and for the particular mum program can make the difference between success and failure. One variety may be absolutely beautiful under certain conditions while another is unsaleable.

Large growers have little trouble in developing a profitable mum program but smaller greenhouses may need to consider some of the options presented below to reduce shipping and labor costs and to stagger the flowering period of a crop. Air freight is a large part of the small grower's cost in purchasing cuttings. More cuttings can be shipped at 1 time for the same total freight cost by planting some cuttings as single stem pots and subjecting them to short days immediately, growing a second group of cuttings on a normal pinched plant schedule, and growing a third group as delayed pinch plants. If half the last group planted is moved to cool conditions once color is evident, the cutting shipment will have been broken up into 4 different flowering dates rather than only a single one.

Staggering the bloom date may be accomplished by manipulating daylength, pinching dates, disbudding methods, storage temperatures at the bloom stage, and variety selection. Multiple bud removal will delay flowering at least 2 weeks over leaving only the terminal bud and 1 week over removing the center bud. The mum program of a small grower may be considerably more complicated than that of a large grower and variety selection will have to be done carefully to fit some of the optional treatments mentioned. Each grower must decide if the extra effort necessary to stagger bloom dates is worthwhile. Plants grown under these conditions are not as uniform as a single cropping regime.

Numerous garden mum varieties can be substituted as pot mums in late summer and fall without resorting to daylength manipulation. This is an easy and profitable program for smaller florists.

Previous references to single stem plants may require an explanation. Some mum varieties, particularly those with large flowers, are suitable to grow as pot plants without pinching. Generally only the terminal bud is left. Single stem 6 inch pots require at least 6 cuttings and preferably 7. Single stem growth usually results in very large exhibition flowers which make up for the lack in numbers. Crop time is shortened by 1 or 2 weeks over pinched plants and this compensates for the extra cuttings required. Labor is reduced because 7 stems are disbudded rather than the 12 to 15 stems on pinched plants. Pinching costs are eliminated.

Small growers may wish to include production of potted spray mums for cut flowers in their program. This option will also increase the number of cuttings shipped at each date and thus reduce freight costs per cutting. Five cuttings for single stem crops or 3 for pinched crops are arranged at the edge of a 6 inch pot. B-9 may or may not be needed. Some support for plants will be needed if long stems are required for the market. Center bud removal is practiced. Standard mums (single large exhibition cut flowers) can be grown in the same manner with normal disbudding but spray mums are much more useful in everyday floral work.

Cineraria

Cinerarias are an important crop in winter and early spring when their ability to prosper at cool temperatures is an advantage over other crops which require more heat. The plants are received by consumers quite well and will last for 2 to 3 weeks in the home at 65^0 F. Cinerarias are very colorful, becoming covered with a mass of daisy like flowers. Blue shades are most common but many other flower colors are encountered. Flowers with "eyes" seem to be more popular than solid colors. The quality of plants begins to suffer as greenhouse temperatures become warmer in late April and May. Well grown cinerarias find a ready market which, combined with their ease of culture, makes them a profitable crop.

Cinerarias require exposure to temperatures of less than 60^0 F for approximately 6 weeks in order to develop flower buds. Temperatures before and after flower initiation may be higher. Typically, seedlings are transplanted to 2 1/4 inch pots and grown at $60\text{-}63^0$ F until they are shifted to 6 inch pots when the temperature is dropped to 50^0 to 55^0 F. After buds have become visible, plants may be forced at $60\text{-}63^0$ F, if necessary, to meet time schedules. Excessive heat will result in soft growth and washed out colors in the flowers. Lighting to provide long days accelerates flowering but growth becomes spindly unless high intensities are provided.

Cinerarias require full sun in winter but will benefit from light shade in early fall and toward the end of April. Late crops are difficult to keep watered on sunny spring days. Heavy plants have a large leaf area and transpire generous quantities of water. Bright, sunny days after periods of dark weather cause cinerarias to wilt even though the soil is saturated, but plants recover overnight and cease to wilt after becoming accustomed to brighter weather.

Cinerarias are heavy feeders and will utilize luxury amounts of fertilizer if it is available in the soil. Being too generous with nitrogen fertilizer and failing to initiate low temperatures early enough can result in extremely large plants which are unprofitable because they occupy too much bench space. This situation most often occurs with early crops because temperatures have not dropped low enough in fall to begin flower initiation. If leaf color is not green enough it may be beneficial to make light applications of chelated iron in conjunction with the regular fertilizer program. Heavy irrigations are necessary when plants have become established but soil should be allowed to dry out somewhat before repeating. Although cinerarias use large quantities of water they do not enjoy wet feet. Constantly wet soil will result in stem and root rot. Inexperienced growers often overwater cinerarias when wilting occurs on sunny days. If the soil is wet, no amount of irrigating will cause plants to become turgid. Only a reduction in sunlight will be of benefit.

Aphids can become very troublesome if early precautions are not taken. Young plants should be treated carefully with a systemic insecticide to eliminate any possibility of these pests becoming well established. Close inspection on the undersides of leaves is required to detect aphid outbreaks early.

If plants become heavily infested, it is best to discard them quickly before pests move to adjoining pots. It is absolutely necessary to have cineraria houses completely free of aphids before the crop is moved in. Careless handling of the aphid problem can lead to an entire crop being unsaleable. If thrips are present in the greenhouse, they can also become a major pest. Plants started in early fall are more likely to become infested with thrips since the weather is warm and dry.

Some growers advocate the use of growth retardants to cut down the size of cineraria plants and allow closer spacing. The same objective can

Cinerarias are a cheery and inexpensive potted flower for winter and early spring production. They like it cool.

be achieved by dropping temperatures earlier to induce flowering and by using straight potassium nitrate fertilizer sooner to reduce vegetative growth. These same cultural procedures can be used if one wishes to grow plants in 4 inch pots for mass market sales. Large 6 inch pots of Improved Festival will be ready in the North for Valentines's Day if seed is sown August 21 and temperatures are raised to 62^0 F after buds are visible in the growing tip. Blooming plants may be ready sooner if earlier maturing varieties are used. If large plants are desired, care must be taken to allow adequate vegetative growth before lowering temperatures on later crops.

Cyclamen

Few potted flowers have undergone such radical changes in growing procedures as have cyclamens in the last decade. Cyclamens have always been popular at Christmas but the market for them has now been extended from early autumn through March. Their increasing popularity can be traced to 2 factors: a general lowering of home temperatures which favors the cyclamen's keeping quality, and a reduction in the time necessary for growing, which makes their price more competitive with other flowers. The first energy crisis in 1973 induced homeowners to lower their thermostats and at the same time spurred growers to emphasize winter crops which could tolerate cooler greenhouse temperatures. New hybrids which flower 7 to 9 months from sowing with careful culture eliminated at least 6 months from the traditional cyclamen schedule.

Cyclamens have a distinctive flower with reflexed petals which is very attractive. Flower color ranges from white through pink, red, and some deep lavender strains. Some strains exhibit 2 tone patterns. Many people consider the leaves of cyclamens almost as attractive as the flowers. Leaves are fleshy and rounded with a green background coloration. Light green or greyish-green zones interrupt the green to produce pleasing patterns. The low, rounded habit of cyclamens makes them a favorite for coffee tables and other locations where a compact form is necessary.

Growers should experiment with several of the many new cyclamen varieties to observe differences in growth, form, and flowering. Sales can be improved significantly by growing only the most attractive types—there really are significant advantages offered by different varieties. The new strains which have ruffled flowers and those which have "eyes" in the center of the flower are especially worth trying. Several dwarf strains have been developed which appeal to the mass market trade.

Cyclamens will tolerate a wide range of temperatures and still produce acceptable crops. The optimum regime for fast crops with F1 hybrids is to carry seedlings at 65^0 F through the spring and summer months until transplanting to 6 inch pots when temperatures are dropped to 60^0 F. Winter crops should be scheduled so that essentially all major growth has taken place by December so that plants may be kept at 50^0 F to save fuel. Colder temperatures do not harm the plants but may subject them to a shock when moved to 65-70^0 F flower shops. If the greenhouse warms up to 60^0 F in the daytime, there should be no problem. Plants grown at cold temperatures must also receive plenty of space for ventilation and be watered carefully. Rotting leaf and flower stems will occur quickly if humidity is not controlled. Although cyclamen are considered a cool season crop, some growers have been able to flower plants well on a year-round schedule if they can control summer heat and light levels adequately.

Cyclamen plants form a roundish, fleshy corm from which leaves and flower stalks originate. The top 1/2 of this corm should be above the soil line when planted so that water does not collect at the base of leaf and flower stems. Soft rot will be troublesome if corms are planted deep, especially at colder temperatures.

Summertime day temperatures over 85^0 F are not conducive to good growth but the intense sunlight is even more damaging. Medium shade is beneficial in high light areas. No shade is recommended from late September through March in the North. Cyclamens prefer a moist but not waterlogged soil; good porosity is therefore essential. Overhead irrigation with water high in mineral salts will result in dull leaves with a mineral film covering their surface. It is best to water from below the leaf surface. Waterings should be thorough but infrequent to lessen the humidity around the crown.

Heavy feeding of cyclamens is not necessary. Young seedlings are especially slow to develop and do not require fertilizer at every irrigation. The same is true once plants are in bud and have ceased to produce significant vegetative growth. Adequate superphosphate is necessary in the soil to compensate for the relatively long crop cycle.

The flowering mechanism is generally of little consequence to commercial growers since plants bloom well in the desired flower season without special treatment. Large growers may benefit by spraying plants 1 or 2 times with gibberllic acid. Flowers are produced in a heavy flush by this treatment and flower stalks become longer to elevate blossoms well above the foliage. Care must be exercised to limit overexposure since flower stalks can become excessively long and fall over. It is reported that crops will flower more speedily and evenly with gibberllic acid applications. Acid treatment can usually be eliminated if the newer varieties are utilized.

With the exception of crown rot, which has been mentioned as being troublesome when humidity levels rise during cold weather, cyclamens are not especially prone to diseases. Spider mites and cyclamen mites can cause serious problems unless growers keep a careful lookout. Both of these pests are likely to cause irreparable damage before being noticed unless a preventive spray program is instituted. Diazinon spray will prevent cyclamen mite infestations. The spray program is best administered when plants are young so that the active ingredient can easily reach all parts of the plant. Treatments when plants are large with a dense leaf cover are ineffective.

The leaves of cyclamen often contribute as much distinction to the plant as do the flowers.

March 1 seedings will produce 6 inch flowering pots by November 1 if fast crop varieties and temperature schedules are utilized. Sowings every 2 to 3 weeks over a 2 1/2 month interval will ensure a progression of bloom dates through March of the next year. Finishing temperatures of second and succeeding plantings are lowered to 50^0 F as winter arrives.

Cyclamen seed is not easy to germinate and the seed of newer F1 hybrid varieties is very expensive. Good germination can be obtained if the following practices are followed. Place seed in a vial of hot tap water and allow to soak overnight; this removes germination inhibitors present in the seedcoat. Plant in rooting mix with 1 inch spacing between seeds. Cover seeds with 1/4 to 1/2 inches of medium; germination will not occur if light penetrates to the seeds. Keep the medium constantly moist at 70^0 F for 45 days. Germination occurs over a period of time but at the end of

3 months approximately 80% success should be obtained. Seedlings are allowed to grow in the flats until they become crowded. Plants are then transplanted to 3 or 4 inch containers with the top half of the corm above the soil. Excessive crowding at any time before the shift to final pots can easily ruin the shape of mature plants.

Some growers offer 4 inch flowering pots for market. Dwarf strains are better for this purpose but regular size varieties can also be used.

Many wholesale greenhouses offer 3 or 4 inch cyclamen plants for sale to other growers as growing on stock in the fall. The beauty of producing plants for this market is that space is occupied almost entirely in the slow summer season when heating costs are low. Small growers may wish to purchase these young plants rather than bother with germinating a few seeds and carrying plants through the summer. Small blooming cyclamen are an ideal addition to winter and early spring gift combination bowls.

Exacum

This excellent potted flower was relatively unknown before 1970 but has since become one of the more popular minor crops. Many small flowers cover these low, mounded plants. The leaves are small and form a dense cover. Most varieties are blue flowered with a yellow or golden eye but white flowered novelty strains are available.

The popularity of exacum is perhaps due mostly to better than average keeping quality and to ease of shipping. It is also one of the few really acceptable potted flowers with a blue color. Most plants are sold in 6 inch pots but 4 and 5 inch pots are not uncommon.

Exacum must have 60-65^0 F temperatures to prosper. Until plants are well established and filling the pot, the higher temperature range will produce plants more easily. Exacum requires light shade in the North from about May through September. Southern growers will often need to shade in all but the darker winter months.

Perhaps the most common cultural problem is rotting of stems and roots from excessive humidity and soil moisture. Excellent ventilation and a very well drained soil will prevent most of these situations if good sanitation is practiced. Preventative fungicide drenches are usually necessary to produce a commercial crop. Spider mites can devastate plants unless preventive action is taken early before plants develop a thick canopy of leaves.

Exacum develop slowly in the early stages, requiring only moderate fertilization. Even when plants are growing most rapidly they do not need high soil nutrient levels.

Plants should not be allowed to wilt but will not tolerate wet feet. Use of a well drained soil mix allows frequent thorough irrigation without overwatering. Exacum seems to naturally grow better during the warmer seasons when plenty of ventilation is possible, thereby avoiding excess water and humidity on or around plants. The plants are not photoperiodic, but winter development is speeded up through the use of additional high intensity lighting. Although most popular exacum varieties produce dense, well shaped plants without pinching or the use of growth retardants, some growers use chemical height control on plants that are being grown under lower light conditions. Summer plants should not need this treatment if they are being grown properly.

The seed of exacum is very small and must be handled carefully to obtain good germination. It comes up readily in 2-3 weeks if sown without covering at 75^0 F. A dome or plastic covering is recommended to provide evenly moist conditions. The seedlings grow slowly and will require about 6 weeks before transplanting to 2 inch pots.

Total production time from sowing is variable with location and season but typically requires 18-20 weeks for northern growers during the warmer months. Many smaller growers purchase well developed 2 inch pots so that they can flower 6 inch material within 6-8 weeks after transplanting This practice limits the risks involved with starting young plants during winter or early spring.

Gloxinia

Gloxinias are a highly profitable crop when grown under proper conditions. Local growers will find a ready market because gloxinias are difficult to ship. The large leaves and delicate flowers damage easily when being sleeved or boxed. A profusion of large, bell shaped flowers make gloxinias very showy. Colors are deep and rich and occur in all shades of red, pink, blue, and white. Two tone colored strains are also available. Gloxinias last well under home conditions due to their tolerance of temperatures over 65^0 F and low light conditions. Traditional florist outlets are particularly fond of gloxinias since they are not commonly found in chain store displays because of their poor shipping characteristics.

Gloxinias are one of the most satisfactory crops for local growers, whether small or large. Excellent quality plants can be flowered year round with no special treatments or complicated environmental manipulations. The only requirement is a house which can be maintained at 65^0 F or higher. Once the crop is potted, there is very little labor involved until market time. The low labor aspect of the crop more than compensates for the higher cost of heating to 65^0 F. For the grower who can provide the temperature requirements and has substantial potential demand locally, there are few crops which will be as suitable for continuous profitable production. Retailers who have not handled large numbers of gloxinias previously may need to be educated as to their desirability when shipping damage is not present. Several orders of beautiful local plants will make regular customers of any doubters.

Seed of gloxinia is very fine and is sown in seed mix which has been lightly firmed on the surface to prevent seeds from falling between soil particles. No covering of soil should be applied. Watering must be done carefully so that seed is not disturbed. Germination takes place easily in 3 to 4 weeks if 75^0 F temperatures and constantly moist soil is maintained. A dome or plastic covering is recommended to maintain evenly moist conditions. Seedlings are slow to develop and are transplanted to 2 1/4 inch containers when their diameter is at least that of a dime. Plants are then shifted to 6 inch pots as they begin to crowd. Excessive crowding at any stage is detrimental to growing dense, well shaped plants. Gloxinias can be grown from tubers more quickly but initial costs are higher and the resulting plants are usually not so attractive as those grown from seed.

Maintaining temperatures no lower than 65^0 F at all stages of growth is absolutely essential to success with gloxinias. Small plants benefit from 70-73^0 F temperatures but more compact growth is obtained when finishing temperatures do not exceed 70^0 F. Development almost ceases at temperatures under 65^0 F and the little growth that is made is yellowish and brittle. Excessive heat is translated into large floppy leaves and elongated flower stalks which may not stand erect. Night temperatures are much more important than day temperatures but if summer days regularly exceed 90^0 F in the greenhouse, the same symptoms may be noted. Plants moved to retail outlets and to consumers' homes in winter must be protected from the cold.

Most authorities cite 2,500 candles as the optimum light intensity for gloxinia growth. Growers may wish to use this as a general guide but test crops grown with higher light intensities may be in order if plants continually develop oversized, soft leaves. Heavy shade is necessary during summer months with little shade being needed in the winter at northern latitudes. Except for brighter days, plants could be grown without shade in mid winter. Some experts recommend the use of mum lighting to speed maturity in gloxinias. Plants become less compact under this type of lighting. Larger gloxinia growers might find that variable shading, depending on light conditions, would result in significantly faster growth. Plants receiving excessive light turn yellow and may be undersized.

Proper spacing is critical to profitable gloxinia production. The high energy costs of this crop dictate that as many plants as possible be raised per square foot. One square foot per plant is entirely adequate if compact varieties are grown with proper levels of heat, fertilizer, and light. One and a half plants per square foot may be harvested if they are sold at first bloom and the market will tolerate a few less than perfect plants. If the latter spacing is used, extremely good air circulation is necessary to prevent various rots and mildews.

Gloxinias will not thrive if allowed to dry out regularly. Irrigation should be heavy and applied before any appreciable water stress takes place. Watering from overhead with cool water does not generally harm quality but water left in the crowns and on leaves for extended periods will result in rotting of the leaves and stems. Healthy gloxinias are reasonably heavy feeders although excessive nitrogen will result in soft growth and large, brittle leaves. Potassium nitrate used alone will result in small plants. Small amounts of iron chelate added to the fertilizer mixture and applied to plants at least 1-2 months before blooming will prevent iron chlorosis. Some damage to leaves may be encountered when 10% iron chelate is applied at rates exceeding 2 ounces per 100 gallons of water. The margins become a dark brownish green color and plants may die if the overdose is severe. Mild cases of toxicity sometimes improve if leaching occurs. Gloxinias will not tolerate a heavy, tight soil. The soil must be well drained and include a large percentage of organic matter.

Diseases are not especially prevalent in gloxinias if air circulation is good and water is not standing on plants or benches. Spider mites, thrips, and cyclamen mites can cause serious damage if not kept in check.

The gloxinia is a regal specimen when grown with careful attention to detail. A low labor plant.

Readers should refer to the preceding discussion of cyclamen culture for information about treating the latter pests.

Some variation in maturity can be expected between varieties but crops sown in the spring may require as little as 4 1/2 months to flower while those seeded in October can take 7 months in the North. Mother's Day is a particularly good market for gloxinias and seed should be planted in mid October to assure flowers for that date. This schedule assumes a high light, northern United States location. In order to produce excellent winter quality, 2 liner plants per 6 inch pot may be required for all crops sown July 15 through November 1. Single plants which flower from mid October through Mother's Day simply do not seem to reach sufficient size to command a premium price. The Ultra series of F1 hybrid varieties produces very nice single flowered plants and seed costs are reasonable. Some double flowered varieties may be added to the program for novelty.

It cannot be emphasized too strongly that gloxinias must be compact to be attractive and profitable. The correct form is achieved by providing adequate light and spacing and by not overdoing nitrogen fertilization and growing temperatures.

Hibiscus

Virtually no other flowering pot plant can be profitably used in so many situations and sizes as the hibiscus. Although it grows most quickly and develops the best shape at higher light intensities, it will flower acceptably under medium shade. The ideal growing temperature seems to be near 62-65°F but 60° or 67°F also produces nice plants if other conditions are favorable. Even lower and higher temperatures can be tolerated but quality definitely begins to suffer at the extremes.

The hibiscus is a tropical or subtropical woody shrub which grows in a wide variety of moisture conditions, ranging from desert to subhumid. Hibiscus appears to adapt to an incredible spectrum of conditions but seems most happy when the light is high, temperatures warm, and nutrients readily available. Under these ideal conditions, growth may become too vigorous and soft to produce compact plants, unless grown outside as a nursery plant or as landscape specimens. Hibiscus is widely used in warmer countries as a perennial flowering shrub.

Harder, more acceptable growth is achieved both by pruning to more mature wood or through the use of growth retardants. Both procedures are often used in conjunction.

Plants which are to be used for larger 6 inch to 12 inch containers will take too long to produce if growth retardants are used. These vigorous larger plants are often used as decorator and foliage type plants. Customers expect them to grow, providing both flowers and greenery. Those plants which are dwarfed with retardants are used mainly as 4 inch and smaller 6 inch potted flowers for the florist trade. They are not generally suited to interior or exterior landscape use since growth will be extremely slow until the effects of the chemical retardant wear off.

Plants not treated with retardant are easier to grow but must be trimmed often in better growth seasons to keep plants within bounds. Cycocel is the growth retardant most often employed. It must be used carefully and at the proper time to produce acceptable results. Growers will want to experiment with different spray concentrations to arrive at the proper dosage for particular conditions and varieties. Excessive concentrations can result in plants which are so dwarfed as to be unusable, often requiring 12 months or longer to grow out of the condition. Cycocel should be applied to plants which already have been pinched and grown to approximately 75% of the desired finish size. This means the plants have many branches which are 2-3 inches in length if they originate 2-4 inches from the soil line. Once Cycocel is applied, only a minimum of further elongation can be expected.

Cycocel treated plants are generally a darker green color and produce more blooms at flowering time. The latter condition may be due to concentration of more stem tips in a smaller size plant rather than to any actual increase in flowering. Blooms on treated or untreated plants generally last only a day or two but are followed by more buds which provide fairly continuous flowers as long as conditions are favorable.

The hibiscus plant flowers more or less continuously after branches have matured and as long as good cultural conditions persist. No photoperiodic or temperature triggers have been reported for flowering although both temperature extremes and very low light levels will cause poor flowering.

Many varieties of hibiscus are available and all commercial strains are propagated by cuttings. The cuttings root within 4-6 weeks under mist or in high humidity tents or domes. The temperatures at root level should be 75-80^0 F. Although double flowered and miniature flowered and variegated leaved plants are available, the normal size single flowered varieties seem most adaptable to commercial production.

Since many varieties of hibiscus are patented and are not especially easy to root, smaller growers often buy rooted cuttings or 4 inch pots to grow on. Needless to say, one must determine if the purchased liners have been treated with retardants.

Aphids, spider mites, and whiteflies can become a real problem in hibiscus culture if preventive action is not taken. These pests become established easily; but if infection sources are not available, the hibiscus does not seem to especially attract any one of them. Hibiscus are seldom bothered by soil or foliage diseases unless sanitation procedures are exceedingly lax. Iron chlorosis may develop in the leaves at the tips of branches if soil conditions are cold or soggy, or if this element is deficient in the soil.

Under northern summer conditions, a single plant hibiscus may take 7 months from cutting to produce a large, flowering 7 inch pot which has not been treated with retardant. A 6 inch treated plant can be produced in the same time frame. Plants grown in the South will generally take less time. Many growers prefer to root several cuttings directly to 6 inch pots or to plant several rooted cuts, thereby eliminating the need to pinch.

A hibiscus grown without the use of growth retardents. The naturally vigorous growth of untreated plants delights consumers who desire a long lasting decorator plant for sunny areas.

Hydrangea

The importance of hydrangeas as a floral crop has been declining for many years. There are several reasons for this decline. Hydrangea production costs are high because the crop requires a good deal of greenhouse space per plant and a previous summer-fall production phase is needed before forcing. Consumer satisfaction is often minimal since plants wilt easily in the home if not watered heavily. Introduction of new varieties and production techniques has been slow compared to the activity with other potted plants such as chrysanthemums, kalanchoes, and poinsettias. The result has been a loss of market by the hydrangea to the other plants.

Hydrangeas are still in fairly strong demand for Easter and Mother's Day, even though a well done plant should retail for 1/3 to 1/2 more than most potted flowers. Lasting quality in the home is excellent if proper directions are given for watering. The flower heads are extremely large and showy when in full bloom. Flower colors are mainly soft blue and pink shades. If the market will accept a price necessary to provide adequate profit margins, growers may wish to produce hydrangeas to include variety in their spring crops.

The summer and fall requirements for hydrangeas will be outlined only so that the ultimate forcer will understand how prior growth and storage conditions may affect greenhouse flowering performance. Most greenhouses, especially smaller ones, order ready to force plants from hydrangea specialists. Cuttings are taken by the specialists from late winter through spring and, after establishment, are generally grown outdoors. Nights below 65^0 F for 6 weeks are required for plants to set flower buds properly. Frost must be avoided to prevent bud injury. After buds are developed, plants are stored at $33\text{-}45^0$ F for another 6 weeks to complete a necessary dormant period. The length and temperature of storage can alter forcing schedules. Failure to develop flowers during forcing can be attributed to several factors during summer and fall preparation: temperatures over 65^0 F, early frosts, severe disease or pest injury, pinching too late in the fall, shifting to cold storage too early, and improper storage temperatures.

Hydrangeas for forcing should be ordered from reputable suppliers to assure proper preconditioning. Dormant plants are started in the greenhouse at approximately 65^0 F until midway through the forcing schedule when temperatures are dropped to $55\text{-}60^0$ F. The lower finishing temperature intensifies flower color but cool temperatures throughout forcing will result in taller plants. Greenhouse forcing requires about 3 months, depending on temperature and variety. Full sun is given until flowers are opening; a light shade is then necessary on bright days in high light areas or some petal burn may occur. Hydrangeas use large amounts of water and will wilt quickly if sufficient supply is not present. They do not, however, tolerate water logged soil; drainage must be good. In general, flower buds should be the size of a pea 8 weeks before flowering, nickel sized 6 weeks before, and show slight color 2 or 3 weeks before well blooming plants are desired. Plants for Mother's Day may develop slightly faster while those for an early Easter could require a few extra days.

If plants are consistently too tall growth retardants may be applied after active growth is well started. Pests are not normally a problem during forcing unless sources of aphids are abundant. Botrytis and mildew can become troublesome if extremely high humidity is present at flowering.

Fertilization of hydrangeas is important not only to proper growth but because management of fertilizer and soil pH greatly influences flower color. Basically, flower color is determined by the amount of available aluminum present in flower cells. High available aluminum results in blue flowers while a low content produces pink or reddish flowers. A medium concentration will cause flowers to be in between; these midway colors are often unsightly but occasional shades may be pleasing. Pink or red is generally assumed to be the natural color of varieties and certain of them are more suitable for color change to blue. White hydrangeas contain essentially no pigment and cannot be changed to either pink or blue.

High levels of phosphorus in the soil make aluminum unavailable to plant roots. A high soil pH accomplishes the same result. If clear pink flowers are wanted, soil should be amended with limestone to a pH of 6.0-7.0 and heavy application of phosphorus made when fertilizing (neutral or basic reaction fertilizers should be used). Blue flowers will be obtained when little or no phosphorus is added to the soil or fertilizer and soil pH is adjusted to 4.5-5.0 (only acid reaction fertilizer should be applied). It may be noted that both potassium nitrate and calcium nitrate fertilizers are not conducive to good blue flower color in hydrangeas.

One cannot normally make blue flowers appear simply by restricting phosphorus and maintaining an acid soil reaction in the soil. Additional aluminum is generally required since most soils do not contain enough of this element to accomplish a distinct color change. If no aluminum has been added to soil prior to receipt of plants for forcing, 5 or more applications of aluminum sulphate will be required. A solution of 1.5 pounds per 10 gallons of water is applied. Maintaining soils at a high pH for pink flower color often results in iron chlorosis. This may be remedied by light applications of chelated iron. Fertilization programs used prior to forcing will affect flower color since dormant plants are normally received with a considerable soil ball and only minimal new soil is added when potting up for forcing.

Kalanchoe

Kalanchoes offer an example of the benefits a strong selection and breeding program can offer. Until a few years ago, kalanchoe production was light and limited to 1 or 2 red varieties around Christmas time. Plants are now flowered heavily from October through Mother's Day and summer crops are not uncommon. Production has not yet reached the stage of truly major crop status but this distinction could be attained within a relatively few years if more attention is given to educating consumers concerning the favorable qualities of kalanchoes. Their blooms are probably the longest lasting of any commercially grown crop and plants will survive under drought conditions which would completely desiccate other potted flowers. The impetus to kalanchoe production has been spearheaded by several large propagators making a major effort to improve the selection of varieties offered as cuttings and small plants on a regular schedule.

The cultural aspects of kalanchoe production are not difficult and very nice plants may be produced if attention is paid to environmental factors and variety selection. Perhaps the biggest mistake which has been made in this crop is that many growers fail to control excessive height through chemical, cultural, and variety selection techniques. Excessive succulence brought about by poor control of fertilizer, heat, and light intensity has also been troublesome at times. The amount of acceptance gained is somewhat surprising in light of the number of tall, floppy plants growers have turned out. The kalanchoe is not inherently especially showy but is quite attractive if grown properly. Poor plants will not sell, as will some potted flowers which have a large colorful flower to cover up defects. The vigor and habit of vegetative growth in kalanchoes must be emphasized particularly since heavy flowering will not obscure imperfections. Perhaps more emphasis should be placed on producing the relatively few superior varieties.

Kalanchoes can be grown under a wide spectrum of temperatures but the most suitable range is 60-65^0 F. When buds are evident and vegetative growth is sufficient, plants may be held back at temperatures as low as 55^0 F. Initiation of flowers is inhibited below 50^0 F and above 86^0 F. Plants stored below 55^0 F will develop a reddish tinge to leaves in some varieties and intense flower colors. Watering needs to be severely reduced at these low temperatures. High temperatures produce washed out flower color. The number of crops necessary may be reduced by subjecting 1/2 of the plants of each crop to cooler temperatures when buds become evident.

Watering must be carefully monitored to obtain adequate and speedy growth but prevent undue succulence or stem rot. Growers should lean toward the dry side since less harm will be caused by intermittent water stress than by overwatering. Heavy but infrequent irrigation will result in much nicer plants than light waterings. Although kalanchoes are succulents, they do not benefit from being kept dry during production.

Kalanchoes are not especially heavy feeders. They may develop excess height and overly succulent, brittle leaves if soil nutrients (particularly nitrogen) are abundant.

Although kalanchoes must be grown as rapidly as possible to insure adequate profits, a better quality and more consistent product can generally be achieved by limiting fertilizer, water, and heat whenever there is real doubt as to the needs of plants in specific situations. More poor kalanchoes have been produced by lush growing conditions than by slight deprivation.

Kalanchoes are grown under full sun but some shade is beneficial when flowers are present in summer. Light shade from May through August will still produce suitable plants in high light areas. Some varieties of kalanchoe may benefit from application of growth retardants under specific conditions; but, in general, retardants are not necessary.

Several pests can become established on kalanchoes but aphids are the most persistent problem. Every effort must be made to prevent infection sources and to clear up any aphid attacks early, the dense growth of larger plants hampers control efforts. Overwatering generally leads to stem and root rot, plants are best left slightly dry if there is any question as to the necessity for irrigation.

The most common method of propagation is by tip cuttings. Seed is seldom used in newer production methods. Cuttings for Christmas crops are taken in early July and will root easily directly in the finishing pot without bottom heat if shade is applied. Three or 4 cuttings per 6 inch pot are sufficient. Cuttings taken after August 15 for later crops will benefit from bottom heat and should be planted 4 per 6 inch pot. The number of cuttings per pot can be reduced if they are taken earlier and pinched to produce a bushy plant. No pinch is necessary with the above Christmas schedule. Short days are initiated August 15 for an early Christmas crop. Stock plants must receive long days at all times of the year if cuttings are to be taken earlier than mid June. Most desirable varieties are patented and require a license to propagate. Excess moisture in the propagation medium

Kalanchoes are practically indestructible if overwatering is avoided. Attractive plants, however, require careful attention to detail.

is a sure route to rotting of cuttings.

Many growers prefer to purchase kalanchoe liners or unrooted cuttings. This eliminates the need to keep stock plants in a vegetative state and to secure propagation rights for patented varieties.

The critical factor in kalanchoe scheduling is daylength. These plants are similar to chrysanthemums in their photoperiod requirements. Varieties will differ somewhat in their response but generally plants should receive a 14 hour dark period each night for 6 weeks to initiate flowering. Plants can then be returned to long days if necessary. Most varieties will flower 10 to 12 weeks after the start of short days in summer and in 14 weeks during winter. Plants should, of course, be given long days until they have reached sufficient size to finish properly. A rule of thumb might be to continue long days until the plant is 1/3 the desired market size. It is generally assumed that days are naturally short enough to initiate flowers in kalanchoes from October 1 to March 1; blackcloth shading is necessary from March 1 through September 30. When vegetative growth is desired, mum lighting schedules may be used from early September to late March. Crops grown without artificial daylengths bloom shortly after Christmas in the northern United States if grown at 60° F (depending upon variety). When temperatures and light levels are high, some varieties may bloom shortly before Christmas under natural daylength.

The following schedules may be used as a guide for fall and winter crops under average conditions: shade with blackcloth July 20 through September 20 for mid-October flowers; shade August 15 through October 1 for early December flowers; shade September 1 through October 20 for Christmas flowers. Of course there is no need for blackcloth shading after October 1 if extraneous nightlight is absent.

Kalanchoes are also popular as 4 inch plants. One cutting per pot without pinching is sufficient if the previous propagation schedule for Christmas is used. Blooming plants in 2 1/4 inch pots will find a ready market from florists at Christmas for use in dish garden arrangements. To prevent overgrowth, these small pots should be subjected to short days as soon as cuttings are taken.

Growers who wish to make kalanchoes a major year-round crop can obtain precise schedules for different varieties by contacting larger suppliers of cuttings.

Lily (Easter)

No crop presents more challenge in timing than does the Easter lily. Not only does the holiday come at a different time each year, but weather in the lily fields the previous fall can also have a significant impact on forcing speed. The relatively short shelf life of lilies is another complicating factor. Supplies of lilies on the market change significantly from year to year. An extremely late Easter will cause many growers to forego lily production in favor of spring bedding plants while some greenhouses may lack sufficient heating facilities to force especially early lily crops. The Easter lily has, in the author's opinion, not shown strong market performance in the flower shop trade in the past decade when compared with other potted flower varieties sold at the same time. Sales of lilies have shifted heavily to mass market outlets at the expense of traditional florists, perhaps to a greater degree than with other potted flowers.

Lily bulbs may be purchased in a precooled state ready for forcing or as raw bulbs which must be conditioned by the grower to force properly. Care should be taken to state specifically which type of bulbs are wanted. Bulbs are graded by the circumference around their girth. In inches, they are termed 6/7, 7/8, 8/9, 9/10, and 10 and up. The lower grades will produce significantly smaller plants with fewer flowers. Only 2 varieties are in widespread use, Ace and Nellie White. Ace lilies are generally not so heavily foliaged and short as Nellie White but occupy slightly less bench space. The Ace variety is generally conceded to be somewhat more tolerant of slight production inadequacies excepting that Ace is more prone to leaf scorch. The 2 varieties are approximately equal to the casual observer in most other respects. Nellie White is increasing in popularity and is now much more frequently grown than Ace. In fact, Ace bulbs may be difficult to find. A new experimental variety which produces more flowers is in development but has not yet been widely tested.

Easter lily bulbs must be exposed to cool treatments to properly initiate flower buds. Floral initiation follows cold exposure by several weeks. Varieties differ slightly in the optimum requirements for floral initiation.

There are 3 widely used methods of preconditioning bulbs for forcing. Regardless of which early treatment is used, the final forcing temperature is approximately 60^0 F. Early Easters may require a higher temperature while late dates could be met with 58^0 F. The first preconditioning method is to subject bulbs to at least 6 weeks of $38\text{-}45^0$ F temperatures in the packing box with slightly moist peat packing. Longer treatments result in bulbs that force faster. These precooled bulbs generally arrive in late November or early December and are placed at forcing temperatures approximately 120 days before Easter. The second preconditioning procedure consists of potting up raw bulbs a few days after they are harvested from the field and placing them in a cool greenhouse or coldframe where temperatures do not rise above 50^0 F. Freezing must be avoided. Forcing conditions and duration are the same as for precooled bulbs.

The third preconditioning method is termed CTF, controlled temperature forcing. Non-precooled bulbs from the field are immediately potted up and placed at 63^0 F for 3 weeks of rooting; the temperature is then dropped to $35\text{-}40^0$ F for Ace and $40\text{-}45^0$ F for Nellie White for approximately 6 weeks. The plants are then subjected to the normal forcing temperature

These Easter lillies are only 1-2 days from flowering at 65⁰ F. A profitable crop but difficult to time properly.

tor about 110 days. A long day treatment is sometimes given to plants after emergence. Growers wishing to use the CTF method should contact their bulb broker for specific details concerning the year in question. The details of CTF will vary from year to year. Early Easters often do not allow enough total time for rooting and cooling, therefore the rooting time may need to be shortened.

Precooled bulbs generally yield a smaller plant with fewer buds than do either of the methods where raw bulbs are potted and then conditioned. A 7/8 precooled bulb is often suitable for mass market sales while a 6/7 bulb which is potted and then conditioned will produce equal quality. Smaller growers will find that case cooled bulbs require less planning time. Large growers can sometimes save money by using CTF; they also are more aware of preconditioning factors which might influence the final forcing schedule.

The most severe scheduling problems occur when bulbs are received late or are not potted on time for an early Easter. It is difficult to make lilies bloom for a late March Easter, even under the best of conditions. A late start often makes it impossible. If close track is kept of the crop, it is much easier to retard an early crop by cooling than it is to speed it up significantly. For late Easters there is generally no problem making the crop; plants should not be brought along too rapidly in these cases.

Lily bulbs left lying around in packing sheds or greenhouses can be damaged by temperature and moisture extremes. They should be potted immediately. Six inch standard rather than azalea depth pots are used so that the bulbs can be covered with several inches of soil. Roots developing on buried stems will add more vigor to plants. Soils must be well drained and uncompacted. Lilies will not flourish in tight soils. Bulbs must be removed from the packing case carefully to avoid injury to shoots which may have formed; they are placed on 1 to 2 inches of soil already in the pot. Covering soil is firmed slightly to prevent bulbs from shifting during movement.

A heavy watering and treatment with fungicide drench is given after potting. No large amounts of fertilizer should be mixed in the soil or given as liquid feed until vigorous growth begins. It has been suggested that tip burn of leaves is associated with high phosphorous levels so phosphorous is normally omitted from liquid feed and incorporated into soils at reduced rates; perhaps 1/3 of normal concentrations.

Lilies initiate flowers in late January and early February. Reducing the forcing temperature to 55-58^0 F at this time increases the bud count appreciably. The temperature must then be raised again to complete forcing. If this technique is followed, additional time is required for plants to flower.

Overwatering must be carefully guarded against, especially before vigorous growth begins. Constantly wet soil can result in crop failure due to severe root rot but the most common result is survival of plants in a state of reduced vigor and loss of lower leaves. If a mistake is to be made, it is better to keep plants slightly on the dry side. Lilies do not wilt easily from water stress and good judgment must be exercised not to dry plants out excessively. Each irrigation should be thorough with light touching up to drier pots in between times.

Lilies are grown under full sun to prevent excessive stem length and to assure maximum growth rates so that flowering schedules are met.

Adequate spacing is also necessary to prevent yellowing of lower leaves. The amount of space given will vary with the size of bulbs, but a rule of thumb might be to allow 1 square foot for each 2 1/2 to 3 plants in northern high light areas. This would assume 8/9 size bulbs are potted. Growers whose greenhouses are oriented east and west will often encounter a bending of some plant stems southward. This crooked stem condition can be alleviated somewhat by turning pots late in the forcing schedule. Greenhouse space is in strong demand at Easter and lilies cannot be grown profitably unless spacing is as close as possible consistent with acceptable quality. Some growers keep plants pot to pot almost until flowering if the light is high.

Problems with root rot are considerably reduced by the post potting fungicide drench recommended earlier. Many growers will apply a second treatment at the mid point in growth. Aphids are the major pest. If greenhouses are clean of these insects, there should be little more than scattered outbreaks, which can be controlled by spot spraying.

Chemical height control is often practiced by using growth retardants. The amount applied will depend on the degree of trouble that has been encountered in controlling height. The DIF temperature control techniques described earlier in this book work effectively with lilies. In general, if plants have been consistently too tall, the difference between night and day temperatures should be narrowed. Nellie White, of course, usually finishes shorter so that growers seldom need apply growth retardants to this variety.

Plants which do not break the soil line in the center of the pot may be shifted by hand in early development. This adds to labor costs but considerably improves the appearance of plants which emerged from the pot extremely crooked.

Each grower must evaluate local conditions to determine the expected deviation in scheduling from the widely accepted 120 day forcing period at 60° F. This 120 day time span does not apply to CTF growing methods. Flowering times may vary considerably depending on geographical location, cultural practices, and condition of greenhouse facilities. Ninety-five days before Easter the shoot should be above the soil, 10 days later it should be 2 to 4 inches tall. Buds should be visible in the growing tip perhaps 50 days before Easter in low light areas while 40 days may be sufficient in higher light localities. Three weeks before Easter the largest bud should begin to turn downward. When it is swollen and creamy white, only a few days remain until blooming. With a late Easter, plants may progress quite rapidly at the end while early Easters present the opposite problem. One holiday with green plants will convince any grower that it is better to be early than late. A more complicated leaf counting method may be utilized to estimate crop progress. Bulb brokers should be contacted to supply details of this method for the year in question.

Careful manipulation of temperature is the most important tool the grower has in timing lily crops. Progress of the crop must be monitored periodically and temperatures turned up or down to speed or slow flowering. Early anticipation of progress is much better than waiting until 2 or 3 weeks before Easter to adjust temperatures drastically. Severe alteration of the temperature is not good for plants but even the most experienced grower will occasionally have need to "sweat" lilies at high temperatures or store them near freezing to assure Easter blooms. During the forcing period, more advanced plants can be sorted out and moved to the cooler spots in the greenhouse. Subjecting lilies to night temperatures over 75^0 F definitely lowers crop quality and can result in abortion of smaller buds. Plants ready too early can be stored at 33^0 F in the dark for approximately 2 weeks. Wilting may occur if these stored plants are returned to bright sunlight or warm temperatures without being acclimatized. Plants to be stored should have 1 or 2 buds which are large and creamy white but none in the open stage. Botrytis and mildew must be guarded against during storage.

Early cold storage of lilies is no substitute for careful growing methods, it should be used only as a last resort rather than being a routine procedure.

Every grower who forces lillies should request a forcing schedule from the bulb supplier and be certain of the type of conditioning given to the bulbs. Lilies will force a little differently each year. The grower, therefore, cannot complacently rely upon published schedules. Constant vigilance concerning progress (and adjustment of temperatures) is necessary. Only those growers who are willing to devote considerable effort to exact timing should bother with lily culture.

Poinsettia

More poinsettias are now grown in the United States than any other potted flower. Their present popularity demonstrates the potential market for other plants when excellent new varieties are introduced and major horticultural firms lead the way in cultural research and promotion of the product. The market for potted flowers, poinsettias in particular, should continue to grow in the Christmas season. Few competing merchandise lines can offer comparable perception as a tasteful, high quality gift for such a low price. A tremendous increase in poinsettia sales has been accomplished even with the large number of substandard plants produced each year.

Poinsettia production would be considerably less were it not for the introduction of long lasting and shorter varieties. Early varieties were tall and lost their leaves shortly after leaving the greenhouse, if not before. At the present time, there is no excuse for informed growers to offer plants which are not acceptable to the consumer in every respect. Introduction of the variety Paul Mikkelsen in 1963 revolutionized poinsettia marketing and culture. It possessed the traits of good foliage retention and stiff stems. The revolution was hardly well established when new, long lasting, shorter varieties known as Eckespoint C-1 and Annette Hegg were made available in the United States in 1968. These later varieties are characterized by the ability to produce plentiful side branches when the growing tip is removed. Thus if a grower wants 4 blooms per pot, a single plant is pinched so that 4 leaf nodes remain. One can readily see the economy of this production technique over the traditional practice of planting 4 plants to obtain 4 blooms.

Both of these original branching type plants are still in limited production, along with several good varieties derived from them. Expanded research has further increased the number of desirable poinsettia types to the point where growers can choose varieties which closely coincide with specific cultural and marketing opportunities available. The choices available in varieties have changed and expanded so dramatically in recent years that it would be useless to recommend particular ones for production. Another more desirable variety might be released tomorrow. There is a good deal of difference between poinsettia varieties in their cultural requirements. Plant appearance and performance also differ significantly.

Growers must evaluate the characteristics of each variety and choose those for production which appear to most closely fulfill the needs at hand. Cultural trials are advisable before any large scale production is undertaken. Although propagators of small plants for growing on can recommend approximate cultural practices for the varieties they offer, deviations from expected performance often occur as plants are grown under varying conditions in hundreds of individual greenhouses.

All poinsettia varieties are similar in that they bloom naturally near Christmas in the northern hemisphere and they grow best under rather warm, sunny conditions. But there are rather important varietal differences which growers must consider, such as: exact flowering date, branching ability, plant height and size, stem strength, flower size and form, color intensity of leaves and flowers, disease resistance, fertility and light and temperature requirements, shipping characteristics, and lasting qualities in the display environment.

It is possible for growers to produce beautiful crops of one variety with particular cultural techniques while another variety might perform poorly under the same conditions. The practical value of variety trials under actual growing conditions cannot be overemphasized.

The keeping quality of poinsettias has progressed so greatly that customers' plants will often still have flowers until Mother's Day. The ability of plants to last a long time and their initial sales appeal is sometimes seriously impaired by shipping conditions. Temperatures under 45^0 F cause wilted looking plants, as will prolonged periods (2 to 5 days) of confinement in shipping containers. Cold temperatures can also result in the plants losing their leaves. The colored bracts (actually leaves) of poinsettias are easily bruised and torn in transit. Bruised spots develop an unsightly black color within a short time. Difficulties encountered in shipping poinsettias make it imperative that handling and packing operations be carefully supervised. Local growers are at a distinct advantage in marketing their crops because these plants are likely to suffer almost no damage and the supply to florists is not subject to shipping delays and mishaps due to weather.

Many bedding plant growers have entered the poinsettia market in recent years with the result that, in some regions, there has been an oversupply. Poinsettia crops fit in very well with bedding plant schedules, especially in the North. A second crop helps defray the cost of equipment and greenhouses. The inexperience of some of these growers with poinsettia culture has led to a wide variation in plant quality. Inadequate facilities for cold weather growing have often contributed to the quality problem. As many of these growers become experienced or decide to eliminate poinsettia production because they lack proper facilities, the quality of poinsettias offered for sale should increase considerably.

The grower who makes poinsettias a major crop should plan growing methods and marketing strategy carefully to assure a profit. Only one

Healthy, attractive poinsettias can be produced under crowded conditions, but they require careful attention to every detail.

chance a year is available and mistakes in culture, timing, or market planning can lead to failure. Colors and varieties should be selected to match the market and growing conditions. Maturity dates need to be in line with expected demand at different periods of the holidays. The intended market, whether retail florist or mass market, will generally influence the amount of space given and number of blooms planned per plant. Above all, planning should be done long in advance. Early orders of cuttings and supplies will often result in appreciable discounts and contacts with customers may assure sales of all or part of the crop before it is planted.

Although breeding work with poinsettias may, upon occasion, involve reproduction by seed; all propagation for commercial crops is done with cuttings.

Poinsettia stock plants are grown through spring and summer and managed so that a large number of cuttings will be available from late June through September. Tip cuttings are rooted with a soil temperature of 70-75^0 F and must be under mist. If adequate bottom heat and mist cannot be supplied, it is fruitless to attempt propagation. Shade is generally required. Cuttings root in 2-4 weeks and should be planted soon afterwards to ensure uninterrupted growth. Shade and mist are gradually reduced as rooting progresses so that the new plants are toughened up to withstand normal greenhouse conditions.

Stock plants must of course be maintained in a vegetative condition, this generally requires no cultural modification during the summer months when cuttings are being taken for the Christmas crop. Long days naturally prevail in the summer season, but some major cutting suppliers still provide additional lighting to assure vegetative growth..

Cuttings which are taken from older stem tips often display a tendency to "split" before flowering. The growing tip splits into several branches without pinching and each of these split stems develops a partial flower. Splitting is thought to increase in frequency whenever cuttings are propagated from branches which possess a heightened tendency to flower (tips of older branches are thought to possess more of a flowering tendency). The splitting phenomenon is variable amongst varieties, some being more prone than others.

Poinsettia propagation is basically no different than taking cuttings for other greenhouse crops but since starting stock plants may conflict with bedding plant production and employee vacations, many growers choose to purchase liners for the Christmas season from specialists.

Poinsettia propagation has become big business for some greenhouses. The efficiency connected with this specialization in one crop generally means that it is more economical for smaller growers to purchase 2 1/4 inch plants rather than becoming involved in propagation. If plants are purchased, investigation into the reliability and integrity of the supplier is a prerequisite so that crop schedules and quality are not compromised by late delivery or poor condition of small plants. Contamination of plants by diseases and pests can be a major problem if suppliers are not chosen carefully. Shortfalls in quality should not be tolerated for any reason since the ultimate profitability of the crop is, in large degree, determined by planting healthy stock.

Planting of the Christmas crop usually takes place in August and September. The date chosen has significant effects upon the quality and size of mature plants. If larger pots are required, the potting date is generally a week or two earlier while the potting date for smaller pots is later.

Poinsettias are short day plants. They initiate flowers when days are shorter than a critical length and proper subsequent development of flowers requires that the days continue to become shorter for a period of time. Photoperiod requirements differ for varieties and can be influenced significantly by temperature. In general, plants initiate flowers at daylengths less than 13 hours. Flower initiation with natural daylengths occurs towards the end of September and early October in most areas of the northern hemisphere. Christmas crops normally require no daylength manipulation but varieties which mature slightly too early can be lighted to delay flowering. Early flowering plants of late varieties can be produced by using blackcloth shade to speed up initiation. Stock plants for propagation must be subjected to a 14 hour photoperiod to maintain vegetative growth. The temperatures plants are subjected to during flower initiation alters the critical daylength. Temperatures higher than 60^0 F generally require shorter photoperiods to initiate flowers. It is common practice to lower temperatures to 60^0 F for 2 or 3 weeks when flower initiation is to take place. Growers must be careful to prevent extraneous light from causing plants to remain vegetative. Busy highways, street lights, and lighted signs can prevent flowering if the intensity is great enough. Although inexperienced growers need not worry themselves about a few street lights or neon signs a block away, new lighting installations in the neighbohood should always be a source of concern.

Propagation and planting of poinsettias must be planned so that plants attain the desired amount of vegetative growth before flowers are initiated. If pinched plants are being grown, they must be pinched prior to floral initiation; the date depending upon how much vegetative growth is needed.

In general, plants propagated and planted earlier will be larger and taller at maturity; plants pinched earlier will also be taller at maturity. The 2 timing factors are somewhat additive but the pinch date is usually more critical in determining height.

Poinsettias were originally potted several plants to a pot (at least in the popular 6 inch size) and grown without pinching. When branching varieties were developed, the majority of growers began to put only 1 pinched plant per 6 inch pot. Single stem culture then became quite infrequent.

But now, single stem plants are making a comeback; mainly because they offer a means of growing premium plants with exceptionally large flowers. Within the same variety and cultural program, pinched plants must be potted slightly earlier to allow time for the growing tip to be removed and new shoots to emerge.

A variety of propagation media are used for rooting poinsettias; it is necessary to take into account the characteristics of this medium as the crop is planted into final pots. Poinsettias rooted in small foam blocks and similar materials must be watered in heavily and kept saturated and shaded until root growth into the final potting medium begins. Plants rooted in larger quantities of more conventional type soil and peat pellets require less constant saturation and shade. In general, the use of smaller, more porous media will necessitate that a higher degree of care be given immediately after potting.

The amount of sunshine and ventilation given to liner plants also influences post potting procedures. Rooted cuttings removed from mist and immediately stuffed in a shipping box will obviously require great care after potting while those which have been hardened off before shipment will need less.

Poinsettia potting soil should be well drained and within reasonable pH limits (generally taken to mean 5.0 to 6.5). Higher values reduce the availability of iron, manganese, and zinc while lower values cause molybdenum, magnesium, and calcium to be less available. A wide variety of soil ingredients have been used successfully with poinsettias but careful attention must be paid to exactly how different ingredients may affect mineral nutrition of the crop.

A problem commonly encountered in poinsettia culture is the phenomenon of ammonium toxicity. This disorder appears to occur more frequently in artificial soil mixes. It is possible that the severity may vary with the proportion of ingredients used to mix media.

Production of quality poinsettia crops is intimately related to management of the total soil chemistry, perhaps more so than with most other crops. This situation is further emphasized by very real differences in the way poinsettia varieties react to soil and nutrient factors. One variety may grow beautifully under a particular soil chemistry regime while another variety exhibits definite disorders.

Before major poinsettia production is begun, growth trials with specific soil and nutrient programs are definitely recommended. Once a successful program is devised, no change should be made without good reason, and only after further testing.

In general, poinsettias in active growth are heavy feeders but early and late stages of production do not require especially high levels of mineral nutrition. Excessive fertilizer levels or the use of water sources with a high soluble salt level can easily burn tender roots. This condition, in its most severe stages may be mistaken for damage caused by root rot or ammonium toxicity; less severe cases cause a general decline in vigor along with reduced plant size.

Specific nutritional programs are difficult to recommend since different soils and varieties may be in use. There are however, several general points which should be addressed in every case: 1) the possibility of ammonium toxicity; 2) the possibility of micronutrient deficiencies, especially molybdenum and magnesium; 3) the likelihood of damage due to high soluble salts in the soil; and 4) the need of actively growing plants for high fertility levels while early and late stages require less.

Other than focusing special attention upon the likelihood of molybdenum deficiencies and ammonium toxicity, the nutritional needs of poinsettias will generally be adequately met with those programs which have proven successful for other moderately fast growing plant species. Only by actually growing plants under rigidly controlled test conditions can a dependable soil and nutritional program be developed for specific varieties.

Since poinsettias are often the largest crop of a single species which growers produce, developing a "cookbook" recipe for soil and mineral nutrition considerably enhances the chances that crops will perform as desired.

The micronutrient needs of poinsettias are usually fulfilled by 1 or 2 applications of a broad spectrum liquid mix during the growing season. Iron, magnesium, and molybdeumn are sometimes required in additional amounts. Micronutrient mixes and iron should be applied with caution to avoid possible toxic effects. Molybdenum reportedly causes no ill effects to poinsettias in luxury amounts (within reason), therefore growers are perhaps better off to make certain it is available in slightly more than anticipated concentrations. Three fluid ounces of molybdenum stock solution in 1000 gallons of water equals slightly more than 0.2 ppm molybdenum. The stock solution is prepared by dissolving 1 pound of sodium or ammonium molybdate in 5 gallons of water. The dilute (0.2

ppm) solution is applied every 3rd or 4th irrigation. Additional magnesium may be applied by adding 6 ounces per 100 gallons magnesium sulphate to the normal fertilizer schedule. This is a low rate and may need to be increased if a documented deficiency is occuring.

The benefits and disadvantages of using slow release fertilizers top dressed or incorporated in the soil mix with poinsettias are similar to those for plants in general which were discussed earlier in the chapter on mineral nutrition. A more than average interest in soil incorporation of slow release fertilizers has perhaps arisen for poinsettias because some authorities have, over the years, stressed that poinsettias are heavy feeders. There now seems to be some realization that this point may have been emphasized too strongly.

Poinsettias grow best at slightly warmer temperatures than most flowering plants and will not tolerate exposure to cold. Varieties differ slightly in the temperatures needed during the vigorous growth stage. For those prefering cooler temperatures, 60-63^0 F is adequate while heat loving varieties do best at up to 68^0 F. When plants have just been pinched it is advisable to raise temperatures 2-3^0 F and increase the humidity for 7-10 days to aid in new shoot emergence. The practice of lowering temperatures during flower initiation has already been mentioned. Once the bracts have colored up well and expanded to near full size it is common practice to lower temperatures 4-5^0 F to intensify color and tone the crop for shipping or to slow down further development.

Holding crops back by lowering temperatures before more or less full bract development has occured is dangerous. The best crops are produced early when light is more abundant. Even with adequate heat it is often difficult to turn out premium flowers after mid December.

If temperatures are lowered drastically on mature crops to prevent further development, the grower must be aware that botrytis on flowers and leaves and root rot may become a real danger. Temperatures below 55^0 F are not recommended for any variety and even this range is too cold for those which prefer warmth.

To summarize the generally accepted temperature regime for poinsettias: start warm for root development and shoot emergence, cool down 7-10 days at the end of September and early October for flower initiation, increase temperatures for vigorous vegetative and floral development, and cool down after bract expansion for color intensification and plant toning.

Each year numerous crops of poinsettias can be seen which have beautiful vegetative growth but lack sufficient color because bracts did not develop fully. In the author's opinion, most of these cases are due to poor light or insufficient heat being applied to the crop during the vigorous growth stage when bracts are expanding. Night temperatures above 75^0 F can seriously delay flowering.

The preferable day temperature for poinsettias is approximately 70-85^0 F. The lower day temperatures tend to produce shorter plants while higher day temperatures produce taller plants (assuming the night temperature in either case is the same). According to the DIF phenomenon explained earlier in this book, even lower day temperatures could be used to shorten plants further if necessary. Day temperatures lower than 70^0 F, however, might require modification of the entire heating schedule to make certain plants will develop quickly enough for market.

After poinsettias are well established in the pots, full sun should be given in most areas of North America. Where light intensities are extremely high, slight shade may be needed when the new shoots are emerging from pinched plants of some varieties and when bracts are in full color. Although acceptable plants can often be produced with less than optimum light intensities, stems are generally weaker and plants require wider spacing. Low light definitely accentuates the problem of plants being too tall.

High light intensities during full bloom have often been blamed for causing tip and edge burn on bracts. While this may be the case, it is likely that the true cause is an inability of mature plants to take up enough water on bright, warm days to prevent desiccation of tips. If the plants are kept well watered and day temperatures are not allowed to get too high, tip burn is reduced.

Spacing the poinsettia crop is very important both to profits and crop quality. Poinsettias are now an extremely competitive crop, and production must be maximized without sacrificing quality. The amount of space given to plants will depend upon several factors: 1) market objectives, 2) pot size and number of blooms, 3) light intensities, 4) date of sale, 5) pinch or no pinch culture, 6) ventilation capabilities, and 7) plant variety.

In a high light area it is possible to produce a quality 6 inch pinched plant with 5-6 blooms in 1 square foot of bench space. This assumes all other factors are conducive to close spacing. The same plant in lower light areas may require 1 1/2 square feet of bench area. Many authorities would regard this spacing as too cramped for quality production, but perhaps they are intent on serving a premium type market rather than the volume market which exists for nice but reasonably priced plants.

Single stem non-pinched 6 inch pots with 3 plants might well require 1 1/2-2 square feet of space even in a high light area if full development of the blooms is expected. But this type of plant is competitive only where quality is the main selling point.

Only by experimenting with different spacing allotments can a grower come up with the most profitable arrangement which fits specific greenhouse conditions and plant markets. Published space requirements can only be used as an approximate guide.

A quality oriented market is the only situation where the wider spacing recommendations could possibly be profitable at the present level of price competition. As the new century dawns, many growers are having trouble making a profit on poinsettias. The market seems poised for a shakeout in which marginally profitable producers or those who are operating at a loss will decide to quit growing poinsettias or reduce the size of their crops. If this happens then perhaps the remaining producers can afford to space plants more generously and emphasize quality.

Irrigation of poinsettias must be carefully monitored, particularly in early and late stages when overwatering is most prevalent. Thorough waterings with a drying out period in between are best. Heavy leaching must take place 2 or 3 times during growth or soluble salts may damage plants. Poinsettias are susceptible to root rot if the soil is overly moist for long periods but plants should never be allowed to wilt for want of water. Watering from overhead when bracts begin to color causes objectionable salt spots on them, particularly red varieties. Heavy irrigations late in the season should be timed to coincide with periods of sunny weather. Plants which are soaked in dark weather may develop serious botrytis problems on the bracts and could lose lower leaves because of mold attacking the petioles. Both diseases thrive under high humidity. If plants are watered heavily and cold, damp weather comes on unexpectedly, the temperature may be turned up for a few days until some drying out takes place. Botrytis and leaf drop make progress with alarming speed and growers must think ahead rather than reacting to damage as it occurs.

Pinching of poinsettias is a critical phase in production of branched plants. The way it is done, the date, and environmental conditions immediately preceding and following the pinch are important to success. Not all current varieties are entirely suitable for pinching and those that are may exhibit a somewhat differing response.

The ideal time to pinch is soon after plants have started rooting vigorously into the final pot. A hard pinch which removes 1/2 inch or more of the growing tip is recommended. Softer pinches may inadvertantly allow more leaf nodes than desirable to be left on the plant; as the distance between leaves at the tip becomes extremely shortened, it is difficult to accurately place the pinch. On most varieties which are suitable for pinching, a new branch can be expected to arise at each leaf node left on the plant. Leaves immediately opposite one another may make only a single branch and leaf nodes at the soil line often do not produce breaks.

If a pinched plant with 4 branches is desired, the pinch would be made above the 4th leaf from the soil line. Many growers in this case would pinch above the 5th leaf in the assumption that some plants would not break reliably at every leaf node. Every leaf attachment point on the stem should be counted as a potential branching area, even if the leaf is not presently attached.

Varieties which do not break reliably from most every leaf node should not be used in a pinched plant program unless they have other desirable qualities which more than compensate for their lack of branching predictability. Plants which are pinched too lightly, leaving many potential branching sites, will have too many flowers for a single plant; even if adequate space were available, most of the branches would be too weak to support a flower.

Poinsettias often become too tall or the stems are not strong enough to hold flowers upright. Pinching closer to the onset of short days is the principal means of reducing finished height. Other ways of reducing height on poinsettia plants are: 1) treat with growth retardants, 2) use lower nitrogen fertilizers, 2) bring day temperatures closer to night temperatures, 4) space to allow maximum light incidence on plants, 5) use shorter growing varieties.

In those cases where growth retardants are deemed necessary, Cycocel is the one most frequently used. Cycocel is applied as a spray or drench. The frequency and concentration of Cycocel applications will vary with the degree of height reduction wanted but the following recommendations may serve as a guideline for medium effects: spray once before October 15 in the North when new shoots are 1 to 2 inches long with 1 quart Cycocel to 10 gallons of water over 2,000 square feet of bench; or drench 6 inch pots with approximately 6 ounces of the same concentration of solution. Southern growers may apply Cycocel until November 1.

Some undesirable effects of Cycocel applications which may occur are reduced bract size, yellowing of leaves, delayed flowering, and marginal leaf burn. Soil drenches are less likely to produce these adverse reactions. The yellowing of leaves caused by spray application generally disappears after a few weeks. Late treatments with Cycocel are more likely to cause plant damage. Many growers are of the opinion that Cycocel eventually makes leaves a deeper green color. Treatment with growth retardants is an added expense and can result in some unwanted side effects. If height can be controlled adequately by cultural methods, then it should be done in that manner.

Diseases and pests can quickly cause havoc with a poinsettia crop. No major problems should be encountered when reasonable care is extended to plants which were clean when potted in disease free soil and containers. Losses to stem and root rot should be minimal if fungicide drenches are applied. A general loss of vigor, leaf yellowing, and leaf drop are characteristic of these diseases but the sudden collapse and subsequent death of plants is also common. Botrytis and sudden lower leaf drop due to mold are caused primarily by high humidity; modification of watering, ventilating, and heating practices to reduce humidity is the only practical solution to these disorders. Botrytis can completely ruin a crop in a few days by disfiguring the bracts. Remedial action must be swift and decisive at the first signs of this disease. Some relief may be gained by the use of fungicides, but one must be certain no damage will result to the bracts from chemical use. Botrytis is characterized on red bracts by blackish or purplish areas caused from rotting of the tissue. This damage can be easily confused with that resulting from bruises or edge burn due to chemical use or high soluble salts in the soil.

In recent years, mildew has become a serious disease of poinsettias; it shows up with alarming speed and can completely devastate crops within a week or two. The best method of dealing with this disease is with preventative sprays through the season. Once mildew actually becomes established, it is often difficult to control. This disease was relatively rare and may have been imported with new poinsettia stock from other countries, or the older varieties of poinsettias may not have been a suitable host.

While many greenhouse pests can become established on poinsettias, whiteflies are the most troublesome. In recent years, the sweet potato whitefly has become more persistent and damaging than the common whitefly. Preventive action is necessary for both of these pests; once well established, they are almost uncontrollable on poinsettia crops. Many chemical control measures can result in plant damage, especially after bracts have colored. Any chemical which is used should be thoroughly tested before the entire crop is treated.

Tomatoes, peppers, fuchsias, and lantanas left over from spring crops are a prime source of whitefly infection. Poinsettia growers must be certain all these plants are removed or completely clean of adult whiteflies and eggs before the crop is planted. Only the most reliable, whitefly free sources of liner plants should be considered as suppliers. No plants are acceptable which have whiteflies or egg chambers on them.

The aim of growers should be to start with plants and premises completely free of whiteflies. This is the only practical means of avoiding costly attempts at control after a dense cover of vegetation on the crop makes effective treatment very difficult.

Latex eruption on tissue surfaces will be noticed on some plants. This phenomenon poses no threat to the health of the plant but extreme cases, especially when located in the flowers, can cause disfigurement. As the latex dries, it turns a greyish brown color and is commonly termed "crud". It is thought that excessive soil moisture and rapid variations in temperatures are the chief causes of this problem.

Bract edge burn at maturity has been reported by numerous growers. This condition is thought to be caused by insufficient calcium in the bracts of certain varieties. Late season sprays with calcium containing compounds reportedly alleviate this condition.

The leaves of poinsettias occasionally exhibit a tendency to yellow and eventually burn. Several causes of this phenomenon are possible. It may result from deficiencies, excesses, or imbalances of several mineral nutrients in the soil; molybdenum deficiency is perhaps the first possibility which should be considered when such a problem is suspected. Ammonium toxicity and high soluble salts in the soil solution are other prime suspects when leaf edge burn is present.

Readers are advised to review chapters in this book concerning fertilizers, soils, and water in order to understand how each one of these cultural factors relate to specific physiological disorders which may be encountered in growing poinsettias.

Another particularly useful source of information about poinsettia nutritional disorders (and poinsettias in general) is *The Poinsettia Manual* published by Paul Ecke Poinsettias, Encinitas, California. Although advance knowledge about the various problems which may be encountered in poinsettia production is helpful, the grower must monitor crops on a constant basis to be aware of unexpected circumstances. In addition to visual inspection, soil and tissue analysis is desirable in assessing the status of crops.

Poinsettias are often classed according to the amount of time required to bloom after short days have been initiated. This classification is only approximate, other cultural factors can be influential. The general range for all varieties from beginning of short days until a crop is market ready is 8 to 12 weeks.

Recently, 2 more or less distinct groups of varieties have been recognized based upon leaf color: 1) The newer darker green leaf varieities; 2) the traditional lighter (or normal) green leaf color. Once the color difference has been observed, it is obvious but rather difficult to transmit in print.

Thus, Freedom Red (perhaps the most popular variety) is classed as an 8 week dark green leaved plant. Other colors in the Freedom family bloom at the same time about the middle of November, although a few plants may be marketable earlier.

Many growers consider the dark green leaved varieties somewhat easier to grow. Particular varieties may not exhibit this general trait, but the Freedom series certainly is an easily grown family. There is also some consensus that the dark green leaved varieties require less fertilizer.

In previous years it has been possible to recommend rather specific poinsettia production schedules if a few qualifying remarks were introduced in order to address the limited number of varieties a grower might encounter. Today, however, the ever growing list of excellent varieties makes such generalization difficult. At the risk of oversimplification, some general scheduling guidelines will be given; the reader must regard these suggestions as only a starting point in formulating a schedule which takes account of the specific environmental conditions in effect and the varieties chosen for culture.

The typical 6 inch pinched poinsettia (a variety which flowers near December 1) would be potted in the North during late August; this date assumes the cutting is well-rooted. As soon as the liner has begun to root well into the final container, it is pinched to the desired number of leaf nodes (varying between 3 and 7, depending upon the grower's preference). The pinch is normally completed near the 1st of September. Five inch pots would be pinched 5-7 days later to 3-5 leaves. Larger pots of 7-8 inches with 2 or 3 plants per pot could be pinched on the same date and in the same manner as 5 inch pots if rather short finished plants are desired. The pinch for 4 inch pots could be done as late as mid-September. Of course, each of these later pinch dates allow growers to delay planting for a proportionate amount of time.

These schedules assume that a medium height variety is being utilized in a northern high light location. Southern growers would likely find they could delay planting and pinching a few days. Shorter growing varieties would need to be potted and pinched a few days earlier in either case to attain the same mature height. Eight week response varieties would, of course, be planted and pinched earlier. The author, for instance, pinches Freedom July 20 for large 6 1/2 inch pots which are grown rather slowly. This is a very early pinch date, but it works well under our conditions.

Poinsettias grown with adequate space in high light areas would possibly need no chemical height control if these pinching schedules are used. The 7-8 inch pots mentioned above would produce a fairly short specimen. Many growers prefer to pinch larger plants such as these about 2 weeks earlier in order to have taller specimens; the latter production scenario may result in plants with weak stems which cannot support large flowers.

Hanging basket poinsettias can be planted on a similar schedule as 4 or 5 inch pots, depending upon the length of stem desired and on the number of plants used.

Large specimen pinched plants (approximately 10-12 inch pots) generally are made from stock plants begun earlier in the summer. The last pinch on these plants must be done near September 1 in the North and include every terminal shoot on the plant in order to produce a well shaped specimen. The pinch should be hard enough to produce only a few strong flowers per stem (the number of total flowers per plant being generally restricted to between 15 and 25).

Poinsettia trees must be started quite early in the summer if 2-3 feet of bare trunk is desired. Basically these plants are produced much as are specimens from stock plants except that the main stem is allowed to develop without pinching until the desired trunk height is reached. As the main stem increases in height, all leaves and side shoots are removed below about 6-8 inches of the newest growth.

In an effort to avoid mass market price competition, some growers are returning to single stem culture of poinsettias, at least for a portion of their crop. The typical single stem 6 inch pot contains 3 plants and could be propagated and potted 7-15 days later than a pinched plant. Thus a 6 inch plant could be produced from the last flush of cuttings removed near September 1 from stock plants. Single stem plants are expensive to grow unless a ready source of cuttings is available. In most cases, single stem culture results in distinctive plants with less effort than do those which are pinched.

Marketing of poinsettias has tended to occur earlier each year. No doubt there will be some point at which this trend slows considerably. Perhaps the week before Thanksgiving is a logical timeframe before which significant numbers of poinsettias are unlikely to be sold. Many businesses and semi-public areas like to take delivery of plants for decoration shortly before Thanksgiving so that the holiday spirit is evident on the biggest of all shopping days which follows on Friday.

Many growers have over 1/2 their poinsettia crop out of the greenhouse by December 1. Moving plants out early is a decided advantage. It not only cuts labor costs and shipping risk but allows for considerable fuel savings.

Early marketing requires that varieties which develop sufficient flower size quickly be utilized. Many growers will wish to grow both early and late varieties so that plants are ready at their peak from mid November until shortly before Christmas.

Although traditional red is the color most widely grown, very significant demand can be expected for pink, white, and multicolored poinsettias. Specialty shops will generally require a higher proportion of non-red colors. Highly novel colors such as yellow are available in poinsettias but find very limited acceptance during the holidays.

Growers are not limited to simply supplying a monotonous array of poinsettias, varying only in size and color. There is a considerable market for poinsettia arrangements; these may be made by combining different colors and types of poinsettias or by mixing poinsettias with other plants.

A final point concerning poinsettias should be made. Statements have been surfacing for years regarding the possibility of humans being poisoned by ingesting poinsettia foliage or flowers. No reliable research to date has confirmed this allegation, in fact tests at major universities have shown that rats are not subject to any ill effects from eating poinsettias. The reactions of rats are widely used to predict human reaction to toxic substances.

Streptocarpus

These warmth loving plants require somewhat similar growing conditions as African violets and gloxinias. However, streptocarpus do seem to prefer temperatures a few degress cooler. A lack of familiarity from both florists and consumers is the chief drawback of these plants. The name is also unflattering. More than one customer has commented to the author that streptocarpus sounds like a disease. The common name of Cape primrose is much more appealing.

Otherwise, streptocarpus is perhaps one of the most suitable flowering plants available for home use and it is easy and profitable for growers to produce. If seed is sown September 1 in the North, flowering 4 inch plants are ready about March 25 at a temperature of 64^0 F. The seed is very small and must not be covered with medium. At $75-80^0$ F seed will germinate easily in 14-21 days if a dome is used to maintain uniformly moist conditions. Some shade is necessary for seedlings in the fall and as plants flower in early spring but full sun can be given in mid winter in low light areas. Southern growers should find a winter crop much easier to produce and can save at least 1 month on production time. Sunny areas of the South will require shade even in mid winter. Six inch pots can be produced on the same schedule by combining 3 plants per pot.

Soil for streptocarpus should be well drained and highly organic. Well drained soils allow thorough irrigation without overwatering. Streptocarpus do not like overly dry soil. Plants will utilize reasonably large amounts of fertilizer during heavy growth stages but only light applications are necessary when plants are young and as they flower.

Streptocarpus continue to bloom well for long periods if old flower stalks are removed at the base. There is no special flowering response to photoperiod or temperature. Plants seem to flower when they have reached a particular stage of growth, not in response to specific trigger mechanisms. Low light seems to limit the blooming capacity. Plants will flower well in summer but if temperatures (both day and night) are too high, the flower stalks often elongate greatly to produce a floppy appearance. The easiest time to produce good blooming plants in the North is early spring or late fall.

The cape primrose is an excellent houseplant because it grows well under reduced light and fairly warm temperatures. It performs much like the African violet but is not so touchy as the latter concerning diseases and water spots on the leaves (a real problem with violets if they experience cool water on the leaf surface). Streptocarpus is more suitable for long term culture than is the gloxinia because it will continue to flower over a longer period and plants maintain a pleasing shape much better than the gloxinia.

Not all streptocarpus varieties are suitable as commercial potted flowers. Only those which produce a pleasing plant shape with decent size flowers elevated well above the foliage are acceptable as a traditional florist plant. The first good commercial varieties were propagated by leaf cuttings but since excellent seed varieties have become available, there is little incentive to purchase or take cuttings. Some older low growing varieties with small flowers are used as small foliage plants and in hanging baskets. These varieties are generally produced from cuttings.

Excessively long, floppy leaves are a common problem of the streptocarpus varieties used as flowering pots. Although this condition is mostly due to genetic factors, it can be emphasized by lush growing conditions. Too much moisture or nitrogen fertilizer or high temperatures can cause a marginally acceptable variety to become unusable.

Florist varieties produce a basal rosette of leaves with many long, bare flower stalks. Several trumpet shaped flowers with an enlarged lower lip are borne on each stalk. Flower colors are predominately blue, dark pink, or white shades. Some varieties have attractive veination patterns in the flowers.

Streptocarpus is a long lasting and beautiful potted flower. Growers and consumers alike should pay it more attention.

Chapter 20

INDOOR FOLIAGE PLANTS

A generalized name for this group of plants is difficult to arrive at. Some of them may exhibit very little foliage and a great number are not tropical in origin. There are three rather broad categories which most foliage plants fall into: those plants originating from tropical forest regions, those native to temperate (cooler) climates, and succulents and cacti which are most often found in dry subtropical deserts. These categories cannot encompass every type of foliage plant but it is useful if growers are familiar with the environmental conditions naturally present in these habitats. Certain plants such as hibiscus and bougainvillea do not fit into a particular category. They are tropical or subtropical in origin and do not flourish particularly well in the forest or desert but rather in conditions somewhat in between. Many other plants will also defy placement in the groups mentioned above.

Those foliage plants native to tropical forests usually prefer low light intensities, organic soils, warm temperatures, and high humidity. Most plants from these areas grow on or near the forest floor and are shaded by a dense canopy of trees. Foliage plants from temperate regions require cooler temperatures; most of them have been collected originally from shady habitats along stream bottoms or in the forest but some temperate zone foliage plants originate from fairly sunny habitats. The majority of cacti and succulents are natives of rather dry, sunny regions where days are hot and nights cool. Optimum growing requirements of the rather diverse group of plants termed "foliage" are quite varied and both the commercial grower and ultimate consumer must realize that a knowledge of each variety's preferences will lead to increased success.

Foliage plants in the home, office, or public place have probably been around since people began constructing shelters to make life more comfortable. The first decorative plants were undoubtedly those which grew naturally in the immediate geographical area and possessed some capability to survive the shady conditions normally present inside a structure. More exotic plants were gradually added to the pool of suitable varieties as Man's knowledge of the world increased through travel for conquest, hunting, and commerce. Interior landscaping very likely progressed little or may have even regressed from the fall of the Roman empire until that period when European discovery opened up the new world and many Pacific regions. A surge of new and exciting foliage plants was then made available for the leisure classes to enjoy.

STATE OF THE FOLIAGE INDUSTRY TODAY

Another great expansion of interest in foliage plants began in the 1970's. This increased interest was brought about primarily because of society's perception that preoccupation with material objects, especially man-made ones, was wrong. Plants became the "natural" way of decorating to enhance the indoor environment. Wholesale foliage plant sales multiplied by more than 10 times from 1970 to 1977, but a general slowdown in demand became apparent toward the end of the decade. Indoor foliage production and sales was rather stagnant during the 1980's, at first decreasing in most areas and then gradually beginning to show new life. Foliage plant sales probably were influenced by the general economy during this decade. A severe recession occurred from about 1980 to 1985 followed by a prolonged but steady increase in business activity.

The early 1990's were a time of mixed opportunity for the indoor foliage industry. Sales in some areas and of some varieties being generally good while remaining stagnant in others. As we enter the new century, no repeat of the 1970's boom has occurred or is anticipated, but business is good and increasingly steady.

Although production and sales of indoor foliage is not now increasing at a rapid pace, this segment of the industry remains a healthy and important aspect of ornamental horticulture. Most conscientious producers and marketers are able to move their product at a profitable price.

If anything, the industry is better off than in the recent past because many marginal producers have left the scene. This development has led to a more stable atmosphere where production and marketing can be carried on with some predictability.

The quality of plants being offered to consumers is generally much better now than it was in times of booming market expansion. Hopefully this quality product will lead to increased customer satisfaction and a continued steady enlargement of the market.

PRODUCTION AND MARKETING CONSIDERATIONS

The majority of foliage production in the United States is centered in Florida and California. Texas is also an important producer. Most large wholesalers are located in warmer states because of the high fuel consumption necessary to keep foliage greenhouses at 65-70⁰ F in northern areas. Growers in the North can profitably produce the types of foliage which require cooler temperatures and those exhibiting fast growth rates. Even tropical foliage may be grown profitably in the North if the majority of development takes place during warm summer months. Summer crops of foliage are an excellent way to fill normally empty benches if a market can be found for them before the onset of winter.

Northern summer production is usually dominated by smaller plants but nice 10 inch specimens of faster growing plants such as scheffleras and Japanese aralia can be grown. Certain local growers may find that foliage production is profitable on a limited scale even in winter. If transport facilities are poor and the area is at considerable distance from southern production areas, a program of heavy summer growing coupled with holding at minimum temperatures through the winter may be the only way of assuring reliable supplies. High fuel costs may be compensated for by avoiding delivery charges from the South and by minimizing damage which normally occurs to plants in shipment. At least 5-10% of a plant's value is lost in routine packing and shipping. This does not include the occasional heavy losses incurred from freezing or heat damage for which many carriers will not assume responsibility.

The benefits of assured supply and quality are added incentives for northern growers to produce their own foliage. One must also consider the labor involved in receiving and unpacking shipments. Growing of most specimen plants in 10 inch containers and larger should generally be left to southern producers but there are a few varieties which can be grown to this size profitably by northern growers in one summer.

Small 2 1/4 inch foliage plants of the faster growing varieties are often economical for northern greenhouse production.

The most common marketing system for foliage plants today is the movement of southern plants to independent local distributing greenhouses north of the growing areas. These distributing greenhouses then sell to chain stores, florists, and smaller greenhouses. Although the distributing greenhouses may produce a considerable amount of the faster growing types and small tropical foliage, their main emphasis is on shipment of material from southern production areas with a quick sale after receipt. Most of the cuttings used for small tropical plants are also imported rather than propagated at the greenhouse. A few of the ultimate retailers may move sufficient quantities of tropical foliage to ship direct from the growing areas rather than obtain their plants from middlemen; this is the route increasingly being utilized by the larger supermarkets and mass merchants. Delivery is made to centralized warehouses and then distributed to individual stores in the chain.

Smaller greenhouses often follow a marketing pattern similar to that of the distributing greenhouses but they are as likely to obtain their plants from distributors as from the initial grower. Any firm acting as a distributor or re-distributor must make certain that an adequate markup is obtained to cover all expenses and yield a suitable profit. An important aspect of this business to remember is that inventory must be turned quickly to compensate for the relatively low markups generally accepted. Some smaller establishments could well be advised to specialize in only those foliage crops which are profitable for them. A certain critical size must be attained by greenhouses before importing cuttings and larger plants becomes feasible.

The type of foliage plant program a greenhouse ultimately settles into will generally vary more greatly than for flowering pot plants and bedding plants. Producers in the later two categories often attempt to grow all plants that are sold on the premises. The foliage grower must evaluate all impinging factors and devise a program of growing and buying plants which is most profitable for the circumstances at hand. The present discussion of foliage plants is mainly oriented towards those greenhouses located outside of the main production areas since growing operations in the latter locations are generally quite large and require more specific cultural information than is possible in this book. Three reference books which will be indispensable to anyone involved appreciably in foliage plants are *Exotica Four-Pictorial Encyclopedia of Exotic Plants, Tropica*, and *Hortica* by Alfred Byrd Graf. Details of identification and culture are well presented in these volumes.

A good number of foliage plant distributors do not even operate a greenhouse. They purchase plants in quantity in the production areas and then deliver to customers along an established truck route. Most such distributors specialize either in mass market outlets or in traditional florist shops.

Whatever approach is taken toward marketing and growing foliage plants, it must be carefully planned ahead and implemented vigorously. Constant vacillation from one hastily contrived plan to another is a waste of effort. Accurate scheduling is certainly as important to profitable foliage plant production as it is in the case of potted flowers and bedding plants. Each crop must be timed so that a steady supply of high quality merchandise is available for market. One must realize that foliage crops reach a point when marketability and profitability interact to produce an optimum marketing period. Plants may sell quickly when they are allowed to become oversized for the price range, but profitability decreases because they remain in the greenhouse too long and are gradually occupying more space. Attempts to market plants before they have reached an acceptable size may increase the profitability of each pot sold, but total profits for the crop will decrease because most customers refuse to purchase an undersized product. Determining the optimum marketing period for foliage plants is not so easy as it is with potted flowers and bedding plants. Most of the latter two crops are sold when flowers appear; prices are calculated for them adjusted according to the amount of time and space consumed in reaching this stage. A definite physical characteristic is usually not apparent in foliage plants to signal the beginning of marketability.

This lack of definite criteria to initiate sales leads many growers into the complacent state of mind that there is no urgent need to work toward a finely tuned balance of sales and production. Their attitude is that if a plant does not sell today it will get larger and be sold in the future. This attitude may be justified somewhat if a higher price is charged for the extra size, but letting crops grow to the next size on a regular basis will upset plans made for larger containers. When plants frequently become too large and must be transplanted to the next size container, efforts should be made toward developing an improved schedule. Continual shortages should be addressed in the same manner.

Foliage plant sales are, in general, less of a feast or famine proposition than are potted flowers and bedding plants. Sales of foliage definitely increase in the winter and spring months but continue at a good pace throughout the year. Production is normally on a more or less regular schedule without the exaggerated peaks and valleys associated with spring plants or potted flowers. Small individual crops are often the result of this marketing pattern since large amounts of each variety are not needed at any one time. No particular method of scheduling foliage plant crops is more correct than another for all situations. The main criterion of suitability is whether or not the scheduling method works to produce plants acceptable for the intended market without serious over supplies or shortages becoming commonplace.

Small local producers may satisfactorily monitor inventory by compiling quick visual estimates of plant varieties and sizes each week or two. New cuttings or shipments can then be scheduled so that a relatively constant supply of material is available.

Growers supervising large wholesale foliage plant greenhouses would be unable to use a manual inventory system efficiently since the time required to inventory crops regularly would be prohibitive. Computerized inventory and marketing records enable large growers to schedule effectively. A system of frequent inventory and crop scheduling works quite well with smaller plants and those which grow rapidly. When large specimen plants and those which grow slowly are considered, it is best to schedule far in advance on the basis of estimated needs. The crop cycle for these plants is so long that growers cannot schedule on the basis of immediate inventories. Most northern greenhouses will be little concerned with growing larger specimens and slow maturing varieties, preferring to purchase them from southern sources.

Foliage plant production is, in some respects, less difficult than other greenhouse crops but the large number of varieties grown and the diverse environmental conditions these various plants require places a burden on the grower to devise cultural programs that can encompass this diversity. It is obvious that different growing environments cannot be created for each variety except in operations where that variety is a major crop. It is incumbent upon the grower to create as few cultural programs as possible which will permit economical growth of the varieties being produced. Limiting the number of cultural requirements, when possible, will increase greenhouse efficiency. A balance must be created between the physical requirements of the plants and a need to simplify growing procedures for the sake of efficiency. Certain varieties may have to be eliminated from the program because their cultural requirements do not coincide with greenhouse conditions.

In major frost free production areas, much foliage plant growing is done outdoors. Some varieties are grown in full sun while others are given some shade. These production facilities may resemble northern tree and shrub nurseries to a great extent. And in some cases they serve the same function; that of providing landscapers and homeowners in these warmer areas with ornamental plants for outdoor decoration. Many of the tropical and subtropical plants which Northerners utilize as indoor foliage are also used freely outdoors in climatic regions where winter freezes are uncommon or do not occur.

Combination pots using several foliage varieties are popular items.

PROPAGATION

Most foliage plants are propagated commercially from cuttings or tissue culture although a significant number are most efficiently started from seed. Cuttings of most varieties root readily and will often exhibit small roots on the stem before they are separated from the mother plant. Seeds of foliage plants are, as a rule, more difficult to germinate than common greenhouse flowers and bedding plants. The time required for germination is often quite long and temperatures needed are perhaps higher than most growers are accustomed to providing. This long germination period leaves more time for occasional improper conditions and practices to eventually reduce the germination percentage. Most growers would be well advised to leave germination of the more difficult varieties to specialists and concentrate their efforts on those such as scheffleras and asparagus fern which are relatively easy. The seed of many foliage varieties loses viability quickly so that it is not advisable to store seed unless it is known to remain viable for a prolonged period. Growers wishing to begin a propagation program for foliage plants should review the earlier chapter on propagation in this book.

A great amount of cuttings and seedlings are started in southern areas and shipped to northern growers for potting up. This is often the most economical method of operation, especially with those varieties which require tropical conditions for excellent growth. Northern growers simply cannot justify the energy costs required to maintain abundant winter growth on tropical mother plants so that cuttings may be taken. Some cuttings may be profitably taken in the North to shape plants as crops grow. Summertime cutting production can be significant from this practice. Greenhouses isolated from main transport arteries and those which are too small to accommodate the minimum shipments often required by suppliers may find that tropical foliage plant propagation is practical on a year around basis if high enough prices can be obtained for the finished merchandise. Those foliage plants which grow well under cooler conditions are, of course, adaptable to propagation in northern greenhouses.

Rooting of plants directly into the finishing container is often practiced with easy to root varieties. This method is particularly well suited to summer crops of cooler growing varieties. No extra heat is usually given. Growers must remember that not all foliage plants thrive under warm conditions and some varieties, such as piggy back plants, will root more readily next to the coolers.

Tissue culture is now of major importance for several large foliage crops and will certainly be used for additional varieties as appropriate techniques are developed. The benefits of tissue culture are mainly that thousands of disease and pest free offspring can be produced from a single mother plant. Thus greatly reducing the space necessary for propagation and the amount of disease and pest control effort required. Many of the newest foliage varieties are propagated primarily by tissue culture.

ENVIRONMENTAL REQUIREMENTS

Greenhouses in which tropical foliage is grown must be capable of maintaining a temperature of at least 65^0 F. Temperatures of 15-20^0 F above this level are not harmful and daytime temperatures in the 90-100°F range are acceptable if the humidity is high. Growth of tropical varieties is negligible below 65°F and plants will begin to yellow. Development is more satisfactory at 70°F and the final appearance of plants will be better. Those varieties which are native to more temperate regions will generally do well at 60-62°F but most of them will also develop into satisfactory merchandise at 65-70°F. Temperatures below 60°F are suitable for some cooler growing varieties although growth is slower and plants may appear hardened. Many small growers have only one shaded greenhouse and must therefore maintain the temperature in a suitable range for tropical foliage if these crops are grown. The 65-70°F temperatures required for tropicals may not be the most economical level for temperate foliage varieties but it is an acceptable compromise in most cases. Cooler areas present in most greenhouses should be reserved for temperate varieties.

An understanding of the light intensities different varieties require is perhaps the most important technical information a grower needs in order to maintain foliage crops in good condition. Light intensity is one environmental factor which can be easily modified within a single greenhouse. If the entire greenhouse is shaded to the point where those plants requiring the most light are happy, additional shade can be applied, inside or outside, to those areas where plants needing low light intensities are located. Low light plants can also be placed in those parts of the greenhouse which naturally receive less sun, such as the north side of greenhouses oriented east and west. Foliage plants requiring full sun can generally be located in potted flower houses. Old greenhouses that no longer transmit sufficient light for full sun crops can be given a new lease on life when transferred to foliage production.

Most foliage plants will make efficient growth in light levels of 1,000-2,000 foot candles. Particular crops such as Chinese evergreens will do better if light intensities are much reduced from this level while hibiscus are happiest in full sun. Light intensities for general foliage production may be allowed to reach 3,000 foot candles during the brightest part of the day but prolonged exposure to this level is normally detrimental. In summer, when natural light intensities are expected to reach 10,000 foot candles in the afternoon, more than 2/3 of the light should be shaded out of the greenhouse. Winter shade should intercept no more than 1/3 of the light in the northern lower light areas. These greenhouse light levels are based on the needs of relatively high light plants and considerably shadier spots must be found for those varieties which prosper under low light. A very heavy shade application is required on the greenhouse to filter out 2/3 of the light rays in summer.

A simple test to determine proper light levels can be administered by observing certain plants carefully. Plants such as scheffleras and aralias which prefer light near the upper production levels mentioned will begin to take on a slight yellowish color when light levels are too high. Chlorophyll in the leaves is being destroyed by excessive light. Leaves will be smaller and harder than those exposed to proper light. If the same plants are subjected to excessive shade they will become tall and spindly with sparse foliage. Chinese evergreens and spathiphyllum, which are low light plants, will exhibit the same yellowing of leaves when light intensity is too high for plants in this group. Light levels which are too low for the latter plants is seldom a concern in the commercial greenhouse unless the plants are located under benches. It should be stressed that the light intensities being suggested are those considered optimum for rapid, profitable commercial production. Most varieties will tolerate much lower light if feeding and watering are reduced and rapid growth is not expected.

The duration of light exposure can, to a certain extent, modify the intensities needed for good growth. Some authors have suggested that 20 hours of 500 foot candles exposure is equivalent to 10 hours of 1,000 foot candles exposure. While the longer exposure can certainly compensate to some degree for reduced intensities, it cannot be considered an equivalent situation. Plants requiring high light levels will generally be taller and spindlier at the reduced intensity for the longer duration, while low light plants may exhibit some leaf yellowing at a higher light intensity with reduced duration.

Light duration is important not only because of its effect on the total energy given to foliage crops but also because it may affect the flowering response in many varieties. Plants native to tropical regions do not normally exhibit such distinct photoperiodic responses as do those from temperate regions. This phenomenon is generally ascribed to the fact that many plants near the equator have not evolved photoperiodic mechanisms simply because the daylength is essentially equal all year long. Most tropical plants are thought to bloom in response to the accumulated amount of radiant energy received, not how short or long the day is. Certain cooler growing plants such as Swedish ivy, wandering Jews and coleus have a distinct flowering period related to daylength. Blooming generally begins in the fall and continues through the winter. Vegetative growth is usually reduced at this time so that a marked decrease in crop production occurs. Growers will be well advised to concentrate on growing strains of these varieties which exhibit a less pronounced flowering tendency. The small but profuse flowers on coleus and Swedish ivy may initially be attractive but soon leave objectionable, bloomed out flower stems cluttering the plant.

The use of the term "foot candles" to describe the light intensities required by foliage plants is rather imprecise but is suitable for most applications, especially when referring to natural sunlight. The imprecision arises when light is filtered through materials which alter the natural proportion of wavelengths or when light is supplied from artificial sources.

Foot candle measurements are based upon visible light wavelengths; however, it is possible to exclude a high proportion of specific visible wavelengths and still have acceptable plant growth. For example, artificial light sources which supply a good deal of light energy in the blue wavelengths and lesser amounts in the red wavelengths are generally acceptable for plant growth while the reverse proportion of wavelengths is not.

In most cases measurement of plant needs can be based upon foot candles but specialized cases (such as artificial light sources) will require more particular reference as to wavelength quality.

Soil for foliage plants should generally be highly organic and drain well. Few foliage plants will tolerate soggy soil. Commercial production of most varieties is generally easier using very coarse soils which do not have a good deal of water holding capacity. With this type of soil, the root ball can be kept more or less saturated without detrimental effects to the plants.

However, when the soil possesses so little water holding capacity as to accomplish this objective, it is generally too porous for effective use in the final interior landscape environment. Plants dry out too quickly and require excessive care to keep watered. A compromise must be reached between ease of production and ease of use in the ultimate environment. Extremely light, porous soils precipitate too much customer dissatisfaction with plant performance. This ultimately discourages further purchases.

The fertilizer requirements for foliage plants in active growth are generally quite similar as for other plant groups described in this book.

But since the production emphasis in foliage is upon lush, dark green vegetation; particular attention must be focused upon providing adequate nitrogen and iron.

Some slower growing foliage varieties and larger specimen plants may be in the greenhouse or nursery for a considerable time, this situation requires that precautions be taken to avoid high soluble salts in the soil solution. This objective is realized by several courses of action: 1) use low salt index fertilizers, 2) avoid fertilizer excess, 3) use water sources known to be low in total dissolved solids, 4) allow periodic leaching of the soil to occur, 5) use soils which drain easily.

Foliage plants which are grown outdoors under sprinkler irrigation are often more easily provided nutrients through incorporation of slow release formulations into the soil.

If growers do not specialize in particular crops of foliage varieties, it will be necessary to develop fertilizer systems which provide acceptable nutrient levels for the total spectrum of crops grown. This approach must also be used by the miscellaneous foliage grower in relation to other environmental factors.

There are special situations, some of which will soon be discussed, where the growth of foliage plants is purposely or incidentally restricted a great deal. In these cases, the application of mineral nutrients should also be reduced to an appropriate level.

Watering of foliage plants is not appreciably different than for any other greenhouse crop. Plants should be irrigated and then allowed to dry to a point where soil aeration is good before further watering occurs. It is essential that a leaching schedule be set up for foliage houses if some leaching does not occur at every watering. The long term nature of some foliage crops and the often piecemeal harvesting of crops can lead to soluble salt buildups in the soil if the grower is not careful. High humidity is beneficial to the growth of most tropical foliage plants but continually high humidity will often lead to an increase in leaf diseases. Some growers make a practice of spraying plants down as they are watered. This is not harmful as long as water does not stand on the leaves for appreciable lengths of time and if the mineral content of the water does not lead to spotting of the leaves. Most water sources, especially if fertilizer is injected, will cause unsightly salt buildup on the foliage when overhead irrigation is used.

In some cases, growers have found that removal of dissolved salts from irrigation water (through reverse osmosis) results in a substantial increase in crop quality. The improvement being brought about by reducing the amount of mineral film and spots deposited on leaves.

Diseases are as common with foliage plants as with any other crop. The same sanitary precautions must be practiced to achieve good results. High humidity in foliage houses often leads to soft rot of leaves. Lowering the humidity slightly will generally reduce the need for fungicidal sprays. Several bacterial and viral diseases can cause leaf spots and there is little the grower can do to control these diseases other than to remove infected tissue and be certain only clean plants are brought into the greenhouse. Root and stem rot are controlled by the use of clean soil and the application of fungicidal drenches when necessary.

The high proportion of foliage plants which are propagated from cuttings makes it imperative that special vigilance be directed toward making sure mother plants are maintained in as disease and pest free state as is practically possible. Poor sanitation and infected mother plants will ensure that diseases and pests are quickly spread through the entire operation.

All greenhouse pests can infest foliage plants but slugs, aphids, spider mites, cyclamen mites, scale, and mealy bugs are especially troublesome. The reader should refer to the chapter on plant pests for detailed discussions of these pests and measures used to control them. It will become readily apparent, with some experience, that certain pests favor particular plants. Efforts at control for individual pests should be concentrated on the appropriate plant varieties.

Foliage plant houses often become pest ridden because unsold plants from previous crops are allowed to remain on the benches and because stock plants are often kept from one year to the next without sufficient vigilance for the pests they may harbor. Timely inspection for and control of pests is especially important in greenhouses when mixed foliage is grown on a continuous schedule.

FOLIAGE PLANTS IN THE HOME OR OFFICE

Greenhouse persons having contact with the consumers of foliage plants will often be subjected to horror stories of how plants died quickly or never performed as they were expected to. It is the responsibility of the horticultural trade to educate consumers concerning the proper care of foliage plants and to provide high quality merchandise which will respond to that care. Plants growing actively in the greenhouse often perform poorly when they are moved quickly to relatively low light and humidity conditions present in the average home. Growth takes place slowly under low light conditions and plants must adjust to this change in growth rate. The adjustment process has come to be referred to as "acclimatization." If consumers are to receive maximum satisfaction from their plant purchases, it is incumbent upon the grower or distributor to make certain acclimatization has taken place before plants are offered for sale.

Acclimatization is accomplished by subjecting foliage plants to lower light, fertilizer, and humidity levels than are optimum for luxuriant growth. The plant is being prepared for the likely conditions to be found in the average home or office. Foliage plants will be better able to face the perils of the world outside if they are placed under 1/2 the light levels necessary for fast growth and fertilized at a reduced rate for approximately 4 weeks prior to sale. A thorough leaching should take place before acclimatization. Plants treated in this manner will be much less likely to begin dropping leaves and turning yellow after the first week or 2 in the home or office.

Foliage plants which do poorly after leaving the greenhouse are often the victims of poor care by their new owners. Improper light, fertilizer, and moisture conditions are the chief culprits responsible for the poor performance of most plants. Consumers must be alerted to the fact that plants will grow slowly in their new environment and consequently will require much less fertilizer. The beneficial effects of a regular leaching program must also be stressed. A slight deficiency of fertilizer elements is preferable to an over supply. Watering practices of consumers are often erratic. The value of thorough irrigation with a drying out period before the next watering must be made obvious. Most consumers would be well advised to maintain foliage plants slightly on the dry side. A regular program of checking for water needs is essential.

The light requirements of different foliage plants are variable and little understood by retailers and customers alike. A concentrated effort by the trade should be made to address this problem. Light levels in the average home will vary dramatically, depending chiefly upon the distance from windows and the size and compass orientation of these windows. Artificial lighting may affect light levels significantly if the duration is long enough and intensity high.

Approximate winter light intensities of locations 1 foot away from North and South windows are 400 foot candles and 5,000 foot candles, respectively, on a bright day. East and west windows exhibit light intensities intermediate to the values mentioned above. These light quantities represent what might be expected in a rather sunny geographical location. Available light drops off quickly as one moves away from the windows. Three feet away from a north window the light intensity could be expected to read only 1/3 of the value registered at a distance of 1 foot.

Many foliage plants will survive quite well at light intensities below 200 foot candles, but most will not grow actively in this situation. Low light plants such as Chinese evergreens, spathiphyllum, cast iron plants, dieffenbachias, philodendrons, dracena marginata, dracena warnecki, and dracena sanderiana will prosper nicely even below 50 foot candles. The trend toward homes with large window expanses and perhaps even atriums or small greenhouses has increased the need for foliage plants which can withstand higher light intensities. Hibiscus and bougainvillea have become very popular for sunny areas in recent years. Jade trees, yucca, citrus trees, crotons, wandering Jews, portulacas, ice plants, cacti and succulents, and asparagus ferns will do fine in well lighted locations. Small flowering plants such as impatiens and begonias will add color if used with these high light plants. A well planned atrium or small greenhouse can accommodate plants which prefer different light levels if high light plants are used as a canopy to filter out bright sunlight.

It must be remembered that light levels will change with the seasons and plants which prospered in one location during winter may receive excessive light during the summer. The duration of light exposure will also change dramatically with seasonal day length. Duration must always be considered when deciding upon the correct placement of plants indoors. As was mentioned, longer durations can make up, to some degree, for low light levels.

In certain situations, foliage plants are placed in locations where only artificial light sources necessary for proper vision are available. Generally, only those plants which tolerate low light levels will prosper under these circumstances. If high light plants were utilized, the light source would likely need to generate 10 or 20 times as much light intensity; resulting in increased installation costs, and perhaps in excessively bright conditions for other uses of the space.

Whenever foliage plants (or any other plants) are to be grown with the aid of artificial light, a good reference text should be consulted to determine the light wavelengths most beneficial to plant growth and the approximate intensities of each needed. A lighting engineer can then suggest the lighting system which most closely meets these requirements in an economical manner.

Reference is often made in the literature to "long lasting" and "temporary" foliage plants. This distinction probably occurs because many plants which prefer relatively high light have performed poorly under the low light conditions of the average home. In truth, they are no more temporary than lower light varieties — they simply have not been grown under proper conditions to ensure long term growth. High light plants often grow vigorously if light is available and they may need frequent pruning and transplanting to remain healthy.

Temperatures encountered in homes and offices are generally suitable for foliage plants if the extremes near doorways, heat vents, and window sills are avoided.

There is some question about the advisability of using leaf polish compounds to remove water spots and other material from leaf surfaces. A few authors are of the opinion that leaf polish can clog the stomates (passages through which air enters the leaf) and prevent proper air entry to the plant. Some concern is expressed that the waxy substances used may collect dust and lint over the long term. Each grower must decide the controversy individually in the absence of definitive evidence. Leaf polish should be tested on each variety before widespread use is begun.

SPECIFIC FOLIAGE PLANT VARIETIES AND FAMILIES

A discussion of all foliage plant varieties is beyond the scope of this book. They have been treated exhaustively in *Exotic Plant Manual and Tropica* by A. B. Graf. A few of the more important families and varieties are described in the following text to acquaint readers with the diversity of material available and to illustrate the conditions necessary for good growth.

No special effort will be made to determine valid scientific species and variety names, at times even scientists specializing in naming plants (taxonomists) cannot agree amongst themselves. Common names are used whenever possible so that the text is useful to practical growers.

Scientific nomenclature is given only when it is felt further clarification will result.

The Aroid Family

Those plants known as aroids are the backbone of the foliage plant industry. They dominate sales and production much as petunias and impatiens do in the bedding plant market. Most aroids are tropical in origin and exemplify what the majority of consumers and growers would consider a good foliage plant. They tolerate the warm, dry, low light conditions found in homes and offices and should be the core of any low light interior landscape. If one is familiar with the distinctive flowers exhibited by anthuriums, calla lilies, spathiphyllum, and caladium it will be easy to visualize the flower characteristics which are the basis of categorizing individual plants into the aroid family. Aroids range in size from those suitable for small pots to large, treelike varieties. They may be of an upright habit or climbing vines. Many aroids make their home climbing through the branches of tropical forest trees and are well suited to hanging basket culture. Perhaps 1,000 species of aroids have been domesticated but the groups listed below account for the vast majority of sales and production within the family.

PHILODENDRON—The most important and diverse group within the aroid family are the philodendrons. Older varieties are familiar to most consumers and will be accepted as dependable performers, although these plants labor under the disadvantage of being considered "old hat" or common. Philodendron cordatum (heart leaf) is particularly common on poles and in small pots and hanging baskets, and it is unchallenged in its ability to survive under the most trying conditions as long as the roots remain on the dry side. The larger varieties of philodendrons are often attached to wooden slabs or grown as bushy floor plants. Many varieties develop long aerial roots in time; these may be removed without danger to the plant if they are considered unsightly. New varieties of philodendron have been introduced but the group as a whole is declining somewhat in popularity relative to other foliage plants simply because many other groups lend themselves to the more "open" light conditions of modern homes and because of the perception of philodendrons as being common. Monstera is a series of philodendron-like varieties which is characterized by perforated or split leaves which lead to the common names of "split leaf" and "Swiss cheese".

DIEFFENBACHIA—Dieffenbachias are broad leaved plants with well defined stems, often becoming treelike. The leaf color is green or variegated with various white patterns. Dieffenbachia is commonly called "dumb cane" since a poison in its tissue will paralyze throat and tongue muscles if plant tissue is ingested. Suffocation can result in extreme cases. The juice from dieffenbachia plants is sometimes extremely irritating to the hands of susceptible workers. Spider mites love dieffenbachias.

Under high light conditions, dieffenbachia leaves tend to become yellowish and may exhibit scorch on the tips and edges. Excessively wet soil often leads to stem rot, so a well drained medium is necessary.

CHINESE EVERGREEN—This group of aroids, known scientifically as *Aglaonema*, is characterized by a bushy habit, tolerance of very low light intensities, and slow growth rates. It was originally popular as a plain green variety, now it is most often cultivated in variegated forms. Chinese evergreens are the premier plant for poor light locations where a plant which will grow within bounds is wanted. The slow growth rate makes them expensive to produce. It is important that interiorscape and holding greenhouses be of a minimum of 65⁰ F. Plants will deteriorate quickly under lower temperatures.

SPATHIPHYLLUM—This is a plant with broad, elongate, green leaves which are born on a long stem originating at the plant base, a definable primary stem is lacking. A graceful, vase-like effect is produced as the leaves flare out from a common origin. This is one of the few tropical plants which is prized as much for flowers as it is for vegetation. The white, Jack in the pulpit type flowers are borne in the same manner as the leaves and are very attractive and long lasting. An excellent floor plant for low light and medium temperature conditions, it can often be substituted in the decor for the more expensive, heat loving Chinese evergreens.

Many new spathiphyllum varieties have recently been introduced. Most are reproduced through tissue culture. These new plants tend to have a bushier, smaller leaved form and often bloom more profusely. Well grown spathiphyllums are perhaps the most popular smaller upright foliage plant at the present time, especially if they are in good bloom.

POTHOS—Pothos, also known as "devil's ivy", is commonly used in small pots, poles, and hanging baskets; this vine is similar to *Philodendron cordatum* in appearance except the foliage is variegated with yellow or white and the stem is coarser. Pothos will not tolerate the extremely low

Spathiphyllum

light conditions under which *Philodendron cordatum* will survive but is otherwise almost as tolerant of adverse conditions.

Pothos like heat and generally will not grow vigorously in northern greenhouses unless constantly warm conditions over 70^0 F can be maintained. The variety with white variegations in the leaf, known as "Marble Queen," is even more demanding of warm conditions.

Pothos is perhaps the most widely grown foliage plant. It is especially adapted to culture in hanging baskets and makes very attractive specimens on a bark slab or poles.

Special large leaved and highly variegated cultivars are available, but these characteristics seldom seem so definitely fixed genetically so as to express themselves under most conditions. These desirable forms more commonly show up under very warm temperatures with slightly higher light conditions. In other words, under situations where vigorous growth is possible.

Diffenbachia

Pothos is particularly difficult to pin a name on. It has been classified as *Scindapsus* in the past and is now scientifically known as *Epipremnum*. *Pothos* is the oldest scientific name and most enduring common label.

ANTHURIUM—Travelers to tropical regions have no doubt seen their share of bright red anthurium flowers displayed in hotel and airport flower shop windows. The waxy texture and bright color combine to give an artificial appearance. Anthurium flowers are important in the cut flower trade but plants have only recently become commonly available as potted specimens. Further detail concerning anthuriums is contained in the potted flower section of this book.

CALADIUM—Known as the Elephant Ears plant because of its characteristic leaf shape. These colorful, warmth loving plants from tubers will prosper indoors on a seasonal basis but perform better if allowed to wither and go dormant during the winter season. More often grown outdoors.

Pothos

SYNGONIUM—Most commonly known as arrowhead plant and used in small containers or hanging baskets, syngonium is sometimes grown on wooden slabs. Varieties with a good deal of white coloration are the most popular. These plants are climbers, although they may not appear so as small plants, and quickly become overgrown unless potted in hanging baskets or provided support. Syngonium may often be referred to in the trade as nephthytis.

Several new varieties have been introduced lately, and this has increased the popularity of these excellent low light plants. Most newer varieties are propagated by tissue culture.

The Lily Family

Plants in the lily family are quite varied in their tolerance to environmental conditions and originate from many widely differing habitats. Several succulents from dry deserts are in the lily family, as are

Syngonium

some dracenas from shaded, moist tropical regions. A few foliage varieties in this family will tolerate fairly cool temperatures with no ill effects. There is some debate whether or not dracenas, cordylines, and sansevieria belong to the lily or to the agave family; this dispute need not concern the present discussion, where all will be treated as lilies. Members of the lily family are often subject to tip burn of the leaves. This condition may be caused by fluorine and chlorine in the soil and water, and some authorities recommend raising of the pH of the soil above 6.5 with limestone to eliminate the problem.

DRACENA—This is perhaps the most important group of lilies used as foliage plants. The leaves are typically long and narrow, originating from a well defined stem. Young plants may be bushy and appear to have no stem until it becomes distinguishable with age. Some varieties develop naked, contorted stems which add character to the plant. Most dracenas will tolerate low light conditions reasonably well. Some contorted dracenas are termed "dragon trees".

Although dracenas are commonly grown into larger specimen plants, many varieties are also useful in pot sizes as small as 2 1/2 inches. Different varieties of dracena have longitudinally stripped leaves with varying color patterns.

Dracena marginata is perhaps the most common variety but Janet Craig, Saunderiana, and Massangeana generally are easier to maintain in the indoor environment, especially under low light conditions.

CHLOROPHYTUM—Chlorophytum is commonly known as the spider or airplane plant. The long narrow leaves of this plant originate at a common source and no main stem is apparent. New satellite stems which elongate from the mother plant are predominantly naked of leaves until the tip, where a small plantlet develops. Spider plants like good diffuse light but will grow well in north windows. Commercial production is most profitable at 60-70^0 F but the plants will prosper at 55^0 F in the home. They are particularly well suited to hanging baskets where the long stems with new plantlets can hang down. Plantlets with air roots forming can be detached and will quickly establish themselves in soil.

Both green and variegated green and white varieties are available. Spider plants are a fast growing crop which is profitable for northern growers. Peak plantlet production can be expected from the fall through late winter. Plantlets become more scarce through the spring and early summer.

SANSEVIERIA—This is an old favorite which has seen the inside of almost every American home. Snake plant and mother-in-law's tongue are the most frequently used common names. Sansevieria will tolerate almost any amount of low light and neglect given to it but is actually native to rather bright habitats. Small plants are not especially useful except in combination dish gardens but large plants with many new lateral plantlets in different stages of growth are very attractive if the leaves are not allowed to become damaged.

ASPARAGUS—The members of this group are most widely used as greenery in spring combination plantings and cut flower arrangements but serve also as inexpensive foliage plants. They will tolerate temperatures of 50^0 F and full summer sun but grow most efficiently at 60-65^0 F with light shade. *Asparagus sprengeri* and *Asparagus plumosus* are the varieties commonly planted from seed. *Asparagus meyeri, falcatus* and *myriocladus* are other useful varieties which are less frequently grown on a commercial basis.

Dracena warneckii

CORDYLINE—These plants closely resemble the dracenas in habit and growing requirements. Several varieties of the Ti plant have been selected which have highly colored leaves.

SUCCULENTS—Many varieties of succulents are members of the lily family. The average person would be hard pressed to see any resemblance between most lily succulents and the more familiar lily type plants of the temperate zone; the flowers, however, are very similar. Succulent lilies are generally residents of dry, sunny regions. Aloes are perhaps the most numerous representatives of this group and include the recently popular aloe vera (burn plant). Several agaves and haworthias are also useful as decorative succulents.

YUCCA—Yuccas have a general appearance much like that of the dracenas but the leaf texture is a good deal heavier and stiffer. Some less commonly used yuccas have very stiff, sharp pointed leaves and could be included as succulents. The green, rather coarse yucca which is widely

Dracena marginata

produced for indoor use today does its best in good light and mildly dry conditions but will survive and remain attractive under low light. Older specimens develop a thick, naked cane with a tuft of vegetation at the top.

ASPIDISTRA—This is a dracena-like plant with tough, leathery foliage. Cast iron plants are renowned for their durability under almost any conditions. They were used frequently in earlier years when homes were dark and likely to be cool but are seldom seen commercially today.

PONY TAIL PALM—Scientifically known as *Beaucanea recurvata*, this is not a common foliage plant but is interesting because of the large bottle shaped stem which is topped by a tuft of long, coarse leaves that are recurved. It is not a member of the palm family but is one of the many exotic lilies.

The Aralia Family

A diverse family which is comprised of both tropical and near temperate varieties. The tropical representatives do not tolerate poor light as does

Chlorophytum

the aroid family. Fifty foot candles of light is the minimum which most varieties will accept and they would generally do much better at several times this intensity. Schaffleras, Japanese aralias, and ivy trees are fast growing in summer daylengths and profitable 10 inch specimen pots can be produced in 1 season by northern growers if small plants are transplanted in late spring.

SCHEFFLERA—The Queensland umbrella tree (*Brassaia actinophylla*) is one of our more important foliage varieties. When given sufficient light it grows as a dense, spreading bush and can become quite large. Specimens subjected to light levels near the minimum 50 foot candles are more open and appear treelike since the lower stems will possess few leaves. If fast growth is not desired, plants may be held on the dry side. Spider mites are particularly fond of schaffleras, as they are of other members of this family, and constant vigilance must be observed to prevent outbreaks. Schaffleras are easily grown from fresh seed; old seed loses viability quickly.

Brassaia arboricola is a smaller, more dense, and greener variety which is perhaps now more popular than the original Queensland umbrella tree. It reputedly will tolerate lower light conditions. Both varieties are utilized in sizes from small seedlings through gigantic specimen trees. Arboricola is also available in variegated forms.

Sansevieria

FATSIA JAPONICA—Japanese aralias share the same general characteristics as scheffleras except they are much wider leaved and even bushier and will tolerate slightly cooler locations. These plants grow quickly from seed but require abundant elbow room to fill out properly. Well grown plants are densely vegetated with large glossy green leaves and make an excellent plant for cool, well lighted situations. Fatsias grown under low light exhibit an open, less desirable appearance.

FATSHEDERA—A hybrid variety with the Japanese aralia and Irish ivy as parents, fatshedera is known in the trade as "ivy tree" or "botanical wonder." It combines the large leaves and vigorous growth of the Japanese aralia with the vining habit of ivies. The predisposition towards vining may not be apparent in young plants or if growth is restricted by pinching and reduced nutrients and water. Older stems are thick and treelike. Ivy trees can be quite attractive if they are given extremely good light and trimmed

Agave

frequently; under these conditions and slightly reduced nutrients, they will develop as trees rather than coarse woody vines. Rooting is more difficult than with ivy but is relatively easy if slightly woody tissue a few inches below the tip is used. Tip cuttings are often too succulent on fast growing plants and wilt immediately when removed from the plant.

DIZYGOTHECA—False aralia, split leaf maple, and spider aralia are common names of this plant. The palmate, brownish-red leaves are very graceful and are borne on woody stems. False aralia has an interesting form and color and should be used more when good light is available. It is easily propagated from fresh seeds and the young plants are well suited for dish garden use. Plants develop into large specimens rather quickly under summer conditions in the northern greenhouse but 10 inch pots can seldom be made in 1 season from seedlings.

POLYSCIAS—A rather slow growing (for this family) group of small

Yucca

woody plants. Also known in horticulture as panax. Perhaps the most widely grown variety is the Ming aralia which has finely divided leaves. It is used where a small oriental looking tree-form is desired. Several other varieties with various leaf shapes and coloration are available.

IVIES—It is difficult to imagine close genetic relationships between large, treelike scheffleras and vining ivies but they are both in the aralia family. Ivies are native of subtropical and temperate regions. Subtropical varieties are more adapted to indoor use since they enjoy warm temperatures. Cooler situations are ideal for the more temperate varieties. Most of the latter are selections of the English ivy (*Hedera helix*) which displays an amazing variety of leaf shapes and color patterns. Ivies are grown the world over as vines and ground cover. Many varieties are available. The problem of growers is to limit their program to a few outstanding selections.

Dwarf schefflera (green), normally propagated from seed

Propagation is easily accomplished from slightly woody cuttings. Every foliage greenhouse should have a steady supply of small pots and hanging baskets as a staple item. English ivies do well at 60-70° F but will not maintain compact growth if light levels are low. Spider mites and cyclamen mites are a continuing problem on ivies unless good preventive measures are an integral part of production methods.

The Fig Family

Plants of this family are especially useful when tree forms are needed for interior landscapes. Light levels of at least 50 foot candles are necessary for maintenance; much higher intensities are required for good growth. Most figs used as ornamentals are in the botanical group *Ficus*. All members of this group have a milky latex for sap which accounts for one of the common names applied to them, "rubber trees." This application applies in particular to the common, broad leaved Ficus elastica and its variants.

Dwarf schefflera (variegated), normally propagated from cuttings.

In modern decor, the weeping fig (*Ficus benjamina*) is replacing the rubber tree (*Ficus elastica*) as the most popular member of the group. Weeping figs are graceful and their small, leathery leaves lend a more refined aspect than is accomplished with the coarser habit of the rubber tree. Weeping figs are sold as multistemmed bushes or they can be trained to a single stem tree. They are notorious for dropping leaves when not properly acclimated to lower indoor light levels before installation. Exposure to sudden cold drafts or extreme drought will sometimes cause total defoliation. New leaves generally grow back after a period of time if suitable conditions for growth are present. When weeping figs have become accustomed to their new home they are durable and maintain an excellent shape. Variegated forms of both the weeping fig and rubber tree are available.

Ficus retusa nitida (Indian laurel tree) is similar to the weeping fig but the branches do not hang and the leaves are not so pointed on the tips. It is attractive when sheared to produce a globe of foliage at the top of a naked stem. *Ficus lyrata* (fiddle leaf fig) has large, generously spaced leaves which resemble a violin and are wavy. This plant is very nice if properly grown but good specimens are seldom seen because leaves are often damaged and stems too weak to support themselves. There are other figs used as ornamentals but their commercial importance is negligible.

The Palm Family

Palms are a large family but only a few varieties are important as indoor specimens. They are often sold in 10 inch or larger containers since their usefulness does not generally emerge until some size is reached. Many people consider them to be the most graceful of all indoor plants. They convey the atmosphere of tropical paradise more readily than any other type of vegetation.

Palm seedlings are popular as small dish garden plants. The neanthe bella palm being most frequently used for this purpose. Rhapis fan palms are sold in smaller container sizes such as 4 inch and 6 inch but are not extensively available since they grow slowly, making production expensive. They are commonly used in oriental theme plantings. A trunk is seldom discernible on smaller palm plants but as they become large most will develop a type of stem which is fibrous rather than woody. The majority of palms produced commercially for interior use prefer shade. They are not, however, considered low light plants. Palms are often categorized by their leaf shape into the feather palms and fan palms. Feather palms have leaflets arranged on either side of a long axis in the manner of a feather while fan palms have the blades radiating out from a central point in the shape of a hand. Many palms which are native to deserts or highland areas will tolerate cooler night temperatures. Some varieties are native at considerable distances from the tropics and many varieties are resident in situations which are not typical of a jungle environment. The following are the more important commercial varieties for indoor use:

    kentia palm (*Howeia forsteriana*)
    neanthe bella palm (*Chamaedorea elegans "bella"*)
    parlor palm (*Chamaedorea elegans*)
    lady palm (*Rhapis excelsa*)
    pygmy date palm (*Phoneix roebelenii*)

False aralia

areca palm (*Chrysalidocarpus lutescens*)

Palms are important for outdoor landscaping in warmer regions of the United States and constitute a considerable crop for nurserymen in those areas.

The Peperomia Family

Perhaps no family of indoor plants is grown so widely for use in small containers as the peperomias. Because of their adaptability to use as small plants, they are a favorite crop in northern greenhouses. Rooted cuttings can be planted in 2 1/4 inch pots and sold in a matter of weeks. Cuttings may be shipped in or taken from stock plants grown at the greenhouse. Most peperomias yield a large number of cuttings per stock plant and are not space hogs so that propagation is often profitable for northern growers. Stock plants which are pinched for cuttings generally regenerate a new flush of growth in several weeks. Peperomias require a 65^0 F temperature but will grow more vigorously at 70^0 F. Unlike philodendrons and pothos which do little more than survive at 65^0 F, the

Rubber tree (*Ficus elastica*)

peperomias will make considerable growth. Light levels for profitable growth should be in the medium range of intensities mentioned earlier for foliage plants. In the home they can be subjected to 50 foot candles and still maintain their appeal.

A limited number of varieties make good hanging baskets and a few are suitable for low profile 6 inch pots. Any variety which is grown in a 2 1/4 inch container will also make acceptable 3 or 4 inch material. The number of cultivars is extensive; the grower is often in the happy circumstance of eliminating varieties which do not perform or sell well under the particular growing program. Peperomias are perhaps the best choice to utilize as the backbone of a 2 1/4 and 4 inch foliage plant program; they grow easily and quickly, propagate economically, are not susceptible to extraordinary pest problems, and will tolerate reasonably low light levels in the home. Many of the other plant groups which can be cultured economically for small pots by northern growers are adapted only to the brighter indoor situations.

Propagation of peperomias is by leaf and stem cuttings and by division of the crown. Stem cuttings are the most common method but certain

Coconut palms

varieties are more profitably reproduced by leaf cuttings. Stem cuttings of most varieties root within 3 to 4 weeks and will make acceptable 2 1/4 inch pots in an equal amount of time after transplanting. Some varieties may attain good size with this schedule when only 1 cutting per pot is used, but the majority will require 2 or 3 cuttings. Leaf cuttings require additional time. Rooting is accomplished easily if the medium is not excessively moist and water is applied only when absolutely necessary. Rotting of stems and leaves is a persistent cause of losses in peperomias during propagation when excessive water is present. Most peperomias will withstand considerable drought; less damage is experienced when cuttings and plants are kept slightly on the dry side than if they are overly moist. Good drainage is essential in soils used for peperomias to avoid excessive rotting of roots, stems, and leaves.

Parlor palm or Neanthe bella

Cleanliness is mandatory for success in propagating peperomias. Experience will soon educate the grower as to which varieties are especially prone to leaf and stem rot. Plants that are intended for 4 inch and larger pots may be established in 2 1/4 inch containers and grown to good size before shifting up so that large, actively growing plants will be capable of utilizing the extra volume of water present in the larger pots.

Certain peperomias are quite sensitive to high soluble salts in the soil solution and will exhibit typical symptoms of leaf edge burn unless lower than normal fertilizer concentrations are applied. Most varieties are not so sensitive and will prosper with the normal fertilizer regime used for other foliage plants. Peperomias are remarkably pest free although almost any insect or mite will establish on them if heavy infestations are present in the greenhouse.

For an extensive description of the numerous varieties of useful peperomias the reader is referred to the *Exotica Series Four* .

Variegated trailing peperomia

Cacti And Succulents

Cacti and succulents come in a wonderful array of forms and colors. While cacti are all members of the Cactaceae family, the succulents are composed of many families. Cacti, especially, produce some of the most beautiful flowers in the plant kingdom when conditions are appropriate for floral initiation and development. Unfortunately, flowering is generally infrequent. The majority of cacti and succulents are native to rather arid regions with hot days, cool nights, and plenty of sunshine. Many varieties will withstand freezing if they are gradually exposed to cooler temperatures since they grow naturally in climates where winter freezes are frequent. There are a few cacti, including the Christmas cactus, which grow as epiphytes (on the branches of trees) in tropical forests. Cacti and succulents are generally grown and sold in 2 1/4 inch pots but 4 inch and larger containers are not uncommon. The slow growth rate of these plants increases the cost of larger sizes tremendously.

The ideal environment for cacti and succulents is one where temperatures are warm, light plentiful, and water available on demand. Although these adaptable plants can survive extreme drought, maximum growth is made when they have all the water they can use consistent with proper soil aeration. Low temperatures, shade, and infrequent irrigation and fertilization may not be conducive to quick growth but they are tolerated with a minimum decrease in quality by most cacti and succulents when they are displayed in an indoor environment. These plants will survive a tremendous amount of abuse but excessive soil moisture is one condition which almost always leads to death. When the soil is waterlogged roots lack enough oxygen to function properly and stem and root rot flourish. Soils must be well drained yet supply adequate mineral nutrition. A sunny south window is an excellent location for these plants. If the window receives no ventilation it may be advisable to provide light shade in summer.

Propagation of most cacti and succulents is easy while others may be extraordinarily difficult. Succulents are often referred to as "soft" varieties and "hard" varieties. The hard ones generally have a much slower growth rate, are more difficult to propagate, and are more sought after by collectors. Soft succulents such as jade plants, kalanchoes, sedums, hen and chicks, and euphorbias root quickly from stem and leaf cuttings and exhibit a reasonably fast growth rate. Production of such varieties can be profitable in northern greenhouses if most growth takes place in the summer so that plants are sold by late fall. Seed, leaf cuttings, stem cuttings, and division of the plant are all commonly used to propagate cacti and succulents. More than one method may be equally feasible, depending on the circumstances. Irrespective of the propagation method, excess water and humidity usually lead to disease and result in failure. Growers must remember that these plants have considerable water stored in their tissues. Leaves or stem portions of some varieties may be observed sprouting roots even when left lying on dry, hot bench surfaces. It should not be surmised that water is not beneficial during propagation—the key word is excess. Any water applied must have ample opportunity to drain off quickly.

Culture of the slower growing cacti and succulents is generally better left to specialists located in areas where fuel consumption is low and good sunlight is assured. Damage during shipment is minimal and transport costs are relatively low due to the small size and durability of the plants. The hard, tough appearance of most cacti and succulents sometimes leads the uninitiated to believe these plants are impervious to attack by pests and diseases. Their susceptibility to root and stem rot when excess moisture is present has already been stressed. Cacti and succulents are not especially prone to pest infestations but they are not immune either. Mealy bugs and spider mites are perhaps the two most frequently troublesome pests. Aphids are often the number one offender on soft succulents.

Illustrations and descriptions of numerous varieties of cacti and succulents are presented in the *Exotic Series Four.* The number of varieties now in use has grown tremendously so that the avid collector or specialist may need to consult even more specialized works than the one mentioned above.

The Fern Family

Ferns are one of the most widely distributed families of ornamental plants. They are found from the Arctic to tropical rain forests. A good fern habitat is usually shaded and damp. Even in the tropics ferns will be found in the cooler locations. Soils are usually highly organic so that even though humidity and moisture are abundant, the root zone is well drained. Ferns are diverse in size and shape. Tree ferns of the tropics may reach heights of 50 feet while smaller varieties of colder regions are no more than a few inches tall. The leaves of staghorn ferns are broad, flat, and leathery while the typical ferns have delicate leaflets arranged on a long axis in the manner of a feather. The beauty of most ferns lies in the delicate arrangement of leaflets into a graceful, airy frond (leaf) which is in turn arranged with other fronds into a refreshing, cool oasis of green.

Although there are many varieties of ferns utilized for indoor landscaping, the vast majority of production is made up of the Boston fern group. The several cultivars of Boston fern originated from selections of the sword fern (*Nephrolepis exaltata*). The most popular members of the group are dwarf Boston, fluffy ruffles, Whitamanii, lace, and Rooseveltii ferns. These descendants of the sword fern have monopolized fern production because they are attractive, are easy to grow, and will thrive under the low humidity conditions found in the average home. Other ferns are produced commercially but their importance is minor. Most of them are difficult to

A diverse group of plants which will tolerate dry conditions. True cacti in the foreground, several taller euphorbias, and a sansevieria just to the right of center.

grow easily unless humidity levels are high.

Boston ferns can be a profitable crop for northern growers if small plants are vigorously growing by July. Good 3 inch plants transplanted at that time 1 per pot to 6 inch containers or 2 to a 10 inch basket will make excellent specimens for Christmas. Temperatures for Boston ferns should be maintained at 60-80° F with light shade in the winter and heavy shade in the summer. Plants are best if allowed to grow pot bound until it is a real necessity to transplant them. Being pot bound allows frequent heavy irrigations without waterlogging the soil. Boston ferns grow vigorously in late spring, summer, and fall but fail to make appreciable progress in northern greenhouses in winter. Unless the crop is made by late fall it seems to stall until spring arrives.

The common dwarf Boston fern has perhaps been overdone in supermarket produce departments. It is offered on a constant basis, often at reduced prices which few northern growers could make a profit. Smaller growers for traditional outlets may find a more exclusive market for lace, feather, and Whitamanii varieties which are not so commonly seen but are just as easy to grow and care for. Large specimen hanging baskets are also an item which is not commonly available at mass outlets.

Jade plant. One of the easiest succulents to propagate and grow.

A relatively recent variety introduction in the Boston fern group has been the Dallas fern. This patented variety is very compact and tolerates lower light levels than the earlier Boston selections. It is easy to grow under similar conditions to those mentioned.

Propagation of ferns is by spores (very tiny reproductive bodies which are analogous to seeds), division of the crown, layering runners, or meristem culture. The brown or black dots which are regularly spaced on the underside of fern leaves at certain periods of the year contain millions of microscopic spores. Spores are released from these small capsules at maturity and will germinate if proper conditions are present. The most persistent problem in obtaining good germination of spores is maintaining adequate humidity. Growers who need only a few Boston type fern plants usually divide the crown of stock plants into sections, each having a small portion of root and vegetation. These are inserted into moist rooting mix and allowed to root and grow until suitable for 2 1/4 or 3 inch pots. Larger

A combination pot of cacti and succulents rooted directly in the pot (top). Dwarf jade similarly propagated (extreme bottom left). The remaining plants arc truc cacti.

growers will generally find that obtaining small pots from specialists who propagate by crown division or meristem culture is preferable to maintaining a supply of stock plants.

Assortments of small ferns from spores are often sold as small 2 1/4 inch plants. These are commonly utilized in terrariums and other specialized plantings. They do not commonly prosper in the usual low humidity present in the average home.

The most persistent pests to attack ferns are the scale insects. Outbreaks are not often encountered if young plants are scrupulously inspected for the pests and if sources of infestation are not present on other crops in the greenhouse. After an outbreak of scale is discovered on larger plants, it is often almost impossible to clear up because of the dense foliage and difficulty in getting control agents to the insects.

Boston fern

The Wandering Jew Family (Commelinaceae)

This family contains some of the most profitable and easily grown foliage plants for the northern grower. Its members are generally well known to the public and have been grown in window sills for generations. The ease of propagation and culture leads many consumers to produce their own plants but there is significant demand for quality, professionally grown specimens. Most members of the wandering Jew family make excellent hanging baskets in a short while and some varieties are marketable as 4 and 6 inch pots. Wandering Jews in the home prefer a sunny spot in winter and light shade in summer. Cool rooms will not cause quality to decline. The best greenhouse specimens are grown at 60º F with full sun in winter and light shade in summer although higher and lower temperatures and light levels will be tolerated with amazing impunity.

Propagation is accomplished by sticking tip cuttings directly to the finishing containers. No bottom heat is required. When cuttings are spaced widely, pinching is essential after establishment if heavy plants are desired. Crops are more uniform and profitable if the finishing container is filled with enough cuttings to result in good plants without pinching. Roots form in 1 to 2 weeks and 4 inch plants can be ready for sale in less than 5 weeks from cuttings when weather is warm and sunny. Many varieties of wandering Jew exist and growers will do well to begin a collection of the more useful types to use as stock plants.

Many wandering Jews exhibit a tendency to flower as winter approaches. This phenomenon is pronounced in certain varieties and almost unnoticed in others. Vegetative growth slows and production may be severely curtailed in those cultivars which bloom profusely. The Tahitian bridal veil plant seems to have the capacity to bloom well in all seasons and vegetative growth does not suffer appreciably. The flowers on bridal veil are the main attraction but flowers on the familiar "inch plant" are unsightly.

Wandering Jews are exceptionally disease and pest free but rotting out of the cuttings can occur if excessive moisture is applied during root formation. Most of these plants will tolerate a surprising degree of drought and freshly harvested cuttings are best left slightly on the dry side.

Moses in a cradle (Rhoeo) is a more upright and coarse featured member of this family. It is often grown for 4 inch and 6 inch pots. A complete variety listing and photographs of different wandering Jews are available in the *Exotic Plant Manual*.

The Pineapple Family

This family is more readily recognized in the floral trade when referred to as "bromeliads." Most members are characterized, as is the pineapple plant, by a basal rosette of tough, fibrous, lanceolate leaves. The central cup formed by these leaves serves as a storage reservoir for water. Bromeliads are seldom grown in northern greenhouses, being shipped in from southern growers in most cases. Their crop time is too long and their culture too specialized for inclusion in most greenhouse programs. The bromeliads exhibit a wide range of attractive leaf colors and flowers. In some varieties the leaf is prized while in others the flower is the object of attention. The cost of growing bromeliads to specimen size is the major factor in limiting their market share. If they could be sold at prices competitive with other indoor plants of similar size they would undoubtedly be very popular.

Bromeliads tolerate a wide range of temperature and light conditions. Even if no growth is made, the tough nature of their tissue prevents any obvious decline in quality from occurring quickly. Ideal conditions would

Purple Wandering Jew

be 65-70⁰ F, filtered sunlight, porous soil, and soil water in adequate supply but never excessive. Water should be kept standing in the central leaf cup. Fertilizer is applied infrequently to match the slow growth and any fertilizer water put in the central cup must be very dilute. Certain members of the family, including pineapples, have no actual need to hold reserve water in the cup.

Wherever cost is not the main objective and plants are desired which are both unusual and easy to maintain, bromeliads should certainly receive consideration. The selection of varieties available is fairly extensive so that plantings of bromeliads may be made quite interesting using different colors and shapes.

The flower spikes of bromeliads are quite unusual and commonly remain attractive for prolonged periods of time.

A specialized group of smaller bromeliads, the tillandsias, have recently become quite popular in the floral trade. Tillandsias are mostly epiphytic on trees in tropical and subtropical areas but will grow upon houses, rocks

Moses-in-a-cradle

or other available material. They do not generally possess a central cup for water storage but they do absorb water through their leaves from the atmosphere or during rainstorms.

The ability of tillandsias to survive without actual root attachment has been used to advantage by florists, who commonly attach these plants onto bark, driftwood, rocks, seashells, or other material by using hot glue guns. A weekly misting with water or dilute fertilizer is all that is needed to keep plants alive.

Tillandsias received into the greenhouse from tropical or subtropical growing centers can be kept in good shape by laying plants on open bottom flats which are elevated above the bench or they can be placed on wire mesh benches. A water shower every week is sufficient unless plants are kept for a long period of time; dilute fertilizer can then be used every month. Water should not be allowed to persist on the plants, it must drain off quickly. Light shade is preferable. The flower spikes of tillandsias are typical of the bromeliad family but generally smaller.

Tillandsia

The Grape Family

This family is represented by only one important group of interior ornamentals, the grape ivies. They are entirely unrelated to commonly known ivies described earlier under aralias. The importance of grape ivy is centered primarily upon one variety (*Cissus rhombifolia*) and its variants which are responsible for the great majority of commercial production. Grape ivy is a favorite plant for hanging baskets, totems, and trellis arrangements. Because of its grasping tendrils, it can be used for indoor arbors and room dividers. It is particularly useful when a very dark green leaf color is desired.

Grape ivy will flourish at temperatures of 60-70° F with medium to heavy shade in summer and light shade in winter. Propagation is by tip or stem cuttings. Seeds are available but seldom used in commercial production.

This plant is perhaps the premier low light vine for production in northern greenhouses. While Pothos and Philodendron barely manage to survive cooler winter temperatures, grape ivy flourishes.

The major drawback of grape ivy is its susceptibility to mildew unless adequate heat and ventilation is provided. Plants grown near the ventilation tubes receive extra air movement and are less likely to develop this disease. Even when advanced cases of mildew are not apparent on plants; an incipient, low level infection may be present and cause deterioration of the leaves and eventual abscission. Chemical preventative sprays for mildew will eliminate the problem.

Leaf drop is common with grape ivy, not only due to the ravages of mildew but also because of extreme water stress, root rot, or high levels of soluble salts in the soil solution. Cuttings are particularly susceptible to leaf drop and must be provided with adequate heat to prevent mildew. Although it is necessary to avoid excess water in the soil and high atmospheric humidity, plants must not be allowed to suffer serious water stress.

Soil for grape ivy must be well drained to prevent soggy conditions and the subsequent development of root rot. Iron chlorosis is also common with wet soils.

The culture of grape ivy in early growth stages is rather exacting but well grown specimens are always in good demand. Although mature plants are also susceptible to mildew, the older, tougher leaves do not contract infection as easily. The grape ivy is a very durable plant in low light situations once established.

The Mint Family

The importance of this family is accounted for by several rather "weedy," easily grown varieties. Coleus, Swedish ivy, candle plant, and silver nettle are grown in almost every general purpose greenhouse in North America. They are highly profitable crops because they grow quickly and easily and enjoy favorable market acceptance. Coleus culture has been described in the bedding plant section of this book.

The mints are considered by many people as temporary plants and perhaps less than full fledged members of the foliage plant fraternity. If they make money for the grower and retailer and satisfy the customer's needs, the debate about legitimacy is unimportant. These plants are no less permanent than others; they simply need different growing conditions and care to remain attractive. Light levels for the mint family in the interior landscape should be good. They will not thrive in dark corners. Cool temperatures of 65^0 F are ideal for compact growth but higher and lower temperatures are tolerated. Regular pruning may be necessary to keep them within bounds.

Grape ivy

Swedish ivy (also called German ivy and creeping Charlie) has become one of the most important modern day foliage plants. Greenhouse production is highly significant and millions of plants are propagated at home. Perhaps no other plant pleases consumers so much, as it roots easily and produces large amounts of attractive vegetation without special care if exposed to strong, filtered light. The demand for it has been tremendous and shows no signs of lessening. Propagation in the home certainly reduces demand for commercially produced plants, but impressive hanging baskets from the greenhouse will always find a ready market. Smaller material also moves at a steady pace.

Greenhouse production is almost fool proof. Tip or stem cuttings will root in 1 to 2 weeks at 70^0 F. Growers may wish to stick cuttings directly to finishing pots in warm weather or resort to rooting in flats with bottom heat in winter. Excellent plants are obtained at $60\text{-}70^0$ F with light shade in winter and medium shade in summer. Large plants require heavy amounts

Swedish ivy. One of the most profitable foliage plants to grow. Demand is also good.

of water in the summer to prevent yellowing of older leaves. Watering at the time of transplanting cuttings must be restricted to prevent losses due to stem rot and root rot. Pinching is necessary unless a sufficient number of cuttings is planted in the container to produce a full plant with single stem growth. The following schedule should serve as a guideline for summer production with direct rooting in the container; 4 inch pots, no pinch-4 weeks; 6 inch pots, no pinch-5 weeks; 10 inch baskets one pinch-9 weeks. Winter schedules should allow 1/3 more growing time if cuttings are rooted with bottom heat. These schedules refer to northern, high light conditions; southern growers should be able to produce plants in somewhat less time.

Swedish ivy grows so quickly during summer that it may suffer from nutrient deficiencies under normal foliage plant fertilizer concentrations. Slow release fertilizers incorporated into the soil can be used to prevent this condition.

Swedish ivy is remarkably pest free. This in itself would recommend the plant to any consumer or grower. Swedish ivy blooms in the northern

United States from November through March. The numerous elongated clusters of small pale blue flowers are quite attractive but can become a nuisance when they drop on plants below or on carpeting in the home. The mature flower stalks are unsightly after flowers have dropped. Flower production reduces the rate of vegetative growth so that cutting production in winter is somewhat restricted.

The variety of Swedish ivy in heaviest production has totally green leaves with a heavy, slightly wrinkled texture. Mature leaves are ovate and generally 1 1/2 to 2 inches broad. A similar cultivar with white variegations in the leaf is also available but maintaining a good variegated pattern is difficult over a period of time. The variegated form grows more slowly. A coarser variety with larger, brownish-purple leaf color enjoys limited sales but it quickly becomes woody and is generally a less desirable plant. Numerous other less important strains are available.

Silver nettle vine or silver lace vine (*Laminum galeobdolon variegatum*) is winter hardy outdoors in most areas of the northern hemisphere but will perform admirably as a foliage plant in the home if given good light at 60-70° F. The leaves are slightly longer than broad and may reach 2 inches in length. They are green with silver markings on either side of the mid rib. Plants in hanging baskets can quickly reach several feet long and frequent pinching is necessary in the early stages of growth to produce a bushy habit. Silver nettle also finds a market in 4 inch pots. These vines make excellent filler in spring flowering baskets when a trailing effect is needed. They will grow in sun or shade when acclimated. Culture and propagation is much the same as for Swedish ivy except that cooler temperatures and more sun will be tolerated. Silver nettle is relatively pest free but cyclamen mites and red spider mites can become serious if infestations are not treated immediately.

Candle plant can be treated in the same manner as Swedish ivy. Moon vine is another dual purpose mint which can be used as a perennial ground cover outside or as a small foliage plant indoors. This plant grows initially in a low mounded form but quickly begins to spread into a semi-vine habit. It has small (3/4-1 1/2 inch) silvery leaves and rosy-pink blooms in season.

The Norfolk Pine Family

These tropical and subtropical trees are closely related to the pine and fir trees of the northern hemisphere. The Norfolk island pine or star pine (*Araucaria excelsa*) is a major foliage variety in the United States, particularly in larger containers. Bunya-bunya or monkey puzzle trees are produced commercially but are not frequently seen. The Norfolk pine looks very much like our pine trees but is perhaps more formal with regularly spaced whorls of 5 to 7 branches on the main stem. The needles are soft and awl-shaped. Monkey puzzle trees have much the same general shape but the needles are much larger, flattened, and quite sharp.

Araucaria trees are generally shipped to northern greenhouses from southern production areas but 6 inch pots can be produced in the greenhouse for Christmas from strong 2 1/4 inch containers if grown through the summer and fall under good conditions. Norfolk pines do well under a wide variety of environmental conditions. They tolerate occasional cold almost to the freezing point if acclimated and will survive light intensities of less than 50 foot candles or almost full sun. Ideal conditions would be light shade at 65-70^0 F. Diseases and pests are seldom a problem but an occasional inspection for spider mites is recommended.

Norfolk pines are generally easy to grow and will please customers if they are cautioned not to allow plants to dry out severely. The lower branches yellow quickly if this happens.

The rather unique form of Norfolk pines is not available in other foliage plants, making it a useful addition to the interior decor. They are very popular as a substitute for traditional Christmas trees.

Norfolk pines are used extensively for outdoor landscaping in warm sections of the United States where winter freezes are uncommon.

Propagation is from seed or tip cuttings. Larger plants are generally derived from cuttings of special strains while 2 1/4 inch and 4 inch pots are grown from common seedlings.

The African Violet Family (Gesneriaceae)

Culture of the more popular members of this family (African violets, streptocarpus, gloxinia) has already been discussed in the chapter devoted to flowering plants.

Several more gesneriad groups are useful as combination foliage and flowering plants in the indoor environment. The two best known and most commonly produced are the lipstick vine and goldfish plant. Both of these durable African violet relatives are easy to grow and produce charming flowers upon occasion.

The leaves of the lipstick vine and goldfish plant are rather leathery and are born on semi woody branches (in contrast to the soft, fleshy growth of most of their close relatives). Both lipstick vine and goldfish plants can be propagated from seed but tip cuttings are easily rooted and save considerable production time. In the North, these plants take up to 1 year for production of 8 inch hanging baskets if several rooted cuttings are planted in each container.

Sinningia, *episcia*, and *achimenes* are some other more or less African violet type plants (at least in their cultural requirements) which are sometimes grown commercially. There are several other, less well known genera which are mainly grown only by hobbyists who specialize in rare flowering plants. Each of these groups of plants contains some very beautiful and unusual varieties which combine both foliage and flowering potential.

The Euphorbia Family

This is of course the family to which poinsettias belong. The characteristic central flowering parts of the poinsettia are common to all members of the Euphorbiaceae but the colorful bracts surrounding the male and female reproductive organs are not universal. Most members of the family also possess milky juice; those varieties which resemble cacti can be quickly differentiated by this characteristic since cacti have watery sap.

Two groups of euphorbias are especially important as foliage plants; the true euphorbias which take on many weird shapes but which, in general, resemble cacti, and the crotons (codiaeum) which are easily recognizable by their large multicolored leathery leaves.

The euphorbias often possess spines but many also produce small leaves (a few have rather large leaves), especially during those times when growing conditions are optimal. There are several species in common use, most being rather tall, stark looking plants. The crown of thorns is in this group, being one of the more leafy representatives. Succulent type euphorbias require only infrequent water availability and, since they grow slowly, do not need heavy fertilization. They thrive best under high light intensity but will tolerate shade if it is not excessive. Plants subjected to extreme drought will loose their leaves, if present, but soon grow them back when water becomes available.

Although euphorbias will tolerate some exposure to cold, they do not thrive if this condition is persistent. Unlike the cacti, cool nights are not conducive to healthy growth.

Propagation is normally by cuttings which root easily if they can be kept

Norfolk pine

from rotting. Cuttings are often allowed to dry at the cut for some time before being stuck. A very well drained rooting medium is necessary so that excess moisture is not held near the cutting. Mature plants also suffer from stem rot near the soil line unless well drained media are used for potting. Injuries on the stems can lead to serious rot, especially if humidity is high in the greenhouse.

The value of euphorbias over cacti is that they can be produced more quickly (thus reducing cost), they will prosper better at higher night temperatures, and the spines are generally not so dangerous on most varieties.

The crotons are certainly widely divergent from the euphorbias in appearance. The colorful leaves of croton have immediate appeal and larger varieties can be very useful in indoor or outdoor landscapes. The croton is not an especially good house plant unless excellent light is available to stimulate bright leaf colors. The leaves of the plants exposed to low light will become almost green in color. Numerous smaller leaved croton varieties are available for combination work in dish gardens.

Some plants for sunny locations

Numerous homes, offices, and public buildings constructed in the last decade have been designed to admit higher levels of daylight. Not only are these structures more airy, but also they often have specific planting areas set aside in sunny locations. As a consequence, there has been a corresponding increase in demand for decorator plants which will thrive under full sun. Several of these varieties have already been described under headings pertaining to other families: Norfolk island pine, aloes, cacti, euphorbias, wandering Jews, and some palms. There are an additional few sun loving plants which deserve special consideration because they are so well adapted to these locations and they are especially striking because of their flowers and/or fruit.

Citrus, bougainvillea, and hibiscus are all excellent plants in full sun. Each of them flower almost year round with short rest periods between heavy bloom production. Temperatures of 60-70°F are most suitable but higher and lower ranges are tolerable. All of these plants seem to benefit from occasional applications of chelated iron. Spider mites are a perennial problem but may easily be eradicated with preventive chemical sprays. Aphids are also troublesome, especially on hibiscus and bougainvillea. These light loving plants make little growth during the northern winter. Commercial production is thus concentrated at these latitudes in the brighter months.

Citrus plants are normally grown in the South and shipped to northern markets. The same procedure is common for bougainvillea and hibiscus but both of the latter can be profitably grown in northern greenhouses as summer crops. Cuttings of hibiscus and bougainvillea can be rooted at any time of the year from half hard wood. The rooting process is slower than for more succulent greenhouse ornamentals but should be accomplished in 6 to 8 weeks. Misting is essential to good results although a 20-30% success rate may be obtained if cuttings are simply sprayed occasionally with a hose and left in the shade. It is important that cuttings be taken at a cool time of day and watered in immediately; wilted cuttings do not recover turgidity easily.

Well branched 6 inch hibiscus plants produce 5 gallon specimens in the North for Christmas if they are transplanted June 1 and pinched hard 1 month later. These will be truly impressive plants and should command

Candelabra plant (Euphorbiaceae)

a premium price. Six inch plants for Christmas must be rooted by June 1 and pinched for the last time by August 1 to attain good size. Commercial production of hibiscus for flowering pot plants has increased tremendously in the last few years and small plants are now available from several specialists. The hibiscus seems to be a plant with an unlimited future if current architectural styles persist.

Production methods for hibiscus plants destined primarily for flowering plant markets may differ from those employed when plants are to be used as foliage specimens. The difference lies in the emphasis placed on height control by chemical means. Hibiscus for flower markets are normally treated with Cycocel to give plants a short, very bushy shape with maximum flower buds per square foot of foliage area. These plants are very attractive but can prove disappointing to the buyer who expects a vigorously growing foliage plant. Experience has shown that it takes about 1 year in the North for the effects of Cycocel to wear off. Plants will not put on appreciable

Croton (Euphorbiaceae)

new growth until that time and are more susceptible to a decrease in quality due to poor growing conditions since they are not in an active metabolic state. Plants intended as actively growing foliage specimens should not be treated with Cycocel. Their height can be controlled sufficiently by allowing plants to suffer slight water stress and by switching to the use of potassium nitrate fertilizer alone to reduce nitrogen uptake.

Hibiscus flowers do not last more than a day or two but are produced constantly over the flowering period. Most varieties have very large flowers. The predominant colors are from pink to red with yellow and white being less common. Few plants can boast a flower which is so striking and yet exquisitely refined. There are many varieties to choose from. One of the major characteristics to be considered when selecting varieties for the greenhouse program is strength and length of stem. Shorter cultivars with strong stems are generally more suitable for both potted flower and foliage plant production. Production of tree forms with a single naked trunk is better left to southern growers since the crop time is greatly extended.

Bougainvilleas are woody shrubs which develop long, slender branches that may sometimes appear almost vining. Growth is rapid under good conditions and plants may be produced under the same schedule as hibiscus except that at least one extra pinch is needed to finish a reasonably bushy plant. One drawback of bougainvilleas in greenhouse production and for home or office is the unwieldy, clambering growth habit. The length of branches can be controlled to some degree by making sure plants have full sun with only enough nutrients and water to sustain healthy growth. Luxuriant production of vegetation does nothing for flower production and increases the tendency of plants to ramble. The use of chemical growth retardants with bougainvillea has not been investigated thoroughly. Dwarf varieties can be grown when smaller sized plants are desired.

Flowers of bougainvillea are inconspicuous; the real color is provided by paper-like leaves surrounding the flower. Numerous groups of these colored leaves are arranged on short stalks at the ends of branches. A bougainvillea in full bloom is perhaps the most striking ornamental plant available. Colors are extremely vivid and some varieties exhibit a neon-like iridescence. The blooms of bougainvillea are long lasting and it is not uncommon for a branch to maintain good color for more than a month. There are many excellent varieties.

Citrus plants offer a unique combination of very fragrant flowers, beautifully glossy foliage and interesting and edible fruits. The wonderful, almost overpowering aroma of citrus plants in bloom is especially enchanting. Northern greenhouses may profit from purchasing large 1 gallon plants in late spring and growing to 8 or 10 inch container size through the summer. Only a moderate amount of growth should be expected and this program is not cost effective unless the starter plants are obtained at excellent prices. Lemon, lime, and orange plants are available in dwarf varieties suitable for container culture. The calamondin orange is far and away the most popular and readily available because it maintains a compact shape and produces fruit and flowers almost continuously through the year. Calamondin fruit is small and tart but edible if allowed to ripen fully; it is more suited for marmalade production. Other varieties yield sweeter fruit and some lime and lemon trees yield full sized fruit of good quality.

An inexpensive water garden.

Systemic insecticides should not be used on citrus plants since the poison may enter the fruit.

Hibiscus, bougainvillea, and citrus can all be grown in outdoor nurseries in warmer regions and are used frequently in outdoor landscaping projects.

Water plants for indoors

There is an increasing market for decorative water plants. Not only are they used in fish aquariums but also in special plant oases. Water plants may live under the water and floating on top with roots attached to the bottom or they may be unattached. Some will live only if moist islands or earth bars are available.

Artificial oxygenation of the water plants is not necessary. Plants actually utilize carbon dioxide and then provide oxygen to the surrounding water.

If the proper varieties are chosen for culture and attention is paid to provide suitable water quality, water gardening indoors is quite easy. Sunlight or artificial light is, of course, necessary as it is for any other plant. Several hours of bright filtered light is generally best. The main problem associated with strong sunlight is not generally excessive intensity to plants but rather the tendency of light energy to heat the water to unacceptable levels.

Acceptable water temperature levels are normally in the 70-80°F range but many species prefer somewhat cooler conditions. The 70-80°F level has been utilized extensively because tropical fish are kept at this temperature; temperatures of 60-70°F for goldfish are more to the liking of most aquatic plants.

Numerous plant varieties are suitable for water gardens. The many beautiful strains of water lily (*Nymphaea*) are perhaps the premier plant of which all fanciers desire at least one specimen. *Cyperus* (papyrus or umbrella palm) is one of the more useful upright plants. Water clover (*Marsilea quadrifolia*) and duckweeed (*Lemna minor*) are commonly used as small floating plants. Madagascar lace-leaf (*Aponogeton fenestralis*) and Parrot's feather (*Myriophyllum proserpinacoides*) are examples of plants which grow well under the water surface.

Several of the unusual carnivorous plants such as cobra plant (*Darlingtonia*), pitcher plant (*Sarracenia*) and sundew (*Drocera*) are adaptable to growth on organic bars or islands in the water garden.

Bonsai plants

Many smaller woody plants which will tolerate indoor conditions are utilized for bonsai training. Plants can be offered as a final product which has been trained, root pruned, and established in an appropriate container or as starter plants upon which consumers can practice their own bonsai skills.

In general, there are two aspects to the bonsai market; those plants which are intended for sale as one of a kind artistic creations (these plants may take years to produce and carry a price tag of over $10000.00), and those which are more or less mass produced for everyday use in interior decoration. The discussion in this book will focus upon the latter aspect although there is no sharp dividing line where artistry leaves off and commercialism begins.

Small junipers are perhaps the most commonly employed plant group for mass production bonsai. They are easy to train, transplant readily, and will tolerate a wide range of conditions without declining in quality. Smaller pines are equally as suitable but they generally are more expensive as starter plants and require somewhat more training to develop unusual shapes. Several juniper species produce a high proportion of young plants with ready made bonsai shapes which require only cosmetic pruning and training before they are acceptable as "authentic mass production bonsai."

Dwarf pomegranates, natal plums (*Carissa*), azaleas, small maples, spruces, rhododendrons, evergreen cypress, cedars, camellias, and pyracanthas are other plant groups which are adaptable to bonsai. No special characteristics other than those mentioned above are necessary for bonsai; if a plant looks good for the purpose it can most likely be utilized for some type of bonsai.

There are several distinct steps which usually occur in commercial production of bonsai. First, the proper size of plant is chosen and then given a preliminary pruning on both the roots and top to begin adapting the plant to small pot culture. Secondly, about 2 months after pruning, the plants should be adapted enough for transplanting to the final decorative container. Slower growing species may require 3 months. Further top and root pruning takes place at this stage, along with basic training of branches to desired configurations.

In the third and final production stage, further cosmetic pruning and branch training are done to finalize plant appearance. Various types of vegetative or artificial ground cover and decorative objects can be introduced to the bonsai arrangement at this time. The third step can be accomplished immediately following transplanting or after a period of establishment. In any case, plants should be allowed to root in for at least 6 weeks after significant root pruning so that retail customers will not experience difficulties.

The schedule elaborated above assumes that a near finished size plant was purchased or grown to start the bonsai process and that the end product will be a well established and reasonably authentic looking reproduction of true artistic creations. The entire mass production schedule is easily accomplished in 6 months for most species. This time frame allows bonsai plants to be started soon after the spring busy season for Christmas sales.

It is assumed that a culling process takes place at each stage of the schedule so that materials and time are not wasted on sickly or poorly shaped plants. Only the better plants should be transplanted to quality bonsai containers (which often are quite expensive).

Culls from the above program or an abbreviated program can be used to produce economy grade bonsais which are made by simply offering the appropriate species in a size which is trimmed to rudimentary shape and placed in an economy container which requires little or no root pruning. For a great number of consumers, this grade of plant is all that is necessary or desired. Purchase price is more important for these people than is artistic form or the underlying adaptation of the plant to small pot culture.

A bonsai crop is easily cultured in greenhouses which produce a broad range of miscellaneous products. Most bonsai species will grow well in a variety of temperature and light conditions so that a specialized environment need not be created. They also help utilize excess summer space and labor. In larger market areas, there may be sufficient demand to support specialists who grow bonsai on a large scale for numerous wholesale customers.

Bonsai production can be very profitable but the grower must carefully define production techniques and marketing objectives. Semi-artistic bonsai cannot bc offered at prices which do not reflect the time and production costs which they require. And neither can a grower expect long term demand for a product which offers little distinction from common nursery ornamentals which could be purchased by consumers for 1/2 the cost.

Miscellaneous foliage plants

There are numerous isolated plant species which are utilized as foliage plants at one time or another. Some of the more important ones are discussed briefly below.

The begonias are an extremely large family in which there are hundreds of varieties suitable for occasional foliage use. Some popular ones such as the Rex and Cleopatra begonias have previously been touched upon under the flowering plant chapter of this book.

Begonias are frequently cultured as much for flowers as for foliage. Vigorous blooming generally occurs in tuberous varieties only once or twice a year. Although the floral display can be beautiful, only a few begonia groups have proven successful commercially when grown primarily for flowers.

Neither have begonias found great acceptance as a large volume foliage crop. They are restricted mainly to a rather low growing habit and they bruise and break quite easily in shipment.

The Cycads are a primitive group of plants which resemble palms or stiff leaved ferns. Although a thick trunk is formed with age, younger specimens of the common Sago palm (cycad) do not usually exhibit one since even mature plants have a very short trunk. Sago palms grow slowly and are an excellent long term foliage plant even though expensive to produce. They are tolerant of a wide range of temperatures and will survive brief exposure to below freezing temperatures if acclimated.

The family Acanthaceae contains several familiar plant varieties: polka dot plants (*Hypoestes*), pachystachys (a not too commonly produced flowering plant, usually with yellow bracts), fittonia (nerve plant) and zebra plant (*Aphelandra*). The zebra plant has been fairly popular in the past because of its colorful flowers and distinctive foliage but does not hold up well under most interior landscape conditions. The polka dot plant was discussed under bedding plants but also has wide use in foliage applications, mostly as a filler plant in situations where light intensity is high but filtered. Hypoestes is fast becoming one of the most commonly utilized inexpensive foliage plants.

Hoyas (wax plants or vines) are a large genus in the milk weed family (*Asclepiadaceae*). They are sold in many sizes of containers but ultimately must be repotted to hanging baskets, trellises, or poles since they form twining vines. The leaves are thick and leathery, sometimes assuming odd shapes such as in the Hindu rope variety. Waxy, almost artificial looking clusters of small flowers appear in selected leaf axils. The flowers are long lasting and although they do not make a gaudy display, are well worth the wait.

Hoyas prefer a somewhat cooler production temperature (60-70° F) than most foliage plants and good light is essential. They may be reproduced by taking slightly woody cuttings. Mealybugs are a constant threat to wax plants.

The saxifrage family contains two plant groups that are frequently grown as small foliage plants which will tolerate lower production and display temperatures (55-65° F). The strawberry begonias (also known as strawberry geraniums, or "mother-of-thousands" are small tufted spreaders which are shaped like strawberry plants and reproduce by runners in a

Rex begonias (top), Cleopatra begonia (bottom).

similar manner to the latter. A predominantly green leaved variety (*Saxifraga sarmentosa*) and a variety with green, white, and rosy pink coloration (*Saxifraga sarmentosa tricolor)* are commonly produced. Both prefer good light. The green variety is more vigorous and easily produced although not generally so showy as "tricolor".

Piggy back plant (*Tolmeiea menziesii*) is another low growing saxifrage which is utilized in small pots and hanging baskets. It is native to shaded, cool areas of the northwestern American coast but it will also flourish in shaded foliage houses at 65° F. The leaves are green (although varieties mottled with yellowish-white are available) and usually 2-4 inches broad. Heavier shade and higher temperatures may result in even larger leaves.

In mature piggy back specimens, small plantlets develop on the upper side of leaves where the base meets the leaf stalk. Small purplish dots then appear at the base of the plantlets (these are actually rudimentary roots). When the purplish dots are apparent, roots will readily form within 2-3 weeks if the dots are covered with moist soil. Rooting is accomplished in a shaded, cool spot; no bottom heat is required and plantlets should be misted daily to maintain turgidity.

The banana family contains several plants which are sometimes utilized as indoor foliage and flowers. Perhaps the best known is the striking bird-

Cycas revoluta. **Known as the Sago palm but not a true palm.**

of-paradise (*Strelitzia reginae*) which comes in many variations. It is moderately easy to grow (once established) if excellent light is available. The foliage is rather unspectacular and unless blooms are present, bird-of-paradise has little value as a decorative.

Certain varieties of smaller true banana plants have some interior landscape value but tend towards a ragged appearance and are generally difficult to grow indoors unless adequate light and warmth are available.

The false bird-of-paradise (*Heliconica*) is another group of banana relations which is used mainly for the striking flowers produced. As the name suggests, the plants resemble true birds-of-paradise a good deal but the leaves are softer and plants will not stand so much abuse.

Gingers (*Zingiber*) resemble some bananas but are generally much smaller in size as a group and more useful as ornamentals. In addition to

Hoya carnosa

the striking flowers produced by certain gingers, some of the plants are quite attractive in their own right.

Several useful ornamental species are members of the nettle family (Urticaceae). The largest group is the pileas which includes artillery plants, aluminum plant, big leaf baby tears (*Pilea depressa*), moon valley, creeping Charlie (*Pilea nummularifolia*), and several friendship plants (*Panamiga*).

The pileas are generally rather small plants which are very useful in combination dishgarden work. In this respect they resemble the peperomia family and are equally easy to propagate in a similar manner .

True baby's tears (*Helxine soleirolii*), is also a member of the nettle family. At the higher temperatures and medium light at which most pileas flourish, baby's tears tends to grow quickly into a ragged tangle. It prefers cooler spots and only light shade if a neat, even carpet of foliage is desired.

Tricolor saxifrage

The tiny roundish leaves form a dense carpet of green, making baby's tears a useful vegetative covering for bonsai specimens or other miniature landscapes which are in cool, well lighted areas.

Other names for baby's tears are Irish moss, Japanese moss, or Corsican curse. Perhaps the latter name is indicative of the invasive character which baby's tears displays when it is allowed to become established on the greenhouse floor as a weed.

Purple passion vine (*Gynura sarmentosa*) and Cambridge ivy (*Senecio macroglossus variegatus*) are both vining members of the sunflower family. Both are vigorous growers, and extensively used in hanging baskets Cambridge ivy or variegated wax ivy, as it is sometimes called, is also useful on totem poles or trellises since it actively twines onto any object.

These vines are easy and profitable to grow but are susceptible especially to aphids. Any infestation will quickly spread. Wax ivy is

Piggyback plant

especcially vigorous and must be pinched often to maintain form. Both vines are easily propagated from half mature stem cuttings without need for mist. A surprisingly strong demand is encountered for purple passion and wax ivy in all smaller pot sizes, indicating that the public is well satisfied with the results they obtain from these rambling plants.

Velvet plant (*Gynura aurantiaca*) is a more upright and larger leaved relative which is less commonly grown than purple passion vine.

The preceding discussion of foliage plants cannot do justice to the myriad varieties which are now available for culture. Especially in the more exploited families, there are numerous strains which simply could not even be mentioned. Anyone who is interested in growing foliage plants commercially must become familiar with the hundreds of useful cultivars in order to intelligently select appropriate subjects for production.

The general overview which has been given will perhaps be useful in steering readers towards promising avenues for further investigation.

Purple passion plant

Cambridge ivy

GLOSSARY

The meaning of some words and terms in this book require clarification if the reader does not possess a botanical or horticultural background. Most of the definitions given below can be found fully explained in the text but the general meaning is more quickly available in this glossary.

Abscission – The process whereby various plant parts become separated or detached from the plant. Abscission usually refers to passive separation due to a modification of cell structure at the separation point rather than an active detachment by man, animals, or other physical causes.

Acclimatize – The process of subjecting plants to environmental conditions in the greenhouse or nursery which will help them withstand being placed in home or garden conditions with as little stress as possible.

Acid – Acid conditions are said to exist when the pH of a solution is below 7.0.

Alkaline – Often used interchangeably with the term basic. This usage is not technically correct but is commonly accepted outside the chemical profession. Alkaline soils or solutions are those which have a high concentration of alkali group chemical elements present and almost always have a basic reaction (pH higher than 7.0).

Ammonium Toxicity – A physiological disorder of plants which arises due to the presence of an excess of ammonium (NH_4^+) forms of nitrogen in the soil. Characterized by scorching of the leaf margins and loss of roots. Occurs more frequently in artificial soil mixes. Different species of plants show a high degree of variability in their reaction to ammonium levels.

Annual – A plant which completes its life cycle and dies after the end of one growing season.

Bareroot – An adjective which describes the roots of trees, shrubs, or other perennials as lacking the major portion or all of the soil substrate they were growing in. This condition refers to live but dormant plants which have been harvested in this fashion for transplanting at a different time or location. Less often used to describe a similar condition in herbaceous annual plants.

Basic – Basic conditions are said to exist when the pH of a solution is above 7.0.

Bedding plants – A common term referring to those plants used in flower beds. An expanded meaning often includes all the herbaceous plants marketed for outdoor or patio use.

Biennial – A plant which requires two years to complete its life cycle. The first growing season is spent in vegetative growth and seed is produced during the second season.

Biological test – A means of determining the effects various treatments have upon plants by actually subjecting a test group to the treatment in question. Tests must be carefully designed so that the effects of the treatment can be separated or segregated from other possible influences. Simple biological tests are usually evaluated by visual observations of the effects a treatment may have upon plants, but numerous other criteria, such as chemical analysis, weight measurement, and patterns of plant development, may be used when visual observation is inadequate or inappropriate.

Bracts – Modified leaf tissue which sometimes appears as if it is a part of the flower. The colored bracts of the poinsettia are commonly referred to as the flower.

Break – A term used to denote the new leaves and branches which arise at leaf nodes after pinching has taken place.

Chlorophyll – A molecule which plays a dominant role in the conversion of light energy into chemical energy during photosynthesis.

Chlorosis – A physiological disorder which is characterized by yellowing of the area between the veins on newer leaves. Tissue near the veins remains a darker green. Chlorosis is due to a lack of available iron. A more general meaning may be applied to chlorosis when it is used to describe the overall yellowing of leaf tissue. In this case the disorder may be due to numerous causes.

Cold frame – An enclosed growing structure which admits natural daylight but normally is not equipped with supplementary heat sources. Larger structures of this sort are perhaps more commonly classed as greenhouses.

Compatibility – Generally refers to the ability of two or more chemicals or fertilizers to be used together without altering the initial intended purpose when used separately. Use together (when compared to use of single ingredients) also does not harm plants.

Container plant – A plant which is grown in a container of some sort rather than in open flats, beds, raised benches, or fields. Usually refers to the status of plants at the marketing stage, not earlier growth stages.

Cultivar – A horticultural term which often is used interchangeably with the more scientific word "variety". "Cultivar" is usually associated with cultivated plants while "variety" is more commonly associated with natural populations. Breeding patterns are generally of little significance in delineating cultivars since many cultivars are vegetatively or asexually reproduced. The terms "variety" and "cultivar" are used interchangeably in this book.

Culture indexed plants – Plants which have been carefully evaluated in a laboratory and declared free of the particular bacterial or fungal diseases for which the indexing procedure was designed.

Cutting mix – A soil mix composed of peat and perlite which is described in this book as a medium for rooting cuttings and germinating coarse seed. Sometimes used as a potting mix for certain species.

Daylength – Refers to the length of light period (either natural or artificial) which is given to plants to induce or prevent flowering in plants. Can also be used in a more general sense to describe the period of irradiation plants are subjected to during a 24 hour time span without any particular connection to the flowering process.

DIF– The abbreviation given to a broad subject area which is concerned primarily with the height characteristics of plants as related to the day/night temperature differential under which plants are grown. The abbreviation is commonly used to denote several specific aspects of the subject area in addition to the more general aspects. A detailed meaning is given in the chapter dealing with temperature.

Dormant stock – Plant material which is in a dormant (alive but not actively growing) state. Plants can be dormant while they still have soil around the roots or they can be in a dormant state while being held bareroot.

Disbudding – The early removal of specific flower buds from plants, usually on flowering pot plants or cut flowers – with a desired goal in mind.

Disease – An impairment to plant health or development caused by fungi, viruses, or bacteria. Various other casual factors may be also occasionally included under this term (various nutrient disorders or hormonal imbalances, for example).

Energy efficient heating – Any means of supplying supplemental heat to horticultural crops which utilizes techniques that reduce the BTU input necessary to achieve desired temperature levels. Methods often are technical improvements but can also be related to better use of existing technology.

EPA – The Environmental Protection Agency of the United States of America. Do not confuse this agency with those administered by state governments.

Fertilizer – In common terms, this designation is applied to all of the essential mineral elements or compounds normally taken into the plant through the roots. No distinction is made, unless appropriate, as to whether fertilizers are derived from natural mineral components, organic sources, or created by manufacturing processes. In a broader sense, fertilizer may be used to describe such gases as CO_2 or other compounds or solutions which potentially enhance plant growth if utilized in a beneficial fashion.

Fixed costs – Those greenhouse and nursery expenses which continue regardless of what crops are being grown. Examples: land and building costs, insurance, and real estate taxes. Certain fixed and variable costs categories may be interchanged depending upon the manager's viewpoint of what category it should be placed in.

Flat – A tray used to hold soil or various sizes and designs of plant containers. Many sizes and configurations are available. The most common flat in present day use is made of plastic and measures approximately 11 1/2 by 21 1/4 inches. It is used primarily for bedding plant production.

Foot candle – A standard measurement of the intensity of visible light. Originally formulated as the light intensity generated by a candle at a distance of one foot.

Genetic – A term encompassing those characteristics of living organisms which are transmitted from one generation to the next by groups of messenger molecules called genes.

Genetic engineering – Human directed altering of the content, structure, or location of genetic material in plants.

Germination – The process through which quiescent or dormant seeds become activated to form seedlings. This process is initiated by specific environmental conditions which may vary somewhat among different species.

Graft – The area on a plant where tissue from two previously separate plants has been joined artificially and allowed to grow together. Grafting is a common procedure in woody plant varieties, especially trees and roses.

Growing on – A commonly used term in the greenhouse and nursery industry meaning the growth of smaller plants on to the desired marketing stage. This term may be used as an adjective.

Growth retardant – Any chemical which is used to restrict the height of ornamental plants.

Hybrid – Technically, a plant which has been produced by mating a male and female from two different species. In horticulture and agriculture it is common to use this term even when more closely related groups of plants, such as varieties of the same species, are mated to produce offspring with characteristics of both parents.

Induction – The process whereby a life function of plants is caused to begin by the presence or absence of a factor or combination of factors.

Initiation – Generally used synonymously with "induction" but may sometimes be used to describe the beginning of life functions which needed no direct causative factor or factors.

Integrated Pest Management (IPM) – A term often employed to denote the use of two or more separate pest control methods together in a program which relates the effects of each method to all others. Also encompasses disease control.

Leach – Application of water or fertilizer solutions in excess of what the soil can hold so that some portion of the applied liquid exits through the drain holes of pots. Dissolved mineral elements are carried out with the drainage. Leaching is important to prevent a buildup of mineral salts in the soil.

Leaf node – That point on the stem of a plant where the leaf is attached.

Life cycle – The total collection of rhythmic patterns of reproduction, growth, development, and dying which plants, animals, insects, microorganisms, and disease organisms go through in completion of their existence as individuals.

Long day – A term used to describe the duration of light required to induce a flowering response in a particular plant variety. Can also be used as an adjective to describe that variety. Plants are termed long day when flowers are initiated as succeeding days become longer after a critical threshold duration is reached.

Medium – As it relates to plants, this noun may mean any environmental background (gaseous, aqueous, etc.) into which plants are introduced. However, it most commonly refers to the soil or soil-like substrate in which the root mass is anchored.

Micronutrients – Those mineral fertilizer elements which are required by plants in very minute quantities.

Mineral elements – When applied to plant growth and development, the term "mineral elements" refers to those necessary or required chemical elements which are normally absorbed by the roots singly or in molecular forms from the soil substrate. In certain circumstances (foliar nutrient application and hydroponic nutrient solutions, for example), the necessary mineral elements are absorbed through other avenues and modified substrates.

Mycorrhizae – A specialized type of plant association between two or more microorganisms or between microorganisms and higher plants. Discussed in further detail in Chapter 12 of this book.

Necrotic – Dead.

Nitrogen depletion – The using up of nitrogen in the soil by microorganisms. Nitrogen depletion occurs when a large supply of undecayed organic matter acts as a source of food for microorganism growth. The organisms also require nitrogen so they use up what is present in the soil and leave little or none for plant growth unless more nitrogen is added than the microorganisms are capable of using.

Nutrient – Usually taken to mean the essential mineral elements which normally enter the plant through the root system (also may mean the same mineral elements when applied as foliar sprays). This term less often is understood to include any substance which is naturally necessary for plant growth and development (e.g. CO_2, H_2O, etc.).

Organic matter – Any substance which contains carbon. In this book usually taken to mean carbonaceous substances derived from dead plant or animal tissue. Most often refers to the dead plant materials which form a part of natural soils or man-made root media.

Packs – A trade term used to describe a generally shallow, rectangular container in which bedding plants are grown and sold. The container may or may not have individual compartments and several packs are usually grouped to fit into a flat.

Pasteurization – The process of subjecting soils to steam heat to kill pests or disease causing organisms in the soil.

Patent – A legal entity issued by the United States government which protects the patent holder from unlawful infringement upon the patentable aspects of a particular plant, process, invention, etc. The prospective patent holder must prove sufficient evidence of originality of the product or process in order to receive protection. Patents are generally valid worldwide, but the intricacies of world law often make enforcement difficult on an international basis.

Plant patents cover asexually produced new creations and selections but do not generally cover those produced by sexual reproductive methods.

Perennial – A plant which does not die within a specified number of growing seasons but maintains the capacity to grow anew each year from dormant tissue.

Petroleum carrier – Oil base compounds which are used to dilute certain pesticides.

Pest – Any plant or animal organism not classified as fungi, bacteria, or virus which impairs plant health or growth. Also commonly refers to any organism living in a location where it is not wanted.

pH – A scale of measurement which denotes the degree of acidity or alkalinity. pH reflects the concentration of hydrogen ions in a solution. Acidity or alkalinity changes by a factor 10 for each unit change in the pH scale. Readings below 7.0 are acid while those above 7.0 are alkaline.

Photo oxidation – The degradation of materials caused by light energy incident upon them.

Photoperiod – The duration of light periods to which plants are subjected.

Photosynthesis – A biochemical reaction which is unique to green plants. Transient light energy is converted to the chemical energy contained in plant compounds.

Physiological drought – A deficiency of water in plants caused by the inability of plants to take up water for various reasons even though sufficient water may be present in the environment.

Phytotoxic – Poisonous to plants.

Pinch – The action of removing the growing tip of plant stems. The actual tip of the stem is removed rather than just the enclosing leaves. Usually performed to promote branching and sometimes to reduce height.

Plant breeding – Usually describes a process by which plants of the same species are sexually mated or "crossed" under controlled conditions. Under exceptional circumstances, even different species may be crossed. However, in the latter situation, very few offspring are normally produced – and very few of these progeny are fertile. "Plant breeding" may also be used to circumscribe the entire concept or field of crop improvement through planning, breeding, selection, testing, and release.

Plug – As it relates to plants, this term generally means any young containerized plant (or sometimes even older ones) which are being grown for eventual transplanting to a larger finishing container. Most commonly the name given to very small bedding or perennial plants grown in multicell packs but not intended for final marketing to consumers in these small containers.

Pollution – Usually refers to a departure from naturally occurring levels for specific measurable environmental components. A very imprecise and often carelessly used word which has greatly differing definitions and connotations to people.

Propagation – The process of producing new plants from the previous generation.

Propagator – A grower who reproduces new plants by seed or vegetative means. This term is generally reserved for those specialists who derive a major portion of their income through supplying starter plants to other growers.

Pruning – The act of eliminating unwanted branches or roots (or portions of them) from a plant. Can be done for several desired effects.

Relative humidity – A measure of the amount of water present as vapor in the air.

Reproduction, asexual – The process of increase in number of individual plants without the union of male and female gametes (no embryo formed). One hundred percent of the genetic material of the offspring is received from the "mother" plant from which divisions, cuttings, bulbs, vegetative cells, or other nonsexual tissue is used to generate new individual plants.

Reproduction, sexual – The process of increase in number of individual plants through the union of male and female gametes (to form seeds or embryos). In this process, approximately 1/2 of the genetic material of offspring is received from the male parent and 1/2 from the female parent.

Respiration – A biochemical reaction in which energy is released through the oxidation or "burning" of chemical compounds by plants and animals.

Return on investment – Profits divided by the total capital invested in a business. The quotient is then expressed as a percentage.

Risk control – A systematically employed method by which adverse possible outcomes for a project are reduced.

Root spiraling – A condition which occurs when plants have been grown in the same restrictive container for extended periods. The roots begin to wind around the container wall in a circular path. Usually thought of as an unhealthy condition which can cause poor growth response in the future.

Rooting mix – The soil mix composed of peat and perlite described in this book for use in rooting cuttings and germinating coarse seed. Occasionally utilized for growing on varieties which require especially well drained soil.

Salt index – A measurement of the amount of soluble salts a fertilizer adds to the soil solution when compared with equal amounts by weight of other fertilizers.

Seed – A specialized structure produced by plants which contains a quiescent juvenile plant stage (embryo) along with various protective coats and food reserves. Seeds are the result of sexual reproduction, whereby male and female gametes from different parents are united.

Seed, modified – Seed which has been altered in some manner in order to enhance the germination process or to facilitate the sowing process. May also refer to various sorting procedures which do not actually alter the seed but merely improve germination by eliminating dead or substandard seed from a batch.

Selection – As it relates to horticulture, plant varieties, or cultivars, selection refers first to the conscious erection of specific criteria for choosing which individual plants are to be allowed to be grown as a crop line and which ones will be removed from the crop line; second, it refers to the actual process of implementing the criteria chosen.

Shade – Refers in general to the condition existing when some portion of the sun's rays are prevented from striking an object. Applied in a more limited sense to the use of blackcloth to alter daylengths for manipulation of the flowering response in plants.

Shadehouse – A structure which prevents the full intensity of natural sunlight from reaching the crops placed in it.

Short day – A term used to describe the duration of light required to induce a flowering response in a particular plant variety. Can also be used as an adjective to describe that variety. Plants are termed short day when flowers are initiated as succeeding days become shorter after a critical threshold duration is reached.

Shrub – The common name given to a rather large group of woody perennial plants which are characterized by being generally smaller than trees and possessing a multi-stemmed growth pattern which originates at or near ground level (as opposed to trees which have a single trunk for a reasonable distance above the soil line).

Single stem – Plants which are not pinched to promote development of side shoots. Only one stem is allowed to grow and flower on each plant.

Soluble salts – The amount of total chemical "salts" dissolved in a solution. Usually refers to water, fertilizer, or soil solutions and is often more accurately termed "total dissolved solids." Can be measured by different methods (such as parts per million or electrical conductivity) which will yield related but different results and is expressed with several different symbols. Workers must be very careful to know both the methods of determination and expression in order to interpret results correctly.

Sow – A term commonly used to denote the entire process of seed planting. Sometimes taken to mean only the operation of placing seed in the germination substrate.

Specialist grower – A horticultural producer who concentrates upon growing a limited range of crops. The limitations may be defined by variety, stage of growth, or other important characteristics. The degree of specialization varies from case to case, therefore allowing the term to be used as an approximation of actual circumstances.

Species – A population of plants which breeds freely amongst members to produce fertile offspring and which shares similar attributes that usually make it more or less easily distinguishable from other related groups. The signal characteristic of a species in the scientific sense is that different species do not breed with one another to produce fertile offspring under the great majority of natural conditions. "Species" is a very controversial and complex concept, the finer points of which are better left out of discussion in this book.

Stock plant – Plants selected to serve as "mothers" for vegetative reproduction, usually chosen for specific desirable characteristics and overall health. Often grown under special sanitary conditions.

Tissue culture – A means of asexual plant reproduction which requires only a small group or a single vegetative mother cell and which requires special laboratory conditions of sanitation and environmental control.

Toxic – Poisonous or harmful to any form of life. Most often used as a term to describe this action upon useful or desirable organisms.

Transplant – The act of removing plants from one rooting medium or container, with all or part of the roots intact, to another medium or container. When used as a noun, this term refers to the actual plant being so moved.

Tree – A woody plant which usually has only one main stalk at or near ground level. Most trees are rather tall in growth habit.

Turgid – Refers to the condition of plant cells when they contain enough water to be in a normal expanded state. When water is lacking to fill the interior of cells the plant becomes wilted.

Turgor pressure – The pressure which water contained in plant cells exerts against the cell wall in an outward direction. Turgor pressure causes cells to be turgid.

Variable cost – Those greenhouse or nursery expenses which change appreciably depending upon the particular crop being grown and upon the level of greenhouse or nursery utilization. Examples: cuttings, seed, soil, chemicals. Certain fixed and variable costs categories may be interchanged depending upon the manager's viewpoint of what category it should be placed in.

Variety – A population of plants which shares similar attributes that usually make it more or less distinguishable from other populations within a species. Unlike different species, varieties within a species generally can easily interbreed to produce fertile offspring when occupying the same or overlapping spatial territories.

Vegetative – Refers to the maintenance of plants in a non-sexually reproductive state. Often used in a general sense to denote the green growth made by plants as opposed to production of flower organs.

Vegetative propagation – Producing new plants by means of cuttings, tissue culture, bulbs, corms, and tubers. The sexual process of mating male and female plants to produce seed is avoided and all resulting new plants are genetically identical.

APPENDIX

USEFUL INFORMATION

Major Horticultural Dates

Category	Holiday	2000	2001	2002	2003	2004
Flowers	St. Valentine's Day	Feb.14	Feb.14	Feb.14	Feb.14	Feb.14
Flowers	Easter Sunday	Apr.23	Apr.15	Mar.31	Apr.20	Apr.11
Flowers & Foliage	Secretary's Day	Apr.26	Apr.25	Apr.24	Apr.23	Apr.21
Trees & Flowers	Mother's Day	May 14	May 13	May 12	May 11	May 9
Trees & Flowers	Memorial Day	May 29	May 28	May 27	May 26	May 31
Trees & Flowers	Father's Day	June 18	June 17	June 16	June 15	June 20
Flowers	Thanksgiving	Nov.23	Nov.22	Nov.28	Nov.27	Nov.25
Flowers, Trees, & Foliage	Christmas	Dec.25	Dec.25	Dec.25	Dec.25	Dec.25
Trees & Shrubs	Earth Day } Arbor Day }	Last 2 weeks in April each year. Either or both may be important in your local area.				

U.S. Cooperative Extension Service

Write to the main office in your state for helpful literature, information on soil testing, and specific information concerning your particular crop. Or call the local office if your county has one.

Alabama
Auburn University
Auburn, AL 36849

Alaska
University of Alaska
Fairbanks, AK 99701

Arizona
University of Arizona
Tucson, AZ 85721

Arkansas
P.O. Box 391
Little Rock, AR 72203

California
University of California
2200 University Ave.
Berkeley, CA 94720

Colorado
Colorado State University
Fort Collins, CO 80523

Connecticut
University of Connecticut
Storrs, CT 06269

Delaware
University of Delaware
Newark, DE 19716

District of Columbia
Federal City College
1424 K. Street NW
Washington, D.C. 20005

Florida
University of Florida
Gainesville, FL 32611

U.S. Cooperative Extension Service (cont.)

Georgia
University of Georgia
Athens, GA 30602

Hawaii
University of Hawaii
Honolulu, HI 96822

Idaho
University of Idaho
Morill Hall
Moscow, ID 83843

Illinois
University of Illinois
Urbana, IL 61801

Iowa
Iowa State University
Ames, IA 50011

Kansas
Kansas State University
Manhattan, KS 66506

Kentucky
University of Kentucky
Lexington, KY 40546

Louisiana
Louisiana State University
Baton Rouge, LA 70803

Maine
University of Maine
Orono, ME 04469

Maryland
University of Maryland
College Park, MD 20742

Massachusetts
University of Mass.
Amherst, MA 48824

Michigan
Michigan State University
East Lansing, MI 48824

Minnesota
University of Minnesota
St. Paul, MN 55455

Mississippi
Mississippi State Univ.
Mississippi State, MS
39762

U.S. Cooperative Extension Service (cont.)

Missouri
University of Missouri
Columbia, MO 65211

Montana
Montana State University
Bozeman, MT 59717

Nebraska
University of Nebraska
Lincoln, NE 68588

Nevada
University of Nevada
Reno, NV 89557

New Hampshire
Univ. of New Hampshire
Taylor Hall
Durham, NH 03824

New Jersey
Rutgers — The State Univ.
New Brunswick, NJ 08903

New Mexico
New Mexico State Univ.
Las Cruces, NM 88003

New York
New York State Col. of Ag.
Ithaca, NY 14853

North Carolina
North Carolina State Univ.
Raleigh, NC 27695

North Dakota
North Dakota State Univ.
Fargo, ND 58105

Ohio
Ohio State University
Columbus, OH 43210

Oklahoma
Oklahoma State Univ.
Stillwater, OK 74078

Oregon
Oregon State University
Corvallis, OR 97331

Pennsylvania
Pennsylvania State Univ.
University Park, PA 16802

U.S. Cooperative Extension Service (cont.)

Puerto Rico
University of Puerto Rico
Rio Piedras, Puerto Rico
00931

Rhode Island
University of Rhode Island
Kingston, RI 02881

South Carolina
Clemson University
Clemson, SC 29634

South Dakota
South Dakota State Univ.
Brookings, SD 57007

Tennessee
University of Tennessee
P.O. Box 1071
Knoxville, TN 37996

Texas
Texas A&M University
College Station, TX 77843

Utah
Utah State University
Logan, UT 84322

Vermont
University of Vermont
Burlington, VT 05405

Virginia
Virginia Polytechnic
Institute and State Univ.
Blacksburg, VA 24601

Washington
Washington State Univ.
Pullman, WA 99164

West Virginia
West Virginia University
Morgantown, WV 26506

Wisconsin
University of Wisconsin
Madison, WI 53706

Wyoming
University of Wyoming
Box 3354, Univ. Station
Laramie, WY 82071

Internet addresses

United States
Department of Agriculture
Cooperative State Research and Extension Service
http://www.reeusda.gov/new/csrees.htm

United States
Department of Agriculture
http://www.usda.gov

United States
Agriculture Statistics
http://www.usda.gov/nass/

United States
Department of Agriculture
Plants Database
http://www.plants.usda.gov/plants/plntmenu.html

U.S. Small Business Administration
http://www.sbaonline.sba.gov

United States
Department of Commerce
http://www.doc.gov

United States
Environmental Protection Agency
http://www.epa.gov

National Weather Service
http://www.nws.noaa.gov

Internet addresses (cont.)

Plant Web
http://www.plantweb.com
(an excellent source for
horticultural links)

American Horticultural Society
http://www.ahs.org/

American Society of Horticultural Science
http://www.ashs.org/

**American Nursery and Landscape
Association**
http://www.anla.org

Associated Landscape Contractors of America
http://www.alca.org

Southern Nursery Association
http://www.sna.org

National Gardening Association
http://www.garden.org/nga/

National Geographic Society
World Maps, features, weather, etc.
http://www.nationalgeographic.com

Parts Per Million (ppm)
Made Easier

Although a conceptual idea of ppm (parts per million) is reasonably easy to visualize and keep in mind (see glossary and chapters on fertilizer and water), accurate expression of this term is particularly devilish. There are several factors which contribute to this situation, namely:

1. There are numerous units of expression.
2. Conversion from unit to unit is confusing and must be done with extreme care.
3. Symbols used for units of expression often sound and look the same but possess minute but important differences.
4. Misapplication and incomplete definition and expression of symbols is common in literature sources.
5. Different information sources often use different figures for approximations of the same theoretical values – therefore leading the novice into much confusion.
6. PPM (total dissolved solids for all practical purposes) and EC (electrical conductivity) are often mistakenly understood to refer to the same value. The terms are sometimes erroneously used interchangeably. They are related but not equal!
7. Literature sources have frequently changed the commonly accepted unit for both ppm and EC over the years, leading to confusion even among purported experts.
8. Ingredient impurities are sometimes not taken into account when ppm figures are calculated. This is especially important with fertilizers.

The author presents a short list of conversion factors and formulas below in the hopes of making life easier for the daily grower. While these figures and expressions have been repeatedly checked, the author does not guarantee them to be the final word or totally error free. Each grower should double check important calculations to make sure both the math and the conceptual understanding are correct. The grower is responsible for making certain that literature sources yield the same answers, and, if not, why they differ.

Parts Per Million (ppm) Made Easier (cont.)

The prefixes u (micro) and m (milli) are related thusly: 1000 umhos = 1 millimhos (or any other measurement designation).

1ppm = $\Big\}$
1 mg/kg by weight (1 milligram per kilogram)
1 ug/g by weight (1 microgram per gram)
1 mg/l weight/volume (1 milligram per liter)
1 ul/l volume/volume (1 microliter per liter)

75ppm = 1 ounce of any 100% pure fertilizer element (totally dissolved) in 100 gallons of water.

– or –

75ppm = 75 (constant) x 1.0 (100% pure)

PPM may be measured directly through weight or volume measures or indirectly through measurement of electrical conductivity of the solution in question. Though EC is related to ppm, it is not equal – the following formula will provide conversion with an error range of approximately 10-20%, depending upon the chemical makeup of the solution. This error range is why literature sources may vary regarding the constant factor used for multiplication.

deciSiemens = ds   milliSiemens = ms   millimhos = mmhos

To estimate total ppm salts in solution (total dissolved salts or TDS), multiply electrical conductivity readings (in ds/m, ms/cm, or mmhos/cm – all can be used interchangeably) by 666. Older instruments may read in umhos/cm (micromhos), in which case ppm is obtained by multiplying umhos by 0.666 (see chapter 7 for further examples).

Area determinations

Triangle

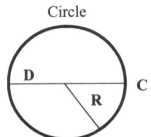

$$A=\frac{W \times H}{2}$$

Rectangle

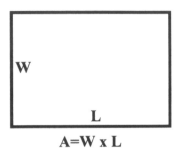

$$A=W \times L$$

Circle

A=3.142 x R xR
C=3.142 x D
R=D÷2
D=2 x R
(Pi=3.142)

Trapezoid

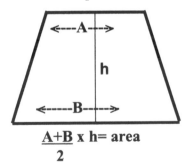

$$\frac{A+B}{2} \times h= area$$

Area determinations (cont.)

Hexagon

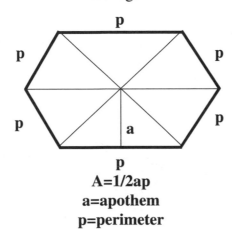

A=1/2ap
a=apothem
p=perimeter

Irregularly shaped area

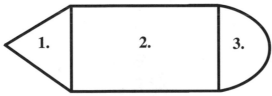

The sum of:
1.area of triangle
2. Area of rectangle
3. Area of circle
divided by 2

Farenheit/Celsius conversion

$$^0F = (1.8 \text{ x} ^0C) + 32$$

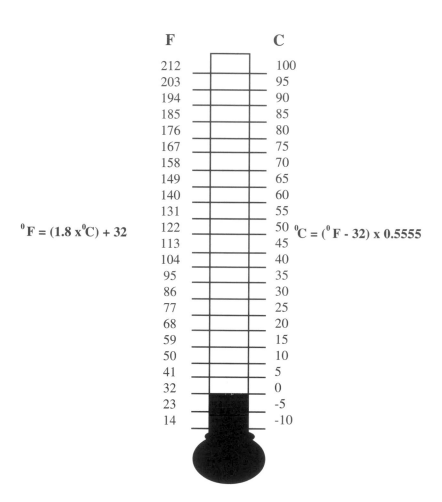

$$^0C = (^0F - 32) \text{ x } 0.5555$$

Decimal gallon/ounce equivalents	
.25 gallon =	32 ounces 1 quart
.5 gallon =	64 ounces 2 quarts
.75 gallon =	96 ounces 3 quarts
1.0 gallon =	128 ounces 4 quarts

Percent to ratio conversions		
2.0%	=	1:50
1.0%	=	1:100
0.8%	=	1:128
0.5%	=	1:200

^ ^ ^

Frequently used fertilizer injection ratios.

Loan repayment table
Term Amount: $10,000 Interest: 7%
5 years: $198.02 per month 10 years: $116.11 15 years: $89.89 20 years: $77.53 25 years: $70.68

Approximate pot volumes	
Pot size	Number filled by 1 cubic yard
4" standard	1,293
4" azalea	1,616
6" standard	397
6" azalea	488.7
8" standard	176

Dry measure

3 level teaspoons	=	1 level tablespoon
16 level tablespoons	=	1 cupful
2 cupfuls	=	1 pint
1 dry pint	=	33.6003 cu. in.
1 dry pint	=	.01994 cu. ft.
1 dry pint	=	.55061 liter
2 pints	=	1 quart
1 dry quart	=	67.2006 cu. in.
8 quarts	=	1 peck
4 pecks	=	1 bushel

Ounces to Grams conversion

Ounces	Grams	Ounces	Grams
1/2	14.175	1/256	.111
1	28.349	1/128	.221
2	56.698	1/64	.443
Seed quantities often measured in these sizes >>		1/32	.886
		1/16	1.772
		1/8	3.544
		1/4	7.087

Liquid measure

1 level tablespoon	3 level teaspoons
1 cupful	.5 pint 8 fluid ounces 16 tablespoons
1 fluid ounce (U.S.)	2 tablespoons 29.57 mililiters
1 pint (U.S.)	16 fluid ounces 2 cupfuls 473.2 mililiters
1 quart (U.S.)	32 fluid ounces 2 pints .9463 liter
1 gallon (U.S.)	128 fluid ounces 8 pints 4 quarts .1337 cubic feet 231 cubic inches 3.785 liter

Media ph
for soilless organic media

Extremely low	4.5 or less
Slightly low	5.0 to 5.1
Optimum	5.2 to 5.5
Slightly high	5.6 to 5.8
Extremely high	6.9 +

Metric equivalent

1 square centimeter	=	.1550 square inches
1 square inch	=	6.452 square centimeters
1 square decimeter	=	.1076 square foot
1 square foot	=	9.2903 sq. decimeters
1 square meter	=	1.196 square yards
1 square yard	=	.8361 square meter
1 acre	=	160 square rods
1 square rod	=	.00625 acre

Approx. Metric equivalents

1 decimeter	=	4 inches
1 meter	=	1.1 yards
1 kilometer	=	5/8 mile
1 kilogram	=	2 1/5 pounds
1 metric ton	=	2,204.6 pounds

Metric vs. English measurement		
1 centimeter	=	.3937 inches
1 inch	=	2.54 centimeters
1 foot	=	30.48 centimeters
1 meter	=	39.37 inches
1 meter	=	100 centimeters
1 meter	=	1.094 yards
1 meter	=	1,000 millimeters
1 yard	=	.914 meters
1 mile	=	1609.344 meters
1 kilometer	=	1000 meters
1 kilometer	=	.62317 miles
1 sq. centimeter	=	.155 sq. inches
1 cubic centimeter	=	.061 cubic inches
1 fluid ounce	=	30 milliliters
1 liter	=	1.057 quarts

Table for small quantities of spray materials from label recommendations quoted at 100 gallonss.

Liquids

Amt. per 100 gal.	Amt per 1 gal.	Approx. dilutions
1 pt	1 tsp	1-800
1 qt	2 tsp	1-400
2 qt	4 tsp	1-200
1 gal	8 tsp	1-100
5 gal	1 cup	1-20

Powder

Amt. per 100 gal.	Amt. per 1 gal.	Approx. dilutions
1/2 lb	3/4 tsp	1-1600
1 lb	1 1/2 tsp	1-800
2 1/2 lb	4 tsp	1-350
5 lb	8 tsp	1-160
10 lb	5 Tbs	1-80

Plant Density for Rectangular Perennial Beds

Size of Bed and Sq. Ft.	Planted 4 inches apart		Planted 6 inches apart		Planted 8 inches apart	
	Plants per Sq. Ft.	Total # Plants	Plants per Sq. Ft.	Total # Plants	Plants per Sq. Ft.	Total # Plants
10x10 Feet = 100 Sq. Ft.	9	900	4	400	2.25	225
10x20 Feet = 200 Sq. Ft.	9	1800	4	800	2.25	450
10x30 Feet = 300 Sq. Ft.	9	2700	4	1200	2.25	675
20x20 Feet = 400 Sq. Ft.	9	3600	4	1600	2.25	900
20x30 Feet = 600 Sq. Ft.	9	5400	4	2400	2.25	1350
30x30 Feet = 900 Sq. Ft.	9	8100	4	3600	2.25	2025

Daylength
(Approx. Dates)

Longest day
Northern hemisphere

———————————————————— June 22

Shortest day
Southern hemisphere

Longest day
Southern hemisphere

———————————————————— December 22

Shortest day
Northern hemisphere

Equinox ——————————————— March 22
                                    September 22

Two equinoxes occur each year. They are the 2 times each year when the sun crosses the equator, hence day and night are everywhere of equal length.

LD$_{50}$ – Probable lethal quanities of orally ingested substances related to various human LD 50 ranges

LD$_{50}$: The lethal dosage for 50% of test animals expressed as milligrams of toxicant per kilogram of body weight.

EPA category rating	EPA pesticide label "signal" word
I. Highly Hazardous	Danger–Poison
II. Moderately Hazardous	Warning
III. Slightly Hazardous	Caution
IV. Relatively nonhazardous	Caution

LD 50 range	Quantity of substance ingested orally
I. 0 to 50 mg.	A taste or a few drops.
II. 50 to 500 mg.	1 teaspoon to 2 tablespoons or 1 ounce.
III. 500 to 5000 mg.	2 tablespoons or 1 ounce to 1 pint or pound.
IV. 5000 mg or over.	Over 1 pint or pound.

Lethal Doses of common substances

Aspirin	1750 mg
Caffeine	200
Nicotine	50
Tylenol	3700

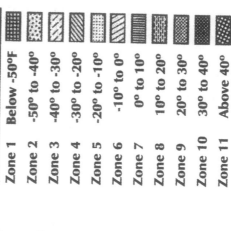

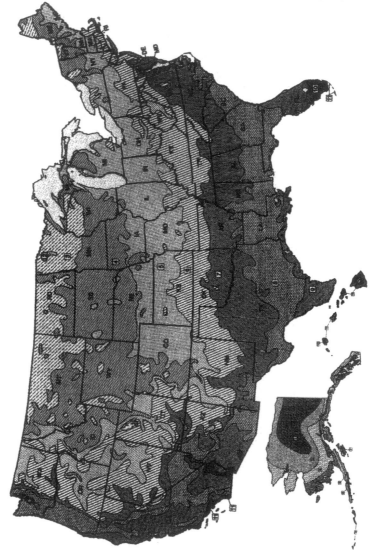

Probable Last Frost Dates

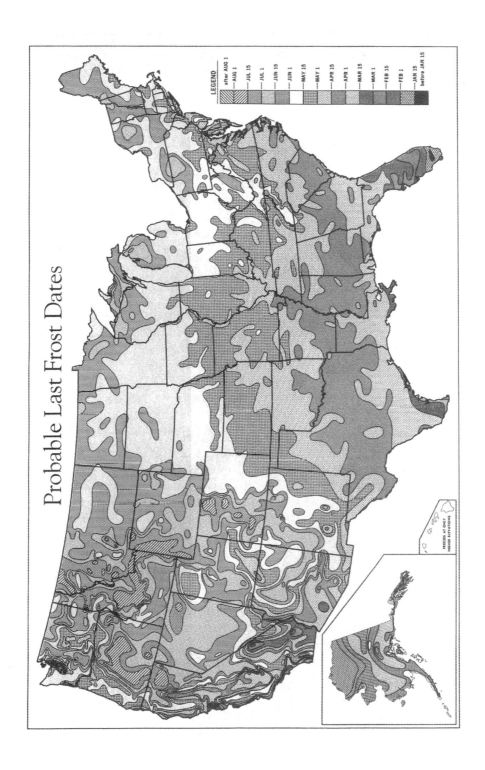

LEGEND

- after AUG 1
- AUG 1
- JUL 15
- JUL 1
- JUN 15
- JUN 1
- MAY 15
- MAY 1
- APR 15
- APR 1
- MAR 15
- MAR 1
- FEB 15
- FEB 1
- JAN 15
- before JAN 15

FREEZE AT ONLY
HIGHER ELEVATIONS

**Step by step
seed sowing for beginners**

The instructions given below have been prepared as an example for seed which is relatively easy to germinate and has no special environmental requirements. They ensure that no detail will be overlooked. Use them as a step-by-step guide. If your seed and materials are of high quality, you can be assured of success on the first try. You may substitute numbers and sizes of materials if they are appropriate but **do not** alter the directions for care either in substance or sequence. Use of raw, untreated seed is assumed.

The illustrations give an idea of the exact materials needed. These requirements should be easily available at local garden shops. If germination containers which fit 6 per flat are not in stock, you can substitute small tinfoil cakepans or styrofoam containers – be sure holes are punched in the bottoms to allow excess water to drain.

When seed is being germinated (sprouted), place it in the soil-filled open containers which fit 6 per flat (the open holding tray). When seed has sprouted and developed into plants ready for transplanting, the small plants should be transplanted to the individual cells in packs which fit 72 cells per flat. The exact numbers in container configurations are unimportant; they refer only to the illustrations given.

A clear dome is placed on top of flats which contain the germination containers. This creates a humid atmosphere surrounding the seed germination containers. Place domes over the seed flats after seed has been planted and watered.

The seed germination formulas described in Chapter 5 (or suitable alternatives) should be used for germination without addition of other ingredients. They can also be used as the soil for transplanting seedlings into later. Keep the soil in closed bags or other containers so that it does not dry out. Do not fill planting containers until shortly before use so that the soil does not dry appreciably. Soil is not actually harmed by drying out, but it does become harder to handle.

If soil accidentally dries out, the easiest way to wet it up again is to add a small amount of water to the bag, mix in, and allow to stand overnight with the top closed. Soil of proper moisture content should ball up when it is compressed as you make a fist, but the ball will easily fall apart when touched. No water should drip from the

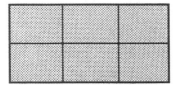

*Top view of germination containers
after placement in flats.*

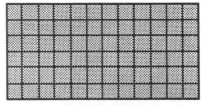

*Top view of transplanting containers
(cell pack) after placement in flats.*

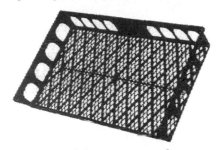

*Flats without containers
inserted.*

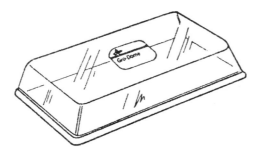

Dome

soil as it is compressed tightly in your fist. If it does, your soil is too wet and should be allowed to dry somewhat by leaving the top of the bag open.

Seed handling stage

- Avoid exposure of seed to temperature extremes. Temperatures above 90° F for extended periods are harmful to many seeds (even when they are still in the seed packets). Cold temperatures are not generally so deleterious.
- Seed should be left in the packets and stored in a dry, cool spot. Any type of moisture (even that in humid air) is harmful to seed if it is exposed before germination is desired.
- Most perennials germinate better if seed is chilled for 2-3 weeks before sprouting. This can be accomplished in the non-freezing portion of a refrigerator. But remember, put at least 2 tightly sealed moisture proof barriers between your seed and the moist refrigerator atmosphere.
- Do not misplace labels included in the seed. It is important to have your plants correctly labeled. Don't open more than 1 seed packet at a time, this will help avoid getting labels confused.
- Protect seed from insects and rodents. One mouse can destroy all your seed within a few minutes.
- Do not store seed in direct sunlight; it is preferable to place it in the dark until it is to be used. Light is essential to proper germination in many species so good light must be allowed when the germination process begins unless labels indicate that dark conditions are necessary.
- Most plant seed can be stored under proper conditions for at least 1 year. There is often a slow loss of vigor but acceptable germination should still occur if good storage procedures have been followed. Only a few plant species show a quick loss of viability (most of these are tropical plants).

Seed germination stage

A. Make sure of what growing and marketing schedule you want to follow.

- Greeen transplants which are ready for the garden plot or for larger pots will usually require about 8 weeks (faster growing species), 10-12 weeks (medium growing species), and 12-16 weeks (slower growing species). This time frame includes the 1-2 weeks necessary for germination to occur. The time schedules just mentioned refer basically to many common annuals and perennials that are easily germinated and grown.

- If you decide to follow a spring sowing schedule, another factor which will help determine when you should sow seed is the date of last frost in your area (you may look this up in locally available weather records or call the county agricultural agent). Unless you intend to protect seedlings from frosty nights, you will want to wait until about 4 weeks before the last frost date to sprout faster growing species. Seeds sown earlier may become too tall and spindly in the indoor heat and shade before you can move them outside without fear of freezes. Add the appropriate amount of extra time for medium (2-4 weeks) and slower (4-8 weeks) growing species. This is a schedule which does not require controlled temperature greenhouse conditions.

  Please note that the above time schedule assumes transplanting to the garden or larger containers will take place before small pots become root bound. Seeds could be planted 2-3 weeks earlier to allow for any problems or less than optimum growing conditions which might be encountered; even if there were no problems, these earlier plants would still be quite usable.

B. Maintain clean conditions in the seed planting area.

C. Prepare labels with the date of sowing and any other information you might wish. Use a pencil or waterproof pen.

D. Fill the small, open seed trays with soil. Lift each tray up with a hand at each end, and drop it on the bench from a height of about 4 inches – this will settle the soil. Then scrape the excess soil from the top of the tray with a small board. If the trays are not completely and evenly full, add some soil by hand and scrape it off evenly with the board.

E. Open the seed packet and arrange it in your fingers so that light taps with your first finger will allow seeds to slowly slide out onto the soil surface prepared previously. Some people prefer to transfer seed to a folded piece of stiff white paper for this operation. Do not clump seed in one area of the flat.

  Deposit about 150 of the seeds of 1 variety evenly onto the surface of 1 small tray (6 open small trays fit into a flat).

F. After the seed has been applied evenly to the soil surface, rub some new soil between the palms of your hands onto the surface so that larger seed is covered by about 1/8 inch of loose soil. **Do not cover seed too heavily**. No covering at all is better than a thick application. Although light is required for best germination in some species, the small amount of soil covering used here will allow adequate germination in most cases.

G. Place a name tag in each seed container after it has been planted.

H. Water the planted seed trays lightly and quickly with a fan sprinkler head about 5 times. *This is a critical operation – practice it a few times before you do it with actual seed containers.* Don't let large water droplets bounce seed around, and don't put water on so quickly as to cause puddles which can cause seed to wash away. Only enough water should be applied to keep the soil moist until seeds germinate – do not soak it until soggy. Overly wet soil prevents the seeds from receiving enough air to sprout.

I. Place the smaller seed trays into larger flats pictured earlier, and cover the flat with a clear dome which should fit closely around the edge of the flat. Make sure the dome fits reasonably tight over the flat and is not held up by labels or other obstructions. If you lack a dome, use loose fitting Saran Wrap or a sheet of plastic.

J. Put the covered seed flats in a place where the temperature stays about 55-75° F, depending upon temperature requirements of the species. Day temperatures of up to 85° F are okay for short periods, but the temperature should cool down at night. Do not place seed flats on top of the TV, refrigerator, or near sunny windows where heat may build up quickly under the dome. **Excess heat can kill seed.** Do not place seed in a completely dark area, some species require light for germination. Look at the planted seed containers every 2 days and give extra water if the soil surface has dried to any extent. The soil surface should never be allowed to dry up.

K. As soon as sprouting occurs, **make sure the dome is removed** and seedlings are placed in bright light. You will want to place sun loving species in direct sunlight the second day after sprouting. Shade species need continued lower light levels.
Leaving seedlings under the dome too long can lead to major disease losses – take the dome off as soon as seed is sprouted! Unless the soil is still extremely wet, a light watering is advisable when the dome is removed.

L. Now allow seedlings to grow indoors under full sunlight, if applicable, and cool night conditions (45-55° F), or they can be placed outdoors in a protected area – they should not be allowed to freeze. Water as necessary when the soil becomes dry. There is no need for fertilizer because the soil formula recommended contains enough for plants at this stage. Poor light, excessive moisture, and too warm conditions are the most common problems encountered in this stage of growth. Keep an inexpensive thermometer handy during germination and seedling stages, this will help you monitor temperature more carefully. Remember, we are interested in the temperature at plant level.

The seedling transplant stage

A. The stage at which transplanting of seedlings takes place varies somewhat with the preference of the grower. It usually occurs soon after seedlings become easy to handle with the fingers but before extensive spread of the root system takes place. Overgrown seedlings will be severely injured in the transplanting operation.

B. Dig under the seedlings with a finger or dibble stick and lift plants out. Then place the seedling in a hole you have poked into the soil present in a small cell pack container. Once the roots are in the hole, press dirt firmly around them so that the roots and soil make good contact. When an entire flat of seedlings has been transplanted, water the plants in lightly. It doesn't hurt to have 2 or 3 seedlings per-pot if you have plenty of them – but 1 will do.

C. If your seedling transplants are to be in an area of bright sun, shade them lightly for 3-4 days and water again only if needed. Then allow plants to have full sun and begin normal irrigation as needed.

D. Now allow plants to grow indoors or outdoors in full sun and cool conditions, if applicable. Light frost will not bother established transplants of most perennial species if they have been gradually acclimated but neither is it useful. It is safest to protect plants when frost is expected if they are outdoors.

E. Fertilizer is not usually necessary at this stage if the germination soil formula is used to fill small containers. Only under the following conditions should plants need additional fertilizer:
  - If a large over supply of water (such as from a heavy storm) has been allowed to soak containers and wash away the natural fertility of the soil.
  - If plants are left in the containers a good deal longer than recommended or a pronounced slow down of growth and yellowing of the foliage occurs, it may indicate a need for

addition of light fertilizer. Fertilizer is most easily applied as a dilute liquid at this time.

F. Plants should be grown in the small cell pack containers until the roots become somewhat congested in the container. At this stage the roots will hold soil firmly together when plants are pushed out of the container with finger pressure from below.

G. Only approximate temperature and light levels have been mentioned since certain species (e.g. Impatiens) prefer rather warm and lower light conditions, while others (e.g. Pansies) prefer high light and cool conditions.

The Worker Protection Standard for Agricultural Pesticides–How To Comply

Quick Reference Guide

This 2-page Quick reference guide to the Worker Protection Standard lists the maximum WP requirements. Fulfilling these maximum requirements is a relatively simple way to comply, but it may cause you to do more than is required in some situations.

The Guide in this unit is presented on 2 pages to allow you to view all the requirements together.

July 1993

QUICK REFERENCE GUIDE TO THE 1992 WORKER PROTECTION STANDARD (WPS)

The WPS is a Federal regulation designed to protect **agricultural workers** (people involved in the production of agricultural plants) and **pesticide handlers** (people mixing, loading, or applying pesticides or doing other tasks involving direct contact with pesticides) (see pp. 14–15). The guide on these two pages presents the **maximum** WPS requirements. It does not include exceptions that may permit you to do less or options that may involve different requirements. **You will be in compliance with the Federal WPS if you make sure that the requirements listed on these two pages are met.** Each section below lists pages in this manual where you can find out about exceptions and options. For more information about your responsibilities, read pp. 12–20. There are some exemptions for owners of agricultural establishments and members of their immediate family (see pp. 91–93).

Duties for All Employers

Anti-Retaliation (p. 19)

Do not retaliate against a worker or handler who attempts to comply with the WPS.

Information at a Central Location (pp. 23–24)

1. In an easily seen central location on each agricultural establishment, display close together:
   - EPA WPS safety poster,
   - name, address, and telephone number of the nearest emergency medical facility,
   - these facts about each pesticide application, [from before each application begins until 30 days after the restricted-entry interval (REI)]:
     - product name, EPA registration number, and active ingredient(s),
     - location and description of treated area,
     - time and date of application, and REI.
2. Tell workers and handlers where the information is posted, and allow them access.
3. Tell them if emergency facility information changes and update the posted information.
4. Keep the posted information legible.

Pesticide Safety Training (pp. 25–28)

Unless they possess a valid EPA-approved training card, train handlers and workers before they begin work and at least once each 5 years:
   - use written and/or audiovisual materials,
   - use EPA WPS handler training materials for training handlers,
   - use EPA WPS worker training materials for training workers,
   - have a certified applicator conduct the training orally and/or or audiovisually in a manner the employees can understand, using easily understood terms, and respond to questions.

Decontamination Sites (pp. 29–31)

1. Establish a decontamination site within 1/4 mile of all workers and handlers. Supply:
   - enough water for routine and emergency whole-body washing and for eyeflushing,
   - plenty of soap and single-use towels,
   - a clean coverall.
2. Provide water that is safe and cool enough for washing, for eyeflushing, and for drinking. Do not use tank-stored water that is also used for mixing pesticides.

3. Provide **handlers** the same supplies where personal protective equipment (PPE) is removed at the end of a task.
4. Provide the same supplies at each mixing and loading site.
5. Make at least 1 pint eyeflush water immediately accessible to each **handler**.
6. Do not put **worker** decontamination sites in areas being treated or under an REI.
7. In areas being treated, put decontamination supplies for **handlers** in enclosed containers.

Employer Information Exchange (pp. 33–34)

1. Before any application, commercial handler employers must make sure the operator of the agricultural establishment where a pesticide will be applied is aware of:
   - specific location and description of all areas on the agricultural establishment where pesticides will be applied or where an REI will be in effect while the commercial handler is on the establishment,
   - time and date of application,
   - product name, EPA registration number, active ingredient(s), and REI,
   - whether the product label requires both oral warnings and treated area posting,
   - all other safety requirements on labeling for workers or other people.
2. Operators of agricultural establishments must make sure any commercial pesticide establishment operator they hire is aware of:
   - location and description of area to be treated,
   - time and date of application.
   - restrictions on entering those areas.

Emergency Assistance (pp. 35–36)

When any handler or worker may have been poisoned or injured by pesticides:
1. Promptly make transportation available to an appropriate medical facility.
2. Promptly provide to the victim and to medical personnel:
   - product name, EPA registration number, and active ingredient(s),
   - all first aid and medical information from label,
   - description of how the pesticide was used,
   - information about victim's exposure.

7/93

Additional Duties for Worker Employers

Restrictions During Applications (p. 45)

1. In areas being treated with pesticides, allow entry only to appropriately trained and equipped handlers.
2. Keep nursery workers at least 100 feet away from nursery areas being treated.
3. Allow only handlers to be in a greenhouse:
   - during a pesticide application,
   - until labeling-listed air concentration level is met or, if no such level, until after 2 hours of ventilation with fans.

(Also see nursery restrictions and greenhouse restrictions) (pp. 51-52, 53-55)

Restricted-Entry Intervals (REI's) (pp. 45-46)

During any REI, do not allow workers to enter a treated area and contact anything treated with the pesticide to which the REI applies.
(Also see early entry by workers) (pp. 46-47, 59-70)

Notice About Applications (pp. 41-44)

1. Orally warn workers and post treated areas if the pesticide labeling requires.
2. Otherwise, either orally warn workers or post entrances to treated areas. Tell workers which method is in effect.
3. Post all greenhouse applications.

Posted Warning Signs:

1. Post legible 14" X 16" WPS-design signs just before application; keep posted during REI; remove before workers enter and within 3 days after the end of the REI.
2. Post signs so they can be seen at all entrances to treated areas, including entrances from labor camps.

Oral Warnings:

1. Before each application, tell workers who are on the establishment (in a manner they can understand):
   - location and description of treated area,
   - REI, and not to enter during REI.
2. Workers who enter the establishment after application starts must receive the same warning at the start of their work period.

Additional Duties for Handler Employers

Application Restrictions and Monitoring (pp. 73-74)

1. Do not allow handlers to apply a pesticide so that it contacts, directly or through drift, anyone other than trained and equipped handlers.
2. Make sight or voice contact at least every 2 hours with anyone handling pesticides labeled with a skull and crossbones.
3. Make sure a trained handler equipped with labeling-specified PPE maintains constant voice or visual contact with any handler in a greenhouse who is doing fumigant-related tasks, such as application or air-level monitoring.

Specific Instructions for Handlers (pp. 75-76)

1. Before handlers do any handling task, inform them, in a manner they can understand, of all pesticide labeling instructions for safe use.
2. Keep pesticide labeling accessible to each handler during entire handling task.
3. Before handlers use any assigned handling equipment, tell them how to use it safely.
4. When commercial handlers will be on an agricultural establishment, inform them beforehand of:
   - areas on the establishment where pesticides will be applied or where an REI will be in effect,
   - restrictions on entering those areas.

(The agricultural establishment operator must give you these facts.)

Equipment Safety (p. 77)

1. Inspect pesticide handling equipment before each use, and repair or replace as needed.
2. Allow only appropriately trained and equipped handlers to repair, clean, or adjust pesticide equipment that contains pesticides or residues.

Personal Protective Equipment (PPE) (pp. 79-83)

(See exceptions to PPE) (pp. 85-87)

Duties Related to PPE:

1. Provide handlers with the PPE the pesticide labeling requires for the task, and be sure it is:
   - clean and in operating condition,
   - worn and used correctly,
   - inspected before each day of use,
   - repaired or replaced as needed.
2. Be sure respirators fit correctly.
3. Take steps to avoid heat illness.
4. Provide handlers a pesticide-free area for:
   - storing personal clothing not in use,
   - putting on PPE at start of task,
   - taking off PPE at end of task.
5. Do not allow used PPE to be worn home or taken home.

Care of PPE:

1. Store and wash used PPE separately from other clothing and laundry.
2. If PPE will be reused, clean it before each day of reuse, according to the instructions from the PPE manufacturer unless the pesticide labeling specifies other requirements. If there are no other instructions, wash in detergent and hot water.
3. Dry the clean PPE before storing, or hang to dry.
4. Store clean PPE away from other clothing and away from pesticide areas.

Replacing Respirator Purifying Elements:

1. Replace dust/mist filters:
   - when breathing becomes difficult,
   - when filter is damaged or torn,
   - when respirator label or pesticide label requires (whichever is shorter), OR
   - at the end of day's work period, in the absence of any other instructions or indications.
2. Replace vapor-removing cartridges/canisters:
   - when odor/taste/irritation is noticed,
   - when respirator label or pesticide label requires (whichever is shorter), OR
   - at the end of day's work period, in the absence of any other instructions or indications.

Disposal of PPE:

1. Discard coveralls and other absorbent materials that are heavily contaminated with undiluted pesticide having a DANGER or WARNING signal word.
2. Follow Federal, State, and local laws when disposing of PPE that cannot be cleaned correctly.

Instructions for People Who Clean PPE:

Inform people who clean or launder PPE:
- that PPE may be contaminated with pesticides,
- of the potentially harmful effects of exposure to pesticides,
- how to protect themselves when handling PPE,
- how to clean PPE correctly.

For more information about the Worker Protection Standard, or if you have questions or concerns about pesticides, contact the agency responsible for regulating pesticides in your area or the EPA Regional Office nearest you.

Region 1 (MA, CT, RI, NH, VT, ME)
U.S. Environmental Protection Agency, Region 1
Pesticides and Toxic Substances Branch (APT)
1 Congress St.
Boston, MA 02203
(617) 565-3273

Region 2 (NY, NJ, PR, VI)
U.S. Environmental Protection Agency, Region 2
Pesticides and Toxic Substances Branch (MS-105)
2890 Woodgridge Ave., Building #10
Edison, NJ 08837-3679
(908) 321-6765

Region 3 (PA, MD, VA, WV, DE)
U.S. Environmental Protection Agency, Region 3
Toxics and Pesticides Branch (3AT-30)
841 Chestnut Building
Philadelphia, PA 19107
(215) 597-8598

Region 4 (GA, NC, SC, AL, MS, KY, FL, TN)
U.S. Environmental Protection Agency, Region 4
Pesticides & Toxic Substances Branch (4-APT-MD)
345 Courtland St., N.E.
Atlanta, GA 30365
(404) 347-5201

Region 5 (IL, MI, MN, IN, OH, WI)
U.S. Environmental Protection Agency, Region 5
Pesticides and Toxic Substances Branch (5SPT)
77 W. Jackson Blvd.
Chicago, IL 60604
(312) 886-6006

Region 6 (TX, OK, AR, LA, NM)
U.S. Environmental Protection Agency, Region 6
Pesticides and Toxics Branch (6T-P)
1445 Ross Ave.
Dallas, TX 75202-2733
(214) 655-7235

Region 7 (MO, KS, IA, NB)
U.S. Environmental Protection Agency, Region 7
Toxics and Pesticides Branch (TOPE)
726 Minnesota Ave.
Kansas City, KS 66101
(913) 551-7020

Region 8 (CO, MT, ND, SD, UT, WY)
U.S. Environmental Protection Agency, Region 8
Toxic Substances Branch (8ART-TS)
One Denver Place, Suite 500
999 18th St.
Denver, CO 80202-2405
(303) 293-1730

Region 9 (CA, NV, AZ, HI, GU)
U.S. Environmental Protection Agency, Region 9
Pesticides and Toxics Branch (A-4)
75 Hawthorne St.
San Francisco, CA 94105
(415) 744-1090

Region 10 (WA, OR, ID, AK)
U.S. Environmental Protection Agency, Region 10
Pesticides and Toxic Substances Branch (AT-083)
1200 Sixth Ave.
Seattle, WA 98191
(206) 553-1918

LITERATURE

American Nurseryman
American Nurseryman Pub. Co.
77 West Washington St. #2100
Chicago, IL 60602
(312)782-5505
1-800-621-5727

American Vegetable Grower
Meister Publishing Co.
37733 Euclid Ave.
Willoughby, OH 44094
(216) 942-2000
1-800-572-774

Floral Mass Marketing
205 Wacker Dr.
Ste. 1040
Chicago, IL 60606
(312) 739-5000

Florist's Review
(312) 782-5505
1-800-621-5727

Flowers
11444 Olympic Blvd.
4th Floor
Los Angeles, CA 90064
(310) 231-9199

Flower News
205 Wacker Dr. Ste. 1040
Chicago, IL 60606
(312) 739-5000

Garden Supply Retailer
One Chilton Way
Radnor, PA 19089
(610) 964-4269

Greenhouse Business
1951 Rohlwing Rd. Ste. B
Rolling Meadows, IL 60008
(847) 870-1576

Greenhouse Grower
Meister Publishing Co.
37733 Euclid Ave.
Willoughby, OH 44094
(216) 942-2000
1-800-572-7740

Greenhouse Product News
Scranton Gillette Comm., Inc.
380 E. Northwest Hwy.
Ste. 200
Des Plaines, IL 60016
(847) 298-6622

Grower Talks
P.O. Box 9
Batavia, IL 60510
(888) 201-1962

Growers Press, Inc.
P.O. Box 189
Princeton, B.C. Canada
VOX 1WO1(250) 295-7755

Herbs for Health, Also Herb Companion. And other Herb books
Interweave Press
201 E. 4th St.
Loveland, CO 80537
(970) 669-7672
1-800-645-3675

Interior Landscape
American Nurseryman Publ. Co.
77 W. Washington St., Ste. 2100
Chicago, IL 60602
(312) 782-5505
1-800-621-5727

Nursery Retailer
Brantwood Publications
2410 Northside Dr.
Clearwater, FL 33761
(727) 796-3877

The Growing Edge
P.O. Box 1027
Corvallis, OR 97339
(541) 757-2511

The Herb Quarterly
P.O. Box 689
San Anselmo, CA 94979
1-800-371-HERB

The Soilless Grower
Hydroponic Society of America
P.O. Box 1183
El Cerito, CA 94530
(510) 743-9605

All the following are publications of :

Branch-Smith Publishing
120 St. Louis Ave.
Fort Worth, TX 76104
(817) 332-8236 or 1-800-433-5612

Garden Center Products & Supplies
Garden Center Merchandising & Management
Greenhouse Management & Production
Nursery Management & Production
SAF Magazine

Horticulture- Magazine of American Gardening
98 N. Washington St.
Boston, MA 02114-1913
(617) 742-5600

Fine Gardening
63 S. Main St.
P.O. Box 5506
Newtown, CT 06470-5506
(203) 426-8171

The American Gardener
American Horticultural Society
7931 E. Boulevard Drive
Alexandria, VA 22308-1300
(703) 768-5700

National Gardening
Magazine of The National Gardening Assoc.
180 Flynn Ave.
Burlington, VT 05401
1-800-538-7476

Entrepreneur Magazine
2392 Morse Ave.
Irvine, CA 92614
(949) 261-2325

Home Business
Magazine
9582 Hamilton Ave.
Suite 368
Huntington Beach, CA 92646
(714) 968-0331

American Horticultural
Therapy Association
9220 Wightman Rd.
Suite 300
Gaithersburg, MD 20879
(303) 331-3862

People Plant Connection
(303) 820-3151

Journal of Theraputic Horticulture
(303) 820-3151

Selected Bibliography

1. Armitage, A. M. *Allan Armitage on Perennials*. Prentice Hall. 1993.
     ISBN: 0-671847-22-8

2. Baker, Kenneth (Ed.). *The University of California System for Producing Healthy Container Grown Plants*. University of California Experimental Station Service. 1957.

3. Ball, Vic. *Ball RedBook*. Ball Publishing. 16th edition. 1997
     ISBN: 1-883052-15-7

4. Bartok, John. *Greenhouse Engineering*. American Nurseryman Publishing. 1994.

5. Bohmont, Bert, L. *The Standard Pesticide User's Guide*. Prentice Hall. 1999.
     ISBN: 0-136791-92-1

6. Boodley, James, William. *The Commercial Greenhouse*. Delmar Publications. 2nd edition. 1998. ISBN: 0-827373-11-2

7. California Fertilizer Association Staff. *Western Fertilizer Handbook: Horticulture Edition*. Interstate Publishers, Inc. 1998.
     ISBN: 0-813431-46-8

8. Capon, Brian. *Botany for Gardeners: An Introduction and Guide*. Timber Press. 1990. ISBN 0-881921-63-7

9. Dirr, Michael, A. *Dirr's Hardy Trees and Shrubs: An Illustrated Encyclopedia*. Timber Press. 1997. ISBN: 0-881924-04-0

10. Ecke, Paul, Jr. *The Poinsettia Manual*. Paul Ecke Poinsettia Publications. 3rd edition. 1990.

11. Environmental Protection Agency. Internet address: www.epa.gov

12. Graf, A. B. *Exotica Series Four: Pictorial Cyclopedia of Exotic plants*. Roehrs Co. 1992. ISBN: 0-911266-15-1

13. Graf, A.B. *Hortica: Color Cyclopedia of Garden Flora in all climates and Exotic Plants Indoors*. Roehrs Co. 1992. ISBN: 0-911266-25-9

14. Graf, A. B. *Tropica: Color Cyclopedia of Exotic Plants and Trees from the Tropics and Subtropics, for Warm Region Horticulture in Cool Climates: The Sheltered Indoors.* Roehrs Co. 1992. ISBN: 0-911266-24-0

15. Griffith, Lynn, P. *Tropical Foliage Plants: A Grower's Guide.* Ball Publishing. 1998.

16. Joiner, Jasper, N. *Foliage Plant Production.* Prentice Hall. 1981.

17. Jozwik, Francis. *Illustrated Guide to Landscape Plants.* Andmar Press. 2000. ISBN: 0-916781-24-0

18. Jozwik, Francis. *How to Make Money Growing Plants, Trees, and Flowers.* Andmar Press. 2000. ISBN:0-916781-22-4

19. Jozwik, Francis. *Perennial Plants for Profit or Pleasure.* Andmar Press. 2000. ISBN: 0-916781-20-8

20. Jozwik, Francis. *Plants for Profit.* Andmar Press. 2000. ISBN: 0-916781-21-6.

21. Jozwik, Francis. *Essentials of Plant Propagation for Profit or Pleasure.* Video. Andmar Press. 1995. ISBN: 0-916781-13-5v

22. Kleyn, John. *Plants from Test Tubes.* Timber Press. 1996. ISBN: 0-881192-361-3

23. Lindquist, Richard. *Identification of Insects and Related Pests: A Pictorial Guide.* Ohio Florists Association. 1999.

24. MacDonald, Bruce. *Practical Woody Plant Propagation for Nursery Growers.* Timber Press. 1987. ISBN: 0-881920-62-2

25. Mallis, Arnold. *Handbook of Pest Control.* Mallis Handbook and Technical Training Company. 1997. ISBN: 1-890561-00-2

26. Maloy, Otis, C. *Plant Disease Control: Principles and Practice.* Wiley, John & Sons. 1993. ISBN: 0-471573-17-5

27. Masterlerz, John. *Bedding Plants: A Manual on the Culture of Bedding Plants as a Greenhouse Crop.* Pennsylvania Flower Growers. 1976.

28. Masterlerz, John. *The Greenhouse Environment.* Penn State University Press. 1977. ISBN: 0-471576-06-9.

29. National Greenhouse Manufacturers Association. *Greenhouse Design Standards.* NGMA. 1996. Internet address: www.ngma.com.

30. National Greenhouse Manufacturers Association. *Greenhouse Glazing.* NGMA. 1996. Internet address: www.ngma.com.

31. Nelson, Paul, V. *Greenhouse Operation and Management.* Prentice Hall. 1997. ISBN: 0-133746-87-9

32. Ohio Cooperative Extension Service. *Tips on Growing Bedding Plants.* Ohio State University. 1989.

33. Ohio Cooperative Extension Service. *Tips on Growing Potted Perennials and Biennials*. Ohio State University. 1989.

34. Phillips, Rodger. *The Random House Book of Perennials: Volume 1 – Early Perennials*. Random House. 1991. ISBN: 0-679737-97-9

35. Phillips, Rodger. *The Random House Book of Perennials: Volume 2 – Late Perennials*. Random House. 1991. ISBN: 0-679737-98-7

36. Powell, Charles, C. *Ball Pest and Disease Manual: Disease, Insect, and Mite Control on Flower and Foliage Crops*. Ball Publishing. 1997. ISBN: 1-883052-13-0

37. Reed, David, W. *A Grower's Guide to Water, Media, and Nutrition for Greenhouse Crops*. Ball Publishing. 1996. ISBN: 1-883052-12-2

38. Resh, Howard, M. *Hydroponic Food Production: A Definitive Guidebook of Soilless Food Growing Methods*. Woodbridge. 1995. ISBN: 0-880072-12-1

39. Shigo, Alex. *Tree basics: What Every Person Needs to Know About Trees*. Shigo. 1996. ISBN: 0-943563-16-X

40. Shigo, Alex. Tree *Pruning: A Worldwide Photo Guide*. Shigo. 1989. ISBN: 0-943563-08-9

41. Snyder, Leon. *Trees and Shrubs for Northern Gardens*. University of Minnesota Press. 1980. ISBN: 0-816609-43-8

42. Thompson, Peter. *Creative Propagation: A Grower's Guide*. Timber Press. 1992. ISBN: 0-881922-51-X

43. United States Department of Agriculture. Agricultural Marketing. Internet address: www.ams.usda.gov.

44. United States Department of Agriculture. Cooperative Extensions. Internet address: www.reeusda.gov.

45. United States Department of Agriculture. Foreign Agricultural Service. Internet address: www. fas.usda.gov.

46. United States Small Business Administration. Internet address: www.sba.gov.

47. Whitcomb, Carl. *Plant Production in Containers*. Lacebark Publications. 1984. ISBN: 0-961310-91-X

48. Yoder Brothers Inc. *Yoder Mums Bulletin*. Ph:1-800-321-9537

Breakdown of literature by chapter

The following list is a chapter by chapter breakdown of the above bibliography. Chapter headings are followed by numbers which correspond to the above publications.

Index

BOOKS BY ANDMAR PRESS

Andmar Press offers the following books by Dr. Jozwik about opportunities and methods in commercial horticulture. Mail order delivery to your door is available. Each purchase is fully guaranteed. Cash refunds are honored for any reason if the original invoice is presented.

The Greenhouse and Nursery Handbook
A Complete Guide to Growing and Selling Ornamental Container Plants.

Everything you need to know about how to grow and sell ornamental plants is clearly presented in this large, illustrated volume. The culture of hundreds of bedding plants, flowering pot plants, foliage plants, trees, shrubs, and perennials is covered from A to Z. Basic environmental factors like fertilizers, moisture, temperature, insects, diseases, and soil are explained in terms everyone can understand. *The Greenhouse and Nursery Handbook* is an absolute must for every horticulturist whether their interests are commercial or recreational. Hardcover $97.00 plus $7.00 shipping. 806 pages.

Perennial Plants for Profit or Pleasure
How to Grow Perennial Flowers and Herbs for Profit or Personal Landscape Use.

This book details the exact methods necessary to set up a low cost business growing perennial plants—literally in your own backyard. Or you can use the system to provide economical perennials for parks, cemeteries, businesses, garden clubs, churches, or home gardens. Every step of production and marketing is clearly pointed out. Convenient sources for supplies are included free. Hardcover. $39.95 plus $5.00 shipping. 300 pages.

How to Make Money Growing Plants, Trees, and Flowers.
A Guide to Profitable Earth-Friendly Ventures.

Outlines the many business opportunities available in horticulture and offers the reader important preliminary information about how to choose a field of interest and how to get started correctly. This book is essential for anyone who needs a concise summary of practical start up advice. Hardcover. $39.95 plus $5.00 shipping. 308 pages.

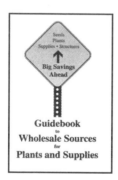

Guidebook to Wholesale Sources for Plants and Supplies

Tells you how to easily obtain beautiful catalogs from leading wholesale horticultural firms. Complete addresses and telephone numbers included to save you time. The companies listed offer a large selection of wholesale supplies and plants which are available only to established professional growers or persons who wish to begin a horticultural business soon. $9.95 plus $3.00 shipping.

Plants for Profit—*Income Opportunities in Horticulture*

A multifaceted book which presents general information about how to start a horticultural business and then examines details of some specific business and employment opportunities. On site field trip forms are included to familiarize you with the industry. Numerous trade publications are cited for further information. Hardcover. $39.95 plus $5.00 shipping. 304 pages.

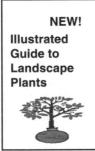

NEW!
Illustrated Guide to Landscape Plants

The Illustrated Handbook of Landscape Plants—*Includes Trees, Shrubs, Annuals and Perennials.*

An indispensable guide to hundreds of North American ornamental species. Illustrated profusely in color to help both professionals and amateurs plan beautiful and ecologically sound landscapes. Details of size, color, and cultural preferences outlined for each variety. Durable 8½ x 11 hardcover notebook style allows professionals to add their own material and drawings for a full open presentation to customers $29.95 plus $5.00 shipping. New!

Visit Our Website:
http://www.andmar.com

ORDER BLANK FOR BOOKS

Please send the following books to me. I understand the total order amount below must be transferred to the reverse side of this page where I will indicate my shipping instructions and deduct any allowable postage discount for orders of more than one title.

Quan.	Title	Price	Shipping	Total
_____	*The Greenhouse and Nursery Handbook* Hardback Deluxe Edition	$97.00	$7.00	$ _____
_____	*Perennial Plants for Profit or Pleasure*	$39.95	$5.00	$ _____
_____	*Make Money Growing Plants, Trees, and Flowers*	$39.95	$5.00	$ _____
_____	*Guidebook to Wholesale Sources for Plants and Supplies*	$9.95	$3.00	$ _____
_____	*Plants for Profit – Income Opportunities in Horticulture*	$39.95	$5.00	$ _____
_____	*The Illustrated Handbook of Landscape Plants*	$29.95	$5.00	$ _____

Total amount due for titles ordered .... $ _____

Canadian and foreign orders must be paid by VISA or MasterCard or by money orders denominated in U.S. dollars. Canadian and U.K. orders add $5.00 additional shipping per order. All other foreign orders add $15.00 additional per order for insured air mail. Orders shipped priority mail where possible.

Please transfer the total order amount to the reverse side of this page and complete all shipping instructions carefully. Enclose full payment by check, credit card, or money order.

FULL MONEY BACK GUARANTEE

SHIPPING AND PAYMENT FORM

Total book order from reverse side of this page .... $ _____

United States and territories customers subtract a
$2.00 postage discount for each title ordered
after the first book .... $ (_____)

Total amount due in U.S. dollars after postage
discount subtracted .... $ _____

Check type of payment enclosed

☐ Visa or MC   ☐ Money Order

☐ Check (drawn on U.S. Branch)

Andmar Press

West Yellowstone Highway
P.O. Box 217
Mills, WY 82644-0217

Please Print or Type Clearly

Name _____

Company _____

Address _____

_____

City _____

State/Zip _____

Phone (_____) _____

VISA or MC
Full Number _____

Expiration Date _____

FULL MONEY BACK GUARANTEE

Please review your order on the reverse side of this page to make sure both the titles and order total are correct.